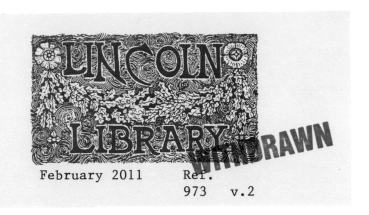

MILESTONE DOCUMENTS IN AFRICAN AMERICAN HISTORY

Exploring the Essential Primary Sources

MILESTONE DOCUMENTS IN AFRICAN AMERICAN HISTORY

Exploring the Essential Primary Sources

Volume 2
1853–1900

Paul Finkelman, Editor in Chief

Schlager Group

Dallas, Texas

Milestone Documents in African American History
Copyright © 2010 by Schlager Group Inc.

Schlager Group Inc.
2501 Oak Lawn Avenue, Suite 440
Dallas, Tex. 75219
USA

You can find Schlager Group on the World Wide Web at
http://www.schlagergroup.com
Text and cover design by Patricia Moritz

Printed in the United States of America

10 9 8 7 6 5 4 3 2 1

ISBN: 978-1-935306-05-4

This book is printed on acid-free paper.

CONTENTS

EDITORIAL AND PRODUCTION STAFF IX
CONTRIBUTORS X
ACKNOWLEDGMENTS XII
READER'S GUIDE XIII
INTRODUCTION XIV

VOLUME 1: 1619–1852

JOHN ROLFE'S LETTER TO SIR EDWIN SANDYS 2
VIRGINIA'S ACT XII: NEGRO WOMEN'S CHILDREN TO SERVE ACCORDING TO THE CONDITION OF THE MOTHER . .17
VIRGINIA'S ACT III: BAPTISM DOES NOT EXEMPT SLAVES FROM BONDAGE 27
"A MINUTE AGAINST SLAVERY, ADDRESSED TO GERMANTOWN MONTHLY MEETING" 36
JOHN WOOLMAN'S *SOME CONSIDERATIONS ON THE KEEPING OF NEGROES* 47
LORD DUNMORE'S PROCLAMATION 63
PETITION OF PRINCE HALL AND OTHER AFRICAN AMERICANS TO THE MASSACHUSETTS GENERAL COURT 72
PENNSYLVANIA: AN ACT FOR THE GRADUAL ABOLITION OF SLAVERY 84
THOMAS JEFFERSON'S *NOTES ON THE STATE OF VIRGINIA* 96
SLAVERY CLAUSES IN THE U.S. CONSTITUTION 112
BENJAMIN BANNEKER'S LETTER TO THOMAS JEFFERSON 130
FUGITIVE SLAVE ACT OF 1793 140
RICHARD ALLEN: "AN ADDRESS TO THOSE WHO KEEP SLAVES, AND APPROVE THE PRACTICE" 151
PRINCE HALL: *A CHARGE DELIVERED TO THE AFRICAN LODGE* 163
OHIO BLACK CODE 175
PETER WILLIAMS, JR.'S "ORATION ON THE ABOLITION OF THE SLAVE TRADE" 187
SAMUEL CORNISH AND JOHN RUSSWURM'S FIRST *FREEDOM'S JOURNAL* EDITORIAL 200
DAVID WALKER'S *APPEAL TO THE COLOURED CITIZENS OF THE WORLD* .213
STATE V. MANN 231
WILLIAM LLOYD GARRISON'S FIRST *LIBERATOR* EDITORIAL 242
THE CONFESSIONS OF NAT TURNER 255
UNITED STATES V. AMISTAD 270
PRIGG V. PENNSYLVANIA 284
HENRY HIGHLAND GARNET: "AN ADDRESS TO THE SLAVES OF THE UNITED STATES OF AMERICA" 306
WILLIAM WELLS BROWN'S "SLAVERY AS IT IS" 320
FIRST EDITORIAL OF THE *NORTH STAR* 338
ROBERTS V. CITY OF BOSTON 351

Fugitive Slave Act of 1850 366

Narrative of the Life of Henry Box Brown, Written by Himself 381

Sojourner Truth's "Ain't I a Woman?" 394

Frederick Douglass's "What to the Slave Is the Fourth of July?" .404

Martin Delany: *The Condition, Elevation, Emigration, and Destiny of the Colored People*
    of the United States 425

Volume 2: 1853–1900

Twelve Years a Slave: Narrative of Solomon Northup 444

Dred Scott v. Sandford 456

John S. Rock's "Whenever the Colored Man Is Elevated, It Will Be by His Own Exertions" 496

Virginia Slave Code 509

Harriet Jacobs's *Incidents in the Life of a Slave Girl* 522

Osborne P. Anderson: *A Voice from Harper's Ferry* 534

Emancipation Proclamation 552

Frederick Douglass: "Men of Color, To Arms!" 564

War Department General Order 143 574

Thomas Morris Chester's Civil War Dispatches 584

William T. Sherman's Special Field Order No. 15 598

Black Code of Mississippi 611

Thirteenth Amendment to the U.S. Constitution 622

Testimony before the Joint Committee on Reconstruction on Atrocities in the
    South against Blacks 633

Fourteenth Amendment to the U.S. Constitution 650

Henry McNeal Turner's Speech on His Expulsion from the Georgia Legislature 662

Fifteenth Amendment to the U.S. Constitution 676

Ku Klux Klan Act 686

United States v. Cruikshank 698

Richard Harvey Cain's "All That We Ask Is Equal Laws, Equal Legislation, and Equal Rights" 715

Civil Rights Cases 728

T. Thomas Fortune: "The Present Relations of Labor and Capital" 762

Anna Julia Cooper's "Womanhood: A Vital Element in the Regeneration and
    Progress of a Race" 772

John Edward Bruce's "Organized Resistance Is Our Best Remedy" 792

John L. Moore's "In the Lion's Mouth" 802

Josephine St. Pierre Ruffin's "Address to the First National Conference
    of Colored Women" 815

Booker T. Washington's Atlanta Exposition Address 824

Plessy v. Ferguson 836

Mary Church Terrell: "The Progress of Colored Women" 858

Ida B. Wells-Barnett's "Lynch Law in America" 872

Volume 3: 1901–1964

George White's Farewell Address to Congress 887

W. E. B. Du Bois: *The Souls of Black Folk* 898

Niagara Movement Declaration of Principles 917

Theodore Roosevelt's Brownsville Legacy Special Message to the Senate 930

Act in Relation to the Organization of a Colored Regiment in the City of New York 944

Monroe Trotter's Protest to Woodrow Wilson 954

Guinn v. United States 964

William Pickens: "The Kind of Democracy the Negro Expects" .981

Thirty Years of Lynching in the United States 992

Cyril Briggs's *Summary of the Program and Aims of the African Blood Brotherhood* 1011

Walter F. White: "The Eruption of Tulsa" 1022

Marcus Garvey: "The Principles of the Universal Negro Improvement Association" 1034

Alain Locke's "Enter the New Negro" 1046

James Weldon Johnson's "Harlem: The Culture Capital" 1063

Alice Moore Dunbar-Nelson: "The Negro Woman and the Ballot" 1077

John P. Davis: "A Black Inventory of the New Deal" 1088

Robert Clifton Weaver: "The New Deal and the Negro: A Look at the Facts" 1102

Charles Hamilton Houston's "Educational Inequalities Must Go!" 1115

Walter F. White's "U.S. Department of (White) Justice" 1128

Mary McLeod Bethune's "What Does American Democracy Mean to Me?" 1140

A. Philip Randolph's "Call to Negro America to March on Washington" 1152

To Secure These Rights 1162

Executive Order 9981 1182

Ralph J. Bunche: "The Barriers of Race Can Be Surmounted" 1192

Sweatt v. Painter 1204

Haywood Patterson and Earl Conrad's *Scottsboro Boy* 1216

Brown v. Board of Education 1234

Marian Anderson's *My Lord, What a Morning* 1246

Roy Wilkins: "The Clock Will Not Be Turned Back" 1260

George Wallace's Inaugural Address as Governor 1270

Martin Luther King, Jr.: "Letter from Birmingham Jail" 1284

John F. Kennedy's Civil Rights Address 1302

Martin Luther King, Jr.: "I Have a Dream" 1316

Civil Rights Act of 1964 1328

Fannie Lou Hamer's Testimony at the Democratic National Convention 1358

Volume 4: 1965–2009

Malcolm X: "After the Bombing" 1370

Moynihan Report 1386

South Carolina v. Katzenbach 1406

Stokely Carmichael's "Black Power" 1424

Bond v. Floyd 1444

Martin Luther King, Jr.: "Beyond Vietnam: A Time to Break Silence" 1460

Loving v. Virginia 1478

Kerner Commission Report Summary 1492

Eldridge Cleaver's "Education and Revolution" 1516

Jesse Owens's *Blackthink: My Life as Black Man and White Man* 1532

Angela Davis's "Political Prisoners, Prisons, and Black Liberation" 1548

Clay v. United States 1566

Jackie Robinson's *I Never Had It Made* 1583

Final Report of the Tuskegee Syphilis Study Ad Hoc Advisory Panel 1600

FBI Report on Elijah Muhammad 1614

Shirley Chisholm: "The Black Woman in Contemporary America" 1630

Thurgood Marshall's Equality Speech 1644

Jesse Jackson's Democratic National Convention Keynote Address 1658

Anita Hill's Opening Statement at the Senate Confirmation Hearing of Clarence Thomas 1674

A. Leon Higginbotham: "An Open Letter to Justice Clarence Thomas from a
   Federal Judicial Colleague" 1686

Colin Powell's Commencement Address at Howard University 1704

Louis Farrakhan's Million Man March Pledge 1716

One America in the 21st Century 1726

Clarence Thomas's Concurrence/Dissent in *Grutter v. Bollinger* 1740

Barack Obama: "A More Perfect Union" 1762

Barack Obama's Inaugural Address 1778

U.S. Senate Resolution Apologizing for the Enslavement and Racial Segregation
   of African Americans 1792

Barack Obama's Address to the NAACP Centennial Convention 1802

Teacher's Activity Guides 1817

List of Documents by Category 1827

Subject Index 1831

MILESTONE DOCUMENTS IN AFRICAN AMERICAN HISTORY

Exploring the Essential Primary Sources

A slave pen in Alexandria, Virginia (Library of Congress)

Twelve Years a Slave: Narrative of Solomon Northup

"Never have I seen such an exhibition of intense, unmeasured, and unbounded grief, as when Eliza was parted from her child."

Overview

Solomon Northup's *Twelve Years a Slave*, published in 1853, stands out as an important piece of literature about slavery because it is written from the perspective of a free man who was captured and forced into bondage and who wrote in great detail about this experience after his release twelve years later. Northup's insights into the workings of the southern slave system reveal the spiritual and physical torment slaves endured. Northup's powerful language describing his capture, his life as a slave, and then his release helps explain why *Twelve Years a Slave* became one of the fastest-selling and most popular narratives of the nineteenth century. Although the authenticity and reliability of slave narratives have been frequently challenged, such narratives are recognized as essential sources for the study of American slavery in the antebellum South.

Prior to Solomon Northup's capture in 1841 at the age of thirty-three, he led a relatively quiet life as a free black man in Saratoga Springs, New York. To care for his wife and three children, he worked in a variety of jobs in agriculture, lumbering, and hotel services. He also used his talent for the violin to earn money throughout his life. In 1841 he met two white men, who overheard him playing the violin and offered to travel with him to New York and later Washington, D.C., where they assured him that he would be able to earn money playing music for a traveling circus. Believing that he would be gone only a short while, Northup did not notify his family. Little did he know that this trip, which would end with his enslavement, would be the beginning of the twelve most difficult years of his life.

Context

The decades before the American Civil War were rife with conflict as sectional discord gripped the nation. Debates over the extension of slavery into newly acquired territory divided the country and would culminate in the secession of the southern states and the war. As early as 1820 Congress grappled with the question of how to appease all sides as slavery extended into the new territories. The Missouri Compromise of 1820 established a dividing line between the free states of the North and the slaveholding states of the South. This, however, would be only a temporary solution to a much larger problem. In 1846 war with Mexico broke out and sparked an explosion of patriotic support in the United States. But by the end of the Mexican-American War in 1848 and the resulting acquisition of new territory, new questions about statehood and the status of slavery arose with the nation now stretching from ocean to ocean. This expansionist agenda created ripple effects nationwide, as political parties shifted, pockets of violence broke out, and Congress wrestled with how to please all sectional interests.

The 1850s have been nicknamed the "Decade of Crisis" by many historians who see the events over these ten years, and responses to them, as thrusting the United States toward civil conflict. The Compromise of 1850 opened the decade by attempting to meet northern, southern, and western interests after the territorial expansions of the 1840s. The most controversial aspect of the 1850 agreement was a new and harsher federal measure called the Fugitive Slave Act, which required federal authorities in the northern states to assist southern slave catchers in returning runaway slaves to their owners. Many northern states responded by enacting personal liberty laws that increased the legal rights of accused fugitives. However, these laws were overturned by the U.S. Supreme Court based on the constitutional premise that federal laws took supremacy over state laws. As a way for the territories of New Mexico and Utah to resolve the question of slavery, the Compromise of 1850 also invoked the controversial idea of popular sovereignty, in which the local population, rather than Congress, decided whether or not to adopt slavery.

In 1854 the Missouri Compromise of 1820 was repealed by the Kansas-Nebraska Act, designed by Senator Stephen A. Douglas of Illinois, in which Congress tried to organize territories carved from the Louisiana Purchase that had been ignored for decades. The two territories of Kansas and Nebraska were formed, and the decision about slavery within them was to be resolved by popular sovereignty. Although Douglas's hope had been to appease all sectional interests, what resulted was an unheard-of level of violence

Time Line

1820	■ The Missouri Compromise establishes 36° 30' as the dividing line between the free states of the North and the slaveholding states of the South.
1841	■ Solomon Northup is kidnapped from the free state of New York and taken to slave territory.
1845	■ The *Narrative of the Life of Frederick Douglass* is published in Boston.
1846–1848	■ The Mexican-American war reopens the issue of the expansion of slavery when new territory is acquired in the peace settlement.
1850	■ The Fugitive Slave Act, passed as part of the Compromise of 1850, requires that federal authorities in the North assist southern slave catchers in returning runaway slaves to their owners.
1852	■ Harriet Beecher Stowe publishes *Uncle Tom's Cabin*.
1853	■ Solomon Northup is released from slavery and publishes his narrative, *Twelve Years a Slave*. ■ *A Key to Uncle Tom's Cabin* is published by Harriet Beecher Stowe to document the information in *Uncle Tom's Cabin* and to refute critics who have argued that it is not authentic.
1854	■ **May 30** The Kansas-Nebraska Act is passed, making the status of slavery in new territories subject to popular sovereignty.
1855–1856	■ Violence breaks out between proslavery and antislavery proponents in "Bleeding Kansas."

over the issue of slavery—and a disaster for the American political system. Horace Greeley, editor of the *New York Tribune*, coined the name "Bleeding Kansas" as he watched proslavery and antislavery gangs attack each other between 1855 and 1856 as they tried to settle the slavery question in these new territories.

One other question regarding slavery in the new territories had to be resolved as masters took their slaves and began to move west with them, often into free territories. In 1857 the Supreme Court declared in *Dred Scott v. Sandford* that blacks, whether enslaved or free, were not citizens of the United States and could not therefore sue in federal courts. Further, because slaves were declared to be property, the Court ruled that freeing Dred Scott would be a clear violation of the Fifth Amendment because it would amount to depriving Sanford, his owner, of his property without due process of law.

While lawmakers and justices debated and decided the fate of slavery and slaves, many individuals embarked on campaigns of their own. Frederick Douglass became one of the most powerful abolitionists and orators of the nineteenth century as he spoke out against the evils of slavery. After spending twenty years in bondage, Douglass published his autobiography, the *Narrative of the Life of Frederick Douglass* (1845), and created an antislavery newspaper titled the *North Star*. Harriet Beecher Stowe's *Uncle Tom's Cabin*, published in 1852, fanned opposition to the Fugitive Slave Act with a graphic story of slavery that evoked empathy and outrage throughout the North. Her picture of Tom's enslaved life and what he suffered at the hands of his evil white overseer, Simon Legree, mobilized not only abolitionists but also many northerners and antislavers around the nation who had been unaware of the level of the atrocities inflicted upon slaves.

It was in this context that the story of Solomon Northup unfolded. When he was kidnapped in 1841, Northup was unaware that his twelve-year episode would coincide with an escalation of sectional discord that would tear the nation apart eight years after his release and the publication of his narrative in 1853.

About the Author

Solomon Northup was born into a free black family in Minerva, New York, in 1808. His father, Mintus, was a freed slave who early in life took the surname Northup from his owner. Mintus Northup worked as a slave in Rhode Island; when his owner moved to Rensselaer County, New York, and took the elder Northup with him, he promised the slave emancipation upon his death. Solomon's father was a man respected for his industry and integrity. Once free, he worked in agriculture and ultimately acquired enough property to entitle him to the right to vote in New York. Mintus Northup felt that it was important to educate his children, so he encouraged Solomon to read when his duties on the family farm were completed. The younger Northup spent many of his leisure hours playing the violin, which gave him amusement and served as consolation for the limited possibilities for blacks to advance in nineteenth-century America.

In 1829, Solomon Northup married Anne Hampton, a mixed-race woman. They had three children, and she supported him as he provided for this family. Northup purchased part of a farm, which he diligently worked for many years, but he was never satisfied with the income produced by agriculture. During the winters he and his family lived in a variety of hotels, where he worked as a carriage driver and relied upon his violin for additional earnings. As he stated in his autobiographical narrative, his life up to this point was nothing unusual. But one day in March 1841, he accepted an offer that would result in the loss of his freedom for the next twelve years.

While he was working in Saratoga Springs, New York, Northup was approached by two white men, Merrill Brown and Abram Hamilton, who offered him a job playing violin for a circus, which was located in Washington, D.C. Northup accepted the offer and first traveled to New York City, where his soon-to-be captors suggested he acquire papers declaring his status as a free black citizen of New York, since he would be traveling to Washington, D.C., where slavery was legal. Believing they were protecting his freedom and looking out for his best interests, Northup cooperated with Brown and Hamilton and even enjoyed their polite company.

When the three men arrived in Washington, D.C., in April 1841, the decision was made to attend the funeral procession of President William Henry Harrison. That afternoon, the three spent time in a local saloon, which is where Northup believed he was drugged with laudanum. He passed out that evening; when he awoke a few days later, he found himself in chains in a prison cell, having been robbed of his documents, money, and ultimately his freedom.

The slave pen Northup woke up in was owned by a man named James H. Burch, a well-known slave dealer in Washington, D.C. To force Northup to cooperate, Burch inflicted multiple beatings with a hardwood paddle and cat-o'-nine-tails and insisted that Northup accept the story that he was a runaway slave from Georgia. This was the first of many brutal treatments Northup endured as a slave. He was eventually sent to a slave pen operated by Burch's partner, Theophilus Freeman, in New Orleans, Louisiana. It was here that Northup realized the extent to which slaves were property, as he became part of a slave auction where slaves were sold to the highest bidder.

Northup spent the next twelve years with three different slave owners, William Ford, John M. Tibeats, and Edwin Epps, as he experienced the horrors of slavery. Early in 1852, a benevolent white man named Bass came to work for his last owner, Edwin Epps. Northup, hearing Bass speak about his hatred for slavery, told Bass his true identity and the story of his enslavement. Bass then agreed to help him send letters to people in New York to try to procure his freedom. One of these letters was forwarded to his wife, Anne, who found a lawyer by the name of Henry B. Northup (a member of the slaveholding

family that had employed his father) to review Northup's case. Once a New York court heard the evidence (since a law existed that stated that free black residents unlawfully taken into captivity must be released), Northup regained his freedom.

After being released from slavery on January 4, 1853, Solomon and Henry Northup left the Epps plantation in Bayou Boeuf, Louisiana, and headed north to New York. None of his captors was ever convicted despite the fact that they all were eventually arrested, and Northup never received legal compensation for the crimes committed against him. With the help of David Wilson, a local lawyer and legislator, he wrote his narrative so that readers could come to their own conclusions about slavery.

Explanation and Analysis of the Document

For many years historians have debated whether slave narratives are reliable sources for historical research. Those who doubt their authenticity, reliability, and usefulness begin with the argument that often these narratives were written by a so-called white amanuensis or recorder who was able to shape the narrative in ways not intended by the slave storyteller. Northup's *Twelve Years a Slave* is considered suspect by some for having been authored by David Wilson, a small-town New York lawyer, former school superintendent, and amateur writer. However, unlike some copyists, Wilson was not an abolitionist and seems to have had no political agenda to promote. Most historians believe that Wilson was faithful to the facts of the story as Northup described them and amply able to capture Northup's sentiments, so Northup's narrative is considered by most to be autobiographical and authentic. Further evidence that Northup's narrative is authen-

Time Line

1856

■ **May 24–25**
John Brown and an antislavery party massacre five proslavery men at Pottawatomie Creek, Kansas.

1857

■ **March 6**
The Supreme Court hands down its decision in *Dred Scott v. Sandford* stating that slaves are not U.S. citizens and that Congress has no jurisdiction over slavery in the territories.

1859

■ **October 16**
John Brown leads a failed raid on a federal arsenal at Harpers Ferry, Virginia, in an attempt to free slaves.

Senator Stephen A. Douglas of Illinois (Library of Congress)

tic is that many scholars have investigated various documents, among them, judicial proceedings, census returns and other such public records, the diaries and letters of whites, and newspaper stories, and deemed it credible. In most narratives, including Northup's *Twelve Years a Slave*, the simple stories of slave life follow consistent themes of escape, life on the plantation, religion and its hypocrisy, survival and deceit, class and color, use and abuse of black women, the role of the white mistress, and mobility. Northup's narrative documents most of these aspects of slave life through a unique perspective as a man who was forcibly removed from a life of freedom in the North to enslavement in the Deep South.

Northup chose to dedicate his narrative, titled *Twelve Years a Slave: Narrative of Solomon Northup, Citizen of New York, Kidnapped in Washington City in 1841 and Rescued in 1853, From a Cotton Plantation Near the Red River, in Louisiana*, to Harriet Beecher Stowe. Some historians believe that Northup's narrative may have attempted to revise aspects of Stowe's novel, *Uncle Tom's Cabin*, since they were published a year apart. Another comparison is frequently made between Northup's narrative and the *Narrative of the Life of Frederick Douglass*, published in 1845. Whereas Douglass uses the model of "rags to riches" as the reader follows his life from his enslavement to his eventual

freedom and economic self-sufficiency, Northup starts with these freedoms and takes his reader on his own downward journey into enslavement. Upon reading Northup's narrative, Douglass stated, "Think of it: For thirty years a *man*, with all a man's hopes, fears and aspirations ... then for twelve years a *thing*, a chattel personal, classed with mules and horses.... Oh! it is horrible. It chills the blood to think that such are."

♦ **The Domestic Slave Trade: Slave Pen and Slave Auction**

Chapter VI in *Twelve Years a Slave* discusses Northup's experience in going from a slave pen to a slave auction after his kidnapping in Washington, D.C. In the opening paragraph, Northup introduces the reader to Mr. Theophilus Freeman, a partner of James H. Burch and keeper of the slave pen in New Orleans. Burch was the slave dealer who bought Northup in Washington, D.C., destroyed his freedom papers, and beat him when he insisted that he was a free man. Burch was also responsible for assigning him his new name, Platt, along with the story that he was an escaped slave from Georgia. The District of Columbia contained many prisons full of slaves without travel passes and free blacks without proper certificates proving their freedom. Even before the Fugitive Slave Act of 1850, state and regional laws permitted slave dealers to round up potential fugitive slaves and offer them for sale to willing slave owners. The penalty was $800, but the fines were no deterrence to slavers. In an earlier chapter, Northup notes the irony of this location as the seat of the national government where such liberties could be denied. As he is being led out of Washington on his way to the slave auction in New Orleans, Northup notes the hypocrisy between the Founders' desire to guarantee the right to life, liberty, and the pursuit of happiness, as found in the Declaration of Independence, and his imminent enslavement.

In the first paragraph of chapter VI, Northup begins with a description of Freeman as amiable and pious-hearted, but he continues with zoo imagery, where Freeman goes "out among his animals" and proceeds to beat them into submission to prepare them to be sold. Northup seems careful to describe the people he encounters. He gives them the benefit of the doubt, by offering both positive and negative descriptions of their behavior toward him and others. Critics of his narrative have suggested that Northup is too gentle in some of his descriptions and therefore fails to adequately illustrate the cruelties of slavery. Others think that he did a good job of illustrating the psychological and physical effects of forced servitude while pointing out the amenities that made his life endurable.

In the third paragraph, Northup describes how he and the rest of those captive in the slave pen are paraded out to impress future owners. He explains how Freeman discovers that Northup can play the violin and then orders him to play so the others might dance. Earlier in the narrative, Northup had described his love for the violin, which he had played since his youth, as a source of amusement, consolation, and income. Now his musical talent is being exploited as part of his own degradation. In later chapters of the narrative, he would explain that once he had settled on the

"I expected to die. Though there was little in the prospect before me worth living for, the near approach of death appalled me. I thought I could have been resigned to yield up my life in the bosom of my family, but to expire in the midst of strangers, under such circumstances, was a bitter reflection."

(Paragraph 12)

"I have seen mothers kissing for the last time the faces of their dead offspring; I have seen them looking down into the grave, as the earth fell with a dull sound upon their coffins, hiding them from their eyes forever; but never have I seen such an exhibition of intense, unmeasured, and unbounded grief, as when Eliza was parted from her child."

(Paragraph 17)

"She was no common slave.... To a large share of intelligence which she possessed, was added a general knowledge and information on most subjects.... She had been lifted up into the regions of a higher life. Freedom—freedom for herself and for her offspring, for many years had been her cloud by day, her pillar of fire by night.... In an unexpected moment she was utterly overwhelmed with disappointment and despair."

(Paragraph 27)

Louisiana plantation, his talent gained him a degree of mobility when he played for dances at neighboring plantations.

In the fourth and fifth paragraphs, Northup portrays the dehumanizing treatment of slaves in the pen and what it felt like to be bartered as someone's property. He describes in detail how they were examined, some of them right down to their naked bodies, and how slave buyers would look for scars on slaves' bodies as a way to gauge their level of rebelliousness. When a gentleman begins bargaining with Freeman, it becomes clear that the more Freeman emphasizes Northup's talents, the higher the price will be for his sale.

♦ **Slave Culture**

Although Northup thinks himself unique among his fellow slaves, his narrative describes a distinct slave culture, as William Nichols puts it, of "close friendships, secret conversations, folk humor, communally shared anger, and what might be called a mythology of escape and rebellion." This culture was shared by all slaves, regardless of where they worked and lived. Northup discusses many aspects of the cultural life of slaves throughout his narrative, but in chapter VI he focuses on the importance of family, health, and religion.

The importance of family becomes evident in Northup's description of a mother's response to her children's sale. In the sixth paragraph, we are reintroduced to two children, Randall and Emily, and their mother, Eliza, who are waiting with Northup to be purchased by southern plantation owners. Despite her pleadings and promises to be "the most faithful slave that ever lived" if she could be sold together with her two children, Freeman refuses to accommodate her, and Randall is sold off separately. Freeman calls her "a blubbering, bawling wench and order[s] her to go to her place, and behave herself.... or he would give her something to cry about." Later, in paragraph 17, with the prospect of the sale of Eliza without Emily, Eliza's "intense, unmeasured, and unbounded grief" causes her to attempt to physically prevent the sale. This action results in Freeman's inflicting "a heartless blow" to Eliza, which does not check her from imploring him to stop the sale. When the prospective owner agrees to purchase Emily also to keep the family together, Freeman, realizing the desirability of Emily and believing that he could receive more money "for such an extra, handsome, fancy piece as Emily would be," refuses to sell the child. Eliza is sold off, never again to hear from either of her children. Northup's detail in describing Eliza's grief and his depiction of her as "no common slave" with her "natural intelligence" helps the reader understand how powerless slaves were even to protect their young children. In the last paragraph of this chapter, Northup connects lack of freedom with a total loss of hope. Eliza stands for all slave mothers who watched their future generations descend into slavery.

From the moment he realizes he has been kidnapped, Northup understands that survival will be his main concern. In the middle of this chapter, in paragraph 12, he describes his bout with smallpox. Brought to a hospital to receive care, his fear was "to expire in the midst of strangers," but he thought that he "could have been resigned to yield up [his] life in the bosom of [his] family." He dwells on the number of coffins being hauled away to the potters' field, never to be mourned by their loved ones.

Most authors of slave narratives describe religious beliefs, frequently as part of their search for spiritual guidance. Northup accepts religious gospel yet sees the hypocrisy of such gospel being spread by the slaveholders of the Deep South. He feels that religion and freedom go hand in hand and speaks about this topic regularly among his fellow slaves. Northup opens his entire narrative with a poem by William Cowper that questions how slavery has been allowed to exist over time, when God created both master and slave as equals. In the last paragraph of chapter VI he further connects freedom to religion when he discusses Eliza's grief over losing her children. He refers to the biblical Mount Pisgah, where Moses climbed to view the "land of promise." Eliza has evidently also seen a promised land, but with the sale of her children to a different owner all promise has been lost. Religion, it seems, was both a source of hope for the slaves and, as in the story of Moses' leading the formerly enslaved Jews out of Egypt, a connection with their own desire for freedom.

◆ Slave versus Master

The relationship between slave and slave master is not directly addressed in this chapter, but Northup provides a glimpse into this relationship when he discusses the slave dealers who brought him from Washington, D.C., to New Orleans and the potential buyers who attend the auction. In the fourth paragraph, Northup describes the first customer as "very loquacious," even as he is looking over their bodies "precisely as a jockey examines a horse which he is about to barter for or purchase." A slave in the South had a dual role—as a commodity and as a producer of more commodities. In paragraph 15, the slave owner who will eventually purchase Northup is described as "a good-looking man ...[with] something cheerful and attractive in his face, and

in his tone of voice." Northup describes those who have power over him as he sees them; he speaks highly of people when it seems fitting to do so, even about those who are contributing to his enslavement.

Audience

Northup wrote *Twelve Years* to inform the general public about the tragic intricacies of slavery. *Uncle Tom's Cabin*, published a year earlier, had such a strong public response that Northup could be perceived by the historians Charles Twitchell Davis and Henry Louis Gates as "riding on Miss Stowe's coattails to share in her immense notoriety." Northup writes that he wanted to repeat the story of his life so that others could determine whether this "peculiar institution" should be allowed to continue. Because of his frustration over the eventual release of his captors, he also probably wanted other citizens of the United States to see the injustice in criminal proceedings that involved the rights of free blacks and slaves. It would not be until the *Dred Scott* case in 1857 that slaves would hear from the Supreme Court that they had no civil liberties because they were considered property.

Impact

Although Northup's narrative did not have an immediate impact on the course of slavery, it succeeded in giving the American public a unique view of slavery as seen through the eyes of a once-free northern black man. The reliability of slave narratives as sources of historical fact has been questioned in the past; however, most historians now believe that such stories as Northup's and those authored by Henry Bibb and William Wells Brown, among others, are authentic autobiographical statements that shed light on the institution of slavery at a time when the nation was heading toward the Civil War. Coming on the heels of *Uncle Tom's Cabin* during the "Decade of Crisis" before the Civil War, Northup's slave narrative added more controversy to the disputes between the North and the South. Whereas earlier authors moderated their stories about slavery to gain credibility with white audiences, Northup provided his readers with the honest and open truth about the horrors of slavery. It is easy to understand its popularity in this context.

See also First Editorial of the *North Star* (1847); Fugitive Slave Act of 1850; *Dred Scott v. Sandford* (1857).

Further Reading

■ Articles

Corrigan, Mary Beth. "Imaginary Cruelties? A History of the Slave Trade in Washington, D.C." *Washington History* 13, no. 2 (Fall/Winter 2001–2002): 4–27.

Nichols, William W. "Slave Narratives: Dismissed Evidence in the Writing of Southern History." *Phylon* 32, no. 4 (1971): 403–409.

Worley, Sam. "Solomon Northup and the Sly Philosophy of the Slave Pen." *Callaloo* 20, no. 1 (Winter 1997): 243–259.

■ **Books**

Davis, Charles Twitchell, and Henry Louis Gates. *The Slave's Narrative*. New York.: Oxford University Press, 1985.

"A Kidnapped Negro's Wife Petitions for His Freedom, 1852." In *A Documentary History of the Negro People in the United States*, ed. Herbert Aptheker. New York: Citadel Press, 1969.

Osofsky, Gilbert, ed. *Puttin' on Ole Massa: The Slave Narratives of Henry Bibb, William Wells Brown, and Solomon Northup*. New York: Harper & Row, 1969.

Stowe, Harriet Beecher. *A Key to Uncle Tom's Cabin: Presenting the Original Facts and Documents upon Which the Story Is Founded*. Boston: J. P. Jewett, 1854.

■ **Web Sites**

"The Kidnapping Case. Narrative of the Seizure and Recovery of Solomon Northup. Interesting Disclosures." Documenting the American South Web site.
    http://docsouth.unc.edu/fpn/northup/support1.html.

"New York and Slavery: Complicity and Resistance." New York State Council for the Social Studies.
    http://www.nyscss.org/resources/publications/new-york-and-slavery.aspx.

"North American Slave Narratives." Documenting the American South Web site.
    http://docsouth.unc.edu/neh/texts.html.

—Wendy Thowdis

Questions for Further Study

1. Why has the decade of the 1850s been called the "Decade of Crisis"?

2. In the early and mid-nineteenth century, slave narratives became a widely read form of literature. Why do you believe Americans were so interested in reading these narratives?

3. Compare Northup's account with that of William Wells Brown in "Slavery As It Is." What experiences did the two men share? Where there any differences in their experiences?

4. What were some of the characteristics of "slave culture"? Why do you think these cultural characteristics among slaves emerged? What function did they serve?

5. What was Northup's attitude to religion, particularly Christianity as it was practiced in the antebellum South?

TWELVE YEARS A SLAVE: NARRATIVE OF SOLOMON NORTHUP

Chapter VI.

The very amiable, pious-hearted Mr. Theophilus Freeman, partner or consignee of James H. Burch, and keeper of the slave pen in New-Orleans, was out among his animals early in the morning. With an occasional kick of the older men and women, and many a sharp crack of the whip about the ears of the younger slaves, it was not long before they were all astir, and wide awake. Mr. Theophilus Freeman bustled about in a very industrious manner, getting his property ready for the sales-room, intending, no doubt, to do that day a rousing business.

In the first place we were required to wash thoroughly, and those with beards, to shave. We were then furnished with a new suit each, cheap, but clean. The men had hat, coat, shirt, pants and shoes; the women frocks of calico, and handkerchiefs to bind about their heads. We were now conducted into a large room in the front part of the building to which the yard was attached, in order to be properly trained, before the admission of customers. The men were arranged on one side of the room, the women on the other. The tallest was placed at the head of the row, then the next tallest, and so on in the order of their respective heights. Emily was at the foot of the line of women. Freeman charged us to remember our places; exhorted us to appear smart and lively,—sometimes threatening, and again, holding out various inducements. During the day he exercised us in the art of "looking smart," and of moving to our places with exact precision.

After being fed, in the afternoon, we were again paraded and made to dance. Bob, a colored boy, who had some time belonged to Freeman, played on the violin. Standing near him, I made bold to inquire if he could play the "Virginia Reel." He answered he could not, and asked me if I could play. Replying in the affirmative, he handed me the violin. I struck up a tune, and finished it. Freeman ordered me to continue playing, and seemed well pleased, telling Bob that I far excelled him—a remark that seemed to grieve my musical companion very much.

Next day many customers called to examine Freeman's "new lot." The latter gentleman was very loquacious, dwelling at much length upon our several good points and qualities. He would make us hold up our heads, walk briskly back and forth, while customers would feel of our hands and arms and bodies, turn us about, ask us what we could do, make us open our mouths and show our teeth, precisely as a jockey examines a horse which he is about to barter for or purchase. Sometimes a man or woman was taken back to the small house in the yard, stripped, and inspected more minutely. Scars upon a slave's back were considered evidence of a rebellious or unruly spirit, and hurt his sale.

One old gentleman, who said he wanted a coachman, appeared to take a fancy to me. From his conversation with Burch, I learned he was a resident in the city. I very much desired that he would buy me, because I conceived it would not be difficult to make my escape from New-Orleans on some northern vessel. Freeman asked him fifteen hundred dollars for me. The old gentleman insisted it was too much, as times were very hard. Freeman, however, declared that I was sound and healthy, of a good constitution, and intelligent. He made it a point to enlarge upon my musical attainments. The old gentleman argued quite adroitly that there was nothing extraordinary about the nigger, and finally, to my regret, went out, saying he would call again. During the day, however, a number of sales were made. David and Caroline were purchased together by a Natchez planter. They left us, grinning broadly, and in the most happy state of mind, caused by the fact of their not being separated. Lethe was sold to a planter of Baton Rouge, her eyes flashing with anger as she was led away.

The same man also purchased Randall. The little fellow was made to jump, and run across the floor, and perform many other feats, exhibiting his activity and condition. All the time the trade was going on, Eliza was crying aloud, and wringing her hands. She besought the man not to buy him, unless he also bought her self and Emily. She promised, in that case, to be the most faithful slave that ever lived. The man answered that he could not afford it, and then Eliza burst into a paroxysm of grief, weeping plaintively. Freeman turned round to her, savagely, with his whip in his uplifted hand, ordering her to stop her noise, or he would flog her. He would not have such work—such snivelling; and unless she ceased that minute, he would take her to the yard and give her a hundred lashes. Yes, he would take the nonsense out of her pretty quick—if he didn't, might he be dead. Eliza shrunk before him, and tried to wipe away her tears, but it was all in vain. She wanted to be with her children, she said, the little time she had to live. All the frowns and threats of Freeman, could not wholly silence the afflicted mother. She kept on begging and beseeching them, most piteously not to separate the three. Over and over again she told them how she loved her boy. A great many times she repeated her former promises—how very faithful and obedient she would be; how hard she would labor day and night, to the last moment of her life, if he would only buy them all together. But it was of no avail; the man could not afford it. The bargain was agreed upon, and Randall must go alone. Then Eliza ran to him; embraced him passionately; kissed him again and again; told him to remember her—all the while her tears falling in the boy's face like rain.

Freeman damned her, calling her a blubbering, bawling wench, and ordered her to go to her place, and behave herself; and be somebody. He swore he wouldn't stand such stuff but a little longer. He would soon give her something to cry about, if she was not mighty careful, and that she might depend upon.

The planter from Baton Rouge, with his new purchases, was ready to depart.

"Don't cry, mama. I will be a good boy. Don't cry," said Randall, looking back, as they passed out of the door.

What has become of the lad, God knows. It was a mournful scene indeed. I would have cried myself if I had dared.

That night, nearly all who came in on the brig Orleans, were taken ill. They complained of violent pain in the head and back. Little Emily—a thing unusual with her—cried constantly. In the morning, a physician was called in, but was unable to determine the nature of our complaint. While examining me, and asking questions touching my symptoms, I gave it as my opinion that it was an attack of smallpox—mentioning the fact of Robert's death as the reason of my belief. It might be so indeed, he thought, and he would send for the head physician of the hospital. Shortly, the head physician came—a small, light-haired man, whom they called Dr. Carr. He pronounced it small-pox, whereupon there was much alarm throughout the yard. Soon after Dr. Carr left, Eliza, Emmy, Harry and myself were put into a hack and driven to the hospital a large white marble building, standing on the outskirts of the city. Harry and I were placed in a room in one of the upper stories. I

became very sick. For three days I was entirely blind. While lying in this state one day, Bob came in, saying to Dr. Carr that Freeman had sent him over to inquire how we were getting on. Tell him, said the doctor, that Platt is very bad, but that if he survives until nine o'clock, he may recover.

I expected to die. Though there was little in the prospect before me worth living for, the near approach of death appalled me. I thought I could have been resigned to yield up my life in the bosom of my family, but to expire in the midst of strangers, under such circumstances, was a bitter reflection.

There were a great number in the hospital, of both sexes, and of all ages. In the rear of the building coffins were manufactured. When one died, the bell tolled—a signal to the undertaker to come and bear away the body to the potter's field. Many times, each day and night, the tolling bell sent forth its melancholy voice, announcing another death. But my time had not yet come. The crisis having passed, I began to revive, and at the end of two weeks and two days, returned with Harry to the pen, bearing upon my face the effects of the malady, which to this day continues to disfigure it. Eliza and Emily were also brought back next day in a hack, and again were we paraded in the sales-room, for the inspection and examination of purchasers. I still indulged the hope that the old gentleman in search of a coachman would call again, as he had promised, and purchase me. In that event I felt an abiding confidence that I would soon regain my liberty. Customer after customer entered, but the old gentleman never made his appearance.

At length, one day, while we were in the yard, Freeman came out and ordered us to our places, in the great room. A gentleman was waiting for us as we entered, and inasmuch as he will be often mentioned in the progress of this narrative, a description of his personal appearance, and my estimation of his character, at first sight, may not be out of place.

He was a man above the ordinary height, somewhat bent and stooping forward. He was a good-looking man, and appeared to have reached about the middle age of life. There was nothing repulsive in his presence; but on the other hand, there was something cheerful and attractive in his face, and in his tone of voice. The finer elements were all kindly mingled in his breast, as any one could see. He moved about among us, asking many questions, as to what we could do, and what labor we had been accustomed to; if we thought we would like to live with him, and would be good boys if he would buy us, and other interrogatories of like character.

After some further inspection, and conversation touching prices, he finally offered Freeman one thousand dollars for me, nine hundred for Harry, and seven hundred for Eliza. Whether the small-pox had depreciated our value, or from what cause Freeman had concluded to fall five hundred dollars from the price I was before held at, I cannot say. At any rate, after a little shrewd reflection, he announced his acceptance of the offer.

As soon as Eliza heard it, she was in an agony again. By this time she had become haggard and hollow-eyed with sickness and with sorrow. It would be a relief if I could consistently pass over in silence the scene that now ensued. It recalls memories more mournful and affecting than any language can portray. I have seen mothers kissing for the last time the faces of their dead offspring; I have seen them looking down into the grave, as the earth fell with a dull sound upon their coffins, hiding them from their eyes forever; but never have I seen such an exhibition of intense, unmeasured, and unbounded grief, as when Eliza was parted from her child. She broke from her place in the line of women, and rushing down where Emily was standing, caught her in her arms. The child, sensible of some impending danger, instinctively fastened her hands around her mother's neck, and nestled her little head upon her bosom. Freeman sternly ordered her to be quiet, but she did not heed him. He caught her by the arm and pulled her rudely, but she only clung the closer to the child. Then, with a volley of great oaths, he struck her such a heartless blow, that she staggered backward, and was like to fall. Oh! how piteously then did she beseech and beg and pray that they might not be separated. Why could they not be purchased together? Why not let her have one of her dear children? "Mercy, mercy, master!" she cried, falling on her knees. "Please, master, buy Emily. I can never work any if she is taken from me: I will die."

Freeman interfered again, but, disregarding him, she still plead most earnestly, telling how Randall had been taken from her—how she never him see him again, and now it was too bad—oh, God! it was too bad, too cruel, to take her away from Emily—her pride—her only darling, that could not live, it was so young, without its mother!

Finally, after much more of supplication, the purchaser of Eliza stepped forward, evidently affected, and said to Freeman he would buy Emily, and asked him what her price was.

"What is her *price*? *Buy* her?" was the responsive interrogatory of Theophilus Freeman. And instantly answering his own inquiry, he added, "I won't sell her. She's not for sale."

The man remarked he was not in need of one so young—that it would be of no profit to him, but since the mother was so fond of her, rather than see them separated, he would pay a reasonable price. But to this humane proposal Freeman was entirely deaf. He would not sell her then on any account whatever. There were heaps and piles of money to be made of her, he said, when she was a few years older. There were men enough in New-Orleans who would give five thousand dollars for such an extra, handsome, fancy piece as Emily would be, rather than not get her. No, no, he would not sell her then. She was a beauty—a picture—a doll—one of the regular bloods—none of your thick-lipped, bullet-headed, cotton-picking niggers—if she was might he be d—d.

When Eliza heard Freeman's determination not to part with Emily, she became absolutely frantic.

"I will *not* go without her. They shall *not* take her from me," she fairly shrieked, her shrieks commingling with the loud and angry voice of Freeman, commanding her to be silent.

Meantime Harry and myself had been to the yard and returned with our blankets, and were at the front door ready to leave. Our purchaser stood near us, gazing at Eliza with an expression indicative of regret at having bought her at the expense of so much sorrow. We waited some time, when, finally, Freeman, out of patience, tore Emily from her mother by main force, the two clinging to each other with all their might.

"Don't leave me, mama—don't leave me," screamed the child, as its mother was pushed harshly forward; "Don't leave me—come back, mama," she still cried, stretching forth her little arms imploringly. But she cried in vain. Out of the door and into the street we were quickly hurried. Still we could hear her calling to her mother, "Come back—don't leave me—come back, mama," until her infant voice grew faint and still more faint, and gradually died away as distance intervened, and finally was wholly lost.

Eliza never after saw or heard of Emily or Randall. Day nor night, however, were they ever absent from her memory. In the cotton field, in the cabin, always and everywhere, she was talking of them—often *to* them, as if they were actually present. Only when absorbed in that illusion, or asleep, did she ever have a moment's comfort afterwards.

She was no common slave, as has been said. To a large share of natural intelligence which she possessed, was added a general knowledge and information on most subjects. She had enjoyed opportunities such as are afforded to very few of her oppressed class. She had been lifted up into the regions of a higher life. Freedom—freedom for herself and for her offspring, for many years had been her cloud by day, her pillar of fire by night. In her pilgrimage through the wilderness of bondage, with eyes fixed upon that hope-inspiring beacon, she had at length ascended to "the top of Pisgah," and beheld "the land of promise." In an unexpected moment she was utterly overwhelmed with disappointment and despair. The glorious vision of liberty faded from her sight as they led her away into captivity. Now "she weepeth sore in the night, and tears are on her cheeks: all her friends have dealt treacherously with her: they have become her enemies."

Glossary

Pisgah	In the Christian Old Testament book of Deuteronomy, the name of a mountain in Palestine, probably Mount Nebo, from which Moses looks out over the "land of promise"
potter's field	a burial place for criminals, paupers, and indigent people
"she weepeth sore in the night …"	from the Christian Old Testament book of Lamentations, chapter 1, verse 2

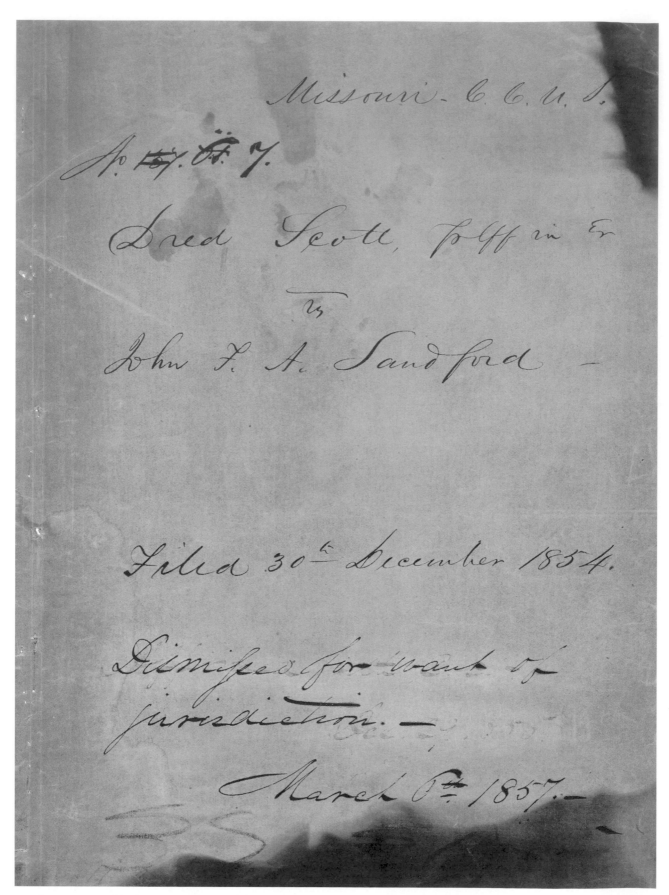

Dred Scott v. Sandford (National Archives and Records Administration)

DRED SCOTT V. SANDFORD

"[African Americans] are not included, and were not intended to be included, under the word 'citizens' in the Constitution."

Overview

In March 1857 Chief Justice Roger B. Taney announced the opinion of the U.S. Supreme Court in *Dred Scott v. John F. A. Sandford*, which was the Court's most important decision ever issued on slavery. The decision had a dramatic effect on American politics as well as law. The case involved a Missouri slave named Dred Scott who claimed to be free because his master had taken him to what was then the Wisconsin Territory and is today the state of Minnesota. In the Missouri Compromise (also known as the Compromise of 1820), Congress declared that there would be no slavery north of the state of Missouri. Thus, Scott claimed to be free because he had lived in a federal territory where slavery was not allowed. In an opinion that was more than fifty pages long, Chief Justice Taney held that Scott was still a slave, that the Missouri Compromise was unconstitutional, and that Congress had no power to ban slavery from a federal territory. In a part of the decision that shocked many northerners, Chief Justice Taney also held that blacks could never be citizens of the United States and that they had no rights under the Constitution. With notorious bluntness, Taney declared that blacks were "so far inferior, that they had no rights which the white man was bound to respect." The decision was criticized by many northerners and led many to support the new Republican Party. While it is an exaggeration to say the case caused the Civil War, Chief Justice Taney's decision certainly inflamed sectional tensions. It also helped lead to the nomination and election of Abraham Lincoln in 1860, which in turn led to secession and the war.

Context

In the Northwest Ordinance of 1787, the Congress, under the Articles of Confederation, banned slavery from all of the territories north and west of the Ohio River. This area, known as the Northwest Territory, would ultimately become the states of Ohio, Indiana, Illinois, Michigan, and Wisconsin. At the time, the western boundary of the United States was the Mississippi River. The territory west of the Mississippi belonged to Spain.

In 1802 Spain ceded its territories north of Mexico to France, and in 1803 the United States acquired all this land through the Louisiana Purchase. Most of the Louisiana Purchase territory was directly west of the Ohio River and north of the point where the Ohio flowed into the Mississippi. In 1812 Louisiana entered the Union as a slave state without any controversy. When Missouri sought admission to the Union in 1818 as a slave state, however, a number of members of Congress from the North objected on the ground that Missouri should be governed by the Northwest Ordinance. This led to a protracted two-year debate over the status of slavery in Missouri. In the end Congress accepted a compromise developed by Representative Henry Clay of Kentucky. Known as the Missouri Compromise, the law allowed Missouri to enter the Union as a slave state and admitted Maine as a free state. The law also prohibited slavery north and west of Missouri.

At the time of these debates Dred Scott was a slave in Virginia. In 1830 his master, Peter Blow, moved to St. Louis, taking Dred Scott with him. In 1832 Peter Blow died, and shortly after that Dred Scott was sold to Captain John Emerson, a U.S. Army surgeon. In 1833 Emerson was sent to Fort Armstrong, which was located on the site of the modern-day city of Rock Island, Illinois. Scott might have claimed his freedom while at Fort Armstrong because Illinois was a free state. Under the accepted rule of law at the time, slaves could usually become free if their masters voluntarily took them to a free state. Indeed, as early as 1824 the Missouri Supreme Court had freed a slave named Winny because her master had taken her to Illinois. In 1836 the Missouri Supreme Court freed another slave woman, Rachel, because her master, who was in the army, had taken her to forts in present-day Michigan and Minnesota. However, Scott, who was illiterate, probably did not know he could be freed, and he made no effort to gain his freedom at this time.

In 1836 the army sent Emerson to Fort Snelling in what is today the city of St. Paul, Minnesota. At the time, this area was called the Wisconsin Territory, and slavery was illegal there under the Missouri Compromise. Once again, Scott might have claimed his freedom because of his resi-

Time Line

1795–1800	■ Dred Scott is born in Virginia. The exact date and year are unknown.
1821	■ Missouri enters the Union as a slave state under the Missouri Compromise, which bans slavery north and west of Missouri.
1830	■ Peter Blow moves to St. Louis with his slave Dred Scott.
1831	■ **January 1** In Boston the abolitionist William Lloyd Garrison begins to publish the *Liberator*, the first successful abolitionist newspaper in the United States. ■ **August 21** In Southampton County, Virginia, Nat Turner leads the bloodiest slave rebellion in American history, leaving white southerners deeply shaken as more than fifty whites and about one hundred blacks die.
1832	■ Peter Blow, Dred Scott's owner, dies in St. Louis. ■ Captain John Emerson, a U.S. Army surgeon, purchases Dred Scott from the estate of Peter Blow.
1833	■ **December 1** Emerson is assigned to Fort Armstrong, on the present-day site of Rock Island, Illinois. He brings Dred Scott with him.
1836	■ **May 4** Emerson transfers to Fort Snelling, bringing Dred Scott with him.
1837	■ **November** Emerson transfers to Fort Jessup in Louisiana, but he leaves Dred Scott and his wife at Fort Snelling, where they are rented out.

dence in a free jurisdiction, but he did not. From 1836 to 1840 Scott lived at Fort Snelling, at Fort Jessup in Louisiana, and then again at Fort Snelling. During this time he married a slave named Harriet, who was then owned by Lawrence Taliaferro, the Indian agent at Fort Snelling. Taliaferro either sold or gave Harriet to Emerson so the newly married couple could be together. In 1838 Emerson married Irene Sanford.

In 1840 Captain Emerson left the Scotts and their two daughters in St. Louis while he went to Florida during the Second Seminole War. In 1842 Emerson left the army and moved to Iowa, a free territory, but he left his slaves and his wife in St. Louis. In 1843 Dr. Emerson died, and ownership of the Scotts passed to Irene Sanford Emerson.

At this point Dred Scott attempted to purchase his freedom with the help of the sons of his former master, Peter Blow. However, Irene Emerson refused to allow Scott to buy his freedom. Thus, in 1846 a lawyer—the first of five who volunteered to help Scott—filed a suit in St. Louis Circuit Court, claiming that he had become free while living in both Illinois and the Wisconsin Territory (Minnesota) and that once free he could not be reenslaved when he returned to Missouri. By this time there had been numerous cases on the issue in the Missouri courts, and usually slaves who had lived in free states or territories were declared free. For technical reasons, however, Dred Scott did not get his hearing until 1850, about four years after he first sued for freedom. At that point a jury of twelve white men, sitting in the slave state of Missouri, declared Scott and his family to be free.

This should have ended the case, but Irene Emerson appealed to the Missouri Supreme Court in an effort to retain her property. The Scotts were a valuable asset. In addition, while the case had been pending, the Court had hired out the Scotts and kept their wages in an account. Thus, Irene Emerson was trying to keep four slaves plus the wages of Dred and Harriet for the previous four years.

Under the existing precedents, Irene Emerson should not have held out much hope that she would win her case. However, a recent amendment to the Missouri Constitution provided for the election of the state supreme court, and in 1851 a new court took office. Two of the new justices were adamantly proslavery. It therefore seemed like the right time for Mrs. Emerson to challenge the decisions that had led to Scott's freedom.

In 1852 the Missouri Supreme Court, by a two-to-one vote, reversed the decision freeing Dred Scott. Reflecting his proslavery sentiments and his hostility to the growing antislavery movement in the North, Justice William Scott (who was not related to Dred Scott) declared that the state would no longer follow its own precedents on slavery. This decision revolutionized Missouri law, but it was consistent with decisions in some Deep South states, which had also abandoned the idea that slaves could become free if they were taken to free states.

Dred Scott's quest for freedom should have ended here, because there was no higher court where he could appeal the decision. Under American law at the time, Scott had no grounds for appealing to the U.S. Supreme Court because no constitutional issue had been raised in the case. The federal courts did not have jurisdiction over the status of slaves within the states.

By this time, however, Mrs. Emerson had moved east and married another physician, Dr. Calvin Chaffee of Springfield, Massachusetts. She could not take her slaves with her because slavery was illegal in Massachusetts. Moreover, her new husband was a firm opponent of slavery, and any discussion of her property interest in the Scotts might have undermined her new marriage. Thus, she either gave or sold the Scotts to her brother, John F. A. Sanford, who lived in New York City but had business interests in both St. Louis and New York. (He spelled his last name Sanford, but the clerk of the U.S. Supreme Court would add an extra "d" to his name, and thus the case would be known as *Dred Scott v. Sandford*.)

Sanford's residence in New York opened up the possibility that Dred Scott could now reopen his case in a federal court. Under the Constitution, citizens of one state are allowed to sue citizens of another state. This is known as diversity jurisdiction because there is a diversity (or difference) in the state citizenship of the people involved in the lawsuit. The framers of the Constitution believed that it was necessary for federal courts to be able to hear suits between citizens of different states because otherwise the people would fear that the courts of one state would favor the state's own citizens. The federal courts presumably would be neutral.

Thus, in 1853 Scott's newest lawyer filed a suit in federal court against John Sanford. Scott alleged that he was a "citizen" of Missouri and sued Sanford for assault and battery, asking for $10,000 in damages. Sanford responded with something called a plea in abatement. In this response Sanford argued that the court should abate (stop) the case immediately because, as Sanford argued, Dred Scott "was not a citizen of the State of Missouri, as alleged in his declaration, being a negro of African descent, whose ancestors were of pure African blood, and who were brought into this country and sold as slaves." In essence, Sanford argued that no black person could be a citizen of Missouri, so even if Dred Scott was free, the federal court did not have jurisdiction to hear the case.

In 1854 U.S. District Judge Robert Wells rejected this argument. He held that *if* Dred Scott was free, then he should be considered a citizen for the purpose of diversity jurisdiction. This was the first and only victory Dred Scott had in the federal courts. After hearing all the evidence, Wells decided that Scott's status had to be determined by applying the law of Missouri. Since the Missouri Supreme Court had already held that Scott was not free, Judge Wells ruled against Scott. This set the stage for the case to go to the U.S. Supreme Court. In the December 1855 term the Supreme Court heard arguments in the case, but in the spring of 1856, with a presidential election looming, the Court declined to decide the case and instead asked for new arguments in the next term, beginning in December 1856, which was after the election.

Time Line

1838

■ **February 6**
Emerson marries Irene Sanford and brings the Scotts to Louisiana.

■ **July**
Emerson is reassigned to Fort Snelling, and the Scotts accompany him.

1840

■ Emerson is reassigned to Florida, and the Scotts are left in St. Louis with Irene Emerson.

1843

■ **December**
Emerson dies, and ownership of the Scotts passes to Irene Emerson.

1846

■ Dred Scott files suit to gain freedom in St. Louis Circuit Court; he loses the suit on a technicality.

1848

■ The Missouri Supreme Court grants Dred Scott the right to have a new trial to test his freedom.

■ **February 2**
The Treaty of Guadalupe Hidalgo ends the Mexican-American War.

1850

■ A jury of twelve white men in St. Louis, Missouri, declares Dred Scott free, based on his residence in Illinois and at Fort Snelling

■ Congress passes a series of statutes collectively known as the Compromise of 1850.

■ **November**
Irene Emerson marries Dr. Calvin Chaffee of Springfield, Massachusetts. Her brother, John F. A. Sanford, continues to defend her claim to Dred Scott.

1852

■ In *Scott v. Emerson*, the Missouri Supreme Court overturns nearly three decades of precedents and reverses Dred Scott's victory in the lower court.

Time Line

1853
- Dred Scott initiates a new suit, against John F. A. Sanford, in the U.S. Circuit Court for Missouri.

1854
- U.S. Judge Robert Wells allows Dred Scott to sue in federal court but then rules against him. Scott remains a slave.

1856
- **December**
The U.S. Supreme Court hears arguments in the Dred Scott case.

1857
- **March 4**
James Buchanan is inaugurated as president. In his address he urges all Americans to support the outcome of the pending case on slavery in the territories (the Dred Scott case).

- **March 6**
Chief Justice Taney announces his decision in *Dred Scott v. Sandford.*

- **May 26**
Taylor Blow, the son of Peter Blow, formally manumits the Scotts, having purchased them from John Sanford after the Supreme Court decision.

1858
- **September 17**
Dred Scott dies in St. Louis from tuberculosis.

While Dred Scott's case was making its way through the courts, slavery had emerged as the central issue of American politics. In 1820 the Missouri Compromise had settled the issue of slavery in the territories. Starting in 1836, however, the Republic of Texas requested to become part of the United States. Presidents Andrew Jackson and Martin Van Buren resisted accepting Texas because they knew that bringing Texas into the Union would reopen the issue of slavery in the West and probably would lead to a war with Mexico. In late 1844 President John Tyler, who was coming to the end of his term, managed to get Congress to accept Texas, which entered the Union in 1845. This immediately let to a confrontation with Mexico, which had never recognized Texas independence. In April 1846 American and Mexican troops clashed, and by May the two nations were at war. The war ended in September 1847, when General Zachary Taylor entered Mexico City.

In the Treaty of Guadalupe Hidalgo, signed on February 2, 1848, Mexico recognized the Texas annexation and ceded all of its northern lands, which included all or part of the present-day states of California, Arizona, New Mexico, Nevada, Utah, and Colorado.

The acquisition of this territory, known as the Mexican Cession, led to a crisis in the Union as the nation debated the status of slavery in the new territories. Congress finally broke the deadlock with a series of statutes collectively known as the Compromise of 1850. These laws allowed slavery in the new territories but admitted California as a free state. This compromise did not satisfy the South, which wanted to repeal the restrictions on slavery in the Missouri Compromise. This was accomplished in 1854 with the passage of the Kansas-Nebraska Act. This law allowed the creation of territorial governments in the territories west and northwest of Missouri—including the present-day states of Kansas, Nebraska, South Dakota, and North Dakota—without regard to slavery. The law allowed the settlers of these territories to decide for themselves whether or not to allow slavery.

The Kansas-Nebraska Act had two immediate results. First was a revolution in politics and the emergence of a new political organization that became the Republican Party. By 1856 it was the dominant party in the North. Its main goal was to prevent the spread of slavery into the territories. Meanwhile, in Kansas a small civil war broke out between supporters and opponents of slavery. Known as Bleeding Kansas, the conflict claimed more than fifty lives in 1855 and 1856.

In 1856 the new Republican Party nominated John C. Frémont for the presidency. Frémont, nicknamed "the Pathfinder," was a national hero for his explorations in the West and his role in securing California during the Mexican-American War. Running on a slogan of "Free Soil, Free Labor, Free Speech, Free Men," Frémont and the new party carried eleven northern states. This was not enough to win but was nevertheless a very impressive showing for a brand-new party. The winning candidate, James Buchanan, was a Pennsylvanian but strongly sympathetic to the South and slavery. He supported opening all of the territories to slavery. In his inaugural address Buchanan declared that the issue of slavery in the territories was a question for the judicial branch and urged Americans to accept the outcome of the Court's pending ruling in the Dred Scott case. Buchanan could so confidently take this position because two justices on the court, Robert C. Grier and John Catron, had told him how the case would be decided. Two days later Chief Justice Taney announced the decision. Rather than settling the issue of slavery in the territories, the decision only made it more troublesome and controversial.

About the Author

Roger Brooke Taney (pronounced "Tawnee") had a long and distinguished career in American politics and law. He was born in 1777 into a wealthy slaveholding family on the eastern shore of Maryland. He served in the Maryland legislature as a Federalist, but in the 1820s he became a supporter of Andrew Jackson. He was attorney general in Jackson's administration and drafted what became Jackson's famous veto in 1831 of the bill to recharter the Second Bank of the United States. As a young lawyer he freed his own slaves because he had no use for them, but he never opposed slavery or favored abolition. As attorney general he prepared a detailed opinion for President Jackson asserting that free blacks were not entitled to passports and could never be considered citizens of the United States. Taney served briefly as secretary of the treasury, overseeing the removal of deposits from the Bank of the United States.

In 1837 Taney became chief justice of the United States, a position he held until 1864, longer than any other chief justice except John Marshall. As chief justice he was a staunch supporter of slavery and the interests of the southern states. By 1857, when he delivered his opinion in Dred Scott's case, Taney was deeply hostile to abolitionism and vigorously proslavery. In 1860 and 1861 he tacitly supported secession and opposed all of President Lincoln's efforts to maintain the Union, suppress the insurrection, and end slavery. When Taney died in 1864, the U.S. Senate refused to authorize a statue for him, as it had for other deceased justices. In arguing against the proposal for a statue, Senator Charles Sumner of Massachusetts declared that Taney had "administered justice at last wickedly, and degraded the judiciary of the country, and degraded the age." He predicted that "the name is to be hooted down the pages of history."

Explanation and Analysis of the Document

All nine justices wrote an opinion in this case. The opinions range in length from Justice Robert C. Grier's half-page concurrence to Justice Benjamin R. Curtis's seventy-page dissent. Chief Justice Taney's "Opinion of the Court" is fifty-four pages long. The nine opinions, along with a handful of pages summarizing the lawyers' arguments, consume 260 pages of *United States Supreme Court Reports*. In his opinion Chief Justice Taney declares that the Missouri Compromise is unconstitutional. This was only the second Supreme Court decision to strike down a federal law. The only other antebellum decision to strike down a federal act—*Marbury v. Madison* (1803)—held unconstitutional a minor portion of the Judiciary Act of 1789. Here the Court struck down a major statute. In his opinion Chief Justice Taney discusses three issues: black citizenship, the constitutionality of the Missouri Compromise, and the power of Congress to ban slavery from the territories. First he examines whether the question of citizenship is legitimately before the Court. The lower federal court had assumed that if Dred Scott was free, he was a citizen of the state where he lived, and he had a right to sue a citizen of another state in federal court. Taney rejects this conclusion. Since the 1830s he had believed that blacks could never be citizens of the United States. Now he had a chance to make his

An 1887 engraving of Dred Scott (Library of Congress)

views the law. Taney bases his argument entirely on race. In a very inaccurate history of the founding period, which ignored the fact that free blacks had voted in a number of states at the time of the ratification of the Constitution, Taney asserts that at the founding of the nation blacks, whether enslaved or free, were without any political or legal rights. He declares that blacks

> are not included, and were not intended to be included, under the word "citizens" in the Constitution, and can therefore claim none of the rights and privileges which that instrument provides for and secures to citizens of the United States. On the contrary, they were at that time [1787] considered as a subordinate and inferior class of beings, who had been subjugated by the dominant race, and, whether emancipated or not, yet remained subject to their authority, and had no rights or privileges but such as those who held the power and the Government might choose to grant them.

In one of the most notoriously racist statement in American law, Taney declares that blacks are "so far inferior, that they had no rights which the white man was bound to respect." He therefore concludes that blacks could never be citizens of the United States, even if they were born in the United States. Taney then turns to the issue of slavery in the territories. Here he discusses the constitutionality of

Justice Roger B. Taney (Library of Congress)

the Missouri Compromise and the status of slavery in the territories. His goal is to settle, in favor of the South, the status of slavery in the territories. To do this, Taney had to overcome two strong arguments in favor of congressional power over slavery in the territories. First was the clause in the Constitution that explicitly gave Congress the power to regulate the territories. Second was the political tradition, dating from the Northwest Ordinance, that Congress had such a power. Taney accomplished this through an examination of two separate provisions of the Constitution: the territories clause and the Fifth Amendment.

The territories clause of the Constitution (Article IV, Section 3, Paragraph 2) provides that "Congress shall have Power to dispose of and make all needful Rules and Regulations respecting the Territory or other Property belonging to the United States." Congress had used this clause to govern the territories, prohibiting slavery in some territories and allowing it in others. As recently as 1854 Congress had passed the Kansas-Nebraska Act, allowing the settlers of a territory to allow or ban slavery as they wished. Almost all Americans assumed that Congress had the power to prohibit slavery in the territories. One American who did not was Chief Justice Taney.

In his opinion Taney interprets the territories clause to apply only to those territories the United States had owned in 1787. Taney writes that the clause is

confined, and was intended to be confined, to the territory which at that time belonged to, or was claimed by, the United States, and was within their boundar-

ies as settled by the treaty with Great Britain, and can have no influence upon a territory afterwards acquired from a foreign Government. It was a special provision for a known and particular territory, and to meet a present emergency, and nothing more.

Few scholars today find this argument even remotely plausible. This was also true in 1857. Justice John Catron, who agreed with Taney on almost every other point, dissented from the claim that Congress could not pass laws to regulate the territories. Nevertheless, Taney asserts that Congress had only the power to provide a minimal government in the territories, but nothing beyond that. Taney implies that allowing Congress to actually govern the territories would be equivalent to "establish[ing] or maintain[ing] colonies bordering on the United States or at a distance, to be ruled and governed at its own pleasure." Taney's argument here is absurd. By 1857 the United States had held some territory (what later became the eastern tip of Minnesota) for the entire period since the adoption of the Constitution without making it a state or treating it as a colony.

The weakness of his argument did not stop Taney, who was determined, as few justices have been, to reach a specific result. His goal was to prohibit the congressional regulation of slavery in the territories, and any argument, it seemed, would do the trick. However, if Congress could not govern the territories, then they would be governed by the settlers. What would happen if the settlers, such as those in Kansas, voted to prohibit slavery? Taney found an answer to this question in the Fifth Amendment to the U.S. Constitution, which prohibits the government from taking private property without due process of law.

Thus, Taney argues that forbidding slavery in the territories violated the due process clause of the Fifth Amendment, which declares that under federal law no person could "be deprived of life, liberty, or property without due process of law." Taney asserts that "an act of Congress which deprives a citizen of the United States of his liberty or property, merely because he came himself or brought his property into a particular Territory of the United States, and who had committed no offence against the laws, could hardly be dignified with the name of due process of law."

This led Taney to assert that slavery was a special form of property with special constitutional protection. Thus he writes:

the right of property in a slave is distinctly and expressly affirmed in the Constitution. The right to traffic in it, like an ordinary article of merchandise and property, was guarantied to the citizens of the United States, in every State that might desire it, for twenty years. And the Government in express terms is pledged to protect it in all future time, if the slave escapes from his owner. This is done in plain words—too plain to be misunderstood. And no word can be found in the Constitution which gives Congress a greater power over slave property, or which entitles property of that kind to less protection than property

"No one, we presume, supposes that any change in public opinion or feeling, in relation to this unfortunate race, in the civilized nations of Europe or in this country, should induce the court to give to the words of the Constitution a more liberal construction in their favor than they were intended to bear when the instrument was framed and adopted."

(Chief Justice Roger Taney, Majority Opinion)

"They [African Americans] are not included, and were not intended to be included, under the word 'citizens' in the Constitution, and can therefore claim none of the rights and privileges which that instrument provides for and secures to citizens of the United States. On the contrary, they were at that time [1787] considered as a subordinate and inferior class of beings, who had been subjugated by the dominant race, and, whether emancipated or not, yet remained subject to their authority, and had no rights or privileges but such as those who held the power and the Government might choose to grant them."

(Chief Justice Roger Taney, Majority Opinion)

"The right of property in a slave is distinctly and expressly affirmed in the Constitution. The right to traffic in it, like an ordinary article of merchandise and property, was guaranteed to the citizens of the United States, in every State that might desire it, for twenty years. And the Government in express terms is pledged to protect it in all future time, if the slave escapes from his owner."

(Chief Justice Roger Taney, Majority Opinion)

"At the time of the ratification of the Articles of Confederation, all free native-born inhabitants of the States of New Hampshire, Massachusetts, New York, New Jersey, and North Carolina, though descended from African slaves, were not only citizens of those States, but such of them as had the other necessary qualifications possessed the franchise of electors, on equal terms with other citizens."

(Justice Benjamin R. Curtis, Dissenting Opinion)

of any other description. The only power conferred is the power coupled with the duty of guarding and protecting the owner in his rights.

This was perhaps Chief Justice Taney's strongest argument. The Constitution of 1787 clearly protected slavery in a number of places. It was an important and unique kind of property, and thus it needed to be protected. Moreover, Taney's argument that all citizens should be able to take their property with them into every federal territory was not wholly wrong. Indeed, the heart of Taney's argument was that slavery was an important part of American society; therefore slave owners had to have equal access to federal lands.

Chief Justice Taney thus declares that any prohibition on slavery in the territories violated the Fifth Amendment. Even the people of a territory could not ban slavery through the territorial legislature. Taney writes, "And if Congress itself cannot do this—if it is beyond the powers conferred on the Federal Government—it will be admitted, we presume, that it could not authorize a Territorial Government to exercise them. It could confer no power on any local Government, established by its authority, to violate the provisions of the Constitution." Like the Missouri Compromise, under Taney's interpretation of the Constitution, popular sovereignty also was unconstitutional.

Six other justices agreed with all or some of Taney's decision. Four were from the South, and two, Samuel Nelson of New York and Robert C. Grier of Pennsylvania, were northern Democrats with southern sympathies. Two justices, John McLean of Ohio and Benjamin R. Curtis of Massachusetts, issued stinging dissents. Both pointed out, at great length, that Taney's history was wrong and that blacks had voted in a number of states at the time of the country's founding. Both justices also pointed out that since African Americans voted for the ratification of the Constitution in 1787, it was hard to argue that they could not be considered citizens of the nation they had helped to create. The dissenters also stressed that since 1787 no one had doubted that Congress could regulate the territories and ban slavery in them. On both grounds they may have had the better historical arguments but not the votes on the Court.

Audience

The main audience for this law was the people of the United States, and particularly the Congress. Chief Justice Taney hoped this decision would forever settle the question of slavery in the territories and stop Congress from trying to ban slavery. He also hoped it would end the conflict in Kansas over slavery, because under this decision the Kansas territorial government could not prohibit slavery.

Impact

Few cases have had such a huge impact on American politics. Most southerners cheered the decision. So did President Buchanan, who hoped the decision would bring peace to Kansas and destroy the Republican Party, since its main platform was prohibiting slavery in the territories. It also undercut Buchanan's rival in the Democratic Party, Senator Stephen A. Douglas. He had been the leading proponent of popular sovereignty in the territories, which would have allowed the settlers in the territories to decide for themselves whether they wanted slavery. This had been the basis of the Kansas-Nebraska Act, which Douglas sponsored. Under *Dred Scott*, however, popular sovereignty was unconstitutional because the territorial governments were prohibited from banning slavery. Douglas would give tacit support for the decision, but it undermined his political strength in the North.

Republicans around the nation attacked the decision. Horace Greeley, the Republican editor of the *New York Tribune*, responded to the decision with outrage, calling Taney's opinion "wicked," "atrocious," and "abominable" and a "collation of false statements and shallow sophistries." The paper's editor thought Taney's decision had no more validity than the opinions that might be expressed in any "Washington bar-room." The *Chicago Tribune* declared that Taney's statements on black citizenship were "inhuman dicta." The black abolitionist Frederick Douglass called it a "devilish decision—this judicial incarnation of wolfishness!" He also believed, however, that the decision would lead more people to oppose slavery. In 1858 Abraham Lincoln, in his "House Divided" speech, attacked the

Questions for Further Study

1. While most Americans find Taney's decision morally wrong, do any of his arguments make sense?

2. Why do you think Dred Scott did not try to gain his freedom when he lived in Illinois or at Fort Snelling?

3. What are the legacies of the decision today? Are there ways in which the ideas of Chief Justice Taney might still be alive in our culture?

decision and warned that if Republicans were not elected to office, the "next Dred Scott decision" would lead to the nationalization of slavery. Lincoln predicted, "We shall *lie down* pleasantly dreaming that the people of *Missouri* are on the verge of making their state *free*; and we shall *awake* to the *reality*, instead that the *Supreme* Court has made *Illinois* a *slave* state." Lincoln was convinced that the "logical conclusion" of Taney's opinion was that "what one master might lawfully do with Dred Scott, in the free state of Illinois, every master might lawfully do with any other *one*, or *one thousand* slaves in Illinois, or in any other free state."

The decision helped make Abraham Lincoln a national figure and led to his nomination and election as president in 1861. The nation would overrule *Dred Scott* with the adoption of the Thirteenth Amendment to the Constitution in 1865, which ended all slavery in the United States, and the Fourteenth Amendment in 1868, which made all people born in the United States citizens of the United States.

See also Thirteenth Amendment to the U.S. Constitution(1865); Fourteenth Amendment to the U.S. Constitution(1868).

Further Reading

■ Books

Ehrlich, Walter. *They Have No Rights: Dred Scott's Struggle for Freedom*. Westport, Conn.: Greenwood Press, 1979.

Fehrenbacher, Don E. *The Dred Scott Case: Its Significance in American Law and Politics*. New York: Oxford University Press, 1978.

Finkelman, Paul. *An Imperfect Union: Slavery, Federalism, and Comity*. Chapel Hill: University of North Carolina Press, 1981.

———. *Slavery in the Courtroom: An Annotated Bibliography of American Cases*. Washington, D.C.: Government Printing Office, 1985.

———. *Dred Scott v. Sandford: A Brief History with Documents*. Boston: Bedford Books, 1997.

———. *The Slaveholding Republic: An Account of the United States Government's Relations to Slavery*. New York: Oxford University Press, 2001.

Lincoln, Abraham. "House Divided Speech." In *Created Equal? The Complete Lincoln-Douglas Debates of 1858*, ed. Paul M. Angle. Chicago: University of Chicago Press, 1958.

—Paul Finkelman

Dred Scott v. Sandford

This case has been twice argued. After the argument at the last term, differences of opinion were found to exist among the members of the court; and as the questions in controversy are of the highest importance, and the court was at that time much pressed by the ordinary business of the term, it was deemed advisable to continue the case, and direct a re-argument on some of the points, in order that we might have an opportunity of giving to the whole subject a more deliberate consideration. It has accordingly been again argued by counsel, and considered by the court; and I now proceed to deliver its opinion. There are two leading questions presented by the record: 1. Had the Circuit Court of the United States jurisdiction to hear and determine the case between these parties? And 2. If it had jurisdiction, is the judgment it has given erroneous or not? The plaintiff in error, who was also the plaintiff in the court below, was, with his wife and children, held as slaves by the defendant, in the State of Missouri; and he brought this action in the Circuit Court of the United States for that district, to assert the title of himself and his family to freedom. The declaration is in the form usually adopted in that State to try questions of this description, and contains the averment necessary to give the court jurisdiction; that he and the defendant are citizens of different States; that is, that he is a citizen of Missouri, and the defendant a citizen of New York. The defendant pleaded in abatement to the jurisdiction of the court, that the plaintiff was not a citizen of the State of Missouri, as alleged in his declaration, being a negro of African descent, whose ancestors were of pure African blood, and who were brought into this country and sold as slaves. To this plea the plaintiff demurred, and the defendant joined in demurrer. The court overruled the plea, and gave judgment that the defendant should answer over. And he thereupon put in sundry pleas in bar, upon which issues were joined; and at the trial the verdict and judgment were in his favor. Whereupon the plaintiff brought this writ of error. Before we speak of the pleas in bar, it will be proper to dispose of the questions which have arisen on the plea in abatement. That plea denies the right of the plaintiff to sue in a court of the United States, for the reasons therein stated. If the question raised by it is legally before us, and the court should be of opinion that the facts stated in it disqualify the plaintiff from becoming a citizen, in the sense in which that word is used in the Constitution of the United States, then the judgment of the Circuit Court is erroneous, and must be reversed. It is suggested, however, that this plea is not before us; and that as the judgment in the court below on this plea was in favor of the plaintiff, he does not seek to reverse it, or bring it before the court for revision by his writ of error; and also that the defendant waived this defence by pleading over, and thereby admitted the jurisdiction of the court. But, in making this objection, we think the peculiar and limited jurisdiction of courts of the United States has not been adverted to. This peculiar and limited jurisdiction has made it necessary, in these courts, to adopt different rules and principles of pleading, so far as jurisdiction is concerned, from those which regulate courts of common law in England, and in the different States of the Union which have adopted the common-law rules.

In these last-mentioned courts, where their character and rank are analogous to that of a Circuit Court of the United States; in other words, where they are what the law terms courts of general jurisdiction; they are presumed to have jurisdiction, unless the contrary appears. No averment in the pleadings of the plaintiff is necessary, in order to give jurisdiction. If the defendant objects to it, he must plead it specially, and unless the fact on which he relies is found to be true by a jury, or admitted to be true by the plaintiff, the jurisdiction cannot be disputed in an appellate court.

Now, it is not necessary to inquire whether in courts of that description a party who pleads over in bar, when a plea to the jurisdiction has been ruled against him, does or does not waive his plea; nor whether upon a judgment in his favor on the pleas in bar, and a writ of error brought by the plaintiff, the question upon the plea in abatement would be open for revision in the appellate court. Cases that may have been decided in such courts, or rules that may have been laid down by common-law pleaders, can have no influence in the decision in this court. Because, under the Constitution and laws of the United

States, the rules which govern the pleadings in its courts, in questions of jurisdiction, stand on different principles and are regulated by different laws.

This difference arises, as we have said, from the peculiar character of the Government of the United States. For although it is sovereign and supreme in its appropriate sphere of action, yet it does not possess all the powers which usually belong to the sovereignty of a nation. Certain specified powers, enumerated in the Constitution, have been conferred upon it; and neither the legislative, executive, nor judicial departments of the Government can lawfully exercise any authority beyond the limits marked out by the Constitution. And in regulating the judicial department, the cases in which the courts of the United States shall have jurisdiction are particularly and specifically enumerated and defined; and they are not authorized to take cognizance of any case which does not come within the description therein specified. Hence, when a plaintiff sues in a court of the United States, it is necessary that he should show, in his pleading, that the suit he brings is within the jurisdiction of the court, and that he is entitled to sue there. And if he omits to do this, and should, by any oversight of the Circuit Court, obtain a judgment in his favor, the judgment would be reversed in the appellate court for want of jurisdiction in the court below. The jurisdiction would not be presumed, as in the case of a common-law English or State court, unless the contrary appeared. But the record, when it comes before the appellate court, must show, affirmatively, that the inferior court had authority, under the Constitution, to hear and determine the case. And if the plaintiff claims a right to sue in a Circuit Court of the United States, under that provision of the Constitution which gives jurisdiction in controversies between citizens of different States, he must distinctly aver in his pleading that they are citizens of different States; and he cannot maintain his suit without showing that fact in the pleadings.

This point was decided in the case of *Bingham v. Cabot*, (in 3 Dall., 382,) and ever since adhered to by the court. And in *Jackson v. Ashton*, (8 Pet., 148,) it was held that the objection to which it was open could not be waived by the opposite party, because consent of parties could not give jurisdiction.

It is needless to accumulate cases on this subject. Those already referred to, and the cases of *Capron v. Van Noorden*, (in 2 Cr., 126,) and *Montalet v. Murray*, (4 Cr., 46,) are sufficient to show the rule of which we have spoken. The case of *Capron v. Van Noorden* strikingly illustrates the difference

between a common-law court and a court of the United States.

If, however, the fact of citizenship is averred in the declaration, and the defendant does not deny it, and put it in issue by plea in abatement, he cannot offer evidence at the trial to disprove it, and consequently cannot avail himself of the objection in the appellate court, unless the defect should be apparent in some other part of the record. For if there is no plea in abatement, and the want of jurisdiction does not appear in any other part of the transcript brought up by the writ of error, the undisputed averment of citizenship in the declaration must be taken in this court to be true. In this case, the citizenship is averred, but it is denied by the defendant in the manner required by the rules of pleading, and the fact upon which the denial is based is admitted by the demurrer. And, if the plea and demurrer, and judgment of the court below upon it, are before us upon this record, the question to be decided is, whether the facts stated in the plea are sufficient to show that the plaintiff is not entitled to sue as a citizen in a court of the United States. We think they are before us. The plea in abatement and the judgment of the court upon it, are a part of the judicial proceedings in the Circuit Court, and are there recorded as such; and a writ of error always brings up to the superior court the whole record of the proceedings in the court below. And in the case of the *United States v. Smith*, (11 Wheat., 172,) this court said, that the case being brought up by writ of error, the whole record was under the consideration of this court. And this being the case in the present instance, the plea in abatement is necessarily under consideration; and it becomes, therefore, our duty to decide whether the facts stated in the plea are or are not sufficient to show that the plaintiff is not entitled to sue as a citizen in a court of the United States.

This is certainly a very serious question, and one that now for the first time has been brought for decision before this court. But it is brought here by those who have a right to bring it, and it is our duty to meet it and decide it.

The question is simply this: Can a negro, whose ancestors were imported into this country, and sold as slaves, become a member of the political community formed and brought into existence by the Constitution of the United States, and as such become entitled to all the rights, and privileges, and immunities, guaranteed by that instrument to the citizen? One of which rights is the privilege of suing in a court of the United States in the cases specified in the Constitution.

It will be observed, that the plea applies to that class of persons only whose ancestors were negroes of the African race, and imported into this country, and sold and held as slaves. The only matter in issue before the court, therefore, is, whether the descendants of such slaves, when they shall be emancipated, or who are born of parents who had become free before their birth, are citizens of a State, in the sense in which the word citizen is used in the Constitution of the United States. And this being the only matter in dispute on the pleadings, the court must be understood as speaking in this opinion of that class only, that is, of those persons who are the descendants of Africans who were imported into this country, and sold as slaves.

The situation of this population was altogether unlike that of the Indian race. The latter, it is true, formed no part of the colonial communities, and never amalgamated with them in social connections or in government. But although they were uncivilized, they were yet a free and independent people, associated together in nations or tribes, and governed by their own laws. Many of these political communities were situated in territories to which the white race claimed the ultimate right of dominion. But that claim was acknowledged to be subject to the right of the Indians to occupy it as long as they thought proper, and neither the English nor colonial Governments claimed or exercised any dominion over the tribe or nation by whom it was occupied, nor claimed the right to the possession of the territory, until the tribe or nation consented to cede it. These Indian Governments were regarded and treated as foreign Governments, as much so as if an ocean had separated the red man from the white; and their freedom has constantly been acknowledged, from the time of the first emigration to the English colonies to the present day, by the different Governments which succeeded each other. Treaties have been negotiated with them, and their alliance sought for in war; and the people who compose these Indian political communities have always been treated as foreigners not living under our Government. It is true that the course of events has brought the Indian tribes within the limits of the United States under subjection to the white race; and it has been found necessary, for their sake as well as our own, to regard them as in a state of pupilage, and to legislate to a certain extent over them and the territory they occupy. But they may, without doubt, like the subjects of any other foreign Government, be naturalized by the authority of Congress, and become citizens of a State, and of the United States;

and if an individual should leave his nation or tribe, and take up his abode among the white population, he would be entitled to all the rights and privileges which would belong to an emigrant from any other foreign people.

We proceed to examine the case as presented by the pleadings.

The words "people of the United States" and "citizens" are synonymous terms, and mean the same thing. They both describe the political body who, according to our republican institutions, form the sovereignty, and who hold the power and conduct the Government through their representatives. They are what we familiarly call the "sovereign people," and every citizen is one of this people, and a constituent member of this sovereignty. The question before us is, whether the class of persons described in the plea in abatement compose a portion of this people, and are constituent members of this sovereignty? We think they are not, and that they are not included, and were not intended to be included, under the word "citizens" in the Constitution, and can therefore claim none of the rights and privileges which that instrument provides for and secures to citizens of the United States. On the contrary, they were at that time considered as a subordinate and inferior class of beings, who had been subjugated by the dominant race, and, whether emancipated or not, yet remained subject to their authority, and had no rights or privileges but such as those who held the power and the Government might choose to grant them.

It is not the province of the court to decide upon the justice or injustice, the policy or impolicy, of these laws. The decision of that question belonged to the political or law-making power; to those who formed the sovereignty and framed the Constitution. The duty of the court is, to interpret the instrument they have framed, with the best lights we can obtain on the subject, and to administer it as we find it, according to its true intent and meaning when it was adopted.

In discussing this question, we must not confound the rights of citizenship which a State may confer within its own limits, and the rights of citizenship as a member of the Union. It does not by any means follow, because he has all the rights and privileges of a citizen of a State, that he must be a citizen of the United States. He may have all of the rights and privileges of the citizen of a State, and yet not be entitled to the rights and privileges of a citizen in any other State. For, previous to the adoption of the Constitution of the United States, every State had the undoubted right to confer on whomsoever it pleased the character of citizen, and to endow him with all its rights. But this character of course was confined to the boundaries of the State, and gave him no rights or privileges in other States beyond those secured to him by the laws of nations and the comity of States. Nor have the several States surrendered the power of conferring these rights and privileges by adopting the Constitution of the United States. Each State may still confer them upon an alien, or any one it thinks proper, or upon any class or description of persons; yet he would not be a citizen in the sense in which that word is used in the Constitution of the United States, nor entitled to sue as such in one of its courts, nor to the privileges and immunities of a citizen in the other States. The rights which he would acquire would be restricted to the State which gave them. The Constitution has conferred on Congress the right to establish an uniform rule of naturalization, and this right is evidently exclusive, and has always been held by this court to be so. Consequently, no State, since the adoption of the Constitution, can by naturalizing an alien invest him with the rights and privileges secured to a citizen of a State under the Federal Government, although, so far as the State alone was concerned, he would undoubtedly be entitled to the rights of a citizen, and clothed with all the rights and immunities which the Constitution and laws of the State attached to that character.

It is very clear, therefore, that no State can, by any act or law of its own, passed since the adoption of the Constitution, introduce a new member into the political community created by the Constitution of the United States. It cannot make him a member of this community by making him a member of its own. And for the same reason it cannot introduce any person, or description of persons, who were not intended to be embraced in this new political family, which the Constitution brought into existence, but were intended to be excluded from it.

The question then arises, whether the provisions of the Constitution, in relation to the personal rights and privileges to which the citizen of a State should be entitled, embraced the negro African race, at that time in this country, or who might afterwards be imported, who had then or should afterwards be made free in any State; and to put it in the power of a single State to make him a citizen of the United States, and endue him with the full rights of citizenship in every other State without their consent? Does the Constitution of the United States act upon him whenever he shall be made free under the laws of a State, and raised there to the rank of a citizen, and immediately clothe him with all the privileges of a citizen in every other State, and in its own courts?

The court think the affirmative of these propositions cannot be maintained. And if it cannot, the plaintiff in error could not be a citizen of the State of Missouri, within the meaning of the Constitution of the United States, and, consequently, was not entitled to sue in its courts.

It is true, every person, and every class and description of persons, who were at the time of the adoption of the Constitution recognised as citizens in the several States, became also citizens of this new political body; but none other; it was formed by them, and for them and their posterity, but for no one else. And the personal rights and privileges guarantied to citizens of this new sovereignty were intended to embrace those only who were then members of the several State communities, or who should afterwards by birthright or otherwise become members, according to the provisions of the Constitution and the principles on which it was founded. It was the union of those who were at that time members of distinct and separate political communities into one political family, whose power, for certain specified purposes, was to extend over the whole territory of the United States. And it gave to each citizen rights and privileges outside of his State which he did not before possess, and placed him in every other State upon a perfect equality with its own citizens as to rights of person and rights of property; it made him a citizen of the United States.

It becomes necessary, therefore, to determine who were citizens of the several States when the Constitution was adopted. And in order to do this, we must recur to the Governments and institutions of the thirteen colonies, when they separated from Great Britain and formed new sovereignties, and took their places in the family of independent nations. We must inquire who, at that time, were recognised as the people or citizens of a State, whose rights and liberties had been outraged by the English Government; and who declared their independence, and assumed the powers of Government to defend their rights by force of arms.

In the opinion of the court, the legislation and histories of the times, and the language used in the Declaration of Independence, show, that neither the class of persons who had been imported as slaves, nor their descendants, whether they had become free or not, were then acknowledged as a part of the people, nor intended to be included in the general words used in that memorable instrument.

It is difficult at this day to realize the state of public opinion in relation to that unfortunate race, which prevailed in the civilized and enlightened portions of the world at the time of the Declaration of Independence, and when the Constitution of the United States was framed and adopted. But the public history of every European nation displays it in a manner too plain to be mistaken.

They had for more than a century before been regarded as beings of an inferior order, and altogether unfit to associate with the white race, either in social or political relations; and so far inferior, that they had no rights which the white man was bound to respect; and that the negro might justly and lawfully be reduced to slavery for his benefit. He was bought and sold, and treated as an ordinary article of merchandise and traffic, whenever a profit could be made by it. This opinion was at that time fixed and universal in the civilized portion of the white race. It was regarded as an axiom in morals as well as in politics, which no one thought of disputing, or supposed to be open to dispute; and men in every grade and position in society daily and habitually acted upon it in their private pursuits, as well as in matters of public concern, without doubting for a moment the correctness of this opinion.

And in no nation was this opinion more firmly fixed or more uniformly acted upon than by the English Government and English people. They not only seized them on the coast of Africa, and sold them or held them in slavery for their own use; but they took them as ordinary articles of merchandise to every country where they could make a profit on them, and were far more extensively engaged in this commerce than any other nation in the world.

The opinion thus entertained and acted upon in England was naturally impressed upon the colonies they founded on this side of the Atlantic. And, accordingly, a negro of the African race was regarded by them as an article of property, and held, and bought and sold as such, in every one of the thirteen colonies which united in the Declaration of Independence, and afterwards formed the Constitution of the United States. The slaves were more or less numerous in the different colonies, as slave labor was found more or less profitable. But no one seems to have doubted the correctness of the prevailing opinion of the time.

The legislation of the different colonies furnishes positive and indisputable proof of this fact.

It would be tedious, in this opinion, to enumerate the various laws they passed upon this subject. It will be sufficient, as a sample of the legislation which then generally prevailed throughout the British colonies, to give the laws of two of them; one being still a large slaveholding State, and the other the first State in which slavery ceased to exist.

The province of Maryland, in 1717, (ch. 13, s. 5,) passed a law declaring "that if any free negro or mulatto intermarry with any white woman, or if any white man shall intermarry with any negro or mulatto woman, such negro or mulatto shall become a slave during life, excepting mulattoes born of white women, who, for such intermarriage, shall only become servants for seven years, to be disposed of as the justices of the county court, where such marriage so happens, shall think fit; to be applied by them towards the support of a public school within the said county. And any white man or white woman who shall intermarry as aforesaid, with any negro or mulatto, such white man or white woman shall become servants during the term of seven years, and shall be disposed of by the justices as aforesaid, and be applied to the uses aforesaid."

The other colonial law to which we refer was passed by Massachusetts in 1705, (chap. 6.) It is entitled "An act for the better preventing of a spurious and mixed issue," &c.; and it provides, that "if any negro or mulatto shall presume to smite or strike any person of the English or other Christian nation, such negro or mulatto shall be severely whipped, at the discretion of the justices before whom the offender shall be convicted."

And "that none of her Majesty's English or Scottish subjects, nor of any other Christian nation, within this province, shall contract matrimony with any negro or mulatto; nor shall any person, duly authorized to solemnize marriage, presume to join any such in marriage, on pain of forfeiting the sum of fifty pounds; one moiety thereof to her Majesty, for and towards the support of the Government within this province, and the other moiety to him or them that shall inform and sue for the same, in any of her Majesty's courts of record within the province, by bill, plaint, or information."

We give both of these laws in the words used by the respective legislative bodies, because the language in which they are framed, as well as the provisions contained in them, show, too plainly to be misunderstood, the degraded condition of this unhappy race. They were still in force when the Revolution began, and are a faithful index to the state of feeling towards the class of persons of whom they speak, and of the position they occupied throughout the thirteen colonies, in the eyes and thoughts of the men who framed the Declaration of Independence and established the State Constitutions and Governments. They show that a perpetual and impassable barrier was intended to be erected between the white race and the one which they had reduced to slavery, and governed as subjects with absolute and despotic power, and which they then looked upon as so far below them in the scale of created beings, that intermarriages between white persons and negroes or mulattoes were regarded as unnatural and immoral, and punished as crimes, not only in the parties, but in the person who joined them in marriage. And no distinction in this respect was made between the free negro or mulatto and the slave, but this stigma, of the deepest degradation, was fixed upon the whole race.

We refer to these historical facts for the purpose of showing the fixed opinions concerning that race, upon which the statesmen of that day spoke and acted. It is necessary to do this, in order to determine whether the general terms used in the Constitution of the United States, as to the rights of man and the rights of the people, was intended to include them, or to give to them or their posterity the benefit of any of its provisions.

The language of the Declaration of Independence is equally conclusive:

It begins by declaring that, "when in the course of human events it becomes necessary for one people to dissolve the political bands which have connected them with another, and to assume among the powers of the earth the separate and equal station to which the laws of nature and nature's God entitle them, a decent respect for the opinions of mankind requires that they should declare the causes which impel them to the separation."

It then proceeds to say: "We hold these truths to be self-evident: that all men are created equal; that they are endowed by their Creator with certain unalienable rights; that among them is life, liberty, and the pursuit of happiness; that to secure these rights, Governments are instituted, deriving their just powers from the consent of the governed."

The general words above quoted would seem to embrace the whole human family, and if they were used in a similar instrument at this day would be so understood. But it is too clear for dispute, that the enslaved African race were not intended to be included, and formed no part of the people who framed and adopted this declaration; for if the language, as understood in that day, would embrace them, the conduct of the distinguished men who framed the Declaration of Independence would

have been utterly and flagrantly inconsistent with the principles they asserted; and instead of the sympathy of mankind, to which they so confidently appealed, they would have deserved and received universal rebuke and reprobation.

Yet the men who framed this declaration were great men—high in literary acquirements—high in their sense of honor, and incapable of asserting principles inconsistent with those on which they were acting. They perfectly understood the meaning of the language they used, and how it would be understood by others; and they knew that it would not in any part of the civilized world be supposed to embrace the negro race, which, by common consent, had been excluded from civilized Governments and the family of nations, and doomed to slavery. They spoke and acted according to the then established doctrines and principles, and in the ordinary language of the day, and no one misunderstood them. The unhappy black race were separated from the white by indelible marks, and laws long before established, and were never thought of or spoken of except as property, and when the claims of the owner or the profit of the trader were supposed to need protection.

This state of public opinion had undergone no change when the Constitution was adopted, as is equally evident from its provisions and language.

The brief preamble sets forth by whom it was formed, for what purposes, and for whose benefit and protection. It declares that it is formed by the people of the United States; that is to say, by those who were members of the different political communities in the several States; and its great object is declared to be to secure the blessings of liberty to themselves and their posterity. It speaks in general terms of the people of the United States, and of citizens of the several States, when it is providing for the exercise of the powers granted or the privileges secured to the citizen. It does not define what description of persons are intended to be included under these terms, or who shall be regarded as a citizen and one of the people. It uses them as terms so well understood, that no further description or definition was necessary.

But there are two clauses in the Constitution which point directly and specifically to the negro race as a separate class of persons, and show clearly that they were not regarded as a portion of the people or citizens of the Government then formed.

One of these clauses reserves to each of the thirteen States the right to import slaves until the year 1808, if it thinks proper. And the importation which it thus sanctions was unquestionably of persons of the race of which we are speaking, as the traffic in slaves in the United States had always been confined to them. And by the other provision the States pledge themselves to each other to maintain the right of property of the master, by delivering up to him any slave who may have escaped from his service, and be found within their respective territories. By the first above-mentioned clause, therefore, the right to purchase and hold this property is directly sanctioned and authorized for twenty years by the people who framed the Constitution. And by the second, they pledge themselves to maintain and uphold the right of the master in the manner specified, as long as the Government they then formed should endure. And these two provisions show, conclusively, that neither the description of persons therein referred to, nor their descendants, were embraced in any of the other provisions of the Constitution; for certainly these two clauses were not intended to confer on them or their posterity the blessings of liberty, or any of the personal rights so carefully provided for the citizen.

No one of that race had ever migrated to the United States voluntarily; all of them had been brought here as articles of merchandise. The number that had been emancipated at that time were but few in comparison with those held in slavery; and they were identified in the public mind with the race to which they belonged, and regarded as a part of the slave population rather than the free. It is obvious that they were not even in the minds of the framers of the Constitution when they were conferring special rights and privileges upon the citizens of a State in every other part of the Union.

Indeed, when we look to the condition of this race in the several States at the time, it is impossible to believe that these rights and privileges were intended to be extended to them.

It is very true, that in that portion of the Union where the labor of the negro race was found to be unsuited to the climate and unprofitable to the master, but few slaves were held at the time of the Declaration of Independence; and when the Constitution was adopted, it had entirely worn out in one of them, and measures had been taken for its gradual abolition in several others. But this change had not been produced by any change of opinion in relation to this race; but because it was discovered, from experience, that slave labor was unsuited to the climate and productions of these States: for some of the States, where it had ceased or nearly ceased to exist, were actively engaged in the slave trade, procuring cargoes on the coast of Africa, and transporting them for sale to those parts of the Union where their labor was found to be profitable, and suited to the climate and productions. And this traffic was openly carried on, and fortunes accumulated by it, without reproach from the people of the States where they resided. And it can hardly be supposed that, in the States where it was then countenanced in its worst form—that is, in the seizure and transportation—the people could have regarded those who were emancipated as entitled to equal rights with themselves.

And we may here again refer, in support of this proposition, to the plain and unequivocal language of the laws of the several States, some passed after the Declaration of Independence and before the Constitution was adopted, and some since the Government went into operation.

We need not refer, on this point, particularly to the laws of the present slaveholding States. Their statute books are full of provisions in relation to this class, in the same spirit with the Maryland law which we have before quoted. They have continued to treat them as an inferior class, and to subject them to strict police regulations, drawing a broad line of distinction between the citizen and the slave races, and legislating in relation to them upon the same principle which prevailed at the time of the Declaration of Independence. As relates to these States, it is too plain for argument, that they have never been regarded as a part of the people or citizens of the State, nor supposed to possess any political rights which the dominant race might not withhold or grant at their pleasure. And as long ago as 1822, the Court of Appeals of Kentucky decided that free negroes and mulattoes were not citizens within the meaning of the Constitution of the United States; and the correctness of this decision is recognized, and the same doctrine affirmed, in 1 Meigs's Tenn. Reports, 331.

And if we turn to the legislation of the States where slavery had worn out, or measures taken for its speedy abolition, we shall find the same opinions and principles equally fixed and equally acted upon.

Thus, Massachusetts, in 1786, passed a law similar to the colonial one of which we have spoken. The law of 1786, like the law of 1705, forbids the marriage of any white person with any negro, Indian, or mulatto, and inflicts a penalty of fifty pounds upon any one who shall join them in marriage; and declares all such marriage absolutely null and void, and degrades thus the unhappy issue of the marriage by fixing upon it the stain of bastardy. And this mark of degradation was renewed, and again impressed upon the race, in the careful and deliberate preparation of their revised code published in 1836. This code forbids any person from joining in marriage any white person with any Indian, negro, or mulatto, and subjects the party who shall offend in this respect, to imprisonment, not exceeding six months, in the common jail, or to hard labor, and to a fine of not less than fifty nor more than two hundred dollars; and, like the law of 1786, it declares the marriage to be absolutely null and void. It will be seen that the punishment is increased by the code upon the person who shall marry them, by adding imprisonment to a pecuniary penalty.

So, too, in Connecticut. We refer more particularly to the legislation of this State, because it was not only among the first to put an end to slavery within its own territory, but was the first to fix a mark of reprobation upon the African slave trade. The law last mentioned was passed in October, 1788, about nine months after the State had ratified and adopted the present Constitution of the United States; and by that law it prohibited its own citizens, under severe penalties, from engaging in the trade, and declared all policies of insurance on the vessel or cargo made in the State to be null and void. But, up to the time of the adoption of the Constitution, there is nothing in the legislation of the State indicating any change of opinion as to the relative rights and position of the white and black races in this country, or indicating that it meant to place the latter, when free, upon a level with its citizens. And certainly nothing which would have led the slaveholding States to suppose, that Connecticut designed to claim for them, under the new Constitution, the equal rights and privileges and rank of citizens in every other State.

The first step taken by Connecticut upon this subject was as early as 1774, when it passed an act forbidding the further importation of slaves into the State. But the section containing the prohibition is introduced by the following preamble:

"And whereas the increase of slaves in this State is injurious to the poor, and inconvenient."

This recital would appear to have been carefully introduced, in order to prevent any misunderstanding of the motive which induced the Legislature to pass the law, and places it distinctly upon the interest and convenience of the white population—excluding the inference that it might have been intended in any degree for the benefit of the other.

And in the act of 1784, by which the issue of slaves, born after the time therein mentioned, were to be free at a certain age, the section is again introduced by a preamble assigning a similar motive for the act. It is in these words:

"Whereas sound policy requires that the abolition of slavery should be effected as soon as may be consistent with the rights of individuals, and the public safety and welfare"

showing that the right of property in the master was to be protected, and that the measure was one of policy, and to prevent the injury and inconvenience, to the whites, of a slave population in the State.

And still further pursuing its legislation, we find that in the same statute passed in 1774, which prohibited the further importation of slaves into the State, there is also a provision by which any negro, Indian, or mulatto servant, who was found wandering out of the town or place to which he belonged, without a written pass such as is therein described, was made liable to be seized by any one, and taken before the next authority to be examined and delivered up to his master—who was required to pay the charge which had accrued thereby. And a subsequent section of the same law provides, that if any free negro shall travel without such pass, and shall be stopped, seized, or taken up, he shall pay all charges arising thereby. And this law was in full operation when the Constitution of the United States was adopted, and was not repealed till 1797. So that up to that time free negroes and mulattoes were associated with servants and slaves in the police regulations established by the laws of the State.

And again, in 1833, Connecticut passed another law, which made it penal to set up or establish any school in that State for the instruction of persons of the African race not inhabitants of the State, or to instruct or teach in any such school or institution, or board or harbor for that purpose, any such person, without the previous consent in writing of the civil authority of the town in which such school or institution might be.

And it appears by the case of *Crandall v. The State*, reported in 10 Conn. Rep., 340, that upon an information filed against Prudence Crandall for a violation of this law, one of the points raised in the defence was, that the law was a violation of the Constitution of the United States; and that the persons instructed, although of the African race, were citizens of other States, and therefore entitled to the rights and privileges of citizens in the State of Connecticut. But Chief Justice Dagget, before whom the case was tried, held, that persons of that description were not citizens of a State, within the meaning of the word citizen in the Constitution of the

United States, and were not therefore entitled to the privileges and immunities of citizens in other States.

The case was carried up to the Supreme Court of Errors of the State, and the question fully argued there. But the case went off upon another point, and no opinion was expressed on this question.

We have made this particular examination into the legislative and judicial action of Connecticut, because, from the early hostility it displayed to the slave trade on the coast of Africa, we may expect to find the laws of that State as lenient and favorable to the subject race as those of any other State in the Union; and if we find that at the time the Constitution was adopted, they were not even there raised to the rank of citizens, but were still held and treated as property, and the laws relating to them passed with reference altogether to the interest and convenience of the white race, we shall hardly find them elevated to a higher rank anywhere else.

A brief notice of the laws of two other States, and we shall pass on to other considerations.

By the laws of New Hampshire, collected and finally passed in 1815, no one was permitted to be enrolled in the militia of the State, but free white citizens; and the same provision is found in a subsequent collection of the laws, made in 1855. Nothing could more strongly mark the entire repudiation of the African race. The alien is excluded, because, being born in a foreign country, he cannot be a member of the community until he is naturalized. But why are the African race, born in the State, not permitted to share in one of the highest duties of the citizen? The answer is obvious; he is not, by the institutions and laws of the State, numbered among its people. He forms no part of the sovereignty of the State, and is not therefore called on to uphold and defend it. Again, in 1822, Rhode Island, in its revised code, passed a law forbidding persons who were authorized to join persons in marriage, from joining in marriage any white person with any negro, Indian, or mulatto, under the penalty of two hundred dollars, and declaring all such marriages absolutely null and void; and the same law was again re-enacted in its revised code of 1844. So that, down to the last-mentioned period, the strongest mark of inferiority and degradation was fastened upon the African race in that State.

It would be impossible to enumerate and compress in the space usually allotted to an opinion of a court, the various laws, marking the condition of this race, which were passed from time to time after the Revolution, and before and since the adoption of the Constitution of the United States. In addition to those already referred to, it is sufficient to say, that Chancellor Kent, whose accuracy and research no one will question, states in the sixth edition of his *Commentaries*, (published in 1848, 2 vol., 258, note b,) that in no part of the country except Maine, did the African race, in point of fact, participate equally with the whites in the exercise of civil and political rights.

The legislation of the States therefore shows, in a manner not to be mistaken, the inferior and subject condition of that race at the time the Constitution was adopted, and long afterwards, throughout the thirteen States by which that instrument was framed; and it is hardly consistent with the respect due to these States, to suppose that they regarded at that time, as fellow-citizens and members of the sovereignty, a class of beings whom they had thus stigmatized; whom, as we are bound, out of respect to the State sovereignties, to assume they had deemed it just and necessary thus to stigmatize, and upon whom they had impressed such deep and enduring marks of inferiority and degradation; or, that when they met in convention to form the Constitution, they looked upon them as a portion of their constituents, or designed to include them in the provisions so carefully inserted for the security and protection of the liberties and rights of their citizens. It cannot be supposed that they intended to secure to them rights, and privileges, and rank, in the new political body throughout the Union, which every one of them denied within the limits of its own dominion. More especially, it cannot be believed that the large slaveholding States regarded them as included in the word citizens, or would have consented to a Constitution which might compel them to receive them in that character from another State. For if they were so received, and entitled to the privileges and immunities of citizens, it would exempt them from the operation of the special laws and from the police regulations which they considered to be necessary for their own safety. It would give to persons of the negro race, who were recognised as citizens in any one State of the Union, the right to enter every other State whenever they pleased, singly or in companies, without pass or passport, and without obstruction, to sojourn there as long as they pleased, to go where they pleased at every hour of the day or night without molestation, unless they committed some violation of law for which a white man would be punished; and it would give them the full liberty of speech in public and in private upon all subjects upon which its own citizens might speak; to hold public meetings upon political affairs, and to keep and carry arms wherever they went. And all of this would be done in the face of the subject race of the same color, both free and slaves, and inevitably producing discontent and insubordination among them, and endangering the peace and safety of the State.

It is impossible, it would seem, to believe that the great men of the slaveholding States, who took so large a share in framing the Constitution of the United States, and exercised so much influence in procuring its adoption, could have been so forgetful or regardless of their own safety and the safety of those who trusted and confided in them.

Besides, this want of foresight and care would have been utterly inconsistent with the caution displayed in providing for the admission of new members into this political family. For, when they gave to the citizens of each State the privileges and immunities of citizens in the several States, they at the same time took from the several States the power of naturalization, and confined that power exclusively to the Federal Government. No State was willing to permit another State to determine who should or should not be admitted as one of its citizens, and entitled to demand equal rights and privileges with their own people, within their own territories. The right of naturalization was therefore, with one accord, surrendered by the States, and confided to the Federal Government. And this power granted to Congress to establish an uniform rule of naturalization is, by the well-understood meaning of the word, confined to persons born in a foreign country, under a foreign Government. It is not a power to raise to the rank of a citizen any one born in the United States, who, from birth or parentage, by the laws of the country, belongs to an inferior and subordinate class. And when we find the States guarding themselves from the indiscreet or improper admission by other States of emigrants from other countries, by giving the power exclusively to Congress, we cannot fail to see that they could never have left with the States a much more important power—that is, the power of transforming into citizens a numerous class of persons, who in that character would be much more dangerous to the peace and safety of a large portion of the Union, than the few foreigners one of the States might improperly naturalize. The Constitution upon its adoption obviously took from the States all power by any subsequent legislation to introduce as a citizen into the political family of the United States any one, no matter where he was born, or what might be his character or condition; and it gave to Congress the power

to confer this character upon those only who were born outside of the dominions of the United States. And no law of a State, therefore, passed since the Constitution was adopted, can give any right of citizenship outside of its own territory.

A clause similar to the one in the Constitution, in relation to the rights and immunities of citizens of one State in the other States, was contained in the Articles of Confederation. But there is a difference of language, which is worthy of note. The provision in the Articles of Confederation was, "that the free inhabitants of each of the States, paupers, vagabonds, and fugitives from justice, excepted, should be entitled to all the privileges and immunities of free citizens in the several States."

It will be observed, that under this Confederation, each State had the right to decide for itself, and in its own tribunals, whom it would acknowledge as a free inhabitant of another State. The term free inhabitant, in the generality of its terms, would certainly include one of the African race who had been manumitted. But no example, we think, can be found of his admission to all the privileges of citizenship in any State of the Union after these Articles were formed, and while they continued in force. And, notwithstanding the generality of the words "free inhabitants," it is very clear that, according to their accepted meaning in that day, they did not include the African race, whether free or not: for the fifth section of the ninth article provides that Congress should have the power "to agree upon the number of land forces to be raised, and to make requisitions from each State for its quota in proportion to the number of white inhabitants in such State, which requisition should be binding."

Words could hardly have been used which more strongly mark the line of distinction between the citizen and the subject; the free and the subjugated races. The latter were not even counted when the inhabitants of a State were to be embodied in proportion to its numbers for the general defence. And it cannot for a moment be supposed, that a class of persons thus separated and rejected from those who formed the sovereignty of the States, were yet intended to be included under the words "free inhabitants," in the preceding article, to whom privileges and immunities were so carefully secured in every State.

But although this clause of the Articles of Confederation is the same in principle with that inserted in the Constitution, yet the comprehensive word inhabitant, which might be construed to include an emancipated slave, is omitted; and the privilege is confined to citizens of the State. And this alteration in words would hardly have been made, unless a different meaning was intended to be conveyed, or a possible doubt removed. The just and fair inference is, that as this privilege was about to be placed under the protection of the General Government, and the words expounded by its tribunals, and all power in relation to it taken from the State and its courts, it was deemed prudent to describe with precision and caution the persons to whom this high privilege was given—and the word citizen was on that account substituted for the words free inhabitant. The word citizen excluded, and no doubt intended to exclude, foreigners who had not become citizens of some one of the States when the Constitution was adopted; and also every description of persons who were not fully recognised as citizens in the several States. This, upon any fair construction of the instruments to which we have referred, was evidently the object and purpose of this change of words.

To all this mass of proof we have still to add, that Congress has repeatedly legislated upon the same construction of the Constitution that we have given. Three laws, two of which were passed almost immediately after the Government went into operation, will be abundantly sufficient to show this. The two first are particularly worthy of notice, because many of the men who assisted in framing the Constitution, and took an active part in procuring its adoption, were then in the halls of legislation, and certainly understood what they meant when they used the words "people of the United States" and "citizen" in that well-considered instrument.

The first of these acts is the naturalization law, which was passed at the second session of the first Congress, March 26, 1790, and confines the right of becoming citizens "to aliens being free white persons."

Now, the Constitution does not limit the power of Congress in this respect to white persons. And they may, if they think proper, authorize the naturalization of any one, of any color, who was born under allegiance to another Government. But the language of the law above quoted, shows that citizenship at that time was perfectly understood to be confined to the white race; and that they alone constituted the sovereignty in the Government.

Congress might, as we before said, have authorized the naturalization of Indians, because they were aliens and foreigners. But, in their then untutored and savage state, no one would have thought of admitting them as citizens in a civilized community. And, moreover, the atrocities they had but recently committed, when they were the allies of Great Britain in the Revolutionary war, were yet fresh in the recollection of the people of the United States, and they were even then guarding themselves against the threatened renewal of Indian hostilities. No one supposed then that any Indian would ask for, or was capable of enjoying, the privileges of an American citizen, and the word white was not used with any particular reference to them.

Neither was it used with any reference to the African race imported into or born in this country; because Congress had no power to naturalize them, and therefore there was no necessity for using particular words to exclude them.

It would seem to have been used merely because it followed out the line of division which the Constitution has drawn between the citizen race, who formed and held the Government, and the African race, which they held in subjection and slavery, and governed at their own pleasure.

Another of the early laws of which we have spoken, is the first militia law, which was passed in 1792, at the first session of the second Congress. The language of this law is equally plain and significant with the one just mentioned. It directs that every "free able-bodied white male citizen" shall be enrolled in the militia. The word white is evidently used to exclude the African race, and the word "citizen" to exclude unnaturalized foreigners; the latter forming no part of the sovereignty, owing it no allegiance, and therefore under no obligation to defend it. The African race, however, born in the country, did owe allegiance to the Government, whether they were slave or free; but it is repudiated, and rejected from the duties and obligations of citizenship in marked language.

The third act to which we have alluded is even still more decisive; it was passed as late as 1813, (2 Stat., 809,) and it provides: "That from and after the termination of the war in which the United States are now engaged with Great Britain, it shall not be lawful to employ, on board of any public or private vessels of the United States, any person or persons except citizens of the United States, or persons of color, natives of the United States." Here the line of distinction is drawn in express words. Persons of color, in the judgment of Congress, were not included in the word citizens, and they are described as another and different class of persons, and authorized to be employed, if born in the United States.

And even as late as 1820, (chap. 104, sec. 8,) in the charter to the city of Washington, the corporation is authorized "to restrain and prohibit the nightly and other disorderly meetings of slaves, free negroes, and mulattoes," thus associating them together in its legislation; and after prescribing the punishment that may be inflicted on the slaves, proceeds in the following words: "And to punish such free negroes and mulattoes by penalties not exceeding twenty dollars for any one offence; and in case of the inability of any such free negro or mulatto to pay any such penalty and cost thereon, to cause him or her to be confined to labor for any time not exceeding six calendar months." And in a subsequent part of the same section, the act authorizes the corporation "to prescribe the terms and conditions upon which free negroes and mulattoes may reside in the city."

This law, like the laws of the States, shows that this class of persons were governed by special legislation directed expressly to them, and always connected with provisions for the government of slaves, and not with those for the government of free white citizens. And after such an uniform course of legislation as we have stated, by the colonies, by the States, and by Congress, running through a period of more than a century, it would seem that to call persons thus marked and stigmatized, "citizens" of the United States, "fellow-citizens," a constituent part of the sovereignty, would be an abuse of terms, and not calculated to exalt the character of an American citizen in the eyes of other nations.

The conduct of the Executive Department of the Government has been in perfect harmony upon this subject with this course of legislation. The question was brought officially before the late William Wirt, when he was the Attorney General of the United States, in 1821, and he decided that the words "citizens of the United States" were used in the acts of Congress in the same sense as in the Constitution; and that free persons of color were not citizens, within the meaning of the Constitution and laws; and this opinion has been confirmed by that of the late Attorney General, Caleb Cushing, in a recent case, and acted upon by the Secretary of State, who refused to grant passports to them as "citizens of the United States."

But it is said that a person may be a citizen, and entitled to that character, although he does not possess all the rights which may belong to other citizens; as, for example, the right to vote, or to hold particular offices; and that yet, when he goes into another State, he is entitled to be recognised there as a citizen, although the State may measure his rights by the rights which it allows to persons of a like character or class resident in the State, and refuse to him the full rights of citizenship.

This argument overlooks the language of the provision in the Constitution of which we are speaking. Undoubtedly, a person may be a citizen, that is, a member of the community who form the sovereignty, although he exercises no share of the political power, and is incapacitated from holding particular offices. Women and minors, who form a part of the political family, cannot vote; and when a property qualification is required to vote or hold a particular office, those who have not the necessary qualification cannot vote or hold the office, yet they are citizens.

So, too, a person may be entitled to vote by the law of the State, who is not a citizen even of the State itself. And in some of the States of the Union foreigners not naturalized are allowed to vote. And the State may give the right to free negroes and mulattoes, but that does not make them citizens of the State, and still less of the United States. And the provision in the Constitution giving privileges and immunities in other States, does not apply to them.

Neither does it apply to a person who, being the citizen of a State, migrates to another State. For then he becomes subject to the laws of the State in which he lives, and he is no longer a citizen of the State from which he removed. And the State in which he resides may then, unquestionably, determine his status or condition, and place him among the class of persons who are not recognised as citizens, but belong to an inferior and subject race; and may deny him the privileges and immunities enjoyed by its citizens.

But so far as mere rights of person are concerned, the provision in question is confined to citizens of a State who are temporarily in another State without taking up their residence there. It gives them no political rights in the State, as to voting or holding office, or in any other respect. For a citizen of one State has no right to participate in the government of another. But if he ranks as a citizen in the State to which he belongs, within the meaning of the Constitution of the United States, then, whenever he goes into another State, the Constitution clothes him, as to the rights of person, with all the privileges and immunities which belong to citizens of the State. And if persons of the African race are citizens of a State, and of the United States, they would be entitled to all of these privileges and immunities in every State, and the State could not restrict them; for they would hold these privileges and immunities under the paramount authority of the Federal Government, and its courts would be bound to maintain and enforce them, the Constitution and laws of the State to the contrary notwithstanding. And if the States could limit or restrict them, or place the party in an inferior grade, this clause of the Constitution would be unmeaning, and could have no operation; and would give no rights to the citizen when in another State. He would have none but what the State itself chose to allow him. This is evidently not the construction or meaning of the clause in question. It guaranties rights to the citizen, and the State cannot withhold them. And these rights are of a character and would lead to consequences which make it absolutely certain that the African race were not included under the name of citizens of a State, and were not in the contemplation of the framers of the Constitution when these privileges and immunities were provided for the protection of the citizen in other States.

The case of *Legrand v. Darnall* (2 Peters, 664) has been referred to for the purpose of showing that this court has decided that the descendant of a slave may sue as a citizen in a court of the United States; but the case itself shows that the question did not arise and could not have arisen in the case.

It appears from the report, that Darnall was born in Maryland, and was the son of a white man by one of his slaves, and his father executed certain instruments to manumit him, and devised to him some landed property in the State. This property Darnall afterwards sold to Legrand, the appellant, who gave his notes for the purchase-money. But becoming afterwards apprehensive that the appellee had not been emancipated according to the laws of Maryland, he refused to pay the notes until he could be better satisfied as to Darnall's right to convey. Darnall, in the mean time, had taken up his residence in Pennsylvania, and brought suit on the notes, and recovered judgment in the Circuit Court for the district of Maryland.

The whole proceeding, as appears by the report, was an amicable one; Legrand being perfectly willing to pay the money, if he could obtain a title, and Darnall not wishing him to pay unless he could make him a good one. In point of fact, the whole proceeding was under the direction of the counsel who argued the case for the appellee, who was the mutual friend of the parties, and confided in by both of them, and whose only object was to have the rights of both parties established by judicial decision in the most speedy and least expensive manner.

Legrand, therefore, raised no objection to the jurisdiction of the court in the suit at law, because he was himself anxious to obtain the judgment of the court upon his title. Consequently, there was nothing

in the record before the court to show that Darnall was of African descent, and the usual judgment and award of execution was entered. And Legrand thereupon filed his bill on the equity side of the Circuit Court, stating that Darnall was born a slave, and had not been legally emancipated, and could not therefore take the land devised to him, nor make Legrand a good title; and praying an injunction to restrain Darnall from proceeding to execution on the judgment, which was granted. Darnall answered, averring in his answer that he was a free man, and capable of conveying a good title.

Testimony was taken on this point, and at the hearing the Circuit Court was of opinion that Darnall was a free man and his title good, and dissolved the injunction and dismissed the bill; and that decree was affirmed here, upon the appeal of Legrand.

Now, it is difficult to imagine how any question about the citizenship of Darnall, or his right to sue in that character, can be supposed to have arisen or been decided in that case. The fact that he was of African descent was first brought before the court upon the bill in equity. The suit at law had then passed into judgment and award of execution, and the Circuit Court, as a court of law, had no longer any authority over it. It was a valid and legal judgment, which the court that rendered it had not the power to reverse or set aside. And unless it had jurisdiction as a court of equity to restrain him from using its process as a court of law, Darnall, if he thought proper, would have been at liberty to proceed on his judgment, and compel the payment of the money, although the allegations in the bill were true, and he was incapable of making a title. No other court could have enjoined him, for certainly no State equity court could interfere in that way with the judgment of a Circuit Court of the United States.

But the Circuit Court as a court of equity certainly had equity jurisdiction over its own judgment as a court of law, without regard to the character of the parties; and had not only the right, but it was its duty—no matter who were the parties in the judgment—to prevent them from proceeding to enforce it by execution, if the court was satisfied that the money was not justly and equitably due. The ability of Darnall to convey did not depend upon his citizenship, but upon his title to freedom. And if he was free, he could hold and convey property, by the laws of Maryland, although he was not a citizen. But if he was by law still a slave, he could not. It was therefore the duty of the court, sitting as a court of equity in the latter case, to prevent him from using its process, as a court of common law, to compel the payment of the purchase-money, when it was evident that the purchaser must lose the land. But if he was free, and could make a title, it was equally the duty of the court not to suffer Legrand to keep the land, and refuse the payment of the money, upon the ground that Darnall was incapable of suing or being sued as a citizen in a court of the United States. The character or citizenship of the parties had no connection with the question of jurisdiction, and the matter in dispute had no relation to the citizenship of Darnall. Nor is such a question alluded to in the opinion of the court.

Besides, we are by no means prepared to say that there are not many cases, civil as well as criminal, in which a Circuit Court of the United States may exercise jurisdiction, although one of the African race is a party; that broad question is not before the court. The question with which we are now dealing is, whether a person of the African race can be a citizen of the United States, and become thereby entitled to a special privilege, by virtue of his title to that character, and which, under the Constitution, no one but a citizen can claim. It is manifest that the case of Legrand and Darnall has no bearing on that question, and can have no application to the case now before the court.

This case, however, strikingly illustrates the consequences that would follow the construction of the Constitution which would give the power contended for to a State. It would in effect give it also to an individual. For if the father of young Darnall had manumitted him in his lifetime, and sent him to reside in a State which recognised him as a citizen, he might have visited and sojourned in Maryland when he pleased, and as long as he pleased, as a citizen of the United States; and the State officers and tribunals would be compelled, by the paramount authority of the Constitution, to receive him and treat him as one of its citizens, exempt from the laws and police of the State in relation to a person of that description, and allow him to enjoy all the rights and privileges of citizenship, without respect to the laws of Maryland, although such laws were deemed by it absolutely essential to its own safety.

The only two provisions which point to them and include them, treat them as property, and make it the duty of the Government to protect it; no other power, in relation to this race, is to be found in the Constitution; and as it is a Government of special, delegated, powers, no authority beyond these two provisions can be constitutionally exercised. The Government of the United States had no right to interfere for any other purpose but that of protecting the rights of the owner, leaving it altogether with the several States

to deal with this race, whether emancipated or not, as each State may think justice, humanity, and the interests and safety of society, require. The States evidently intended to reserve this power exclusively to themselves.

No one, we presume, supposes that any change in public opinion or feeling, in relation to this unfortunate race, in the civilized nations of Europe or in this country, should induce the court to give to the words of the Constitution a more liberal construction in their favor than they were intended to bear when the instrument was framed and adopted. Such an argument would be altogether inadmissible in any tribunal called on to interpret it. If any of its provisions are deemed unjust, there is a mode prescribed in the instrument itself by which it may be amended; but while it remains unaltered, it must be construed now as it was understood at the time of its adoption. It is not only the same in words, but the same in meaning, and delegates the same powers to the Government, and reserves and secures the same rights and privileges to the citizen; and as long as it continues to exist in its present form, it speaks not only in the same words, but with the same meaning and intent with which it spoke when it came from the hands of its framers, and was voted on and adopted by the people of the United States. Any other rule of construction would abrogate the judicial character of this court, and make it the mere reflex of the popular opinion or passion of the day. This court was not created by the Constitution for such purposes. Higher and graver trusts have been confided to it, and it must not falter in the path of duty.

What the construction was at that time, we think can hardly admit of doubt. We have the language of the Declaration of Independence and of the Articles of Confederation, in addition to the plain words of the Constitution itself; we have the legislation of the different States, before, about the time, and since, the Constitution was adopted; we have the legislation of Congress, from the time of its adoption to a recent period; and we have the constant and uniform action of the Executive Department, all concurring together, and leading to the same result. And if anything in relation to the construction of the Constitution can be regarded as settled, it is that which we now give to the word "citizen" and the word "people."

And upon a full and careful consideration of the subject, the court is of opinion, that, upon the facts stated in the plea in abatement, Dred Scott was not a citizen of Missouri within the meaning of the Constitution of the United States, and not entitled as such to sue in its courts; and, consequently, that the Circuit Court had no jurisdiction of the case, and that the judgment on the plea in abatement is erroneous.

We are aware that doubts are entertained by some of the members of the court, whether the plea in abatement is legally before the court upon this writ of error; but if that plea is regarded as waived, or out of the case upon any other ground, yet the question as to the jurisdiction of the Circuit Court is presented on the face of the bill of exception itself, taken by the plaintiff at the trial; for he admits that he and his wife were born slaves, but endeavors to make out his title to freedom and citizenship by showing that they were taken by their owner to certain places, hereinafter mentioned, where slavery could not by law exist, and that they thereby became free, and upon their return to Missouri became citizens of that State.

Now, if the removal of which he speaks did not give them their freedom, then by his own admission he is still a slave; and whatever opinions may be entertained in favor of the citizenship of a free person of the African race, no one supposes that a slave is a citizen of the State or of the United States. If, therefore, the acts done by his owner did not make them free persons, he is still a slave, and certainly incapable of suing in the character of a citizen.

The principle of law is too well settled to be disputed, that a court can give no judgment for either party, where it has no jurisdiction; and if, upon the showing of Scott himself, it appeared that he was still a slave, the case ought to have been dismissed, and the judgment against him and in favor of the defendant for costs, is, like that on the plea in abatement, erroneous, and the suit ought to have been dismissed by the Circuit Court for want of jurisdiction in that court.

But, before we proceed to examine this part of the case, it may be proper to notice an objection taken to the judicial authority of this court to decide it; and it has been said, that as this court has decided against the jurisdiction of the Circuit Court on the plea in abatement, it has no right to examine any question presented by the exception; and that anything it may say upon that part of the case will be extra-judicial, and mere obiter dicta.

This is a manifest mistake; there can be no doubt as to the jurisdiction of this court to revise the judgment of a Circuit Court, and to reverse it for any error apparent on the record, whether it be the error of giving judgment in a case over which it had no jurisdiction, or any other material error; and this, too, whether there is a plea in abatement or not.

The objection appears to have arisen from confounding writs of error to a State court, with writs of error to a Circuit Court of the United States. Undoubtedly, upon a writ of error to a State court, unless the record shows a case that gives jurisdiction, the case must be dismissed for want of jurisdiction in this court. And if it is dismissed on that ground, we have no right to examine and decide upon any question presented by the bill of exceptions, or any other part of the record. But writs of error to a State court, and to a Circuit Court of the United States, are regulated by different laws, and stand upon entirely different principles. And in a writ of error to a Circuit Court of the United States, the whole record is before this court for examination and decision; and if the sum in controversy is large enough to give jurisdiction, it is not only the right, but it is the judicial duty of the court, to examine the whole case as presented by the record; and if it appears upon its face that any material error or errors have been committed by the court below, it is the duty of this court to reverse the judgment, and remand the case. And certainly an error in passing a judgment upon the merits in favor of either party, in a case which it was not authorized to try, and over which it had no jurisdiction, is as grave an error as a court can commit.

The plea in abatement is not a plea to the jurisdiction of this court, but to the jurisdiction of the Circuit Court. And it appears by the record before us, that the Circuit Court committed an error, in deciding that it had jurisdiction, upon the facts in the case, admitted by the pleadings. It is the duty of the appellate tribunal to correct this error; but that could not be done by dismissing the case for want of jurisdiction here—for that would leave the erroneous judgment in full force, and the injured party without remedy. And the appellate court therefore exercises the power for which alone appellate courts are constituted, by reversing the judgment of the court below for this error. It exercises its proper and appropriate jurisdiction over the judgment and proceedings of the Circuit Court, as they appear upon the record brought up by the writ of error.

The correction of one error in the court below does not deprive the appellate court of the power of examining further into the record, and correcting any other material errors which may have been committed by the inferior court. There is certainly no rule of law—nor any practice—nor any decision of a court—which even questions this power in the appellate tribunal. On the contrary, it is the daily practice of this court, and of all appellate courts where they reverse the judgment of an inferior court for error, to correct by its opinions whatever errors may appear on the record material to the case; and they have always held it to be their duty to do so where the silence of the court might lead to misconstruction or future controversy, and the point has been relied on by either side, and argued before the court.

In the case before us, we have already decided that the Circuit Court erred in deciding that it had jurisdiction upon the facts admitted by the pleadings. And it appears that, in the further progress of the case, it acted upon the erroneous principle it had decided on the pleadings, and gave judgment for the defendant, where, upon the facts admitted in the exception, it had no jurisdiction.

We are at a loss to understand upon what principle of law, applicable to appellate jurisdiction, it can be supposed that this court has not judicial authority to correct the last-mentioned error, because they had before corrected the former; or by what process of reasoning it can be made out, that the error of an inferior court in actually pronouncing judgment for one of the parties, in a case in which it had no jurisdiction, cannot be looked into or corrected by this court, because we have decided a similar question presented in the pleadings. The last point is distinctly presented by the facts contained in the plaintiff's own bill of exceptions, which he himself brings here by this writ of error. It was the point which chiefly occupied the attention of the counsel on both sides in the argument—and the judgment which this court must render upon both errors is precisely the same. It must, in each of them, exercise jurisdiction over the judgment, and reverse it for the errors committed by the court below; and issue a mandate to the Circuit Court to conform its judgment to the opinion pronounced by this court, by dismissing the case for want of jurisdiction in the Circuit Court. This is the constant and invariable practice of this court, where it reverses a judgment for want of jurisdiction in the Circuit Court.

It can scarcely be necessary to pursue such a question further. The want of jurisdiction in the court below may appear on the record without any plea in abatement. This is familiarly the case where a court of chancery has exercised jurisdiction in a case where the plaintiff had a plain and adequate remedy at law, and it so appears by the transcript when brought here by appeal. So also where it appears that a court of admiralty has exercised jurisdiction in a case belonging exclusively to a court of common law. In these cases there is no plea in abatement. And for the same reason, and upon the same principles, where the defect of jurisdiction is patent on the record, this court is bound to reverse the judgment, although the defendant has not pleaded in abatement to the jurisdiction of the inferior court.

The cases of *Jackson v. Ashton* and of *Capron v. Van Noorden*, to which we have referred in a previous part of this opinion, are directly in point. In the last-mentioned case, Capron brought an action against Van Noorden in a Circuit Court of the United States, without showing, by the usual averments of citizenship, that the court had jurisdiction. There was no plea in abatement put in, and the parties went to trial upon the merits. The court gave judgment in favor of the defendant with costs. The plaintiff thereupon brought his writ of error, and this court reversed the judgment given in favor of the defendant, and remanded the case with directions to dismiss it, because it did not appear by the transcript that the Circuit Court had jurisdiction.

The case before us still more strongly imposes upon this court the duty of examining whether the court below has not committed an error, in taking jurisdiction and giving a judgment for costs in favor of the defendant; for in *Capron v. Van Noorden* the judgment was reversed, because it did not appear that the parties were citizens of different States. They might or might not be. But in this case it does appear that the plaintiff was born a slave; and if the facts upon which he relies have not made him free, then it appears affirmatively on the record that he is not a citizen, and consequently his suit against Sandford was not a suit between citizens of different States, and the court had no authority to pass any judgment between the parties. The suit ought, in this view of it, to have been dismissed by the Circuit Court, and its judgment in favor of Sandford is erroneous, and must be reversed.

It is true that the result either way, by dismissal or by a judgment for the defendant, makes very little, if any, difference in a pecuniary or personal point of view to either party. But the fact that the result would be very nearly the same to the parties in either form of judgment, would not justify this court in sanctioning an error in the judgment which is patent on the record, and which, if sanctioned, might be drawn into precedent, and lead to serious mischief and injustice in some future suit.

We proceed, therefore, to inquire whether the facts relied on by the plaintiff entitled him to his freedom. The case, as he himself states it, on the record brought here by his writ of error, is this:

The plaintiff was a negro slave, belonging to Dr. Emerson, who was a surgeon in the army of the United States. In the year 1834, he took the plaintiff from the State of Missouri to the military post at Rock Island, in the State of Illinois, and held him there as a slave until the month of April or May, 1836. At the time last mentioned, said Dr. Emerson removed the plaintiff from said military post at Rock Island to the military post at Fort Snelling, situated on the west bank of the Mississippi river, in the Territory known as Upper Louisiana, acquired by the United States of France, and situate north of the latitude of thirty-six degrees thirty minutes north, and north of the State of Missouri. Said Dr. Emerson held the plaintiff in slavery at said Fort Snelling, from said last-mentioned date until the year 1838.

In the year 1835, Harriet, who is named in the second count of the plaintiff's declaration, was the negro slave of Major Taliaferro, who belonged to the army of the United States. In that year, 1835, said Major Taliaferro took said Harriet to said Fort Snelling, a military post, situated as hereinbefore stated, and kept her there as a slave until the year 1836, and then sold and delivered her as a slave, at said Fort Snelling, unto the said Dr. Emerson hereinbefore named. Said Dr. Emerson held said Harriet in slavery at said Fort Snelling until the year 1838.

In the year 1836, the plaintiff and Harriet intermarried, at Fort Snelling, with the consent of Dr. Emerson, who then claimed to be their master and owner. Eliza and Lizzie, named in the third count of the plaintiff's declaration, are the fruit of that marriage. Eliza is about fourteen years old, and was born on board the steamboat Gipsey, north of the north line of the State of Missouri, and upon the river Mississippi. Lizzie is about seven years old, and was born in the State of Missouri, at the military post called Jefferson Barracks.

In the year 1838, said Dr. Emerson removed the plaintiff and said Harriet, and their said daughter Eliza, from said Fort Snelling to the State of Missouri, where they have ever since resided.

Before the commencement of this suit, said Dr. Emerson sold and conveyed the plaintiff, and Harriet, Eliza, and Lizzie, to the defendant, as slaves, and the defendant has ever since claimed to hold them, and each of them, as slaves.

In considering this part of the controversy, two questions arise: 1. Was he, together with his family, free in Missouri by reason of the stay in the territory of the United States hereinbefore mentioned? And 2. If they were not, is Scott himself free by reason of his removal to Rock Island, in the State of Illinois, as stated in the above admissions?

We proceed to examine the first question.

The act of Congress, upon which the plaintiff relies, declares that slavery and involuntary servitude, except as a punishment for crime, shall be forever prohibited in all that part of the territory ceded by France, under the name of Louisiana, which lies north of thirty-six degrees thirty minutes north latitude, and not included within the limits of Missouri. And the difficulty which meets us at the threshold of this part of the inquiry is, whether Congress was authorized to pass this law under any of the powers granted to it by the Constitution; for if the authority is not given by that instrument, it is the duty of this court to declare it void and inoperative, and incapable of conferring freedom upon any one who is held as a slave under the have of any one of the States.

The counsel for the plaintiff has laid much stress upon that article in the Constitution which confers on Congress the power "to dispose of and make all needful rules and regulations respecting the territory or other property belonging to the United States;" but, in the judgment of the court, that provision has no bearing on the present controversy, and the power there given, whatever it may be, is confined, and was intended to be confined, to the territory which at that time belonged to, or was claimed by, the United States, and was within their boundaries as settled by the treaty with Great Britain, and can have no influence upon a territory afterwards acquired from a foreign Government. It was a special provision for a known and particular territory, and to meet a present emergency, and nothing more.

A brief summary of the history of the times, as well as the careful and measured terms in which the article is framed, will show the correctness of this proposition.

It will be remembered that, from the commencement of the Revolutionary war, serious difficulties existed between the States, in relation to the disposition of large and unsettled territories which were included in the chartered limits of some of the States. And some of the other States, and more especially Maryland, which had no unsettled lands, insisted that as the unoccupied lands, if wrested from Great Britain, would owe their preservation to the common purse and the common sword, the money arising from them ought to be applied in just proportion among the several States to pay the expenses of the war, and ought not to be appropriated to the use of the State in whose chartered limits they might happen to lie, to the exclusion of the other States, by whose combined efforts and common expense the territory was defended and preserved against the claim of the British Government.

These difficulties caused much uneasiness during the war, while the issue was in some degree doubtful, and the future boundaries of the United States yet to be defined by treaty, if we achieved our independence.

The majority of the Congress of the Confederation obviously concurred in opinion with the State of Maryland, and desired to obtain from the States which claimed it a cession of this territory, in order that Congress might raise money on this security to carry on the war. This appears by the resolution passed on the 6th of September, 1780, strongly urging the States to cede these lands to the United States, both for the sake of peace and union among themselves, and to maintain the public credit; and this was followed by the resolution of October 10th, 1780, by which Congress pledged itself, that if the lands were ceded, as recommended by the resolution above mentioned, they should be disposed of for the common benefit of the United States, and be settled and formed into distinct republican States, which should become members of the Federal Union, and have the same rights of sovereignty, and freedom, and independence, as other States.

But these difficulties became much more serious after peace took place, and the boundaries of the United States were established. Every State, at that time, felt severely the pressure of its war debt; but in Virginia, and some other States, there were large territories of unsettled lands, the sale of which would enable them to discharge their obligations without much inconvenience; while other States, which had no such resource, saw before them many years of heavy and burdensome taxation; and the latter insisted, for the reasons before stated, that these unsettled lands should be treated as the common property of the States, and the proceeds applied to their common benefit.

The letters from the statesmen of that day will show how much this controversy occupied their thoughts, and the dangers that were apprehended from it. It was the disturbing element of the time, and fears were entertained that it might dissolve the Confederation by which the States were then united.

These fears and dangers were, however, at once removed, when the State of Virginia, in 1784, voluntarily ceded to the United States the immense tract of country lying northwest of the river Ohio, and which was within the acknowledged limits of the State. The only object of the State, in making this cession, was to put an end to the threatening and exciting controversy, and to enable the Congress of that time to dispose of the lands, and appropriate the proceeds as a common fund for the common benefit of the States. It was not ceded, because it was inconvenient to the State to hold and govern it, nor from any expectation that it could be better or more conveniently governed by the United States.

The example of Virginia was soon afterwards followed by other States, and, at the time of the adoption of the Constitution, all of the States, similarly situated, had ceded their unappropriated lands, except North Carolina and Georgia. The main object for which these cessions were desired and made, was on account of their money value, and to put an end to a dangerous controversy, as to who was justly entitled to the proceeds when the lands should be sold. It is necessary to bring this part of the history of these cessions thus distinctly into view, because it will enable us the better to comprehend the phraseology of the article in the Constitution, so often referred to in the argument.

Undoubtedly the powers of sovereignty and the eminent domain were ceded with the land. This was essential, in order to make it effectual, and to accomplish its objects. But it must be remembered that, at that time, there was no Government of the United States in existence with enumerated and limited powers; what was then called the United States, were thirteen separate, sovereign, independent States, which had entered into a league or confederation for their mutual protection and advantage, and the Congress of the United States was composed of the representatives of these separate sovereignties, meeting together, as equals, to discuss and decide on certain measures which the States, by the Articles of Confederation, had agreed to submit to their decision. But this Confederation had none of the attributes of sovereignty in legislative, executive, or judicial power. It was little more than a congress of ambassadors, authorized to represent separate nations, in matters in which they had a common concern.

It was this Congress that accepted the cession from Virginia. They had no power to accept it under the Articles of Confederation. But they had an undoubted right, as independent sovereignties, to accept any cession of territory for their common benefit, which all of them assented to; and it is equally clear, that as their common property, and having no superior to control them, they had the right to exercise absolute dominion over it, subject only to the restrictions which Virginia had imposed in her act of cession. There was, as we have said, no Government of the United States then in existence with special enumerated and limited powers. The territory belonged to sovereignties, who, subject to the limitations above mentioned, had a right to establish any form of government they pleased, by compact or treaty among themselves, and to regulate rights of person and rights of property in the territory, as they might deem proper. It was by a Congress, representing the authority of these several and separate sovereignties, and acting under their authority and command, (but not from any authority derived from the Articles of Confederation,) that the instrument usually called the ordinance of 1787 was adopted; regulating in much detail the principles and the laws by which this territory should be governed; and among other provisions, slavery is prohibited in it. We do not question the power of the States, by agreement among themselves, to pass this ordinance, nor its obligatory force in the territory, while the confederation or league of the States in their separate sovereign character continued to exist.

This was the state of things when the Constitution of the United States was formed. The territory ceded by Virginia belonged to the several confederated States as common property, and they had united in establishing in it a system of government and jurisprudence, in order to prepare it for admission as States, according to the terms of the cession. They were about to dissolve this federative Union, and to surrender a portion of their independent sovereignty to a new Government, which, for certain purposes, would make the people of the several States one people, and which was to be supreme and controlling within its sphere of action throughout the United States; but this Government was to be carefully limited in its powers, and to exercise no authority beyond those expressly granted by the Constitution, or necessarily to be implied from the language of the instrument, and the objects it was intended to accomplish; and as this league of States would, upon the adoption of the new Government, cease to have any power over the territory, and the ordinance they had agreed upon be incapable of execution, and a mere nullity, it was obvious that some provision was necessary to give the new Government sufficient power to enable it to carry into effect the objects for which it was ceded, and the compacts and agreements which the States had made with each other in the exercise of their powers of sovereignty. It was necessary that the lands should be sold to pay the war debt; that a Government and system of jurisprudence should be maintained in it, to protect the citizens of the United States who should migrate to the territory, in their rights of person and of property. It was also necessary that the new Government, about to be adopted, should be authorized to maintain the claim of the United States to the unappropriated lands in North Carolina and Georgia, which had not then been ceded, but the cession of which was confidently anticipated upon some terms that would be arranged between the General Government and these two States. And, moreover, there were many articles of value besides this property in land, such as arms, military stores, munitions, and ships of war, which were the common property of the States, when acting in their independent characters as confederates, which neither the new Government nor any one else would have a right to take possession of, or control, without authority from them; and it was to place these things under the guardianship and protection of the new Government, and to clothe it with the necessary powers, that the clause was inserted in the Constitution which give Congress the power "to dispose of and make all needful rules and regulations respecting the territory or other property belonging to the United States." It was intended for a specific purpose, to provide for the things we have mentioned. It was to transfer to the new Government the property then held in common by the States, and to give to that Government power to apply it to the objects for which it had been destined by mutual agreement among the States before their league was dissolved. It applied only to the property which the States held in common at that time, and has no reference whatever to any territory or other property which the new sovereignty might afterwards itself acquire.

The language used in the clause, the arrangement and combination of the powers, and the somewhat unusual phraseology it uses, when it speaks of the political power to be exercised in the government of the territory, all indicate the design and meaning of the clause to be such as we have mentioned. It does not speak of any territory, nor of Territories, but uses language which, according to its legitimate meaning, points to a particular thing. The power is given in relation only to the territory of the United States—that is, to a territory then in existence, and then known or claimed as the territory of the United States. It begins its enumeration of powers by that of disposing, in other words, making sale of the lands, or raising money from them, which, as we have already said, was the main object of the cession, and which is accordingly the first thing provided for in the article. It then gives the power which was necessarily associated with the disposition and sale of the lands—that is, the power of making needful rules and regulations respecting the territory. And whatever construction may now be given to these words, every one, we think, must admit that they are not the words usually employed by statesmen in giving supreme power of legislation. They are certainly very unlike the words used in the power granted to legislate over territory which the new Government might afterwards itself obtain by cession from a State, either for its seat of Government, or for forts, magazines, arsenals, dock yards, and other needful buildings.

And the same power of making needful rules respecting the territory is, in precisely the same language, applied to the other property belonging to the United States—associating the power over the territory in this respect with the power over movable or personal property—that is, the ships, arms, and munitions of war, which then belonged in common to the State sovereignties. And it will hardly be said, that this power, in relation to the last-mentioned objects, was deemed necessary to be thus specially given to the new Government, in order to authorize it to make needful rules and regulations respecting the ships it might itself build, or arms and munitions of war it might itself manufacture or provide for the public service.

No one, it is believed, would think a moment of deriving the power of Congress to make needful rules and regulations in relation to property of this kind from this clause of the Constitution. Nor can it, upon any fair construction, be applied to any property but that which the new Government was about the receive from the confederated States. And if this be true as to this property, it must be equally true and limited as to the territory, which is so carefully and precisely coupled with it—and like it referred to as property in the power granted. The concluding words of the clause appear to render this construction irresistible; for, after the provisions we have mentioned, it proceeds to say, "that nothing in the Constitution shall be so construed as to prejudice any claims of the United States, or of any particular State."

Now, as we have before said, all of the States, except North Carolina and Georgia, had made the cession before the Constitution was adopted, according to the resolution of Congress of October 10, 1780. The claims of other States, that the unappropriated lands in these two States should be applied to the common benefit, in like manner, was still insisted on, but refused by the States. And this member of the

clause in question evidently applies to them, and can apply to nothing else. It was to exclude the conclusion that either party, by adopting the Constitution, would surrender what they deemed their rights. And when the latter provision relates so obviously to the unappropriated lands not yet ceded by the States, and the first clause makes provision for those then actually ceded, it is impossible, by any just rule of construction, to make the first provision general, and extend to all territories, which the Federal Government might in any way afterwards acquire, when the latter is plainly and unequivocally confined to a particular territory; which was a part of the same controversy, and involved in the same dispute, and depended upon the same principles. The union of the two provisions in the same clause shows that they were kindred subjects; and that the whole clause is local, and relates only to lands, within the limits of the United States, which had been or then were claimed by a State; and that no other territory was in the mind of the framers of the Constitution, or intended to be embraced in it. Upon any other construction it would be impossible to account for the insertion of the last provision in the place where it is found, or to comprehend why, or for what object, it was associated with the previous provision.

This view of the subject is confirmed by the manner in which the present Government of the United States dealt with the subject as soon as it came into existence. It must be borne in mind that the same States that formed the Confederation also formed and adopted the new Government, to which so large a portion of their former sovereign powers were surrendered. It must also be borne in mind that all of these same States which had then ratified the new Constitution were represented in the Congress which passed the first law for the government of this territory; and many of the members of that legislative body had been deputies from the States under the Confederation—had united in adopting the ordinance of 1787, and assisted in forming the new Government under which they were then acting, and whose powers they were then exercising. And it is obvious from the law they passed to carry into effect the principles and provisions of the ordinance, that they regarded it as the act of the States done in the exercise of their legitimate powers at the time. The new Government took the territory as it found it, and in the condition in which it was transferred, and did not attempt to undo anything that had been done. And, among the earliest laws passed under the new Government, is one reviving the ordinance of 1787, which had become inoperative and a nullity upon the adoption of the Constitution. This law introduces no new form or principles for its government, but recites, in the preamble, that it is passed in order that this ordinance may continue to have full effect, and proceeds to make only those rules and regulations which were needful to adapt it to the new Government, into whose hands the power had fallen. It appears, therefore, that this Congress regarded the purposes to which the land in this Territory was to be applied, and the form of government and principles of jurisprudence which were to prevail there, while it remained in the Territorial state, as already determined on by the States when they had full power and right to make the decision; and that the new Government, having received it in this condition, ought to carry substantially into effect the plans and principles which had been previously adopted by the States, and which no doubt the States anticipated when they surrendered their power to the new Government. And if we regard this clause of the Constitution as pointing to this Territory, with a Territorial Government already established in it, which had been ceded to the States for the purposes hereinbefore mentioned—every word in it is perfectly appropriate and easily understood, and the provisions it contains are in perfect harmony with the objects for which it was ceded, and with the condition of its government as a Territory at the time. We can, then, easily account for the manner in which the first Congress legislated on the subject—and can also understand why this power over the territory was associated in the same clause with the other property of the United States, and subjected to the like power of making needful rules and regulations. But if the clause is construed in the expanded sense contended for, so as to embrace any territory acquired from a foreign nation by the present Government, and to give it in such territory a despotic and unlimited power over persons and property, such as the confederated States might exercise in their common property, it would be difficult to account for the phraseology used, when compared with other grants of power—and also for its association with the other provisions in the same clause.

The Constitution has always been remarkable for the felicity of its arrangement of different subjects, and the perspicuity and appropriateness of the language it uses. But if this clause is construed to extend to territory acquired by the present Government from a foreign nation, outside of the limits of any charter from the British Government to a colony, it would be difficult to say, why it was deemed necessary to give the Government the power to sell any vacant lands belonging to the sovereignty which might be found within it; and if this was necessary, why the grant of this power should precede the power to legislate over it and establish a Government there; and still more difficult to say, why it was deemed necessary so specially and particularly to grant the power to make needful rules and regulations in relation to any personal or movable property it might acquire there. For the words, other property necessarily, by every known rule of interpretation, must mean property of a different description from territory or land. And the difficulty would perhaps be insurmountable in endeavoring to account for the last member of the sentence, which provides that "nothing in this Constitution shall be so construed as to prejudice any claims of the United States or any particular State," or to say how any particular State could have claims in or to a territory ceded by a foreign Government, or to account for associating this provision with the preceding provisions of the clause, with which it would appear to have no connection.

The words "needful rules and regulations" would seem, also, to have been cautiously used for some definite object. They are not the words usually employed by statesmen, when they mean to give the powers of sovereignty, or to establish a Government, or to authorize its establishment. Thus, in the law to renew and keep alive the ordinance of 1787, and to re-establish the Government, the title of the law is: "An act to provide for the government of the territory northwest of the river Ohio." And in the Constitution, when granting the power to legislate over the territory that may be selected for the seat of Government independently of a State, it does not say Congress shall have power "to make all needful rules and regulations respecting the territory;" but it declares that "Congress shall have power to exercise exclusive legislation in all cases whatsoever over such District (not exceeding ten miles square) as may, by cession of particular States and the acceptance of Congress, become the seat of the Government of the United States."

The words "rules and regulations" are usually employed in the Constitution in speaking of some particular specified power which it means to confer on the Government, and not, as we have seen, when granting general powers of legislation. As, for example, in the particular power to Congress "to make rules for the government and regulation of the land and naval forces, or the particular and specific power to regulate commerce;" "to establish an uniform rule of naturalization;" "to coin money and regulate the value thereof." And to construe the words of which we are speaking as a general and unlimited grant of sovereignty over territories which the Government might afterwards acquire, is to use them in a sense and for a purpose for which they were not used in any other part of the instrument. But if confined to a particular Territory, in which a Government and laws had already been established, but which would require some alterations to adapt it to the new Government, the words are peculiarly applicable and appropriate for that purpose. The necessity of this special provision in relation to property and the rights or property held in common by the confederated States, is illustrated by the first clause of the sixth article. This clause provides that "all debts, contracts, and engagements entered into before the adoption of this Constitution, shall be as valid against the United States under this Government as under the Confederation." This provision, like the one under consideration, was indispensable if the new Constitution was adopted. The new Government was not a mere change in a dynasty, or in a form of government, leaving the nation or sovereignty the same, and clothed with all the rights, and bound by all the obligations of the preceding one. But, when the present United States came into existence under the new Government, it was a new political body, a new nation, then for the first time taking its place in the family of nations. It took nothing by succession from the Confederation. It had no right, as its successor, to any property or rights of property which it had acquired, and was not liable for any of its obligations. It was evidently viewed in this light by the framers of the Constitution. And as the several States would cease to exist in their former confederated character upon the adoption of the Constitution, and could not, in that character, again assemble together, special provisions were indispensable to transfer to the new Government the property and rights which at that time they held in common; and at the same time to authorize it to lay taxes and appropriate money to pay the common debt which they had contracted; and this power could only be given to it by special provisions in the Constitution. The clause in relation to the territory and other property of the United States provided for the first, and the clause last quoted provided for the other. They have no connection with the general powers and rights of sovereignty delegated to the new Government, and can neither enlarge nor diminish them. They were inserted to meet a present emergency, and not to regulate its powers as a Government.

Indeed, a similar provision was deemed necessary, in relation to treaties made by the Confederation; and when in the clause next succeeding the one of which we have last spoken, it is declared that treaties shall be the supreme law of the land, care is taken to include, by express words, the treaties made by the confederated States. The language is: "and all treaties made, or which shall be made, under the authority of the United States, shall be the supreme law of the land."

Whether, therefore, we take the particular clause in question, by itself, or in connection with the other provisions of the Constitution, we think it clear, that it applies only to the particular territory of which we have spoken, and cannot, by any just rule of interpretation, be extended to territory which the new Government might afterwards obtain from a foreign nation. Consequently, the power which Congress may have lawfully exercised in this Territory, while it remained under a Territorial Government, and which may have been sanctioned by judicial decision, can furnish no justification and no argument to support a similar exercise of power over territory afterwards acquired by the Federal Government. We put aside, therefore, any argument, drawn from precedents, showing the extent of the power which the General Government exercised over slavery in this Territory, as altogether inapplicable to the case before us.

But the case of the *American and Ocean Insurance Companies v. Canter* (1 Pet., 511) has been quoted as establishing a different construction of this clause of the Constitution. There is, however, not the slightest conflict between the opinion now given and the one referred to; and it is only by taking a single sentence out of the latter and separating it from the context, that even an appearance of conflict can be shown. We need not comment on such a mode of expounding an opinion of the court. Indeed it most commonly misrepresents instead of expounding it. And this is fully exemplified in the case referred to, where, if one sentence is taken by itself, the opinion would appear to be in direct conflict with that now given; but the words which immediately follow that sentence show that the court did not mean to decide the point, but merely affirmed the power of Congress to establish a Government in the Territory, leaving it an open question, whether that power was derived from this clause in the Constitution, or was to be necessarily inferred from a power to acquire territory by cession from a foreign Government. The opinion on this part of the case is short, and we give the whole of it to show how well the selection of a single sentence is calculated to mislead.

The passage referred to is in page 542, in which the court, in speaking of the power of Congress to establish a Territorial Government in Florida until it should become a State, uses the following language:

"In the mean time Florida continues to be a Territory of the United States, governed by that clause of the Constitution which empowers Congress to make all needful rules and regulations respecting the territory or other property of the United States. Perhaps the power of governing a Territory belonging to the United States, which has not, by becoming a State, acquired the means of self-government, may result, necessarily, from the facts that it is not within the jurisdiction of any particular State, and is within the power and jurisdiction of the United States. The right to govern may be the inevitable consequence of the right to acquire territory. Whichever may be the source from which the power is derived, the possession of it is unquestionable."

It is thus clear, from the whole opinion on this point, that the court did not mean to decide whether the power was derived from the clause in the Constitution, or was the necessary consequence of the right to acquire. They do decide that the power in Congress is unquestionable, and in this we entirely concur, and nothing will be found in this opinion to the contrary. The power stands firmly on the latter alternative put by the court—that is, as "the inevitable consequence of the right to acquire territory."

And what still more clearly demonstrates that the court did not mean to decide the question, but leave it open for future consideration, is the fact that the case was decided in the Circuit Court by Mr. Justice Johnson, and his decision was affirmed by the Supreme Court. His opinion at the circuit is given in full in a note to the case, and in that opinion he states, in explicit terms, that the clause of the Constitution applies only to the territory then within the limits of the United States, and not to Florida, which had been acquired by cession from Spain. This part of his opinion will be found in the note in page 517 of the report. But he does not dissent from the opinion of the Supreme Court; thereby showing that, in his judgment, as well as that of the court, the case before them did not call for a decision on that particular point, and the court abstained from deciding it. And in a part of its opinion subsequent to the passage we have quoted, where the court speak of the legislative

power of Congress in Florida, they still speak with the same reserve. And in page 546, speaking of the power of Congress to authorize the Territorial Legislature to establish courts there, the court say: "They are legislative courts, created in virtue of the general right of sovereignty which exists in the Government, or in virtue of that clause which enables Congress to make all needful rules and regulations respecting the territory belonging to the United States."

It has been said that the construction given to this clause is new, and now for the first time brought forward. The case of which we are speaking, and which has been so much discussed, shows that the fact is otherwise. It shows that precisely the same question came before Mr. Justice Johnson, at his circuit, thirty years ago—was fully considered by him, and the same construction given to the clause in the Constitution which is now given by this court. And that upon an appeal from his decision the same question was brought before this court, but was not decided because a decision upon it was not required by the case before the court.

There is another sentence in the opinion which has been commented on, which even in a still more striking manner shows how one may mislead or be misled by taking out a single sentence from the opinion of a court, and leaving out of view what precedes and follows. It is in page 546, near the close of the opinion, in which the court say: "In legislating for them," (the territories of the United States,) "Congress exercises the combined powers of the General and of a State Government." And it is said, that as a State may unquestionably prohibit slavery within its territory, this sentence decides in effect that Congress may do the same in a Territory of the United States, exercising there the powers of a State, as well as the power of the General Government.

The examination of this passage in the case referred to, would be more appropriate when we come to consider in another part of this opinion what power Congress can constitutionally exercise in a Territory, over the rights of person or rights of property of a citizen. But, as it is in the same case with the passage we have before commented on, we dispose of it now, as it will save the court from the necessity of referring again to the case. And it will be seen upon reading the page in which this sentence is found, that it has no reference whatever to the power of Congress over rights of person or rights of property—but relates altogether to the power of establishing judicial tribunals to administer the laws constitutionally passed, and defining the jurisdiction they may exercise.

The law of Congress establishing a Territorial Government in Florida, provided that the Legislature of the Territory should have legislative powers over "all rightful objects of legislation; but no law should be valid which was inconsistent with the laws and Constitution of the United States."

Under the power thus conferred, the Legislature of Florida passed an act, erecting a tribunal at Key West to decide cases of salvage. And in the case of which we are speaking, the question arose whether the Territorial Legislature could be authorized by Congress to establish such a tribunal, with such powers; and one of the parties, among other objections, insisted that Congress could not under the Constitution authorize the Legislature of the Territory to establish such a tribunal with such powers, but that it must be established by Congress itself; and that a sale of cargo made under its order, to pay salvors, was void, as made without legal authority, and passed no property to the purchaser. It is in disposing of this objection that the sentence relied on occurs, and the court begin that part of the opinion by stating with great precision the point which they are about to decide.

They say: "It has been contended that by the Constitution of the United States, the judicial power of the United States extends to all cases of admiralty and maritime jurisdiction; and that the whole of the judicial power must be vested 'in one Supreme Court, and in such inferior courts as Congress shall from time to time ordain and establish.' Hence it has been argued that Congress cannot vest admiralty jurisdiction in courts created by the Territorial Legislature."

And after thus clearly stating the point before them, and which they were about to decide, they proceed to show that these Territorial tribunals were not constitutional courts, but merely legislative, and that Congress might, therefore, delegate the power to the Territorial Government to establish the court in question; and they conclude that part of the opinion in the following words: "Although admiralty jurisdiction can be exercised in the States in those courts only which are established in pursuance of the third article of the Constitution, the same limitation does not extend to the Territories. In legislating for them, Congress exercises the combined powers of the General and State Governments."

Thus it will be seen by these quotations from the opinion, that the court, after stating the question it was about to decide in a manner too plain to be misunderstood, proceeded to decide it, and announced, as the opinion of the tribunal, that in organizing the judicial department of the Government in a Territory of the United States, Congress does not act under, and is not restricted by, the third article in the Constitution, and is not bound, in a Territory, to ordain and establish courts in which the judges hold their offices during good behaviour, but may exercise the discretionary power which a State exercises in establishing its judicial department, and regulating the jurisdiction of its courts, and may authorize the Territorial Government to establish, or may itself establish, courts in which the judges hold their offices for a term of years only; and may vest in them judicial power upon subjects confided to the judiciary of the United States. And in doing this, Congress undoubtedly exercises the combined power of the General and a State Government. It exercises the discretionary power of a State Government in authorizing the establishment of a court in which the judges hold their appointments for a term of years only, and not during good behaviour; and it exercises the power of the General Government in investing that court with admiralty jurisdiction, over which the General Government had exclusive jurisdiction in the Territory.

No one, we presume, will question the correctness of that opinion; nor is there anything in conflict with it in the opinion now given. The point decided in the case cited has no relation to the question now before the court. That depended on the construction of the third article of the Constitution, in relation to the judiciary of the United States, and the power which Congress might exercise in a Territory in organizing the judicial department of the Government. The case before us depends upon other and different provisions of the Constitution, altogether separate and apart from the one above mentioned. The question as to what courts Congress may ordain or establish in a Territory to administer laws which the Constitution authorizes it to pass, and what laws it is or is not authorized by the Constitution to pass, are widely different—are regulated by different and separate articles of the Constitution, and stand upon different principles. And we are satisfied that no one who reads attentively the page in Peters's Reports to which we have referred, can suppose that the attention of the court was drawn for a moment to the question now before this court, or that it meant in that case to say that Congress had a right to prohibit a citizen of the United States from taking any property which he lawfully held into a Territory of the United States.

This brings us to examine by what provision of the Constitution the present Federal Government, under its delegated and restricted powers, is authorized to acquire territory outside of the original limits of the United States, and what powers it may exercise therein over the person or property of a citizen of the United States, while it remains a Territory, and until it shall be admitted as one of the States of the Union.

There is certainly no power given by the Constitution to the Federal Government to establish or maintain colonies bordering on the United States or at a distance, to be ruled and governed at its own pleasure; nor to enlarge its territorial limits in any way, except by the admission of new States. That power is plainly given; and if a new State is admitted, it needs no further legislation by Congress, because the Constitution itself defines the relative rights and powers, and duties of the State, and the citizens of the State, and the Federal Government. But no power is given to acquire a Territory to be held and governed permanently in that character.

And indeed the power exercised by Congress to acquire territory and establish a Government there, according to its own unlimited discretion, was viewed with great jealousy by the leading statesmen of the day. And in the Federalist, (No. 38,) written by Mr. Madison, he speaks of the acquisition of the Northwestern Territory by the confederated States, by the cession from Virginia, and the establishment of a Government there, as an exercise of power not warranted by the Articles of Confederation, and dangerous to the liberties of the people. And he urges the adoption of the Constitution as a security and safeguard against such an exercise of power.

We do not mean, however, to question the power of Congress in this respect. The power to expand the territory of the United States by the admission of new States is plainly given; and in the construction of this power by all the departments of the Government, it has been held to authorize the acquisition of territory, not fit for admission at the time, but to be admitted as soon as its population and situation would entitle it to admission. It is acquired to become a State, and not to be held as a colony and governed by Congress with absolute authority; and as the propriety of admitting a new State is committed to the sound discretion of Congress, the power to acquire territory for that purpose, to be held by the United States until it is in a suitable condition to become a State upon an equal footing with the other States, must rest upon the same discretion. It is a question for the political department of the Government, and not the judicial; and whatever the political departent of the Government shall recog-

nise as within the limits of the United States, the judicial department is also bound to recognise, and to administer in it the laws of the United States, so far as they apply, and to maintain in the Territory the authority and rights of the Government, and also the personal rights and rights of property of individual citizens, as secured by the Constitution. All we mean to say on this point is, that, as there is no express regulation in the Constitution defining the power which the General Government may exercise over the person or property of a citizen in a Territory thus acquired, the court must necessarily look to the provisions and principles of the Constitution, and its distribution of powers, for the rules and principles by which its decision must be governed.

Taking this rule to guide us, it may be safely assumed that citizens of the United States who migrate to a Territory belonging to the people of the United States, cannot be ruled as mere colonists, dependent upon the will of the General Government, and to be governed by any laws it may think proper to impose. The principle upon which our Governments rest, and upon which alone they continue to exist, is the union of States, sovereign and independent within their own limits in their internal and domestic concerns, and bound together as one people by a General Government, possessing certain enumerated and restricted powers, delegated to it by the people of the several States, and exercising supreme authority within the scope of the powers granted to it, throughout the dominion of the United States. A power, therefore, in the General Government to obtain and hold colonies and dependent territories, over which they might legislate without restriction, would be inconsistent with its own existence in its present form. Whatever it acquires, it acquires for the benefit of the people of the several States who created it. It is their trustee acting for them, and charged with the duty of promoting the interests of the whole people of the Union in the exercise of the powers specifically granted.

At the time when the Territory in question was obtained by cession from France, it contained no population fit to be associated together and admitted as a State; and it therefore was absolutely necessary to hold possession of it, as a Territory belonging to the United States, until it was settled and inhabited by a civilized community capable of self-government, and in a condition to be admitted on equal terms with the other States as a member of the Union. But, as we have before said, it was acquired by the General Government, as the representative and trustee of the people of the United States, and it must therefore be held in that character for their common and equal benefit; for it was the people of the several States, acting through their agent and representative, the Federal Government, who in fact acquired the Territory in question, and the Government holds it for their common use until it shall be associated with the other States as a member of the Union.

But until that time arrives, it is undoubtedly necessary that some Government should be established, in order to organize society, and to protect the inhabitants in their persons and property; and as the people of the United States could act in this matter only through the Government which represented them, and the through which they spoke and acted when the Territory was obtained, it was not only within the scope of its powers, but it was its duty to pass such laws and establish such a Government as would enable those by whose authority they acted to reap the advantages anticipated from its acquisition, and to gather there a population which would enable it to assume the position to which it was destined among the States of the Union. The power to acquire necessarily carries with it the power to preserve and apply to the purposes for which it was acquired. The form of government to be established necessarily rested in the discretion of Congress. It was their duty to establish the one that would be best suited for the protection and security of the citizens of the United States, and other inhabitants who might be authorized to take up their abode there, and that must always depend upon the existing condition of the Territory, as to the number and character of its inhabitants, and their situation in the Territory. In some cases a Government, consisting of persons appointed by the Federal Government, would best subserve the interests of the Territory, when the inhabitants were few and scattered, and new to one another. In other instances, it would be more advisable to commit the powers of self-government to the people who had settled in the Territory, as being the most competent to determine what was best for their own interests. But some form of civil authority would be absolutely necessary to organize and preserve civilized society, and prepare it to become a State; and what is the best form must always depend on the condition of the Territory at the time, and the choice of the mode must depend upon the exercise of a discretionary power by Congress, acting within the scope of its constitutional authority, and not infringing upon the rights of person or rights of property of the citizen who might go there to reside, or for any other lawful purpose. It was acquired by the exercise of this discretion, and it must

be held and governed in like manner, until it is fitted to be a State.

But the power of Congress over the person or property of a citizen can never be a mere discretionary power under our Constitution and form of Government. The powers of the Government and the rights and privileges of the citizen are regulated and plainly defined by the Constitution itself. And when the Territory becomes a part of the United States, the Federal Government enters into possession in the character impressed upon it by those who created it. It enters upon it with its powers over the citizen strictly defined, and limited by the Constitution, from which it derives its own existence, and by virtue of which alone it continues to exist and act as a Government and sovereignty. It has no power of any kind beyond it; and it cannot, when it enters a Territory of the United States, put off its character, and assume discretionary or despotic powers which the Constitution has denied to it. It cannot create for itself a new character separated from the citizens of the United States, and the duties it owes them under the provisions of the Constitution. The Territory being a part of the United States, the Government and the citizen both enter it under the authority of the Constitution, with their respective rights defined and marked out; and the Federal Government can exercise no power over his person or property, beyond what that instrument confers, nor lawfully deny any right which it has reserved.

A reference to a few of the provisions of the Constitution will illustrate this proposition.

For example, no one, we presume, will contend that Congress can make any law in a Territory respecting the establishment of religion, or the free exercise thereof, or abridging the freedom of speech or of the press, or the right of the people of the Territory peaceably to assemble, and to petition the Government for the redress of grievances.

Nor can Congress deny to the people the right to keep and bear arms, nor the right to trial by jury, nor compel any one to be a witness against himself in a criminal proceeding.

These powers, and others, in relation to rights of person, which it is not necessary here to enumerate, are, in express and positive terms, denied to the General Government; and the rights of private property have been guarded with equal care. Thus the rights of property are united with the rights of person, and placed on the same ground by the fifth amendment to the Constitution, which provides that no person shall be deprived of life, liberty, and property, without due process of law. And an act of Congress which deprives a citizen of the United States of his liberty or property, merely because he came himself or brought his property into a particular Territory of the United States, and who had committed no offence against the laws, could hardly be dignified with the name of due process of law.

So, too, it will hardly be contended that Congress could by law quarter a soldier in a house in a Territory without the consent of the owner, in time of peace; nor in time of war, but in a manner prescribed by law. Nor could they by law forfeit the property of a citizen in a Territory who was convicted of treason, for a longer period than the life of the person convicted; nor take private property for public use without just compensation.

The powers over person and property of which we speak are not only not granted to Congress, but are in express terms denied, and they are forbidden to exercise them. And this prohibition is not confined to the States, but the words are general, and extend to the whole territory over which the Constitution gives it power to legislate, including those portions of it remaining under Territorial Government, as well as that covered by States. It is a total absence of power everywhere within the dominion of the United States, and places the citizens of a Territory, so far as these rights are concerned, on the same footing with citizens of the States, and guards them as firmly and plainly against any inroads which the General Government might attempt, under the plea of implied or incidental powers.

And if Congress itself cannot do this—if it is beyond the powers conferred on the Federal Government—it will be admitted, we presume, that it could not authorize a Territorial Government to exercise them. It could confer no power on any local Government, established by its authority, to violate the provisions of the Constitution.

It seems, however, to be supposed, that there is a difference between property in a slave and other property, and that different rules may be applied to it in expounding the Constitution of the United States. And the laws and usages of nations, and the writings of eminent jurists upon the relation of master and slave and their mutual rights and duties, and the powers which Governments may exercise over it, have been dwelt upon in the argument.

But in considering the question before us, it must be borne in mind that there is no law of nations standing between the people of the United States and their Government, and interfering with their relation to each other. The powers of the Government, and the rights of the citizen under it, are positive and practical regulations plainly written down. The people of the United States have delegated to it certain enumerated powers, and forbidden it to exercise others. It has no power over the person or property of a citizen but what the citizens of the United States have granted. And no laws or usages of other nations, or reasoning of statesmen or jurists upon the relations of master and slave, can enlarge the powers of the Government, or take from the citizens the rights they have reserved. And if the Constitution recognises the right of property of the master in a slave, and makes no distinction between that description of property and other property owned by a citizen, no tribunal, acting under the authority of the United States, whether it be legislative, executive, or judicial, has a right to draw such a distinction, or deny to it the benefit of the provisions and guarantees which have been provided for the protection of private property against the encroachments of the Government.

Now, as we have already said in an earlier part of this opinion, upon a different point, the right of property in a slave is distinctly and expressly affirmed in the Constitution. The right to traffic in it, like an ordinary article of merchandise and property, was guarantied to the citizens of the United States, in every State that might desire it, for twenty years. And the Government in express terms is pledged to protect it in all future time, if the slave escapes from his owner. This is done in plain words—too plain to be misunderstood. And no word can be found in the Constitution which gives Congress a greater power over slave property, or which entitles property of that kind to less protection than property of any other description. The only power conferred is the power coupled with the duty of guarding and protecting the owner in his rights.

Upon these considerations, it is the opinion of the court that the act of Congress which prohibited a citizen from holding and owning property of this kind in the territory of the United States north of the line therein mentioned, is not warranted by the Constitution, and is therefore void; and that neither Dred Scott himself, nor any of his family, were made free by being carried into this territory; even if they had been carried there by the owner, with the intention of becoming a permanent resident.

We have so far examined the case, as it stands under the Constitution of the United States, and the powers thereby delegated to the Federal Government.

But there is another point in the case which depends on State power and State law. And it is contended, on the part of the plaintiff, that he is made free by being taken to Rock Island, in the State of Illinois, independently of his residence in the territory of the United States; and being so made free, he was not again reduced to a state of slavery by being brought back to Missouri.

Our notice of this part of the case will be very brief; for the principle on which it depends was decided in this court, upon much consideration, in the case of *Strader et al. v. Graham*, reported in 10th Howard, 82. In that case, the slaves had been taken from Kentucky to Ohio, with the consent of the owner, and afterwards brought back to Kentucky. And this court held that their status or condition, as free or slave, depended upon the laws of Kentucky, when they were brought back into that State, and not of Ohio; and that this court had no jurisdiction to revise the judgment of a State court upon its own laws. This was the point directly before the court, and the decision that this court had not jurisdiction turned upon it, as will be seen by the report of the case.

So in this case. As Scott was a slave when taken into the State of Illinois by his owner, and was there held as such, and brought back in that character, his status, as free or slave, depended on the laws of Missouri, and not of Illinois.

It has, however, been urged in the argument, that by the laws of Missouri he was free on his return, and that this case, therefore, cannot be governed by the case of *Strader et al. v. Graham*, where it appeared, by the laws of Kentucky, that the plaintiffs continued to be slaves on their return from Ohio. But whatever doubts or opinions may, at one time, have been entertained upon this subject, we are satisfied, upon a careful examination of all the cases decided in the State courts of Missouri referred to, that it is now firmly settled by the decisions of the highest court in the State, that Scott and his family upon their return were not free, but were, by the laws of Missouri, the property of the defendant; and that the Circuit Court of the United States had no jurisdiction, when, by the laws of the State, the plaintiff was a slave, and not a citizen.

Moreover, the plaintiff, it appears, brought a similar action against the defendant in the State court of Missouri, claiming the freedom of himself and his family upon the same grounds and the same evidence upon which he relies in the case before the court. The case was carried before the Supreme Court of the State; was fully argued there;

and that court decided that neither the plaintiff nor his family were entitled to freedom, and were still the slaves of the defendant; and reversed the judgment of the inferior State court, which had given a different decision. If the plaintiff supposed that this judgment of the Supreme Court of the State was erroneous, and that this court had jurisdiction to revise and reverse it, the only mode by which he could legally bring it before this court was by writ of error directed to the Supreme Court of the State, requiring it to transmit the record to this court. If this had been done, it is too plain for argument that the writ must have been dismissed for want of jurisdiction in this court. The case of *Strader and others v. Graham* is directly in point; and, indeed, independent of any decision, the language of the 25th section of the act of 1789 is too clear and precise to admit of controversy.

But the plaintiff did not pursue the mode prescribed by law for bringing the judgment of a State court before this court for revision, but suffered the case to be remanded to the inferior State court, where it is still continued, and is, by agreement of parties, to await the judgment of this court on the point. All of this appears on the record before us, and by the printed report of the case.

And while the case is yet open and pending in the inferior State court, the plaintiff goes into the Circuit Court of the United States, upon the same case and the same evidence, and against the same party, and proceeds to judgment, and then brings here the same case from the Circuit Court, which the law would not have permitted him to bring directly from the State court. And if this court takes jurisdiction in this form, the result, so far as the rights of the respective parties are concerned, is in every respect substantially the same as if it had in open violation of law entertained jurisdiction over the judgment of the State court upon a writ of error, and revised and reversed its judgment upon the ground that its opinion upon the question of law was erroneous. It would ill become this court to sanction such an attempt to evade the law, or to exercise an appellate power in this circuitous way, which it is forbidden to exercise in the direct and regular and invariable forms of judicial proceedings.

Upon the whole, therefore, it is the judgment of this court, that it appears by the record before us that the plaintiff in error is not a citizen of Missouri, in the sense in which that word is used in the Constitution; and that the Circuit Court of the United States, for that reason, had no jurisdiction in the case, and could give no judgment in it. Its judgment for the defendant must, consequently, be reversed, and a mandate issued, directing the suit to be dismissed for want of jurisdiction.

jurisdiction	the power or right of a court to hear a case
mulatto	a person of mixed European and African ancestry; technically, a mulatto was considered half European and half African, but the term was more loosely used to describe all people with some African and some European ancestry.

Martin Van Buren and Charles Francis Adams in the presidential race of 1848 (Library of Congress)

John S. Rock's "Whenever the Colored Man Is Elevated, It Will Be by His Own Exertions"

"When the white man was created, nature was pretty well exhausted."

Overview

First delivered in Boston's Faneuil Hall in March 1858, "Whenever the Colored Man Is Elevated, It Will Be by His Own Exertions" was an address given by the black physician and abolitionist John Swett Rock. Coming one year after the Supreme Court's pronouncement in *Dred Scott v. Sandford* that African Americans lacked all legal rights, Scott's speech was at once a challenge to the Court and a plea for blacks to shift their emphasis away from formal legal equality and toward economic power. Although African Americans had endorsed racial nationalism earlier, Rock differed from proponents of self-help like Martin Delany by rejecting the idea that African Americans should return to Africa, as proposed by the American Colonization Society in 1817.

Instead, Rock prefigured the self-help arguments that would be made by later black leaders like Booker T. Washington, who declared in the 1890s that African American interests would be better served by replacing the quest for legal rights with a more pragmatic quest for technical education and property accumulation. Yet Rock went further than Washington even, by hinting at the idea that African Americans might actually be superior to whites in certain regards. Foreshadowing the Afrocentric arguments of the 1960s, Rock publicly declared African Americans to be more physically appealing than whites, a claim that roundly rejected the white racist views dominant in both the North and the South at the time.

Notable for both its racial claims and its eloquence, Rock's address stands out among contemporary abolitionist statements primarily for its anticipation of trends in black politics that would not come to fruition until the 1960s and 1970s. Rock also outlined a relatively sophisticated analysis of the social construction of race, observing that many of the inferior characteristics that whites seemed to find endemic to blacks were actually the direct result of the oppression and deprivation that African Americans suffered at white hands.

Context

John Rock's Boston address came near the tail end of over a century of abolitionist activity in the North. Per-

haps the first sign of such activity emerged in Philadelphia, where the Quaker minister John Woolman took a public stand against slavery in his 1754 tract *Some Considerations on the Keeping of Negroes*. Working off Quaker theology, Woolman posited that slavery actually corrupted slave owners, distancing them from God. By 1780, Woolman's work culminated in a Pennsylvania statute calling for the gradual abolition of slavery in the state. Seven years later, delegates to the Constitutional Convention in Philadelphia debated whether the slave trade should be terminated by constitutional provision, with some delegates, even some from southern states, declaring the trade a scourge.

Nine years after the importation of slaves was abolished, in 1817, opponents of slavery in Virginia formed the American Colonization Society (ACS), arguably the first abolitionist organization in the country, which aimed to free black slaves and return them to Africa. In 1822 the ACS had established its first colony, Liberia, which would become an independent nation in 1846. Despite the ACS's hope that slave owners could be paid to manumit their slaves and those slaves then transported outside of the United States, few took advantage of the agency's services, creating a vacuum that would be filled by more radical opponents of slavery, such as William Lloyd Garrison.

Garrison, who initially belonged to the ACS, grew frustrated with the organization and suspected that it was secretly trying to prolong slavery by reducing the number of free blacks in the South. Increasingly convinced that slavery should be abolished outright, Garrison went to work for an antislavery newspaper run by Quakers, only to grow frustrated with their gradualist approach. In 1831 he established his own weekly newspaper, *The Liberator*, an antislavery publication that propounded a markedly different view from the one espoused by John Woolman in 1754. Rather than focus on the negative effect that slavery had on white owners, Garrison chose to emphasize the harm that slavery caused African Americans, using that harm as a justification for ending slavery immediately. Electrified by the message that blacks should be manumitted immediately and granted full political rights, northern readers of *The Liberator* became so numerous that Garrison founded the New England Anti-Slavery Society in 1832 and, one year later, the American Anti-Slavery Society. By 1838 more

Time Line

1825	■ **October 13** John S. Rock is born in Salem, New Jersey.
1831	■ William Lloyd Garrison begins publishing *The Liberator*.
1833	■ **December** The American Anti-Slavery Society is founded.
1852	■ **July 5** Frederick Douglass delivers his oration "What to the Slave Is the Fourth of July?"
1854	■ The Kansas-Nebraska Act leads to violence on the Missouri-Kansas border.
1857	■ **March 6** *Dred Scott v. Sandford* is decided by the Supreme Court, effectively denying citizenship to all blacks.
1858	■ **March 5** John S. Rock delivers his Faneuil Hall address.
1859	■ **October 16** The abolitionist John Brown leads an assault on a federal arsenal at Harpers Ferry, Virginia.
1861	■ **April 12** Civil War breaks out over the secession crisis.
1865	■ **February 1** John S. Rock becomes the first black man admitted to practice before the Supreme Court. ■ **April 9** The Civil War ends with the Confederate surrender at Appomattox Court House.
1866	■ **December 3** John S. Rock dies.

than one thousand branches of the American Anti-Slavery Society had been founded, and its membership numbered over two hundred fifty thousand.

Of course, whites like Garrison were not the only Americans to oppose slavery. African Americans fought slavery from both within and without. Slave revolts began as early as 1739 in Stono, South Carolina; continued through the eighteenth century; and culminated in the rebellion of Nat Turner, a Virginia slave who, purportedly acting upon God's command, roused sixty of his peers and killed over fifty whites, sending tremors of fear across the South. Less violent forms of revolt emerged in the North, many led by Frederick Douglass, a Maryland slave who escaped to Massachusetts in 1838. Like Garrison, Douglass also founded an abolitionist newspaper, the *North Star*, and allied himself with other reformist causes, among them women's suffrage. However, he became best known for his autobiography, a riveting account of the evils of slavery published in 1845.

In a manner that would come to be representative of abolitionists generally, Douglass and Garrison split in the 1830s, Garrison actually going down the more radical path of criticizing not only southern slavery but also the national government and even the Constitution. Declaring America's founding document a "covenant with death," Garrison succeeded in fracturing his own organization, the American Anti-Slavery Society, contributing to a larger dissonance in the abolitionist movement. Although Douglass charted a more moderate path, eventually becoming an influential figure in the Republican Party, other black abolitionists followed the more radical, Garrisonian road. Indeed, by the early 1850s, abolitionist sentiment had intensified in the North, producing the first hints of black nationalism. In 1852, for example, the black journalist Martin R. Delany announced that black elevation would come only from "self-efforts"—a claim that John Rock would reiterate six years later—and called for black colonization of Central and South America. Even Frederick Douglass—who advocated working for change from within American society—took an increasingly critical stance on the national implications of slavery. In 1852 he delivered a scathing address arguing that the Fourth of July had little significance for blacks, a charge extending the usual abolitionist emphasis on the South northward, to include liberal elites in Boston, New York, and Philadelphia.

Amid such calumny, larger historical forces pushed the country toward civil war. Perhaps foremost among them was westward settlement. Northern settlers, or homesteaders, flooded into the Ohio River Valley during the early years of the nineteenth century and, by 1820, had crossed the Mississippi in sufficient numbers to request that Congress admit Missouri as an independent state, albeit one tolerating slavery. The Missouri Compromise, enacted that year, limited slavery to all places south of Missouri's southern border, an arrangement that seemed to keep North and South satisfied until 1848, when American victory in the Mexican-American War raised the question of whether the South was entitled to establish slave plantations in Arizona, New Mexico, Texas, and southern California, pursuant to the Missouri Compromise. After heated debate between northern and southern leaders in Congress, a new series of compromises was introduced, including the Compromise of 1850 and the Kansas-Nebraska Act of 1854. This last act declared that the newly formed states of Kansas and Nebraska could decide for themselves, by popular vote, whether they were to be slave or free, essentially nullifying the Missouri Compromise of 1820.

Almost immediately, violence erupted along the Kansas-Missouri border, as proslavery settlers clashed with free-soil advocates, leading to insurgent warfare. Convinced that the Supreme Court should intervene to settle the slave question once and for all, Chief Justice Roger Taney agreed to hear a case brought by a slave who had left Missouri to live in free territory, only to then return to St. Louis and sue for his freedom. In *Dred Scott v. Sandford*, decided in 1857, the Court ruled the Missouri Compromise unconstitutional, opening much of the West to proslavery settlers. The Court also declared that no African American, whether slave or free, had constitutional rights that the Court was "bound to respect," an added barb that did much to set the stage for John S. Rock's speech at Boston's Faneuil Hall one year later.

Organized by the black abolitionist William Cooper Nell, the Faneuil Hall event was designed to commemorate the death of the black patriot Crispus Attucks during the Boston Massacre of 1770, meanwhile providing a platform for abolitionists to refute the Supreme Court's recent ruling in *Dred Scott v. Sandford*. Among those invited were John S. Rock and Theodore Parker, a white Unitarian minister and radical abolitionist who was active in the protection of fugitive slaves but who was also a firm believer in Anglo-Saxon racial superiority. Parker's racial paternalism angered black abolitionists like Douglass and Rock, who took the Faneuil Hall event as an opportunity to engage his white peer.

About the Author

Born a free black on October 13, 1825, in Salem, New Jersey, John Swett Rock became known early in life for being studious. Noticing that their son rarely went anywhere without a book, Rock's parents encouraged him, at age nineteen, to become a schoolteacher in his hometown of Salem. The yearning for further education goaded him onward to spend his free time studying, in the hope of becoming a physician. Two local doctors, both white, allowed him to use their libraries, and though he took quickly to the material, he failed to gain admittance to medical school in Massachusetts on account of his color. Undaunted, Rock sought out a related profession that did not require formal training, dentistry, and was able to persuade a white dentist to hire him as a servant and tutor him in his off-hours. Open to anyone who completed an apprenticeship, dentistry provided Rock with a potentially more lucrative profession than teaching.

Consequently, once his apprenticeship was over, he opened his own office and even won a medal for his ability to make dentures. However, he quickly learned that only African Americans would seek out his services, and most

Faneuil Hall in the nineteenth century (Library of Congress)

of them did not have enough money to provide him with a good living. Even after moving to Philadelphia in the hope of finding more black clients, Rock struggled, eventually taking up teaching again, though he taught only part time at an evening school for African Americans.

Unwilling to give up his original dream, Rock returned to his medical books and, with the help of well-connected white associates, was able to gain admission to the American Medical College in Philadelphia. After two years of work, Rock attained his medical degree, only to then find himself, as one of the few black professionals in the city, increasingly caught up in the abolitionist movement. Blessed with a compelling speaking style, Rock became sought after as a public speaker and, sensing a new calling, left Philadelphia for Boston, the hub of abolitionist politics. Once there, Rock began to attract attention as a lyceum lecturer, delivering talks on race, slavery, and black life and even gaining notice in William Lloyd Garrison's *The Liberator*, which praised Rock as a "first class" lecturer who could dazzle audiences both in the formal setting of the lyceum and on the stump.

Although he is remembered for his lectures on race, Rock also addressed other popular reform topics, including temperance and women's rights. In fact, one of his most popular speeches advocated the political and intellectual equality of women, a subject that he became interested in after visiting the influential literary salon of Madame de Staël in Paris in 1858. Impressed by de Staël's literary prowess, Rock proceeded to compare her with Napoléon, whom he deemed to be de Staël's intellectual inferior. Intrigued,

"Nothing but superior force keeps us down."

"Sooner or later, the clashing of arms will be heard in this country, and the black man's services will be needed."

"When I contrast the fine tough muscular system, the beautiful, rich color, the full broad features, and the gracefully frizzled hair of the Negro, with the delicate physical organization, wan color, sharp features and lank hair of the Caucasian, I am inclined to believe that when the white man was created, nature was pretty well exhausted."

"The colored man, by dint of perseverance and industry, educates and elevates himself, prepares the way for others, gives character to the race, and hastens the day of general emancipation."

reformers in Massachusetts invited Rock to address the Massachusetts legislature, which he did in 1860.

As he became increasingly well known for his speeches, Rock decided to abandon medicine and commence the study of law. By 1861 he had learned enough to impress the Massachusetts Superior Court, gaining admission to the state bar. That same year, he opened his own law office and gained employment as the justice of the peace for Boston County, a promotion noted by Garrison's *Liberator*. In 1864 Rock applied for and gained admission to practice before the Supreme Court of the United States, a feat aided by Charles Sumner—the same abolitionist senator who (in a notorious incident in 1856 on the Senate floor) had been caned by the proslavery South Carolinian Preston Brooks—and by Supreme Court Justice Salmon Chase. Although he never argued a case before the Court, Rock's admission made him the first African American admitted to practice there, a feat that did much to undermine the still persuasive legal authority of *Dred Scott v. Sandford*, which had denied all rights to African Americans. Two years after this singular accomplishment, Rock died of consumption, only forty-one years old.

Explanation and Analysis of Document

Rock begins by refuting white claims that African Americans were "cowards" too afraid to resist their own enslavement. Ironically, Rock's target in this attack was a white abolitionist named Theodore Parker, who had recently argued before the Massachusetts legislature that white Anglo-Saxons were naturally more courageous than their black counterparts, who were by nature pacifist and cowardly. Even Native Americans, Parker contended, were more warlike than Africans, which explained their freedom from enslavement.

Incensed, Rock asserts that unlike Indians, Africans were brought to the New World unarmed and bound in chains, conditions that made their plight different from the Indian, who possessed "armies," "battle-grounds," and "places of retreat" and whom whites often cited for bravery. If whites dared engage black people only on their home terrain, whether in Africa or "Hayti," then they would meet a very different foe. As it was, however, black submission to slavery was not cowardice but common sense, a survival mechanism that whites themselves would resort to if they found themselves enslaved in Africa. Indeed, posits Rock, a form of white slavery did exist, in Europe, where peasants suffered under the "iron heel of oppression" but did not dare "protest against it." Moreover, such slavery went back to Roman times, when Romans had enslaved "Anglo-Saxon" tribes from northern Europe, despite the fact that leading citizens like Cicero cautioned against it on account of Anglo-Saxon "stupidity."

In contrast to Anglo-Saxons and subservient European peasants, Rock invokes the legendary slave rebellion in Haiti, led by Toussaint-Louverture, during which "blacks whipped the French and the English" and proceeded to establish an independent black nation, even overcoming the opposition of Napoléon ("that villainous First Consul"). Rock also invokes the black soldiers who fought in the American Revolution, the War of 1812, and the Mexican-American War. Such historical examples of black militancy enable Rock to undermine a more recent claim made by his fellow black abolitionist Reverend Theodore Parker, who just a "few weeks" before had argued that slavery could have been ended long ago with a black "stroke of the axe." To Rock's mind, Parker did not fully understand the challenges to black armed revolt in the United States, nor did he recognize the role that "superior force" played in maintaining the slave system. Despite claims by white southerners that slaves were content in the South, Rock held the more accurate view that slaves existed in a state of perpetual resistance, disciplined by fear and threats of violence.

Precisely because African Americans had proved their military capabilities in the past, so, too, Rock believes they can be relied upon in the future. Anticipating the Civil War, Rock notes that "sooner or later, the clashing of arms will be heard in this country" and, upon such notice, "150,000 freemen capable of bearing arms," together with "three quarters of a million slaves" will be eager to "strike a genuine blow for freedom." Even the racist pronouncements of *Dred Scott* supporters like Supreme Court Justice Roger Taney or Attorney General Caleb Cushing would not discourage blacks from fighting, their ultimate allegiance going not so much to nation as to race. "Will the blacks fight? Of Course they will…. No man shall cause me to turn my back upon my race. With it I will sink or swim."

Race pride here surges to the fore, pushing Rock not only to defend black courage in battle but also to extol black beauty. Conceding admiration for "the talents and noble characters" of many whites, he confesses to being generally disappointed by "their physical appearance." To him, whites possess "sharp features," "lank hair," and a "wan color," that was far less attractive than the "fine tough muscular system," "full broad features," and "gracefully frizzled hair of the Negro." An ironic reversal of white claims that it was blacks who were unattractive, Rock's celebration of black features is at once reactionary and forward looking. Reactionary in the sense that he had clearly not transcended racialist thinking but simply cobbled together his own form of black supremacism. Forward looking precisely because black radicals would make similar claims over a century later in the 1960s, advancing a "black is beautiful" aesthetic.

In close conjunction with his aesthetic views, Rock proceeds to outline a theory of uplift that hinges not on white magnanimity but on black ingenuity and hard work. Prefiguring Booker T. Washington by almost half a century, Rock argues that the future of black advancement lies not in abolitionist politics (what he terms making "brilliant speeches") but in "work," "perseverance," and "industry." Whites can help in this regard, says Rock, by removing "the obstacles which prevent our elevation," but blacks must not "rely on them." Again foreshadowing Washington, Rock focuses not on the acquisition of civil rights for blacks so much as the importance of economics and, in particular, business for black advancement. "Money is the great sympathetic nerve which ramifies" American society. Therefore, only when "the avenues to wealth are opened to us," would blacks truly gain equality.

Black economic success, Rock concludes, would have a transformative effect on white attitudes. "Then, and not till then," he concludes, "will the tongue of slander be silenced, and the lip of prejudice sealed." This is because economic success would have a transformative effect on African Americans themselves. Wealth "will make our jargon, wit—our words, oracles; flattery will then take the place of slander, and you will find no prejudice in the Yankee whatever." By arguing that money would transform black jargon, reducing white prejudice in the process, Rock is essentially making a prescient analysis of race as a social construct rather than an innate characteristic, that is, a product of legal repression and economic deprivation, not of blood. Although he is clearly unafraid to argue that some aspects of racialism are positive, Rock seems to believe that, ultimately, the most significant racial categories are contrived by society. What whites cited as black inferiority, he argues, is in fact a logical result of circumstance, not heredity.

Audience

John S. Rock's immediate audience consisted of black and white abolitionists at Faneuil Hall as well as abolitionist readers of *The Liberator*. Aware that abolitionists varied from moderate to extreme in their views, however, he specifically targeted increasingly militant white abolitionists who had impugned the honor of African Americans by implying that they lacked courage and could have ended slavery earlier had they only risen up violently against their masters. Perhaps foremost among these abolitionists was Reverend Theodore Parker, a Unitarian minister from Lexington, Massachusetts, cited by name in the speech, who had became increasingly convinced that violence was justified in the struggle against slavery. Parker personally declared that blacks could have ended slavery themselves had they only resorted to the "axe," but were too afraid to do so. Their fear, Parker maintained, was attributable to their racial inferiority.

Outraged, Rock sought to discredit Parker's racial views before Boston's abolitionist community, a bold move given that many African Americans and whites alike supported

Parker's work, particularly his success at protecting fugitive slaves. Rock risked abolitionist admonishment in order to make a case for black military honor, a strategic move given that abolitionist thinking was assuming a more militant form. Parker himself had provided weapons to free militias in Kansas, even joining a subversive organization, the "Secret Six," who supported the insurgent plans of the renegade abolitionist John Brown. Brown rejected the pacifism of abolitionist leaders like William Lloyd Garrison and Frederick Douglass, even orchestrating the brutal murder of five proslavery settlers in Pottawatomie, Kansas, in 1856.

Despite the cold-blooded nature of Brown's attack, radical abolitionists in the North hailed him as a hero, marking the rise of a new, decidedly martial strain of abolitionist thought. Although he refuted Parker on the question of black cowardice, Rock identified himself with this assertive strain of thinking, spending much of his 1858 speech extolling black potential in combat. Yet Rock did not himself engage in violence, nor did he show much interest in funneling money to radicals like Brown. Instead, his militant stance remained largely rhetorical, a muscular complement to his larger emphasis on black self-help.

By endorsing self-help—and refuting Parker—Rock successfully pressed the abolitionist community in Boston to come to terms with its own often patronizing views toward blacks. At the time, even the most fervent white abolitionists tended to consider African Americans to be their racial inferiors. Still, few blacks dared to challenge them, partly out of a strategic apprehension that these white advocates might abandon the abolitionist cause, cease to help fugitive slaves, and turn to other reform struggles. For this very reason, Rock's targeting of white abolitionists was important, an intellectual challenge that exposed fault lines within the abolitionist movement, even as it shamed whites into accepting blacks as their intellectual equals.

Of course, Rock's speech also aimed to reach African Americans, warning them not to rely on the support of people who did not truly accept them as equals and also to work to gain financial independence and success on their own. Like Booker T. Washington, in his controversial Atlanta Exposition Address of 1895, Rock charged African Americans to become self-reliant, particularly in economic matters. Once blacks were economically successful, argued Rock, white attitudes would change automatically, something that could otherwise take centuries. Indeed, by positing that African Americans were superior to whites in certain respects, Rock offered a message that was both a barb to his white listeners and an inspirational note to the black members of his audience.

Impact

Although Rock would never become as influential as abolitionists like Douglass, Garrison, or even Theodore Parker, his speech did have an immediate effect in Boston. Many white listeners confessed to being persuaded by his argument, particularly his allusion to black armed re-

Questions for Further Study

1. How did Rock's views on black nationalism differ from those expressed by Martin Delany in *The Condition, Elevation, Emigration, and Destiny of the Colored People of the United States* (1852)?

2. How did Rock's address anticipate the debate about economic versus political power that took place later in the century and into the twentieth century between such advocates as Booker T. Washington and W. E. B. Du Bois?

3. In the later years of the nineteenth century, numerous key documents in African American history were written by men: John S. Rock, Frederick Douglass, Martin R. Delany, Richard Cain, T. Thomas Fortune, John E. Bruce, John L. Moore, and others. By the end of the century, though, the voices of numerous women were being heard: Anna Julia Cooper, Josephine St. Pierre Ruffin, Mary Church Terrell, and Ida B. Wells-Barnett. What changes, if any, in social, economic, or political circumstances provided women with a wider platform at the end of the century?

4. In what ways did Rock's address prefigure the black nationalism of such twentieth-century figures as Stokely Carmichael, as manifested in his "Black Power" speech (1966)?

5. Describe the events surrounding John Brown's raid on Harpers Ferry, Virginia, and Rock's relationship to those events. What do these events tell you about the attitudes and tensions in the African American community on the eve of the Civil War?

volt in Haiti, which they agreed refuted Parker's charges that blacks were cowardly and inherently nonviolent. This alone was significant, for racial attitudes in the North were already beginning to crystallize under newly emerging scientific theories about ethnology and human development, theories that, by the end of the nineteenth century would lead most Americans, northerners and southerners alike, to accept the theory of black inferiority.

Rock's speech may have had a dramatic effect. The day after the Faneuil Hall event, Theodore Parker met with the militant abolitionist John Brown at the American House Hotel in Boston, agreeing to raise funds for his efforts. While Parker would normally have scoffed at plans for an armed insurrection (out of his conviction that blacks were congenital cowards), John Rock's speech seems to have convinced even him that African Americans would rise up against their owners and bring about their own liberation. Of course, John Brown's plan, which resulted in the raid on Harpers Ferry, Virginia, on October 16 of the following year, went horribly awry after Brown fired on a Baltimore & Ohio train traveling through the town. It is certainly possible that Parker's support of the mission derived from Rock's strident words.

Perhaps the ultimate significance of Rock's speech would not become manifest until a century later, when young black activists like Stokely Carmichael tired of the pacifist stance of the civil rights movement and lobbied for Black Power. Calls for armed self-defense by Carmichael and others seemed to echo Rock's words, as would an emerging Afrocentrism that rejected white, Eurocentric models of beauty and fashion in favor of black alternatives. While there is relatively little evidence that the Black Panthers and others were reading Rock, black scholars like Manning Marable and Leith Mullings would recover his words, entering him into the canon of black political writings in the United States.

See also John Woolman's *Some Considerations on the Keeping of Negroes* (1754); Pennsylvania: An Act for the Gradual Abolition of Slavery (1780); Slavery Clauses in the U.S. Constitution (1787); *The Confessions of Nat Turner* (1831); William Lloyd Garrison's First *Liberator* Editorial (1831); Martin Delany: *The Condition, Elevation, Emigration, and Destiny of the Colored People of the United States* (1852); Frederick Douglass's "What to the Slave Is the Fourth of July?" (1852); *Dred Scott v. Sandford* (1857); Booker T. Washington's Atlanta Exposition Address (1895); Stokely Carmichael's "Black Power" (1966).

Further Reading

■ Articles

Levesque, George A. "Boston's Black Brahmin: Dr. John S. Rock." *Civil War History* 26 (1980): 326–346.

Link, Eugene P. "The Civil Rights Activities of Three Great Negro Physicians (1840–1940)." *Journal of Negro History* 52 (1967): 169–184.

Teed, Paul E. "Racial Nationalism and Its Challengers: Theodore Parker, John Rock, and the Antislavery Movement." *Civil War History* 41 (1995): 142–160.

■ Books

Foner, Eric. *Reconstruction: America's Unfinished Revolution, 1863–1877.* New York: Harper & Row, 1988.

Quarles, Benjamin. *The Black Abolitionists.* New York: Oxford University Press, 1970.

—Anders Walker

John S. Rock's "Whenever the Colored Man Is Elevated, It Will Be by His Own Exertions"

You will not expect a lengthened speech from me to-night. My health is too poor to allow me to indulge much in speech-making. But I have not been able to resist the temptation to unite with you in this demonstration of respect for some of my noble but misguided ancestors.

White Americans have taken great pains to try to prove that we are cowards. We are often insulted with the assertion, that if we had had the courage of the Indians or the white man, we would never have submitted to be slaves. I ask if Indians and white men have never been slaves? The white man tested the Indian's courage here when he had his organized armies, his battle-grounds, his places of retreat, with everything to hope for and everything to lose. The position of the African slave has been very different. Seized a prisoner of war, unarmed, bound hand and foot, and conveyed to a distant country among what to him were worse than cannibals; brutally beaten, half-starved, closely watched by armed men, with no means of knowing their own strength or the strength of their enemies, with no weapons, and without a probability of success. But if the white man will take the trouble to fight the black man in Africa or in Hayti, and fight him as fair as the black man will fight him there—if the black man does not come off victor, I am deceived in his prowess. But, take a man, armed or unarmed, from his home, his country or his friends, and place him among savages, and who is he that would not make good his retreat? "Discretion is the better part of valor," but for a man to resist where he knows it will destroy him, shows more fool-hardiness than courage. There have been many Anglo-Saxons and Anglo-Americans enslaved in Africa, but I have never heard that they successfully resisted any government. They always resort to running indispensables.

The courage of the Anglo-Saxon is best illustrated in his treatment of the negro. A score or two of them can pounce upon a poor negro, tie and beat him, and then call him a coward because he submits. Many of their most brilliant victories have been achieved in the same manner. But the greatest battles which they have fought have been upon paper. We can easily account for this; their trumpeter is dead. He died when they used to be exposed for sale in the Roman market, about the time that Cicero cautioned his friend Atticus not to buy them, on account of their stupidity. A little more than half a century ago, this race, in connection with their Celtic neighbors, who have long been considered (by themselves, of course,) the bravest soldiers in the world, so far forgot themselves, as to attack a few cowardly, stupid negro slaves, who, according to their accounts, had not sense enough to go to bed. And what was the result? Why, sir, the negroes drove them out from the island like so many sheep, and they have never dared to show their faces, except with hat in hand.

Our true and tried friend, Rev. Theodore Parker, said, in his speech at the State House, a few weeks since, that "the stroke of the axe would have settled the question long ago, but the black man would not strike." Mr, Parker makes a very low estimate of the courage of his race, if he means that one, two or three millions of these ignorant and cowardly black slaves could, without means, have brought to their knees five, ten, or twenty millions of intelligent, brave white men, backed up by a rich oligarchy. But I know of no one who is more familiar with the true character of the Anglo-Saxon race than Mr. Parker. I will not dispute this point with him, but I will thank him or any one else to tell us how it could have been done. His remark calls to my mind the day which is to come, when one shall chase a thousand, and two put ten thousand to flight. But when he says that "the black man *would not* strike," I am prepared to say that he does us great injustice. The black man is not a coward. The history of the bloody struggles for freedom in Hayti, in which the blacks whipped the French and the English, and gained their independence, in spite of the perfidy of that villainous First Consul, will be a lasting refutation of the malicious aspersions of our enemies. The history of the struggles for the liberty of the U.S. ought to silence every American calumniator. I have learned that even so late as the Texan war, a number of black men were silly enough to offer themselves as living sacrifices for our country's shame. A gentleman who delivered a lecture before the New York Legislature, a few years since, whose name I do not now remember, but whose language I give with some precision, said, "In the Revolution, colored soldiers fought side by side with you in your struggles for liberty, and there is not a battle-field from Maine to Georgia that has not been crimsoned with their blood, and whitened with their bones." In 1814, a bill passed the Legislature of New York, accepting the services of 2000 colored volunteers. Many black men served under Com. McDonough when he conquered on Lake Champlain. Many were in the battles of Plattsburgh and Sackett's Harbor, and General Jackson called out colored troops from Louisiana and Alabama, and in a solemn proclamation attested to their fidelity and courage.

The white man contradicts himself who says, that if he were in our situation, he would throw off the yoke. Thirty millions of white men of this proud Caucasian race are at this moment held as slaves, and bought and sold with horses and cattle. The iron heel of oppression grinds the masses of all European races to the dust. They suffer every kind of oppression, and no one dares to open his mouth to protest against it. Even in the Southern portion of this boasted land of liberty, no white man dares, advocate so much of the Declaration of Independence as declares that "all men are created free and equal, and have an inalienable right to life, liberty," &c.

White men have no room to taunt us with tamely submitting. If they were black men, they would work wonders; but, as white men, they can do nothing. "O, Consistency, thou art a jewel!"

Now, it would not be surprising if the brutal treatment which we have received for the past two centuries should have crushed our spirits. But this is not the case. Nothing but a superior force keeps us down. And when I see the slaves rising up by hundreds annually, in the majesty of human nature, bidding defiance to every slave code and its penalties, making the issue Canada or death, and that too while they are closely watched by paid men armed with pistols, clubs and bowie-knives, with the army and navy of this great Model Republic arrayed against them, I am disposed to ask if the charge of cowardice does not come with ill-grace.

But some men are so steeped in folly and imbecility; so lost to all feelings of their own littleness; so destitute of principle, and so regardless of humanity, that they dare attempt to destroy everything which exists in opposition to their interests or opinions which their narrow comprehensions cannot grasp.

We ought not to come here simply to honor those brave men who shed their blood for freedom, or to protest against the Dred Scott decision, but to take counsel of each other, and to enter into new vows of duty. Our fathers fought nobly for freedom, but they were not victorious. They fought for liberty, but they

got slavery. The white man was benefitted, but the black man was injured. I do not envy the white American the little liberty which he enjoys. It is his right, and he ought to have it. I wish him success, though I do not think he deserves it. But I would have all men free. We have had much sad experience in this country, and it would be strange indeed if we do not profit by some of the lessons which we have so dearly paid for. Sooner or later, the clashing of arms will be heard in this country, and the black man's services will be needed: 150,000 freemen capable of bearing arms, and not all cowards and fools, and three quarters of a million slaves, wild with the enthusiasm caused by the dawn of the glorious opportunity of being able to strike a genuine blow for freedom, will be a power which white men will be "bound to respect." Will the blacks fight? Of course they will. The black man will never be neutral. He could not if he would, and he would not if he could. Will he fight for this country, right or wrong? This the common sense of every one answers; and when the time comes, and come it will, the black man will give an intelligent answer. Judge Taney may outlaw us; Caleb Cushing may show the depravity of his heart by abusing us; and this wicked government may oppress us; but the black man will live when Judge Taney, Caleb Cushing and this wicked government are no more. White man may despise, ridicule, slander and abuse us; they may seek as they always have done to divide us, and make us feel degraded; but no man shall cause me to turn my back upon my race. With it I will sink or swim.

The prejudice which some white men have, or affected to have, against my color gives me no pain. If any man does not fancy my color, that is his business, and I shall not meddle with it. I shall give myself no trouble because he lacks good taste. If he judges my intellectual capacity by my color, he certainly cannot expect much profundity, for it is only skin deep, and is really of no very great importance to any one but myself. I will not deny that I admire the talents and noble characters of many white men. But I cannot say that I am particularly pleased with their physical appearance. If old mother nature had held out as well as she commenced, we should, probably, have had fewer varieties in the races. When I contrast the fine tough muscular system, the beautiful, rich color, the full broad features, and the gracefully frizzled hair of the Negro, with the delicate physical organization, wan color, sharp features and lank hair of the Caucasian, I am inclined to believe that when the white man was created, nature was pretty well exhausted—but determined to keep up appearances, she pinched up his features, and did the best she could under the circumstances.

I would have you understand, that I not only love my race, but am pleased with my color; and while many colored persons may feel degraded by being called negroes, and wish to be classed among other races more favored, I shall feel it my duty, my pleasure and my pride, to concentrate my feeble efforts in elevating to a fair position a race to which I am especially identified by feelings and by blood.

My friends, we can never become elevated until we are true to ourselves. We can come here and make brilliant speeches, but our field of duty is elsewhere. Let us go to work—each man in his place, determined to do what he can for himself and his race. Let us try to carry out some of the resolutions which we have made, and are so fond of making. If we do this, friends will spring up in every quarter, and where we least expect them. But we must not rely on them. They cannot elevate us. Whenever the colored man is elevated, it will be by his own exertions. Our friends can do what many of them are nobly doing, assist us to remove the obstacles which prevent our elevation, and stimulate the worthy to persevere. The colored man who, by dint of perseverance and industry, educates and elevates himself, prepares the way for others, gives character to the race, and hastens the day of general emancipation. While the negro who hangs around the corners of the streets, or lives in the grog-shops or by gambling, or who has no higher ambition than to serve, is by his vocation forging fetters for the slave, and is "to all intents and purposes" a curse to his race. It is true, considering the circumstances under which we have been placed by our white neighbors, we have a right to ask them not only to cease to oppress us, but to give us that encouragement which our talents and industry may merit. When this is done, they will see our minds expand, and our pockets filled with rocks. How very few colored men are encouraged in their trades or business! Our young men see this, and become disheartened. In this country, where money is the great sympathetic nerve which ramifies society, and has a ganglia in every man's pocket, a man is respected in proportion to his success in business. When the avenues to wealth are opened to us, we will then become educated and wealthy, and then the roughest looking colored man that you ever saw, or ever will see, will be pleasanter than the harmonies of Orpheus, and black will be a very pretty color. It will make our jargon, wit—our words, oracles; flattery will then take the place of slander, and you will find no prejudice

Glossary

Anglo-Saxons	the Germanic tribes that overran Europe and the British Isles after the collapse of the Roman Empire; used loosely to refer to white northern Europeans
"bound to respect"	a quotation from the U.S. Supreme Court's decision in *Dred Scott v. Sandford*, which stated that blacks "had no rights which the white man was bound to respect."
bowie-knives	fixed-blade knives named after Colonel James Bowie, a frontiersman who fought and died at the Battle of the Alamo during the Texas War of Independence
Caleb Cushing	a U.S. attorney general and member of the U.S. House of Representatives from Massachusetts
Celtic	a reference to the Celts, widespread European ethnic group; used loosely in modern times to refer to the peoples of Ireland, Scotland, Brittany, Wales, and Cornwall
Cicero	Marcus Tullius Cicero, an ancient Roman historian, philosopher, and statesman and the biographer and close friend of Titus Pomponius Atticus
Com. McDonough	Commander Thomas McDonough, the leader of U.S. naval forces that won a decisive victory at the Battle of Lake Champlain, also called the Battle of Plattsburgh, during the War of 1812

in the Yankee whatever. We do not expect to occupy a much better position than we now do, until we shall have our educated and wealthy men, who can wield a power that cannot be misunderstood. Then, and not till then, will the tongue of slander be silenced, and the lip of prejudice sealed. Then, and hot till then, will we be able to enjoy true equality, which can exist only among peers.

Glossary

"Discretion is the better part of valor"	common misquotation from Shakespeare's *Henry IV*, Part 1, act 5, scene 4; the correct quotation is "The better part of valor is discretion."
Dred Scott decision	the decision of the U.S. Supreme Court in *Dred Scott v. Sandford* (1857)
General Jackson	Andrew Jackson, the seventh U.S. president and a military commander best known for the U.S. victory at the Battle of New Orleans during the War of 1812
Hayti	Haiti, the site of a revolution that ended slavery in the late eighteenth and early nineteenth centuries
Judge Taney	Roger Taney, chief justice of the United States, who delivered the Court's decision in *Dred Scott v. Sandford*
"O, Consistency, thou art a jewel!"	a traditional proverb of unknown origin
Orpheus	a Greek god associated with, among other things, music
Sackett's Harbor	Sackets Harbor, New York, the site of a battle during the War of 1812
Texan war	the Texas War of Independence (from Mexico) in 1835–1836
Theodore Parker	a white abolitionist and Unitarian minister
villainous First Counsel	Napoléon Bonaparte, the ruler of France and its colonies
Yankee	a common nickname for northerners

"If a free person ... maintain that owners have not right of property in their slaves, he shall be confined in jail."

Overview

Virginia's legal defense of slave ownership began in 1662 and ended in 1865, so Virginia statutes concerning slaves reflected two centuries of lawmaking. In the nineteenth century, these statutes were incorporated into the much broader *Code of Virginia.* Thus, to refer to a single "slave code" is a bit of a misnomer, for the "Virginia Slave Code" consisted in fact of provisions that were made part of the 1860 version of the *Code of Virginia,* which was in turn the "second edition" of the 1849 revised code. The fact that none of the many slave revolts over the centuries ever fully succeeded testifies to the lawmakers' role in perpetuating the "peculiar institution." As in other slaveholding societies, white Virginians were continually alert to any signs of slave rebelliousness, and they modified their laws accordingly.

Context

The Virginia Slave Code of 1860 reflected a deep history. The mother country had shipped an estimated one hundred fourteen thousand Africans to the Old Dominion (as King Charles II fondly called the prized colony of Virginia) between 1619 and 1778, when the state government outlawed the importation of Africans. Virginians were not the first Europeans to impose lifetime servitude in the Americas. Dutch, French, Portuguese, and Spanish slave traders and planters had sent approximately twelve million enslaved Africans into their New World settlements from the 1500s to the 1800s. To maintain control over their African servants, the county governments of Virginia began to rely on court decisions and statutes created by the colonial assembly, the House of Burgesses. These judicial and legislative developments, based sometimes on English laws and court decisions in English Caribbean colonies, buttressed the successful slave society that Old Dominion planters created.

Many English people assumed that Africans were to be treated not only as servants but also as "lesser" human beings. Two statutes especially prepared the way for legally protected slavery. The first, passed in 1662, declared that children of enslaved African women and European men in Virginia were slaves from their birth (slave status being passed through the female line). Such children inherited legal debasement as soon as they were born. The second statute (1667) pronounced, lest anyone had doubts, that Christian baptism would not emancipate any slave. This law, having denied freedom to newborn black Christians, went on to declare that masters could now "carefully endeavor the propagation of Christianity by permitting children, though slaves, or those of greater growth if capable to be admitted to that sacrament."

From 1700 to 1865, diverse white Virginians relied on themselves, on their employees, and on laws and courts to protect their investment in and to maintain their control over their increasing numbers of slaves. The white leaders mostly succeeded. Despite the Virginia government's 1778 decision to outlaw African importation and increased sales of slaves out of the Old Dominion, the state's enslaved population grew steadily from 1790 to 1860. During this period the slave population increased by 68 percent and the free white population by 137 percent. By 1860 the enslaved population of the Old Dominion was 490,865. This steady growth of human bondage required diverse legal revisions, innovations, and many court cases—local, county, and state.

Virginia leaders and legislators developed the law of slavery over two centuries—from the 1660s until 1860. The slave laws in the second edition of the *Code of Virginia* differed to some extent from seventeenth-century slave laws, but there was continuity as well. At first, the royal governors joined with plantation owners to secure what would later be called the "peculiar institution." And English monarchs, members of Parliament, government officials, writers, and other leaders defended human bondage—that is, enslavement of Africans and of Native Americans as well. The laws enacted by the House of Burgesses under Governor William Berkeley in 1662 and 1667 protected slave owners' legal rights for years to come. Berkeley and his immediate successors all had some military experience, unlike many later governors. That experience helped when rebellious people challenged slaveholders.

Time Line

1676	■ At least eighty enslaved Africans join Bacon's Rebellion but are eventually captured and punished.
1680	■ The Virginia House of Burgesses passes An Act for Preventing Negroes Insurrections, citing the "frequent meeting of considerable numbers of negroe slaves" as justification for prohibiting slaves' carrying arms.
1687	■ A failed black conspiracy in Tidewater, Virginia, leads authorities to find new ways to control the African population.
1692	■ An Act for the More Speedy Prosecution of Slaves Committing Capitall Crimes prescribes hanging as the penalty for insurrection.
1705	■ An Act concerning Servants and Slaves becomes the first comprehensive statute concerning slavery in Virginia.
1710– 1732	■ A period of vigorous prosecutions in Virginia leads to at least twenty convictions relating to insurrection by 1732.
1748	■ The Virginia burgesses enact An Act Directing the Trial of Slaves Committing Capital Crimes; and for the More Effectual Punishing Conspiracies and Insurrections of Them; and for the Better Government of Negroes, Mulattoes, and Indians, Bond or Free.
1765	■ The Virginia burgesses pass An Act for Amending the Act Entitled An Act Directing the Trial of Slaves Committing Capital Crimes; and for the More Effectual Punishing Conspiracies and Insurrections of Them; and for the Better Government Of Negroes, Mulattoes, and Indians, Bond or Free.

Later royal governors wrestled not only with property law but also with rebellious slaves. Bacon's Rebellion of 1674–1676, an uprising of aggrieved frontier settlers, had the support of some indentured servants and slaves, who presumably hoped to gain their freedom amid the havoc of revolt. Many of the African men were ultimately killed or punished, but white leaders undoubtedly remembered the specter of bondsmen attaining temporary freedom. In 1680, Governor Thomas Culpeper and the House of Burgesses were clearly aware of this possibility when they declared in 1680 that "the frequent meeting of considerable numbers of negroe slaves under pretence of feasts and burials is judged of dangerous consequence." Therefore no African should carry any weapon, nor should any leave his master's land without a certificate from his "master, mistress or overseer."

Judicial power gradually became more important as a means of controlling bondspeople. In April 1692, Lieutenant Governor Francis Nicholson and the burgesses created the oyer and terminer (hearing and determining) courts, in which local judges would try slaves for capital criminal offenses. (These courts were separate from other oyer and terminer courts in Virginia.) Courts of oyer and terminer had existed for centuries in England to try cases of treason, felony, and misdemeanors. In Virginia, these courts would be called as needed in all counties from April 1692 to April 1865—173 years. Was it logical to deny trial by jury to enslaved men and women? Who would have been a jury of their peers? Numerous slaves were hanged upon condemnation by an oyer and terminer court. Others were transported out of the Old Dominion or whipped. And some were found not guilty. The judges did not have absolute power. From 1692 to 1765, the courts required authorization from the colonial governor to carry out an execution. Afterward, state governors could authorize or block executions. Eventually, lawyers were allowed to represent enslaved defendants. Clemency petitions sometimes gained relief for slaves.

Laws concerning slavery were harsh and fearsome from many enslaved people's point of view—and properly strong as far as slave owners were concerned. Still, over time, some owners tried to alleviate the burden that enslaved people carried. Thomas Jefferson's famous statement in his *Notes on the State of Virginia*—"I tremble for my country when I reflect that God is just: that his justice cannot sleep for ever"—reflected his conscience. But such thoughts resulted in relatively few people being freed. Some later commentators advocated a rational approach to enslaved people. Among the most effective efforts to employ rational jurisprudence with respect to Virginia's Slave Code was the work of St. George Tucker, who, in addition to serving on the Virginia Court of Appeals, published an edition of Blackstone's *Commentaries on the Laws of England* in 1803 that included judges' opinions and Tucker's discussion of slave law. Virginia Supreme Court opinions also parsed the practical legal questions related to slavery in Virginia. On the whole, however, judges and legislators continued to support restrictive laws related to enslaved people under their jurisdiction. In turn, the oyer and terminer judges found slaves innocent or guilty and rarely recorded their reasoning.

There were occasions when judges tried to persuade the state governor and council to make exceptions concerning capital punishment for some condemned men and women. Judges sometimes argued with one another about a person condemned to death for conspiracy to rebel, taking into account extenuating circumstances. Finally, during the aftermath of slave plots or rebellions, occasionally the state government concluded that, as happened after Gabriel's conspiracy of 1800, there had been enough public hangings. On September 15, 1800, Governor James Monroe told the presidential candidate Thomas Jefferson that "when to arrest the hand of the Executioner, is a question of great importance." On September 20, Jefferson responded, "There is a strong sentiment that there has been hanging enough." Twenty men had been hanged by September 22; thereafter only six rebels, including Gabriel, went to their deaths on the gallows. A few months later, with President Jefferson's help, Governor Monroe persuaded the Virginia legislators to pass a law that allowed the transportation out of Virginia and away from the United States of enslaved men and women condemned to death but granted mercy. Soon the Virginia government transported nine men held in jail after being convicted of conspiring with Gabriel, including Jack Bowler, a plot leader. After Nat Turner's revolt in 1831, eighteen men convicted of rebellion were transported. It should be noted that transportation (usually to the West Indies) offered only partial mitigation of a death sentence, since the harsh conditions of Caribbean slavery ensured a far higher mortality rate than existed in Virginia. Some of those condemned to transportation still sought to escape. They clearly did not regard transportation as merciful.

Various events likely prompted Virginia to further revise its slave laws in 1860. One was no doubt the Fugitive Slave Act of 1850, which established federal protection and remedies for slave owners—and which had the unintended effect of increasing traffic on the Underground Railroad so that a growing number of people took part in providing safe houses, guides, and routes for escaped slaves. The Kansas-Nebraska Act of 1854 attempted, and failed, to settle the growing sectional dispute between North and South over the issue of slavery. Some states would have liked to have seen a federal slave code, but sectional divisions made agreement on such a code extremely unlikely. In 1857 the U.S. Supreme Court issued its landmark decision in *Dred Scott v. Sandford*, holding that neither a state nor the federal government had the authority to ban slavery in the Territories. In 1858, Abraham Lincoln, in challenging Stephen A. Douglas for his seat as senator from Illinois, gave his famous "House Divided" speech in which he said that the nation could not exist half slave and half free. Then, in 1859, the abolitionist John Brown led an abortive raid on the federal arsenal at Harpers Ferry, Virginia, further inflaming passions over the slavery issue. By 1860, when Virginia amended its code, it was clear that the nation was on a course that would lead to civil war.

Time Line

1775
- At one of the Virginia Conventions, held after the House of Burgesses was dissolved by the royal governor, Lord Dunmore, delegates accuse Lord Dunmore of arming slaves against "the good people of this colony."

1800
- Gabriel and twenty-five other enslaved men in and near Richmond are hanged for conspiring to rebel.

1802
- Ten men are executed and four transported amid an insurrection plot.

1816
- Five men are hanged and another six transported when George Boxley's Spotsylvania County plot is discovered.

1819
- *The Revised Code of the Laws of Virginia, 1819* includes An Act, Reducing into One the Several Acts Concerning Slaves, Free Negroes and Mulattos, authorizing the suppression of slave rebels.

1831
- Nat Turner's Rebellion results in sixty white deaths and the hanging of twenty-three slaves.

1833
- Laws concerning slave rebellion are restated in the *Supplement to the Revised Code of Laws of Virginia:— Being a Collection of All the Acts of the General Assembly ... Passed Since the Year 1819.*

1849
- The *Code of Virginia* includes revised laws concerning insurrectionary slaves.

1859
- **October 16** John Brown launches his raid on the federal arsenal at Harpers Ferry, Virginia.

1860
- The *Code of Virginia, Second Edition, Including Legislation to the Year 1860* codifies previous legislation.

About the Author

Hundreds of Virginia leaders debated and legislators wrote the law of slavery for over two centuries—from the 1660s until 1860. (While no enslaved people wrote laws, white lawmakers' actions and legislation were frequently responses to slaves' actions.) George Wythe Munford (1802–1882), secretary of the Commonwealth of Virginia, led the writers who created the 1860 *Code of Virginia*. Munford had graduated from the College of William and Mary and worked as a clerk of the Virginia House of Delegates, secretary of the Virginia Convention of 1829, and secretary of the Commonwealth of Virginia until 1865. A staunch Democrat, he was most proud of compiling the *Code of Virginia* of 1860. The publication revised many parts of the 1849 *Code of Virginia*. House of Delegates members, such as John M. Patton, Conway Robinson, and Robert G. Scott, also contributed, and the Virginia General Assembly members voted in favor of the revisions. Ten thousand copies of the 1860 *Code of Virginia* were published and distributed to legislators and libraries. (About two hundred copies are now in major libraries.) Many, perhaps all, of the 1860 legislators were proslavery; they adamantly and sometimes bitterly opposed Abraham Lincoln's 1860 presidential candidacy and later his election, and they eventually supported Virginia's secession from the United States and the creation of the Confederate States of America.

Explanation and Analysis of the Document

The provisions added to the *Code of Virginia* in 1860 touched on a number of issues. One was the disposition of slaves who were under a sentence of death. A second was the establishment of courts, jails, and other legal apparatus for dealing with slaves. A third called for the breaking up of assemblies of African Americans, which were a source of fear among white Virginians in the climate of the 1850s. A key set of provisions dealt specifically with the issue of runaway slaves. The Virginia legislature also included provisions having to do with the residence of freed blacks in the commonwealth, writings and other activities urging slaves to rebel or escape, and aiding runaway slaves.

◆ Title 10

CHAPTER XVII The "Executive Functions" law empowered Virginia's governor to transport slaves convicted of insurrection or other major crimes out of Virginia and the United States. There had to be a conscious decision to transport some enslaved convicts rather than execute them. The code also specified that the governor could contract for the sale of slaves under a death sentence and provides details as to how that was to be done. Another provision gave the governor the power to imprison for a term of years any slave under sentence of death who would have been entitled to his or her freedom at some point in the future. Any such slave, though, was required to leave the state at the end of the prison term.

◆ Title 11

CHAPTER XXII The militia could be, and often was, called up to suppress slave rebellions. A properly led militia could capture alleged criminals and protect them from mob violence so they could be tried in a court. This provision states that every able-bodied white male between the ages of eighteen and forty-five and resident in the state is subject to military duty.

◆ Title 16

CHAPTER L This provision required each town and county to maintain a courthouse, jail, whipping posts, and stocks—that is, timber frames in which the hands and feet of a prisoner could be locked so that he could be exhibited publicly. The required racial separation in jails certainly was meant to maintain white people's intrinsic social superiority and to enforce African American social inferiority. But black and white inmate interaction in jail could also lead to slave revolts or other problems. While interracial conspiracies were improbable in jails, given the separation of the prisoners, lawmakers still tried to prevent any chance of conspiracy.

◆ Title 28

CHAPTER XCVIII The purpose of this provision was to impede the free movement of slaves and to prevent any assemblies of slaves that might be called to foment rebellion. The provision authorized militia commanders to establish patrols to visit "negro quarters and other places suspected of having therein unlawful assemblies."

◆ Title 30

CHAPTER CV The body of laws concerning fugitive slaves indicates the state's concern about people who had escaped and could not be captured. From the 1820s until the 1860s Virginia legislators passed and revised law after law about fugitives. Some new laws took into account the interstate activity of slaves who had disappeared and abolitionists who had sometimes helped them. The most famous Virginia case was Henry "Box" Brown's successful escape. He shipped himself out of Richmond in a box addressed to an abolitionist in Philadelphia, Pennsylvania. Virginia authorities condemned this and any other alleged violation of Virginia or U.S. laws (specifically the Fugitive Slave Act of 1793 and the Fugitive Slave Act of 1850, which penalized the escapee and anyone who assisted the escapee). While most escapees from slavery were not involved in any rebellion, their successful escapes began to undermine human bondage in Virginia. Such men and women were sometimes suspected of conspiring with other people to rebel.

Accordingly, Chapter CV of Title 30 deals with the capture of runaway slaves, who were to be taken before a justice. The justice then was to make provisions for the safekeeping of the slave. Anyone who captured a runaway slave was entitled to a reward. Captured slaves were to be returned to their owners, and whenever a slave was captured, the jailor was required to distribute an advertisement so that the owner could reclaim the slave. If no

Illustration of African Americans escaping from slavery (LIbrary of Congress)

one claimed the slave, the county was authorized to sell the person.

CHAPTER CVII Emancipated people often left Virginia to build a new life. But some risked re-enslavement to collaborate with rebellious black people in Virginia. That is one reason why Virginia lawmakers decreed that emancipated slaves must move elsewhere. Of course, nothing prevented freedpeople from moving to a nearby free state such as Pennsylvania or Ohio, where they could help to plan rebellion with Virginian conspirators. The new provisions of the Virginia code mandated that an emancipated slave could remain in the commonwealth after a year only with permission. The provision then established the procedures to be followed in obtaining that permission, which could be revoked for any cause. Meanwhile, any free African American in the commonwealth had to be registered—clearly a means by which Virginia would be able to keep tabs on emancipated slaves in the event of any unrest or rebellion.

♦ **Title 54**

CHAPTER CXC This provision of the code, defining treason and the punishment for treason, and further indicating that advising or conspiring with slaves to "make insurrection" was an act of treason, had a long history. In late 1775, Lord Dunmore, Virginia's royal governor, officially proclaimed freedom as a reward for enslaved people who would bear

arms for the king and help Dunmore suppress the American Revolutionaries. That threat having ended, there were later scattered instances of white men who attempted to foment slave rebellion, but they mostly failed. Virginia courts sentenced to death at least two alleged insurrectionists, one in 1775 and the other in 1777. By the 1800s, Virginia lawmakers reacted to the growing number of northern (and southern) abolitionists who challenged human bondage. In early 1816 George Boxley, a white Virginian who lived near Fredericksburg in Spotsylvania County, plotted with several enslaved men. Five enslaved men were tried and executed in connection with this conspiracy, and another six suspects were transported to unknown locations. (Boxley himself, one of very few recorded white conspirators, lived in Indiana until his death in 1865 despite bounty agents' attempts to capture him.) Virginia's government invoked the same law to prosecute John Brown and other conspirators after the raid on Harpers Ferry in 1859. The law passed in the late 1790s, which appeared in every edition of the Virginia code, made very clear the Virginia legislature's position concerning white people who conspired with slave rebels. Responding to President Lincoln's Emancipation Proclamation, Governor John Letcher threatened to prosecute Union troops for allegedly violating the Virginia law.

CHAPTER CXCII In response to such activities as the Underground Railroad and other efforts to free slaves, the

"Every such jail shall be well secured, and sufficient for the convenient accommodation of those who may be confined therein, so that convicts and slaves not convicts, may be in apartments separate from each other and from the other prisoners."

(Title 16)

"The commander of each regiment of the militia, may, when necessary, appoint one or more patrols … to patrol and visit … all negro quarters and other places suspected of having therein unlawful assemblies, or such slaves as may stroll from one plantation to another without permission."

(Title 28)

"No negro, emancipated since the first day of May eighteen hundred and six, or hereafter,… shall, after being twenty-one years of age, remain in this state more than one year without lawful permission."

(Title 30)

"If a free person advise or conspire with a slave to rebel or make insurrection, or with any person, to induce a slave to rebel or make insurrection, he shall be punished with death."

(Title 54)

"If a free person, by speaking or writing, maintain that owners have not right of property in their slaves, he shall be confined in jail not more than one year and fined not exceeding five hundred dollars. He may be arrested, and carried before a justice, by any white person."

(Title 54)

Virginia legislature made it against the law for any free person to help a slave escape. Doing so was punishable by a stiff fine and a term in jail. This portion of the code extended as well to commanders of ships at sea who might take on board a runaway slave. Anyone who provided a runaway with money, passes, clothes, provisions, and so on would likewise be guilty of a crime punishable by imprisonment. Further, anyone who kept a ferry or bridge and allowed a slave to escape by that means would also be subject to imprisonment. To white authorities, twenty slaves were property, and twenty acres and a mule were also property. It was not just property that was at stake in this law. An escaped slave could be a future rebel, especially if such a person left Virginia and associated with abolitionists. White people who helped slaves to escape were legally thieves of human beings.

CHAPTER CXCVIII The law regarding seditious speech made free people's mere spoken and written antislavery opinions grounds for incarceration and a fine, but only if such opinion was meant to incite slaves to rebel. The lawmakers obviously intended to protect free Virginians from insurrection. The free-speech controversy inflamed the slavery controversy in the United States between the 1820s and 1865. But Old Dominion lawmakers held to their belief that antislavery speech, publications, and even mail could lead to insurrection and therefore must be censored. Thus, it was against the law to oppose the "right of property" in slaves in speech and writing and to write any materials that incited slave insurrection. Postmasters were required to inform the authorities of any antislavery materials being sent through the mail and to burn such materials. The code made "assemblage of negroes for the purpose of religious worship" against the law if the service was led by an African American. It was also against the law to assemble blacks for the purpose of teaching them to read and write. The law established stiff penalties for any white person who violated these provisions.

These provisions, too, had a long history. White authorities feared the outcome if enslaved people learned how to read—even to read the Bible. Shortly after Gabriel's conspiracy of 1800, the Virginia legislature passed a law to control slaves' gatherings of any kind. Such gatherings had always raised suspicion of rebelliousness, but in some whites' perception Gabriel and his confederates had imbibed dangerous opinions about spiritual equality with whites. What was more, Gabriel could read and write. "Look at the result," some concluded. Soon after the 1800 and 1802 Virginia conspiracies, lawmakers focused expressly on any assembly of black people, even for religious reasons. They were aware that some conspirators in 1800 had discussed rebellion directly after attending a "preachment." Religious motivation figured in the 1802 conspiracy as well. After Nat Turner's Rebellion in 1831, more laws were passed to control religious assemblies. But it should not be assumed that no one taught enslaved black people to read and write. Some slave owners taught their own human property to read the Bible and even to write. Ministers found a way to do the same. Some enslaved people even taught themselves.

CHAPTER CC The law required rigorous punishment of any slave convicted of conspiring to rebel. Note that Title 54 does not explicitly mention actual rebellion. There was no need. Any slave convicted of conspiracy would have been implicitly judged by a court to have rebelled. The point of conspiring to rebel was to rebel, but this law ensured that convicted slaves could be executed even if their conspiracy was blocked. The later clauses of Title 54 yoke punishments of free blacks to punishments of slaves. But the confusing conditional statements relate to alleged crimes other than rebellion. Thus, a black could be punished by whipping for such offenses as using "provoking language or menacing gestures to a white person," furnishing a slave with a pass or similar document without authority, keeping or carrying firearms, rioting, assembling unlawfully, or making a seditious speech.

Audience

The audience for the 1860 *Code of Virginia Code*, like any legal code, consisted of judges, attorneys, law enforcement authorities, and anyone who might be a slave owner or involved with the capture of escaped slaves. Beyond the legal community were the people of Virginia. The news of frequent slave conspiracies created a public audience that wanted assurance that the laws would enable authorities to suppress an insurrectionary spirit among the enslaved. Many other people took the opportunity to read at least part of the slave code. Among them could be some free and enslaved African Americans, despite attempts to prevent them from learning how to read.

Impact

The Virginia oyer and terminer justices who tried allegedly felonious enslaved people were required to decide on the guilt or innocence of slaves. That almost all oyer and terminer judges were slave owners does not necessarily mean that they would be either too hard or too soft on slaves tried for crimes. While not all Virginia court records have survived, data from accessible trial records make it possible to estimate how rigorous slave trial judges were when they sat on slave rebellion trials.

It is possible to estimate the number of enslaved people who were hanged in Virginia for insurrection and conspiracy from 1706 to 1785. Between 1706 and 1800, all people convicted of conspiracy and insurrection were supposed to be executed. However, some judges or slave owners found private ways to "show mercy." Many trial records have been lost, but those that survive (1706–1785) contain records of twenty-eight insurrection trials. Twenty-five of the accused, or 89 percent, were convicted. From 1785 to 1834, the period of the largest number of detected rebellious conspiracies, of the 243 people accused of conspiracy to rebel, 142 (nearly 60 percent) were convicted—a percentage markedly lower than resulted from the trials in the 1706–1785 period. Because transportation became a legal "act of mercy" in early 1801, those thereafter convicted of conspiracy and insurrection experienced diverse fates. Seventy-six were hanged; thirteen were pardoned; forty-six were transported; four were given corporal punishment. The numbers indicate that judges had more sentencing leeway from 1801 to 1865. The Civil War and especially the Emancipation Proclamation of 1863 gained new opponents for 1860 Virginia Slave Code. Many who had trod carefully concerning slavery now saw hundreds, and ultimately thousands, of enslaved people ignoring the slave codes wherever the Union soldiers prevailed. This dire turn of events undoubtedly stiffened slaveholders' resolve. Even after April 1865 and the constitutional ratification of the final emancipation—the Thirteenth Amendment—notorious "black laws" were passed by white legislators seeking to maintain control of now free African Americans.

See also Virginia's Act XII: Negro Women's Children to Serve according to the Condition of the Mother (1662); Virginia's Act III: Baptism Does Not Exempt Slaves from Bondage (1667); Lord Dunmore's Proclamation (1775); Thomas Jefferson's *Notes on the State of Virginia* (1784); Fugitive Slave Act of 1793; *The Confessions of Nat Turner* (1831); Fugitive Slave Act of 1850; *Narrative of the Life of Henry Box Brown, Written by Himself* (1854); Emancipation Proclamation (1863); Thirteenth Amendment to the U.S. Constitution (1865).

Further Reading

■ Books

Billings, Warren M., ed. *The Old Dominion in the Seventeenth Century: A Documentary History of Virginia, 1606–1700*. Rev. ed. Chapel Hill: University of North Carolina Press, 2007.

Bodenhamer, David J., and James W. Ely, eds. *Ambivalent Legacy: A Legal History of the South*. Jackson: University Press of Mississippi, 1984.

Catterall, Helen Tunnicliff. *Judicial Cases concerning American Slavery and the Negro*. 5 vols. New York: Octagon Books, 1968.

Miller, Randall M., and John David Smith, eds. *Dictionary of Afro-American Slavery*. Westport, Conn.: Praeger, 1997.

Morris, Thomas D. *Southern Slavery and the Law, 1619–1860*. Chapel Hill: University of North Carolina Press, 1996.

Schwarz, Philip J. *Twice Condemned: Slaves and the Criminal Laws of Virginia*. Baton Rouge: Louisiana State University Press, 1988.

———. *Slave Laws in Virginia*. Athens: University of Georgia Press, 2010.

■ Web Sites

Goodell, William. *The American Slave Code in Theory and Practice: Its Distinctive Features Shown by Its Statutes, Judicial Decisions, and Illustrative Facts*. Dinsmore Documentation Web Site. http://www.dinsdoc.com/goodell-1-0a.htm.

Hening, William Waller, comp. *Hening's Statutes at Large*.
    http://vagenweb.org/hening/index.htm
"Jefferson's Letter to James Monroe." PBS's Africans in America Resource Bank Web site.
    http://www.pbs.org/wgbh/aia/part3/3h492.html.

"Official Records—Virginia Laws." Geography of Slavery in Virginia Web site.
    http://www2.vcdh.virginia.edu/gos/laws.html.

St. George Tucker, ed. *Blackstone's Commentaries*.
    http://www.constitution.org/tb/tb-0000.htm.
"Selected Virginia Statutes relating to Slavery." Virtual Jamestown Web Site.
    http://www.virtualjamestown.org/slavelink.html.

"Slavery and the Law in Virginia." Colonial Williamsburg Web Site.
    http://www.history.org/History/teaching/slavelaw.cfm.

—Philip J. Schwarz

Questions for Further Study

1. In 1860 slavery had existed in Virginia for almost two centuries, and a body of law pertaining to slavery already existed. What circumstances prompted the commonwealth's legislators to pass yet further slavery laws?

2. Virginia's legislators, along with legislators throughout the South, were particularly concerned about two things: the ability of slaves to read and write and religious assemblies led by African Americans. Why were they so concerned about these specific matters?

3. Read this document in conjunction with Osborne P. Anderson's *A Voice from Harper's Ferry*. What impact do you think John Brown's 1859 raid on Harpers Ferry had on the thinking of Virginia's legislators in 1860?

4. Think of the Fugitive Slave Act of 1850 and the Virginia Slave Code as "bookends" for what some historians have called the decade of crisis. How did these two documents, taken together, define the issues that would divide the nation during the Civil War?

5. Slavery is often mistakenly thought of as a U.S. institution, but until the nineteenth century numerous other European powers participated in the slave trade and maintained slavery in their colonies. Why do you think slavery persisted in the United States for a half century or more after it had ended in many other places?

VIRGINIA SLAVE CODE

Title 10 ...

◆ Chapter XVII ...

§18 In the case of a slave under sentence of death, the governor may without any petition or assent by him, or on his behalf, order a commutation of the punishment.... The governor may direct that such slave be sold to be transported beyond the limits of the *United States*, and never allowed to return into this state ... or the slave may be directed to undergo such other punishment, neither cruel nor unusual, in lieu of that to which he was sentenced, as the governor may deem proper.

§19 Where slaves who are under sentence of death are to be sold, the governor may either contract for the sale therof, or appoint an agent to sell the same.

§20 Upon every such sale of any slave, the purchaser before delivery to him of the slave shall pay into the treasury, the price agreed to be paid, and shall enter into bond with one or more sufficient sureties, in the penalty of one thousand dollars, payable to the commonwealth of *Virginia*, conditioned that the slave shall within three months be transported beyond the limits of the *United States*, and shall never afterwards return into this state.

§21 In the case of a person under sentence of death, who is a slave only for a term of years, or for the life of another, and after the expiration of such term or life estate would be entitled to freedom, if the case be one in which had the person been a slave for his own life, the governor would have directed him to be sold to be transported beyond the *United States*, he shall instead of giving such direction, order that he be imprisoned in the penitentiary for a term not less than five nor more than ten years, and that after the expiration of such term of imprisonment he depart out of this state....

Title 11 ...

◆ Chapter XXII ...

§1 Every able bodied white male citizen between the ages of eighteen and forty-five, resident within this state, and not exempt from serving in the militia by the laws of the *United States* or of this state, shall be subject to military duty....

Title 16 ...

◆ Chapter L ...

§1 There shall be provided by the court of every county and by the council of each town wherein there is a corporation court, a courthouse and jail, pillory, whipping post and stocks....

§2 Every such jail shall be well secured, and sufficient for the convenient accommodation of those who may be confined therein, so that convicts and slaves not convicts, may be in apartments separate from each other and from the other prisoners.... The jail shall be kept in good repair....

Title 28 ...

◆ Chapter XCVIII ...

§1 The commander of each regiment of the militia, may, when necessary, appoint one or more patrols, consisting of an officer, either commissioned or noncommissioned, and so many privates as he may think requisite, to patrol and visit, within the bounds of such regiment, as often as he shall require, all negro quarters and other places suspected of having therein unlawful assemblies, or such slaves as may stroll from one plantation to another without permission....

§9 Such patrols shall take any persons found in an unlawful assembly, or any slaves found strolling as aforesaid, before some justice near the place of capture, to be dealt with according to law; and said patrols, when in search of fire arms or other weapons, under warrant from a justice, may force open the doors of free negroes, or of slaves in the absence of their masters, if access be denied....

Title 30 ...

◆ Chapter CV ...

§1 Every slave arrested as a runaway, shall be taken before a justice, and if there be reasonable cause to suspect that such slave is a runaway, the justice shall give a certificate thereof ....

§2 The justice giving the certificate ... shall command the person applying for the same, forthwith to deliver the slave for safe keeping ... to the jailor of his county or corporation....

§4 Every person who may arrest a runaway slave, and deliver him to the owner, or his agent, or to some jailor at his jail, with the certificate of a justice ... shall be entitled to demand of such owner a reward....

§7 The court of the county or corporation in which a runaway slave may be confined ... may order such slave to be delivered to the owner or his agent upon payment to the jailor of all lawful charges incident upon his arrest....

§9 When a runaway slave is committed to jail, the jailor shall forthwith set up an advertisement, describing the slave and his apparel, at the door of the courthouse of his county or corporation. If no owner claim him within one month, the jailor shall cause like advertisement to be published for six weeks in some newspaper in the city of *Richmond....* He shall also endeavor to ascertain the owner's name and address....

§10 If such runaway be not claimed by the owner within four months after the advertisement aforesaid is ended, the county or corporation ... shall order its officer to sell the slave....

◆ Chapter CVII ...

§1 No negro, emancipated since the first day of May eighteen hundred and six, or hereafter,... shall, after being twenty-one years of age, remain in this state more than one year without lawful permission.

§2 Any such negro may be permitted by the court of any county or corporation to remain in this state, and reside in such county or corporation only, but the order granting the permission shall be void, unless it shew that all the acting justices were summoned, and a majority of them present and voting on the question,... that notice of the application for such permission was posted at the courthouse door for at least two months immediately preceding,... and that the applicant produced satisfactory proof of his being of good character, sober, peaceable, orderly and industrious. Such permission shall not be granted to any person who, having removed from this state, shall have returned into it. Nor shall any such permission, granted to a female negro, be deemed a permission to the issue of such female, whether born before or after it was granted....

§3 The court granting such permission may, for any cause which seems to it sufficient, revoke the same....

§6 Every free negro shall, every five years, be registered and numbered in a book to be kept by the clerk of the court of the county or corporation where such free negro resides; which register shall specify his name, age, colour and stature, with any apparent mark or scar ... , by what instrument he was emancipated, and when and where it was recorded; or that he was born free, and in what country or place....

Title 54 ...

◆ Chapter CXC ...

§1 Treason shall consist only in levying war against the state, or adhering to its enemies, giving them aid and comfort, or establishing without authority of the legislature any government within its limits, separate from the existing government ... and such treason ... shall be punished with death....

§4 If a free person advise or conspire with a slave to rebel or make insurrection, or with any person, to induce a slave to rebel or make insurrection, he shall be punished with death, whether such rebellion or insurrection be made or not....

◆ Chapter CXCII ...

§24 Any free person who shall carry or cause to be carried out of any county or corporation any slave, without the consent of his owner, or of the guardian or committee of the owner, with intent to defraud or deprive the owner of such slave, shall be prosecuted therefor, in such county or corporation, and confined in the penitentiary not less than two nor more than ten years, and shall, moreover ... forfeit to the owner double the value of the slave, and pay him all reasonable expenses incurred by him in regaining or attempting to regain such slave.

§25 Any master of a vessel having a slave on board, and going with him beyond the limits of any county, without the consent aforesaid, and any free person travelling by land, who shall aid any slave to escape out of any county or corporation, shall be considered as carrying off such slave....

§26 If the master or skipper of any vessel knowingly receive on board any runaway slave, and permit him to remain on board without proper effort to apprehend him, he shall be confined in the penitentiary not less than two nor more than five years; and if such slave be on board such vessel after leaving port, the master or skipper shall be presumed to have knowingly received him.

§27 If a free person advise any slave to abscond from his master, or aid such slave to abscond, by procuring for or delivering a pass ... or furnishing him money, clothes, provisions, or other facility, he shall be confined in the penitentiary not less than two nor more than five years.

§28 If any owner or keeper of a ferry or bridge across a water course separating this from another state, knowingly permit a slave to pass at such ferry or bridge without the consent of his master, he shall pay to the party injured twenty-five dollars, and all damages occasioned thereby; and if the slave … escape, such owner or keeper shall moreover be confined in the penitentiary not less than one nor more than five years.…

♦ **Chapter CXCVIII** …

§22 If a free person, by speaking or writing, maintain that owners have not right of property in their slaves, he shall be confined in jail not more than one year and fined not exceeding five hundred dollars. He may be arrested, and carried before a justice, by any white person.

§23 If a free person write, print, or cause to be written or printed, any book or other writing with intent to advise or incite negroes in this state to rebel or make insurrection, or inculcating resistance to the right of property of masters in their slaves, or if he shall, with intent to aid the purpose of any such book or writing, knowingly circulate the same, he shall be confined in the penitentiary not less than one nor more than five years.

§24 If a postmaster, or deputy postmaster, know that any such book or other writing has been received at his office in the mail, he shall give notice thereof to some justice, who shall enquire into the circumstances and have such book or writing burned in his presence; if it appear to him that the person to whom it was directed subscribed therefor, knowing its character, or agreed to receive it for circulation to aid the purposes of abolitionists, the justice shall commit such person to jail. If any postmaster, or deputy postmaster, violate this section, he shall be fined not exceeding two hundred dollars.

§25 Any judge or justice, before whom any person may be brought for the offence mentioned in the previous section, shall cause him to enter into a recognizance, with sufficient surety, to appear before the circuit court having jurisdiction of the offence, at the next term thereof, and, in default of such recognizance, shall commit him to jail.…

§31 Every assemblage of negroes for the purpose of religious worship, when such worship is conducted by a negro, and every assemblage of negroes for the purpose of instruction in reading or writing, or in the night time for any purpose, shall be an unlawful assembly. Any justice may issue his warrant to any officer or other person, requiring him to enter any place where such assemblage may be, and seize any negro therein; and he, or any other justice, may order such negro to be punished with stripes.

§32 If a white person assemble with negroes for the purpose of instructing them to read or write, or if he associate with them in an unlawful assembly, he shall be confined in jail not exceeding six months and fined not exceeding one hundred dollars; and any justice may require him to enter into a recognizance,

Glossary

balls	bullets
commonwealth	the official name of four U.S. states: Virginia, Massachusetts, Pennsylvania, and Kentucky
pillory	a framework with holes for the head and feet, used to expose criminals to public humiliation
recognizances	recorded obligations entered before a court to appear in court at a particular time or pay a penalty
Richmond	the capital city of Virginia
shew	an antique spelling of "show"
stocks	a framework on which a criminal was subjected to public humiliation
stripes	whipping
sureties	persons who promise to pay a sum of money in the event that another person fails to fulfill an obligation

with sufficient security, to appear before the circuit, county or corporation court, of the county or corporation where the offence was committed, at its next term, to answer therefor, and in the mean time to keep the peace and be of good behaviour....

♦ **Chapter CC** ...

§4 If a slave plot or conspire to rebel or make insurrection, or commit an offense for the commission of which a free negro, at the time of committing the same, is punishable with death or by confinement in the penitentiary for not less than three years, he shall be punished with death. But unless it be an offence for which a free white person ... might have been

punished with death, such slave ... may, at the discretion of the court, be punished by sale or transportation beyond the limits of the *United States*....

§8 A negro shall be punished with stripes:

First, If he use provoking language or menacing gestures to a white person:

Secondly, If he furnish a slave, without the consent of his master or manager, any pass, permit or token of his being from home with authority:

Thirdly, If he keep or carry fire arms, sword or other weapon, or balls or ammunition; besides forfeiting to the state, any such articles in his possession:

Fourthly, If he be guilty of being in a riot, rout, unlawful assembly, or making seditious speeches.

A spring house on Cooling Springs Farm in Adamstown, Maryland, used to shelter runaway slaves on the Under-ground Railroad (AP/Wide World Photos)

HARRIET JACOBS'S
INCIDENTS IN THE LIFE OF A SLAVE GIRL

1861

"I was, in fact, a slave in New York, as subject to slave laws as I had been in a Slave State."

Overview

Harriet Jacobs's *Incidents in the Life of a Slave Girl: Written by Herself* (1861) is a personal narrative published as the author was approaching fifty years of age on the cusp of the Civil War. Jacobs was born into slavery in North Carolina, but she managed to escape and gain her freedom as well as the freedom of her two children. While the book is autobiographical, it changes the names of the participants, with Jacobs writing under the pseudonym Linda Brent. Her narrative details her life as a young slave girl, focusing on the unrelenting sexual advances she endured from her master. She surveys the time that she spent as a fugitive, including seven years hiding in her grandmother's attic. In detailing her time spent in the North while she was still a fugitive, she emphasizes her efforts to keep her children, who were born into slavery, out of the hands of slave catchers. Chapter XL of Jacobs's book, "The Fugitive Slave Law," details the effect that the 1850 law had on her, her family, and the black community in New York City.

The book originally began appearing in serial form in the *New York Tribune*, a newspaper run by the abolitionist Horace Greeley. Many of the incidents of sexual abuse, however, as well as Jacobs's out-of-wedlock motherhood, were regarded as too shocking for newspaper readers, so Greeley suspended publication before the narrative was completed. It was eventually published in book form in Boston. The narrative went on to find a wide audience, particularly in England, and ranks with Harriet Beecher Stowe's novel *Uncle Tom's Cabin* (1852) as one of the most moving accounts of the conditions of slavery published prior to the Civil War. The book is classed within the slave narrative genre and as such has earned a place beside other influential slave narratives, including the one published by the famed abolitionist and orator Frederick Douglass, *Narrative of the Life of Frederick Douglass, an American Slave* (1845).

Context

Jacobs's narrative was published in 1861, the year that the sectional conflict dividing the United States erupted into war. For decades the nation had been grappling with the slavery issue. In 1820, when Jacobs was yet a young girl, Congress had tried to appease both sides in the slavery debate through the Missouri Compromise, which created a dividing line between the free northern states and the southern slaveholding states. The compromise, though, proved to be only a temporary solution. After the United States acquired new territories as a result of the Mexican-American War of 1846–1848, the nation stretched from coast to coast, raising anew questions about the status of slavery in the new territories.

The events of the 1850s, when Jacobs gained her freedom and began writing her narrative, thrust the nation toward civil war. A key event was the passage of the Compromise of 1850, a package of legislation that included a new Fugitive Slave Act, designed to strengthen the Fugitive Slave Act of 1793. The earlier act had laid the responsibility for capturing fugitive slaves on the state from which they escaped. The new law was highly controversial because it required federal authorities in the northern states, as well as citizens, to help southern slave catchers in returning runaway slaves to their owners. In many northern states the response to the Fugitive Slave Act was the enactment of personal liberty laws designed to increase the legal rights of accused fugitives and prevent the kidnapping of free blacks. The U.S. Supreme Court, however, overturned these laws, arguing that federal law took precedence over state laws. Meanwhile, abolitionist societies had sprung up in the North. While some of them were created and run by African Americans, many were the work of whites, particularly Quakers, who had long had a strong religious aversion to slavery. The abolitionist movement shared many of the goals of the incipient women's rights and suffrage movement, so some women, such as Jacobs's friend Amy Post, played key roles in the opposition to slavery and deliberately flouted the law by hiding escaped slaves and giving them aid. The Underground Railroad, a secretive network of meeting points, safe houses, and escape routes, conducted runaway slaves north and, in many instances, to Canada; Philadelphia, Jacobs's destination after leaving North Carolina, was one of the main "depots." By some estimates, as many as a hundred thousand slaves had escaped via this network by 1850; thenceforth, the Fugitive Slave Act made

Time Line

1813	■ **February 11** Harriet Ann Jacobs is born in Edenton, North Carolina.
1825	■ Jacobs is willed to the niece of her mistress, coming under the control of Dr. James Norcom, who harassed her with sexual advances for a decade.
1835	■ Jacobs escapes from slavery to hide out in her grandmother's attic.
1842	■ Jacobs escapes to Philadelphia.
1845	■ *Narrative of the Life of Frederick Douglass* is published in Boston.
1850	■ **September 18** Congress passes the Fugitive Slave Act as part of the Compromise of 1850, requiring federal authorities in the North to assist southern slave catchers in returning runaway slaves to their owners.
1852	■ Harriet Beecher Stowe publishes *Uncle Tom's Cabin*.
1853	■ Solomon Northup, a free black who was kidnapped into bondage, publishes his narrative, *Twelve Years a Slave*; around this time, Jacobs begins writing her own narrative.
1854	■ **May 30** President Franklin Pierce signs into law the Kansas-Nebraska Act, allowing for popular sovereignty to determine whether new states would permit slavery.
1861	■ Jacobs's *Incidents in the Life of a Slave Girl: Written by Herself* is published in Boston; the Civil War begins on April 12 with the Confederacy's bombardment of Fort Sumter in South Carolina.
1897	■ **March 7** Jacobs dies in Cambridge, Massachusetts.

the work of the Underground Railroad more crucial—and more productive.

In 1854, shortly after Jacobs is presumed to have begun composing her narrative, the Kansas-Nebraska Act was passed to repeal the Missouri Compromise. The new act, the work of the Illinois senator Stephen A. Douglas, was an attempt to deal with slavery in the new states being carved out of the Louisiana Purchase. In essence, the act held that the question of slavery in those states would be settled by popular vote, but the law proved disastrous, leading to extraordinary bloodshed as proslavery and antislavery settlers clashed. Horace Greeley, the *New York Tribune* editor and initial publisher of portions of Jacobs's book, coined the term "Bleeding Kansas" as politically opposed gangs attacked each other in the mid-1850s. One of the most notorious acts of violence was the sacking of Lawrence, Kansas, by proslavery forces in May 1856. In retaliation, John Brown—best known for his later raid on the federal arsenal at Harpers Ferry, Virginia, in 1859—led a band of abolitionists that murdered a group of proslavery settlers in Kansas in what came to be called the Pottawatomie Massacre. Adding insult to injury was the Supreme Court's decision in *Dred Scott v. Sandford* (1857), which held that presently or formerly enslaved African Americans, as well as their descendants, were not citizens of the United States and thus not entitled to the protection of federal law.

During this period, many people mounted their own campaigns against slavery. Prominent among them was Frederick Douglass, who became one of the nation's most powerful abolitionists and orators as he railed against the evils of slavery. After spending some twenty years as a slave, Douglass escaped, and seven years later he published an autobiography, *Narrative of the Life of Frederick Douglass* (1845). He also created an antislavery newspaper called the *North Star*, which would evolve into a succession of newspapers bearing Douglass's name. Fanning the flames of opposition to the Fugitive Slave Act was Harriet Beecher Stowe's 1852 novel *Uncle Tom's Cabin*, a graphic depiction of slavery that evoked sympathy and outrage throughout the North. Stowe's depiction of Tom's enslaved life under his cruel white overseer, Simon Legree, mobilized abolitionists and others who had perhaps until then given little thought to the issue. Joining these writers was Solomon Northup, a free man who was captured and forced into slavery and who in 1853 published *Twelve Years a Slave*, an account of his time in bondage. During these years numerous other slave narratives were published, among them *The Life of John Thompson, a Fugitive Slave* (1856); *The Kidnapped and the Ransomed: Being the Personal Recollections of Peter Still and his Wife "Vina," after Forty Years of Slavery* (1856), authored by Kate E. R. Pickard; and *Running a Thousand Miles for Freedom; or, The Escape of William and Ellen Craft from Slavery* (1860). Thus, by the time Jacobs published *Incidents in the Life of a Slave Girl* in 1861, a vibrant market for these kinds of books had already been established.

Harriet Ann Jacobs was born into slavery in Edenton, North Carolina, in 1813. Her father was a carpenter named Elijah Knox, a mulatto who was probably the son of a white farmer, Henry Jacobs, and a slave named Athena Knox; her mother was Delilah Horniblow. Harriet had a brother, John S. Jacobs. After her mother's death in about 1819, Harriet Jacobs lived with her mother's mistress, Margaret Horniblow, where she learned to read and write and became an accomplished seamstress. Margaret Horniblow died in 1825, apparently leaving Harriet, now twelve years old, to her five-year-old niece (although there are questions about the legitimacy of the codicil to the will that made this bequest, which Horniblow did not sign). The result was that the niece's father, Dr. James Norcom, became in effect Jacobs's master—and her tormentor for nearly a decade, alternatively threatening and cajoling her in making advances; he never did resort to using force. Jacobs, in an effort to escape his unwanted attentions, paired herself with a white lawyer, Samuel Sawyer, and the two had two children, Joseph and Louisa. Norcom yet threatened to force the children to work on a plantation as slaves if Jacobs did not submit to him. Determined not to let this happen, Jacobs escaped in 1835, to spend seven years hiding out in the attic of her grandmother, Molly Horniblow, a free black who operated a bakery out of her home. Norcom, as Jacobs had predicted, no longer had any use for the children, so he sold them to Sawyer, who granted them their freedom and then arranged for Jacobs and the children to flee to the North.

In 1842 Jacobs was able to escape to Philadelphia, where members of the Vigilant Committee of Philadelphia, an antislavery group, took her in. In 1845 the group helped her get to New York, where she found work as a nursemaid in the home of a prominent writer, Nathaniel Parker Willis, and his wife, Mary. After Mary died, Jacobs remained with Willis and even traveled with him to England. Upon her return to the United States she left Willis's employment and went first to Boston to be with her children and then to Rochester, New York, to be with her brother, John, who had opened a local antislavery reading room and was an abolitionist lecturer. There she became friends with Amy Post, a Quaker and staunch abolitionist who had recently attended the women's rights convention in Seneca Falls, New York. Jacobs joined the American Anti-Slavery Society, raising money for the reading room by giving lectures.

When the Fugitive Slave Act was passed in 1850, Jacobs and her brother began to fear for their safety, for Norcom had been unrelenting in his efforts to find her. John decided to join the California gold rush, principally because California was not enforcing the act. By this time, Jacobs was back in New York City, where she was informed that the husband of her legal owner had checked into a hotel. Fearing that she would be kidnapped, she returned to the Willis family. In 1852 the new Mrs. Willis purchased Jacobs's freedom for $300. Jacobs was grateful, but at the same time she expressed her dismay at having to gain her freedom by being "purchased." She wrote that

Horace Greeley, editor of the New York Tribune
(Library of Congress)

she felt she had been deprived of a victory in gaining her freedom this way.

Sometime around 1852 or 1853, Post suggested that Jacobs write her life story. Jacobs favored the idea, and over the next several years she wrote while living at the Willis home, named Idlewild, in Cornwall, New York. She completed the manuscript in 1858 but was initially unable to find a publisher. One publisher agreed to publish the book only if the well-known writer Lydia Maria Child would pen an introduction for it. Child agreed, but before the book could be published, the firm went out of business. Finally, the book was published privately in 1861. During the Civil War, Jacobs used her newfound celebrity to raise funds to help southern blacks who had fled the Confederacy. After a stay in Savannah, Georgia, she returned north in 1866, to spend her final decades with her daughter in Cambridge, Massachusetts. She died, having survived into her mid-eighties, on March 7, 1897.

Explanation and Analysis of the Document

Chapter XL in *Incidents in the Life of a Slave Girl* is titled "The Fugitive Slave Law" and is the book's penultimate chapter. Earlier chapters detail Jacobs's life from her

"But while fashionables were listening to the thrilling voice of Jenny Lind in Metropolitan Hall, the thrilling voices of poor hunted colored people went up, in an agony of supplication, to the Lord, from Zion's church. Many families, who had lived in the city for twenty years, fled from it now."

(Paragraph 3)

"What a disgrace to a city calling itself free, that inhabitants, guiltless of offence, and seeking to perform their duties conscientiously, should be condemned to live in such incessant fear, and have nowhere to turn for protection!"

(Paragraph 4)

"When a man has his wages stolen from him, year after year, and the laws sanction and enforce the theft, how can he be expected to have more regard to honesty than has the man who robs him?"

(Paragraph 9)

"I was, in fact, a slave in New York, as subject to slave laws as I had been in a Slave State. Strange incongruity in a State called free!"

(Paragraph 10)

"He remonstrated with her for harboring a fugitive slave ... and asked her if she was aware of the penalty. She replied, 'I am very well aware of it. It is imprisonment and one thousand dollars fine. Shame on my country that it is so! I am ready to incur the penalty. I will go to the state's prison, rather than have any poor victim torn from my house, to be carried back to slavery.'"

(Paragraph 13)

girlhood in North Carolina through her flight to her grandmother's home, her escape to Philadelphia, her time with the Willis family, her freedom, and other events. Throughout the narration the names of the characters are changed, such that she herself is "Linda Brent," her brother is "William Brent," her children are "Benjamin" (or "Benny") and "Ellen," Dr.

Norcom is named "Dr. Flint," Samuel Sawyer is "Mr. Sands," Nathaniel Parker Willis is "Mr. Bruce," and Willis's second wife, who bought Jacobs's freedom, is "Cornelia Bruce."

By the first paragraph of Chapter XL, the narration has reached the time when William Brent decides to head to California to take part in the gold rush and agrees that Benjamin, Linda Brent's son, will go with him. Left alone, the narrator decides to return to New York and to the Bruce family, where she was previously employed. Mr. Bruce has taken a new wife, Cornelia, whom the narrator describes as "aristocratic" but also as heartily opposed to slavery and resistant to any of the "sophistry" used by southerners to defend it. In the third paragraph, the narrator makes reference to an event of "disastrous import to the colored people"— the passage of the Fugitive Slave Act of 1850. She refers to a slave by the name of Hamlin who was hunted down by the "bloodhounds" of the North and South in New York. In describing the impact of the law on New Yorkers, she refers to the "short and simple annals of the poor." This is a line originally from Thomas Gray's famous poem "Elegy Written in a Country Churchyard" (1751) and later used by Abraham Lincoln in 1859 to describe his childhood. The paragraph also makes reference to Jenny Lind, a Swedish opera singer known in America as the "Swedish Nightingale." The narrator makes the point that while "fashionables" were listening to opera, "the thrilling voices of poor hunted colored people went up … from Zion's church," a reference to the city's African Methodist Episcopal Zion Church. Because of the new law, many blacks who had found homes in the city had little choice but to flee, perhaps to Canada; many wives and husbands discovered that their spouses were fugitive slaves and liable to capture. Making matters worse was the fact that children born to a slave mother were themselves legally slaves, so fathers faced the prospect of losing not only their wives but also their children to slave catchers.

In paragraph 4 the narrator refers to the discussions she and her brother had before he left for California, pointing out his anger at the new law. The narrator then goes on to describe how she and others had to go about the city through back streets and byways, living in constant fear of being taken by slave catchers. Vigilance committees were formed to keep tabs on the activities of slave catchers, and New York's blacks kept their eyes on newspapers that reported the arrival of southerners at the city's hotels. The phrases "running to and fro" and "knowledge should be increased" are from the book of Daniel in the King James Bible.

In paragraphs 5–9, the narrator tells the story of a slave named Luke whom she had known as a child. Luke had been owned by a particularly cruel master who depended on Luke for his care but beat him constantly—or called on the town constable to do so for him. After the master died, Luke hid some of the man's money in the pocket of the pants in which he would be buried. At the time of the burial, Luke asked for the pants, in this way getting funds that enabled him to flee to New York with the goal of reaching Canada—where he would have joined an estimated twenty thousand New York African Americans who fled to Canada after the law was passed. The narrator encounters Luke in New York and learns of his plans. Luke refers to "speculators," men who purchased the rights to runaway slaves so as to catch them and then sell them to the highest bidder. The narrator concludes this portion of the account by noting that Luke's tale offered an example of how the slave system corrupted morals: "When a man has his wages stolen from him, year after year, and the laws sanction and enforce the theft, how can he be expected to have more regard to honesty than has the man who robs him?"

With paragraph 10, the narrator returns to her own experiences, again stressing how anxious she was that she could be caught, especially with the approach of summer. She reflects on the irony that she was in a "free" state but still felt like a slave. Her anxiety was well advised, for she learned that Dr. Flint was on the hunt for her and had learned from informants about her mode of dress. In point of fact, the real-life Norcom placed newspaper ads in which he offered a reward of $100 for information about her. The ads stressed that "being a good seamstress, she has been accustomed to dress well, has a variety of very fine clothes, made in the prevailing fashion, and will probably appear, if abroad, tricked out in gay and fashionable finery." When she informed Mrs. Bruce of the danger she was in, Mrs. Bruce offered to allow the narrator to carry her daughter about so that if the narrator were caught, the authorities would have to return the Bruce child to her mother. In this way Mrs. Bruce could learn of the capture and take action to help. In paragraph 13 the narrator notes that Mrs. Bruce had a proslavery relative who questioned her decision to harbor a fugitive slave. When he asked her whether she knew the penalty for doing so, she acknowledged that she did but expressed her willingness to go to jail "rather than have any poor victim torn from *my* house, to be carried back to slavery." The narrator concludes the account by noting that she went to the safety of Massachusetts to avoid capture. The Massachusetts senator referred to by the narrator was probably Robert Rantoul, Jr., an outspoken opponent of the Fugitive Slave Act who provided a legal defense for Thomas Sims, the first purported slave captured under the new act in Massachusetts.

Audience

The most pertinent audience for *Incidents in the Life of a Slave Girl* consisted of those Americans who still needed convincing that the slave system had to be eradicated. Shortly after the book's publication, Jacobs and Lydia Maria Child began writing letters to newspaper editors, bookstore owners, and anyone else they could think of who would advertise and promote the book. Jacobs's brother John, now living in London, published a condensed version of the book under the title *A True Tale of Slavery*, leaving out the sexual elements to make it more palatable to English readers. The book achieved some popularity with its British audience and fueled more intense opposition to slavery in England.

In particular, Jacobs and Child saw middle-class Christian white women as a primary audience for the book, hoping that the sexual harassment Jacobs endured would motivate Christian women to take up the cudgel against slavery after feeling its corrupting moral influence. In this regard, a passage from Child's introduction provides insight into the writer's intention:

I am well aware that many will accuse me of indecorum for presenting these pages to the public; for the experiences of this intelligent and much-injured woman belong to a class which some call delicate subjects, and others indelicate. This peculiar phase of Slavery has generally been kept veiled; but the public ought to be made acquainted with its monstrous features, and I willingly take the responsibility of presenting them with the veil withdrawn. I do this for the sake of my sisters in bondage, who are suffering wrongs so foul, that our ears are too delicate to listen to them. I do it with the hope of arousing conscientious and reflecting women at the North to a sense of their duty in the exertion of moral influence on the question of Slavery, on all possible occasions.

Incidents in the Life of a Slave Girl found a new audience in the twentieth century and beyond as feminists and literary critics began to discover the literary merit of slave narratives and thus directed attention to documents giving voice to the disenfranchised rather than works by prominent New England authors. During the Great Depression, the Works Projects Administration, one of the federal agencies created as part of Franklin Roosevelt's New Deal, put unemployed researchers and writers to work in the Federal Writers' Project. One of the project's major undertakings entailed writers' interviewing surviving African Americans who had been slaves prior to the passage of the Thirteenth Amendment, which abolished slavery, and documenting their stories. From 1936 to 1938 the project's writers recorded the stories of more than twenty-three hundred former slaves, to be presented in a series of volumes, with each volume focusing on the narratives of former slaves in particular states. Jacobs's North Carolina was featured in the project's 1939 volume These Are Our Lives. In the twenty-first century, Americans have learned more about Jacobs through a successful Broadway play by Lydia Diamond titled Harriet Jacobs.

Impact

Jacobs confessed in letters to her friend Post that she felt some reticence about committing her life story to paper, largely because it would deal with the sexual exploitation of slaves and because she would have to make known her own status as an unwed mother. It was for these reasons that she created the fictional persona Linda Brent, who narrates the story. The book differed from other slave narratives of the era in its focus on two major themes regarding the female narrator's life, as that of a "fallen woman" and as that of a heroic woman who keeps her children from falling prey to chattel slavery. Notably, the book accordingly uses two different styles: When Jacobs is discussing her efforts on behalf of her children, she writes in a direct, pointed style. When the subject turns to sexual exploitation and her own sexual history, the style becomes more indirect and elevated, similar to the style of much popular fiction from the time. The fact that Jacobs's narrative was written by a wom-

an was alone a distinguishing factor. The slave narratives of writers such as Frederick Douglass and Solomon Northup focus on the largely solitary efforts of a heroic man. Jacobs, on the other hand, embedded her narrative in more of a social context that includes family relationships and friendships both within and outside the black community.

Some readers found the book too unbelievable to be true and accused the author of exaggerating and fictionalizing for sensational effect. Some thought that the book had to have been written by a white woman, and some scholars continue to suggest that Child had more of hand in shaping and even writing the book than she admitted. Jacobs, though, tried to counter these reactions by insisting on its veracity. In an appendix, Post bore witness to the book's truth. So, too, did an African American Bostonian named George W. Lowther, who after the Civil War would be elected to the Massachusetts House of Representatives and who wrote of the book,

> However it may be regarded by the incredulous, I know that it is full of living truths. I have been well acquainted with the author from my boyhood. The circumstances recounted in her history are perfectly familiar to me. I knew of her treatment from her master; of the imprisonment of her children; of their sale and redemption; of her seven years' concealment; and of her subsequent escape to the North.

See also Fugitive Slave Act of 1793; First Editorial of the North Star(1847); Fugitive Slave Act of 1850; Dred Scott v. Sandford(1857); Twelve Years a Slave: Narrative of Solomon Northup (1853); Thirteenth Amendment to the U.S. Constitution (1865).

Further Reading

■ Articles

Cutter, Martha J. "Dismantling 'The Master's House': Critical Literacy in Harriet Jacobs' Incidents in the Life of a Slave Girl." Callaloo 19, no. 1 (Winter 1996): 209–225.

Miller, Jennie. "Harriet Jacobs and the 'Double Burden' of American Slavery." International Social Science Review 78 (June 2003): 31–41.

■ Books

Federal Writers' Project. North Carolina Slave Narratives: A Folk History of Slavery in North Carolina from Interviews with Former Slaves. Bedford, Mass.: Applewood Books, 2006.

Fisch, Audrey, ed. The Cambridge Companion to the African American Slave Narrative. Cambridge, U.K.: Cambridge University Press, 2007.

Garfield, Deborah M., and Rafia Zafar, eds. *Harriet Jacobs and "Incidents in the Life of a Slave Girl": New Critical Essays*. Cambridge, U.K.: Cambridge University Press, 1996.

Heglar, Charles J. *Rethinking the Slave Narrative: Slave Marriage and the Narratives of Henry Bibb and William and Ellen Craft*. Westport, Conn.: Greenwood Press, 2001.

Johnson, Yvonne. *The Voices of African American Women: The Use of Narrative and Authorial Voice in the Works of Harriet Jacobs, Zora Neale Hurston, and Alice Walker*. New York: Peter Lang, 1998.

Shockley, Ann Allen, ed. *Afro-American Women Writers, 1746–1933: An Anthology and Critical Guide*. New Haven, Conn.: Meridian Books, 1989.

Taylor, Yuval, ed. *I Was Born a Slave: An Anthology of Classic Slave Narratives*. Chicago: Lawrence Hill Books, 1999.

Washington, Mary Helen. "Meditations on History: The Slave Narrative of Linda Brent." In *Invented Lives: Narratives of Black Women, 1860–1960*, ed. Mary Helen Washington. New York: Doubleday, 1987.

Yellin, Jean Fagan. *Harriet Jacobs: A Life*. Cambridge, Mass.: Basic Civitas Books, 2004.

———, ed. *The Harriet Jacobs Family Papers*. Chapel Hill: University of North Carolina Press, 2008.

■ Web Sites

Child, Lydia Maria. Introduction to *Incidents in the Life of a Slave Girl, Written by Herself*. Documenting the American South, University of North Carolina at Chapel Hill Web site.
   http://docsouth.unc.edu/fpn/jacobs/jacobs.html.

"Harriet Jacobs." Harriet Jacobs Web site.
   http://www.harrietjacobs.org.

Lowther, George W. Appendix to *Incidents in the Life of a Slave Girl, Written by Herself*. Documenting the American South, University of North Carolina at Chapel Hill Web site.
   http://docsouth.unc.edu/fpn/jacobs/jacobs.html.

—Michael J. O'Neal

Questions for Further Study

1. What impact did the Mexican-American War have on the issue of slavery in the decade before the Civil War?

2. Most slave narratives published during this era were written by men. How do you think Jacobs's narrative might differ from those because of her experiences as a woman?

3. By the time Jacobs was born, the Fugitive Slave Act of 1793 was already on the books. What made the Fugitive Slave Act of 1850 more frightening for her and her children?

4. What was "Bleeding Kansas"? What part did it play in the sectional divide that led to the Civil War?

5. Compare this document with *Twelve Years a Slave: Narrative of Solomon Northup*. What similar experiences did the authors have? How were their experiences different?

HARRIET JACOBS'S
INCIDENTS IN THE LIFE OF A SLAVE GIRL

My brother, being disappointed in his project, concluded to go to California; and it was agreed that Benjamin should go with him. Ellen liked her school, and was a great favorite there. They did not know her history, and she did not tell it, because she had no desire to make capital out of their sympathy. But when it was accidentally discovered that her mother was a fugitive slave, every method was used to increase her advantages and diminish her expenses.

I was alone again. It was necessary for me to be earning money, and I preferred that it should be among those who knew me. On my return from Rochester, I called at the house of Mr. Bruce, to see Mary, the darling little babe that had thawed my heart, when it was freezing into a cheerless distrust of all my fellow-beings. She was growing a tall girl now, but I loved her always. Mr. Bruce had married again, and it was proposed that I should become nurse to a new infant. I had but one hesitation, and that was my feeling of insecurity in New York, now greatly increased by the passage of the Fugitive Slave Law. However, I resolved to try the experiment. I was again fortunate in my employer. The new Mrs. Bruce was an American, brought up under aristocratic influences and still living in the midst of them; but if she had any prejudice against color, I was never made aware of it; and as for the system of slavery, she had a most hearty dislike of it. No sophistry of Southerners could blind her to its enormity. She was a person of excellent principles and a noble heart. To me, from that hour to the present, she has been a true and sympathizing friend. Blessings be with her and hers!

About the time that I reentered the Bruce family, an event occurred of disastrous import to the colored people. The slave Hamlin, the first fugitive that came under the new law, was given up by the bloodhounds of the north to the bloodhounds of the south. It was the beginning of a reign of terror to the colored population. The great city rushed on in its whirl of excitement, taking no note of the "short and simple annals of the poor." But while fashionables were listening to the thrilling voice of Jenny Lind in Metropolitan Hall, the thrilling voices of poor hunted colored people went up, in an agony of supplication, to the Lord, from Zion's church. Many families, who had lived in the city for twenty years, fled from it now. Many a

poor washerwoman, who, by hard labor, had made herself a comfortable home, was obliged to sacrifice her furniture, bid a hurried farewell to friends, and seek her fortune among strangers in Canada. Many a wife discovered a secret she had never known before—that her husband was a fugitive, and must leave her to insure his own safety. Worse still, many a husband discovered that his wife had fled from slavery years ago, and as "the child follows the condition of its mother," the children of his love were liable to be seized and carried into slavery. Every where, in those humble homes, there was consternation and anguish. But what cared the legislators of the "dominant race" for the blood they were crushing out of trampled hearts?

When my brother William spent his last evening with me, before he went to California, we talked nearly all the time of the distress brought on our oppressed people by the passage of this iniquitous law; and never had I seen him manifest such bitterness of spirit, such stern hostility to our oppressors. He was himself free from the operation of the law; for he did not run from any Slaveholding State, being brought into the Free States by his master. But I was subject to it; and so were hundreds of intelligent and industrious people all around us. I seldom ventured into the streets; and when it was necessary to do an errand for Mrs. Bruce, or any of the family, I went as much as possible through back streets and by-ways. What a disgrace to a city calling itself free, that inhabitants, guiltless of offence, and seeking to perform their duties conscientiously, should be condemned to live in such incessant fear, and have nowhere to turn for protection! This state of things, of course, gave rise to many impromptu vigilance committees. Every colored person, and every friend of their persecuted race, kept their eyes wide open. Every evening I examined the newspapers carefully, to see what Southerners had put up at the hotels. I did this for my own sake, thinking my young mistress and her husband might be among the list; I wished also to give information to others, if necessary; for if many were "running to and fro," I resolved that "knowledge should be increased."

This brings up one of my Southern reminiscences, which I will here briefly relate. I was somewhat acquainted with a slave named Luke, who belonged to a wealthy man in our vicinity. His master died, leaving a son and daughter heirs to his large fortune. In the division of the slaves, Luke was included in the son's portion. This young man became a prey to the vices growing out of the "patriarchal institution," and when he went to the north, to complete his education, he carried his vices with him. He was brought home, deprived of the use of his limbs, by excessive dissipation. Luke was appointed to wait upon his bed-ridden master, whose despotic habits were greatly increased by exasperation at his own helplessness. He kept a cowhide beside him, and, for the most trivial occurrence, he would order his attendant to bare his back, and kneel beside the couch, while he whipped him till his strength was exhausted. Some days he was not allowed to wear any thing but his shirt, in order to be in readiness to be flogged. A day seldom passed without his receiving more or less blows. If the slightest resistance was offered, the town constable was sent for to execute the punishment, and Luke learned from experience how much more the constable's strong arm was to be dreaded than the comparatively feeble one of his master. The arm of his tyrant grew weak, and was finally palsied; and then the constable's services were in constant requisition. The fact that he was entirely dependent on Luke's care, and was obliged to be tended like an infant, instead of inspiring any gratitude or compassion towards his poor slave, seemed only to increase his irritability and cruelty. As he lay there on his bed, a mere disgraced wreck of manhood, he took into his head the strangest freaks of despotism; and if Luke hesitated to submit to his orders, the constable was immediately sent for. Some of these freaks were of a nature too filthy to be repeated. When I fled from the house of bondage, I left poor Luke still chained to the bedside of this cruel and disgusting wretch.

One day, when I had been requested to do an errand for Mrs. Bruce, I was hurrying through back streets, as usual, when I saw a young man approaching, whose face was familiar to me. As he came nearer, I recognized Luke. I always rejoiced to see or hear of any one who had escaped from the black pit; but, remembering this poor fellow's extreme hardships, I was peculiarly glad to see him on Northern soil, though I no longer called it *free* soil. I well remembered what a desolate feeling it was to be alone among strangers, and I went up to him and greeted him cordially. At first, he did not know me; but when I mentioned my name, he remembered all about me. I told him of the Fugitive Slave Law, and

asked him if he did not know that New York was a city of kidnappers.

He replied, "De risk ain't so bad for me, as 'tis fur you. 'Cause I runned away from de speculator, and you runned away from de massa. Dem speculators vont spen dar money to come here fur a runaway, if dey ain't sartin sure to put dar hans right on him. An I tell you I's tuk good car 'bout dat. I had too hard times down dar, to let 'em ketch dis nigger."

He then told me of the advice he had received, and the plans he had laid. I asked if he had money enough to take him to Canada. "'Pend upon it, I hab," he replied. "I tuk car fur dat. I'd bin workin all my days fur dem cussed whites, an got no pay but kicks and cuffs. So I tought dis nigger had a right to money nuff to bring him to de Free States. Massa Henry he lib till ebery body vish him dead; an ven he did die, I knowed de debbil would hab him, an vouldn't vant him to bring his money 'long too. So I tuk some of his bills, and put 'em in de pocket of his ole trousers. An ven he was buried, dis nigger ask fur dem ole trousers, an dey gub 'em to me." With a low, chuckling laugh, he added, "You see I didn't *steal* it; dey *gub* it to me. I tell you, I had mighty hard time to keep de speculator from findin it; but he didn't git it."

This is a fair specimen of how the moral sense is educated by slavery. When a man has his wages stolen from him, year after year, and the laws sanction and enforce the theft, how can he be expected to have more regard to honesty than has the man who robs him? I have become somewhat enlightened, but I confess that I agree with poor, ignorant, much abused Luke, in thinking he had a *right* to that money, as a portion of his unpaid wages. He went to Canada forthwith, and I have not since heard from him.

All that winter I lived in a state of anxiety. When I took the children out to breathe the air, I closely observed the countenances of all I met. I dreaded the approach of summer, when snakes and slaveholders make their appearance. I was, in fact, a slave in New York, as subject to slave laws as I had been in a Slave State. Strange incongruity in a State called free!

Spring returned, and I received warning from the south that Dr. Flint knew of my return to my old place, and was making preparations to have me caught. I learned afterwards that my dress, and that of Mrs. Bruce's children, had been described to him by some of the Northern tools, which slaveholders employ for their base purposes, and then indulge in sneers at their cupidity and mean servility.

I immediately informed Mrs. Bruce of my danger, and she took prompt measures for my safety. My place as nurse could not be supplied immediately, and this generous, sympathizing lady proposed that I should carry her baby away. It was a comfort to me to have the child with me; for the heart is reluctant to be torn away from every object it loves. But how few mothers would have consented to have one of their own babes become a fugitive, for the sake of a poor, hunted nurse, on whom the legislators of the country had let loose the bloodhounds! When I spoke of the sacrifice she was making, in depriving herself of her dear baby, she replied, "It is better for you to have baby with you, Linda; for if they get on your track, they will be obliged to bring the child to me; and then, if there is a possibility of saving you, you shall be saved."

This lady had a very wealthy relative, a benevolent gentleman in many respects, but aristocratic and pro-slavery. He remonstrated with her for harboring a fugitive slave; told her she was violating the laws of her country; and asked her if she was aware of the penalty. She replied, "I am very well aware of it. It is imprisonment and one thousand dollars fine. Shame on my country that it *is* so! I am ready to incur the penalty. I will go to the state's prison, rather than have any poor victim torn from *my* house, to be carried back to slavery."

The noble heart! The brave heart! The tears are in my eyes while I write of her. May the God of the helpless reward her for her sympathy with my persecuted people!

I was sent into New England, where I was sheltered by the wife of a senator, whom I shall always hold in grateful remembrance. This honorable gentleman would not have voted for the Fugitive Slave Law, as did the senator in "Uncle Tom's Cabin;" on the contrary, he was strongly opposed to it; but he was enough under its influence to be afraid of having me remain in his house many hours. So I was sent into the country, where I remained a month with the baby. When it was supposed that Dr. Flint's emissaries had lost track of me, and given up the pursuit for the present, I returned to New York.

Glossary

Benjamin	the fictional name Jacobs gives to her son, Joseph
"the child follows the condition of its mother"	a reference to the fact that under the law, the children of a slave mother were automatically born as slaves
Dr. Flint	the fictional name Jacobs gives to her master and tormentor, Dr. James Norcom
Fugitive Slave Law	the Fugitive Slave Act of 1850
Jenny Lind	a famous Swedish opera singer
Linda	Linda Brent, the persona Jacobs adopts in her narrative
Mr. Bruce	the fictional name Jacobs gives to Nathanial Parker Willis, the New Yorker who took her in
"running to and fro" ... "knowledge should be increased"	quotations from the book of Daniel in the King James Bible
"short and simple annals of the poor"	a line originally from Thomas Gray's 1751 poem "Elegy Written in a Country Churchyard," later used by Abraham Lincoln to describe his childhood
speculator	a person who purchased the rights to runaway slaves so as to catch them and then sell them to the highest bidder
Uncle Tom's Cabin	the widely read antislavery novel by Harriet Beecher Stowe
wife of a Senator	probably a reference to Robert Rantoul, Jr., an outspoken opponent of the Fugitive Slave Act
William	the fictional name Jacobs gives her brother John

John Brown (Library of Congress)

OSBORNE P. ANDERSON:
A VOICE FROM HARPER'S FERRY

"We visited the plantations and acquainted the slaves with our purpose to effect their liberation."

Overview

In 1861 Osborne Anderson published *A Voice from Harper's Ferry: A Narrative of Events at Harper's Ferry; With Incidents Prior and Subsequent to Its Capture by Captain Brown and His Men* to present his eyewitness account of events during and revolving around John Brown's raid on the federal arsenal at Harpers Ferry, Virginia (now West Virginia), of October 16–18, 1859. After the capture and execution of the other raiders, Anderson was the only one left alive who had been present in Harpers Ferry during the raid; because he believed that southern accounts were biased, he felt compelled to give an account of the event from the raiders' perspective. The book's publication, accomplished by the author with the aid of antislavery Bostonians, was announced in William Lloyd Garrison's newspaper *The Liberator* on January 11, 1861, and in Frederick Douglass's *Monthly* in the February 1861 issue. The book became an important source for historians and biographers of the renowned abolitionist Brown.

Context

Despite the fact that he was born free in the northern United States, Osborne Anderson, an African American, lived in a world in which he was considered a nonperson. The movement to abolish slavery was very much alive, but it had primarily succeeded in creating a hostile relationship between northern and southern states. The Compromise of 1850, which included the new Fugitive Slave Act of 1850, decreeing that those who helped fugitive slaves would be prosecuted and ordering northerners to aid in the capture and return of fugitive slaves to their masters, only served to deepen that hostile relationship. Subsequently, Harriet Beecher Stowe's antislavery novel *Uncle Tom's Cabin*, published in 1852, fanned the flames of northern hatred for slavery and encouraged northerners to flout the Fugitive Slave Act by aiding fugitive slaves. While Stowe was attempting to persuade southerners to eschew slavery based on an appeal to emotion and religious beliefs, she

succeeded only in making many southerners feel personally angry. The Kansas-Nebraska Act of 1854 prolonged the debate over slavery by allowing the residents of the two new territories to decide for themselves via the ballot box whether they would enter the union as slave states or free states.

John Brown was a white man who had always been opposed to slavery, but in November 1837, following the murder of Elijah P. Lovejoy, editor of an antislavery newspaper in Alton, Ohio, Brown publicly declared his personal war on slavery and committed himself to its destruction. He had come to believe that the only way to end slavery was through the use of violence. Thus, in 1855, Brown joined with five of his sons in an attempt to help bring the Kansas Territory into the Union as a free state. With antislavery and proslavery factions battling for control of the land and of the vote, "Bleeding Kansas" became a microcosm of the future Civil War; in the end, Kansas emerged as a free state (incorporated on January 29, 1861). By then, Brown had made himself a legend and a wanted man primarily because of his actions following the sack of Lawrence, Kansas, by proslavery factions on May 21, 1856. To avenge the murders of five Lawrence residents, Brown ordered and carried out the murder of five proslavery men who lived along the banks of the Pottawatomie Creek. This incident came to be known as the Pottawatomie Massacre.

Rendered a fugitive, Brown became a hero to white and black abolitionists alike. Fleeing to the East, he was welcomed and sheltered, and he gained financial backers, including the "Secret Six"—a group of wealthy, white abolitionists who approved of his plans to use violence to end slavery. Also known as the "Committee of Six," the group included Thomas Wentworth Higginson, minister and author; Samuel Gridley Howe, physician, social reformer, and philanthropist; Theodore Parker, Unitarian minister and social reformer; Franklin Sanborn, journalist, educator, and biographer of John Brown (1885); Gerrit Smith, philanthropist and politician; and George Luther Stearns, a wealthy industrialist. Brown's original plan involved rescuing slaves from the slave states a few at a time, but it eventually escalated into plans for a slave insurrection. In order to follow through on either plan, he felt that he needed the help of free blacks; thus, he attempted to gain the support

Time Line	
1800	■ **May 9** John Brown is born in Torrington, Connecticut.
1830	■ **July 27** Osborne Anderson is born in West Fallowfield, Pennsylvania.
1850	■ **September 18** As part of the Compromise of 1850, the Fugitive Slave Act of 1850 is passed, by which northerners are forbidden to help fugitive slaves escape and ordered to aid in their return to their owners.
1854	■ **May 30** Through the Kansas-Nebraska Act, residents of the two new territories are allowed to vote on whether their territory will enter the Union as a slave state or a free state; five of Brown's sons subsequently move to Kansas to help ensure that it enters as a free state.
1856	■ **May** Following the sack of Lawrence, Kansas, by proslavery forces, Brown orders the murder of five proslavery settlers at Pottawatomie Creek; Brown becomes a wanted man and leaves Kansas in September.
1857	■ Brown travels throughout New England recruiting financial backers for his planned raid, including the Secret Six; he orders one thousand pikes in Connecticut for the purpose of arming slaves.
1858	■ **April** Anderson meets Brown during the latter's first visit to Chatham, Canada West, in preparation for the Chatham Convention. ■ **May 8–10** Brown, Anderson, Martin Delany, and other abolitionists attend the Chatham Convention.

of prominent black abolitionists such as Frederick Douglass, Harriet Tubman, and Martin Delany.

Brown's attempts to recruit black assistance led to his planning a conference at Chatham, in Canada West (now Ontario, Canada), where he recruited Osborne Anderson. Brown paid his first visit to Chatham in April 1858 in preparation for the Chatham Convention of May 8–10, 1858. While in town, Brown stayed with members of the Shadd family, which was also sheltering Anderson; they offered Brown the use of their printing press to record and spread his ideas. His goal was to recruit black Canadian abolitionists to take part in his planned slave insurrection in the South. Thirty-four blacks from the local area attended the convention; Brown brought twelve of his followers—eleven white and one black. Delany organized the convention and served as chairman; Anderson served as secretary. Brown used the convention to lay out his "Provisional Constitution and Ordinances for the People of the United States," with the purpose of establishing his credibility as a careful planner and highlighting his differences from other leaders of slave insurrections, such as Nat Turner.

Although Brown gained the support of black Canadian abolitionists at the convention, he was unwilling to reveal many specific details about his plans. But by the summer of 1859, his plans were in place, and John Brown, Jr., returned to Chatham in August 1859 to issue a call to arms among those who had attended the convention. Unfortunately for Brown, over a year had gone by, and support for his plans had dwindled. Mary Ann Shadd, however, felt that someone needed to represent the Chatham contingent, and Anderson volunteered. Thus, he became one of only two Canadians to take part in the raid (the other being Stewart Taylor).

Brown led the raid of the arsenal at Harpers Ferry, Virginia, on October 16, 1859. He then had only twenty-one followers, including five blacks and sixteen whites. He led eighteen of them into Harpers Ferry, and they quickly captured two bridges, the arsenal, the rifle factory, and the engine house. But by noon on October 17, militia groups arrived from nearby locales and attacked Brown's men who were holding the Baltimore and Ohio Railroad bridge. Thus, Brown and his men were cut off from their major escape route. After an attack on the engine house and on Brown's men at the rifle factory, it seemed clear that all was lost. The local militia was later joined by Colonel Robert E. Lee and ninety U.S. marines. On the morning of October 18, Brown was asked to surrender; following his refusal, Lee's marines attacked the engine house, capturing Brown and those of his men who were still alive. Anderson and Albert Hazlett were the only two men to escape from Harpers Ferry itself (as the other five accomplices who escaped were not in Harpers Ferry). Anderson and Hazlett made their way back toward Chambersburg, Pennsylvania, but separated before they reached their goal. Anderson made it to Chambersburg and from there proceeded to York, to Philadelphia, and thence to Canada. Hazlett, on the other hand, was captured near Newville, Pennsylvania, and returned to Virginia, where he was tried, convicted, and hanged. As for Brown, he was captured on October 18; convicted of murder, treason, and inciting a slave insurrection on November 2 at the Charles Town courthouse; and hanged on December 2, to be buried on his farm in North Elba, New York.

Anderson was thus the only one of Brown's men to witness the events at Harpers Ferry and live to tell about them. With the assistance of Shadd, Anderson then wrote *A Voice from Harper's Ferry*, published in Boston in 1861. Subsequent to Brown's raid, the South, believing itself more and more threatened by northern abolitionists, began to arm; eighteen months later, the Civil War began.

About the Author

Osborne Perry Anderson was an abolitionist, author, and political activist and one of five black raiders who followed John Brown in his attack on the arsenal at Harpers Ferry in 1859. He was born free in West Fallowfield, Pennsylvania. His father, Vincent Anderson, moved the family to West Goshen (near West Chester) around 1850. There Anderson met the Shadds, a family of black abolitionists. In the early 1850s he followed them to Chatham, Canada West, one of several Canadian communities in which free blacks and fugitive slaves from the United States could find a haven. Blacks could be full citizens in Canada, and it is estimated that forty to fifty thousand African Americans had moved there by 1850. Anderson lived with the Shadd family and became a printer's apprentice at the *Provincial Freeman*, a newspaper founded by Mary Ann Shadd, the first black woman editor on the continent. Thus, Anderson was in Chatham when Brown planned and held his convention there.

Unlike many other recruits, Anderson paid his own way to the rally point of Chambersburg, Pennsylvania, arriving on September 16, 1859. There, he stayed with a local black barber named Henry Watson, and on September 24 he walked (by night) from Chambersburg to meet Brown near the Kennedy Farm in Maryland, a place that Brown had rented to be used as a staging area for the raid. The raid on the federal arsenal at Harpers Ferry, Virginia, began on October 16, 1859, and ended two days later. Anderson, being the only one of Brown's men to witness the raid and live to tell the story, proceeded to write *A Voice from Harper's Ferry*, which was edited by Shadd, his mentor, and published in 1861. Along with an estimated fifty thousand other Canadians, Anderson went south to the United States when the Civil War began. While some historians believe that he served in the army, there is no record of such service; he did, however, work as a recruiter for the Union army's U.S. Colored Troops.

Following the war, Anderson resided in the United States, where he had trouble supporting himself. He revisited Harpers Ferry a year before his death, pointing out strategic scenes to Richard Hinton, who would author *John Brown and His Men: With Some Account of the Roads They Traveled to Reach Harper's Ferry* (1894). In 1872, Anderson died penniless in Washington, D.C., and was buried in a pauper's grave. Because of his abolitionist activities, Anderson is claimed by Canada as a national hero.

Time Line

1859

- **October 16**
  The raid at Harpers Ferry begins, ending in Brown's defeat and capture two days later.

- **December 2**
  Convicted of murder, treason, and inciting a slave insurrection, Brown is hanged.

1861

- **January**
  Anderson publishes *A Voice from Harper's Ferry*.

- **April 12**
  Fort Sumter, in Charleston, South Carolina, is fired upon by Confederate forces, marking the beginning of the Civil War.

1863

- **January 1**
  Abraham Lincoln's Emancipation Proclamation abolishes slavery in the southern slave states.

1865

- **December 18**
  The Thirteenth Amendment to the U.S. Constitution abolishes slavery in the United States.

1872

- **December 13**
  Anderson dies in Washington, D.C.

Explanation and Analysis of the Document

In *A Voice from Harper's Ferry* (in which the author, as have others, added an apostrophe to the town's name), Anderson narrates his participation in Brown's raid on Harpers Ferry of October 1859, including events leading up to the raid and his escape afterward. Anderson journeyed to Chambersburg, Pennsylvania, in September 1859 and from there to the Kennedy Farm in Maryland, the final staging area for the raid. He gives details of life at the Kennedy Farm and the final council meeting on October 16, when Brown gave eleven specific orders to the raiders regarding their duties during the raid. He next describes the raid itself, including the capture of prisoners, the engine house, the armory, the two bridges, and the rifle factory. The arming of slaves occurred on October 17, as did the attack on Brown's men by federal troops. After describing Brown's capture, Anderson relates his escape with Albert Hazlett, Hazlett's capture, and the fate of the other five raiders who escaped. Like Hazlett, John Cook escaped but was captured and returned to Virginia for trial. Thus, only five of Brown's men survived the raid. Anderson's final chapter details the

Gerrit Smith, one of the Secret Six (Library of Congress)

responses of slaves during the raid and their participation in and support of the raid. The book ends with a series of poems praising Brown.

◆ Preface

Because he was an eyewitness of the events of October 16 and 17, 1859, during the raid on Harpers Ferry, Anderson feels compelled to give an account of those events. He establishes his credibility by arguing that no one can question the fact that he was one of Brown's raiders; after all, he points out that he is a wanted man. He also notes that only two raiders escaped from Harpers Ferry—he himself and Hazlett. But since Hazlett was later captured in Pennsylvania, returned to Virginia, and hanged, Anderson is the only one left alive who can give a true account of what happened from the point of view of the raiders. In fact, five other raiders escaped, but they were not in Harpers Ferry itself. Owen Brown, F. J. Merriam, and Barclay Coppic had remained at the Kennedy Farm in Maryland to guard the arms stored there; Cook and Charles P. Tidd had been in Harpers Ferry early on October 16 but were ordered by Brown to go to the Kennedy Farm to aid in moving arms closer to Harpers Ferry.

◆ Chapter X

In Chapter X, Anderson begins with the entry of the raiders into the town of Harpers Ferry and shows how easily Brown and eighteen of his men captured the two bridges into and out of town, the engine house, the arsenal, and the rifle factory. (Three of the twenty-one raiders meanwhile remained at the Kennedy Farm to guard the weapons.) Three watchmen were taken prisoner along with several townspeople who were walking about. Anderson announces proudly, "These places were all taken, and the prisoners secured, without the snap of a gun, or any violence whatever."

Anderson is intent on showing the fear and cowardice of some of the southerners who were taken prisoner. For example, the watchman at the bridge "asked them to spare his life." The watchman guarding the engine-house yard at Harpers Ferry refused to open the gate but "commenced to cry," and when the raiders took Colonel Lewis Washington prisoner, he begged for his life and "cried heartily when he found he must submit." Colonel Washington was also "taken aback" when told to present to Anderson "the famous sword formerly presented by Frederic [the Great] to his illustrious kinsman, George Washington"; Frederick the Great, the king of Prussia, was an admirer of Washington and reportedly had sent the sword to him in 1780. When John Allstadt, another plantation owner, was taken prisoner, "he went into as great a fever of excitement as Washington had done." Evidently, awareness of previous slave insurrections convinced these men that they were doomed. Nat Turner's 1831 rebellion, for example, was still fresh in the memory of Virginia's slave owners, since it had occurred in Southampton County, Virginia, and had resulted in the deaths of some fifty-five white people. Perhaps because he understood this fear and wished to show the difference between Brown's insurrection and previous ones, Anderson makes a point of telling his readers that each prisoner was assured by his captors that he would not be harmed.

In this chapter, Anderson also discusses encounters with local blacks who were asked to "circulate the news," with the result that "many colored men gathered to the scene of action." He also reports the first death: Ironically, a free black who worked as a baggage handler, Heyward Shepherd (referred to as "Haywood"), was shot by the raiders at the bridge—before he could be identified as black—because he refused an order to halt.

◆ Chapter XI

Anderson records the spread of terror and fear among the residents of Harpers Ferry and among the prisoners. More prisoners were taken, and Brown ordered Tidd, Cook, and William Leeman, along with fourteen armed slaves, to begin moving the secured arms from the Kennedy Farm to a schoolhouse near the ferry. Brown also ordered Anderson to begin passing out pikes, from Brown's wagon, to the slaves from the Washington and Allstadt plantations as well as to other blacks who had arrived on the scene.

As in Chapter X, Anderson dwells on the cowardice of white southerners: "The cowardly Virginians submitted like sheep, without resistance, … until the marines came

U.S. Marines storming the engine house at Harpers Ferry (Library of Congress)

down." He also introduces a new topic—Brown's desire to make arrangements about the prisoners, which causes some delay, though, as Anderson points out, it was "no part of the original plan." According to Anderson, "This tardiness ... was eventually the cause of our defeat."

♦ Chapter XII

Anderson, who was stationed in the arsenal—his being in that location saved his life—reports on the initial triumph of Brown's men over the armed troops who arrived to put down the insurrection. Brown ordered his men out into the street, and they fired upon the troops, scattering them. Anderson declares that "they seemed not to realize, at first, that we would fire upon them," and he notes their hasty retreat to the bridge, where they awaited reinforcements. He mentions the death of Dangerfield Newby, shot by a man hiding in a store. The "cowardly murderer" was quickly brought down by Shields Green.

During a lull in the fighting, Brown's prisoners requested breakfast, and he obliged by ordering food from the Wager House, a nearby hotel. Anderson attempts to set the record straight regarding the legend that Brown ordered food for his men in the heat of the conflict; rather, Anderson asserts that the Wager House offered food to Brown and his men, but he suspected the food might have been poisoned and refused it. Similarly, Anderson spends a good deal of time in this chapter further attempting to set the record straight about the myth of

southern chivalry and the alleged bravery of white plantation owners. He points to the fact that the white lower classes and marines fought the raiders, while slave owners held back. He also points to the shootings of Watson Brown and A. D. Stevens, who were wounded while carrying flags of truce.

♦ Chapter XIII

In this chapter, Anderson again discusses the lack of honor that he witnessed among the raiders' opponents, especially in regard to the flags of truce and "the brutal treatment of Captain Brown and his men in the charge by the marines on the engine house." Although Brown was not captured until early Tuesday morning, October 18, when a contingent of marines commanded by Robert E. Lee stormed the engine house, while apparently Anderson and Hazlett escaped late on Monday, October 17, Anderson writes that he "saw the charge upon the engine house with the ladder" leading to "Brown's capture," which he describes in some detail. Anderson pays lofty tribute to Green, one of the black raiders who was captured by the marines: "Wiser and better men no doubt there were, but a braver man never lived than Shields Green."

♦ Chapter XIV

It is clear that Anderson feels that he either has been or may be accused of cowardice for having left Harpers Ferry; thus, he attempts to explain why he and Hazlett did not remain. Since

"Monday, the 17th of October… Gray dawn and yet brighter daylight revealed great confusion, and as the sun arose, the panic spread like wildfire. Men, women, and children could be seen leaving their homes in every direction; some seeking refuge among residents, and in quarters further away, others climbing up the hillsides, and hurrying off in various directions, evidently impelled by a sudden fear, which was plainly visible in their countenances or in their movements."

(Chapter XI)

"Hardly the skin of a slaveholder could be scratched in open fight; the cowards kept out of the way until danger was passed, sending the poor whites into the pitfalls, while they were reserved for the bragging, and to do the safe but cowardly judicial murdering afterwards."

(Chapter XII)

"On the Sunday evening of the outbreak, we visited the plantations and acquainted the slaves with our purpose to effect their liberation, the greatest enthusiasm was manifested by them—joy and hilarity beamed from every countenance. One old mother, white-haired from age and borne down with the labors of many years in bond, when told of the work in hand, replied: 'God bless you! God bless you!'"

(Chapter XIX)

"John Brown did not only capture and hold Harper's Ferry for twenty hours, but he held the whole South. He captured President Buchanan and his Cabinet, convulsed the whole country, killed Governor Wise, and dug the mine and laid the train which will eventually dissolve the union between Freedom and Slavery."

(Chapter XIX)

out of the six men originally stationed at the arsenal, he and Hazlett were the only ones left and felt that they could do nothing, they decided to escape while they still could, in order to fight another day. As they escaped, they captured a prisoner who told them that seventy "citizens" had been killed. Again, Anderson is trying to counter subsequent southern claims—in this instance, that Brown's raiders had killed only twenty southerners.

After their prisoner begged for his life and assured them that he would not inform on them, Hazlett and Anderson let him go—but having second thoughts, they soon concealed themselves. Sure enough, troops pursued them, but the two raiders fought them off, killing a few, and the troops returned to Harpers Ferry. Once more, Anderson records the lack of honor among southerners and the cowardice of the enemy.

♦ **Chapter XV**

Anderson admired the wisdom and courage of John Kagi, Brown's second in command, and although he does not openly criticize Brown here, Anderson notes that Kagi foresaw the danger that they were in and urged Brown early on to leave Harpers Ferry, to no avail. As the man was a participant in the assault on Kagi's position, Anderson learns from the prisoner taken by himself and Hazlett the details of Kagi's death. Anderson describes the courage of Kagi, John Copeland, Sherrard Lewis Leary, "and three colored men from the neighborhood," who defended the rifle factory against "as many as five hundred" men in all.

♦ **Chapter XIX**

In conventional rhetorical fashion, Anderson saves the most controversial subject for last: the actions of local slaves during the Harpers Ferry raid. In order to counter the claims of southerners "that the slaves were cowardly," he gives numerous examples to prove that they were not. They indeed supported the raid, and Brown told him that he was "agreeably disappointed in the behavior of the slaves; for he did not expect one out of ten to be willing to fight." Anderson projects, based on the examples he gives, "that hundreds of slaves were ready, and would have joined in the work, had Captain Brown's sympathies not been aroused in favor of the families of his prisoners." Again, there is a note of criticism in his appraisal of Brown's actions as commander.

Audience

Anderson's target audience consisted of both whites and blacks. He particularly wanted to show white southerners, as well as northerners, that the southerners whom Brown's party encountered at Harpers Ferry were cowards. But Anderson's most immediate audience was black. On January 1, 1861, for example, a meeting of black citizens was held at the Twelfth Street Baptist Church in Boston to promote Anderson's book. Excerpts from the book were read aloud, and a collection was taken up for Anderson, who was still a wanted man and in dire financial straits. The book, which sold for fifteen cents, was available for purchase at the Anti-Slavery Office in Boston. The book later became and remains an excellent source for biographers of Brown and historians writing about the raid on Harpers Ferry.

Questions for Further Study

1. Based on what you know about John Brown and his raid on Harpers Ferry, do you believe that he was a hero, a crazed fanatic, or perhaps a bit of both? Would your opinion change or remain the same if you knew that Virginia governor Henry Wise, a staunch southerner, personally interviewed Brown and found him to be sane and eloquent?

2. What impact did Brown's raid and the attendant publicity surrounding the event have on the course of the nation toward civil war?

3. Compare Brown's raid with the rebellion led by Nat Turner early in the century, as recounted in *The Confessions of Nat Turner* (1831). Do you see any similarities between the events and their impact? How were they different?

4. Try to imagine yourself living in 1850s Virginia. Do you think you would have advocated violence to end the slave system? Why or why not?

5. In the modern era, some groups resort to violent acts because they believe such acts serve a higher purpose. An example would be "eco-terrorists" who destroy logging equipment or laboratories where animal experimentation takes place. Do you think that the motives behind and effectiveness of these contemporary actions are similar to or different from those of John Brown?

Impact

Brown's raid has often been referred to as the "catalyst of the Civil War" because it widened the breach between the North and South. In the North, the philosopher and essayist Ralph Waldo Emerson and the naturalist and writer Henry David Thoreau spoke out in Brown's defense, justifying his violent acts, labeling him a hero, and comparing him to Christ because he had sacrificed his life for the slaves. Even northerners, who disapproved of Brown's violent means, believed that his end—the destruction of slavery—was ultimately good. Indeed, on the day of Brown's execution, northern church bells tolled for the martyred hero. While Brown's belief that violence was required to destroy slavery had not yet gained universal approval among northerners, his actions and his much-quoted antislavery testimony during the trial had given them food for thought; thus, his ideas began gaining support.

In the South, of course, Brown's actions were universally condemned, but, more important, southerners lived in fear of similar future attacks. Before Brown's raid, slave owners had focused on the threats posed by northern abolitionists who had established the Underground Railroad to aid runaway slaves and on their attempts to keep new states from being admitted to the Union as slave states. After Brown's raid, slave owners feared abolitionists who would arm their slaves and lead them in slave insurrections. Such fears led many southerners to support South Carolina's Governor William Henry Gist when, in November 1859, he called for what he believed was the only possible solution to the threat posed by Brown's raid: secession from the Union and the establishment of a confederacy of southern states.

Anderson's book seems to have had minimal impact on any general audience in its own day, and indeed it almost disappeared. But it has become a popular source among historians of today who focus on black studies and the abolitionist movement, particularly those seeking to establish proof of participation by local blacks in the raid on Harpers Ferry.

See also *The Confessions of Nat Turner* (1831); Fugitive Slave Act of 1850; Emancipation Proclamation (1863); Thirteenth Amendment to the U.S. Constitution (1865).

Further Reading

■ Books

Du Bois, W. E. B. *John Brown*. New York: International Publishers, 1962.

Finkelman, Paul, ed. *His Soul Goes Marching On: Responses to John Brown and the Harpers Ferry Raid*. Charlottesville: University Press of Virginia, 1995.

Hinton, Richard J. *John Brown and His Men: With Some Account of the Roads They Traveled to Reach Harper's Ferry*. 1894. Reprint. New York: Arno Press, 1968.

Libby, Jean. *Black Voices from Harpers Ferry: Osborne Anderson and the John Brown Raid*. Palo Alto, Calif.: Libby, 1979.

McCarthy, Timothy P., and John Stauffer, eds. *Prophets of Protest: Reconsidering the History of American Abolitionism*. New York: New Press, 2006.

Oates, Stephen B. *To Purge This Land with Blood: A Biography of John Brown*. 2nd ed. Amherst: University of Massachusetts Press, 1985.

Quarles, Benjamin. *Allies for Freedom: Blacks and John Brown*. New York: Oxford University Press, 1974.

Russo, Peggy A., and Paul Finkelman, eds. *Terrible Swift Sword: The Legacy of John Brown*. Athens: Ohio University Press, 2005.

Sanborn, Franklin B. *The Life and Letters of John Brown: Liberator of Kansas and Martyr of Virginia*. 1885. Reprint. New York: Negro Universities Press, 1969.

Stowe, Harriet Beecher. *Uncle Tom's Cabin*. New York: Signet Classics, 2008.

Villard, Oswald Garrison. *John Brown, 1800–1859: A Biography Fifty Years After*. New York: Alfred A. Knopf, 1943.

■ Web Sites

"John Brown's Provisional Constitution." University of Missouri–Kansas City School of Law "Famous Trials" Web site. http://www.law.umkc.edu/faculty/projects/Ftrials/johnbrown/brownconstitution.html.

—Peggy A. Russo

OSBORNE P. ANDERSON: *A VOICE FROM HARPER'S FERRY*

Preface

My sole purpose in publishing the following Narrative is to save from oblivion the facts connected with one of the most important movements of this age, with reference to the overthrow of American slavery. My own personal experience in it, under the orders of Capt. Brown, on the 16th and 17th of October, 1859, as the only man alive who was at Harper's Ferry during the entire time the unsuccessful groping after these facts, by individuals, impossible to be obtained, except from an actor in the scene and the conviction that the cause of impartial liberty requires this duty at my hands alone have been the motives for writing and circulating the little book herewith presented.

I will not under such circumstances, insult nor burden the intelligent with excuses for defects in composition, nor for the attempt to give the facts. A plain unadorned, truthful story is wanted, and that by one who knows what he says, who is known to have been at the great encounter, and to have labored in shaping the same. My identity as a member of Capt. Brown's company cannot be questioned, successfully, by any who are bent upon suppressing the truth; neither will it be by any in Canada or the United States familiar with John Brown and his plans, as those know his men personally, or by reputation, who enjoyed his confidence sufficiently to know thoroughly his plans.

The readers of this narrative will therefore keep steadily in view this main point that they are perusing a story of events which have happened under the eye of the great Captain, or are incidental thereto, and not a compendium of the "plans" of Capt. Brown; for as his plans were not consummated, and as their fulfilment is committed to the future, no one to whom they are known will recklessly expose all of them to the public gaze. Much has been given as true that never happened; much has been omitted that should have been made known; many things have been left unsaid, because, up to within a short time, but two could say them; one of them has been offered up, a sacrifice to the Moloch, Slavery; being that other one, I propose to perform the duty, trusting to that portion of the public who love the right for an appreciation of my endeavor. O.P.A....

Chapter X. The Capture of Harper's Ferry—Col. A. D. Stevens and Party Sally Out To the Plantations—What We Saw, Heard, Did, Etc.

As John H. Kagi and A. D. Stevens entered the bridge, as ordered in the fifth charge, the watchman, being at the other end, came toward them with a lantern in his hand. When up to them, they told him he was their prisoner, and detained him a few minutes, when he asked them to spare his life. They replied, they did not intend to harm him; the object was to free the slaves, and he would have to submit to them for a time, in order that the purpose might be carried out.

Captain Brown now entered the bridge in his wagon, followed by the rest of us, until we reached that part where Kagi and Stevens held their prisoner, when he ordered Watson Brown and Stewart Taylor to take the positions assigned them in order sixth, and the rest of us to proceed to the engine house. We started for the engine house, taking the prisoner along with us. When we neared the gates of the engine-house yard, we found them locked, and the watchman on the inside. He was told to open the gates, but refused, and commenced to cry. The men were then ordered by Captain Brown to open the gates forcibly, which was done, and the watchman taken prisoner. The two prisoners were left in the custody of Jerry Anderson and Adolphus Thompson, and A. D. Stevens arranged the men to take possession of the Armory and rifle factory. About this time, there was apparently much excitement. People were passing back and forth in the town, and before we could do much, we had to take several prisoners. After the prisoners were secured, we passed to the opposite side of the street and took the Armory, and Albert Hazlett and Edwin Coppic were ordered to hold it for the time being.

The capture of the rifle factory was the next work to be done. When we went there, we told the watchman who was outside of the building our business, and asked him to go along with us, as we had come to take possession of the town, and make use of the Armory in carrying out our object. He obeyed the command without hesitation. John H. Kagi and John Copeland were placed in the Armory, and the prisoners taken to the engine house. Following the capture of the Armory, Oliver Brown and William Thompson were ordered to take possession of the bridge leading out of town, across the Shenandoah river, which they immediately did. These places were all taken, and the prisoners secured, without the snap of a gun, or any violence whatever.

The town being taken, Brown, Stevens, and the men who had no post in charge, returned to the engine house, where council was held, after which Captain Stevens, Tidd, Cook, Shields Green, Leary and myself went to the country. On the road, we met some colored men, to whom we made known our purpose, when they immediately agreed to join us. They said they had been long waiting for an opportunity of the kind. Stevens then asked them to go around among the colored people and circulate the news, when each started off in a different direction. The result was that many colored men gathered to the scene of action. The first prisoner taken by us was Colonel Lewis Washington. When we neared his house, Capt. Stevens placed Leary and Shields Green to guard the approaches to the house, the one at the side, the other in front. We then knocked, but no one answering, although females were looking from upper windows, we entered the building and commenced a search for the proprietor. Col. Washington opened his room door, and begged us not to kill him. Capt. Stevens replied, "You are our prisoner," when he stood as if speechless or petrified. Stevens further told him to get ready to go to the Ferry; that he had come to abolish slavery, not to take life but in self-defence, but that he must go along. The Colonel replied: "You can have my slaves, if you will let me remain." "No," said the Captain, "you must go along too; so get ready." After saying this, Stevens left the house for a time, and with Green, Leary and Tidd proceeded to the "Quarters," giving the prisoner in charge of Cook and myself. The male slaves were gathered together in a short time, when horses were tackled to the Colonel's two-horse carriage and four-horse wagon, and both vehicles brought to the front of the house.

During this time, Washington was walking the floor, apparently much excited. When the Captain came in, he went to the sideboard, took out his whiskey, and offered us something to drink, but he was refused. His fire-arms were next demanded, when he brought forth one double-barreled gun, one small rifle, two horse-pistols and a sword. Nothing else was asked of him. The Colonel cried heartily when he found he must submit, and appeared taken aback when, on delivering up the famous sword formerly presented by Frederic to his illustrious kinsman, George Washington, Capt. Stevens told me to step forward and take it. Washington was secured and placed in his wagon, the women of the family making great outcries, when the party drove forward to Mr. John Allstadt's. After making known our business to him, he went into as great a fever of excitement as Washington had done. We could have his slaves, also, if we would only leave him. This, of course, was contrary to our plans and instructions. He hesitated, puttered around, fumbled and meditated for a long time. At last, seeing no alternative, he got ready, when the slaves were gathered up from about the quarters by their own consent, and all placed in Washington's big wagon and returned to the Ferry.

One old colored lady, at whose house we stopped, a little way from the town, had a good time over the message we took her. This liberating the slaves was the very thing she had longed for, prayed for, and dreamed about, time and again; and her heart was full of rejoicing over the fulfilment of a prophecy which had been her faith for long years. While we were absent from the Ferry, the train of cars for Baltimore arrived, and was detained. A colored man named Haywood, employed upon it, went from the Wager House up to the entrance to the bridge, where the train stood, to assist with the baggage. He was ordered to stop by the sentinels stationed at the bridge, which he refused to do, but turned to go in an opposite direction, when he was fired upon, and received a mortal wound. Had he stood when ordered, he would not have been harmed. No one knew at the time whether he was white or colored, but his movements were such as to justify the sentinels in shooting him, as he would not stop when commanded. The first firing happened at that time, and the only firing, until after daylight on Monday morning.

Chapter XI. The Events of Monday, Oct. 17— Arming The Slaves—Terror. In the Slaveholding Camp—Important Losses to Our Party—The Fate of Kagi—Prisoners Accumulate—Workmen at the Kennedy Farm, Etc.

Monday, the 17th of October, was a time of stirring and exciting events. In consequence of the movements of the night before, we were prepared for commotion and tumult, but certainly not for more than we beheld around us. Gray dawn and yet brighter daylight revealed great confusion, and as the sun arose, the panic spread like wildfire. Men, women and children could be seen leaving their homes in every direction; some seeking refuge among residents, and in quarters further away, others climbing up the hillsides, and hurrying off in various directions, evidently impelled by a sudden fear which was plainly visible in their countenances or in their movements.

Capt. Brown was all activity, though I could not help thinking that at times he appeared somewhat puzzled. He ordered Sherrard Lewis Leary, and four slaves, and a free man belonging in the neighborhood, to join John Henry Kagi and John Copeland at the rifle factory, which they immediately did. Kagi, and all except Copeland, were subsequently killed, but not before having communicated with Capt. Brown, as will be set forth further along.

As fast as the workmen came to the building or persons appeared in the street near the engine house, they were taken prisoners, and directly after sunrise, the detained train was permitted to start for the eastward. After the departure of the train, quietness prevailed for a short time; a number of prisoners were already in the engine house, and of the many colored men living in the neighborhood, who had assembled in the town, a number were armed for the work.

Capt. Brown ordered Capts. Charles P. Tidd, Wm. H. Leeman, John E. Cook, and some fourteen slaves, to take Washington's four-horse wagon, and to join the company under Capt. Owen Brown, consisting of F. J. Merriam and Barclay Coppic, who had been left at the Farm the night previous, to guard the place and the arms. The company, thus reinforced, proceeded, under Owen Brown, to move the arms and goods from the Farm down to the school-house in the mountains, three-fourths of a mile from the Ferry.

Capt. Brown next ordered me to take the pikes out of the wagon in which he rode to the Ferry, and to place them in the hands of the colored men who had come with us from the plantations, and others who had come forward without having had communication with any of our party. It was out of the circumstances connected with the fulfilment of this order, that the false charge against "Anderson" as leader, or "ringleader," of the negroes, grew.

The spectators, about this time, became apparently wild with fright and excitement. The number of prisoners was magnified to hundreds, and the judgment-day could not have presented more terrors, in its awful and certain prospective punishment to the justly condemned for the wicked deeds of a life-time, the chief of which would no doubt be slaveholding, than did Capt. Brown's operations.

The prisoners were also terror-stricken. Some wanted to go home to see their families, as if for the last time. The privilege was granted them, under escort, and they were brought back again. Edwin Coppic, one of the sentinels at the Armory gate, was fired at by one of the citizens, but the ball did not reach him, when one of the insurgents close by put up his rifle, and made the enemy bite the dust.

Among the arms taken from Col. Washington was one double-barrel gun. This weapon was loaded by Leeman with buckshot, and placed in the hands of an elderly slave man, early in the morning. After the cowardly charge upon Coppic, this old man was ordered by Capt. Stevens to arrest a citizen. The old man ordered him to halt, which he refused to do, when instantly the terrible load was discharged into him, and he fell, and expired without a struggle.

After these incidents, time passed away till the arrival of the United States troops, without any further attack upon us. The cowardly Virginians submitted like sheep, without resistance, from that time until the marines came down. Meanwhile, Capt. Brown, who was considering a proposition for release from his prisoners, passed back and forth from the Armory to the bridge, speaking words of comfort and encouragement to his men. "Hold on a little longer, boys," said he, "until I get matters arranged with the prisoners." This tardiness on the part of our brave leader was sensibly felt to be an omen of evil by some us, and was eventually the cause of our defeat. It was no part of the original plan to hold on to the Ferry, or to parley with prisoners; but by so doing, time was afforded to carry the news of its capture to several points, and forces were thrown into the place, which surrounded us.

At eleven o'clock, Capt. Brown dispatched William Thompson from the Ferry up to Kennedy Farm with the news that we had peaceful possession of the town, and with directions to the men to continue on moving the things. He went; but before he could get back, troops had begun to pour in and the general encounter commenced.

Chapter XII. Reception to the Troops—They Retreat to the Bridge—A Prisoner—Death of Dangerfield Newby—William Thompson—The Mountains Alive—Flag of Truce—The Engine House Taken.

It was about twelve o'clock in the day when we were first attacked by the troops. Prior to that, Capt. Brown, in anticipation of further trouble, had girded to his side the famous sword taken from Col. Lewis Washington the night before, and with that memorable weapon, he commanded his men against General Washington's own State.

When the Captain received the news that the troops had entered the bridge from the Maryland side, he, with some of his men, went into the street, and sent a message to the Arsenal for us to come forth also. We hastened to the street as ordered, when he said "The troops are on the bridge, coming into town; we will give them a warm reception." He then walked around amongst us, giving us words of encouragement, in this wise:—"Men! be cool! Don't waste your powder and shot! Take aim, and make every shot count!" "The troops will look for us to retreat on their first appearance; be careful to shoot first." Our men were well supplied with firearms, but Capt. Brown had no rifle at that time; his only weapon was the sword before mentioned.

The troops soon came out of the bridge, and up the street facing us, we occupying an irregular position. When they got within sixty or seventy yards, Capt. Brown said, "Let go upon them!" which we did, when several of them fell. Again and again the dose was repeated.

There was now consternation among the troops. From marching in solid martial columns, they became scattered. Some hastened to seize upon and bear up the wounded and dying,—several lay dead upon the ground. They seemed not to realize, at first, that we would fire upon them, but evidently expected we would be driven out by them without firing. Capt. Brown seemed fully to understand the matter, and hence, very properly and in our defence, undertook to forestall their movements. The consequence of their unexpected reception was, after leaving several of their dead on the field, they beat a confused retreat into the bridge, and there stayed under cover until reinforcements came to the Ferry.

On the retreat of the troops, we were ordered back to our former post. While going, Dangerfield Newby, one of our colored men, was shot through the head by a person who took aim at him from a brick store window, on the opposite side of the street, and who was there for the purpose of firing upon us. Newby was a brave fellow. He was one of my comrades at the Arsenal. He fell at my side, and his death was promptly avenged by Shields Green, the Zouave of the band, who afterwards met his fate calmly on the gallows, with John Copeland. Newby was shot twice; at the first fire, he fell on his side and returned it; as he lay, a second shot was fired, and the ball entered his head. Green raised his rifle in an instant, and brought down the cowardly murderer, before the latter could get his gun back through the sash.

There was comparative quiet for a time, except that the citizens seemed to be wild with terror. Men, women and children forsook the place in great haste, climbing up hillsides and scaling the mountains. The latter seemed to be alive with white fugitives, fleeing from their doomed city. During this time, Wm. Thompson, who was returning from his errand to the Kennedy Farm, was surrounded on the bridge by the railroad men, who next came up, taken a prisoner to the Wager House, tied hand and foot, and, at a late hour of the afternoon, cruelly murdered by being riddled with balls and thrown headlong on the rocks.

Late in the morning, some of his prisoners told Capt. Brown that they would like to have breakfast, when he sent word forthwith to the Wager House to that effect, and they were supplied. He did not order breakfast for himself and men, as was currently but falsely stated at the time, as he suspected foul play; on the contrary, when solicited to have breakfast so provided for him, he refused. Between two and three o'clock in the afternoon. armed men could be seen coming from every direction; soldiers were marching and counter-marching; and on the mountains. a host of blood-thirsty ruffians swarmed, waiting for their opportunity to pounce upon the little band. The fighting commenced in earnest after the arrival of fresh troops. Volley upon volley was discharged, and the echoes from the hills, the shrieks of the townspeople, and the groans of their wounded and dying, all of which filled the air, were truly frightful. The Virginians may well conceal their losses, and Southern chivalry may hide its brazen head, for their boasted bravery was well tested that day, and in no way to their advantage. It is remarkable, that except that one fool-hardy colored man was reported buried, no other funeral is mentioned, although the Mayor and other citizens are known to have fallen. Had they reported the true number, their disgrace would have been more apparent; so they wisely (?) concluded to be silent.

The fight at Harper's Ferry also disproved the current idea that slaveholders will lay down their lives for their property. Col. Washington, the representative of the old hero, stood "blubbering like a great calf at supposed danger"; while the laboring white classes and non-slaveholders, with the marines (mostly gentlemen from "furrin" parts), were the men who faced the bullets of John Brown and his men. Hardly the skin of a slaveholder could be scratched in open fight; the cowards kept out of the way until danger was passed, sending the poor whites into the pitfalls, while they were reserved for the bragging, and to do the safe but cowardly judicial murdering afterwards.

As strangers poured in, the enemy took positions round about, so as to prevent any escape, within shooting distance of the engine house and Arsenal. Capt. Brown, seeing their manouevres, said: "We will hold on to our three positions, if they are unwilling to come to terms, and die like men."

All this time, the fight was progressing; no powder and ball were wasted. We shot from under cover, and took deadly aim. For an hour before the flag of truce was sent out, the firing was uninterrupted, and one and another of the enemy were constantly dropping to the earth.

One of the Captain's plans was to keep up communication between his three points. In carrying out this idea, Jerry Anderson went to the rifle factory, to see Kagi and his men. Kagi, fearing that we would be overpowered by numbers if the Captain delayed leaving, sent word by Anderson to advise him to leave the town at once. This word Anderson communicated to the Captain, and told us also at the Arsenal. The message sent back to Kagi was, to hold out for a few minutes longer, when we would all evacuate the place. Those few minutes proved disastrous, for then it was that the troops before spoken of came pouring in, increased by crowds of men from the surrounding country. After an hour's hard fighting, and when the enemy were blocking up the avenues of escape, Capt. Brown sent out his son Watson with a flag of truce, but no respect was paid to it; he was fired upon, and wounded severely. He returned to the engine house, and fought bravely after that for fully an hour and a half, when he received a mortal wound, which he struggled under until the next day. The contemptible and savage manner in which the flag of truce had been received, induced severe measures in our defence, in the hour and a half before the next one was sent out. The effect of our work was, that the troops ceased to fire at the buildings, as we clearly had the advantage of position.

Capt. A. D. Stevens was next sent out with a flag, with what success I will presently show. Meantime, Jeremiah Anderson, who had brought the message from Kagi previously, was sent by Capt. Brown with another message to John Henrie, but before he got far on the street he was fired upon and wounded. He returned at once to the engine house, where he survived but a short time. The ball, it was found, had entered the right side in such manner that death necessarily ensued speedily.

Capt. Stevens was fired upon several times while carrying his flag of truce, and received severe wounds, as I was informed that day, not being myself in a position to see him after. He was captured, and taken to the Wager House, where he was kept until the close of the struggle in the evening, when he was placed with the rest of our party who had been captured.

After the capture of Stevens, desperate fighting was done by both sides. The marines forced their way inside the engine-house yard, and commanded Capt. Brown to surrender, which he refused to do, but said in reply, that he was willing to fight them, if they would allow him first to withdraw his men to the second lock on the Maryland side. As might be expected, the cowardly hordes refused to entertain such a proposition, but continued their assault, to cut off communication between our several parties. The men at the Kennedy Farm having received such a favorable message in the early part of the day, through Thompson, were ignorant of the disastrous state of affairs later in the day. Could they have known the truth, and come down in time, the result would have been very different; we should not have been captured that day. A handful of determined men, as they were, by taking a position on the Maryland side, when the troops made their attack and retreated to the bridge for shelter, would have placed the enemy between two fires. Thompson's news prevented them from hurrying down, as they otherwise would have done, and thus deprived us of able assistance from Owen Brown, a host in himself, and Tidd, Merriam and Coppic, the brave fellows composing that band.

The climax of murderous assaults on that memorable day was the final capture of the engine house, with the old Captain and his handful of associates. This outrageous burlesque upon civilized warfare must have a special chapter to itself, as it concentrates more of Southern littleness and cowardice than is often believed to be true.

Chapter XIII. The Capture of Captain John Brown at the Engine House.

One great difference between savages and civilized nations is the improved mode of warfare adopted by the latter. Flags of truce are always entitled to consideration, and an attacking party would make a wide departure from military usage, were they not to give opportunity for the besieged to capitulate, or to surrender at discretion. Looking at the Harper's Ferry combat in the light of civilized usage, even where one side might be regarded as insurrectionary, the brutal treatment of Captain Brown and his men in the charge by the marines on the engine house is deserving of severest condemnation, and is one of those blood-thirsty occurrences, dark enough in depravity to disgrace a century.

Captain Hazlett and myself being in the Arsenal opposite, saw the charge upon the engine house with the ladder, which resulted in opening the doors to the marines, and finally in Brown's capture. The old hero and his men were hacked and wounded with indecent rage, and at last brought out of the house and laid prostrate upon the ground, mangled and bleeding as they were. A formal surrender was required of Captain Brown, which he refused, knowing how little favor he would receive, if unarmed, at the hands of that infuriated mob. All of our party who went from the Farm, save the Captain, Shields Green, Edwin Coppic and Watson Brown (who had received a mortal wound some time before), the men at the Farm, and Hazlett and I, were either dead or captured before this time; the particulars of whose fate we learned still later in the day, as I shall presently show. Of the four prisoners taken at the engine house, Shields Green, the most inexorable of all our party, a very Turco in his hatred against the stealers of men, was under Captain Hazlett, and consequently of our little band at the Arsenal; but when we were ordered by Captain Brown to return to our positions, after having driven the troops into the bridge, he mistook the order, and went to the engine house instead of with his own party. Had he remained with us, he might have eluded the vigilant Virginians. As it was, he was doomed, as is well known, and became a free-will offering for freedom, with his comrade, John Copeland. Wiser and better men no doubt there were, but a braver man never lived than Shields Green.

Chapter XIV. Setting for the Reasons Why O.P. Anderson and A. Hazlett Escaped from the Arsenal, Instead of Remaining, When They Had Nothing to Do—Took a Prisoner, and What Resulted to Them, And to this Narrative, Therefrom—Pursuit, When Somebody Got Killed, And Other Bodies Wounded.

Of the men assigned a position in the arsenal by Captain Brown, four were either slain or captured; and Hazlett and myself, the only ones remaining, never left our position until we saw, with feelings of intense sadness, that we could be of no further avail to our commander, he being a prisoner in the hands of the Virginians. We therefore, upon consultation, concluded it was better to retreat while it was possible, as our work for the day was clearly finished, and gain a position where in the future we could work with better success, than to recklessly invite capture and brutality at the hands of our enemies. The charge of deserting our brave old leader and of fleeing from danger has been circulated to our detriment, but I have the consolation of knowing that, reckless as were the half-civilized hordes against whom we contended the entire day, and much as they might wish to disparage his men, they would never have thus charged us. They know better. John Brown's men at Harper's Ferry were and are a unit in their devotion to John Brown and the cause he espoused. To have deserted him would have been to belie every manly characteristic for which Albert Hazlett, at least, was known by the party to be distinguished, at the same time that it would have endangered the future safety of such deserter or deserters. John Brown gave orders; those orders must be obeyed, so long as Captain Brown was in a position to enforce them; once unable to command, from death, being a prisoner, or otherwise, the command devolved upon John Henry Kagi. Before Captain Brown was made prisoner, Captain Kagi had ceased to live, though had he been living, all communication between our post and him had been long cut off. We could not aid Captain Brown by remaining. We might, by joining the men at the Farm, devise plans for his succor; or our experience might become available on some future occasion.

The charge of running away from danger could only find form in the mind of some one unwilling to encounter the difficulties of a Harper's Ferry campaign, as no one acquainted with the out-of-door and in-door encounters of that day will charge anyone with wishing to escape danger, merely. It is well enough for men out of danger, and who could not be induced to run the risk of a scratching, to talk flippantly about cowardice, and to sit in judgment upon the men who went with John Brown and who did not fall into the hands of the Virginians; but to have been there, fought there, and to understand what did transpire there, are quite different. As Capt. Brown had all the prisoners with him, the whole force of the enemy was concentrated there, for a time, after the capture of the rifle factory. Having captured our commander, we knew that it was but little two of us could do against so many, and that our turn to be taken must come; so Hazlett and I went out at the back part of the building, climbed up the wall, and went upon the railway. Behind us, in the Arsenal were thousands of dollars, we knew full well but that wealth had no charms for us, and we hastened to communicate with the men sent to the Kennedy Farm. We traveled up the Shenandoah along the railroad, and overtook one of the citizens. He was armed, and had been in the fight in the afternoon. We took him prisoner, in order to facilitate our escape. He submitted without resistance, and quietly gave up his gun. From him we learned substantially of the final struggle at the rifle factory, where the noble Kagi commanded. The number of citizens killed was, according to his opinion, much larger than either Hazlett or I had supposed, although we knew there were a great many killed and wounded together. He said there must be at least seventy killed, besides wounded. Hazlett had said there must be fifty, taking into account the defence of the three strong positions. I do not know positively, but would not put the figure below thirty killed, seeing many fall as I did, and knowing the "dead aim" principle upon which we defended ourselves. One of the Southern published accounts, it will be remembered, said twenty citizens were killed, another said fifteen. At last it got narrowed down to five, which was simply absurd, after so long an engagement. We had forty rounds apiece when we went to the Ferry, and when Hazlett and I left, we had not more than twenty rounds between us. The rest of the party were as free with their ammunition as we were, if not more so. We had further evidence that the number of dead was larger than published, from the many that we saw lying dead around.

When we had gone as far as the foot of the mountains, our prisoner begged us not to take his life, but to let him go at liberty. He said we might keep his gun; he would not inform on us. Feeling compassion for him, and trusting to his honor, we suffered him to go, when he went directly into town, and finding every thing there in the hands of our enemies, he informed on us, and we were pursued. After he had left us, we crawled or climbed up among the rocks in the mountains, some hundred yards or more from the spot where we left him, and hid ourselves, as we feared treachery, on second thought. A few minutes before dark, the troops came in search of us. They came to the foot of the mountains, marched and counter-marched, but never attempted to search the mountains; we supposed from their movements that they feared a host of armed enemies in concealment. Their air was so defiant, and their errand so distasteful to us, that we concluded to apply a little ammunition to their case, and having a few cartridges on hand, we poured from our excellent position in the rocky wilds, some well-directed shots. It was not so dark but that we could see one bite the dust

now and then, when others would run to aid them instantly, particularly the wounded. Some lay where they fell, undisturbed, which satisfied us that they were dead. The troops returned our fire, but it was random shooting, as we were concealed from their sight by the rocks and bushes. Interchanging of shots continued for some minutes, with much spirit, when it became quite dark, and they went down into the town. After their return to the Ferry, we could hear the drum beating for a long time; an indication of their triumph, we supposed. Hazlett and I remained in our position three hours, before we dared venture down.

Chapter XV. The Encounter at the Rifle Factory.

As stated in a previous chapter, the command of the rifle factory was given to Captain Kagi. Under him were John Copeland, Sherrard Lewis Leary, and three colored men from the neighborhood. At an early hour, Kagi saw from his position the danger in remaining, with our small company, until assistance could come to the inhabitants. Hence his suggestion to Captain Brown, through Jeremiah Anderson, to leave. His position, being more isolated than the others, was the first to invite an organized attack with success; the Virginians first investing the factory with their hordes, before the final success at the engine house. From the prisoner taken by us who had participated in the assault upon Kagi's position, we received the sad details of the slaughter of our brave companions. Seven different times during the day they were fired upon, while they occupied the interior part of the building, the insurgents defending themselves with great courage, killing and wounding with fatal precision. At last, overwhelming numbers, as many as five hundred, our informant told us, blocked up the front of the building, battered the doors down, and forced their way into the interior. The insurgents were then forced to retreat the back way, fighting, however, all the time. They were pursued, when they took to the river, and it being so shallow, they waded out to a rock, mid-way, and there made a stand being completely hemmed in, front and rear. Some four or five hundred shots, said our prisoner, were fired at them before they were conquered. They would not surrender into the hands of the enemy, but kept on fighting until every one was killed, except John Copeland. Seeing he could do no more, and that all his associates were murdered, he suffered himself to be captured. The party at the rifle factory fought desperately till the last, from their perch on the rock. Slave and free, black and white, carried out the special injunction of the brave old Captain, to make sure work of it. The unfortunate targets for so many bullets from the enemy, some of them received two or three balls. There fell poor Kagi, the friend and adviser of Captain Brown in his most trying positions, and the cleverest man in the party; and there also fell Sherrard Lewis Leary, generous-hearted and companionable as he was, and in that and other difficult positions, brave to desperation. There fought John Copeland, who met his fate like a man. But they were all "honorable men," noble, noble fellows, who fought and died for the most holy principles. John Copeland was taken to the guard-house, where the other prisoners afterwards were, and thence to Charlestown jail. His subsequent mockery of a trial, sentence and execution, with his companion Shields Green, on the 16th of December—are they not part of the dark deeds of this era, which will assign their perpetrators to infamy, and cause after generations to blush at the remembrance? ...

Chapter XIX. The Behavior of the Slaves—Captain Brown's Opinion.

Of the various contradictory reports made by slaveholders and their satellites about the time of the Harper's Ferry conflict, none were more untruthful than those relating to the slaves. There was seemingly a studied attempt to enforce the belief that the slaves were cowardly, and that they were really more in favor of Virginia masters and slavery, than of their freedom. As a party who had an intimate knowledge of the conduct of the colored men engaged, I am prepared to make an emphatic denial of the gross imputation against them, They were charged especially with being unreliable, with deserting Captain Brown at the first opportunity, and going back to their masters; and with being so indifferent to the work of their salvation from the yoke, as to have to be forced into service by the Captain, contrary to their will.

On the Sunday evening of the outbreak, we visited the plantations and acquainted the slaves with our purpose to effect their liberation, the greatest enthusiasm was manifested by them—joy and hilarity beamed from every countenance, One old mother, white-haired from age and borne down with the labors of many years in bond, when told of the work in hand, replied: "God bless you! God bless you!" She then kissed the party at her house, and requested all to kneel, which we did, and she offered prayer to God

for His blessing on the enterprise, and our success. At the slaves' quarters, there was apparently a general jubilee, and they stepped forward manfully, without impressing or coaxing. In one case, only, was there any hesitation. A dark-complexioned free-born man refused to take up arms. He showed the only want of confidence in the movement, and far less courage than any slave consulted about the plan. In fact, so far as I could learn, the free blacks in the South are much less reliable than the slaves, and infinitely more fearful. In Washington City, a party of free colored persons offered their services to the Mayor, to aid in suppressing our movement. Of the slaves who followed us to the Ferry, some were sent to help remove stores, and the others were drawn up in a circle around the engine-house, at one time, where they were, by Captain Brown's order, furnished by me with pikes, mostly, and acted as a guard to the prisoners to prevent their escape, which they did.

As in the war of the American Revolution, the first blood shed was a black man's, Crispus Attuck's, so at Harper's Ferry, the first blood shed by our party, after the arrival of the United States troops, was that of a slave. In the beginning of the encounter, and before the troops had fairly emerged from the bridge, a slave was shot. I saw him fall. Phil, the slave who died in prison, with fear, as it was reported, was wounded at the Ferry, and died from the effects of it. Of the men shot on the rocks, when Kagi's party were compelled to take to the river, some were slaves, and they suffered death before they would desert their companions, and their bodies fell into the waves beneath. Captain Brown, who was surprised and pleased by the promptitude with which they volunteered, and with their manly bearing at the scene of violence, remarked to me, on that Monday morning, that he was agreeably disappointed in the behavior of the slaves; for he did not expect one out of ten to be willing to fight. The truth of the Harper's Ferry "raid," as it has been called, in regard to the part taken by the slaves, and the aid given by colored men generally, demonstrates clearly: First, that the conduct of the slaves is a strong guarantee of the weakness of the institution, should a favorable opportunity occur; and, secondly, that the colored people, as a body, were well represented by numbers, both in the fight, and in the number who suffered martyrdom afterward.

The first report of the number of "insurrectionists" killed was seventeen, which showed that several slaves were killed; for there were only ten of the men that belonged to the Kennedy Farm who lost their lives at the Ferry, namely: John Henri Kagi, Jerry Anderson, Watson Brown, Oliver Brown, Stewart Taylor, Adolphus Thompson, William Thompson, William J. Leeman, all eight whites, and Dangerfield Newby and Sherrard Lewis Leary, both colored. The rest reported dead, according to their own showing, were colored. Captain Brown had but seventeen with him, belonging to the Farm, and when all was over, there were four besides himself taken to Charlestown, prisoners, viz: A. D. Stevens, Edwin Coppic, white; John A. Copeland and Shields Green, colored. It is plain to be seen from this, that there was a proper percentage of colored men killed at the Ferry, and executed at Charlestown. Of those that escaped from the fangs of the human bloodhounds of slavery, there were four whites, and one colored man, myself being the sole colored man of those at the Farm.

That hundreds of slaves were ready, and would have joined in the work, had Captain Brown's sympathies not been aroused in favor of the families of his prisoners, and that a very different result would have been seen, in consequence, there is no question. There was abundant opportunity for him and the party to leave a place ill which they held entire sway and possession, before the arrival of the troops. And so cowardly were the slaveholders, proper, that from Colonel Lewis Washington, the descendant of the Father of his Country,

General George Washington, they were easily taken prisoners. They had not pluck enough to fight, or to use the well-loaded arms in their possession, but were concerned rather in keeping a whole skin by parleying, or in spilling cowardly tears, to excite pity, as did Colonel Washington, and in that way escape merited punishment. No, the conduct of the slaves was beyond all praise; and could our brave old Captain have steeled his heart against the entreaties of his captives, or shut up the fountain of his sympathies against their families—could he, for the moment, have forgotten them, in the selfish thought of his own friends and kindred, or, by adhering to the original plan, have left the place, and thus looked forward to the prospective freedom of the slave—hundreds ready and waiting would have been armed before twenty-four hours had elapsed. As it was, even the noble old man's mistakes were productive of great good, the fact of which the future historian will record, without the embarrassment attending its present narration. John Brown did not only capture and hold Harper's Ferry for twenty hours, but he held the whole South. He captured President Buchanan and his Cabinet, convulsed the whole country, killed Governor Wise, and dug the mine and laid the train which will eventually dissolve the union between Freedom and Slavery. The rebound reveals the truth. So let it be!

Glossary

Crispus Attuck	Crispus Attucks, an African American killed in the Boston Massacre of 1770 and sometimes regarded as the first casualty of American Revolution
engine house	a structure where train engines are housed and repaired
furrin	dialect pronunciation of "foreign"
Governor Wise	Henry Wise of Virginia, who personally interviewed John Brown after his arrest and, with some reluctance, ordered his execution
Kennedy Farm	a Maryland farm Brown rented as a staging area for the raid
Moloch	an ancient god associated with costly sacrifices, often by fire
parleying	talking, from the French *parler* meaning "to talk" or "to speak"
pitfalls	in combat, concealed holes in the ground, dug with the purpose of impeding or injuring attacking troops
President Buchanan	James Buchanan, the fifteenth U.S. president
Wager House	a hotel in Harpers Ferry
Zouave	originally, a North African soldier who served with the French army but by the time of the Civil War any soldier who adopted the colorful uniform and elaborate drill maneuvers of the Zouaves

By the President of the United States of America.

A Proclamation.

Whereas, on the twenty-second day of September, in the year of our Lord one thousand eight hundred and sixty-two, a proclamation was issued by the President of the United States, containing, among other things, the following, to wit:

"That on the first day of January, in the "year of our Lord one thousand eight hundred "and sixty-three, all persons held as slaves within "any State or designated part of a State, the people "whereof shall then be in rebellion against the "United States, shall be then, thenceforward, and "forever free; and the Executive Government of the "United States, including the military and naval "authority thereof, will recognize and maintain "the freedom of such persons, and will do no act

Emancipation Proclamation (National Archives and Records Administration)

EMANCIPATION PROCLAMATION

"Upon this act, ... I invoke the considerate judgment of mankind, and the gracious favor of Almighty God."

Overview

The Emancipation Proclamation freed all slaves in the states that constituted the Confederacy. The document emphasizes that this action was a "war measure," taken, in part, to protect the slaves who were being offered refuge in Union forts, garrisons, and vessels. The proclamation was also offered as a moral statement, as an "act of justice" in accordance with the U.S. Constitution, and as a "military necessity." That President Abraham Lincoln was addressing not merely his countrymen and the rebels but the world and his maker as well is clear from the document's parting statement: "I invoke the considerate judgment of mankind, and the gracious favor of Almighty God."

Context

Lincoln issued the Emancipation Proclamation on September 22, 1862, freeing forever those slaves in the Confederate states. (The proclamation would take effect on January 1, 1863.) At that time the Civil War, begun in the spring of 1861, had yet to turn decisively in the North's favor, although Lincoln was beginning to envisage victory at long last after the Union army's success in the Battle of Antietam. He had been elected to office pledging to keep the Union together, and when the South seceded, his main task became that of reuniting his nation. Although he was opposed to slavery and its extension into new states and territories, Lincoln never advocated complete, let alone immediate, abolition of what was known as the "peculiar institution." During the early stages of the war, he successfully kept border slave states like Maryland and Missouri in the Union by not issuing statements that might have driven them toward the Confederacy. Even with this proclamation, slaves in the border states within the Union remained the property of their owners.

Pressure on Lincoln to issue this proclamation had been building for some time. He had not been opposed to emancipation in principle once the war was in progress, but he thought the timing of such an act would be crucial; it would have to come at a time when it would foster respect and inspire his troops. Lincoln had rescinded an earlier proclamation of emancipation issued by John Frémont, one of the Union's commanders, in Missouri. Lincoln viewed Frémont's proclamation not only as premature but also as insubordinate, since it was the commander in chief's duty to make such a declaration. Moreover, Lincoln wanted to issue a very carefully worded document that would limit the scope of emancipation. Indeed, fervent abolitionists criticized Lincoln for not going so far as to liberate all slaves.

Lincoln's aim, however, was to cause disruption behind Confederate lines. He hoped that his proclamation would inspire slaves to desert their masters and join the Union cause. He also hoped that the dramatic act would prevent England and France from recognizing the legitimacy of the Confederacy and supporting rebel forces. While the Emancipation Proclamation was primarily a political and diplomatic document as well as a military measure, it nevertheless acquired enormous symbolic meaning because, for the first time, it made slavery itself one of the primary issues of the war. The ideological precedent this document set led to the enlistment of some two hundred thousand soldiers and sailors in the Union army and navy.

About the Author

Abraham Lincoln, born on February 12, 1809, in a one-room log cabin in southeastern Kentucky, grew up in a frontier environment. He had little formal education but was a prodigious reader, favoring the Bible, Shakespeare, and biographies. As a young man he studied law. At age twenty-three he ran unsuccessfully for a seat in the Illinois General Assembly, to which state his family had moved when he was nine. He served briefly in the Black Hawk War before being elected to the state legislature in 1834. Admitted to the bar in 1837, Lincoln proved to be a successful attorney, admired for his ability to argue on his feet in court cases.

In 1842 Lincoln married Mary Todd, daughter of a prominent southern family. The couple had four children, but only one, Robert, survived into adulthood. Quarrelsome but proud of her husband, Mary supported Lincoln's political ambitions. He was elected for one term in the

1860

■ **November 6**
Abraham Lincoln is elected
president.

■ **December 20**
South Carolina becomes the
first southern state to secede
following the election of
Lincoln as president.

1861

■ **March 4**
Lincoln is inaugurated as
president.

■ **April 13**
Fort Sumter, in South Carolina,
surrenders to Confederate
forces, beginning the Civil
War.

■ **April 17**
Virginia secedes from the
Union.

■ **May 16–June 8**
Arkansas, North Carolina, and
Tennessee secede.

■ **August 6**
Congress approves the first
Confiscation Act, declaring
Confederate slaves seized by
the Union army to be free.

■ **August 30**
John C. Frémont, then
commander of the Western
Department, stationed in
Missouri, proclaims the slaves
in that state "forever free."
Lincoln promptly rescinds
Frémont's proclamation.

1862

■ **July 17**
Congress approves the
second Confiscation Act,
declaring slaves taking refuge
behind Union lines to be free.

■ **September 17**
The Union is victorious at
Antietam.

■ **September 22**
Lincoln issues the
Emancipation Proclamation,
to take effect in one hundred
days.

U.S. House of Representatives and made a notable speech opposing the Mexican-American War; the speech proved unpopular, however, and he did not run for reelection. Indeed, Lincoln's political career then seemed over not only because of his own politics but also because he had linked his future with that of the Whig Party, which steadily lost ground to the Democrats in the 1850s.

Lincoln's political prospects actually rose in 1854 when a new party, the Republicans, took control of the Illinois legislature. Lincoln was the Republican candidate for senator in the famous 1858 election, when he debated Stephen Douglas, the incumbent Democratic senator and a politician with a national profile and the ambition to be president. Although Lincoln's outstanding performance in the debates drew national attention, his party lost the statewide election, and Douglas retained his seat as senator.

During those debates, Lincoln enunciated his position on the sensitive issue of slavery. Douglas attempted to portray Lincoln as supporting equality for blacks and whites, knowing full well that the electorate would reject such a position. Douglas himself advocated "popular sovereignty"—that is, allowing each state to vote on whether to accept or reject slavery. Lincoln objected, making no attempt to hide his rejection of slavery but promising not to oppose the institution where it already existed. Lincoln did emphasize that he opposed "Slave Power"—that is, the political position of those states intent on spreading slavery to the territories in the West—as he wanted to contain the peculiar institution within its current southern borders.

Even though Lincoln's position on slavery was not radical, the southern states made clear that they would not remain in the Union should he be elected president. This threat of secession notwithstanding, Lincoln was genuinely surprised when the South made good on its warning; his objective then was to prosecute a war that would preserve the Union. In fact, Lincoln wished to prioritize the Union even if that meant retaining slavery in the South, although he also intended to consider abolition or partial emancipation if those actions would have the effect of reuniting the country. Lincoln's role as a symbol of northern dominance that secessionists could not abide culminated in his assassination in April 1865 by the southern sympathizer John Wilkes Booth.

Explanation and Analysis of the Document

In the summer of 1862, Lincoln concluded that freeing the slaves was essential if the Union was to emerge victorious from the war. Up until then, Lincoln had opposed the national government's interference with the present institution of slavery. He had only reluctantly signed into law the two Confiscation Acts, the first (1861) freeing Confederate slaves seized by the Union army and the second (1862) freeing slaves who had taken refuge behind Union lines. He was concerned about the seizure of property without due legal process, but he decided that the acts were temporary measures taken in time of war, and the Supreme Court declared the acts constitutional.

Radical Republicans like William Graham Sumner had been urging the president to free the slaves—an act he could then take because the Union was at war with the Confederacy. In addition to Frémont's proclamation freeing the slaves, General David Hunter, in command of the Military Department of the South, proclaimed that "slavery and martial law in a free country are altogether incompatible" and declared that slaves in Florida, Georgia, and South Carolina were "forever free." Lincoln voided both decrees, asserting that only he, as commander in chief, could order such sweeping action; he did also note that he saw no constitutional reason why he could not issue an emancipation proclamation.

As early as July 1862, Lincoln began to draft the wording of just such an emancipation edict. He proceeded cautiously, uncertain whether the restrained document he proposed to his cabinet would have the desired effect of bolstering the Union's fortunes in the war. One early draft offered compensation to Confederate states if they would cease their rebellion. But subsequent drafts deleted such conciliatory language and focused specifically on the fate of slaves in the rebellious states.

The final version of the Emancipation Proclamation reads like a legal document drafted by Lincoln the lawyer. It is a carefully couched, formal piece of writing devoid of most of the president's gift for somber yet inspiring rhetoric. Because Lincoln was taking a momentous step in American history, he was extraordinarily mindful of setting limits upon what would be denoted by the word *emancipation*, which means, of course, "setting free or the condition of being free." The primary thrust of Lincoln's decree was that he was liberating only those slaves in the areas engaged in rebellion; he was setting them free from their southern masters.

The first paragraph of the document provides the date and the authority under which the proclamation is being made. The formal language harks back to the earliest proclamations in history—the kind that were announced in the Roman Forum, although the phrase "in the year of our Lord" emphasizes that this historic declaration is rooted in the Christian era. The effort to be absolutely precise and measured is one of the hallmarks of this edict.

The next paragraph states the main purpose of the document, which is to announce that on January 1, 1863, all slaves in the rebellious areas "shall be, then, thenceforward, and forever free." The wording is essential, because late in the Civil War certain slave states were considering liberating slaves who would agree to fight for the Confederacy. With Lincoln's proclamation, however, freedom was not contingent; southern slaves needed to do nothing in particular in order to gain their freedom. In other words, whatever else might have been stated in the document, it extended an unequivocal grant of freedom to a certain segment of slaves. Moreover, this grant of freedom was not merely a matter of words, as the proclamation specifies that the U.S. government, including its military organizations, would be obligated not only to recognize but also to "maintain" that freedom. Thus, Lincoln set the precedent for the

Time Line

1863

- **January 1**
  The Emancipation Proclamation takes effect.

- **July 1–3**
  The Battle of Gettysburg is fought, and Robert E. Lee's invasion of the North fails.

1865

- **April 9**
  Lee surrenders to Ulysses S. Grant, and the Civil War is ended.

- **April 14**
  John Wilkes Booth shoots Lincoln; the president dies the following day.

- **December 18**
  The Thirteenth Amendment abolishes slavery.

federal government's being responsible for the security of the freed men and women. He also added the proviso that the "military and naval" authorities would do nothing to "repress" the efforts of former slaves to secure their "actual freedom." Commanders in the battlefield, engaged in occupying enemy territory, would be prohibited from taking any actions that would make it harder for "such persons" to escape bondage. In being used as a term referring to slaves and former slaves, the word *persons* accorded a measure of respect for a group that had been fully repressed, to the extent that each slave was counted as three-fifths of a person in the U.S. Constitution. Still, Lincoln stopped short of ordering the armed forces to actively secure the freedom of "such persons." In many cases, Union commanders had already deliberately assisted and even proclaimed the liberation of slaves, but the president held back from making such actions an explicit war aim.

In the midst of the war, Lincoln could not be sure which states or groups of states might be in rebellion as of January 1, 1863. That is why in the third paragraph he stipulates that the executive (Lincoln himself) would proclaim on a certain date which areas remained in rebellion. Thus, Lincoln left open the possibility that states in rebellion as of September 22, 1862, might return to the Union before January 1, 1863. Provided that a majority of the qualified voters in such states elected representatives to Congress and that no "strong countervailing testimony" indicated that the states had not fully determined to rejoin the Union, the executive would no longer consider them in rebellion. The implications of this statement are striking: In effect, Lincoln suggested that southern slave states might return to the Union and keep their slaves. The likelihood at that point of a Confederate state returning to the Union was remote, but in the 100 days leading up to January 1, 1863, the fortunes of war might have brought

Abraham Lincoln (Library of Congress)

some surprises. Indeed, Lincoln was leaving open a way for the rebellious states to return to the Union without sacrificing what they considered their property—that is, the slaves. Passages like this one constitute one reason why the Emancipation Proclamation disappointed some abolitionists and was attacked by others.

The fourth paragraph, like the first, states Lincoln's formal authority as commander in chief to issue the Emancipation Proclamation. He emphasizes that his declaration is a "fit and necessary war measure" and that it was undertaken only because of the exigencies of an "armed rebellion." Lincoln knew full well that the North would have offered little support for the unequivocal, absolute, and immediate liberation of all slaves, and he did not want his efforts to win the arduous, costly, and tragic war to be conflated with the agitations of abolitionists. An announcement of the complete abolition of slavery everywhere in the North and South alike would have signaled a drastic change in Lincoln's objectives in fighting the war—and might have caused border states with slaves to secede from the Union.

Paragraph 5 names the states in rebellion but also specifies "excepted parts" of those states (like the parishes in Louisiana) that were under Union control. In those parts no longer considered in rebellion, the proclamation would have no effect; they would be left "precisely as if this proclamation were not issued." The sixth paragraph reiterates

in legal language that the slaves in the states and parts of states named in the fifth paragraph were now liberated "for the purpose aforesaid" (that is, as a war measure), and the freedom of "said persons" was to be recognized and maintained by military and naval authorities.

Lincoln addresses the former slaves in the seventh paragraph, enjoining them not to take up violence, except for their own protection, and to work "faithfully for reasonable wages." This curious statement was the result of discussions about what would happen to the masses of people who would suddenly be freed. How would they defend themselves? How would they find employment and be paid for it? Before the Civil War, considerable public argument took place over how slave labor depressed the wages of free men, and Lincoln's statement here seems to allude to that concern. The newly freed slaves, in other words, were to make sure not to be exploited, such as by working for unreasonably low wages offered by employers seeking to take advantage of a cheap—and impoverished—new labor pool.

Lincoln broke new ground in paragraph 8, stipulating that former slaves could become part of the war effort, though only in a supportive capacity at garrisons, in forts, aboard ships, and so on. In other words, conspicuously absent from this declaration is an invitation to former slaves to enlist in the army and navy as combatants. Doubts existed that slaves could make effective frontline soldiers, particularly that they would stand up to enemy fire. Lincoln had also needed to consider the fact that northern troops might object to serving beside former slaves. Regardless of the aims of the war, the idea of equality between whites and African Americans was not one that the majority of whites entertained. Even Lincoln himself, at this point, was not prepared to acknowledge such equality, let alone put it into practice by integrating former slaves into the armed forces. Nevertheless, this paragraph represents a step forward in Lincoln's thinking, as he envisioned an enlarged role for the freed slaves. In fact, they would eventually be recruited to fight on the front lines of the war.

Although Lincoln repeats in paragraph 10 that the proclamation is an act of "military necessity," that phrase is encircled by his assertion that it is an "act of justice" and that he invokes the "considerate judgment of mankind, and the gracious favor of Almighty God." In cloaking the largely political and military action in moral and even religious terms—and however painstakingly he dressed the document up as a legal one forged for limited purposes in a time of war—Lincoln made his proclamation a symbolic statement. Acts of justice, in other words, are far more than matters of "military necessity," and Lincoln was looking not only to the opinions of his fellow Americans but also to the "considerate" (that is, mindful or thoughtful) judgment of humankind as well as to the blessing of his creator. This note of humility—of subjecting himself to the verdict of history, so to speak, and to God's approval—was Lincoln's way of transforming his deed into an act of universal significance.

Lincoln ends the proclamation by noting that he has had the seal of the United States affixed to the document and

An engraving copied from an 1864 painting, done at the White House, titled
The First Reading of the Emancipation Proclamation before the Cabinet (Library of Congress)

by again specifying the date and the fact that it represents the eighty-seventh year of the country's independence. In this way, Lincoln reaffirmed his faith in the Union without explicitly saying so.

Secretary of State William H. Seward, at one time Lincoln's rival for the presidency, witnessed the document. Seward was sympathetic to the abolitionists but became a trusted and shrewd adviser to the president. Although he worried that the proclamation might cause deep divisions in the North and a slave rebellion in the South that would complicate the war effort, he backed Lincoln's strategy, and most of Lincoln's cabinet did so as well. The appearance of Seward's name on the proclamation surely communicated a message to those who wanted the complete abolition of slavery; in witnessing the document, Seward was implying that this measure was as much as could be expected at that point in the war.

Given its limited scope, the Emancipation Proclamation certainly could not have been the last word on the abolition of slavery. Lincoln understood as much, but as a politician and war leader he believed that the document was as bold a declaration as he could then make. He undoubtedly realized that pressures to accomplish more, such as to more fully involve the former slaves in the war—even to grant them citizenship—had to be withstood; further issues would have to be confronted in the near future. Lincoln believed that for

the present, a temporizing message was as much as he and the nation could countenance. Although critics might have deemed the proclamation indecisive or evasive, Lincoln saw it as a way to come to terms with the current state of public opinion, to gain time, and to advance the state of public consciousness about a controversial issue.

Audience

Although Lincoln's intended audience actually was not blacks or former slaves, he was acutely conscious of the profound significance of the Emancipation Proclamation for the people who would be freed from bondage. Shortly after signing the document, he gave it to an associate to read to a group of blacks assembled on Pennsylvania Avenue near the White House. As they listened to the words, they shouted, clapped, and sang in a robust demonstration of their approval.

Lincoln's proclamation was aimed primarily at northern soldiers and voters who would see in the edict a strengthening of their moral authority and at the southern nonslave populace as well as governments abroad that might hesitate to declare support for a Confederacy that remained dedicated to "Slave Power." After all, the British nation had abolished slavery, and although members of

"That on the first day of January, in the year of our Lord one thousand eight hundred and sixty-three, all persons held as slaves within any State or designated part of a State, the people whereof shall then be in rebellion against the United States, shall be then, thenceforward, and forever free."

(Paragraph 2)

"And I hereby enjoin upon the people so declared to be free to abstain from all violence, unless in necessary self-defence; and I recommend to them that, in all cases when allowed, they labor faithfully for reasonable wages."

(Paragraph 7)

"And upon this act, sincerely believed to be an act of justice, warranted by the Constitution, upon military necessity, I invoke the considerate judgment of mankind, and the gracious favor of Almighty God."

(Paragraph 10)

the British government might have held a certain sympathy for the traditional, quasi-aristocratic South, Lincoln's "act of justice" would make it difficult for them to take sides against the Union.

Impact

The first wave of response to the Emancipation Proclamation varied by population but was generally favorable, drawing positive comments from such observers as the prominent abolitionist leader William Lloyd Garrison, the former slave and abolitionist leader Frederick Douglass, and the writer Ralph Waldo Emerson. Lincoln's political party, the Republicans, likewise welcomed the proclamation. Democrats, on the other hand, denounced Lincoln's decree as unconstitutional and later nominated General George McClellan to oppose Lincoln in the 1864 presidential election. McClellan vowed not to fight a war to free slaves. Southerners, meanwhile, charged Lincoln with fomenting a slave revolt. Abroad, the response was mixed, with some British newspapers hailing Lincoln's humanitarian action and others supporting the South and criticizing the proclamation. Regardless of such criticism, the British

government delayed consideration of a proposal to recognize the Confederacy, which meant that Lincoln had gained his objective of buying time with the proclamation.

A second wave of response to the document turned quite negative. In November 1862 northern voters returned Democratic majorities in several states that had voted for Lincoln in 1860, although Lincoln's party still held a slim majority in Congress. In the words of the historian Thomas Keneally, Lincoln's critics pointed out that all he had done was "liberate the slaves his armies had not so far encountered. He realized that this could leave the proclamation open to mockery, and some abolitionists at one end of the scale and many Democratic newspapers and orators at the other end obliged him."

While many historians emphasize that northern public opinion was against making the abolition of slavery a war issue, the biographer Richard Carwardine notes that the proclamation had a profound impact on Union soldiers. Many felt their moral conviction strengthened by the decree; they indeed believed that they were fighting for a just cause. The historian Doris Kearns Goodwin notes that the proclamation "superseded legislation on slavery and property rights that had guided policy in eleven states for nearly three-quarters of a century. Three and a half million blacks who had lived enslaved for generations were promised freedom." Although Lincoln worried over the immediate reactions to the proclamation, he had his eye on posterity, noting that his place in history would likely be secured by the Emancipation Proclamation. He considered the decree the crowning achievement of his administration.

See also War Department General Order 143 (1863).

Further Reading

■ Books

Carwardine, Richard. *Lincoln: A Life of Purpose and Power*. New York: Alfred A. Knopf, 2006.

Donald, David Herbert. *Lincoln*. New York: Simon & Schuster, 1995.

Gienapp, William E. *Abraham Lincoln and Civil War America: A Biography*. New York: Oxford University Press, 2002.

Goodwin, Doris Kearns. *Team of Rivals: The Political Genius of Abraham Lincoln*. New York: Simon & Schuster, 2005.

Guelzo, Allen C. *Abraham Lincoln: Redeemer President*. Grand Rapids, Mich.: W. B. Eerdmans, 1999.

Keneally, Thomas. *Abraham Lincoln*. New York: Lipper/Viking, 2003.

McClure, A. K. *Abraham Lincoln and Men of War-Times: Some Personal Recollections of War and Politics during the Lincoln Administration*. Lincoln: University of Nebraska Press, 1997.

Neely, Mark E., Jr. *The Last Best Hope of Earth: Abraham Lincoln and the Promise of America*. Cambridge, Mass.: Harvard University Press, 1993.

Oates, Stephen B. *With Malice toward None: The Life of Abraham Lincoln*. New York: Harper & Row, 1977.

Paludan, Phillip Shaw. *The Presidency of Abraham Lincoln*. Lawrence: University Press of Kansas, 1994.

Thomas, Benjamin P. *Abraham Lincoln: A Biography*. New York: Knopf, 1952.

Questions for Further Study

1. While drafting the Emancipation Proclamation, Lincoln replied to an editorial in the *New York Tribune* attacking him for paying too much deference to border states with slaves and arguing that he should act on emancipation. Lincoln responded by noting that his highest priority was to save the Union, not to free the slaves. He went on to say that if he could save the Union by freeing some slaves or by freeing all of them, he would do so. What do Lincoln's sentiments reveal about his state of mind and his political calculations, considering that he was trying to stay true to his principles as well as to take into account northern attitudes toward blacks?

2. Some critics have described the Emancipation Proclamation as lacking the emotion and vigor of some of Lincoln's other writings and speeches. Allen Guelzo, however, explains why Lincoln did not publish a more comprehensive or inspiring document: A proclamation with broader scope—say, freeing all slaves in the North and South alike—would have been challenged by the Supreme Court, which was still headed by Chief Justice Roger Taney, a former slaveholder. Research Taney's infamous opinion in the case *Dred Scott v. Sandford* (1857); then consider the political and moral issues that Lincoln had to confront and why he ultimately decided to offer the proclamation as a war measure.

3. Compare and contrast Lincoln's response to the decision in *Dred Scott v. Sandford* (1857) with his decision to issue the Emancipation Proclamation.

4. Compare and contrast Lincoln's position on slavery in his First and Second Inaugural Addresses.

■ **Web Sites**

"Civil War Harper"s Weekly, September 14, 1861: Fremont's Slave Proclamation." Civil War Web site.
   http://www.sonofthesouth.net/leefoundation/civil-war/1861/september/slave-proclamation.htm.

McRae, Bennie J. "Major Generals John C. Fremont and David Hunter versus President Abraham Lincoln." Lest We Forget Web site.
   http://www.coax.net/people/lwf/FHL_POL.HTM

"Suggested Lincoln Sources." History Now Web site.
   http://www.historynow.org/12_2005/ask2b.html.

   —Carl Rollyson

EMANCIPATION PROCLAMATION

By the President of the United States of America:

A Proclamation.

Whereas, on the twenty-second day of September, in the year of our Lord one thousand eight hundred and sixty-two, a proclamation was issued by the President of the United States, containing, among other things, the following, to wit:

"That on the first day of January, in the year of our Lord one thousand eight hundred and sixty three, all persons held as slaves within any State or designated part of a State, the people whereof shall then be in rebellion against the United States, shall be then, thenceforward, and forever free; and the Executive Government of the United States, including the military and naval authority thereof, will recognize and maintain the freedom of such persons, and will do no act or acts to repress such persons, or any of them, in any efforts they may make for their actual freedom.

"That the Executive will, on the first day of January aforesaid, by proclamation, designate the States and parts of States, if any, in which the people thereof, respectively, shall then be in rebellion against the United States; and the fact that any State, or the people thereof, shall on that day be, in good faith, represented in the Congress of the United States by members chosen thereto at elections wherein a majority of the qualified voters of such State shall have participated, shall, in the absence of strong countervailing testimony, be deemed conclusive evidence that such State, and the people thereof, are not then in rebellion against the United States."

Now, therefore I, Abraham Lincoln, President of the United States, by virtue of the power in me vested as Commander-in-Chief, of the Army and Navy of the United States in time of actual armed rebellion against the authority and government of the United States, and as a fit and necessary war measure for suppressing said rebellion, do, on this first day of January, in the year of our Lord one thousand eight hundred and sixty-three, and in accordance with my purpose so to do publicly proclaimed for the full period of one hundred days, from the day first above mentioned, order and designate as the States and parts of States wherein the people thereof respectively, are this day in rebellion against the United States, the following, to wit:

Arkansas, Texas, Louisiana, (except the Parishes of St. Bernard, Plaquemines, Jefferson, St. John, St. Charles, St. James Ascension, Assumption, Terrebonne, Lafourche, St. Mary, St. Martin, and Orleans, including the City of New Orleans) Mississippi, Alabama, Florida, Georgia, South Carolina, North Carolina, and Virginia, (except the forty-eight counties designated as West Virginia, and also the counties of Berkley, Accomac, Northampton, Elizabeth City, York, Princess Ann, and Norfolk, including the cities of Norfolk and Portsmouth), and which excepted parts, are for the present, left precisely as if this proclamation were not issued.

And by virtue of the power, and for the purpose aforesaid, I do order and declare that all persons held as slaves within said designated States, and parts of States, are, and henceforward shall be free; and that the Executive government of the United States, including the military and naval authorities thereof, will recognize and maintain the freedom of said persons.

And I hereby enjoin upon the people so declared to be free to abstain from all violence, unless in necessary self-defence; and I recommend to them that, in all cases when allowed, they labor faithfully for reasonable wages.

And I further declare and make known, that such persons of suitable condition, will be received into the armed service of the United States to garrison

Glossary

emancipation	the act of freeing, the act of setting free from certain restrictions, or the condition of being free
proclamation	a formal government announcement

forts, positions, stations, and other places, and to man vessels of all sorts in said service.

And upon this act, sincerely believed to be an act of justice, warranted by the Constitution, upon military necessity, I invoke the considerate judgment of mankind, and the gracious favor of Almighty God.

In witness whereof, I have hereunto set my hand and caused the seal of the United States to be affixed.

Done at the City of Washington, this first day of January, in the year of our Lord one thousand eight hundred and sixty three, and of the Independence of the United States of America the eighty-seventh.

By the President: ABRAHAM LINCOLN
WILLIAM H. SEWARD, Secretary of State.

Two soldiers of the Twenty-third New York Infantry—one black and one white—sit in front of a tent during the Civil War. (Library of Congress)

FREDERICK DOUGLASS: "MEN OF COLOR, TO ARMS!"

1863

"The iron gate of our prison stands half open. One gallant rush from the North will fling it wide open."

Overview

Frederick Douglass, a prominent African American who had escaped from bondage and became an outspoken abolitionist, delivered his speech "Men of Color, To Arms!" before a crowd in his hometown of Rochester, New York, in 1863. In this speech Douglass encourages free blacks in the North to see the Civil War as the means of ending the system of human bondage that was still thriving in the American South. These African Americans continued to encounter discrimination, as they were denied citizenship and were often consigned to low-paying menial labor, but in Douglass's eyes, blacks could overcome such prejudice by performing heroically on the battlefield. His Rochester speech has since been considered one of the clearest appeals for the enlistment of African Americans in the Union army, and it serves as an excellent example of Douglass's talent for oratory and his position as the leading black intellectual of his day.

Context

African Americans had been a vital part of the American armed forces long before the Civil War. Black soldiers fought in the American Revolution and defended New Orleans in 1815, but a federal law passed in 1792 prohibited them from serving in state militias or the regular army. When the Civil War broke out in 1861, public opinion in the United States was generally not in favor of using African American troops. Some critics feared that blacks lacked the courage necessary for combat, while others resented any action that would raise blacks' position in the racial hierarchy and challenge white supremacy. Likewise, some African Americans in the North were skeptical that black enlistment would truly lead to more equality for blacks within the military or among civilian society more generally.

Some white and black abolitionists, however, understood that African Americans could provide an essential contribution to the northern war effort. Former slaves and other free blacks in the North swelled with the same patriotism that encouraged white men to join the military; these men also felt a special burden to aid their brothers who still languished under the cruel slave system. Abolitionists believed that black troops would disprove negative criticisms and help African Americans become further integrated into northern society. Likewise, slaves in the South, who began flocking to Union lines in staggering numbers after the attack on Fort Sumter, South Carolina, in April 1861, presented Union commanders with a dilemma: Since the Confederacy had no qualms about using slave laborers to aid its military actions, why should the Union refuse to use black soldiers to bolster its own war effort? Union general Benjamin Butler was the first to use these refugees—whom he called "contrabands"—to build defensive trenches, serve as camp cooks, and perform other menial labor at Fortress Monroe, the coastal Union bastion near Hampton, Virginia. These escaped slaves were pursued by their owners, but after the passage of the First Confiscation Act on August 6, 1861, army commanders were not obligated to return slave owners' property. Other leading military officials, like Secretary of War Simon Cameron, spoke publicly about the benefits of black enlistment. General John C. Frémont, commander of the Department of the West based in Saint Louis, Missouri, went a step further and issued a proclamation on August 30, 1861, declaring that the slaves of any Missourian who was disloyal would be freed. His proclamation received support from many northerners, but it complicated President Abraham Lincoln's efforts to bring southern states back into the fold.

Lincoln's attitude toward black troops would change over the course of the Civil War, but at the beginning of the conflict his greatest concern was to keep the border slaveholding states (Missouri, Kentucky, Maryland, and Delaware) in the Union, and to demonstrate to the Confederacy that reunion was still a viable possibility. He illustrated his intentions by making clear that emancipation was not a war aim of the Lincoln administration (thus tacitly promising slaveholders that their human property was safe). Early in 1861 he directed Union officials to send slaves who hid behind army lines back to their owners, an action that emphasized Lincoln's ultimate plan to preserve the Union. However, when Union forces increasingly found themselves on the defensive,

1861

■ **April 12**
Confederate forces fire on Fort Sumter in South Carolina, officially beginning the Civil War.

■ **August 6**
Congress passes the First Confiscation Act, authorizing Union forces to seize any property (including slaves) from defeated Confederates.

1862

■ **July 17**
Congress passes the Second Confiscation Act, mandating the surrender and freedom of slaves in the service of the Confederate government.

■ **September 22**
President Abraham Lincoln and his advisers release the preliminary draft of the Emancipation Proclamation, which gives the Confederate states until January 1, 1863, to surrender.

■ **September 27**
The Louisiana Native Guards is the first African American regiment (with whites as senior officers) to be officially mustered into the Union Army.

1863

■ **January 1**
The Emancipation Proclamation goes into effect, freeing all slaves living in the states still in rebellion (that is, the Confederacy).

■ **February**
Frederick Douglass begins to recruit for the Fifty-fourth Massachusetts. Two of his sons, Lewis Douglass and Charles Douglass, enlist in the regiment.

■ **March 2**
Douglass delivers his speech "Men of Color, To Arms!" before a crowd in Rochester, New York.

■ **July 17–18**
Black troops fight in two of their most significant battles of the war: The First Kansas Colored Volunteer Infantry repels a Confederate force near Honey Springs, Indian Territory (Oklahoma), and the 54th Massachusetts assaults Fort Wagner, South Carolina.

Lincoln began to alter his stance on black recruitment and supported the passage of the First Confiscation Act, which he signed on August 6, 1861. Heavy casualties contributed to this change of heart. He also worked closely with his advisers to create a preliminary draft of the Emancipation Proclamation, which was released in September 1862, shortly after the Union victory at Antietam; this signaled his shift toward making slavery's abolition an official goal of the administration.

With Lincoln's strategy changing, and public opinion in the North moving increasingly toward support of black enlistment, Congress passed the Second Confiscation Act on July 17, 1862. This act mandated that all slaves who belonged to Confederate masters would be free and that any black person who was employed by the Union forces was also free. The first black unit to be officially mustered into the army was the Louisiana Native Guards, initially brought into service by Benjamin Butler in his General Order No. 63, published on August 22, 1862. Meanwhile, General James Lane, an ardent abolitionist (and U.S. senator) in the new state of Kansas, began the recruitment of black troops to protect Kansas citizens from Confederate guerrillas clustered along the Kansas-Missouri border. His actions were technically not sanctioned by Lincoln or the army's leading generals, but after the issuance of the Emancipation Proclamation in 1863, the only remaining barrier to the use of black troops disintegrated. The Emancipation Proclamation declared that all slaves living in a state in rebellion were free. This made the Civil War a war of emancipation as well as a war to reunite the Union, since advancing Union armies stood to gain support from the newly freed slaves in conquered territory. Lane's troops were the first black regiment to encounter Confederates on the battlefield at a skirmish in Bates County, Missouri; these troops were officially mustered into the service in 1863 as the First Kansas Colored and Second Kansas Colored.

The governor of Massachusetts, John A. Andrew, also sought permission to raise two regiments of black troops. The War Department authorized this recruitment, and Andrews solicited Frederick Douglass, the former slave and noted abolitionist, to assist in locating free black men willing to fight for the cause of freedom. Douglass began recruiting for the Fifty-fourth Massachusetts Regiment of the United States Colored Troops in February 1863. The Bureau of Colored Troops, the government body assigned to administer the recruitment and organization of these units, was created by the War Department on May 1, 1863.

About the Author

Frederick Douglass was a prominent abolitionist and outspoken advocate for black equality, who had himself been born into slavery on a Maryland plantation sometime in February 1818, under the name Frederick Augustus Washington Bailey. His mother was enslaved, and his father was an unknown white man, who at one point Douglass believed may have been his mother's owner. As a child he was separated from his mother, living instead with various other relatives. At age eight he moved to Baltimore to work for a carpenter named Hugh Auld, and it was in Baltimore that he first learned to read and encountered abolitionist newspapers that would inspire him to make an escape.

After enduring harsh whippings and other mistreatment at the hands of white overseers and slave owners—including an infamous encounter with a cruel slave breaker named Edward Covey—the twenty-year-old Douglass finally made his escape on September 3, 1838. He fled by steamboat and then by train to New York City, and from there he settled in Massachusetts to begin his new life as a free man, taking the new name "Frederick Douglass." While he was in Massachusetts, he cultivated a friendship with his fellow abolitionist William Lloyd Garrison, who published an influential and controversial newspaper called *The Liberator*, the same paper that had first inspired him to seek freedom in the North. With Garrison's encouragement, in 1841 Douglass delivered his first public lecture in Nantucket, to a packed crowd that had assembled for the annual convention of the Massachusetts Anti-Slavery Society.

His experience at that abolitionist meeting set him on a course that would make him a leading national advocate of emancipation; he began a widespread lecture tour that made him a prominent voice in the movement thanks to his personal experiences as a slave. The attendant publicity (both negative and positive), however, made Douglass fearful that his former owner might capture him, so in 1845 he moved to Britain, where he spent two years making connections with British supporters of black equality; he returned to the United States in 1847, after English abolitionists purchased his freedom. After settling in Rochester, New York, he established a series of abolitionist newspapers, including *The North Star* (1847–1851), *Frederick Douglass' Paper* (1851–1860), and *Douglass' Monthly* (1858–1863). When full-scale civil war broke out in 1861, Douglass eagerly suggested that free blacks be allowed to fight and help free their enslaved brethren who lived in the South. He assisted with the recruitment of the Fifty-fourth Massachusetts, encouraging two of his sons Lewis and Charles to join the regiment. During the war Douglass consulted with the Lincoln administration and was a constant advocate for black equality. He continued to proclaim his support of black troops until the war's end in 1865, at which point he could easily have been described as the most famous African American of his time. He worked for full racial equality until his death in Washington, D.C., on February 20, 1895.

Douglass authored several books, including three versions of his autobiography, in addition to numerous editorials and newspaper articles in many of the leading abolitionist papers like *The Liberator*, the *Anti-Slavery Advocate*, and other publications. The best known of these works was his first autobiography, the *Narrative of the Life of Frederick Douglass, an American Slave*, published in 1845. This narrative is still considered one of the most moving accounts of slave life in the American South.

Time Line

1863

■ **August 10**
Douglass visits President Lincoln at the White House to plead for equal treatment of black soldiers.

1864

■ **April 12**
Confederate general Nathan Bedford Forrest massacres approximately three hundred Union soldiers, including African Americans, near Fort Pillow, Tennessee.

1865

■ **April 9**
Union general Ulysses S. Grant and Confederate general Robert E. Lee meet at Appomattox Court House, where Lee surrenders. The Civil War comes to an end.

■ **December 6**
The Thirteenth Amendment, which abolishes slavery, is ratified.

Explanation and Analysis of the Document

In the opening lines of his speech, Douglass grounds his arguments in his prophetic belief that this war will bring about great advances in the struggle for racial equality. After establishing that black troops would eventually be used, regardless of the northern public's criticisms, Douglass turns to an examination of how the ongoing Civil War is not merely a war over states' rights; it is a war to determine whether or not slavery would be part of the American legal, political, economic, and social system. Here he advances his first main point: The only logical response to southerners' perpetuation of slavery is to enlist black troops in the war effort; anyone should have been able to see that "the arm of the slave was the best defense against the arm of the slaveholder."

Douglass had been a vocal proponent of black enlistment throughout the war, but it was not until 1863 that the Emancipation Proclamation created a path that could fulfill his dreams. Influencing the government's position on this matter had been a slow (even tedious) process, but in the next section of his speech he encourages the audience not to revisit the history of black enlistment. The war effort could not be delayed any longer: "Action! Action! not criticism, is the plain duty of this hour. Words are now useful only as they stimulate to blows." Although Douglass had always advocated the use of violence to free slaves, the ongoing war had convinced him that this was the perfect time for northern blacks—whether they had been born free or slave—to accept this challenge.

General Nathan Bedford Forrest (Library of Congress)

Next, Douglass addresses the black critics of black enlistment, methodically dismantling the fallacies behind their reluctance to fight. He even calls these critics "weak and cowardly men.... They tell you this is the 'white man's war'; and you will be 'no better off after than before the war.'" Some black northerners' resistance to enlistment, according to Douglass, stemmed from their fear that white officers would carelessly place them on the front lines to be sacrificed "on the first opportunity." As Douglass and his audience were aware, even northerners who supported the war effort and believed that slavery was an immoral system did not necessarily support full racial equality, and this prejudiced attitude could engender resentment among the ranks of white officers who commanded black regiments. Douglass did not want such negativity to discourage black men who were willing to perform their civic duty on the battlefield, since "liberty won by white men would lose half its luster." Instead of giving credence to these objections leveled by "cowards," he encouraged black men to prove their bravery by enlisting. Lest anyone suspect that he had not given this matter due consideration, Douglass reassured the audience that "the counsel I give comes of close observation of the great struggle now in progress, and of the deep conviction that this is your hour and mine."

The previous points all serve as an introduction to the heart of Douglass's argument: that after much thought he is confident enough in his convictions to use plain language and "call and counsel you to arms." He links blacks' involvement in the military directly to the furtherance of black rights in the United States, declaring, "I urge you to fly to arms, and smite with death the power that would bury the government and your liberty in the same hopeless grave." The destiny of African Americans is here tied directly to the continuation of the Union.

Who will lead this fight? In paragraph 2 he presents the practical implications of this call to arms and announces how Massachusetts is poised to take the lead in black enlistment. Massachusetts harbors only a small population of free blacks, but Douglass encourages those in Rochester to "go quickly and help fill up the first colored regiment from the North." Douglass had been in contact with the governor of Massachusetts, John A. Andrews, in addition to other key political and military figures in the days and weeks leading up to this speech. He reassures the audience that he is an authorized spokesperson who knows the details of the enlistment process and that any black men who enlisted would be accorded the same wages and treatment as white soldiers. Although he does not state whether the officers would be white or African American, he promises that these leaders would treat all their recruits equally and without discrimination.

The closing section of Douglass's speech includes the most powerfully inspiring rhetoric of the entire presentation, and it is also the richest in terms of historical references. Douglass suggests an analogy to the audience, observing that the slave system in the South is a prison and that those African Americans who are already free now have the responsibility to save their brethren who still labor in bondage. He calls to mind some of the great black revolutionaries in American history as a reminder that this current conflict is only an extension of a battle that had been raging in the hearts of African Americans for centuries. First he names Denmark Vesey, a former slave in Charleston, South Carolina, who planned a rebellion against slaveholders in 1822; before Vesey and his compatriots could implement their plan, word got out to the local white community and a full-scale panic erupted in the countryside. Vesey was executed in 1822. Douglass then references Nathaniel (Nat) Turner, a Virginia slave who launched a full-scale rebellion in 1831 that ended with the deaths of at least fifty-five whites and most members of the rebellion (including Turner himself). Last, he recalls that two former slaves—Shields Green and John Anthony Copeland—had participated in John Brown's raid on the federal arsenal at Harpers Ferry, Virginia, in October 1859. Green had spent some time in Rochester, the site of Douglass's speech, prior to his involvement with Brown, so his name would have been familiar to the audience. Both Green and Copeland were executed in Charles Town, Virginia (now West Virginia), on December 16, 1859, for their involvement in the raid. These men had paved the way for black involvement in the military. According to Douglass this was the perfect opportunity for northern blacks to combat slavery and "win for ourselves the gratitude of our country, and the best blessings of our posterity through all time."

"A war undertaken and brazenly carried on for the perpetual enslavement of colored men, calls logically and loudly for colored men to help suppress it."

"Action! Action! not criticism, is the plain duty of this hour. Words are now useful only as they stimulate to blows. The office of speech now is only to point out when, where, and how to strike to the best advantage. There is no time to delay."

"The iron gate of our prison stands half open. One gallant rush from the North will fling it wide open, while four millions of our brothers and sisters shall march out into liberty. The chance is now given you to end in a day the bondage of centuries, and to rise in one bound from social degradation to the place of common equality with all other varieties of men"

"This is our golden opportunity. Let us accept it, and forever wipe out the dark reproaches unsparingly hurled against us by our enemies. Let us win for ourselves the gratitude of our country, and the best blessings of our posterity through all time."

Audience

Douglass delivered this speech in Rochester, New York, but in broader terms, by titling his speech "Men of Color, To Arms!" Douglass was speaking to the entire free black population of the North. He knew this message would be printed and would function as a rallying cry to encourage blacks' involvement in the Union effort; additionally, his speech reinforced the convictions of the many northern blacks who had been vocalizing their desires to enlist, pressing against Lincoln's unsupportive policies since the beginning of the conflict in 1861. In addition, Douglass fully understood that white critics of black enlistment would read his speech, and as a result, they might become more comfortable with the concept of black soldiers. His fervent call for blacks to fight for the Union cause was, in effect, distributed to a national audience.

Impact

After the publication of this speech in *Douglass' Monthly*, the great abolitionist's beliefs about blacks' fitness for military duty and their opportunity to bring about the freedom of their people were disseminated not only to his readership but also, through republication in other northern newspapers, to a wider audience. Thanks to this speech, the American public was exposed to Douglass's impassioned rhetoric in favor of emancipation and the use of black troops, and as the war progressed, more northerners came to agree with his position. Douglass had himself been disenchanted with Lincoln's policies, but in this speech he made clear to the black public that their involvement in the military effort would reinforce the importance of equal treatment of all individuals, regardless of race. Douglass's established place as a leading voice for racial equality guaranteed that his speeches and publications would generate conversation and debate among both northerners and southerners. For modern readers of this transcript, Douglass's position illustrates how freed blacks and abolitionists were an integral part of the effort to recruit black troops. Historians today acknowledge that Douglass's "To Arms" describes in vivid language how African American soldiers could aid in the Union's triumph and, more important, prove their right to equality and their readiness to become full citizens of American society.

Despite (or perhaps because of) the North's hesitance to arm former slaves and other free blacks, African American regiments thoroughly proved their mettle on the battlefield. Perhaps the most famous episode of blacks in combat was the Fifty-fourth Massachusetts's assault on Fort Wagner, near Charleston, South Carolina, in July 1863, which has been memorialized by Augustus Saint-Gaudens's sculpture in the Boston Common (1897) and by the movie *Glory* (1989). The commander of the Fifty-fourth, Robert Gould Shaw, was killed, and 271 of his men were killed, wounded, or taken prisoner. From a military perspective the engagement failed, but after that night the Fifty-fourth became a symbol of how African American regiments could perform with valor and determination in the face of fierce opposition. William H. Carney, who had distinguished himself at Fort Wagner, was the first African American to earn the highest military decoration, the Medal of Honor. Just one day earlier, in Indian Territory, the First Kansas Colored had beaten off a far larger force of Texas Confederates at the Battle of Honey Springs. By 1863, thanks to the Fifty-fourth Massachusetts and other black regiments, African Americans' place in the military was generally accepted both by the Lincoln administration and many members of the northern public.

Black troops did, however, continue to encounter racism and discrimination from government officials, military officers, and the general public. Lingering concerns regarding blacks' ability to serve, combined with continued discrimination from whites, required that black regiments be commanded only by white officers. Key leaders in the administration maintained that since most black soldiers were inexperienced, it made sense to have white officers, who could effectively teach new recruits how to drill and how to perform in battle. These arguments did little to assuage the apprehension of black recruits who feared that such a policy could foster widespread discrimination, but as the tide of public opinion turned in favor of black regiments, the army adjusted its policy and granted some officers' commissions to surgeons. By some estimations, there were around one hundred black officers who received commissions during the Civil War.

In addition to fighting prejudice at home in the North, black troops faced even greater challenges on the battlefield. Confederate officers resented the Union's use of black troops and often mistreated blacks who were captured or who surrendered. In Missouri, James Williams, commander of the 1st Kansas Colored, found that some members of his scouting party had been captured by Confederate guerrillas; although Williams attempted to arrange for a prisoner ex-

change, the guerrillas refused and executed one of the black prisoners. Williams reciprocated by executing one of the captured Confederate soldiers, showing that racial recrimination would not be tolerated. Situations such as this were not uncommon in other black regiments. On April 12, 1864, a force of about 2,500 Confederates under the command of Nathan Bedford Forrest assaulted Fort Pillow, in Tennessee. There were some six hundred Union men garrisoned at the fort, about half of them former slaves. Forrest's men violated the terms of the flag of truce and overran the fort, brutally massacring most of the black men within. (Over 60 percent of the blacks were killed.) After this cruelty, a rallying cry among other black troops was "Remember Fort Pillow!"

Black soldiers received less pay than white troops, even though the first black regiments to formally enlist (which included the First South Carolina and the Fifty-fourth and Fifty-fifth Massachusetts) had all been promised equal pay by the War Department. Black soldiers received $10 per month, with $3 of that taken for their clothing allowance; meanwhile, white soldiers received $13 per month, plus $3.50 for clothes. It was not until June 15, 1864, that Congress finally passed legislation ensuring that black soldiers would receive equal pay. A problem arose, however, over the matter of retroactive wages. The adjutant general's office maintained that only men who were legally free after April 19, 1861, would receive back pay, which excluded some recruits and consequently damaged the black regiments' morale. Finally—after much protest on the part of black soldiers, white officers, and recruiters—legislation passed on March 3, 1865, guaranteed that retroactive equal pay would be given to all African American regiments that had been promised equal treatment by the military. Although this had been a years-long struggle, by war's end black troops were on a more equal footing with their white comrades, illustrating how revolutionary the Civil War period was in terms of altering the racial hierarchy present in the North.

By war's end, approximately 178,892 black soldiers had served in the Union army, making up a little more than 12 percent of the armed forces. Of that number, more than one-third died either as the result of injuries sustained in battle or of disease. When the hostilities ceased in 1865, most black regiments were mustered out of active service. Some of these troops stayed on with the army and went to military outposts in the West, gaining the nickname "Buffalo Soldiers." African Americans throughout both the North and the South were officially emancipated with the Thirteenth Amendment, which was ratified on December 6, 1865. Less than five years later, black men won the right to vote with the passage of the Fifteenth Amendment. Since that time, blacks have served honorably in every major military conflict in American history.

See also *The Confessions of Nat Turner* (1831); First editorial of the *North Star* (1847); Emancipation Proclamation (1863); War Department General Order 143 (1863); Thomas Morris Chester's Civil War Dispatches (1864) Thirteenth Amendment to the U.S. Constitution (1865); Fifteenth Amendment to the U.S. Constitution (1870).

Further Reading

■ Books

Blight, David W. *Frederick Douglass' Civil War: Keeping Faith in Jubilee*. Baton Rouge: Louisiana State University Press, 1989.

Cornish, Dudley Taylor. *The Sable Arm: Black Troops in the Union Army, 1861–1865*. 2nd ed. Lawrence: University Press of Kansas, 1987.

Douglass, Frederick. *The Life and Times of Frederick Douglass: His Early Life as a Slave, His Escape from Bondage, and His Complete History*. New York: Dover Publications, 2003.

Foner, Eric. *Forever Free: The Story of Emancipation and Reconstruction*. New York: Alfred A. Knopf, 2005.

Glatthaar, Joseph T. *Forged in Battle: The Civil War Alliance of Black Soldiers and White Officers*. New York: Free Press, 1990.

McPherson, James. *The Struggle for Equality: Abolitionists and the Negro in the Civil War and Reconstruction*. Princeton, N.J.: Princeton University Press, 1964.

Manning, Chandra. *What This Cruel War Was Over: Soldiers, Slavery, and the Civil War*. New York: Alfred A. Knopf, 2007.

■ Web Sites

"The Fight for Equal Rights: Black Soldiers in the Civil War." National Archives "Teaching with Documents" Web site.
http://www.archives.gov/education/lessons/blacks-civil-war/.

"Frederick Douglass National Historic Site, Virtual Museum Exhibit." National Park Service Web site.
http://www.nps.gov/history/museum/exhibits/douglass/.

—Kristen K. Epps

Questions for Further Study

1. Explain how President Abraham Lincoln's views regarding the enlistment of black troops during the Civil War changed. Why do you think he altered his views?

2. Compare this document with Thomas Morris Chester's Civil War Dispatches (1864). How did the actions of black troops that Chester wrote about help to realize the views that Douglass expressed?

3. Douglass expressed great optimism about the Civil War and what he believed its impact would be on racial issues and the position of African Americans. Do you believe that after the Civil War he felt vindicated or disappointed?

4. In the twentieth century, numerous black writers urged African Americans to resist the military draft and refuse to fight in the nation's wars, particularly World War I, World War II, and the Vietnam War. Yet Douglass urged African Americans to take up arms. Why do you think attitudes changed from the nineteenth to the twentieth centuries?

5. Read this entry in conjunction with War Department General Order 143 (1863). What do you think Douglass's reaction to this order was? Why?

FREDERICK DOUGLASS: "MEN OF COLOR, TO ARMS!"

When first the rebel cannon shattered the walls of Sumter and drove away its starving garrison, I predicted that the war then and there inaugurated would not be fought out entirely by white men. Every month's experience during these dreary years has confirmed that opinion. A war undertaken and brazenly carried on for the perpetual enslavement of colored men, calls logically and loudly for colored men to help suppress it. Only a moderate share of sagacity was needed to see that the arm of the slave was the best defense against the arm of the slaveholder. Hence with every reverse to the national arms, with every exulting shout of victory raised by the slaveholding rebels, I have implored the imperiled nation to unchain against her foes, her powerful black hand. Slowly and reluctantly that appeal is beginning to be heeded. Stop not now to complain that it was not heeded sooner. It may or it may not have been best that it should not. This is not the time to discuss that question. Leave it to the future. When the war is over, the country is saved, peace is established, and the black man's rights are secured, as they will be, history with an impartial hand will dispose of that and sundry other questions. Action! Action! not criticism, is the plain duty of this hour. Words are now useful only as they stimulate to blows. The office of speech now is only to point out when, where, and how to strike to the best advantage. There is no time to delay. The tide is at its flood that leads on to fortune. From East to West, from North to South, the sky is written all over, "Now or never." Liberty won by white men would lose half its luster. "Who would be free themselves must strike the blow." "Better even die free, than to live slaves." This is the sentiment of every brave colored man amongst us. There are weak and cowardly men in all nations. We have them amongst us. They tell you this is the "white man's war"; and you will be "no better off after than before the war"; that the getting of you into the army is to "sacrifice you on the first opportunity." Believe them not; cowards themselves, they do not wish to have their cowardice shamed by your brave example. Leave them to their timidity, or to whatever motive may hold them back. I have not thought lightly of the words I am now addressing you. The counsel I give comes of close observation of the great struggle now in progress, and of the deep conviction that this is your hour and mine. In good earnest then, and after the best deliberation, I now for the first time during this war feel at liberty to call and counsel you to arms. By every consideration which binds you to your enslaved fellow—countrymen, and the peace and welfare of your country; by every aspiration which you cherish for the freedom and equality of yourselves and your children; by all the ties of blood and identity which make us one with the brave black men now fighting our battles in Louisiana and in South Carolina, I urge you to fly to arms, and smite with death the power that would bury the government and your liberty in the same hopeless grave. I wish I could tell you that the State of New York calls you to this high honor. For the moment her constituted authorities are silent on the subject. They will speak by and by, and doubtless on the right side; but we are not compelled to wait for her. We can get at the throat of treason and slavery through the State of Massachusetts. She was the first in the War of Independence; first to break the chains of her slaves; first to make the black man equal before the law; first to admit colored children to her common schools, and she was first to answer with her blood the alarm cry of the nation, when its capital was menaced by rebels. You know her patriotic governor, and you know Charles Sumner. I need not add more.

Massachusetts now welcomes you to arms as soldiers. She has but a small colored population from which to recruit. She has full leave of the general government to send one regiment to the war, and she has undertaken to do it. Go quickly and help fill up the first colored regiment from the North. I am authorized to assure you that you will receive the same wages, the same rations, and the same equipments, the same protection, the same treatment, and the same bounty, secured to the white soldiers. You will be led by able and skillful officers, men who will take especial pride in your efficiency and success. They will be quick to accord to you all the honor you shall merit by your valor, and see that your rights and feelings are respected by other soldiers. I have assured myself on these points, and can speak with authority. More than twenty years of unswerving devotion to our common cause may give me some humble claim to be trusted at this momentous crisis. I will not argue. To do so implies hesitation and doubt, and you do not hesitate. You do not doubt. The day dawns; the morning star is bright upon the horizon! The iron gate of our prison stands half open. One gallant rush from the North will fling it wide open, while four millions of our brothers and sisters shall march out into liberty. The chance is now given you to end in a day the bondage of centuries, and to rise in one bound from social degradation to the place of common equality with all other varieties of men. Remember Denmark Vesey of Charleston; remember Nathaniel Turner of Southampton; remember Shields Green and Copeland, who followed noble John Brown, and fell as glorious martyrs for the cause of the slave. Remember that in a contest with oppression, the Almighty has no attribute which can take sides with oppressors. The case is before you. This is our golden opportunity. Let us accept it, and forever wipe out the dark reproaches unsparingly hurled against us by our enemies. Let us win for ourselves the gratitude of our country, and the best blessings of our posterity through all time. The nucleus of this first regiment is now in camp at Readville, a short distance from Boston. I will under take to forward to Boston all persons adjudged fit to be mustered into the regiment, who shall apply to me at any time within the next two weeks.

Glossary

Charles Sumner	a U.S. senator from Massachusetts and a leader of the abolition movement
Denmark Vesey	the leader of a planned slave revolt in South Carolina in 1822
John Brown	the white abolitionist who led an unsuccessful raid on the U.S. arsenal at Harpers Ferry, Virginia, in 1859
Nathaniel Turner	commonly called Nat Turner, the leader of a slave revolt in Virginia in 1831
patriotic governor	Governor John A. Andrew of Massachusetts, who backed the recruitment of black troops
Sumter	Fort Sumter in South Carolina, the site of the first hostilities of the Civil War

GENERAL ORDERS, }   WAR DEPARTMENT,
ADJUTANT GENERAL'S OFFICE,
No. 143.   *Washington, May 22, 1863.*

I..A Bureau is established in the Adjutant General's Office for the record of all matters relating to the organization of Colored Troops. An officer will be assigned to the charge of the Bureau, with such number of clerks as may be designated by the Adjutant General.

II..Three or more field officers will be detailed as Inspectors to supervise the organization of colored troops at such points as may be indicated by the War Department in the Northern and Western States.

III..Boards will be convened at such posts as may be decided upon by the War Department to examine applicants for commissions to command colored troops, who, on application to the Adjutant General, may receive authority to present themselves to the board for examination.

IV..No persons shall be allowed to recruit for colored troops except specially authorized by the War Department; and no such authority will be given to persons who have not been examined and passed by a board; nor will such authority be given any one person to raise more than one regiment.

V..The reports of Boards will specify the grade of commission for which each candidate is fit, and authority to recruit will be given in accordance. Commissions will be issued from the Adjutant General's Office when the prescribed number of men is ready for muster into service.

VI..Colored troops may be accepted by companies, to be afterwards consolidated in battalions and regiments by the Adjutant General. The regiments will be numbered *seriatim*, in the order in which they are raised, the numbers to be determined by the Adjutant General. They will be designated: "—— Regiment of U. S. Colored Troops."

VII..Recruiting stations and depôts will be established by the Adjutant General as circumstances shall require, and officers will be detailed to muster and inspect the troops.

War Department General Order 143 (National Archives and Records Administration)

"No persons shall be allowed to recruit for colored troops except specially authorized by the War Department."

Overview

The U.S. War Department issued General Order 143 on May 22, 1863, to organize and provide uniform recruitment and governance of black troops. The order established the Bureau of U.S. Colored Troops, and after that date most existing and all newly recruited African American units were incorporated and administered with the bureau's supervision.

One of the biggest controversies during the American Civil War revolved around the role that African Americans should play in the Union war effort. From the onset of the conflict, African Americans such as Frederick Douglass and other abolitionists urged President Abraham Lincoln to make ending slavery a war aim. African Americans also demanded a more active role in fighting the war. President Lincoln was hesitant to include black troops for several reasons. Racial prejudice was deep-seated in the northern states, and many, including Lincoln, feared that white soldiers would not fight side by side with African Americans. Many northerners held that African Americans were incapable of making good soldiers because they believed that blacks were too servile or cowardly.

Even before the Emancipation Proclamation brought slavery to the forefront of the conflict, blacks strove for inclusion in the ranks of the U.S. military despite the attitudes of northern whites. Both free blacks in the northern states and newly freed slaves in the southern areas under Union control were eager to contribute. Some Union generals began raising black units in occupied areas of the South in 1862, but recruitment began in earnest after formal announcement of the Emancipation Proclamation on January 1, 1863. The first black units were organized as volunteer units of the states. General Order 143 formalized these efforts.

Context

In April 1861, a mere few days after the Civil War had begun when the Confederates fired on Fort Sumter in the harbor at Charleston, South Carolina, a group of African Americans in Cleveland, Ohio, gathered to pledge their support for the Union cause. As they put it, "As colored citizens of Cleveland, desiring to prove our loyalty to the Government, [we] feel that we should adopt measures to put ourselves in a position to defend the government of which we claim protection." They continued: "That to-day, as in the times of '76, and the days of 1812, we are ready to go forth and do battle in the common cause of the country." Although African Americans had taken up arms during the American Revolution and during the War of 1812, federal law had prohibited the enlistment of blacks in state militias and the U.S. Army since 1792. At the beginning of the Civil War there were no black soldiers in the regular army, and most white northerners hoped to keep it that way.

African Americans recognized at the war's outset that this conflict had the potential to rid the United States of slavery, and they were eager to push for their inclusion in the fight. Abraham Lincoln's administration and the mainstream press were careful to declare that the war was about restoring the Union and emphatically denied that the issue of slavery had any role in the conflict. Northern public opinion, at least early in the war, was not prepared to consider challenging the racial balance that placed African Americans at the bottom of the social ladder. Prominent blacks and abolitionists, however, began pushing for the enlistment of black troops almost immediately, and many realized the implications of those fears. Perhaps Frederick Douglass most clearly outlined the fear of white northerners with regard to black military participation. In August 1861 he editorialized in his newspaper, *Douglass' Monthly*, "Once let the black man get upon his person the brass letters, U.S., let him get an eagle on his button, and a musket on his shoulder and bullets in his pocket, and there is no power on earth which can deny that he has earned the right to citizenship in the United States." Lincoln recognized that military service for blacks would indeed place African Americans in a position to demand the rights of citizenship, including suffrage. He also feared that the presence of black soldiers would discourage white enlistments. Another concern was maintaining the loyalty of the border states, including Maryland, Kentucky, Missouri, and Delaware. Although these were slave states, they had not joined the Confederacy, and the president wanted them to remain part of the Union.

1861

■ **April 12**
The Civil War begins following the firing on Fort Sumter at Charleston, South Carolina.

■ **May**
General Benjamin F. Butler declares escaped slaves to be the property of the Union and puts them to work behind Union lines.

■ **August 6**
Congress passes the first Confiscation Act authorizing the seizure of property, including slaves, used to aid the Confederate war effort.

1862

■ **July 17**
Congress passes the second Confiscation Act, authorizing federal courts to free the slaves of those fighting against the Union, and the Militia Act, authorizing President Abraham Lincoln to enroll African American troops in the Union army.

■ **September 27**
The First Louisiana Native Guards becomes the first black unit to be recognized by the War Department.

1863

■ **January 1**
The Emancipation Proclamation takes effect, declaring an end to slavery in the Confederate states under rebellion.

■ **January**
The First Kansas Volunteer Colored Infantry is mustered into service as the first regiment of African American troops raised in a northern state.

■ **January**
Governor John A. Andrew of Massachusetts is granted permission to raise an African American regiment, the Fifty-fourth Massachusetts Infantry.

■ **May 22**
The War Department issues General Order 143, creating the U.S. Colored Troops.

Despite these concerns, pressures to allow black military enlistment mounted from several directions. From early in the war the Confederate army employed free black and slave labor to perform much of the manual work required for the military. Eventually, the Confederate army requisitioned slaves from their masters in much the same way it appropriated food or other necessary supplies. Throughout the war African Americans not only raised much of the food that fed the Confederate troops but also built many of the fortifications and entrenchments that protected troops in the field. The Union general Benjamin F. Butler, in command of troops at Fortress Monroe in Virginia, was one of the earliest advocates of using African Americans in the Union cause. In May 1861 he declared escaped slaves who had labored on behalf of the Confederate war effort as "contraband of war" and refused to return them to their masters. Reasoning that returning the slaves to their masters would benefit the enemy, Butler put them to work behind Union lines. Although the policy was controversial, Lincoln allowed Butler's action to stand. Before the summer of 1861 ended, Congress would pass legislation to more clearly define how the Union army should treat the large numbers of slaves who sought freedom behind Union lines.

Realizing the importance of slave labor to the Confederacy, in August 1861 Congress passed the frst Confiscation Act, permitting the seizure of any property, including slaves, used to aid the Confederate war effort. This provided legitimacy to Butler's ad hoc contraband policy, and over the duration of the war some two hundred thousand "contrabands" worked for the Union army. Although the act sidestepped the issue of emancipation, it did introduce the concept of manumission into federal policy. The same month, General John C. Frémont was bolder in declaring free the slaves of Confederates in Missouri. As commander in charge of the Department of the West in St. Louis, Frémont's emancipation declaration was a part of a larger plan to bring Missouri under closer control of the Union.

Alarmed that the action might lead Missouri and the other border states to join the Confederacy, Lincoln quickly rescinded the order and eventually removed Frémont from his post. Lincoln's action angered abolitionists such as the radical Parker Pillsbury, who condemned the president's act as "cowardly submission to southern and border slave state dictation." Some prominent northern politicians, including Massachusetts governor John A. Andrew and Kansas senator James H. Lane, urged Lincoln to arm African Americans. Along with the generals John W. Phelps and David Hunter, they argued that blacks were eager to fight for the nation. Although Lincoln was not prepared to support a radical emancipation policy in 1861, by midyear 1862, at the urging of these men, he was beginning to see the value of including African Americans in the military. It was also becoming clear that emancipation would necessarily result if African Americans were allowed to enlist in the U.S. Army.

In July 1862 Congress passed two bills that tied emancipation to military enlistment. The second Confiscation Act authorized northern courts to free the slaves of those "engaged in rebellion" and authorized Lincoln to employ "as many persons of African descent as he may deem necessary and proper for the suppression of this rebellion, and for this purpose he may organize and use them in such manner as he may judge best for the public welfare." The Militia Act granted freedom to slaves who worked for the U.S. Army and gave Lincoln the authority to "to receive into the service of the United States, for the purpose of constructing intrenchments, or performing camp service, or any other labor, or any military or naval service which they may be found competent, persons of African descent." While Lincoln and many northerners remained skeptical about arming African Americans, Congress had clearly paved the way for the enlistment of blacks with these two acts. During the summer of 1862 Lincoln also began secretly drafting a proclamation that would emancipate slaves in the Confederate states that had not fallen under Union control.

The public would not learn of the Emancipation Proclamation until September 1862, when it was announced following the Union victory at the Battle of Antietam. Not knowing Lincoln's plan, some northerners attacked his failure to fully execute the emancipation clause of the second Confiscation Act. Douglass proclaimed in an editorial, "The signs of the times indicate that the people will have to take this war into their own hands and dispense with the services of all who by their incompetency give aid and comfort to the destroyers of the country." Horace Greeley, editor of the *New York Tribune*, complained that Lincoln was too worried about the border states and urged him to enforce the new acts. In the summer and fall of 1862, as Lincoln cautiously danced around the full implementation of the second Confiscation Act, more radical military leaders in the field took it to heart.

The first African Americans to take up arms for the Union cause during the Civil War did so in the South. Empowered by the second Confiscation Act and the Militia Act, commanders in the field were willing and sometimes eager to begin enlisting black units. One of the first to do so was General Butler, who by mid-1862 commanded occupation forces in Louisiana. As his earlier contraband policy might suggest, Butler had no problem employing African Americans to fill a shortfall in the number of Union soldiers available to defend New Orleans. On September 27 he mustered into service the First Louisiana Native Guards. Although blacks had been placed in defensive roles in several small units, this was the first sanctioned regiment of African American soldiers in the Union army. Pleased with the result, Butler organized two additional regiments, the Second and Third Louisiana Native Guards, by November 1862. Other early African American regiments were raised in South Carolina, including the First South Carolina Volunteer Infantry (African Descent), commanded by the abolitionist Thomas Wentworth Higginson. In Kansas, before he had official authorization, Senator James H. Lane began recruiting for the First Kansas Volunteer Colored Infantry, which became the first black regiment recruited in the northern states. All African American

Time Line

1864

- **June**
Congress grants equal pay to soldiers in the U.S. Colored Troops.

1865

- The Civil War ends in April, and in December the Thirteenth Amendment to the Constitution abolishes slavery in the United States.

1866

- **July 28**
Congress authorizes two permanent African American regiments, the Ninth and Tenth United States Cavalry, who would gain renown as the Buffalo Soldiers.

units were headed by white commissioned officers, although eventually black soldiers could aspire to the rank of corporal or sergeant, and more than a hundred gained commissioned ranks. By the end of 1862 between three thousand and four thousand black men were serving in five regiments. When first recognized by the War Department, the soldiers in black regiments received $10 monthly pay, $3 less than their white counterparts.

Following the issuance of the final Emancipation Proclamation on January 1, 1863, black enlistment became a major priority and a central part of Lincoln's emancipation program. That month Massachusetts governor John A. Andrew was authorized to raise the Fifty-fourth Massachusetts Infantry, and prominent New England abolitionists rushed to help recruit. Secretary of War Edwin Stanton also authorized Rhode Island and Connecticut to begin recruiting black regiments. Black abolitionists, including Frederick Douglass, Martin R. Delany, Henry McNeal Turner, and John Mercer Langston, recruited broadly across the northern and midwestern states. In March 1863 the army's adjutant general, Lorenzo Thomas, was ordered to the South to head an enlistment drive.

Thomas's southern travels took him to the Mississippi Valley, where he was charged not only with recruiting African American troops but also with finding qualified officers to lead the newly forming regiments. The enlistment drive was successful, as Thomas found many freedmen eager to serve. Thomas's 1863 recruiting resulted in raising twenty black regiments but also pointed to the need for a more ordered system of recruitment and organization to govern the new troops. Issued on May 22, 1863, General Order 143 provided the mechanism for organizing all black regiments under the newly created Bureau of Colored Troops.

Assistant Adjutant General Charles W. Foster was appointed to lead the bureau, and he primarily supervised black enlistment and recruitment in both the North and South for the remainder of the war. Following the creation

Lorenzo Thomas (Library of Congress)

of the United States Colored Troops, African American regiments with state names, with only a few exceptions, were renamed and designated units of the U.S. Colored Troops. Exceptions were made for a few regiments from Connecticut, Massachusetts, and Louisiana. The significance of renaming the First Kansas Colored Volunteer Infantry as the Seventy-ninth U.S. Colored Infantry or the First Louisiana Native Guards the Seventy-third U.S. Colored Infantry was that instead of being mustered into a state unit, the black soldiers became agents of the U.S. Army. In June 1864, a year after the creation of the Bureau of Colored Troops, Congress granted equal pay to African American soldiers. The Bureau of Colored Troops offered a professional, organized, and well-ordered chain of command and bureaucratic structure that enabled African Americans to gain a permanent place in the military and to stand and fight for the freedom guaranteed by the U.S. government.

About the Author

General Order 143 was a directive issued by the War Department and as such does not have an author of record. However, the army's adjutant general, Lorenzo Thomas, most likely had a hand in authoring the order. In March 1863 Secretary of War Edwin Stanton ordered Thomas to the Mississippi Valley to recruit and muster regiments of African American troops.

Lorenzo Thomas was born in New Castle, Delaware, in 1804. An 1823 graduate of the U.S. Military Academy at West Point, Thomas was a career army officer who was appointed adjutant general of the army in the early months of the Civil War. In this post he was the person primarily responsible for recruitment and staffing of the army. It was under his watch that large-scale recruitment of black troops began. He was not known as an abolitionist or Radical Republican, who were critical of Lincoln's slowness in freeing the slaves and supporting their legal equality. Instead, as a moderate he was able to convince many of the necessity of enlisting African Americans in the army. Although Thomas did not favor black officers for the new regiments, he was a firm believer that the African American troops should not be relegated to general labor but rather should be given combat assignments. It was during his recruitment drive through Kentucky, Arkansas, Louisiana, Mississippi, and Tennessee in 1863 that Thomas came to realize that a new organizational system was required, resulting in General Order 143 creating the U.S. Colored Troops.

Following the Civil War, Thomas remained in the adjutant general's post, although his relationship with Secretary Stanton was somewhat tenuous and the secretary reportedly doubted Thomas's loyalty. Perhaps Stanton's concern had some foundation. In 1868, President Andrew Johnson briefly appointed Thomas interim secretary of war to replace Stanton. It was this action that led Congress to declare Johnson in violation of the Tenure of Office Act, resulting in his impeachment. During the impeachment proceedings both Thomas and Stanton claimed to be the secretary of war. After successfully avoiding conviction, Johnson failed to appoint Thomas permanently to the post. Thomas retired from the army with the rank of major general in February 1869. He died in 1875.

Explanation and Analysis of the Document

General Order 143 is divided into nine sections. Section I establishes a separate bureau within the War Department to administer and organize African American regiments, officially called Colored Troops. The order provides for an administrative officer and a number of supporting clerks to be appointed by the adjutant general. Section II authorizes the appointment of three or more inspectors to oversee the organization of regiments within the U.S. Colored Troops. These inspectors could be sent anywhere within the northern states under the authorization of the War Department.

Section III attends to the recruitment of white commissioned officers to command units within the Colored Troops. The order authorizes an examining board or boards to evaluate and select among applicants for commissioned posts in command of the newly raised regiments. Section IV restricts recruitment agents to those individuals authorized by the War Department. Recruiters were required to pass the evaluation of a specially created board, and each was permitted to raise only one regiment of Colored Troops.

Members of the 107th U.S. Colored Infantry, shown with musical instruments (Library of Congress)

Sections V and VI link an officer's rank to the number of troops he is authorized to recruit. Once the prescribed number of men was recruited, the adjutant general would grant the appropriate officer's commission. Recruitment could be into companies of about one hundred soldiers, which would then be incorporated into regiments that included up to ten companies. Instead of having regiments that bore a number tied to their locus of recruitment, such as the Fifty-fourth Massachusetts, regiments of the U.S. Colored Troops would be numbered separately in the order in which they were raised. The first unit organized under General Order 143 would be the First U.S. Colored Troops, the next the Second U.S. Colored Troops, and so forth. Section VII authorizes the establishment of recruiting depots and stations and provides for officers to oversee the inspection and mustering of the Colored Troops regiments.

Section VIII concerns the recruitment of noncommissioned officers, generally sergeants and corporals, from within the ranks of the African American members of each regiment. While the commanding commissioned officers of the Colored Troops were drawn from the white army population, African Americans could advance to noncommissioned officer status. An important distinction was made on the basis of responsibility. Commissioned officers enjoyed the responsibility of ultimate command of the regiment, but noncommissioned officers exercised more limited control over men within the unit. Noncommissioned officers were selected based on merit, and those who showed an aptitude for leading could be promoted, as from corporal to sergeant. Each company generally included four sergeants and four corporals, so opportunities to advance to officer status were not common. The final section of the order establishes procedures for directing correspondence and inquiries regarding the Colored Troops. It directs that applications for officer appointments be made directly to the chief of the Bureau of Colored Troops.

Audience

General Order 143 is a military directive whose immediate audience was the Union army. It was especially aimed at those responsible for the administration and recruitment of African American troops. Those recruiting black enlistments outside the auspices of the army were another potential audience of the order. Ultimately, General

"A Bureau is established in the Adjutant General's Office for the record of all matters relating to the organization of Colored Troops."

(Section I)

"No persons shall be allowed to recruit for colored troops except specially authorized by the War Department."

(Section IV)

"The non-commissioned officers of colored troops may be selected and appointed from the best men of their number in the usual mode of appointing non-commissioned officers."

(Section VIII)

143 was aimed at the nation, as it laid the foundation for organizing and administering the participation of African American soldiers in the Union war effort. Beyond establishing procedures and an administrative structure, the order indicated clearly that African Americans would have a stake in American society.

Impact

By the end of the Civil War in April 1865, the Union army had recruited 178,975 African American soldiers into its ranks. Black troops made up 133 infantry regiments, 4 independent companies, 7 cavalry regiments, 12 heavy artillery regiments, and 10 companies of light infantry. Most of the black Union soldiers were former slaves, although a significant number were drawn from the ranks of the northern free black community. African Americans made up nearly 10 percent of all Union troops serving in the war.

The creation of the Bureau of Colored Troops had implications beyond the Civil War. In establishing a military bureau and administrative structure, General Order 143 set the precedent for permanent inclusion of African Americans in the military. By October 1865 the regiments of the U.S. Colored Troops began demobilizing, but this was not the end to black military participation. On July 28, 1866, Congress authorized the creation of two African American regiments for the regular army. The Ninth and Tenth U.S.

Cavalry later gained recognition as the Buffalo Soldiers as they performed important service in the American West in the late 1800s. Although blacks would never again be denied entrance to the military, the U.S. Colored Troops also established the segregation of African Americans into separate units led by white commissioned officers. The U.S. military remained segregated through World War II. Racial separation in the military ended in July 1948 when President Harry S. Truman signed Executive Order 9981 ending segregation in the armed forces.

See also Emancipation Proclamation (1863); Frederick Douglass: "Men of Color, To Arms!" (1863).

Further Reading

■ Books

Douglass, Frederick. "The Proclamation and a Negro Army." In *The Frederick Douglass Papers*, Series 1: *Speeches, Debates, and Interviews*, Vol. 3: *1855–63*, ed. John Blassingame and John R. McKivigan. New Haven, Conn.: Yale University Press, 1985.

Fisher, Ernest F. *Guardians of the Republic: A History of the Non-commissioned Officer Corps of the U.S. Army.* New York: Stackpole Books, 2001.

Higginson, Thomas Wentworth. *Army Life in a Black Regiment.* 1870. Reprint. New York: Collier Books, 1962.

McPherson, James M. *The Negro's Civil War: How American Blacks Felt and Acted during the War for the Union*. 1965. Reprint. New York: Ballantine Books, 1991.

Smith, John David, ed. *Black Soldiers in Blue: African American Troops in the Civil War Era*. Chapel Hill: University of North Carolina Press, 2002.

Trudeau, Noah Andre. *Like Men of War: Black Troops in the Civil War, 1862–1865*. Boston: Little, Brown, 1998.

■ **Web Sites**

"The Fight for Equal Rights: Black Soldiers in the Civil War." National Archives "Teaching with Documents" Web site. http://www.archives.gov/education/lessons/blacks-civil-war/.

—L. Diane Barnes

Questions for Further Study

1. Explore how War Department General Order 143 fit into the struggle of African Americans to gain full citizenship and civil rights in the United States. What rights, if any, do you believe African Americans gained from serving in the U.S. Army during the Civil War?

2. General Order 143 was issued several months after the Emancipation Proclamation. Explore the connection between these two documents. How did freeing slaves in the Confederate areas under rebellion tie to the recruitment of African American troops for the Union army?

3. African American troops complained about getting less pay than white soldiers until Congress granted pay equity in June 1864. What arguments were used to justify paying African Americans less? What arguments were used to support equal pay? Can you think of examples in today's society when certain groups or classes of people receive unequal compensation for equal work?

War Department General Order 143

May 22, 1863

I—A Bureau is established in the Adjutant General's Office for the record of all matters relating to the organization of Colored Troops. An officer will be assigned to the charge of the Bureau, with such number of clerks as may be designated by the Adjutant General.

II—Three or more field officers will be detailed as Inspectors to supervise the organization of colored troops at such points as may be indicated by the War Department in the Northern and Western States.

III—Boards will be convened at such posts as may be decided upon by the War Department to examine applicants for commissions to command colored troops, who, on Application to the Adjutant General, may receive authority to present themselves to the board for examination.

IV—No persons shall be allowed to recruit for colored troops except specially authorized by the War Department; and no such authority will be given to persons who have not been examined and passed by a board; nor will such authority be given any one person to raise more than one regiment.

V—The reports of Boards will specify the grade of commission for which each candidate is fit, and authority to recruit will be given in accordance. Commissions will be issued from the Adjutant General's Office when the prescribed number of men is ready for muster into service.

VI—Colored troops may be accepted by companies, to be afterward consolidated in battalions and regiments by the Adjutant General. The regiments will be numbered seriatim, in the order in which they are raised, the numbers to be determined by the Adjutant General. They will be designated: "—Regiment of U. S. Colored Troops."

VII—Recruiting stations and depots will be established by the Adjutant General as circumstances shall require, and officers will be detailed to muster and inspect the troops.

VIII—The non-commissioned officers of colored troops may be selected and appointed from the best men of their number in the usual mode of appointing non-commissioned officers. Meritorious commissioned officers will be entitled to promotion to higher rank if they prove themselves equal to it.

IX—All personal applications for appointments in colored regiments, or for information concerning them, must be made to the Chief of the Bureau; all written communications should be addressed to the Chief of the Bureau, to the care of the Adjutant General,

BY ORDER OF THE SECRETARY OF WAR:
E. D. TOWNSEND, Assistant Adjutant General.

Glossary

adjutant general	the chief administrative officer of a military unit or army
regiment	unit of military organization including up to ten companies

The storming of Fort Wagner by the Fifty-fourth Massachusetts (Library of Congress)

MILESTONE DOCUMENTS IN AFRICAN AMERICAN HISTORY

Thomas Morris Chester's Civil War Dispatches

"The colored troops fully sustained the most exalted opinion which their ardent friends could possibly entertain."

Overview

Thomas Morris Chester pursued a number of careers, including teaching, law, and journalism. As the first and only African American journalist to cover the Civil War for a major daily American newspaper— the *Philadelphia Press*—he filed dispatches about the progress of the war. In them, including the two from August 1864 reproduced here, he emphasized the exploits of "colored troops," that is, African American soldiers who fought during the later stages of the Civil War. As such, his reports became important documents in the ongoing debate about the place of African Americans in American society, whether they should be allowed to defend the nation's interests as members of the military, and what their future would be after the war. Chester's dispatches from Virginia, specifically from near Richmond, the Confederate capital, and Petersburg, a vital city to its south, give the modern reader a ground's-eye view of the progress of the war and the part that African American troops played in it.

Context

In January 1865, General Robert E. Lee, the commander of the Confederacy's Army of Northern Virginia, contacted the administration of President Jefferson Davis to request that the troop-starved Confederacy recruit African Americans. He wrote:

> Such an interest we can give our negroes by giving immediate freedom to all who enlist, and freedom at the end of the war to the families of those who discharge their duties faithfully (whether they survive or not), together with the privilege of residing at the South. To this might be added a bounty for faithful service.

Some black regiments were, in fact, mustered, but none ever fought in the war, though some individual blacks took up arms and fought where they could on behalf of the Confederacy.

In the North, however, a different decision was made. The question of whether African Americans, who had been allowed to fight against the British in the Revolutionary War, would be allowed to serve in the Union cause was raised early on. African Americans had offered to serve at least from the time of the Confederacy's attack at Fort Sumter in 1861—the start of the war—but it was not until January 1863, after President Abraham Lincoln issued the Emancipation Proclamation, that Secretary of War Edwin Stanton acceded to Massachusetts governor John Andrew's fervent requests and authorized the creation of an African American volunteer regiment.

The result was the formation of the Fifty-fourth Massachusetts Volunteer Infantry under the leadership of Colonel Robert Gould Shaw, a white officer. So many men volunteered for the black regiment that officials were able to make physical requirements more stringent, creating a regiment that was as fit and able-bodied as any in the Union army, if not more so. Additionally, the large number of volunteers led to the creation of a sister regiment, the Fifty-fifth Massachusetts Volunteer Infantry. Chester, a native of Harrisburg, Pennsylvania, spearheaded recruitment efforts in the Harrisburg area and by June 1863 was able to enlist 135 African American volunteers in the Fifty-fifth.

Harrisburg was under threat of imminent attack, with Confederate forces camped just outside, on the western bank of the Susquehanna River. At the same time, many African Americans displaced by the war were flooding into the city, which previously had been known as a refuge and a stop on the Underground Railroad. Many of them served as laborers to build the city's defenses along the river. Meanwhile, a number of African American volunteers from Philadelphia were rejected by the governor of Pennsylvania and the general in charge of the city's defense, Darius Crouch. In response, Secretary of War Stanton informed Crouch that he should accept volunteers without regard to their race. Two companies of African American recruits were formed from Harrisburg and Philadelphia, one of which was led by Chester, who had been a captain. However, neither company saw action, as the battle for Harrisburg did not take place. Instead, the Confederate troops abandoned their position in order to join the campaign that led to the Battle of Gettysburg in July. Ultimately, the Fifty-fourth

1834
- **May 11**
Thomas Morris Chester is born in Harrisburg, Pennsylvania.

1850
- **September 18**
The federal Fugitive Slave Act is passed.

1853
- Chester briefly teaches high school in Monrovia, Liberia (the first of several visits to the new nation).

1858
- **November**
Chester returns to Liberia and starts an independent newspaper, the *Star of Liberia*.

1861
- **March 4**
Abraham Lincoln is inaugurated as U.S. president.

- **April 12**
Confederate forces attack Fort Sumter, South Carolina, starting the Civil War.

1862
- **September 22**
Abraham Lincoln issues the preliminary Emancipation Proclamation.

1863
- **January**
Secretary of War Edwin Stanton agrees to allow Massachusetts governor John Andrew to form an African American volunteer military unit, the Fifty-fourth Massachusetts Regiment.

- **June**
Chester recruits 135 African American volunteers to join the Fifty-fourth's sister regiment, the Fifty-fifth Massachusetts Volunteer Infantry.

- **June**
Two companies of African American recruits, one commanded by Chester, are formed in Harrisburg and Philadelphia.

- **July 18**
The Fifty-fourth Massachusetts spearheads an unsuccessful assault on Fort Wagner in South Carolina.

Massachusetts would go on to spearhead an assault on Fort Wagner, outside Charleston, South Carolina, on July 18, 1863, its major engagement in the war.

From the Confederate point of view, news from the battlefronts was relentlessly dispiriting during the summer of 1864. Because the war was going so badly, and because many people in the South were coming to regard Jefferson Davis as a tyrant for suspending the writ of habeas corpus (giving authorities the power to make arrests and hold people without charge), the governor of Georgia had pulled his state's troops from the field, and the state threatened to secede from the Confederacy. The Confederate Army of Tennessee was in full retreat. Union troops had a Fourth of July picnic for African Americans on the grounds of Davis's home in Mississippi. In August, Union warships blockaded Mobile Bay off the coast of Alabama, cutting off the last port open to the South. Great Britain, which had remained officially neutral during the war but continued to buy southern cotton and supply the South with ships, severed relations with the South and seized the ships being built for the Confederacy in British shipyards. That month, too, the Union general William Tecumseh Sherman completed his famous "march to the sea" across Georgia, cutting the Confederacy in half, laying waste everything in his path, and capturing Atlanta. Meanwhile, the Confederate army had at most one hundred twenty-five thousand weary, starving troops in the field. The rate of desertion was high, as many soldiers simply threw down their weapons and set off for home. Starved for troops, the Confederacy employed "dog-catchers" in the cities to press into service boys as young as fourteen and men as old as sixty (many of them wounded veterans walking with crutches).

By the summer of 1864, the strategy of the northern generals was to wear down the Confederacy by circling in on Richmond, which lay on the James River just a hundred miles south-southwest of Washington, D.C. The Army of the James, led by General Benjamin Butler, was to move on Richmond from the south and east; the Army of the Potomac, led by General George Meade, was to approach from the north. In what was called the Overland Campaign, a series of bloody engagements took place in Virginia, but they all resulted in a stalemate. From May 8 to May 21, 1864, the battle at Spotsylvania Court House claimed a total of thirty thousand casualties on both sides, almost a fifth of the combatants. The Battle of Cold Harbor, from May 31 to June 12, claimed nearly thirteen thousand Union casualties.

These and other frontal assaults on the capital failed to dislodge the Confederate defenses, so General Ulysses S. Grant, the Union commander, decided on a different tack: to ignore Richmond and focus on Petersburg, a vital railroad hub to the south through which food, supplies, and war matériel passed. The siege of Petersburg, which lasted some 290 days until the spring of 1865, was intended to choke the Confederacy into submission. To resist this siege, the Confederacy, using troops and slave labor, constructed multiple defensive trenches in concentric rings around both cities. One of the major battles of the siege was the Battle of the Crater on July 30. The Union, seeking to break

---

the defensive line around Petersburg, had tunneled underneath and packed the tunnel with four tons of explosives. When the powder blew, a huge crater was formed, into which Union forces stormed; after several hours of fighting, the Union had lost some four thousand troops, compared with just fifteen hundred Confederates. Again, the battle was a stalemate.

In August attention shifted to the area around the James River. Beginning on August 13, Union troops moved into an area called Deep Bottom in an effort to draw Confederate troops away from Petersburg. Over the next week, during the Second Battle of Deep Bottom (a first having been fought in June), the armies skirmished, once again with no clear victor. Union losses were heavy, with many troops dying of heatstroke. Union troops remained bottled up, and many military historians blame the bungling and hesitancy of General Butler for the failure to break through. The battle did succeed, though, in stretching Lee's forces. These and other assaults weakened the Confederate army in much the same way that repeated battering breaks down a door. Thomas Chester was on hand with the Army of the James to witness events around Petersburg and Richmond. He filed a story on August 18 from the Headquarters of the Tenth Corps and then filed a story on August 22 from the Headquarters of the Second Brigade, Third Division of the Eighteenth Army Corps.

About the Author

Thomas Morris Chester (also known as T. Morris Chester) was born in Harrisburg, Pennsylvania, on May 11, 1834. His mother was a former slave; his father was a restaurateur whose establishment was a center of African American social and political activity and the sole location in the area where William Lloyd Garrison's abolitionist newspaper, *The Liberator*, could be bought. Although little is known of Chester's early life, it is clear that early on he was determined to become a lawyer and that he placed a high value on education. At age sixteen he began studies at the Allegheny Institute outside Pittsburgh. These were particularly difficult times for African Americans in the North, particularly escaped slaves, as 1850 marked the passage of the federal Fugitive Slave Act. Under this law, which was designed to appease the South, slave owners or their agents were authorized to capture their escaped slaves and return them to bondage in the South. The threat of this practice (as well as occasional kidnapping of free blacks) decimated the Pittsburgh area's African American population as many blacks fled to locales farther north.

In 1853, Harrisburg's African Americans were engaged in the debate over whether emigration was the best course. Chester was a noteworthy participant in debates about whether freed slaves should remain in the United States or immigrate to the African state of Liberia, founded in part by the American Colonization Society (or, more formally, the Society for the Colonization of Free People of Color of America) in 1821–1822 as a haven for freed slaves. Chester

Time Line	
1864	■ **August 14** Chester is hired by the *Philadelphia Press* and begins his coverage of the war in Virginia. ■ **August 18** Chester files the dispatch "Ten Miles from Richmond." ■ **August 22** Chester files the dispatch "Before Petersburg."
1865	■ **April 9** Confederate general Robert E. Lee surrenders to Union general Ulysses S. Grant at Appomattox Court House, Virginia, ending the Civil War.
1870	■ **April** Chester becomes the first African American to be called to the English bar.
1873	■ Chester becomes the first African American to be admitted to the Louisiana bar.
1884	■ Chester assumes the presidency of the Wilmington, Wrightsville, and Onslow Railroad.
1892	■ **September 30** Chester dies in Harrisburg.

argued in favor of emigration and finally announced his intention to move to Africa. During the 1850s he traveled on three occasions to Liberia, where he taught and, in 1858, founded the newspaper the *Star of Liberia*. By 1859 he was back in central Pennsylvania promoting emigration. After yet another trip to Liberia (1860–1863), he returned to the United States, which was in chaos amid the Civil War. He helped muster troops for the war effort, but he became disenchanted with the federal government's unwillingness to give equal status to African American recruits, so in 1863 he left the United States for Great Britain, where he lectured on abolition and in support of the Union cause in Britain.

Frustrated with his inability to raise enough money to fund his legal education, Chester returned to Pennsylvania in 1864, where his life took another turn. John Russell Young, the editor of the *Philadelphia Press*, hired Chester

Confederate entrenchments near Spotsylvania Court House, showing felled trees placed in trenches (Library of Congress)

to cover the war as what would today be called an embedded reporter with the Army of the James, led by General Benjamin Butler. He ended his reporting career at the beginning of Reconstruction and returned to Harrisburg, but soon he returned to England, where he studied law and, in 1870, became the first African American to be called to the English bar. That year he returned to the United States, eventually settling in Louisiana, where he took part in local politics and, in 1873, became the first African American to be admitted to the Louisiana bar. He was also made a brigadier general in the Louisiana State Militia, and in 1878 he was appointed as U.S. commissioner for New Orleans. In 1884 his life took an odd turn when he assumed the presidency of the Wilmington, Wrightsville, and Onslow Railroad, a North Carolina company owned by African Americans. In 1892 he returned to his mother's home in Harrisburg, where he died on September 30.

Explanation and Analysis of the Document

Chester began reporting on the operations of the Army of the James and Potomac on August 14, 1864. At that time the opposing armies were entrenched around Richmond and Petersburg. Chester sent dispatches through the fall of Richmond and the early occupation and Reconstruction of the South, with the last dispatch dated June 12, 1865. Reproduced here are two of his early dispatches.

♦ "Headquarters 10th Army Corps Ten Miles from Richmond, August 18, 1864"

Chester begins his dispatch by noting a Union victory. He carefully praises both African American and white troops: "The troops, white and black, covered themselves with undying fame. Their conduct could not have been sur-

passed." Chester consistently praises the African American troops but is careful to avoid doing so at the expense of white troops, although white officers who treated African American troops as less than equals were not spared his opprobrium. Then, in the second paragraph, he outlines for readers the progression of events. He makes reference to David Bell Birney, the commander of the Tenth Army Corps and a prominent Union general who had taken part in several major battles, including Gettysburg, Chancellorsville, and the Second Battle of Bull Run. Perhaps exercising a bit of wishful thinking, he states, "A few more exhibitions of loyalty and bravery, as evinced during the past few days in this Corps, will soon eradicate the last vestige of prejudice and oppression from the grand Army of the Potomac." He goes on to describe the events surrounding the Battle of Deep Bottom, again extolling the bravery of the African American troops in their assault on Confederate rifle pits in a kind of trench warfare that presaged the massive slaughter of World War I. Many of the Confederate defensive works were highly ingenious. One tactic was to fell trees and place them whole in trenches with their branches pointing toward the direction from which Union troops would assault; the branches, then, would impede troop movement. The result was a large number of skirmishes and hand-to-hand fighting, with Union troops making progress and being pushed back. Chester then describes the actual combat episode, noting that there were between fifty and sixty African American troops killed and wounded. In fact, more than one-third of all African American troops would die in the war, a number approaching sixty thousand.

In the same paragraph, Chester makes reference to General William Birney, the older brother of David Birney. The brothers were the sons of abolitionists, and William played a major role in the recruitment of African Americans. He recruited seven regiments of black soldiers and was appointed to the position of superintendent of enlistment for black troops. Two of these regiments were the Seventh United States Colored Troops and the Ninth United States Colored Troops, both of which had seen action before being transferred to the Tenth Corps.

Chester then describes a cease-fire ("flag of truce") called to allow both sides to gather their dead. He noted that there was evidence that the Union dead had been searched and their valuables taken, commenting that "this act of ineffable meanness has nerved the hearts and strengthened the arms of the defenders of the Union, who will sweep from existence these enemies of God and civilization." In point of fact, Union troops would also seize booty from fallen Confederate troops, though typically the Confederate dead had little of value on them. For their part, the Confederates were often able to find U.S. currency, which was much more valuable than the greatly eroded Confederate money; throughout the South, black market transactions were almost always conducted with U.S. rather than Confederate currency. Chester concludes his dispatch with the ironic note that some Confederates in retreat had been forced to leave behind slave manacles, "which illustrate their character and humanity."

Union seaborne expedition landing on the Atlantic Coast near Deep Bottom, Virginia (Library of Congress)

♦ **"Headquarters 2d Brigade, 3d Division, 18th Army Corps; Before Petersburg, August 22, 1864"**

In the second dispatch, Chester describes an attack outside Petersburg. The goal of Union troops during the summer and fall of 1864 was to sever all of the town's connecting railroad lines. These rail lines, including the Weldon railroad, were vital to Lee's forces and the city of Richmond, some thirty miles to the north. They were the Confederate capital's only link with the Deep South, providing foodstuffs, supplies, and troops. Union forces engaged in numerous battles and skirmishes in their efforts to seize these rail lines, often tearing up tracks to prevent trains from entering the city. Their efforts were aided by many local Union sympathizers, who took part in nighttime sabotage of tracks, locomotives, and water tanks. Some southern train operators would even lose paperwork to delay troop movements and otherwise undermine the Confederate war effort. The battle that Chester describes took place in the wake of the Union's seizure of the Weldon railroad.

In the section titled "The Negro Troops before Petersburg," Chester notes that there were "many regiments of colored troops." In fact, there were fifteen such regiments in the Eighteenth Corps and a total of twenty-five black regiments in the Army of the James. During the Civil War, a regiment typically consisted of ten companies of soldiers, or a total of a thousand to fifteen hundred men (and occasion-

"Another battle has been fought, and a decided advantage has been gained. The troops, white and black, covered themselves with undying fame. Their conduct could not have been surpassed. The colored troops fully sustained the most exalted opinion which their ardent friends could possibly entertain."
("Ten Miles from Richmond")

"There was neither wavering nor straggling; but presenting a fearless front to the enemy, their conduct elicited especial remark, and excited admiration. A few more exhibitions of loyalty and bravery, as evinced during the past few days in this Corps, will soon eradicate the last vestige of prejudice and oppression from the grand Army of the Potomac."
("Ten Miles from Richmond")

"The colored troops were the last to retire, which they did with unwavering firmness and in obedience to orders; not, however, before they gave three cheers, which evinced their dauntless spirit."
("Ten Miles from Richmond")

"The hearts of the colored soldiers in this vicinity have been gladdened by the good news from the extreme left of the Army of the Potomac. Yesterday, about the time the church bells were inviting the inhabitants of your city to renew the assurances of their Christianity, the loud report of cannon announced that once more the defenders of the Union had met its enemies in mortal combat."
("Before Petersburg")

"What Gen. Birney has done others may accomplish, if they do not regard it as humiliating to treat a negro patriot as a man, who offers himself a willing sacrifice upon his country's altar."
("Before Petersburg")

"There is not a day but what some brave black defender of the Union is made to bite the dust by a rebel sharpshooter or picket, but his place is immediately and cheerfully filled by another."
("Before Petersburg")

ally women who had disguised themselves as young men so that they could enlist). Chester goes on to praise General William Birney, who commanded African American troops from Maryland. Reinforcing one of the themes of his dispatches, Chester states,

> The secret of Gen. Birney's success is, that he treats his men as any other gallant officer would regard the defenders of the Union.... What Gen. Birney has done others may accomplish, if they do not regard it as humiliating to treat a negro patriot as a man, who offers himself a willing sacrifice upon his country's altar.

Finally, Chester alludes to the Confederate treatment of captured African American soldiers. He states that "between the negroes and the enemy it is war to the death." Captured African Americans were naturally returned to slavery; at the very least they were treated worse than white prisoners, and in some cases they were reportedly killed as they attempted to surrender. Although Jefferson Davis had issued a decree that captured African Americans were to be returned to their masters, it was widely believed among black troops that they and their white officers were to be put to death. Rumors abounded that entire black regiments had been slaughtered. In response, Lincoln threatened to retaliate, and the issue of the treatment of captured black soldiers contributed to the suspension of prisoner exchanges between North and South in the spring of 1864—a strategic move on the North's part to deplete Confederate forces. Despite the danger not just from combat but from capture, tens of thousands of African Americans volunteered to fight for the Union.

Audience

Chester wrote primarily for the *Philadelphia Press*. The newspaper is perhaps best known for first publishing in serial form Stephen Crane's classic novel *The Red Badge of Courage* a year before its 1895 publication in book form. It is notable that Chester was published in this white-owned newspaper in a city where the news media generally offered little news concerning African Americans. Morris's target audiences were manifold: free African Americans of the city, white Philadelphians, military leaders, and even the president. His dispatches sought to promote not only the increased use of African American troops but also their equal treatment in such issues as pay and promotion to officers' ranks.

Impact

There was a slow but steady shift in the viewpoint of the military hierarchy and the Lincoln administration regarding the use of African American troops. At first, blacks were relegated to such roles as digging trenches and defensive earthworks. Then they were armed and eventually allowed to fight. Chester's dispatches highlighted the bravery and

successes of the African American troops and must have helped convince a skeptical white public and administration that armed former slaves fighting for the Union cause posed no threat, other than to the Confederacy. By the end of the war some one hundred eighty-six thousand African Americans had served in the Union cause, fully 12 percent of the total of the Union's land forces—though it must be acknowledged that many were forced to "volunteer" at the point of a bayonet, for there was a bounty of $100 for every soldier an officer "recruited." The troops were segregated. The officers who commanded them were largely whites (only a hundred African Americans were commissioned as officers), and for the most part the African American soldiers received reduced pay compared to that of their white counterparts; oddly, African Americans who joined the Confederate army were given equal pay and equal rations. Nevertheless, Chester's dispatches from the Virginia front served as a constant reminder that African Americans were willing and able to participate in a war that would secure their freedom.

After the war, African American soldiers continued to provide meritorious service as the "Buffalo Soldiers," the name given to two cavalry regiments and two infantry regiments that took part in the Indian wars, built roads and forts in the West, escorted the mail, served as park rangers, and fought in the Spanish-American War. In all, the Buffalo Soldiers earned twenty-three Congressional Medals of Honor during the Indian wars. Black soldiers and sailors continued to be segregated through World War I and World War II until 1948, when President Harry S. Truman issued Executive Order 9981 desegregating the military.

See also Fugitive Slave Act of 1850; Frederick Douglass: "Men of Color, To Arms!" (1863); Emancipation Proclamation (1863); Executive Order 9981 (1948).

Further Reading

■ Articles

Eggert, Gerald G. "'Two Steps Forward a Step and a Half Back': Harrisburg's African American Community in the Nineteenth Century." *Pennsylvania History* 58, no. 1 (1991). Reprinted in Joe William Trotter, Jr., and Eric Ledell Smith, eds. *African Americans in Pennsylvania: Shifting Historical Perspectives.* University Park: Pennsylvania State University Press, 1997.

Finkelman, Paul. "Not Only the Judges' Robes Were Black: African-American Lawyers as Social Engineers." *Stanford Law Review* 47 (1994): 161–209.

■ Books

Blackett, R. J. M. *Thomas Morris Chester, Black Civil War Correspondent: His Dispatches from the Virginia Front.* 1989. Reprint, New York: Da Capo Press, 1991.

Cornish, Dudley Taylor. *The Sable Arm: Black Union Troops in the Union Army, 1861–1865*. Lawrence: University Press of Kansas, 1987.

Scott, John Weldon, and Eric Ledell Smith. *African Americans of Harrisburg*. Charleston, S.C.: Arcadia, 2005.

Slotkin, Richard. *No Quarter: The Battle of the Crater, 1864*. New York: Random House, 2009.

■ **Web Sites**

"Robert E. Lee's Position on Arming the Slaves." Son of the South Web site.
http://www.sonofthesouth.net/leefoundation/LettersAndrew-Hunter.htm.

—Keith E. Sealing

Questions for Further Study

1. What was the overall military strategy of the North in the final months of the Civil War? How did northern generals execute this strategy? How successful was it?

2. Imagine that you are at a gathering at which someone asserts that blacks should have fought in the Civil War, since the war was fought in large part to end slavery. How would you set the person straight? Be specific.

3. Some readers of Chester's dispatches might regard them as a form of "cheerleading." Although he criticized commanders who treated black troops poorly, overall his dispatches are filled with praise for both black and white troops. Do you believe he was perhaps exaggerating? If so, how would you justify that?

4. Chester was a proponent of the immigration of blacks to Africa and left the United States on several occasions. Yet he always returned. Why do you think he remained drawn to the United States?

5. Compare this document to Frederick Douglass's "Men of Color, To Arms!" Taken together, what picture of African Americans during the Civil War do the documents produce?

Thomas Morris Chester's Civil War Dispatches

Headquarters 10th Army Corps; Ten Miles from Richmond, August 18, 1864

Another step has been taken toward the rebel capital. Another warning has again disturbed the heavily-burdened consciences of the arch conspirators. Lieut. Gen. Grant is rapidly negotiating peace "on this line," and is daily despatching messengers towards Richmond, and into Petersburg, whose powerful reasonings even Jeff Davis will not be able to resist much longer.

Another battle has been fought, and a decided advantage has been gained. The troops, white and black, covered themselves with undying fame. Their conduct could not have been surpassed. The colored troops fully sustained the most exalted opinion which their ardent friends could possibly entertain. Major General Birney, commanding the 10th Army Corps remarked yesterday, without, however, wishing to do any injustice to the whites, that his colored soldiers had done handsomely. There was neither wavering nor straggling; but presenting a fearless front to the enemy, their conduct elicited especial remark, and excited admiration. A few more exhibitions of loyalty and bravery, as evinced during the past few days in this Corps, will soon eradicate the last vestige of prejudice and oppression from the grand Army of the Potomac. The circumstances which gave the colored troops, in conjunction with the others, the opportunity of a passage into public favor, are as follows: On the night of the 13th inst., in accordance with the masterly strategy of General Grant, a part of the 10th Corps crossed the James river at Deep Bottom, and on the 14th moved out on the Darbytown road, and, as a necessary precaution, indulged in skirmishing during the day. About 4 P.M., Brigadier General Wm. Birney commanding a division, sent seven companies of the 7th U. S. C. T., supported by a part of the 9th Regiment U. S. C. T., to retake a line of rifle pits on our left, which had been captured by Brigadier General Terry in the morning, and afterwards abandoned voluntarily by a mistake and reoccupied by the enemy. They sent up a shout of confidence, and, under the inspiration of their beloved commander, General Wm. Birney, the colored troops charged through a corn field and drove the rebels out of the rifle-pits. The enemy poured a heavy fire upon them, but was obliged to yield to their bravery. He was driven out, and we occupied them as a part of our defences. In this assault our loss was between fifty and sixty killed and wounded.

That night our forces moved from Deep Bottom, and took the position which they now occupy. It is an onward to Richmond movement, and thus far is regarded as a success. As speculations always tend to acquaint the enemy with our movements, I will add nothing more than the cheering prospect which now animated this grand army. The crowning act of the Commander-in-Chief may be the reduction of Richmond and Petersburg at the same time.

On the 16th, General Terry was directed to attack the line of the enemy's works on our left, and to drive him from his position. Brigadier General Birney was ordered to hold his division as a support to Brigadier General Terry. General Terry advanced, and drove the enemy out of the first line of rifle-pits, and then stormed the strong line of breastworks, suffering severe loss, but driving the enemy from his position. The rebs rallied, however, in overpowering numbers, to force General Terry to retreat in confusion. Finding himself gradually driven back by a greatly superior force his men acquitting themselves grandly amid a galling fire, Brigadier General Birney moved forward to his support, and with his troops, which consisted of the 2d and 3d Brigades of the 10th Corps, and the 9th U.S. colored troops, he advanced to the enemy's breastworks. The rebels then appeared in great numbers, advancing upon Gens. Birney's and Terry's forces, and a brisk fire was opened and continued on both sides. The enemy in attempting to take the breast works were repeatedly driven back with severe loss. The rebels finally succeeded, however, by moving their troops to our left; a portion of the breast works which had extended beyond our lines, and had not been carried by our forces. By this manoeuvre, they were enabled to pour a galling fire upon our flank and rear, and under which the men on the left were obliged to withdraw, not because they were whipped, but that the position was, under the circumstances, untenable.

General William Birney, after having twice filled the gaps caused by the giving way on the left, was unable to do so again without exposing his lines at other and more vital points. He gave the order to fall back to the first line of rifle-pits, which were captured from the enemy, which was accomplished in good order and without any confusion. The colored troops were the last to retire, which they did with unwavering firmness and in obedience to orders; not, however, before they gave three cheers, which evinced their dauntless spirit.

During this fighting the 3d Brigade, 21 Division, 10th A. C, lost one hundred and forty-eight men and officers, killed, wounded, and missing.

Colonel F. A. Osborn, 21th Massachusetts, was slightly wounded; Major Walroth, 115th New York, wounded in the side; Captain F. W. Parker, 4th N. H., wounded in the face. These officers were wounded while each was temporary commander of the 3d Brigade.

The 4th Regiment N. H. Volunteers lost three killed, thirty-two wounded, and fourteen missing. The killed are Corp. David W. Knox, Joseph Appleyard, and First Sergt. Edmund T. McNell.

The 115th N. Y. Volunteers lost four killed: Sergt. Frank M. Conner, Co. D.; Corp. Abort C. Meisgrove, Corp. J. H. Haynes, and First Sergt. F. W. Francisco; forty wounded, and fifteen missing.

The whole loss in this brigade is thirteen killed, ninety-one wounded, and forty-four missing, making a total of one hundred and forty-eight

♦ **Trophies**

The 10th Army Corps has captured during this flanking campaign four 8-inch siege guns, six colors, and over five hundred prisoners.

♦ **Flag of Truce**

Major General Birney requested, yesterday, a cessation of hostilities to allow him to recover his wounded and bury his dead, which were near the enemy's breastworks. It was conceded, and the time was fixed from four to six o'clock P.M. Major J. C. Briscoe and Captain Sweet, aide-de-camp to Major General Birney, and Lieut. Pancoast, ambulance officer, carried the flag of truce. It was received by Captain Rand, aide to General Ewell. Major Briscoe delivered the body of the rebel Gen. Chambliss, killed and remaining within our lines. The Major received our dead. During the existence of the flag of truce the rebel officers manifested no inclination to communicate with our officers. Their countenances wore an aspect of anxiety, not unmingled with chagrin and disappointment. The interchanging was of that formal nature which convinced the Union officers that the enemy was not in the enjoyment of good spirits, or were indulging in pleasing prospects.

♦ **Stripping the Union Dead**

As the hour approached for the cessation of hostilities, I mounted and advanced to the outer line of our works, to witness the bearing in of our honored dead. Two rows of men, several deep, extending far into the dense forest, formed a passage through which their comrades were now borne on stretchers. As each fallen hero was carried along this passage of brave men, even the solemnity of the scene could not restrain the indignation of the soldiers, as they witnessed the Union dead returned to them stripped of their shoes, coats, pants, and, in some instances, of their shirts. Those who were returned in their pants gave unmistakable evidence of having their pockets rifled—the pockets of which were turned inside out. The mutterings of the men were deep, and their feelings emphatically expressed on witnessing the respected dead dishonored. This act of ineffable meanness has nerved the hearts and strengthened the arms of the defenders of the Union, who will sweep from existence these enemies of God and civilization.

♦ **The Enemy Repulsed**

Last evening, just after the flag of truce returned, the enemy advanced in line of battle, and made a vigorous effort to turn our left flank, but were forced to retire. Later in the evening an effort was made to drive in our skirmishers, but without success. The firing was so severe for a few minutes that it much resembled the opening of a grand battle.

♦ **Slave Manacles**

The hurried manner in which the worshippers of the patriarchal institution were obliged to leave these parts for Richmond, compelled them to leave behind several articles which illustrate their character and their humanity. I am, through their haste, able to add to some one's collection two pair of manacles for the wrists, and one iron collar for the neck, which is fastened with a padlock, to which are several links of a chain to be attached, if necessary, to a similar necklace on an individual, by which means quite a number of men and women could be yoked together, single file, for any desirable length.

Headquarters 2d Brigade, 3d Division, 18th Army Corps; Before Petersburg, August 22, 1864

The hearts of the colored soldiers in this vicinity have been gladdened by the good news from the extreme left of the Army of the Potomac. Yesterday, about the time the church bells were inviting the inhabitants of your city to renew the assurances of their

Christianity, the loud report of cannon announced that once more the defenders of the Union had met its enemies in mortal combat.

◆ The Enemy Moving to the Left

As soon as the attack began, the enemy, plainly visible to the vigilant black troops in our front, began to hurry off troops to support the attempt which he had undertaken on our left. This information was, no doubt, duly attended to by the authorities.

◆ The Attack

The Weldon railroad having been severed, the enemy, finding an important advantage was gained by the commander-in-chief, sought, by a desperate assault, to drive him from his position, and permit, as heretofore, uninterrupted supplies to reach his army in and around Richmond and Petersburg. The enemy, by a well-conceived piece of strategy, manoeuvered to advance on our flank and rear. Insomuch they had gained an advantage, but the 5th Corps, under the immediate supervision of General Warren, fought with an unwavering firmness that withstood the several assaults of the enemy, and drove him into his jungle to mourn over his disaster—not, however, before three stand of colors and six hundred prisoners were captured.

Another attempt was made last night with renewed vigor, to force our army from its gained position, and in order that the enemy might obtain possession of the important rail communication which he lost. He was repulsed with severer loss than in the morning. Several stand of colors and one brigade were captured.

The rebels during Sunday morning and night fought desperately and furiously, and were only checked by the stubborn resistance which they encountered. General Grant, without weakening any part of his lines, has sent forward sufficient reinforcements to hold his position, and advance when he deems it necessary. A division of negro troops has also been given a position where the enemy will have an opportunity of testing their mettle, should he attempt again to recapture the Weldon railroad. Our losses in the engagements of yesterday were comparatively small, as later dates will corroborate.

◆ The Negro Troops before Petersburg

In General Butler's army there are many regiments of colored troops, who, thus far, have inspired confidence in their officers by the discipline and bearing which they have evinced under the incessant fire of the enemy, along the lines, and the handsome manner in which they have borne themselves whenever opportunity placed them in front of the rebels. It would not be extravagant to predict that they will yet accomplish more brilliant achievements. Their success will depend much on the character of the officers in immediate command. If the men are attached to them for their kindness and consideration on their behalf there is no doubt but what they will follow wherever their superiors may lead. So long as they are commanded by such accomplished gentlemen as Col. A. G. Draper, 36th U.S. Colored Troops, Lieut. Colonel Pratt, of the same regiment, and many other excellent officers whom I will credit when I shall speak of the regiments separately, there is not the least doubt but what they will fully meet public expectation.

In this connection it may not be inappropriate to speak, for the guidance of others, of the enthusiastic admiration of the colored troops under Gen. Wm. Birney for that gallant officer. They are all from Maryland, and were taken from the plantations of their former owners by the General, whom they regard as their deliverer. The General has implicit confidence in their fighting qualities. The highest praise that can be bestowed upon them is, that he prefers them rather than white troops. This is not a mental preference, for he has had the opportunity of electing, and chose to command colored soldiers. The secret of Gen. Birney's success is, that he treats his men as any other gallant officer would regard the defenders of the Union.

There are other colored troops from Maryland, obtained in the same way, but under a different class of officers, in the Army of the Potomac. I trust they will do all that is expected of them, but fear that the kind of men who command them has tended to demoralize rather than to inspire them. What Gen. Birney has done others may accomplish, if they do not regard it as humiliating to treat a negro patriot as a man, who offers himself a willing sacrifice upon his country's altar.

Those before Petersburg have the good fortune to be commanded by good men—though there are some black sheep among them—who are laboring to bring this branch of the service to the highest state of perfection. The kindness of the officers is reflected in the unflinching mettle of the men in the trying positions where duty calls them. There is not a day but what some brave black defender of the Union is made to bite the dust by a rebel sharpshooter or picket, but his place is immediately and cheerfully filled by another under the inspiring glance of such commanders as Colonels Wright, Pratt, and Acting

Brigadier General A. G. Draper. They are ever on the alert to catch a glimpse of a rebel, to whom they send their compliments by means of a leaden messenger. Between the negroes and the enemy it is war to the death. The colored troops have cheerfully accepted the conditions of the Confederate Government, that between them no quarter is to be shown. Those here have not the least idea of living after they fall into the hands of the enemy, and the rebels act very much as if they entertained similar sentiments with reference to the blacks. Even deserters fear to come into our lines where colored troops may be stationed. Not unfrequently have they asked if there are any black troops near, and if there were the rebs have entreated that they should not be permitted to harm them.

Such has been the effect of Jeff Davis' proclamation for the wholesale massacre of our colored troops, and such will it continue to be until the rebels shall treat all the defenders of the Union as prescribed by the rules of civilized warfare.

The military situation never was more encouraging. The Army of the Potomac during the past few days has successfully performed several strategic movements, which surprised the enemy and gave to us many important advantages. The successful "onward to Richmond," the severing of the Weldon railroad, by means of which the enemy has received all his supplies from the South, and the threatening demonstrations against Petersburg, each one of which is a grand campaign in itself, can be regard-

Glossary

Army of the Potomac	the Union force led by General George Meade, referring to the Potomac River
breastwork	any temporary fortification, such as walls or mounds of dirt, that is approximately breast high
Brigadier General Terry	Alfred Howe Terry, who later would assume command of the Tenth Corps when General David Birney died
Brigadier General Wm. Birney	William Birney, General David Birney's older brother and a commander of black troops
colors	the flag(s) carried by a military unit into battle
Deep Bottom	a colloquial name for an area in Virginia surrounded by a horseshoe bend in the James River
General Butler's army	the Army of the James, referring to the James River, commanded by General Benjamin Butler
General Warren	Gouverneur Kemble Warren, a former teacher of mathematics who had a reputation for bringing analytic calculation to his military command and who had played a key role in the Battle of Gettysburg
inst.	an abbreviation of "instant," meaning "this month"
Jeff Davis	Jefferson Davis, the president of the Confederate States of America
Lieut. Gen. Grant	Ulysses S. Grant, the commander of Union forces
Major General Birney	David Bell Birney, the commander of the Tenth Army Corps
Petersburg	a vital railroad hub to the south of Richmond, Virginia
rebel capital	Richmond, Virginia, the capital of the Confederacy during the Civil War
rebs	a common abbreviation of "rebel" applied to Confederates
U.S.C.T.	United States Colored Troops

ed as nothing less than the successful accomplishment of a masterly mind. When or where next the commander-in-chief will suddenly appear is a matter which, under the circumstances, should be left to the development of his strategy. Advancing on several points at the same time will effectually checkmate the enemy. One of his principal means of maintaining his position in different parts of the country has been the celerity with which he has been able to move great bodies of troops to places which our army was about to attack. Everything betokens success. The army is in the best of spirits. The colored soldiers are not only ready, but are anxious to meet the rebels.

GENERAL WILLIAM T. SHERMAN.

William Tecumseh Sherman (Library of Congress)

WILLIAM T. SHERMAN'S SPECIAL FIELD ORDER NO. 15

1865

"Each family shall have a plot of not more than

(40) forty acres of tillable ground."

Overview

On January 16, 1865, three months before General Robert E. Lee's surrender at Appomattox Court House, Virginia, Major General William Tecumseh Sherman, commander of the Military Division of the Mississippi in Savannah, Georgia, issued his controversial Special Field Order No. 15. The field order was inspired principally by the Union general's determination to rid his army of the large number of escaped, destitute, and homeless slaves who accompanied his army's flanks as it marched across Georgia during his famous raid to the sea of the autumn of 1864. Sherman's order set aside "the islands from Charleston, south, the abandoned rice fields along the rivers for thirty miles back from the sea, and the country bordering the St. Johns River, Florida," for the exclusive settlement of slave refugees. Sherman instructed Brigadier General Rufus Saxton to make available to each head of a black family forty acres of land and to "furnish ... subject to the approval of the President of the United States, a possessory title." The army was also to supply the freedpeople with farm animals.

Context

Southern slavery deteriorated as an institution during the Civil War as Union troops enveloped the Confederacy, forever changing the South's economic and social landscape. Because of a lack of consistent reporting and conflicting or nonexistent sources, historians cannot compute accurately the number of African Americans set in motion by the federal invasion and occupation, but they know that by early 1865 as few as five hundred thousand and as many as a million fugitive slaves and free black refugees sought the protection of Union troops and resided within Union lines. Contemporaries termed these people "contrabands" or "freedmen." They participated in large numbers in federally sponsored activities in occupied territory, toiling as soldiers, laborers, residents of contraband camps, and urban workers, and on farms and plantations under federal supervision. Based on the approximation of one million displaced

persons, refugees are estimated to have numbered 13,000 on the Eastern Shore of Virginia; 70,000 throughout Virginia's Tidewater region; 17,300 in North Carolina; 25,000 in South Carolina; 106,000 in Louisiana; and 770,000 in the Mississippi Valley.

In the late fall of 1864, as General Sherman and his 62,000-man force marched southeastward from Atlanta to Savannah, the number of black refugees accompanying his army multiplied quickly. According to the historian Willie Lee Rose, "Behind his army followed an ever-increasing throng of liberated Negroes, seeking freedom and security somewhere beyond the confines of the home plantation, perhaps on the coastal islands, waiting quietly in the declining autumn sunlight." Sherman discouraged the refugees, especially the old, young, and sick, from following his army, believing that caring for the indigent would slow his progress, prove deleterious to his soldiers' morale, and compromise his soldiers' effectiveness as a fighting force.

In correspondence dated January 11, 1865, the general lectured Secretary of the Treasury Salmon P. Chase, who had chided Sherman for treating the freedpeople "as a set of pariahs, almost without rights." Responding to this charge, Sherman explained that as he approached Savannah, his force was encumbered by "the crowds of helpless negros that flock after our armies." He complained that "at least 20,000 negros" were "clogging my roads, and eating up our subsistence." Sherman professed that he was unbiased toward blacks, asserting that he would treat white and black refugees equally in the case of their posing "a military weakness."

No racial egalitarian, Sherman defined the role of the army as being to suppress the slaveholders' rebellion and treason, not to emancipate slaves or to provide humanitarian relief to freedpeople. While he was not opposed to the freeing of the South's slaves per se, Sherman nonetheless objected to what he considered the inordinate influence of political abolitionism and abolitionists on President Abraham Lincoln and his administration. Sherman also was among the most vocal of military men to oppose the employment of African Americans as armed soldiers. He reasoned that once black men served as soldiers they would demand full equality, a condition that Sherman considered a threat to white supremacy. At best he favored using black soldiers as "surplus" troops, in labor battalions. Like many

WILLIAM T. SHERMAN'S SPECIAL FIELD ORDER NO. 15   **599**

Time Line

1863

■ **January 1**
President Abraham Lincoln issues the final Emancipation Proclamation, declaring free all slaves in territory remaining in a state of rebellion.

1864

■ **December 21**
After marching his army across Georgia, General William T. Sherman captures Savannah, Georgia, for the Union.

1865

■ **January 16**
Sherman issues Special Field Order No. 15, on the resettlement of freedpeople.

■ **March 3**
Congress establishes the Bureau of Refugees, Freedmen, and Abandoned Lands, known as the Freedmen's Bureau.

■ **April 9**
General Robert E. Lee surrenders the Confederacy's major army at Appomattox Court House, Virginia, to General Ulysses S. Grant.

■ **April 14**
John Wilkes Booth shoots President Lincoln, who dies the next day.

■ **April 15**
Vice President Andrew Johnson becomes president.

■ **September 12**
As ordered by President Johnson, the Freedmen's Bureau commissioner General Oliver O. Howard issues a circular retracting land contracts to blacks and restoring land to pardoned insurgents.

1866

■ **June 21**
Congress passes the Southern Homestead Act, making public land available for sale at low prices.

■ **July 16**
Congress passes the second Freedmen's Bureau Act over President Johnson's veto, ensuring continued land availability.

---

whites of his day, the general perceived the freedmen and women as inferiors and as "problems," as distractions who impeded his work and complicated his military objectives. Whenever possible, Sherman put tools, not weapons, in the hands of black men. He preferred having them work as baggage handlers, ditch diggers, fatigue laborers, fortification builders, lumbermen, servants, and stevedores—not as soldiers. Sherman employed black women as cooks, laundresses, nurses, and servants.

Although Sherman and his men shunned the role of "liberators," the freedpeople of Georgia and South Carolina nonetheless considered the Yankees an army of liberation. They crowded the Union lines for protection from their Confederate masters and relief from fatigue, hunger, sickness, winter cold, and rain. In January the general boasted to Treasury Secretary Chase that far from viewing him as a devil, the freedmen and women "regard me as a second Moses or Aaron. I treat them as free, and have as much trouble to protect them against the avaricious recruiting agents of New England States as against their former masters."

Through March almost one hundred new black refugees would reach the coast each day, adding ten thousand freedpeople to an already swollen and impoverished African American population requiring clothing, food, medicine, shelter, and firewood. Northern observers, largely abolitionists and missionaries, reported numerous cases of Sherman's white soldiers abusing, cheating, and robbing the vulnerable freedpeople, whom they considered ignorant "niggers." "Sherman and his men," reported Arthur Sumner, a teacher-turned-plantation superintendent, "are impatient of darkies, and annoyed to see them so pampered, petted, and spoiled, as they have been here."

On January 11, 1865, responding to reports of the refugees' destitution and the mistreatment of freedpeople by Sherman's troops, Secretary of War Edwin M. Stanton arrived in Savannah to assess the situation for himself. Brusque, businesslike, and unawed by, if not resentful of, powerful military officers like Sherman, Stanton underscored the sovereignty of civilian authority over the army. The two men had tangled previously over Sherman's opposition to the arming of blacks as soldiers. Upon arriving in Savannah, Stanton insisted on interviewing an array of black leaders to gain a clear sense of the social conditions and status of the coastal freedpeople, to assess Sherman's humanitarian efforts on behalf of the freedpeople in his charge, and to gauge the degree to which Sherman protected the blacks' rights. To accomplish this, the secretary of war spoke with African American clergymen, plantation foremen, barbers, pilots, and sailors to gain their perspectives on the conditions of the thousands of refugees who crowded coastal South Carolina and Georgia.

The black leaders shared their concerns candidly with Stanton, informing him that they preferred settling in black communities apart from whites. Sherman later recalled that the freedpeople claimed to favor living in black settlements, "for there is a prejudice against us in the South that it will take years to get over." The secretary of war also polled the blacks regarding their attitude to-

---

MILESTONE DOCUMENTS IN AFRICAN AMERICAN HISTORY

Sketch of contrabands accompanying the line of Sherman's march through Georgia, from Frank Leslie's Illustrated Newspaper of March 1865 (Library of Congress)

ward Sherman, specifically whether or not the general had manifested "an almost *criminal* dislike" of people of color and had cruelly undermined their efforts to accompany his army's trek across Georgia.

For his part, Sherman dismissed Stanton as an errand boy of the Lincoln administration, at best a political hack. Writing to his wife on January 15, a day before issuing his Special Field Order No. 15, the general remarked, "Stanton has been here and is cured of that Negro nonsense which arises not from a love of the negro but a desire to dodge Service." Sherman opposed arming blacks, he wrote, because he wanted "soldiers made of the best bone & muscle in the land and wont attempt military feats with doubtful materials." Sherman continued: "I have said that Slavery is dead and the Negro free and want him treated as free & not hunted & badgered to make a soldier of when his family is left back on the plantation. I am right & wont Change."

In his *Memoirs* Sherman remarked,

It certainly was a strange fact that the great War Secretary should have catechized negroes concerning the character of a general who had commanded a hundred thousand men in battle, had captured cities, conducted sixty-five thousand men successfully across four hundred miles of hostile territory, and had just brought tens of thousand of freedmen to a place of security.

No doubt to Stanton's great surprise and utter disappointment, the black leaders praised Sherman's work with the freedpeople, stating their "inexpressible gratitude" for his efforts on their behalf. Soon after, on January 16, Sherman issued, with Stanton's imprimatur, Special Field Order No. 15.

About the Author

William Tecumseh Sherman was born on February 8, 1820, in Lancaster, Ohio. He graduated from the U.S. Military Academy at West Point, in New York, in 1840. After serving in Florida and South Carolina, Sherman left the military to tour the southern states, gaining especially rich knowledge of the geography of the Mississippi Valley and Georgia. After rejoining the army, Sherman served during the Mexican-American War and in the Pacific Division before resigning again to work as a banker, as a lawyer, and in real estate. In 1859 Sherman assumed the superintendency of the Louisiana State Seminary of Learning and Military Academy.

Following the Confederacy's attack on Fort Sumter in April 1861, Sherman once again returned to the army, rising by May 1862 from colonel to major general of volunteers and serving at the First Battle of Bull Run, in the defense of Kentucky, and at the Battle of Shiloh, in Tennessee. Sherman next commanded the defenses of Memphis

> *"The three parties named will subdivide the land, under the supervision of the Inspector, among themselves ... so that each family shall have a plot of not more than (40) forty acres of tillable ground, ... with not more than 800 feet water front, in the possession of which land the military authorities will afford them protection, until ... they can protect themselves, or until Congress shall regulate their title."*
>
> (Clause III)

> *"In order to carry out this system of settlement, a general officer will be detailed as Inspector of Settlements and Plantations, whose duty it shall be to visit the settlements, to regulate their police and general management, and who will furnish personally to each head of a family, subject to the approval of the President of the United States, a possessory title in writing, giving as near as possible the description of boundaries."*
>
> (Clause V)

and fought at Chickasaw Bayou, Arkansas Post, and Vicksburg before assuming leadership of the Army of the Tennessee in October 1863 and then overall command of western troops in March 1864. From March 1864 to June 1865 Sherman led the Military Division of the Mississippi and orchestrated the attack from lower Tennessee into Georgia that culminated in the fall of Atlanta on September 2. This victory occasioned Sherman's promotion to major general in the regular army.

After resting his troops for ten weeks, Sherman dispatched part of his force under Major General George H. Thomas to engage Confederate forces in Tennessee. On November 15, Sherman oversaw a march southeast across Georgia by two columns of infantry and cavalry that covered 250 miles in twenty-six days. With the army traversing central Georgia in a forty- to sixty-mile-wide front, Sherman's men left a swath of destruction in their wake, disrupting communications, destroying government buildings, laying waste crops, and desolating railroads and agricultural equipment. Unquestionably his use of "hard" war—employing the selective destruction of military and civilian targets and psychological warfare in his Georgia and later Carolinas campaigns—helped break the Confederates' will to fight. Sherman's famous "March to the Sea" ended on December 21, when he and his troops entered Savannah. This campaign left white Georgians angry and stunned, while black Georgians stood emancipated and hungry for the fruits of freedom.

Following the war Sherman remained in the army and openly sympathized with the fate of white southerners, not blacks; he opposed the granting of civil and political rights to freedpeople. Sherman commanded the Military Division of the Mississippi, provided military support for the construction of the transcontinental railroad, and participated in the campaigns waged against American Indians. In 1866 Sherman was promoted to lieutenant general and placed in temporary command of the U.S. Army. Following Ulysses S. Grant's assuming the presidency in 1869, Sherman was promoted to full general and appointed commanding general of the army. He retired in 1884 and died on February 14, 1891. Historians continue to debate Sherman's contributions to "total" or "modern" warfare and rely upon his frank, two-volume *Memoirs of General William T. Sherman* (1875) as an important primary source.

Although he was an Ohio native, Sherman shared the conservative, antiblack, proslavery views of many of his southern friends and comrades in the army, holding contempt multilaterally for African Americans, abolitionists, and southern disunionists. According to the historian Louis Gerteis, the general "despised blacks and secessionists equally" and "scornfully dismissed Northern humanitarian concerns with the freedmen's welfare." Seemingly unabashed, he publicly opposed the Emancipation Proclamation, the recruitment of African American soldiers, and what Sherman considered the granting of special privileges to people of color. The Reverend Henry M. Turner, a free black man from South Carolina who served as chaplain in the U.S. Colored Troops and later as a state congressman in Georgia, dubbed a commander who shared what he termed the general's "ignoble prejudice" to be nothing more than a "*Shermanized* officer."

Sherman expressed his antipathy toward blacks in general and escaped bondsmen in particular early in the war in his personal correspondence. In July 1862, while commanding in Memphis, Tennessee, he complained to his wife of being bombarded by loyal masters who sought military assistance in tracking down their escaped slaves. "As to freeing the negros," Sherman continued,

> I don't think the time is come yet—when Negros are liberated either they or their masters must perish. They cannot exist together except in their present relation, and to expect negros to change from Slaves to masters without one of those horrible convulsions which at times Startle the world is absurd.

A year later Sherman explained to his brother that blacks proved unreliable as servants and he opposed their recruitment as armed soldiers. "I wont trust niggers to fight yet," he said, "but dont object to the Government taking them from the Enemy, & making such use of them as experience may suggest."

Writing in September 1864, Sherman summarized his attitude toward the granting of civil rights to African Americans: "I like niggers *well enough* as niggers, but when fools & idiots try & make niggers better than ourselves, I have an opinion." When asked rhetorically whether blacks might not stop Confederate bullets as well as whites, the general retorted: "Yes, and a sand bag is better; but can a negro do our skirmishing and picket duty? … Can they improvise roads, bridges, sorties, flank movements, etc. like the white man? I say no." Shortly after the war, in May 1865, Sherman found himself embroiled in a controversy over the surrender terms he had offered Confederate troops in North Carolina; the general wrote his wife, "Stanton wants to kill me because I do not favor his scheme of declaring the Negroes of the South, now free, to be loyal voters, whereby politicians may manufacture just so much pliable electioneering material."

Explanation and Analysis of the Document

Despite Sherman's antipathy toward blacks and their rights, his Special Field Order No. 15 represented an overarching, positive, and radical step toward settling the freedpeople on abandoned plantation lands. Ironically, as Gerteis explains, "the most thoroughgoing program for blacks" along coastal South Carolina and Georgia "came not from Radicals or self-proclaimed friends of the freedmen, but from … Sherman, a battlefield general with an ill-concealed distaste for blacks and for those laboring among them." The scholar Paul Cimbala explains that Sherman, "no philanthropist or reformer, was primarily concerned with pursu-

ing Confederates into South Carolina. He needed to rid his army of the thousands of slaves who had marched along in its train." A third historian, John Syrett, maintains that although Sherman issued the field orders, "Stanton and Saxton were doubtless chiefly responsible for their content." Regardless, the order incorporated a multitiered solution to solving what Sherman judged a "Negro problem" resulting from emancipation.

From Sherman's perspective, the resettlement of the freedpeople on abandoned plantations offered several advantages. First, so doing would free his army from what he considered the logistical annoyance posed by the thousands of black refugees burdening his troops and crowding along the southeastern Atlantic coast. Second, allowing the freedpeople to occupy abandoned plantations would shift the cost of supporting the newly free men and women from the federal government to their former masters. Third, settling the freedpeople on coastal land would render them (and U.S. forces) less vulnerable to attacks by Confederate cavalry and guerrillas. Finally, a positive, fostering program for the freedpeople would serve to assuage Sherman's critics on the race question. While Sherman was no doubt influenced by pressure from Chase, Stanton, and black leaders to accommodate the freedpeople, his special order stemmed largely from his determination to liberate himself from dealing with the freedpeople, which he considered a military necessity. Accordingly, in the order of January 16, Sherman opens by declaring in clause I that the Sea Island region, extending from Charleston, South Carolina, south to the Saint Johns River in northern Florida, and the coastal lands thirty miles inland along rivers were to be reserved solely for African American settlers. Thousands of acres of additional abandoned land would thus be available to black refugees.

Clause II reserved exclusively for people of color the Sea Islands between Charleston and Jacksonville as well as other settlements carved out in the newly established reservation. Sherman's order also specified that blacks would manage their own affairs in their communities, subject only to the army and the U.S. Congress. This clause underscored the blacks' freedom and stated that the freedmen could not be coerced into military units without specific orders from the president or congress. Nevertheless, Sherman's field order stated that young freedmen were to be encouraged to enlist in units of the U.S. Colored Troops and receive bounties upon enlistment.

In clause III, Sherman articulated the process by which freedmen could settle and establish agricultural operations. In order to do so, "three respectable negroes, heads of families" would petition government officials for a license and then subdivide the land in plots no larger than forty acres of tillable ground and, if bounding water, no more than eight hundred feet of waterfront. Precedent for the forty-acre limitation stemmed from President Lincoln's directive of December 31, 1863, to South Carolina's Direct Tax Commission. The military would protect the freedmen, if necessary, until they could protect themselves and until Congress would legitimize their land titles. The military also would make ships available to the freedmen to assist them in supplying themselves and selling their crops.

Clause IV stated that families of men serving in the U.S. Colored Troops, aboard gunboats, or engaged in commercial fishing or as pilots could settle on plots in the Sherman reservation. According to the fifth clause of the special field order, the blacks were to receive temporary "possessory" title to the abandoned land until the government could uphold their permanent ownership of the land. Clause VI appointed General Saxton to oversee the blacks' settlement of what became known as the Sherman Reserve.

Audience

Sherman's field order held foremost significance to the freedpeople along the coast who hoped that freedom would translate into land ownership and more than the right to labor for others. Like the freed black men and women, Radical Republicans, former abolitionists, and sympathetic military commanders interpreted the general's field order, followed by the land provisions of the 1865 Freedmen's Bureau Act and the 1866 Southern Homestead Act, as confiscating the rich estates of former rebels and redistributing them to their former slaves. The *New York Tribune*, however, a supporter of emancipation, opposed Sherman's edict based on the fact that it segregated blacks from whites. Southern whites uniformly condemned Sherman's order and sought to reclaim their property through legal means. In the years since Sherman issued Special Field Order No. 15, black activists from W. E. B. Du Bois to contemporary reparationists have identified the order as a promise of "forty acres and a mule"—their rallying cry for compensation for their ancestors' centuries of bondage and institutionalized degradation.

Impact

Despite the assertion in Sherman's Special Field Order No. 15 that freedpeople would be granted "possessory" titles to land, the land provision in the March 1865 Freedmen's Bureau Act made clear that the freedpeople could occupy and rent—but not receive as reparation—up to forty acres of abandoned and occupied land for three years. The refugees could purchase the land based on whatever titles could be provided. In June 1865, General Saxton reported that approximately forty thousand blacks had settled on about 485,000 acres of land. The Freedmen's Bureau then controlled approximately 858,000 acres of land—only roughly 1 percent of the land in the Confederacy.

Sherman's linguistic vagueness encouraged contemporary blacks and their white friends to believe that the government would ultimately grant the freedpeople the land they occupied. But two essential factors—the ambiguity of Sherman's reference to "possessory" titles and President Andrew Johnson's insistence in September 1865 that confiscated land in the Sherman Reserve (except that sold under a court decree) be restored to pardoned former Confeder-

ates—undercut all but the symbolic meaning of Sherman's order. Indeed, not surprisingly, Sherman's murky language left contemporary white southerners hopeful of reclaiming their land, through legal action if necessary. In 1866 the process of restoring land to white claimants began, as the freedpeople proved unsuccessful in providing valid "possessory titles" in line with the wording of Sherman's order. On January 31, 1866, the Freedmen's Bureau held only about 464,000 acres of land; by February 1866, bureau officials had already restored 393,000 acres to whites who had received presidential pardons and had successfully proved prior ownership.

Thus, few of the freedpeople who claimed farms in the Sherman Reserve were ultimately allowed to retain their land. Upon General Saxton fell the burden of informing the freedpeople that they would have to surrender the land they occupied. According to the general, by reneging on its promise to distribute land to the freedpeople, the government was violating a solemn pledge. He observed that the former slaves' "love of the soil and desire to own farms amounts to a passion—it appears to be the dearest hope of their lives." For his part, in February 1866 Sherman informed the president,

I knew of course we could not convey title to land and merely provided 'possessory titles' to be good so long as war and our Military Power lasted. I merely aimed to make provision for the negroes who were absolutely dependent on us, leaving the value of their possessions to be determined by after events or legislation.

In his postwar memoirs Sherman recalled that

the military authorities at that day ... had a perfect right to grant the possession of any vacant land to which they could extend military protection, but we did not undertake to give a fee-simple title; and all that was designed by these special field orders was to make temporary provisions for the freedmen and their families during the rest of the war, or until Congress should take action in the premises.

Sherman added that Stanton approved his field order before he announced it. As W. E. B. Du Bois lamented in 1935, Sherman thus had literally given the freedpeople on the Sherman Reserve "only possessory titles, and in the end, the government broke its implied promise and drove them off the land."

Two later pieces of Reconstruction-era legislation continued the "implied promise" of government land grants and complicated understanding of Sherman's field order for generations. First, the Southern Homestead Act of June 1866 set aside public land in Alabama, Arkansas, Florida, Louisiana, and Mississippi for purchase by freedpeople for a five-dollar fee. The available land, however, was generally of inferior quality, and freedmen lacked sufficient capital to purchase implements and to farm the land properly. When Congress repealed the act in 1876, blacks had cultivated only several thousand acres, mostly in Florida. Second, the July 1866 Freedmen's Bureau Act essentially authorized the government to lease, though not grant outright, twenty-acre lots on government-controlled lands with a six-year option to buy the land. Only some fourteen hundred persons took advantage of this option. By August 1868 the Freedmen's Bureau controlled less than 140,000 acres of land. At best, then, the federal government's Reconstruction-era land policy amounted to an opportunity for former slaves to lease family farms with the later option to buy the property.

In the end, for all of the controversy Sherman's field order generated, it resulted in frightfully little land distributed to freedpeople. In November 1867, General Oliver O. Howard reported that 1,980 heads of families in Beaufort, South Carolina, had paid the government $31,000 for 19,040 acres. Many blacks who settled on their forty acres refused to surrender their claims to the white landowners and ultimately were removed forcibly by the Freedmen's Bureau and the army. Others squatted on marginal land, determined to scratch out a living on unimproved soil. Most black refugees on the Sherman Reserve surrendered their claims and moved elsewhere to work on shares or as tenants on land owned by whites. Writing in 1893, a former missionary to the freedpeople, Elizabeth Hyde Botume, recalled that the freed slaves "regarded the return of the former owners as an inauguration of the old slavery times, with the worst consequences."

Ever since Reconstruction, misreadings and distortions of Sherman's Special Field Order No. 15 by historians and polemicists have fueled demands for reparations by African Americans and their white allies. Repeatedly and erroneously, reparationists have cited Sherman's order as the origin of the U.S. government's alleged promise of "forty acres and a mule." In fact, Sherman's order was never intended to award land to the freedpeople. At best it was the general's short-term strategy to alleviate what he considered the military problem of dealing with the burden of thousands of freedpeople in his army's midst.

Confusion over the awarding of "land for the freedmen" continues today. Proponents of reparations maintain that the government reneged on its wartime pledge to compensate the former slaves for their centuries of bondage with land and animals. Many persons still believe that the so-called promise of "forty acres and a mule" justifies African Americans' appeals for a broad range of compensation—from cash payments to tax credits—for the descendants of America's four million black slaves. They point to Sherman's Special Field Order No. 15 and "forty acres and a mule" as symbols of the government's broken promises and the freed slaves' shattered dreams.

See also Emancipation Proclamation (1863).

Questions for Further Study

1. Describe Sherman's attitude toward African Americans. Was he simply a racist, a liberator, or something between the two? To what extent do you believe his attitude might have been similar to that of many northerners?

2. Sherman opposed the employment of black troops. Compare this document with Thomas Morris Chester's Civil War Dispatches and the events surrounding it. Do you believe that Sherman might have been convinced by Chester's reports?

3. In your opinion, did Sherman's order represent genuine progress or just a symbolic victory for African Americans in the wake of the Civil War?

4. Some northern abolitionists criticized Sherman's order because it created segregated black communities. Others, however, saw it as a form of reparations for slavery. Which do you believe is the more defensible position?

5. Throughout history, invading armies have attracted large numbers of camp followers, including prostitutes, destitute people, curious onlookers, and those who hoped to earn money or subsistence by performing services for the armies. What made the problem of camp followers of Sherman's army unique?

Further Reading

■ Articles

Cox, LaWanda. "The Promise of Land for the Freedmen." *Mississippi Valley Historical Review* 45 (December 1958): 413–440.

Drago, Edmund L. "How Sherman's March through Georgia Affected the Slaves." *Georgia Historical Quarterly* 57 (Fall 1973): 361–375.

Pope, Christie Farnham. "Southern Homesteads for Negroes." *Agricultural History* 44 (April 1970): 201–212.

Smith, John David. "The Enduring Myth of 'Forty Acres and a Mule.'" *Chronicle of Higher Education*, February 21, 2003, p. B11.

Westley, Robert. "Many Billions Gone: Is It Time to Reconsider the Case for Black Reparations?" *Boston College Law Review* 40 (December 1998): 429–476.

■ Books

Berlin, Ira, ed. *Freedom: A Documentary History of Emancipation, 1861–1867*, Series 1, Vol. 2: *The Wartime Genesis of Free Labor: The Upper South*. Cambridge, U.K.: Cambridge University Press, 1993.

Botume, Elizabeth Hyde. *First Days amongst the Contrabands*. 1893. Reprint. New York: Arno Press, 1968.

Cimbala, Paul A. *The Freedmen's Bureau: Reconstructing the American South after the Civil War*. Malabar, Fla.: Krieger Publishing, 2005.

Du Bois, W. E. B. *Black Reconstruction in America: An Essay toward a History of the Part Which Black Folk Played in the Attempt to Reconstruct Democracy in America, 1860–1880*. 1935. Reprint. New York: Atheneum, 1973.

Gerteis, Louis S. *From Contraband to Freedman: Federal Policy toward Southern Blacks, 1861–1865*. Westport, Conn.: Greenwood Press, 1973.

Marszalek, John F. *Sherman: A Soldier's Passion for Order*. New York: Free Press, 1993.

———. *Sherman's Other War: The General and the Civil War Press*. Memphis, Tenn.: Memphis State University Press, 1981.

Oubre, Claude F. *Forty Acres and a Mule: The Freedmen's Bureau and Black Land Ownership*. Baton Rouge: Louisiana State University Press, 1978.

Rose, Willie Lee. *Rehearsal for Reconstruction: The Port Royal Experiment*. New York: Vintage Books, 1967.

Sherman, William Tecumseh. *Memoirs of General W. T. Sherman*. 2 vols. New York: Library of America, 1990.

Simpson, Brooks D., and Jean V. Berlin, eds. *Sherman's Civil War: Selected Correspondence of William T. Sherman, 1860–1865*. Chapel Hill: University of North Carolina Press, 1999.

Syrett, John. *The Civil War Confiscation Acts: Failing to Reconstruct the South*. New York: Fordham University Press, 2005.

Westwood, Howard C. *Black Troops, White Commanders, and Freedmen during the Civil War*. Carbondale: Southern Illinois University Press, 1992.

—John David Smith

WILLIAM T. SHERMAN'S SPECIAL FIELD ORDER NO. 15

I. The islands from Charleston, south, the abandoned rice fields along the rivers for thirty miles back from the sea, and the country bordering the St. Johns River, Florida, are reserved and set apart for the settlement of the negroes now made free by the acts of war and the proclamation of the President of the United States.

II. At Beaufort, Hilton Head, Savannah, Fernandina, St. Augustine and Jacksonville, the blacks may remain in their chosen or accustomed vocations—but on the islands, and in the settlements hereafter to be established, no white person whatever, unless military officers and soldiers detailed for duty, will be permitted to reside; and the sole and exclusive management of affairs will be left to the freed people themselves, subject only to the United States military authority and the acts of Congress. By the laws of war, and orders of the President of the United States, the negro is free and must be dealt with as such. He cannot be subjected to conscription or forced military service, save by the written orders of the highest military authority of the Department, under such regulations as the President or Congress may prescribe. Domestic servants, blacksmiths, carpenters and other mechanics, will be free to select their own work and residence, but the young and able-bodied negroes must be encouraged to enlist as soldiers in the service of the United States, to contribute their share towards maintaining their own freedom, and securing their rights as citizens of the United States.

Negroes so enlisted will be organized into companies, battalions and regiments, under the orders of the United States military authorities, and will be paid, fed and clothed according to law. The bounties paid on enlistment may, with the consent of the recruit, go to assist his family and settlement in procuring agricultural implements, seed, tools, boots, clothing, and other articles necessary for their livelihood.

III. Whenever three respectable negroes, heads of families, shall desire to settle on land, and shall have selected for that purpose an island or a locality clearly defined, within the limits above designated, the Inspector of Settlements and Plantations will himself, or by such subordinate officer as he may appoint, give them a license to settle such island or district, and afford them such assistance as he can to enable them to establish a peaceable agricultural settlement. The three parties named will subdivide the land, under the supervision of the Inspector, among themselves and such others as may choose to settle near them, so that each family shall have a plot of not more than (40) forty acres of tillable ground, and when it borders on some water channel, with not more than 800 feet water front, in the possession of which land the military authorities will afford them protection, until such time as they can protect themselves, or until Congress shall regulate their title. The Quartermaster may, on the requisition of the Inspector of Settlements and Plantations, place at the disposal of the Inspector, one or more of the captured steamers, to ply between the settlements and one or more of the commercial points heretofore named in orders, to afford the settlers the opportunity to supply their necessary wants, and to sell the products of their land and labor.

IV. Whenever a negro has enlisted in the military service of the United States, he may locate his family in any one of the settlements at pleasure, and acquire a homestead, and all other rights and privileges of a settler, as though present in person. In like manner, negroes may settle their families and engage on board the gunboats, or in fishing, or in the navigation of the inland waters, without losing any claim to land or other advantages derived from this system. But no one, unless an actual settler as above defined, or unless absent on Government service, will be entitled to claim any right to land or property in any settlement by virtue of these orders.

V. In order to carry out this system of settlement, a general officer will be detailed as Inspector of Settlements and Plantations, whose duty it shall be to visit the settlements, to regulate their police and general management, and who will furnish personally to each head of a family, subject to the approval of the President of the United States, a possessory title in writing, giving as near as possible the description of boundaries; and who shall adjust all claims or conflicts that may arise under the same, subject to the like approval, treating such titles altogether as possessory. The same general officer will also be charged with the enlistment and organization of the negro recruits, and protecting their interests while absent from their settlements; and will be governed by the rules and regulations prescribed by the War Department for such purposes.

VI. Brigadier General R. SAXTON is hereby appointed Inspector of Settlements and Plantations, and will at once enter on the performance of his duties. No change is intended or desired in the settlement now on Beaufort [Port Royal] Island, nor will any rights to property heretofore acquired be affected thereby.

By Order of Major General W. T. Sherman

"Every freedman, free negro and mulatto shall ... have a lawful home or employment, and shall have written evidence thereof."

Overview

In 1865 the Mississippi state legislature passed a series of related laws known as the Black Code. These laws, written within months of the conclusion of the Civil War and styled after the state's antebellum slave code, represented the first effort by white Mississippians to define what freedom and citizenship would mean to recently freed slaves and others of African descent. As the Black Code reveals, the initial legal definition that whites offered suggests that they intended the condition of freedom for blacks to differ little from enslavement.

The Mississippi Black Code was the most extreme example of similar codes that sought to nullify the freedom of former slaves and to define their citizenship as virtual enslavement. The laws consequently offer an example of the attitudes of whites toward freedpeople and other people of African descent; they also testify to the persistence of those attitudes across time. Finally, the Black Code is significant because its existence proved to the U.S. Congress that southern states needed a more thoroughgoing reconstruction than that called for by President Andrew Johnson. A year after the passage of the Black Code, Congress assumed authority over Reconstruction in the southern states.

Context

In April 1865, after four years of fighting and deprivation, the Civil War ended. The cessation of fighting, however, did not firmly settle the end of their social system in white southerners' minds. The lack of commitment to black freedom in Washington, D.C., and among white southerners meant that former slaves could not easily acquire citizenship. By the conclusion of 1865, Mississippi, abetted by the U.S. president, offered firm evidence that white southerners, while reluctantly granting the abolition of slavery, refused to grant African Americans equality before the law.

An assassin took the life of President Abraham Lincoln within days of the war's end. Lincoln's generous plan for ensuring the return of the southern states to the Union fell into the hands of his successor, Andrew Johnson. The new president, a native of east Tennessee, significantly modified Lincoln's plan for Reconstruction by adding provisions intended to punish the elite planters of the South, whom he blamed for the secession crisis and the Civil War. In addition to depriving wealthy southerners and certain former Confederates of the right to citizenship, Johnson insisted that before southern states reenter the Union they repeal their secession ordinances and ratify the Thirteenth Amendment to the U.S. Constitution, which ended slavery.

Johnson's plan for Reconstruction, however, was ultimately undemanding. Even though he wished to punish certain Confederate officials and officers as well as wealthy planters, he refused to require that southern states embrace liberal notions of African American citizenship. In an August 1865 letter to Mississippi's provisional governor, William Sharkey, Johnson encouraged him to lead the state constitutional convention, which was meeting at the time, to grant the right to vote only to individuals who could read and write and to owners of property valued at a minimum of $250. Since few, if any, former slaves or African Americans living in Mississippi owned taxable property (real estate) of any sort and few could read and write, Johnson's vision of voting rights in the post-Emancipation era did not include extension of suffrage to more than a handful of blacks. Regarding suffrage, the 1865 constitutional convention chose to replicate the Constitution of 1832; it limited the right to vote to white males over the age of twenty-one.

Two other matters that the president demanded be addressed, the secession ordinance and the abolition of slavery, occupied the 1865 convention delegates. After much wrangling, the delegates declared the ordinance of session "null, and of no binding force." Convention delegates rejected other language that accomplished the same task, lest signers of the 1861 ordinance find themselves subject to prosecution as traitors. Delegates debated vigorously even the abolition of slavery. Foolishly hoping that the federal government might offer former slave owners compensation for the loss of their human property, the convention eventually declared that the state ended the institution of slavery not voluntarily but under duress. Albert T. Morgan, a white northerner who went south during Reconstruction, rightly argued that through such language the delegates intended

1860

■ **December 20**
South Carolina secedes from the Union.

1861

■ **January 9**
Mississippi secedes from the Union.

■ **April 12**
The first shots of the Civil War are fired at Fort Sumter in the harbor at Charleston, South Carolina.

1865

■ **April 9**
Robert E. Lee surrenders the bulk of the Confederate army at Appomattox Court House, Virginia, effectively ending the Civil War.

■ **April 15**
President Abraham Lincoln dies after being shot the previous day, and Andrew Johnson becomes president.

■ **November 25**
The Mississippi legislature passes the Black Code.

1867

■ **March 26**
General E. O. C. Ord arrives in Mississippi as military governor, signaling the start of congressional Reconstruction in the state.

1875

■ **November 10**
The election of the Democrat John Marshal Stone signals the end of the Reconstruction in Mississippi and the beginning of a slow but certain retreat from the recognition of the fullness of African American citizenship.

governed, reformed and guided by higher instincts, minds and morals higher and holier than theirs." Benjamin Grubb Humphreys, who was elected governor after the convention, embraced the convention report when he told the first postwar legislature: "The purity and progress of both races require that caste must be maintained." Perhaps not surprisingly, the first Mississippi legislature to convene after the Civil War embraced the Black Code.

About the Author

A number of legislators contributed to the authorship of the Mississippi Black Code. While Governor Benjamin Grubb Humphreys probably did not write a word of the laws, he was singularly responsible for pushing the bill through the legislature. Debate over the code consumed an inordinate amount of time in the first postwar session of the legislature. The law was finally approved only when Humphreys offered a compromise between legislators, some of whom wanted to appease Republicans in Washington and thereby to avoid a more stringent Reconstruction process, and some of whom wished to ignore the demands of the federal government and the significance of the Confederacy's military defeat.

Humphreys (1808–1882) was a native of Claiborne County, Mississippi, and a brigadier general in the Confederate army. Before the war, he attended the U.S. Military Academy at West Point, though his participation in a rowdy demonstration, which led to a riot, caused him to be expelled. After his dismissal, he returned to Mississippi, where he became a cotton planter and politician in Sunflower County, the heart of the Mississippi Delta. In 1865 white Mississippians elected him governor, and in 1867 they reelected him. By that time, congressional Reconstruction had begun, and he resigned his office in 1868 soon after being sworn in, rather than operate under the supervision of a military governor. For almost ten years he worked for an insurance company in Jackson, Mississippi, before retiring back to his Sunflower County home.

Explanation and Analysis of the Document

The document consists of three parts: "An Act to Confer Civil Rights on Freedmen, and for Other Purposes"; "An Act to Regulate the Relation of Master and Apprentice, as Relates to Freedmen, Free Negroes, and Mulattoes"; and "An Act to Amend the Vagrant Laws of the State."

♦ "An Act to Confer Civil Rights on Freedmen, and for Other Purposes"

In this first section of the Black Code, African Americans were granted the right to buy and sell property other than real estate. By denying blacks the ability to own real property, the legislature attempted to ensure that they would remain dependent laborers. Indeed, Section 1 of the

that their heirs know that "slavery had not been destroyed." Former slaves viewed the 1865 constitution in a similar manner. A group of former bondsmen meeting at Vicksburg predicted that soon the state of Mississippi would try to enslave blacks again or force them from the state.

At the conclusion of the constitutional convention, delegates filed a report with the newly elected state legislature. The report called for the body to withhold from former slaves "some unbridled privileges for the present." According to the report, "the wayward and vicious, idle and dishonest, the lawless and reckless, the wicked and improvident, the vagabond and meddler must be smarted, law permits blacks to rent property in cities and towns only if local government expressly allows them to do so. In this way, the legislature was trying to keep blacks in the country, close to agricultural labor, the only labor whites assumed that blacks could perform.

Further attempts to control the labor of blacks appear in Sections 5 through 9. In those sections, African Americans were required to have a legally validated address and employment at the start of each new year, typically the same time that labor contracts were signed. Although blacks received certain protections in the execution of contracts, they were not permitted to break their contracts without "good cause." Doing so would result in prosecution in the courts. The sections of the law addressing those who breached contracts resemble the sections of the separate act that regulated relations between masters and apprentices. By subjecting individuals who broke their contracts to treatment and punishment similar to those meted out to runaway apprentices, the legislature evinced its belief that African Americans could not be trusted to perform their labor.

The act also regulated the social rights of African Americans. While slaves never had the legal right to marry, the Black Code recognized that they could marry as long as they married someone of their own race. The code also allowed former slaves who lived with someone in a spousal relationship to record their relationship as married in the county records. To further clarify who classified as black and was thus prohibited from marrying a white person, the law defined a mulatto as someone with a single "negro" great-grandparent.

Section 4 of the law states that former slaves and others of African descent could testify in civil cases against other African Americans. In criminal proceedings, they could testify against a white person accused of committing a crime against a black person. The restriction on blacks' testimony in the court reflects restrictions that appear in the antebellum slave code.

♦ "An Act to Regulate the Relation of Master and Apprentice, as Relates to Freedmen, Free Negroes, and Mulattoes"

This section of the Mississippi Black Code may be the best known, as it provides ample evidence that lawmakers were reluctant to wholly abolish slavery. The first section of the law required that officers of county courts twice annually file a report listing the names of African Americans under the age of eighteen who were orphans or whose parents could not provide proper care for them. According to the law, juveniles listed on the report would then be apprenticed to a "competent and suitable person." Not only would the treatment provided to orphaned or neglected African Americans differ from the treatment provided to white orphans but former owners of orphaned or poorly cared-for children would also be the preference when the court searched for a suitable master for the child. Apprenticed children would be subject to "moderate" corporal punishment and protected from cruel or inhumane treatment.

Governor Benjamin Grubb Humphreys was responsible for pushing the Black Code through the Mississippi legislature. (Library of Congress)

Gender determined the term of an orphaned or neglected child's indenture. Males would be apprentices until they reached the age of twenty-one; females could achieve release from their indenture upon their eighteenth birthdays. Further, the law allowed the "recapture" of apprentices who fled before their term of service ended, and it permitted punishment of apprentices who refused to return to their masters. Apprentices could, however, challenge their masters' rights to retain them against their will. If a county court judged the apprentice to have good cause for desiring an end to his or her indenture, the court could release the apprentice and fine the master up to $100. Any fine collected would be used for the benefit of the apprentice.

This section of the law also prohibited any white person from helping an apprentice escape his or her master or from enticing an apprentice to accept employment. Individuals convicted of violating the law would be subject to punishment.

♦ "An Act to Amend the Vagrant Laws of the State"

This section of the law defined a broad swath of behavior, including juggling, gambling, and the habitual drinking of alcoholic beverages, as indicative of vagrancy. The law also classified individuals (regardless of color)

> *"Every freedman, free negro and mulatto shall, on the second Monday of January, one thousand eight hundred and sixty-six, and annually thereafter, have a lawful home or employment, and shall have written evidence thereof."*
>
> (Section 5, An Act to Confer Civil Rights on Freedmen, and for Other Purposes)

> *"All rouges and vagabonds, idle and dissipated persons, beggars, jugglers, or persons practicing unlawful games or plays, runaways, common drunkards, common night-walkers, pilferers, lewd, wanton, or lascivious persons, in speech or behavior, common railers and brawlers, persons who neglect their calling or employment, misspend what they earn, or do not provide for the support of themselves or their families, or dependents, and all other idle and disorderly persons, including all who neglect all lawful business, habitually misspend their time by frequenting houses of ill-fame, gaming-houses, or tippling shops, shall be deemed and considered vagrants."*
>
> (Section 1, An Act to Amend the Vagrant Laws of the State)

who did not work, misspent their money, or did not properly care for themselves or their dependents as vagrants. Prostitutes and gambling house operators, as well as all manner of citizens who obtained their income from illegal or immoral acts, are here classified by the law as vagrants. Individuals who were convicted of vagrancy were to be fined up to $100 and could be sentenced to jail for up to ten days.

African Americans were subject to additional penalties for vagrancy, as were whites who commonly associated with African Americans. Section 2 of the amendment clearly echoes Mississippi's antebellum slave code. Specifically, the section prohibited unemployed blacks from free assembly and white males from assembling with African Americans or from having sexual relations with black women. Blacks convicted of vagrancy under Section 2 of the amendment would be subject to a $50 fine and ten days in jail; white men would be subject to a $200 fine and six months in jail. If convicted, African Americans who could not pay their fines were to be hired out by the county sheriff to labor until their fine was paid. If a black vagrant was too old or infirm to be hired out, then the sheriff could treat the vagrant as a pauper. According to the law, African Americans eighteen to sixty-five years old were required to pay a $1 poll tax to fund the "Freedman's Pauper Fund" in each county. (White paupers were cared for through other means of taxation,

not a special pauper's tax.) Refusal or inability to pay the tax caused an African American to be classified as a vagrant and to be hired out to anyone who was willing to pay the tax for the vagrant.

Audience

Public laws are written, in part, to shape behavior. Consequently, the audience to whom the Mississippi Black Code was addressed included all of Mississippi's residents and visitors. However, few Mississippians, including lawyers, law enforcement officials, and judges, would have read the actual text of the law.

Impact

Passage of the Black Code immediately provoked two reactions in the nation. In the South other state legislators emulated the Mississippi Black Code, yet in the North the laws alerted Republicans in Congress to the fact that white southerners would not voluntarily embrace black liberty. While testifying before Congress in 1865, Colonel Samuel Thomas, an official with the Bureau of Refugees, Freedmen, and Abandoned Lands, noted the persistence of such attitudes:

The whites esteem the blacks their property by natural right, and however much they may admit that the individual relations of masters and slaves have been destroyed by the war and the President's emancipation proclamation, they still have an ingrained feeling that the blacks at large belong to the whites at large, and whenever opportunity serves they treat the colored people just as their profit, caprice or passion may dictate.

Taken together with President Andrew Johnson's alleged violation of laws and his disdain for Republican measures directed toward ensuring the liberty of former slaves, Congress exerted its authority in 1866 and took over the reins of Reconstruction. With a military governor placed in charge of Reconstruction in Mississippi, the state convened a new constitutional convention, a body elected in the first biracial, statewide election. The constitution that eventually emerged granted the full measure of citizenship to African Americans and thereby removed the Mississippi Black Code from the law books. Despite the code's brief life span, its impact reverberated broadly and throughout the course of Reconstruction.

See also Thirteenth Amendment to the U.S. Constitution (1865); Fourteenth Amendment to the U.S. Constitution (1868); Fifteenth Amendment to the U.S. Constitution (1870).

Andrew Johnson (Library of Congress)

Further Reading

■ Books

Bond, Bradley G. *Political Culture in the Nineteenth-Century South: Mississippi, 1830–1900*. Baton Rouge: Louisiana State University Press, 1995.

———, ed. *Mississippi: A Documentary History*. Jackson: University Press of Mississippi, 2003.

Harris, William C. *Presidential Reconstruction in Mississippi*. Baton Rouge: Louisiana State University Press, 1967.

———. *The Day of the Carpetbagger: Republication Reconstruction in Mississippi*. Baton Rouge: Louisiana State University Press, 1979.

Journal of the Proceedings and Debates in the Constitutional Convention of the State of Mississippi, August, 1865. Ann Arbor: University of Michigan Library, 2005.

Morgan, A. T. *Yazoo; or, On the Picket Line of Freedom in the South: A Personal Narrative*. 1884. Reprint. New York: Russell and Russell, 1968.

Wharton, Vernon Lane. *Negro in Mississippi, 1865–1890*. Chapel Hill: University of North Carolina Press, 1947.

Questions for Further Study

1. Compare the Mississippi Black Code with the state's antebellum slave code.

2. How did the Mississippi Black Code differ from the Louisiana Black Code? How might those differences be explained?

3. Describe the restrictions placed upon African Americans by the Mississippi Black Code and by formal laws and ordinances enforced during the epoch of Jim Crow.

■ **Web Sites**

"African American Voices." Digital History Web site.
    http://www.digitalhistory.uh.edu/black_voices/voices_display.
    cfm?id=82.

"Louisiana Black Codes." About.com "African-American History"
Web site.
    http://afroamhistory.about.com/library/bllouisiana_blackcodes.htm.

"Race, Racism, and the Law." University of Dayton School of Law Web site.
    http://academic.udayton.edu/race/02rights/jcrow02.htm.

"Reconstruction in Mississippi, 1865–1876." Mississippi History
Now Web site.
    http://teacherexchange.mde.k12.ms.us/MHNLP/reconstruc
    tionlp.htm.

—Bradley G. Bond

BLACK CODE OF MISSISSIPPI

An Act to Confer Civil Rights on Freedmen, and for Other Purposes

◆ Section 1.

All freedmen, free negroes and mulattoes may sue and be sued, implead and be impleaded, in all the courts of law and equity of this State, and may acquire personal property, and chooses in action, by descent or purchase, and may dispose of the same in the same manner and to the same extent that white persons may: Provided, That the provisions of this section shall not be so construed as to allow any freedman, free negro or mulatto to rent or lease any lands or tenements except in incorporated cities or towns, in which places the corporate authorities shall control the same.

◆ Section 2.

All freedmen, free negroes and mulattoes may intermarry with each other, in the same manner and under the same regulations that are provided by law for white persons: Provided, that the clerk of probate shall keep separate records of the same.

◆ Section 3.

All freedmen, free negroes or mullatoes who do now and have herebefore lived and cohabited together as husband and wife shall be taken and held in law as legally married, and the issue shall be taken and held as legitimate for all purposes; and it shall not be lawful for any freedman, free negro or mulatto to intermarry with any white person; nor for any person to intermarry with any freedman, free negro or mulatto; and any person who shall so intermarry shall be deemed guilty of felony, and on conviction thereof shall be confined in the State penitentiary for life; and those shall be deemed freedmen, free negroes and mulattoes who are of pure negro blood, and those descended from a negro to the third generation, inclusive, though one ancestor in each generation may have been a white person.

◆ Section 4.

In addition to cases in which freedmen, free negroes and mulattoes are now by law competent witnesses, freedmen, free negroes or mulattoes shall be competent in civil cases, when a party or parties to the suit, either plaintiff or plaintiffs, defendant or defendants; also in cases where freedmen, free negroes and mulattoes is or are either plaintiff or plaintiffs, defendant or defendants. They shall also be competent witnesses in all criminal prosecutions where the crime charged is alleged to have been committed by a white person upon or against the person or property of a freedman, free negro or mulatto: Provided, that in all cases said witnesses shall be examined in open court, on the stand; except, however, they may be examined before the grand jury, and shall in all cases be subject to the rules and tests of the common law as to competency and credibility.

◆ Section 5.

Every freedman, free negro and mulatto shall, on the second Monday of January, one thousand eight hundred and sixty-six, and annually thereafter, have a lawful home or employment, and shall have written evidence thereof as follows, to wit: if living in any incorporated city, town, or village, a license from that mayor thereof; and if living outside of an incorporated city, town, or village, from the member of the board of police of his beat, authorizing him or her to do irregular and job work; or a written contract, as provided in Section 6 in this act; which license may be revoked for cause at any time by the authority granting the same.

◆ Section 6.

All contracts for labor made with freedmen, free negroes and mulattoes for a longer period than one month shall be in writing, and a duplicate, attested and read to said freedman, free negro or mulatto by a beat, city or county officer, or two disinterested white persons of the county in which the labor is to performed, of which each party shall have one: and said contracts shall be taken and held as entire contracts, and if the laborer shall quit the service of the employer before the expiration of his term of service, without good cause, he shall forfeit his wages for that year up to the time of quitting.

◆ Section 7.

Every civil officer shall, and every person may, arrest and carry back to his or her legal employer any freedman, free negro, or mulatto who shall have quit the service of his or her employer before the expiration of his or her term of service without good cause; and said officer and person shall be entitled to receive for arresting and carrying back every deserting employee aforesaid the sum of five dollars, and ten cents per mile from the place of arrest to the place of delivery; and the same shall be paid by the employer, and held as a set off for so much against the wages of said deserting employee: Provided, that said arrested party, after being so returned, may appeal to the justice of the peace or member of the board of police of the county, who, on notice to the alleged employer, shall try summarily whether said appellant is legally employed by the alleged employer, and has good cause to quit said employer. Either party shall have the right of appeal to the county court, pending which the alleged deserter shall be remanded to the alleged employer or otherwise disposed of, as shall be right and just; and the decision of the county court shall be final.

♦ **Section 8.**

Upon affidavit made by the employer of any freedman, free negro or mulatto, or other credible person, before any justice of the peace or member of the board of police, that any freedman, free negro or mulatto legally employed by said employer has illegally deserted said employment, such justice of the peace or member of the board of police issue his warrant or warrants, returnable before himself or other such officer, to any sheriff, constable or special deputy, commanding him to arrest said deserter, and return him or her to said employer, and the like proceedings shall be had as provided in the preceding section; and it shall be lawful for any officer to whom such warrant shall be directed to execute said warrant in any county in this State; and that said warrant may be transmitted without endorsement to any like officer of another county, to be executed and returned as aforesaid; and the said employer shall pay the costs of said warrants and arrest and return, which shall be set off for so much against the wages of said deserter.

♦ **Section 9.**

If any person shall persuade or attempt to persuade, entice, or cause any freedman, free negro or mulatto to desert from the legal employment of any person before the expiration of his or her term of service, or shall knowingly employ any such deserting freedman, free negro or mulatto, or shall

knowingly give or sell to any such deserting freedman, free negro or mulatto, any food, raiment, or other thing, he or she shall be guilty of a misdemeanor, and, upon conviction, shall be fined not less than twenty-five dollars and not more than two hundred dollars and costs; and if the said fine and costs shall not be immediately paid, the court shall sentence said convict to not exceeding two months imprisonment in the county jail, and he or she shall moreover be liable to the party injured in damages: Provided, if any person shall, or shall attempt to, persuade, entice, or cause any freedman, free negro or mulatto to desert from any legal employment of any person, with the view to employ said freedman, free negro or mulatto without the limits of this State, such costs; and if said fine and costs shall not be immediately paid, the court shall sentence said convict to not exceeding six months imprisonment in the county jail.

♦ **Section 10.**

It shall be lawful for any freedman, free negro, or mulatto, to charge any white person, freedman, free negro or mulatto by affidavit, with any criminal offense against his or her person or property, and upon such affidavit the proper process shall be issued and executed as if said affidavit was made by a white person, and it shall be lawful for any freedman, free negro, or mulatto, in any action, suit or controversy pending, or about to be instituted in any court of law equity in this State, to make all needful and lawful affidavits as shall be necessary for the institution, prosecution or defense of such suit or controversy.

♦ **Section 11.**

The penal laws of this state, in all cases not otherwise specially provided for, shall apply and extend to all freedman, free negroes and mulattoes....

An Act to Regulate the Relation of Master and Apprentice, as Relates to Freedmen, Free Negroes, and Mulattoes

♦ **Section 1.**

It shall be the duty of all sheriffs, justices of the peace, and other civil officers of the several counties in this State, to report to the probate courts of their respective counties semiannually, at the January and July terms of said courts, all freedmen, free negroes, and mulattoes, under the age of eighteen, in their respective counties, beats, or districts, who are orphans, or whose parent or parents have not the means or who refuse to provide for and support said minors; and thereupon it shall be the duty of said probate court to order the clerk of said court to apprentice said minors to some competent and suitable person on such terms as the court may direct, having a particular care to the interest of said minor: Provided, that the former owner of said minors shall have the preference when, in the opinion of the court, he or she shall be a suitable person for that purpose.

♦ **Section 2.**

The said court shall be fully satisfied that the person or persons to whom said minor shall be apprenticed shall be a suitable person to have the charge and care of said minor, and fully to protect the interest of said minor. The said court shall require the said master or mistress to execute bond and security, payable to the State of Mississippi, conditioned that he or she shall furnish said minor with sufficient food and clothing; to treat said minor humanely; furnish medical attention in case of sickness; teach, or cause to be taught, him or her to read and write, if under fifteen years old, and will conform to any law that may be hereafter passed for the regulation of the duties and relation of master and apprentice: Provided, that said apprentice shall be bound by indenture, in case of males, until they are twenty-one years old, and in case of females until they are eighteen years old.

♦ **Section 3.**

In the management and control of said apprentices, said master or mistress shall have the power to inflict such moderate corporeal chastisement as a father or guardian is allowed to infliction on his or her child or ward at common law: Provided, that in no case shall cruel or inhuman punishment be inflicted.

♦ **Section 4.**

If any apprentice shall leave the employment of his or her master or mistress, without his or her consent, said master or mistress may pursue and recapture said apprentice, and bring him or her before any justice of the peace of the county, whose duty it shall be to remand said apprentice to the service of his or her master or mistress; and in the event of a refusal on the part of said apprentice so to return, then said justice shall commit said apprentice to the jail of said county, on failure to give bond, to the next term of the county court; and it shall be the duty of said

court at the first term thereafter to investigate said case, and if the court shall be of opinion that said apprentice left the employment of his or her master or mistress without good cause, to order him or her to be punished, as provided for the punishment of hired freedmen, as may be from time to time provided for by law for desertion, until he or she shall agree to return to the service of his or her master or mistress: Provided, that the court may grant continuances as in other cases: And provided further, that if the court shall believe that said apprentice had good cause to quit his said master or mistress, the court shall discharge said apprentice from said indenture, and also enter a judgment against the master or mistress for not more than one hundred dollars, from the use and benefit of said apprentice, to be collected on execution as in other cases.

♦ **Section 5.**

If any person entice away any apprentice from his or her master or mistress, or shall knowingly employ an apprentice, or furnish him or her food or clothing without the written consent of his or her master or mistress, or shall sell or give said apprentice spirits without such consent, said person so offending shall be guilty of a misdemeanor, and shall, upon conviction there of before the county court, be punished as provided for the punishment of person enticing from their employer hired freedmen, free negroes or mulattoes.

♦ **Section 6.**

It shall be the duty of all civil officers of their respective counties to report any minors within their respective counties to said probate court who are subject to be apprenticed under the provisions of this act, from time to time as the facts may come to their knowledge, and it shall be the duty of said court from time to time as said minors shall be reported to them, or otherwise come to their knowledge, to apprentice said minors as hereinbefore provided....

♦ **Section 9.**

It shall be lawful for any freedman, free negro, or mulatto, having a minor child or children to apprentice the said minor child or children, as provided for by this act.

♦ **Section 10.**

In all cases where the age of the freedman, free negro, or mulatto cannot be ascertained by record testimony, the judge of the county court shall fix the age....

An Act to Amend the Vagrant Laws of the State

✦ Section 1.

All rogues and vagabonds, idle and dissipated persons, beggars, jugglers, or persons practicing unlawful games or plays, runaways, common drunkards, common night-walkers, pilferers, lewd, wanton, or lascivious persons, in speech or behavior, common railers and brawlers, persons who neglect their calling or employment, misspend what they earn, or do not provide for the support of themselves or their families, or dependents, and all other idle and disorderly persons, including all who neglect all lawful business, habitually misspend their time by frequenting houses of ill-fame, gaming-houses, or tippling shops, shall be deemed and considered vagrants, under the provisions of this act, and upon conviction thereof shall be fined not exceeding one hundred dollars, with all accruing costs, and be imprisoned, at the discretion of the court, not exceeding ten days.

✦ Section 2.

All freedmen, free negroes and mulattoes in this State, over the age of eighteen years, found on the second Monday in January, 1866, or thereafter, with no lawful employment or business, or found unlawfully assembling themselves together, either in the day or night time, and all white persons assembling themselves with freedmen, free negroes or mulattoes, or usually associating with freedmen, free negroes or mulattoes, on terms of equality, or living in adultery or fornication with a freed woman, freed negro or mulatto, shall be deemed vagrants, and on conviction thereof shall be fined in a sum not exceeding, in the case of a freedman, free negro or mulatto, fifty dollars, and a white man two hundred dollars, and imprisonment at the discretion of the court, the free negro not exceeding ten days, and the white man not exceeding six months.

✦ Section 3.

All justices of the peace, mayors, and aldermen of incorporated towns, counties, and cities of the several counties in this State shall have jurisdiction to try all questions of vagrancy in their respective towns, counties, and cities, and it is hereby made their duty, whenever they shall ascertain that any person or persons in their respective towns, and counties and cities are violating any of the provisions of this act, to have said party or parties arrested, and brought before them, and immediately investigate said charge, and, on conviction, punish said party or parties, as provided for herein. And it is hereby made the duty of all sheriffs, constables, town constables, and all such like officers, and city marshals, to report to some officer having jurisdiction all violations of any of the provisions of this act, and in case any officer shall fail or neglect any duty herein it shall be the duty of the county court to fine said officer, upon conviction, not exceeding one hundred dollars, to be paid into the county treasury for county purposes.

✦ Section 4.

Keepers of gaming houses, houses of prostitution, prostitutes, public or private, and all persons who derive their chief support in the employments that militate against good morals, or against law, shall be deemed and held to be vagrants.

✦ Section 5.

All fines and forfeitures collected by the provisions of this act shall be paid into the county treasury of general county purposes, and in case of any freedman, free negro or mulatto shall fail for five days after the imposition of any or forfeiture upon him or her for violation of any of the provisions of this act to pay the same, that it shall be, and is hereby, made the duty of the sheriff of the proper county to hire out said freedman, free negro or mulatto, to any person who will, for the shortest period of service, pay said fine and forfeiture and all costs: Provided, a preference shall be given to the employer, if there be one, in which case the employer shall be entitled to deduct and retain the amount so paid from the wages of such freedman, free negro or mulatto, then due or to become due; and in case freedman, free negro or mulatto cannot hire out, he or she may be dealt with as a pauper.

✦ Section 6.

The same duties and liabilities existing among white persons of this State shall attach to freedmen, free negroes or mulattoes, to support their indigent families and all colored paupers; and that in order to secure a support for such indigent freedmen, free negroes, or mulattoes, it shall be lawful, and is hereby made the duty of the county police of each county in this State, to levy a poll or capitation tax on each and every freedman, free negro, or mulatto, between the ages of eighteen and sixty years, not to exceed the sum of one dollar annually to each person so taxed, which tax, when collected, shall be paid into the county treasurer's hands, and constitute a fund to be called the Freedman's Pauper Fund, which shall be applied by the commissioners of the poor for the maintenance of the poor of the freedmen, free negroes and mulattoes of this State, under such regulations as may be established by the boards of county police in the respective counties of this State.

♦ **Section 7.**

If any freedman, free negro, or mulatto shall fail or refuse to pay any tax levied according to the provisions of the sixth section of this act, it shall be *prima facie* evidence of vagrancy, and it shall be the duty of the sheriff to arrest such freedman, free negro, or mulatto, or such person refusing or neglecting to pay such tax, and proceed at once to hire for the shortest time such delinquent taxpayer to any one who will pay the said tax, with accruing costs, giving preference to the employer, if there be one.

♦ **Section 8.**

Any person feeling himself or herself aggrieved by judgment of any justice of the peace, mayor, or alderman in cases arising under this act, may within five days appeal to the next term of the county court of the proper county, upon giving bond and security in a sum not less than twenty-five dollars nor more than one hundred and fifty dollars, conditioned to appear and prosecute said appeal, and abide by the judgment of the county court; and said appeal shall be tried *de novo* in the county court, and the decision of the said court shall be final.

Glossary

freedmen	former slaves who had been emancipated at the conclusion of the Civil War
free negroes	blacks who had been emancipated by their owners, or the children of parents emancipated prior to the start of the Civil War
mulatto	a general term used to refer to people of mixed race, though it specifically refers to anyone who had at least one great-grandparent who was black
pauper	a term used mainly before the twentieth century to refer to a poor or indigent person
tippling shops	businesses that sold liquor by either the glass or the bottle

Thirty-Eighth Congress of the United States of America;

At the Second Session,

Begun and held at the City of Washington, on Monday, the *fifth* day of December, one thousand eight hundred and sixty-*four*.

A RESOLUTION

Submitting to the legislatures of the several States a proposition to amend the Constitution of the United States.

Resolved by the Senate and House of Representatives of the United States of America in Congress assembled, (two-thirds of both houses concurring), That the following article be proposed to the legislatures of the several States as an amendment to the Constitution of the United States, which, when ratified by three-fourths of said Legislatures, shall be valid, to all intents and purposes, as a part of the said Constitution, namely: Article XIII. Section 1. Neither slavery nor involuntary servitude, except as a punishment for crime whereof the party shall have been duly convicted, shall exist within the United States, or any place subject to their jurisdiction. Section 2. Congress shall have power to enforce this article by appropriate legislation.

Schuyler Colfax
Speaker of the House of Representatives.

H. Hamlin
Vice President of the United States,
and President of the Senate

Approved, February 1. 1865.

Abraham Lincoln

The Thirteenth Amendment (National Archives and Records Administration)

THIRTEENTH AMENDMENT TO THE U.S. CONSTITUTION

1865

"Neither slavery nor involuntary servitude ... shall exist within the United States."

Overview

The Thirteenth Amendment to the U.S. Constitution legally ended slavery in the United States. It was passed by Congress and ratified by the required three-fourths of the states in 1865. President Abraham Lincoln had issued the Emancipation Proclamation in 1862, declaring slaves in areas in rebellion against the government to be freed by executive decree. Afterward, Lincoln and many of his fellow Republicans had believed that more permanent legislation in the form of a constitutional amendment prohibiting slavery would be needed to ensure that the Emancipation Proclamation could not be subsequently ruled either unconstitutional or a temporary war measure. The Thirteenth Amendment was the first constitutional amendment to be adopted in more than sixty years, and it initiated a series of subsequent amendments, including the Fourteenth and Fifteenth Amendments, with which it is often associated. Those two Reconstruction-era amendments guaranteed citizenship and voting rights to African Americans and, along with the Thirteenth Amendment, represented a crucial step in the broadening of the American legal definitions and conceptions of freedom and equality.

Context

Early in the Civil War, the North was divided on the issue of emancipation. The Republican Party and its leader, President Lincoln, opposed the expansion of slavery into the western territories but generally conceded that the Constitution protected the "peculiar institution" in the states where it already existed. A vocal minority of abolitionists within the party called for immediate emancipation, although they differed even among themselves about whether this desirable outcome could best be achieved by executive, legislative, or judicial action. The Democratic Party generally opposed emancipation, although as the war wore on many of its members grudgingly came to accept that the measure in some form might be necessary—to win the conflict, to remove the underlying cause

and prevent its recurrence, and to punish the recalcitrant southern slave owners for their continued, and immensely destructive, defiance.

During the "secession winter" of 1860–1861, before the outbreak of the war, Lincoln and other Republicans announced their support for a proposed amendment that would have guaranteed that the federal government could never abolish slavery in the southern states; Lincoln and his fellow Republicans were even willing to make this amendment unamendable in the future. Confederate leaders, convinced that secession and an independent southern nation would prove to be the best means of protecting slavery, scorned this offer. (Ironically for them, the true Thirteenth Amendment, which went into effect at the end of the war, took a form much less favorable to slave owners.) In July 1861 Congress passed, with overwhelming support, the Crittenden-Johnson Resolution, stating that the northern war aims would include the restoration of the Union but not the emancipation of southern slaves.

In the same cautious spirit, Lincoln resisted overt action against slavery in 1861 and for much of 1862. Concerned with maintaining support for the Union in the conflict-ridden border slave states (Maryland, Kentucky, Missouri, and tiny Delaware), the president overruled early emancipation declarations by General David Hunter in South Carolina and General John C. Frémont in Missouri. Lincoln encouraged the leaders of border states to adopt policies of voluntary, compensated emancipation, but without success. General Benjamin F. Butler adopted an effective expedient in May 1861 when he began refusing to return runaway slaves to their masters, characterizing them essentially as spoils of war. By thus treating slaves as property, he avoided the controversy associated with an announced policy of emancipation; while this did not entirely satisfy abolitionists, it was accepted by most northerners as a useful and clever compromise. The influx over Union lines of large numbers of African Americans fleeing slavery and seeking refuge put considerable additional pressure on government leaders to come up with a solution to this colossal problem, with huge moral and practical implications for the future of the nation's existence. Legislators were eventually bombarded with petitions and letters from constituents demanding action to end slavery. Congress essentially af-

1857

■ **March 6**
In the *Dred Scott v. Sandford* decision, the Supreme Court rules that Congress has no authority to prohibit slavery in the western territories.

1860

■ **December 20**
South Carolina becomes the first southern state to secede following the election of the northern Republican Abraham Lincoln as president.

1861

■ **April 12**
The Confederate firing on Fort Sumter begins the American Civil War.

■ **March 2**
Congress passes a proposed amendment, which is never ratified, barring Congress from interfering with slavery in states where the institution exists.

1862

■ **April 16**
Slavery is abolished in the District of Columbia.

■ **September 22**
President Abraham Lincoln issues the Emancipation Proclamation.

1863

■ **January 1**
The Emancipation Proclamation goes into effect.

1865

■ **January 31**
Congress proposes the Thirteenth Amendment to the states.

■ **April 9**
The Confederate general Robert E. Lee surrenders to the Union general Ulysses S. Grant, effectively ending the Civil War.

■ **December 18**
Secretary of State William H. Seward issues proclamation announcing that the Thirteenth Amendment has been ratified by the necessary three-quarters of the states.

1995

■ **March 6**
Mississippi ratifies the Thirteenth Amendment, 130 years after initially rejecting it.

firmed Butler's policy with the passage of the first Confiscation Act in August 1861, authorizing representatives of the federal government to confiscate the slaves of disloyal citizens used in support of the rebellion.

The emancipation question was inseparable from the problem of precisely how to reconstruct southern state governments and oversee their restoration to the Union after the war. Ensuring that these states would be free of slavery seemed essential to many (though not all) northerners, but how to accomplish that aim was less obvious. Congress began to take more aggressive steps against slavery in 1862, while radicals like the Massachusetts senator Charles Sumner both publicly and privately maintained pressure on President Lincoln to use his war powers as commander in chief to do likewise. The second Confiscation Act, of July 1862, provided for the forfeiture of slaves as well as other property belonging to those supporting the Confederacy. The lack of effective enforcement mechanisms, along with doubts held by Lincoln and others regarding the act's constitutionality, made the act somewhat irrelevant, but it did represent another tentative step toward a federal emancipation policy.

The most famous but not the final blow against American slavery was struck on September 22, 1862, when President Lincoln, shortly following the Union victory at the Battle of Antietam, issued his famous Emancipation Proclamation, freeing all the slaves in areas of the South not occupied by federal troops as of the coming January 1. As this proclamation did not apply to the border slave states that had not seceded—and might ultimately have been regarded by the courts as a temporary war measure only—Lincoln and many of his fellow Republicans recognized that further action would be needed to end slavery and remove the root cause of the conflict between the North and the South. Although many Americans were reluctant to alter the text of the Constitution, which had not been amended for over sixty years and was widely regarded as permanent and sacred, an emancipation amendment seemed to offer the best and most definitive solution to this troublesome issue. As early as 1839 the staunch slavery opponent John Quincy Adams had introduced such a constitutional amendment to bring about abolition; although his proposal had made no headway at the time, the idea had been percolating among his successors in the political antislavery movement.

In December 1863 competing antislavery amendments were introduced in the House of Representatives by the Republican congressmen James M. Ashley of Ohio and James F. Wilson of Iowa. Both men introduced their bills in the context of ongoing debate over how to reconstruct the southern states and bring them back into the Union. They advocated a constitutional amendment barring slavery as a means to ensure republican government in those states. Wilson's proposed amendment included an enforcement clause, empowering Congress to pass legislation to ensure compliance. In this session, however, the House passed neither an emancipation amendment nor any of the envisioned supplemental legislation intended to protect civil rights.

Charles Sumner initially took the lead in pushing for an abolition amendment in the Senate. He hoped not just to end slavery but also to ensure full legal and practical equality for African Americans. Even many fellow members of the Republican Party hesitated to push so far, worrying that the party's fragile wartime coalition of different ideological factions, as bolstered by an important bloc of Democrats who supported the war effort, might be damaged by overly radical legislation. On February 8, 1864, Sumner introduced a constitutional amendment outlawing slavery, hoping that it would be referred to a committee that he chaired on issues related to slavery and freedmen. Following standard legislative practice, however, the amendment was instead referred to the Judiciary Committee, chaired by Lyman Trumbull of Illinois. Trumbull, a less radical Republican than Sumner, oversaw the crafting of a document with less explicit guarantees that former slaves would be granted full citizenship rights and protections.

Sumner's arrogant, humorless personality made it difficult for him to win colleagues over to his more radically egalitarian vision of the proposed amendment. Trumbull, meanwhile, insisted during debate that the more neutral language in his committee's version (much of it borrowed from the well-known Northwest Ordinance) would fully accomplish the same object of ensuring equality for all regardless of race. This claim was likely disingenuous, however. Trumbull and other Senate Republicans were hoping to avoid charges of favoring excessive and revolutionary social and political upheaval on the order of the French Revolution. One senator even expressed the fear that Sumner's amendment's promise that all individuals would be equal before the law could be applied to women, a measure that did not have widespread political support, at least among the men who held a monopoly on voting rights at the time.

The proposed antislavery amendment provoked extensive congressional debate. Intended more to inspire supporters back in home districts who would later read published accounts of the speeches than to convince the fellow members, who rarely listened to colleagues' speeches in any event. As 1864 was an election year, the amendment was a particularly potent political issue, and with Lincoln's approval it became part of the Republican Party's campaign platform. The amendment passed the Senate on April 6, 1864, by a vote of 38 to 4; after a fierce struggle and considerable lobbying at the president's behest, it passed the House of Representatives on January 31, 1865, by a vote of 119 to 56, with enough Democrats joining with the Republican majority to ensure the measure's victory. Lincoln enthusiastically indicated his pleasure at this outcome by signing the amendment when it was presented to him, although he was not legally required to do so for it to go into effect.

One of the most difficult issues facing the supporters of the Thirteenth Amendment was that of ratification. Constitutional amendments needed to be ratified by three-quarters of the states in order to take effect. Would the seceded states be counted toward this total? Most Republicans, following the lead of Lincoln, argued that secession was il-

Congressman James Mitchell Ashley (Library of Congress)

legal and that the states had not technically left the Union. This presented a dilemma, as some southern states would then have to vote for the abolition amendment in order for it to go into effect. Charles Sumner proposed leaving the Confederate states out of the ratification calculations, but Trumbull and other Republicans successfully opposed this plan, as some worried that the amendment might seem to lack legitimacy if the southern states were not included in the ratification process. In one of his final speeches, only a few days before his assassination, Lincoln indicated that he agreed that all of the states must be allowed the opportunity to ratify the amendment. His successor, Andrew Johnson, implored conventions in the southern states to meet and voluntarily ratify the amendment, and, indeed, enough states ratified the amendment for it to become law. Ominously, however, several of the ratification conventions in the former Confederate states warned that they did not accept the legitimacy of the clause giving Congress the right to pass supplemental legislation ensuring civil rights for

African Americans. This significant distinction, generally overlooked by the administration and congressional leaders at the time, suggested that many southern whites were determined to prevent the establishment of equality for African Americans, despite the Thirteenth Amendment's promise of freedom.

About the Author

The Thirteenth Amendment had no single author. Some of its key congressional creators and supporters were James M. Ashley, James F. Wilson, Lyman Trumbull, and Charles Sumner.

James M. Ashley was born in Pennsylvania in 1824. The mostly self-educated young man moved west to Ohio in 1848, where he became the editor of a Democratic newspaper and a close political ally of the antislavery leader and future Supreme Court chief justice Salmon P. Chase. Ashley was first elected to Congress in 1858, representing the Republican Party. During the Civil War, he played a leading role in winning support for the emancipation of slaves in the District of Columbia before helping push for the Thirteenth Amendment. He would also favor a punitive Reconstruction policy, including confiscating the property of supporters of the Confederacy and taking away their political rights, which sometimes put him at odds with President Lincoln, who favored a more moderate and generous policy aimed at facilitating reconciliation and reunion. Ashley worked closely with Lincoln, however, in winning support among wavering members of both parties in order to ensure congressional passage of the Thirteenth Amendment. Following the war, Ashley was one of the leaders in the movement to impeach President Andrew Johnson for obstructing Reconstruction, and he aired wild accusations that Johnson had been complicit in Lincoln's murder. He later served as territorial governor of Montana and as a railroad president. He died in 1896.

James F. Wilson, born in Ohio in 1828, was a Republican congressman from Iowa during the Civil War. He had moved to Iowa and begun practicing law and involving himself in politics in the early 1850s, and in 1856 he participated in the convention that revised the state's constitution. Wilson was first elected to Congress in 1861 when his district's former representative, Samuel R. Curtis, resigned to accept an appointment as a general in the Union Army. Once in the Republican-controlled House of Representatives, Wilson was appointed chairman of the Judiciary Committee despite the seniority of other party members on the committee, a compliment to Wilson's legal knowledge, ability, and work ethic. Like Ashley, he also helped win support for ending slavery in the District of Columbia. Following the Civil War, he served in both the Senate and the House of Representatives and as director of the Union Pacific Railroad. Wilson once reputedly turned down an offer of the prestigious position of secretary of state by President Ulysses S. Grant, possibly a wise move given the scandals and misfortune that tarnished the Grant cabinet. Wilson

died in 1895, having occupied a prominent place in the Iowa and national Republican leadership for forty years.

Lyman Trumbull of Illinois, a Democrat turned Republican and one of the party's most forceful and respected national leaders during the Civil War era, was born in 1813. He was first elected to the Senate in 1855, triumphing over his rival, Abraham Lincoln, in one of the most bitter setbacks in the career of "Honest Abe." Although Lincoln and Trumbull had an uneasy personal relationship following this contest—and Mary Todd Lincoln afterward refused to speak to Trumbull's wife, Julia, her former friend—the two men put aside their differences to champion Republican policies, including the Thirteenth Amendment, during the Civil War. Feisty and bespectacled, Trumbull broke with Radical Republicans over Reconstruction and voted against the impeachment of Andrew Johnson in 1868. Thereafter, he variously supported the short-lived Liberal Republican movement, returned to the Democratic fold, and even advocated the Populist Party (defending the Socialist labor leader Eugene V. Debs at a trial for the appeal of his conviction for violating a federal antistrike injunction). Trumbull died in 1896.

Charles Sumner first took his seat as a senator from Massachusetts in 1851 at the age of forty, representing first the Free-Soil Party and subsequently the Republican Party. He gained fame for his scholarly oratory and zealous abolitionism as well as for suffering a savage beating from a stout cane wielded by the proslavery South Carolina congressman Preston Brooks on the floor of the Senate in 1856. This famous incident led Sumner to become, in the eyes of many northerners, a heroic symbol of freedom of speech and opponent of southern proslavery barbarism. Sumner did not return to take his Senate seat for several years, though his physical injuries healed relatively quickly. He exercised particular clout in foreign affairs issues owing to his knowledge and wide circle of acquaintances abroad, and he both chaired the Senate Foreign Affairs Committee and served as an adviser to Lincoln on international issues, often much to the annoyance of his long-time political rival Secretary of State William H. Seward. Sumner was one of the Thirteenth Amendment's first and most consistent advocates, and he remained committed to civil rights causes—often finding himself at odds with his fellow Republicans—until his death in 1874.

Explanation and Analysis of the Document

The Thirteenth Amendment announces that slavery will no longer be legally permitted in the United States or its territories, with the significant exception that "involuntary servitude" may be imposed on those who have been convicted of crimes. This loophole, to which Charles Sumner strongly objected, permitted those serving jail terms, often African Americans convicted on petty or false charges, to be used as a source of cheap, brutally coerced labor in many southern states well into the twentieth century. The amendment does not specify what the legal status of the former

"Neither slavery nor involuntary servitude, except as a punishment for crime whereof the party shall have been duly convicted, shall exist within the United States, or any place subject to their jurisdiction."

(Section 1)

"Congress shall have the power to enforce this article by appropriate legislation."

(Section 2)

"In passing this amendment we do not confer upon the negro the right to vote. We give him no right except his freedom, and leave the rest to the states."

(Republican Senator John Henderson, *Congressional Globe*, April 6, 1864, p. 1438)

"But this amendment is a king's cure-all for all the evils. It winds the whole thing up. He [Lincoln] would repeat that it was the fitting, if not the indispensable, adjunct to the consummation of the great game we are playing."

(Nicolay, p. 475)

slaves would be or if they would be fully entitled to the rights of American citizens. The document also includes an enforcement clause, giving Congress the power to pass laws to enforce emancipation. Unfortunately, lack of political will and Supreme Court decisions leaving most issues of interpretation and enforcement to the states undermined the impact of this clause.

Audience

The Thirteenth Amendment was designed to appeal to northern Republicans and Democrats alike in order to keep both groups behind the war effort; partly for that reason, the authors avoided addressing controversial issues of enforcement, citizenship, and voting rights for the former slaves, which later amendments would address. As the amendment had to be ratified by some southern states as well, its shapers had further incentive to keep its language and provisions as uncontroversial as possible. Moreover, the uncertain question of how it would be read and interpreted by the courts, then and in the future, loomed large.

President Lincoln, like other northern leaders during the Civil War, was also acutely conscious that steps to end slavery in America would be lauded and appreciated by another very meaningful audience: posterity. "We of this Congress and this administration will be remembered in spite of ourselves," he had assured legislators in his annual message to Congress of December 1, 1862. "In giving *freedom* to the *slave*, we *assure* freedom to the *free*—honorable alike in what we give, and what we preserve.... The way is plain, peaceful, generous, just—a way which, if followed, the world will forever applaud, and God must forever bless." Indeed, the Thirteenth Amendment, like the Emancipation Proclamation, continues to garner laurels for those associated with it, as Lincoln hoped and expected it would.

Impact

The Thirteenth Amendment was widely hailed upon its passage and ratification for effectively ending slavery and bringing the United States into closer proximity to its ideals of freedom and democracy. The decree left open, however, the questions of whether former slaves would possess the full rights of citizenship and of what precisely those rights were. Lincoln's successor, Andrew Johnson, felt that no further federal civil rights legislation was necessary. On the other hand, congressional Republicans, who were displeased with the slow pace of change in the postwar southern states—and with those states' implementation of racist black codes in attempts to create slavery-like status for African Americans—increasingly used the enforcement clause of the Thirteenth Amendment to justify further action to ensure that slavery would be fully abolished. Among the first legislative efforts along these lines were the Freedmen's Bureau Acts, passed in 1865 and 1866, and the Civil Rights Act, passed in 1866—all aimed at ensuring that the former Confederate states did not violate the rights of African Americans. Johnson vetoed the two 1866 bills, breaking decisively with his former Republican allies on Reconstruction and civil rights, but Congress overrode both vetoes. The Civil Rights Act represented an attempt by Republicans to define just what the freedom they had offered the former slaves in the Thirteenth Amendment would look like. The Civil Rights Act defined all native-born Americans as citizens of the United States, negating the Supreme Court's suggestion in the 1857 *Dred Scott* case that African Americans could not lay claim to citizenship rights. These rights, as envisioned in the Civil Rights Act, did not necessarily include voting rights.

Subsequent constitutional amendments would go further to define the legal rights of African Americans. Ratified in 1868, the Fourteenth Amendment specified that, as citizens, African Americans were entitled to due process and the equal protection of the law; ratified in 1870, the Fifteenth Amendment outlawed the use of race to disqualify citizens from voting. Together, the Thirteenth Amendment and its two successors were truly revolutionary, laying the foundation for a more egalitarian and democratic nation. Widespread resistance to implementing these amendments among white southerners—and their continued use of force, intimidation, and other extralegal methods of denying civil rights to African Americans—ultimately led to the collapse of the Reconstruction state governments in the South by 1877. Afterward came the gradual restoration of white supremacy in the form of a new system of discriminatory segregation. This Jim Crow era lasted for the better part of a century, with the promise of the Thirteenth Amendment left unfulfilled, until the civil rights movement of the 1950s and 1960s.

Indeed, for decades after its passage, as segregation was brutally imposed on African Americans, the Thirteenth Amendment was rarely cited by the courts. Generally, in the late nineteenth century the Supreme Court defined the freedom offered by the Thirteenth Amendment very narrowly and was reluctant to concede to the federal government sufficient power to enforce it. In 1872 the Court ruled in *Blyew v. United States* that states could refuse to allow African Americans to deliver trial testimony. The 1873 Slaughter-House Cases ruling gave states virtually free rein in defining what the rights of state citizenship for African

Americans consisted of, taking the teeth out of the Thirteenth and Fourteenth Amendments. The *Plessy v. Ferguson* decision of 1896 allowed segregation, in a notorious phrase, as long as the facilities offered to African Americans were "separate but equal." The ruling was ominously silent on how this "equality" would be determined and enforced. Further, in the 1906 case of *Hodges v. United States*, the Court averred that state courts would have the sole responsibility of identifying and addressing violations of the Thirteenth Amendment, a power that, needless to say, Jim Crow–era southern states were not aggressive in exercising.

Ultimately, a late-twentieth-century Supreme Court case resurrected the dormant amendment. In the *Jones v. Alfred H. Mayer Company* ruling of 1968, the Court insisted that the constitutional rights of an African American man had been violated when he was barred from buying property in a private housing development owing to his race. The Thirteenth Amendment, the court ruled, had given African Americans freedom and the same status as all other Americans, making such discrimination illegal. Coming in the wake of other judicial and legislative civil rights rulings of the 1950s and 1960s, this case suggested that the full promise of the Thirteenth Amendment would finally be fulfilled.

See also *Dred Scott v. Sandford* (1857); Emancipation Proclamation (1863); Fourteenth Amendment to the U.S. Constitution (1868); Fifteenth Amendment to the U.S. Constitution (1870); *Plessy v. Ferguson* (1896).

Further Reading

■ Articles

Belz, Herman. "The Civil War Amendments to the Constitution: The Relevance of Original Intent." *Constitutional Commentary* 5 (1988): 115–141.

Zuckert, Michael P. "Completing the Constitution: The Thirteenth Amendment." *Constitutional Commentary* 4 (1987): 259–284.

■ Books

Basler, Roy P., ed. *The Collected Works of Abraham Lincoln*. 9 vols. New Brunswick, N.J.: Rutgers University Press, 1953–1955.

Belz, Herman. *Abraham Lincoln, Constitutionalism, and Equal Rights in the Civil War Era*. New York: Fordham University Press, 1998.

Berlin, Ira, et al., eds. *Freedom: A Documentary History of Emancipation, 1861–1867*. 4 vols. Cambridge, U.K.: Cambridge University Press, 1982–1993.

Blassingame, John W., et al., eds. *The Frederick Douglass Papers*. 5 vols. New Haven: Yale University Press, 1979–1992.

Blight, David W., and Brooks D. Simpson, eds. *Union and Emancipation: Essays on Politics and Race in the Civil War Era*. Kent, Ohio: Kent State University Press, 1997.

Bogue, Allan G. *The Earnest Men: Republicans of the Civil War Senate*. Ithaca, N.Y.: Cornell University Press, 1981.

Cox, Samuel S. *Eight Years in Congress, from 1857 to 1865*. New York: D. Appleton, 1865.

Dana, Charles A. *Recollections of the Civil War: With the Leaders at Washington and in the Field in the Sixties*. New York: D. Appleton, 1898.

Du Bois, W. E. B. *Black Reconstruction in America: An Essay toward a History of the Part Which Black Folk Played in the Attempt to Reconstruct Democracy in America, 1860–1880*. New York: Russell and Russell, 1963.

Hyman, Harold M. *A More Perfect Union: The Impact of the Civil War and Reconstruction on the Constitution*. New York: Knopf, 1973.

Merrill, Walter M., ed. *The Letters of William Lloyd Garrison*. 6 vols. Cambridge, Mass.: Belknap Press of Harvard University Press, 1971–1981.

Nicolay, John G. *A Short Life of Abraham Lincoln*. New York: Century, 1902.

Paludan, Phillip S. *A Covenant with Death: The Constitution, Law, and Equality in the Civil War Era*. Urbana: University of Illinois Press, 1975.

Vorenberg, Michael. *Final Freedom: The Civil War, the Abolition of Slavery, and the Thirteenth Amendment*. Cambridge, U.K.: Cambridge University Press, 2001.

■ **Web Sites**

"Annual Message to Congress, Abraham Lincoln, December 1, 1862." Teaching American History Web site.
  http://www.teachingamericanhistory.org/library/index.asp?document=1065.

"Documents from *Freedom: A Documentary History of Emancipation, 1861–1867*." University of Maryland Web site.
  http://www.history.umd.edu/Freedmen/sampdocs.htm.

"The End of Slavery: The Creation of the 13th Amendment." Harp-Week Web site.
  http://13thamendment.harpweek.com/.

"From Slavery to Freedom: The African-American Pamphlet Collection, 1822–1909." Library of Congress "American Memory" Web site.
  http://memory.loc.gov/ammem/aapchtml/aapchome.html.

—Michael Thomas Smith

Questions for Further Study

1. Why might some Americans have voted for the Thirteenth Amendment in 1865? Why might some have voted against it?

2. President Lincoln regarded the Thirteenth Amendment as a "king"s cure-all for all the evils" of slavery, but following his death Congress passed two more amendments in an attempt to complete the work of ensuring freedom and equality for freedmen. Compare and contrast the Thirteenth Amendment with the Fourteenth and Fifteenth Amendments. Which do you think did the most to advance civil rights, and why do you think so?

3. Historians continue to argue about who should receive the most credit for ending slavery: President Lincoln, Congress, the army, or the slaves themselves. Which of these parties do you think played the most crucial role in this process, and why do you think so?

4. The great African American historian and political activist W. E. B. Du Bois wrote in his 1935 book *Black Reconstruction in America* that "slavery was not abolished even after the Thirteenth Amendment." To what extent and in what ways was this true? How was this possible, once the amendment had become law? What does this suggest about the power of the Constitution?

Thirteenth Amendment to the U.S. Constitution

◆ **Section 1.**

Neither slavery nor involuntary servitude, except as a punishment for crime whereof the party shall have been duly convicted, shall exist within the United States, or any place subject to their jurisdiction.

◆ **Section 2.**

Congress shall have power to enforce this article by appropriate legislation.

"We feel in danger of our lives, of our property, and of everything else."

Overview

The testimony taken by the Joint Committee on Reconstruction consists of a series of interviews conducted after the Civil War to determine the condition of society in the former Confederacy. The Joint Committee, formed by both Senate and House members of the Thirty-ninth Congress in December 1865, investigated reports of violence toward white Unionists and freed slaves in order to determine the extent of federal intervention needed in the South. Opposed to President Andrew Johnson's policy of quick restoration of the southern states to their prewar status, also known as "Presidential Reconstruction," the Joint Committee interviewed 144 people about their experiences in the postwar South, asking specifically about white southerners' treatment of freedpeople and white Unionists as well as their attitudes toward the federal government. Upon the conclusion of its investigation, the committee issued a report summarizing its findings on March 5, 1866, which included transcripts of witnesses' testimony. The testimony largely supported the belief held by Johnson's opponents, the Radical Republicans, that greater oversight was needed to ensure that freedpeople's rights were protected and that the old power structures that had supported slavery and secession were not reestablished. The testimony gave Radical Republicans the proof they needed to wrest control away from Johnson and institute a set of policies known as "Radical Reconstruction," which included a period of military governance, disfranchisement of white Confederates, the extension of the Freedmen's Bureau, and the passage of the Fourteenth and Fifteenth Amendments to the U.S. Constitution.

Context

Although the Confederate general Robert E. Lee surrendered what remained of his army to Ulysses S. Grant on April 9, 1865, the official cessation of armed conflict left many unresolved questions. Paramount among them was what would become of the former Confederate states and their leaders. Should the two sections immediately be reunited and set

about the work of healing and forgiving, or should the South remain separate, under federal control, until its people could demonstrate that they had been thoroughly reconstructed? Could southern whites be trusted to oversee their own affairs, and, most important, respect the rights of the newly freed? Although many rejoiced that the war was over, these troubling questions loomed large on the political horizon.

President Andrew Johnson favored a policy of quick restoration of the southern states to their prewar status. A native of Tennessee and an ardent Unionist, Johnson assumed the presidency upon Abraham Lincoln's death on April 15, 1865. At first, Johnson's well-known dislike for slaveholders and their aristocratic pretensions led many Republicans to believe that his treatment of the South would be much harsher than that of his predecessor, who had urged charity toward errant southerners. Johnson's initial plans to deprive wealthy southerners and high-ranking Confederate leaders of citizenship, along with his demands that the southern states repeal their secession ordinances and ratify the Thirteenth Amendment before being readmitted to the Union, pleased the more radical members of his party. Soon, however, it became apparent that Johnson would do little else to ensure a peaceful transition from slavery to freedom in the South.

Following what he believed would have been President Lincoln's course of action, Johnson issued a general amnesty proclamation in May 1865, effectively relieving Confederates of any fear of criminal prosecution or other retributive measures the government might take against them. He appointed provisional governors to the southern states, many of whom had Confederate sympathies. He also removed federal troops from the South upon request from the provisional governors and in 1866 vetoed key measures aimed at protecting freed slaves, namely the renewal of the Freedmen's Bureau and enactment of a bill on civil rights. (Congress overrode both vetoes.)

Johnson's plans were unpopular among many within his own party, who favored greater federal intervention in the South and a longer, more sustained plan of Reconstruction. Known as Radical Republicans, these men came from an antislavery background and had struggled to make emancipation the primary war aim. While Lincoln hesitated, fearing that such a move would alienate the border states and push them out of the Union, men like Massachusetts sena-

Time Line

1860

■ **December**
Southern states begin to secede from the Union.

1861

■ **April 12**
The first shots of the Civil War are fired at Fort Sumter, South Carolina.

1865

■ **April 9**
Robert E. Lee surrenders to Ulysses S. Grant at the village of Appomattox Court House, Virginia.

■ **April 15**
President Abraham Lincoln dies from wounds received the previous evening at the hands of John Wilkes Booth; Andrew Johnson becomes president.

■ **May 29**
President Johnson issues a general amnesty proclamation restoring rights and property to most southern rebels once they have taken a loyalty oath, but which excludes civil and diplomatic officials, military officers, and those who left judicial or political offices to join the Confederacy.

■ **November**
The Mississippi state legislature passes its Black Code; other southern states follow suit.

■ **December 3**
The Thirty-ninth Congress meets in Washington, D.C. Among its newly elected members are many former Confederates elected by unreconstructed state legislatures, whom Republicans refuse to seat.

■ **December 13**
The Joint Committee on Reconstruction is formed by a joint resolution of Congress to investigate the condition of affairs in the southern states and the effects of Johnson's leniency toward former rebels.

■ **December 19**
The Thirteenth Amendment is ratified, officially abolishing slavery in the United States.

tor Charles Sumner and Pennsylvania congressman Thaddeus Stevens urged the president to see that emancipation was not only a military necessity but also a moral imperative. Their leadership on the issue eventually secured the Thirteenth Amendment (December 1865), which abolished slavery forever. However, Radical Republicans felt that more needed to be done in order to ensure that freedpeople's rights would be firmly established and protected.

Former Confederates responded to Johnson's leniency by passing laws aimed at curtailing black freedom. Known as Black Codes, these state laws attempted to regulate labor relations between white employers and black workers by making it illegal to break an employment contract. The laws enacted fines and jail time for vagrancy, thereby forcing black people to sign contracts with whites, who were often their former owners. The laws also required the apprenticeship of minor children. The Black Codes also forbade freedpeople from owning or carrying firearms, so as to limit their ability to defend themselves against assault or coercion. They instituted curfews and sometimes required blacks to carry passes in order to travel off the plantation, just as they formerly had to do as slaves. The Black Codes criminalized a variety of personal behaviors, such as using insulting language or gestures or otherwise being "insolent." White southerners proudly declared their intention to establish "a white man's country," and the Black Codes aimed to do just that.

White southerners elected former Confederate leaders to positions of political power. Candidates running for office would print on their tickets "late of the Confederate army," and former Confederate officers often wore their old uniforms. In Alabama, a man accused of murdering a Union general was elected sheriff. The unreconstructed state legislatures sent high-ranking Confederate leaders, including their former vice president, Alexander H. Stephens of Georgia, to Congress. They also called state constitutional conventions that valorized the southern war effort and refused to repudiate secession. President Johnson advised provisional governors against such acts of open defiance, but his advice fell on deaf ears. Ultimately, the former Confederates overplayed their hand. Their disloyal behavior and attacks against freedpeople caused Johnson much embarrassment and fueled Radical criticisms against him.

It was in this context that the Joint Committee on Reconstruction was established by the Thirty-Ninth Congress on December 13, 1865, to investigate and report on conditions in the former Confederate states and to propose necessary legislation. Nine representatives and six senators composed the committee: the senators William Pitt Fessenden of Massachusetts, James W. Grimes of Iowa, Ira Harris of New York, Jacob M. Howard of Michigan, Reverdy Johnson from Maryland, and George H. Williams of Oregon and the representatives Thaddeus Stevens of Pennsylvania, Elihu B. Washburne of Illinois, Justin S. Morrill of Vermont, Kentuckian Henry Grider, John A. Bingham from Ohio, Roscoe Conkling of New York, George S. Boutwell from Massachusetts, Missourian Henry T. Blow, and Andrew J. Rogers of New Jersey. Radical Republicans were a minority on the committee, as most of its members were moderate Republicans. There were only three Democrats.

For several months in 1866 four subcommittees took testimony in Washington, D.C., from a variety of sources: among them, U.S. military officers and Freedmen's Bureau officials; former Confederate leaders, including General Robert E. Lee and the Confederate vice president, Alexander H. Stephens; northerners who had spent time in the South; southern Unionists, and black southerners. Only 7 of the 144 witnesses called before the Joint Committee were black. There would have been no blacks testifying at all, except for the fact that a freedmen's rights convention coincided with the hearings in Washington, D.C., and the Virginia delegates to the convention petitioned to appear before the committee. The men were Daniel Norton, a free black man from New York trained as a physician; the Reverend William Thornton, a former slave and minister in Hampton; Madison Newby, a free black landowner from Norfolk who had worked as a boat pilot for Union forces during the war; Richard R. Hill, a former slave also living in Hampton; Alexander Dunlop, a free black before the war and trustee of the First Baptist Church in Williamsburg; Thomas Bain, a fugitive slave living in Massachusetts until emancipation, when he returned to Virginia; and Edmund Parsons, a house servant before the war living in Williamsburg. Based on the overall testimony (most of which was taken in February), the committee issued its report in March of 1866.

About the Author

The seven black men who testified before the Joint Committee came from diverse backgrounds. Their ages ranged from twenty-six to fifty. Some were freeborn, and others had been enslaved until the Emancipation Proclamation set them free. Two came from the North but had ties to Virginia. Despite these differences, however, all the men held positions of respect and authority in their local communities and acted as representatives both at the hearings of the Joint Committee and at a freedmen's convention that took place concurrently with the hearings in Washington, D.C.

Daniel Norton, twenty-six and the youngest among the black Virginians, was a physician from New York State who had come south either during or immediately after the war to aid the freed population. Although he was born in Williamsburg, it is not known whether Norton had been a slave or free or at what age he went to New York. Unlike Norton, the Reverend William Thornton, forty-two, had been a slave until 1863, when the Emancipation Proclamation went into effect. Madison Newby, thirty-three and from Surrey County, had been free before the war and owned his own house and land. Richard Hill, thirty-four, was a former slave from Hampton. Alexander Dunlop, forty-eight, was also a free black before the war, worked as a blacksmith, and was a trustee of the First Baptist Church in Williamsburg. Thomas Bain, forty, was a freedman who had escaped Virginia on the Underground Railroad and was living in

Time Line

1866

■ **January**
The Joint Committee begins to form four subcommittees to take testimony in Washington, D.C., relating to the condition of the South.

■ **February 3**
Seven black Virginians testify before the Joint Committee.

■ **March 5**
The Joint Committee issues its report to Congress and orders the findings and testimony printed for publication.

■ **April 9**
The Civil Rights Act of 1866 is passed by Congress over presidential veto; the bill guarantees equal protection to all citizens regardless of color.

■ **June 13**
Fearing that the Civil Rights Act might face a constitutional challenge, Congress proposes the Fourteenth Amendment to the U.S. Constitution.

■ **July 16**
The bill extending the Freedmen's Bureau is passed over presidential veto.

1868

■ **February 24**
The House of Representatives votes to impeach President Johnson over conflicts related to Reconstruction policy.

■ **July 9**
The Fourteenth Amendment is ratified, granting national citizenship "to all persons born or naturalized in the United States" and guaranteeing to them the rights of due process and equal protection.

1870

■ **February 3**
The Fifteenth Amendment is ratified, guaranteeing universal suffrage to all male citizens.

Massachusetts at the time of emancipation in 1863, when he returned to Virginia as a missionary. Edmund Parsons, who at fifty was the oldest of the men, had been a house slave in Williamsburg. These men's testimony reveals the attitudes of whites toward their former slaves and their efforts to reassert their domination and supremacy in all areas of life. The testimony provides an important view into life

The surrender of Robert E. Lee to Ulysses S. Grant, ending the Civil War (Library of Congress)

in the immediate postwar South and the struggles between freedpeople and southern whites to define freedom there. It also gives insight into the problems of establishing a system of wage labor after slavery and freedpeople's efforts to gain economic as well as political independence.

Explanation and Analysis of Document

The most powerful testimony came from the small group of black men who testified before the committee. Although they received some condescending questions from some Committee members (particularly Democrats opposed to the whole process), who asked if they had any "white blood" or could read and or write, the black deponents responded patiently and with great detail about freedpeople's desire to live peaceably and build a better life.

They testified to the mistreatment of freedpeople by white southerners and the need for increased federal protection. The physician Daniel Norton, living in Yorktown, Virginia, testified that he believed freedpeople would be "hunted and killed" if federal troops were removed. As a doctor working among the black community, he was in a position to observe their relationship with local whites. He related how numerous freedmen had not been paid their wages and how their white employers threw them off the land and sold the crops that the freedmen had raised. The

employers then dared the freedmen to complain to the government. He insisted that freedpeople were "law-abiding citizens" who loved the federal government and wanted nothing more than to work hard and be productive.

Like Norton, the Reverend William Thornton told of the violence freedpeople endured from whites. In his testimony, Thornton recalled how a white man became enraged at his mention of Abraham Lincoln's assassination in a sermon and told Thornton that once the troops and the Freedmen's Bureau were gone, "we will put you to rights" and promised to break up the black churches. Thornton also recounted how a white man shot a neighboring black man who had unintentionally trespassed on the white man's property.

The black witnesses also negated the contentions of many southern deponents that blacks were lazy and indolent and that they committed breaches of the peace by drinking, carrying weapons, and acting aggressively toward whites. Madison Newby, a landowner, related how he had gone to the county courthouse to pay his taxes but found no federal agent there to take them, so he held on to the money, fearing that disloyal southerners would pocket it. He insisted that blacks wanted to work and would work diligently for decent pay. He reminded the committee that as slaves, blacks were used to hard work. He said that in Surrey County whites would tie blacks up by the thumbs if they did not consent to work for low wages. Newby also testified that whites continued to patrol black neighborhoods, searching their houses, confiscating valuables, and terrorizing the residents.

Richard Hill, a former slave from Hampton, reassured the committee that blacks had no intentions of "amalgamating" with the whites. However, Hill did point out that during the years of slavery, white men frequently had sexual relations with black women, and he suspected that this would continue. White southerners and opponents of Radical Reconstruction argued that interracial marriage would result from extending civil and political rights to freedpeople.

Alexander Dunlop had aided Union troops by giving them information about the local area and had suffered because of it. He was considered a "Union man" and targeted for special abuse by former Confederates. He insisted that freedpeople were anxious to get an education. Because they were poor, however, and whites threatened teachers and drove them away, they needed assistance from the government.

Thomas Bain, living and working as a Methodist missionary in Norfolk, told how whites tricked freedpeople into believing that the military officials had ordered them to punish blacks. Because they did not want to disobey the government, Bain said, freedpeople often submitted to being whipped. Like the others, however, Bain also spoke of freedpeople's eagerness for education and independence.

Finally, Edmund Parsons, formerly a slave, testified that before he was emancipated he always felt "secure" with whites but that now he stood in fear of them. He testifies to the threats that had been made against him and describes how he had been evicted from his house. He also indicates that the African Americans he knows would like to become educated and are grateful for any education they receive.

A caricature of Reconstruction under Andrew Johnson, showing an acrobat with legs stretched between the head of ***Thaddeus Stevens*** (Library of Congress)

Audience

As part of a Congressional investigation, the Joint Committee's report and testimony aimed to persuade members of Congress to vote in favor of the Radical Republicans' measures and thereby override President Johnson's vetoes of the Freedmen's Bureau and Civil Rights bills. Upon publication, the report and testimony created a public record justifying federal intervention in the South and amending the Constitution to guarantee citizenship rights to African Americans. Northern newspapers reported on the committee's investigation and excerpted testimony, thereby broadening the documents' scope beyond the walls of Congress. In the end, the black Virginians who testified were speaking directly to Congress and the nation.

Impact

After hearing the testimony, the Joint Committee issued a lengthy report and made recommendations to Congress.

The report consists of three parts: the majority report, the minority report, and the testimony. The testimony is divided into three parts. Part I contains the testimony from Tennessee; Part II contains that from Virginia, North Carolina, and South Carolina; and Part III contains testimony from Georgia, Alabama, Mississippi, Arkansas, Florida, Louisiana, and Texas. In the majority report, Republican members of the committee made their case against President Johnson's quick restoration of the southern states and called for tougher measures, including continued use of federal troops, the extension of the Freedmen's Bureau, and passage of the Fourteenth Amendment. Citing testimony given to the committee regarding former Confederates' abuse of freedpeople and white Unionists, the report argued that the southern states remained in a state of open rebellion. The minority report, signed by Reverdy Johnson, Henry Grider, and Andrew Rogers, the Democrats on the committee, countered the majority's conclusions by accusing them of stacking the witness pool in their favor and ignoring evidence presented that proved the South was peaceable and that any violence committed

"Question. Do they find any difficulty in obtaining employment at fair wages? … Answer. They do find some difficulty. The slaveholders, who have owned them, say that they will take them back, but cannot pay them any wages. Some are willing to pay a dollar a month, and some less, and some are only willing to give them their clothing and what they eat. They are not willing to pay anything for work."

(Dr. Daniel Norton)

"Question. Do you feel any danger? … Answer. We feel in danger of our lives, of our property, and of everything else."

(Alexander Dunlop)

"Question. Are the black people there anxious for education and to go to school? Answer: Generally they are; but in my neighborhood they are afraid to be caught with a book"

(Madison Newby)

"Question. How are the black people treated in Virginia by the whites since the close of hostilities? Answer. The only hope the colored people have is in Uncle Sam's bayonets."

(Thomas Bain)

was the work of outside agitators or freedmen themselves. The minority report supported President Johnson's lenient policy toward the South. The testimony consists of transcripts of the interviews conducted during the committee's investigation, mostly with white witnesses.

The majority report placed the blame for southern violence squarely on President Johnson's shoulders. At the end of the war, the southern states, according to the report, "were in a state of utter exhaustion," but Johnson had missed a golden opportunity to remake southern society for the better. The report charged Johnson with neglecting his obligation to preserve the life and property of loyal citizens: As "commander-in-chief of a victorious army it was his duty, under the law of nations … to restore order, to preserve property, and to protect the people against violence from any quarter until provision should be made by law for their government." The report argued that Johnson had violated his duty by withdrawing military authority and re-

instating disloyal leaders. He had ignored evidence of continued disloyalty, hostility to the government, and violence against freedpeople and loyal whites. Furthermore, he had acted unconstitutionally by assuming unilateral power to reorganize the governments of the southern states, a task the report claimed belonged not to the president but to Congress. By portraying Johnson as not simply inept but criminally negligent, the majority report laid the foundations for his future impeachment.

The report's aggressive tone reflected not only the level of animosity that existed between Radical Republicans and President Johnson but also the importance of controlling the war's meaning for the Republican Party. Radical Republicans remained committed to the emancipationist vision of the war. The report rejected the legality of secession and labeled the Confederate war effort as treasonous as well as murderous.

The minority report claimed that once the war ceased, so too did Congress's war power. Therefore, Johnson's policy of restoration was both expedient and constitutional. They believed that Radical Republicans were driven by greed and revenge. Yet an additional concern animated the minority's opposition to Radical Reconstruction: economics. Not only would it be very expensive to oversee such an expansive Reconstruction effort, it also might delay the South's reemergence as the world's primary producer of cotton.

Whatever the minority objections, the testimony of the seven black men compelled Congress to act on behalf of freedpeople. The Joint Committee's report helped persuade moderate Republicans, who were skeptical of increasing federal intervention, to take a more vigorous path to southern Reconstruction. This shift enabled Radical Republicans to wrest control from President Johnson and eventually led to his impeachment for efforts to circumvent Congress. As a result of the Joint Committee's investigation, Congress extended the Freedmen's Bureau and passed the Civil Rights Act of 1866. The report introduced the Fourteenth Amendment and paved the way for the Fifteenth Amendment, granting universal suffrage to all men regardless of color.

The Joint Committee's report was one of a flurry of such reports and other documents that were issued in 1866. Among them was Carl Schurz's *The Condition of the South: Extracts from the Report of Major-General Carl Schurz, on the States of South Carolina, Georgia, Alabama, Mississippi and Louisiana: Addressed to the President*. Schurz's conclusion was that in

his travels throughout the South (at the request of President Johnson), he saw little in the way of national feeling; instead, the war was seen as the result of the perfidy of the Yankees. He noted, too, that while the South fought against the Union, blacks did all they could to aid the Union.

Also in 1866, Secretary of War Edwin Stanton wrote *Murder of Union Soldiers in North Carolina*, a report issued to the U.S. House of Representatives detailing atrocities committed against Union loyalists and any persons or organizations that aided blacks. Stanton noted that churches and schools were favorite targets and that the South was relying on Johnson and a Democratic Congress to keep blacks in subordinate positions. On July 25, 1866, Elihu Benjamin Washburne, a congressional representative from Illinois and a member of the Select Committee on the Memphis Riots, issued a report, *Memphis Riots and Massacres*, to Congress. The riot had taken place in May of that year and was one of the events that prompted Congress to assume control of Reconstruction. During the riot, white mobs attacked a black shantytown in Memphis and killed nearly fifty people in an early show of white southern rejection of emancipation. Meanwhile, after the First Convention of Colored Men of Kentucky, held in Lexington, Kentucky, in March 1866, the group issued its proceedings, asserting the place of African Americans in the body politic. Later that year, in October, the Freedmen held a convention in Raleigh, North Caroli-

Questions for Further Study

1. What was the distinction between "Presidential Reconstruction" and "Radical Reconstruction"? What do you think might have been the effects if Presidential Reconstruction had continued to be the policy of the Union?

2. What do you think were President Andrew Johnson's motives in treating the rebellious South with leniency in the immediate aftermath of the Civil War? Do you believe he was right or wrong? Explain.

3. Throughout the Civil War, numerous people living in the Confederacy were loyal to the Union at heart and, in some instances, did what they could to aid the Union by, for example, providing information to Union generals. What do you think the position of these Union loyalists would have been in the months and years following the war? How vulnerable to reprisals do you think they would have been?

4. Even in the twenty-first century, debates continue to rage about the legacy of the Confederacy and its role in the Civil War. Some people continue to regard the Confederacy—and the Confederate flag—as a symbol of a way of life and of an attitude toward state and regional interests versus federal interests. What is your position on this matter?

5. In the years immediately following the Civil War, many African Americans felt a sense of hope, despite the dangers and abuses they suffered. The Emancipation Proclamation had freed slaves, the Thirteenth Amendment abolished slavery, and numerous African Americans were elected to Congress. What happened? Why did this hope collapse in later years?

na, and through published minutes continued to agitate for equal rights and the vote. These documents, together with the Joint Committee report, gave the president, Congress, and the American public a vivid portrait of southern intransigence in the months following the Civil War.

See also Emancipation Proclamation (1863); Black Code of Mississippi (1865); Thirteenth Amendment to the U.S. Constitution (1865); Fourteenth Amendment to the U.S. Constitution (1868); Fifteenth Amendment to the U.S. Constitution (1870).

Further Reading

■ Articles

Lowe, Richard. "The Joint Committee on Reconstruction: Some Clarifications." *Southern Studies* 3 (Spring 1992): 55–65.

■ Books

Foner, Eric. *Reconstruction: America's Unfinished Revolution, 1863–1877.* New York: Harper & Row, 1988.

Franklin, John Hope. *Reconstruction after the Civil War.* 2nd ed. Chicago: University of Chicago Press, 1994.

Kendrick, Benjamin B. *The Journal of the Joint Committee of Fifteen on Reconstruction, 39th Congress, 1865–1867.* 1914. Reprint. New York: Negro Universities Press, 1969.

Report of the Joint Committee on Reconstruction at the First Session, Thirty-ninth Congress. Washington, D.C.: Government Printing Office, 1866.

Trefousse, Hans L. *The Radical Republicans: Lincoln's Vanguard for Racial Justice.* New York: Alfred A. Knopf, 1969.

Wilbur, W. Allan. "Joint Committee on Reconstruction, 1865." In *Congress Investigates: A Documented History, 1792–1974,* ed. Arthur M. Schlesinger, Jr., and Roger Bruns. New York: Chelsea House, 1975.

—Carole Emberton

TESTIMONY BEFORE THE JOINT COMMITTEE ON RECONSTRUCTION ON ATROCITIES IN THE SOUTH AGAINST BLACKS

Washington, February 3, 1866.

Dr. Daniel Norton (colored) sworn and examined.

By Mr. Howard:

Question. Where do you reside?

Answer. I reside in Yorktown, Virginia.

Question. How old are you?

Answer. About 26 years old.

Question. Are you a regularly licensed physician?

Answer. I am.

Question. Where were you educated?

Answer. In the State of New York. I studied privately under Dr. Warren.

Question. How long have you resided at Yorktown?

Answer. About two years.

Question. Are you a native of Virginia?

Answer. Yes, sir; I was born in Williamsburg, Virginia.

Question. What is the feeling among the rebels in the neighborhood of Yorktown towards the government of the United States?

Answer. They do not manifest a very cordial feeling toward the government of the United States. There are some, of course, who do, but the majority do not seem to manifest a good spirit or feeling.

Question. How are they disposed to treat you?

Answer. Me, as a man, they are generally disposed to treat well, but there are others of my fellow-men whom they do not treat as well.

Question. Are you employed as a physician in white families?

Answer. I have not been employed in any white families, except in one case, since I have been there. I principally practice among the colored.

Question. How do the returned rebels treat the colored people?

Answer. They have in some cases treated them well, but in more cases they have not. A number of persons living in the country have come into Yorktown and reported to the Freedmen's Bureau that they have not been treated well; that they worked all the year and had received no pay, and were driven off on the first of January. They say that the owners with whom they had been living rented out their places, sold their crops, and told them they had no further use for them, and that they might go to the Yankees.

Question. What is the condition of the colored people in that neighborhood?

Answer. They are poor, sir. There is a large settlement near Yorktown, called Slabtown, settled by the government during the war with those who came within the lines. The colored people there are doing such work as they can get to do, oystering, &c.

Question. Are not their old masters ready to employ them for wages?

Answer. There have been some sent for, and in several cases they received such bad treatment that they came back again. (Witness related several instances of this kind.)

Question. Are the colored people in your neighborhood willing to work for fair wages?

Answer. They are, sir.

Question. Do they find any difficulty in obtaining employment at fair wages?

Answer. They do find some difficulty. The slaveholders, who have owned them, say that they will take them back, but cannot pay them any wages. Some are willing to pay a dollar a month, and some less, and some are only willing to give them their clothing and what they eat. They are not willing to pay anything for work.

Question. Are the colored people generally provided with houses in which they can eat and sleep?

Answer. Yes, sir; such houses as they have built themselves, slab-houses.

Question. How do the colored people feel toward the government of the United States?

Answer. They feel determined to be law-abiding citizens. There is no other feeling among them.

Question. Are you a delegate sent to the city of Washington by some association?

Answer. I am. I was sent by three counties; I represent, perhaps, something like fifteen or twenty thousand people. The great trouble, in my opinion, is, that the colored people are not more disposed to return to their former homes on account of the treatment which those who have gone back have received.

Question. State generally whether or not the treatment which these colored people receive at the hands of their old white masters is kind or unkind?

Answer. It is not what I would consider kind or good treatment. Of course I do not mean to be understood that there are not some who treat them kindly, but I mean generally; they do not treat them kindly.

Question. In case of the removal of the military force from among you, and also of the Freedmen's Bureau, what would the whites do with you?

Answer. I do not think that the colored people would be safe. They would be in danger of being hunted and killed. The spirit of the whites against the blacks is much worse than it was before the war; a white gentleman with whom I was talking made this remark: he said he was well disposed toward the colored people, but that, finding that they took up arms against him, he had come to the conclusion that he never wanted to have anything to do with them, or to show any spirit of kindness toward them. These were his sentiments.

Washington, February 3, 1866.

Reverend William Thornton (colored) sworn and examined.

By Mr. Howard:

Question. What is your age?

Answer. Forty-two, sir.

Question. Where were you born?

Answer. In Elizabeth City county, Virginia.

Question. What degree of education have you received?

Answer. My education is very narrowly limited; I have not had the advantages of a first-rate education.

Question. You can read and write?

Answer. Yes, sir.

Question. Can you read the Bible?

Answer. Oh, yes, sir.

Question. Can you read ordinary newspapers?

Answer. Yes, sir.

Question. Can you write a letter on business?

Answer. Yes, sir.

Question. Were you ever a slave?

Answer. Yes, sir.

Question. When were you made free?

Answer. I was made free under the proclamation.

Question. Where do you reside?

Answer. Hampton, Elizabeth City county, Virginia.

Question. How do the old rebel masters down there feel toward your race?

Answer. The feeling existing there now is quite disagreeable.

Question. Do they not treat the colored race with kindness down there?

Answer. No, sir.

Question. What acts of unkindness can you mention?

Answer. I was asked the other day if I did not know I was violating the law in celebrating marriages. I did not know that that was the case, and I went up to the clerk's office to inquire; I said nothing out of the way to the clerk of the court; I only asked him if there had been any provision for colored people to be lawfully married. Said he, "I do not know whether there is or not, and if they are granting licenses you can't have any; that is my business, not yours." After I found I was violating the law, I went to the Freedmen's Bureau and stated the case. A provision was afterwards made in the bureau granting licenses, and authorizing me to marry. Some days after that an old gentleman named Houghton, a white man living in the neighborhood of my church, was in the church. In my sermon I mentioned the assassination of Mr. Lincoln. Next day I happened to meet Houghton, who said to me, "Sir, as soon as we can get these Yankees off the ground and move that bureau, we will put you to rights; we will break up your church, and not one of you shall have a church here." Said I, "For what? I think it is for the safety of the country to have religious meetings, and for your safety as well as everybody else's." "We will not have it, sir," said he, and then he commenced talking about two classes of people whom they intended to put to rights, the colored people and the loyal white men. I asked him in what respect be was going to put them to rights; said he, "That is for myself."

Question. Is he a man of standing and condition in the neighborhood?

Answer. He owns property there.

Question. Is he a rebel?

Answer. Oh, yes.

Question. Can you speak of any acts of violence committed by the whites upon the blacks?

Answer. Yes, sir; about three weeks ago a colored man got another one to cut some wood for him, and sent him into the woods adjoining the property of a Mr. Britner, a white man. The colored man, not knowing the line between the two farms, cut down a tree on Britner's land, when Britner went into the woods and deliberately shot him as he would shoot a bird.

Question. Was he not indicted and punished for that?

Answer. They had him in prison.

Question. Is he not in prison now?

Answer. I heard that they had let him out last Sunday morning.

Question. Do you know any other instances of cruelty?

Answer. I have church once a month in Matthews county, Virginia, the other side of the bay. The last time I was over there an intelligent man told me that just below his house a lady and her husband, who had been at the meeting, received thirty-nine lashes for being there, according to the old law of Virginia, as if they had been slaves. This was simply because they were told not to go to hear a Yankee darkey talk. They said he was not a Yankee but was a man born in Virginia, in Hampton,

Question. Why did they not resist being flogged?

Answer. They are that much down.

Question. Did they not know that they had a right to resist?

Answer. They dare not do it.

Question. Why?

Answer. I do not know. On the 1st of January we had a public meeting there, at which I spoke. The next night when I was coming from the church, which is about a mile and a half from my house, I met a colored man who told me that there was a plot laid for me; I went back to the church and got five of my church members to come with me. I afterwards learned that a fellow named Mahon, a white man, had determined, for my speech that day, to murder me the first chance.

Question. Did that come to you in so authentic a form as to leave no doubt upon your mind?

Answer. I believe he made the threat. The next day he said to me, "We hope the time will come that these Yankees will be away from here, and then we will settle with you preachers." That gave me to understand that the threat was made.

Question. Do you wish to state any other instances?

Answer. These are as many as I care to speak of.

Question. You are up here as a delegate to make representations to the President in reference to the condition of the colored people?

Answer. Yes, sir.

Question. Are you a regularly ordained minister of the gospel?

Answer. Yes, sir.

Question. In what church?

Answer. In the Baptist church.

Washington, February 3, 1866.

Madison Newby (colored) sworn and examined.
By Mr. Howard:
Question. Have you any white blood in you?
Answer. No, sir.

Question. Where were you born?
Answer. In Surrey county, Virginia.
Question. How old are you?
Answer. Thirty-three.
Question. Can you read and write?
Answer. I cannot write; I can read a little.
Question. Can you read the Testament?
Answer. A little.
Question. Have you a family?
Answer. Yes, sir.
Question. Have you been a slave before the war?
Answer. No, sir; I never was a slave.
Question. How do the rebel white people treat you since the war?
Answer. They do not allow me to go where I came from, except I steal in there.
Question. Why not?
Answer. They say I am a Yankee. I have been there, but was driven away twice; they said I would not be allowed to stay there, and I had better get away as quick as possible. I had gone down to look after my land.
Question. Do you own land there?
Answer. Yes.
Question. How much?
Answer. One hundred and fifty acres.
Question. Did you pay for it?
Answer. Yes.
Question. Do you stand in fear of the rebel white men?
Answer. Yes, sir, I do. If all the Union men that are down there would protect us we would not be so much afraid. I went down there to pay my taxes upon my land, but I could not see any person to pay them to; I didn't want to pay any but the United States government; and finally, they told me at the courthouse that I had better let it alone until I could see further about it.
Question. What is your land worth?
Answer. I gave $700 for it.
Question. Is there a house on it?
Answer. Yes.
Question. Do the colored people down there love to work?
Answer. They work if they can get anything for it; but the rebel people down there who have got lands will not let the colored people work unless they work for their prices, and they drive them away. They expect colored people down there to work for ten or eighteen cents a day. Six or eight dollars a month is the highest a colored man can get; of course he gets his board, but he may have a family of six to support on these wages, and of course he cannot do it.

Question. How do you get your living?

Answer. I am living in Norfolk at present. I piloted the Union forces there when they first came to Surrey; and afterwards the rebels would not let me go back.

Question. Were you impressed by the Union forces, or did you voluntarily act as a guide?

Answer. I was impressed. I told the Union forces when they came that unless they were willing to protect me I did not want them to take me away, because my living was there; and they promised they would see to me.

Question. Did they pay you for your services?

Answer. No, sir.

Question. They gave you enough to eat and drink?

Answer. They gave me plenty to eat when I was travelling, but nothing to drink except water.

Question. Now that the blacks are made free, will they not, if left to themselves without the protection of the whites, become strollers and rovers about the country and live in idleness, and pilfer and misbehave generally?

Answer. No, sir.

Question. Why not?

Answer. Because they have all been used to work, and will work if they can get anything to do.

Question. Do they not want to go away from the old places where they have been accustomed to live and go off west somewhere?

Answer. No, sir; we want to stay in our old neighborhoods, but those of us who have gone away are not allowed to go back. In Surrey county they are taking the colored people and tying them up by the thumbs if they do not agree to work for six dollars a month; they tie them up until they agree to work for that price, and then they make them put their mark to a contract.

Question. Did you ever see a case of that kind?

Answer. Yes, sir, I did.

Question. How many cases of that kind have you ever seen?

Answer. Only one; I have heard of several such, but I have only seen one.

Question. What is the mode of tying up by the thumbs?

Answer. They have a string tied around the thumbs just strong enough to hold a man's weight, so that his toes just touch the ground; and they keep the man in that position until he agrees to do what they say. A man cannot endure it long.

Question. What other bad treatment do they practice on the blacks? Do they whip them?

Answer. Yes, sir; just as they did before the war; I see no difference.

Question. Have you seen them whipped since the war?

Answer. Several times.

Question. By their old masters?

Answer. By the old people around the neighborhood; the old masters get other people to do it.

Question. Do they whip them just as much as they did before the war?

Answer. Just the same; I do not see any alteration in that. There are no colored schools down in Surrey county; they would kill any one who would go down there and establish colored schools. There have been no meetings or anything of that kind. They patrol our houses just us formerly.

Question. What do you mean by patrolling your houses?

Answer. A party of twelve or fifteen men go around at night searching the houses of colored people, turning them out and beating them. I was sent here as a delegate to find out whether the colored people down there cannot have protection. They are willing to work for a living; all they want is some protection and to know what their rights are; they do not know their rights; they do not know whether they are free or not, there are so many different stories told them.

Question. Where did you learn to read?

Answer. I first picked up a word from one and then from another.

Question. Have you ever been at school?

Answer. Never in my life.

Question. Are the black people there anxious for education and to go to school?

Answer. Generally they are; but down in my neighborhood they are afraid to be caught with a book.

Washington, February 3, 1866.

Richard R. Hill (colored) sworn and examined.

By Mr. Howard:

Question. Where do you live?

Answer. Hampton, Virginia.

Question. That is where President Tyler used to live?

Answer. Yes, sir.

Question. Did you know him?

Answer. Yes, I knew him pretty well.

Question. Can you read and write?

Answer. Yes, sir.

Question. How old are you?

Answer. About thirty-four years.

Question. Were you ever a slave?

Answer. Yes, sir.

Question. When did you become free?

Answer. When the proclamation was issued. I left Richmond in 1863.

Question. Did you serve in the rebel army?

Answer. No, sir.

Question. Or in the Union army?

Answer. No, sir.

Question. How do the rebels down there, about Hampton, treat the colored people?

Answer. The returned rebels express a desire to get along in peace if they can. There have been a few outrages out upon the roadside there. One of the returned Union colored soldiers was met out there and beaten very much.

Question. By whom was he beaten?

Answer. It was said they were rebels; they had on Union overcoats, but they were not United States soldiers. Occasionally we hear of an outrage of that kind, but there are none in the little village where I live.

Question. What appears to be the feeling generally of the returned rebels towards the freedmen; is it kind or unkind?

Answer. Well, the feeling that they manifest as a general thing is kind, so far as I have heard.

Question. Are they willing to pay the freedmen fair wages for their work?

Answer. No, sir; they are not willing to pay the freedmen more than from five to eight dollars a month.

Question. Do you think that their labor is worth more than that generally?

Answer. I do, sir; because, just at this time, everything is very dear, and I do not see how people can live and support their families on those wages.

Question. State whether the black people down there are anxious to go to school?

Answer. Yes, sir; they are anxious to go to school; we have schools there every day that are very well filled; and we have night schools that are very well attended, both by children and aged people; they manifest a great desire for education.

Question. Who are the teachers; white or black?

Answer. White, sir.

Question. How are the white teachers treated by the rebels down there?

Answer. I guess they are not treated very well, because they have very little communication between each other. I have not heard of any threatening expression in regard to them.

Question. Did you ever hear any threats among the whites to reduce your race to slavery again?

Answer. They have said, and it seems to be a prevalent idea, that if their representatives were received in Congress the condition of the freedmen would be very little better than that of the slaves, and that their old laws would still exist by which they would reduce them to something like bondage. That has been expressed by a great many of them.

Question. What has become of your former master?

Answer. He is in Williamsburg.

Question. Have you seen him since the proclamation?

Answer. Yes, sir.

Question. Did he want you to go back and live with him?

Answer. No, sir; he did not ask me to go back, but he was inquiring of me about another of his slaves, who was with him at the evacuation of Williamsburg by the rebels.

Question. How do you feel about leaving the State of Virginia and going off and residing as a community somewhere else?

Answer. They do not wish to leave and go anywhere else unless they are certain that the locality where they are going is healthy and that they can get along.

Question. Are they not willing to be sent back to Africa?

Answer. No, sir.

Question. Why not?

Answer. They say that they have lived here all their days, and there were stringent laws made to keep them here; and that if they could live here contented as slaves, they can live here when free.

Question. Do you not think that to be a very absurd notion?

Answer. No, sir; if we can get lands here and can work and support ourselves, I do not see why we should go to any place that we do not want to go to.

Question. If you should stay here, is there not danger that the whites and blacks would intermarry and amalgamate?

Answer. I do not think there is any more danger now than there was when slavery existed. At that time there was a good deal of amalgamation.

Question. Amalgamation in Virginia?

Answer. There was no actual marrying, but there was an intermixture to a great extent. We see it very plainly. I do not think that that troubles the colored race at all.

Question. But you do not think that a Virginia white man would have connexion with a black woman?

Answer. I do, sir; I not only think so, but I know it from past experience. It was nothing but the stringent laws of the south that kept many a white man from marrying a black woman.

Question. It would be looked upon as a very wicked state of things, would it not, for a while man to marry a black woman?

Answer. I will state to you as a white lady stated to a gentleman down in Hampton, that if she felt disposed to fall in love with or marry a black man, it was nobody's business but hers; and so I suppose, that if the colored race get all their rights, and particularly their equal rights before the law, it would not hurt the nation or trouble the nation.

Question. In such a case do you think the blacks would have a strong inclination to unite with the whites in marriage?

Answer. No, sir; I do not. I do not think that the blacks would have so strong an inclination to unite with the whites as the whites would have to unite with the blacks.

Washington, D. C. February 3, 1866.

Alexander Dunlop (colored) sworn and examined.
By Mr. Howard:
Question. How old are you?
Answer. Forty-eight years.
Question. Where do you reside?
Answer. In Williamsburg, Virginia. I was born there.
Question. Have you ever been a slave?
Answer. Never, sir.
Question. Are you able to read and write?
Answer. No, sir; I can read some. That was not allowed me there.
Question. Can you read the Bible?
Answer. Yes, sir.
Question. Do you belong to a church?
Answer. Yes; I belong to the First Baptist church of Williamsburg. I am one of the leading men and trustees.
Question. About how many are included in the church?
Answer. Our minutes show seven hundred and thirty-six.
Question. Do you own the church building?
Answer. We do.
Question. Are you a delegate to the President of the United States?
Answer. Yes, sir; I was sent by my people convened at a large mass meeting.
Question. For what purpose?
Answer. My purpose was to let the government know our situation, and what we desire the government to do for us if it can do it. We feel down there without any protection.
Question. Do you feel any danger?
Answer. We do.
Question. Danger of what?
Answer. We feel in danger of our lives, of our property, and of everything else.
Question. Why do you feel so?
Answer. From the spirit which we see existing there every day toward us as freedmen.
Question. On the part of whom?
Answer. On the part of the rebels. I have a great chance to find out these people. I have been with them before the war. They used to look upon me as one of the leading men there. I have suffered in this war; I was driven away from my place by Wise's raid; and so far as I, myself, am concerned, I do not feel safe; and if the military were removed from there I would not stay in Williamsburg one hour, although what little property I possess is there.
Question. In case of the removal of the military, what would you anticipate?
Answer. Nothing shorter than death; that has been promised to me by the rebels.
Question. Do they entertain a similar feeling toward all the freedmen there?
Answer. I believe, sir, that that is a general feeling, I ask them, sometimes, "Why is it? we have done you no harm." "Well," they say, "the Yankees freed you, and now let the Yankees take care of you: we want to have nothing to do with you." I say to them, "You have always been making laws to keep us here, and now you want to drive us away— for what?" They say, "We want to bring foreign immigration here, and drive every scoundrel of you away from here." I told them that I was born in Virginia, and that I am going to die in Virginia. "There is but one thing that will make me leave Virginia," I say, "and that is, for the government to withdraw the military and leave me in your hands; when it does that, I will go."
Question. Has your property been destroyed by the rebels?
Answer. I had not much, except my blacksmith's shop. I carried on a large business there. The rebels and the northern men destroyed everything I had; what the one did not take, the other did; they did not leave me even a hammer.
Question. Have you a family?
Answer. Yes, sir; a wife, but no children; I bought my wife.
Question. How much did you give for her?

Answer. I gave four hundred and fifty dollars for my wife, and seven hundred dollars for my wife's sister. After I bought my wife, they would not let me set her free. I paid the money, and got the bill of sale.

Question. What hindered her being free?

Answer. It was the law, they said. She had to stand as my slave.

Question. How extensive is this feeling of danger on the part of colored people there?

Answer. I believe, sincerely, that it is the general feeling.

Question. Did you ever see a black rebel, or hear of one?

Answer. I must be honest about that. I believe that we have had some as big rebel black men as ever were white.

Question. Many?

Answer. No, sir; they are "few and far between;" but I believe that any man who, through this great trouble that we have had, would do anything to stop the progress of the Union army, was a rebel. When Wise made his raid into Williamsburg, I just had time to leave my house and make my escape. They broke up everything I had; they took their bayonets and tore my beds all to pieces. All they wanted was Aleck Dunlop; they wanted to hang him before his own door. One day, since the fall of Richmond, I met General Henry A. Wise at Norfolk. He spoke to me, and asked me how I was. I said, "I am doing a little better than could be expected." Said he, "Why?" Said I, "Them devils of yours did not catch me; I was too smart for them that morning." "Do you think," said he, "they would have hurt you?" "No," said I, "I don't think so, but I know it; they had orders to hang me."

Question. Did Wise admit it?

Answer. He did not say so; but he turned and went off. The day that Wise's men were there, my wife asked them what had I done that they wanted to hang me in preference to anybody else? They said it was because I was a Union man. I had worked for the rebels from the time the war broke out until General McClellan moved up; and then they concocted a scheme to get me to Richmond; but when I saw the wagon coming for me, I went off in the opposite, direction. When General Hooker and General Kearney came there, they sent for me, within three hours of their arrival, and asked me about the country, and what I knew. I gave them all the information I could; that, through a colored friend, got to the secessionists and embittered them against me. The next Union officer who came there was Colonel Campbell, of the 5th Pennsylvania cavalry; and I believe he was as great a rebel as Jeff. Davis. He was governor there for a long time. They captured him, and carried him to Richmond.

Question. The rebels never caught you?

Answer. They have never caught me yet.

Question. How do the black people down there feel about education?

Answer. They want it, and they have a desire to get it; but the rebels use every exertion to keep teachers from them. We have got two white teachers in Williamsburg, and have got to put them in a room over a colored family.

Question. Do the black people contribute liberally to the support of their own schools?

Answer. They are not able, sir. The rebels made many raids there, and destroyed everything they could get their hands on belonging to colored people—beds and clothing.

Washington, February 3, 1866.

Thomas Bain (colored) sworn and examined.

By Mr. Howard:

Question. Where do you reside?

Answer. Norfolk, Virginia.

Question. How old are you?

Answer. I think about forty.

Question. Have you ever been a slave?

Answer. Yes.

Question. When were you made free?

Answer. When emancipation came, I was in Massachusetts; I had got there on the underground railroad. I went back to Virginia after the proclamation, and sent my child away to Massachusetts; I have been down there ever since.

Question. Can you read and write?

Answer. Yes, sir.

Question. Can you write a letter on business?

Answer. Yes, sir.

Question. Can you read the Bible?

Answer. Yes, sir.

Question. And newspapers?

Answer. Yes, sir; I subscribe to newspapers.

Question. What is your business?

Answer. Dentist.

Question. Did you ever start to be a dentist?

Answer. Yes, sir; I was raised in the business.

Question. Where?

Answer. In Norfolk. I spent ten years at it in Norfolk, and ten years in Massachusetts.

Question. Have you a family?

Answer. My wife died some time after I was married; I have one child—a daughter.

Question. Are you here as a delegate from the colored people of Norfolk?

Answer. Yes, sir.

Question. To make representations to the President?

Answer. Yes, sir.

Question. Have you had an interview with him?

Answer. No, sir.

Question. What is the feeling on the part of white rebels at Norfolk towards the colored people?

Answer. Their feelings are very hard—terrible. I have had a chance to travel around some, preaching.

Question. Do you preach?

Answer. Yes, sir; I am a volunteer missionary—a self-sustaining one. The church, under whose auspices I act, is not taxed for my services; neither are the people; I make my practice as I go along; just enough to support me; I can reach most of them in that way; I have a permanent office; and then I travel about the State and preach.

Question. To what denomination do you belong?

Answer. The Wesleyan Methodist.

Question. You preach to the colored people?

Answer. Yes; I have had occasion, of course, to visit a great many.

Question. How are the black people treated in Virginia by the whites since the close of hostilities?

Answer. The only hope the colored people have is in Uncle Sam's bayonets; without them, they would not feel any security; and what is true of the colored people in that respect, is also true of the Union men; the secessionists do not seem to discriminate between them; they do not seem to care whether a northern man is with us or not with us; if he is a Yankee, that is enough; they hardly wait to examine what his views are; it is not uncommon to hear such threats as this: "We will kill one negro, at least, for every rebel soldier killed by them."

Question. Did you, yourself, over hear such a threat as that made?

Answer. I have heard it at night, in the streets of Norfolk. (Witness related some incidents going to show how much afraid the colored people there are of ill treatment from the whites.) Last June there was a threat by a white citizen of Norfolk to get up a riot.

Question. Did he get one up?

Answer. Yes; they got one up.

Question. What did it result in?

Answer. It resulted in three colored men being shot. One white man got shot through the shoulder; had his arm amputated, and died. It was got up to attack the colored people, and clear all the negroes out of the city.

Question. Are the colored people whipped now as they used to be?

Answer. Not in my vicinity; I only hear reports of that.

Question. Have you heard of cases of whipping by white men?

Answer. Yes, sir.

Question. During the summer?

Answer. Yes, sir.

Question. Many cases?

Answer. Yes, sir; and it is not so much that the colored people are afraid of the white people, as it is that they are a law-abiding people.

Question. Do they submit to be whipped?

Answer. They do, in places near where there are military men. They fool the colored people into believing that the military ordered them to be whipped; they do not want to resist the government.

Question. Are the black people down there fond of education?

Answer. I think that they are excelled by no people in an eagerness to learn.

Washington, February 3, 1866.

Edmund Parsons (colored) sworn and examined.
By Mr. Howard:
Question. How old are yon?
Answer. A little over fifty.
Question. Where do you reside?
Answer. In Williamsburg, Virginia.
Question. Can you read and write?
Answer. I can read a little. I have been a regular house-servant, and I had a chance to turn my attention to it.
Question. Have you ever been a slave?
Answer. Yes, sir. I have been a slave from my childhood up to the time I was set free by the emancipation proclamation.
Question. How do the black people in your neighborhood feel toward the rebels?
Answer. I did think myself always secure with the whites; but it is very different now sir, very different.
Question. Do you stand in fear of them?
Answer. Yes, sir.
Question. What have you to be afraid off
Answer. When the Union forces came there first a good many officers became attached to me and my wife, and we felt perfectly secure; but now the rebels

use the officers that are there "to pull the chestnuts out of the fire."

Question. Have you heard threats of violence by white rebels against the blacks?

Answer. Yes.

Question. What do they threaten to do?

Answer. They threaten to do everything they can. My wife died about a year ago. I had a house, where I had been living for twenty years. A lawyer there went and got the provost marshal to send a guard and put me out of my house. They broke my things up, and pitched them out, and stole a part of them.

Question. The Union guard?

Answer. Yes, sir; it is a positive fact. They put me out of my own house. That was January, 1866.

Question. What was the pretext for putting you out?

Answer. My wife had been left free. She had a half-sister and a half-brother; and they pretended to be owners of the property where I had been living all my lifetime.

Question. Who was the provost marshal?

Answer. Reynolds.

Question. Do the returned rebels threaten to commit violence on the colored people there?

Answer. I can hear people complaining of that; but I have really been so mortified at the bad treatment I received, that I have not paid much attention.

Question. How do the colored people feel in regard to education?

Answer. They are very anxious to get education, and feel grateful for it.

Question. Are you a member of a church?

Answer. Yes, sir. I have been deacon of the Baptist church for years. It is pretty much my living.

Question. Are you willing to go away and leave old Virginia?

Answer. No, sir.

Question. Why not?

Answer. I would rather stay in Virginia.

Glossary

Colonel Campbell	Colonel Thomas Campbell, the provost marshal for Williamsburg, Virginia
Freedmen's Bureau	The Bureau of Refugees, Freedmen, and Abandoned Lands, established in 1865 to aid newly emancipated African Americans
General Hooker	Joseph Hooker, a major general in the Union army
General Kearney	Philip Kearny, Jr., a brigadier general in the Union army
General McClellan	George McClellan, the commander of all Union forces early in the Civil War
Jeff. Davis	Jefferson Davis, the president of the Confederate States of America during the Civil War
President Tyler	John Tyler, the tenth U.S. president
proclamation	the Emancipation Proclamation of 1863
slab-houses	houses sided with rough-hewn planks of lumber
"to pull the chestnuts out of the fire"	to rescue someone
Uncle Sam	a common nickname for the United States
underground railroad	the informal system of routes, safe houses, and guides who led slaves to the North prior to the Civil War
Wise's raid	a raid by the Confederate cavalry led by General Henry A. Wise on a Union command post in Williamsburg, Virginia, in 1862
Yankees	a common nickname for northerners

H.Res.127.

Thirty-ninth Congress of the United States, at the first Session, begun and held at the City of Washington, in the District of Columbia, on Monday the fourth day of December, one thousand eight hundred and sixty-five.

Joint Resolution proposing an amendment to the Constitution of the United States.

Be it resolved by the Senate and House of Representatives of the United States of America in Congress assembled, (two-thirds of both Houses concurring,) That the following article be proposed to the legislatures of the several States as an amendment to the Constitution of the United States, which, when ratified by three-fourths of said legislatures, shall be valid as part of the Constitution, namely:

Article XIV.

Section 1. All persons born or naturalized in the United States, and subject to the jurisdiction thereof, are citizens of the United States and of the State wherein they reside. No State shall make or enforce any law which shall abridge the privileges or immunities of citizens of the United States; nor shall any State deprive any person of life, liberty, or property, without due process of law; nor deny to any person within its jurisdiction the equal protection of the laws.

Section 2. Representatives shall be apportioned among the several States according to their respective numbers, counting the whole number of persons in each State, excluding Indians not taxed. But when the right to vote at any election for the choice of electors for President and Vice President of the United States, Representatives in Congress, the Executive and Judicial officers of a State, or the members of the Legislature thereof, is denied to any of the male inhabitants of such State, being twenty-one years of age, and citizens of the United States, or in any way abridged, except for participation in rebellion, or other crime, the basis of representation therein shall be reduced in the proportion which the

The Fourteenth Amendment (National Archives and Records Administration)

FOURTEENTH AMENDMENT TO THE U.S. CONSTITUTION

"No State shall make or enforce any law which shall abridge the privileges or immunities of citizens of the United States."

Overview

Even before the Civil War ended, President Abraham Lincoln wrestled with Congress over how to reconstruct the Union. After Lincoln's assassination, President Andrew Johnson initiated a minimalist program that offended many northerners. The Thirty-ninth Congress, after failing to reach a compromise with Johnson, proposed a constitutional amendment to solve the most pressing issues.

The Fourteenth Amendment extended citizenship and rights to the freed slaves and excluded many prominent former Confederates from government. It revised the formula for congressional reapportionment and settled the status of wartime debts. The Fourteenth Amendment, approved by Congress in June 1866, was pronounced ratified by the states on July 28, 1868. Although today three of its five sections are nonfunctional, the first section of the amendment has been used, especially since the mid-1900s, to expand significantly the rights of African Americans and other groups in society. Accompanying these developments, the powers of the Supreme Court and federal government have increased at the expense of the states. Debate rages to the present day about the ultimate boundaries of the Fourteenth Amendment.

Context

In 1861 the Lincoln administration and Congress declared that the goal of the Civil War was to restore the Union and that slavery was not to be disturbed. By mid-1862 President Lincoln had changed his mind, to the delight of abolitionists and the grudging acceptance of many frustrated northerners. His Emancipation Proclamation and the subsequent Thirteenth Amendment ended the institution. Nevertheless, with the capitulation of the Confederacy in the spring of 1865, the government faced numerous unprecedented questions that the Constitution was unable to answer. Foremost among the uncertainties were, first, the requirements and procedures for readmitting the Confederate states into the Union and, second,

the status of the freed slaves. The absence of the politically astute Abraham Lincoln complicated the resolution of these problems.

President Andrew Johnson certainly did not shy away from the task, but his stubbornness allowed for little consultation with Republican congressional leaders. The former Democrat from Tennessee demanded that southern states renounce their Confederate debts and ratify the Thirteenth Amendment. He had little interest in any other steps to assist the freed slaves and was content to leave their progress to state action. Johnson also used presidential pardons to restore some prominent Confederates to political life. He then permitted the obedient former Confederate states to elect state officials as well as representatives and senators to Congress.

The Republican-dominated Thirty-ninth Congress, which first met December 4, 1865, would have none of this. Individual southern states aggravated the situation by enacting so-called Black Codes, which significantly circumscribed the economic and social freedoms of former slaves. At this time political rights were not contemplated by many in the North or South. To counter the Black Codes, Congress passed the Freedmen's Bureau Bill and the Civil Rights Act in February 1866 to give the freed slaves educational and economic opportunities and to guarantee basic civil rights. Johnson vetoed both. Although Congress overrode both vetoes, Republican congressmen concluded that they needed to take a greater initiative to restore the Union and protect African Americans. A constitutional amendment (or series of amendments) seemed the most effective device to remedy the situation and to prevent future legislation from undermining their gains.

About the Author

The Fourteenth Amendment has many authors. It was legislation of the first session of the Thirty-ninth Congress following the recommendation of the Joint Committee on Reconstruction. In general, the Republican majority in Congress was responsible for its major features and success. The criticisms of the Democratic minority did little to reshape the amendment.

Time Line

1861

- **April 12**
  The Confederates bombard Fort Sumter, beginning the Civil War.

1862

- **September 17**
  The Battle of Antietam (Maryland) is a draw, but Robert E. Lee's Army of Northern Virginia is forced to retreat.

- **September 22**
  With the preliminary Emancipation Proclamation, Lincoln warns seceded states of the impending emancipation of slaves.

1863

- **January 1**
  Using his war powers to issue the Emancipation Proclamation, Lincoln frees the slaves in ten states.

1865

- **April 9**
  Lee surrenders at Appomattox Court House, Virginia.

- **April 14**
  Lincoln is shot at Ford's Theatre in Washington, D.C., and dies the next morning.

- **December 18**
  The Thirteenth Amendment is ratified, ending slavery in the United States.

1866

- **March 27**
  President Johnson vetoes the Civil Rights Act.

- **April 6–9**
  The Senate and House of Representatives override the veto of the Civil Rights Act.

- **June 8–13**
  The Senate and House of Representatives pass the final version of the Fourteenth Amendment.

1868

- **July 28**
  The Fourteenth Amendment is pronounced ratified.

John A. Bingham, a Republican representative from Ohio, is usually credited with the wording of the crucial first section of the Fourteenth Amendment. He was born in Mercer, Pennsylvania, on January 21, 1815. He attended Franklin College in Ohio and later studied law. Bingham was admitted to the bar in 1840 and served as district attorney for Tuscarawas County, Ohio, from 1846 to 1849. He was known for his antislavery sentiments and had advocated for the rights of free blacks. In 1854, following the political turmoil of the Kansas-Nebraska Act, Bingham was elected to Congress. Although Bingham was defeated in the 1862 congressional election, Lincoln employed his talents in the Bureau of Military Justice and then as solicitor in the U.S. Court of Claims. In the spring of 1865 he was a judge advocate in the commission that tried the Lincoln assassination conspirators. Bingham was returned to Congress, taking his seat in December 1865. In the Joint Committee on Reconstruction, Bingham played an active role, especially in composing draft after draft of what would become the Fourteenth Amendment. Ironically, he was one of the few Republicans who agreed with President Johnson that the Civil Rights Act of 1866 was unconstitutional. Bingham, however, felt that the true solution was a constitutional amendment legitimizing the federal government's protection of black rights. In 1868 Bingham was instrumental in the impeachment of President Johnson. He failed to be renominated in 1872. President Ulysses S. Grant appointed the former congressman to be minister to Japan in 1873, where he served for twelve years. Bingham died in Cadiz, Ohio, on March 19, 1900.

Thaddeus Stevens, a Republican representative from Pennsylvania, led a vigorous opposition to President Johnson's Reconstruction program. His motion created the Joint Committee on Reconstruction to investigate whether southern congressmen should be seated and to propose guidelines for the states' restoration. Stevens, who served as cochair of the Joint Committee, strove to secure maximum punishment of the former Confederates and maximum rights for the freedmen. Born in Danville, Vermont, on April 4, 1792, Thaddeus Stevens graduated from Dartmouth College in 1814 and moved to Pennsylvania that same year. He was admitted to the bar in 1816 and established a law practice in Gettysburg and later in Lancaster. He defended many fugitive slaves without taking a fee. Stevens served in the Pennsylvania legislature and the convention to revise the state constitution. He refused to sign the constitution because it restricted suffrage to white men. From 1849 to 1853 Stevens served in Congress as a Whig who opposed the extension of slavery. He returned to the House of Representatives in March 1859 as a Republican and represented Pennsylvania there until his death on August 11, 1868.

Stevens was the leader of the Radical Republicans in the House during and after the war. He was a vocal critic of Lincoln's moderation on slavery and Reconstruction. He felt that the former Confederate states were conquered territories and that Congress had primary responsibility to supervise such territories. Stevens pushed as hard as he could to secure black suffrage and to disfranchise all Confederates, whom he classified as traitors. Unlike some radicals, however, Stevens had a pragmatic streak. When leading the debate in favor of the passage of the Fourteenth Amendment, he responded to his fellow radicals that he was disappointed with the proposed amendment, but as to why he would "accept so imperfect a proposition? I answer, because I live among men and not among angels." Stevens continued to advocate black suffrage as a condition of readmission to the Union. Two years later he demanded the impeachment of President Johnson, but he was fatally ill at the time and left the matter in the hands of others, including Bingham.

The members of the Joint Committee on Reconstruction conducted the early debates on the Fourteenth Amendment. In January 1866 alone they received more than fifty proposals for constitutional amendments. From the House, in addition to Stevens and Bingham, were Elihu B. Washburne of Illinois, Roscoe Conkling of New York, George S. Boutwell of Massachusetts, Justin S. Morrill of Vermont, Henry T. Blow of Missouri, Henry Grider of Kentucky, and Andrew J. Rogers of New Jersey. The Senate appointed William Pitt Fessenden of Maine, James W. Grimes of Iowa, Jacob M. Howard of Michigan, Ira Harris of New York, George H. Williams of Oregon, and Reverdy Johnson of Maryland. Rogers, Grider, and Johnson were the only Democrats on the committee. Although he was often ill, Fessenden acted as a moderate counterbalance to Stevens's designs.

Explanation and Analysis of the Document

♦ Section 1

The least controversial part of Section 1 is the first sentence, which makes it clear that the former slaves are now citizens of the United States and citizens of the states in which they live. National citizenship is thus defined for the first time. This pointedly overturns the *Dred Scott* decision of 1857. In that Supreme Court case, Chief Justice Roger Taney denied Dred Scott, a slave, his freedom in part on the ground that a black might be a citizen of a state but not of the United States. Therefore, Scott had no right to sue in a federal court. In 1866, however, Republicans wanted to prevent former slaves from slipping into a half-free position by explicitly granting them citizenship and at least the promise of federal protection.

The lengthy second sentence contains three distinctive clauses; the meaning of each remains controversial today. Each prohibits certain state actions. First, the Fourteenth Amendment guarantees to every citizen privileges and immunities; second, all "persons" are protected from a loss of life, liberty, and property without "due process"; and, third, all are to enjoy the "equal protection of the laws." At a minimum, congressmen were determined to stop the southern states from enacting Black Codes that recreated a form of near-slavery. Many, including John Bingham, specifically declared that their intention was to constitutionalize the

Time Line

1869

■ March 4
Ulysses S. Grant is inaugurated as president.

1870

■ July 15
Georgia is readmitted to the Union, becoming the final former Confederate state to be reconstructed.

1873

■ April 14
With their decision in the Slaughter-House Cases, the Supreme Court significantly restricts the scope of the Fourteenth Amendment.

1883

■ October 15
With their decision in the Civil Rights Cases, the Supreme Court limits enforcement of the Fourteenth Amendment by declaring the Civil Rights Act of 1875 unconstitutional.

1896

■ May 18
With the *Plessy v. Ferguson* decision, the Supreme Court permits "separate but equal" facilities for African Americans.

Civil Rights Act of 1866. Former abolitionists had long wanted to extend to African Americans the natural rights that are celebrated in the Declaration of Independence. The vagueness of Section 1 emerges from the "the difficulties inherent in any attempt to incorporate a natural law concept into a constitution or public law, especially in a federal system," as Harold Hyman and William M. Wiecek put it. "No legal authorities supplied neat definitions of civil rights; none does today, or can."

John Bingham, the principal author of Section 1, took the terms "privileges and immunities" from Article IV, Section 2, of the U.S. Constitution. He and Senator Jacob Howard argued that the phrase embraced not only the rights that the states created for their citizens but also the Bill of Rights. Many scholars today agree with Bingham that the federal government has the power to enforce the Bill of Rights in the states. This represented a huge expansion of federal power in the 1860s. Some of Bingham's colleagues and later scholars disputed this broad interpretation. They observed that privileges and immunities preceded the Bill of Rights and the wording simply meant that citizens visiting from another state would enjoy the same rights as the citizens of that state. These rights might include freedom of movement, property rights, and

John A. Bingham (Library of Congress)

freedom to make contracts. In essence, the privileges and immunities clause guarantees equality within a state. In the Slaughter-House Cases (1873) the Supreme Court declined to apply the privileges or immunities clause to a Louisiana state law. While most constitutional scholars see this as a poor decision, it would have the real effect of negating whatever meaning the phrase had.

Section 1 guarantees every person "due process of law." Bingham took this phrase from the Fifth Amendment, which says that the federal government cannot deny due process. The Fourteenth Amendment dictates that a state may not do so either. The accepted interpretation of due process is simply that the legal rules, proceedings, and customs of a state are available to all persons in that state, again with an emphasis on equality for all. Later in the nineteenth century, the Supreme Court would expand the meaning of due process by examining how laws and regulations affected the life, liberty, or property of persons.

Finally, Section 1 restricts states from denying "to any person ... the equal protection of the laws." In the 1860s this was another assertion of equal justice and that states could not discriminate against groups of individuals by selectively enforcing laws. As such, it is a subset of rights contained in the privileges and immunities clause. For decades the clause had little impact, to the point where Justice Oliver Wendell Holmes ridiculed it as "the last refuge of a lawyer with no other arguments to make." Again, in time,

the meaning of the equal protection clause would change. Because of the confusion over the meaning of "privileges or immunities," the interpretation of what constitutes "equal laws" resulted in a vast expansion of rights and government-enforced toleration of minority groups in society.

♦ **Section 2**

The Thirteenth Amendment ended slavery, but it remained unclear how to apportion members of Congress in the absence of the three-fifths clause (Article I, Section 2, of the Constitution). On one level the Fourteenth Amendment's answer is not surprising; apportionment is based on the total number of people, excluding Native Americans on reservations and tribal areas. According to Section 2, if a state discriminates against any group of adult males by preventing them from voting for federal or state offices, the state would be punished by losing representation. The total number of people would be reduced in proportion to the group of voters that is excluded. In other words, a state could not benefit with a full representation in Congress if they refused to let some of their male citizens vote.

This section represents a complicated compromise. Radical Republicans like Thaddeus Stevens and Charles Sumner of Massachusetts demanded black suffrage. While most northerners wanted protection for African Americans in the South, they generally were not prepared to give them the right to vote in either the South or the North. On the other hand, if blacks were to be counted as full persons, not three-fifths persons, the southern states would gain approximately ten to twelve representatives. It seemed ironic that because of four years of bloodletting, white southerners would increase their presence in Congress without recognizing the needs and rights of the freedmen. At that time, northern states had small black populations, so excluding them made no difference in their congressional delegations. Senator James Grimes proposed the solution to forgo black suffrage but to prevent the increase of the southern delegation in the House of Representatives. If a former slave state wanted to grant its black male citizens the vote, then the apportionment would change. The Fifteenth Amendment granting suffrage to African Americans would make this section largely moot.

Despite the protests of Elizabeth Cady Stanton, Susan B. Anthony, and other leaders of the women's rights movement, the word *male* is used here for the first time in the Constitution. There would be no penalty for denying women the right to vote.

♦ **Section 3**

The Fourteenth Amendment prevented some Confederates from serving in federal and state offices. This section was also a product of compromise. Radicals wanted to disfranchise anyone who had aided the Confederacy, but this move was seen as too draconian, if not impractical. If blacks were denied political rights, the former Confederate states would be in turmoil for decades. Instead, Congress came up with a much milder punishment. If one had held state or federal office before the Civil War but

MENDING THE FAMILY KETTLE.

In this 1866 engraving, Andrew Johnson holds a leaking kettle labeled "The Reconstructed South" toward a woman representing liberty and carrying a baby who represents the newly approved Fourteenth Amendment. (Library of Congress)

then renounced loyalty to the United States, that person was to be forbidden to hold federal or state office, with two exceptions. First, anyone who received a presidential pardon before the ratification of the Fourteenth Amendment could hold office. Second, the amendment allowed Congress to pardon, in effect, an individual by a two-thirds vote in each house.

Northerners were upset by two patterns in the months following the end of the war. First, President Johnson was increasingly lenient to wealthy former slaveholders who came to plead for mercy or who sent their spouses to do

so. Second, as Johnson's approved state governments came into operation, former Confederate military officers and political leaders were filling positions in state government and being sent to Washington, D.C., to assume seats in Congress. The South's leaders were not showing sufficient sorrow for the death and destruction they had caused.

A substantial amount of the debate recorded in the *Congressional Globe* surrounds this section and its earlier drafts. Some like Stevens wanted severe penalties for all Confederates. Others wanted disfranchisement until 1870 or 1876. The compromise was to deny political power

> *"No State shall make or enforce any law which shall abridge the privileges or immunities of citizens of the United States; nor shall any State deprive any person of life, liberty, or property, without due process of law; nor deny to any person within its jurisdiction the equal protection of the laws."*
>
> (Section 1)

> *"Representatives shall be apportioned among the several States according to their respective numbers, counting the whole number of persons in each State, excluding Indians not taxed."*
>
> (Section 2)

> *"No person shall be a Senator or Representative in Congress, or elector of President and Vice-President, or hold any office, civil or military, under the United States, or under any State, who, having previously taken an oath, as a member of Congress, or as an officer of the United States, or as a member of any State legislature, or as an executive or judicial officer of any State, to support the Constitution of the United States, shall have engaged in insurrection or rebellion against the same."*
>
> (Section 3)

to as many established southern leaders as possible with the hope that new white leaders would emerge with more conciliatory views. As crucial as Section 1 was for the future, Stevens concluded one of his last speeches about the Fourteenth Amendment by exclaiming, "Give us the third section or give us nothing."

♦ **Section 4**

The Fourteenth Amendment makes it clear that all the debts the United States incurred in prosecuting the war, including soldiers' bounties for enlisting and their pensions, war bonds, greenback currency, and other debts, were legitimate. All Confederate debts, including their paper money and bonds, were worthless. Furthermore, slave owners would not be reimbursed for the loss of their slaves. This section is largely obvious to all. Some Radical Republicans tried to scare the northern public into thinking that if President Johnson had his way and if the Democratic Party gained control of Congress, northern creditors would not be paid in full but Confederates *would* be paid in full. This was nonsense, or perhaps it was just a ploy to get votes.

This section, however, reassured the Union's backers—both foreign and domestic. British shipbuilders who had financed and supplied Confederate blockade-runners, on the other hand, were out of luck. Finally, there was some concern that the Emancipation Proclamation and the Thirteenth Amendment conflicted with the Fifth Amendment, since no one, not even slaveholders, could have their property taken from them without due process of law. Section 4 resolves the issue by explicitly stating that slaveholders would not be compensated for freed slaves.

♦ **Section 5**

The single sentence of Section 5 repeats Section 2 of the Thirteenth Amendment almost verbatim. Congress would have the authority to defend the rights outlined in Section 1. When Congress passed the Freedmen's Bureau Bill and the Civil Rights Act of 1866, many Republicans felt they had the authority under this provision of the Thirteenth Amendment. President Johnson disagreed, and Republicans feared that the Supreme Court might back the president's interpretation. By reemphasizing

Congress's authority in the Fourteenth Amendment, Republicans thought that the problem could be avoided. The Ku Klux Klan Act of 1871 (also called the Civil Rights Act of 1871) and the Civil Rights Act of 1875 are just two manifestations of that belief.

Audience

As an addition to the Constitution this legislation was addressed to the entire nation. Each supporter of the amendment in Congress had his own opinion as to how the balance of federal and state powers was changed to the advantage of the former. All agreed that the rights of all citizens were being expanded.

More specifically, the Fourteenth Amendment was a message to four distinct audiences who had very different interests. First, the amendment told President Johnson that Congress was taking charge of Reconstruction policy. If the southerners (with Johnson's silent consent) were not going to protect the lives and rights of African Americans, Congress would do so. Section 3 struck at Johnson's liberal pardoning policies. President Johnson, of course, would not accept this message and took on the Republicans as they campaigned for Congress in the fall of 1866.

Second, the Fourteenth Amendment was addressed to the former Confederate states. Southern whites were being told to heed Congress if they wished to reenter the Union. They would need a new political leadership, and their Black Codes were unacceptable. Originally, there was a provision that would have admitted a state's delegation to Congress upon its ratification of the Fourteenth Amendment. That measure was tabled. Here the Radical Republicans had their way. Tennessee quickly ratified the amendment and was readmitted, but this move clearly did not set a precedent. It was presumed by many, however, that ratification would substantially advance the states toward readmission. Section 2 also prodded the southern states to adopt black suffrage. Unfortunately, President Johnson encouraged southerners to reject the amendment. With no clear promise of readmission and the drastic consequences of the amendment, white southerners balked.

Third, the message sent to northern voters was that Republicans in Congress, not the president, had their interests at heart. Although it is difficult to measure public opinion, it is safe to say that northerners wanted the South to pay and to express sorrow for what they had done. They also wanted some degree of protection for southern blacks. Johnson and white southerners had utterly disappointed them. Republicans gave the northern electorate hope. By avoiding black suffrage directly, punishing Confederate leaders, and guaranteeing the payment of debts, the Fourteenth Amendment was a rallying issue for Republicans in the 1866 and succeeding elections.

Fourth, for oppressed southern blacks, struggling to make their way amid a hostile and humiliated white population, the Fourteenth Amendment held much promise. Should they ever get the right to vote, the party of Lincoln would be their destination. In the meantime, southern blacks relied upon Congress for protection. The Joint Committee on Reconstruction published a report too late to be used by Congress, but it documented the plight of the freedmen and, of course, appealed to the northern public to aid them.

Impact

Politically the Fourteenth Amendment struck a positive chord with the northern electorate. Not surprisingly, President Johnson misjudged public sentiment. The congressional elections of 1866 produced decisive Republican majorities in both the Senate and the House. The North trusted Congress with the responsibility of Reconstruction, which President Johnson might resist at his own peril.

The Fourteenth Amendment required the ratification of twenty-eight of the thirty-seven states. Connecticut was the first to ratify (June 25, 1866), followed quickly by New Hampshire (July 6) and Tennessee (July 19). Ratification became complicated when, in early 1868, New Jersey and Ohio tried to rescind their approvals. By July 28, 1868, Secretary of State William Seward certified that twenty-eight states had ratified the Fourteenth Amendment, allowing it to go into operation.

The Fourteenth Amendment, and particularly Section 1, has had a complicated history. Supreme Court justices and constitutional scholars have read the intentions of its authors in different ways. The legal scholar Alexander Bickel concludes that Section 1 fulfilled the moderate Republicans' objective of striking down the Black Codes but speculates that perhaps there was a compromise to create language that "was sufficiently elastic to permit reasonable future advances." Thus, the debate about how far to stretch the Fourteenth Amendment continues to rage.

In the Slaughter-House Cases (1873), the Supreme Court pulled away from an expansive application of Section 1 of the Fourteenth Amendment. The state of Louisiana had the right to create "reasonable" laws, and "reasonable" was defined as applying equally to all. The federal government had no responsibility to supervise the states and should concern itself with fundamental rights. The Court's majority refused to explore the meaning of "privileges or immunities." In the Civil Rights Cases (1883), the Supreme Court struck down the Civil Rights Act of 1875, which prevented discrimination in public accommodations and by private individuals. The Court claimed that the Fourteenth Amendment dealt only with discrimination by state governments. Sadly, the Court's majority in Plessy v. Ferguson (1896) reached the conclusion that "separate but equal" facilities were constitutional.

The concept of due process evolved in important ways. In several cases the Supreme Court examined the substance of state laws to determine whether individuals' liberty and property were unfairly impinged on. In Munn v. Illinois (1876) the Court declared that the State of Illinois could serve the public good by imposing maximum rates charged by grain-storage operators, even though those operators might lose profits. In *Santa Clara County v. Southern Pacific Railroad Company* (1886) the Court broadened the definition of person to include corporations, who then sought relief from state regulations as an infringement of their property under due process. The Supreme Court began to inspect the details of laws, not just the procedures. This is termed "substantive due process." Such an approach led to the striking down of state regulation of businesses, including laws setting maximum work hours or improving working conditions. *Lochner v. New York* (1905) is often cited as the classic statement of the doctrine. Amid the massive distress caused by the Great Depression, applying substantive due process to economic regulation was discredited. What is significant is that substantive due process shifted to the "equal protection of the laws" portion of the Fourteenth Amendment.

In the late 1930s Justice Hugo Black suggested that the equal protection clause meant that the federal government had the responsibility to impose the Bill of Rights on the states. The so-called doctrine of incorporation, whereby the Fourteenth Amendment incorporates the liberties in the Bill of Rights and allows the courts to apply them to state laws, is quite controversial. Cases involving gay rights and affirmative action rely on Section 1 of the Fourteenth Amendment. The Supreme Court in *Griswold v. Connecticut* (1965) said the Bill of Rights and the Fourteenth Amendment created a zone of privacy for individuals against government intrusion. As such, in *Roe v. Wade*

(1973) the Supreme Court ruled that state laws forbidding abortion represented a violation of a woman's right to privacy and were unconstitutional.

In today's society Section 1 has made it clear that the ways in which states treat their own citizens is a question of federal law. The responsibility of interpreting the Fourteenth Amendment has fallen into the hands of the federal judiciary and has significantly shifted the balance of power in our federal system. The debate over what rights the Fourteenth Amendment protects and the extent of substantive due process to investigate state laws will continue well into the future.

The fates of the other sections of the Fourteenth Amendment were relatively anticlimactic. The Fifteenth Amendment, which allows black suffrage, largely supplanted Section 2. Furthermore, despite decades of regulations in southern states inhibiting black voting, Section 2 was never invoked. No attempt was made to diminish southern congressional delegations. By the late 1890s those former Confederates who were adversely affected by Section 3 were either dead or had been pardoned by Congress. In a symbolic vote in 1978 Congress removed the political disability of Jefferson Davis and Robert E. Lee. With regard to Section 4 the status of the debts of the Union and Confederacy was never in doubt.

See also Emancipation Proclamation (1863); Black Code of Mississippi (1865); Thirteenth Amendment to the U.S. Constitution (1865); Fifteenth Amendment to the U.S. Constitution (1870); *Plessy v. Ferguson* (1896).

Questions for Further Study

1. How does the Fourteenth Amendment respond to the concerns of President Johnson in his veto of the Civil Rights Act of 1866? To what extent are the goals of the Civil Rights Act contained in the Fourteenth Amendment?

2. Does the Fourteenth Amendment undermine the federal system set up by the Constitution by subverting the rights of the states? Does it delegate too much power to the central government? Has this readjustment of powers been taken too far in our current society?

3. Does the Fourteenth Amendment undermine democracy by overemphasizing equality at the expense of majority rule and the predominant values of American society?

4. Constitutional scholars and Supreme Court justices debate whether the Fourteenth Amendment incorporates the Bill of Rights. To what degree does the Bill of Rights conflict with or complement the intention of Section 1 of the Fourteenth Amendment?

Further Reading

■ Articles

Aynes, Richard L. "On Misreading John Bingham and the Fourteenth Amendment." *Yale Law Journal* 103, no. 1 (October 1993): 57–104.

Bickel, Alexander M. "The Original Understanding and the Segregation Decision." *Harvard Law Review* 69, no. 1 (November 1955): 1–65.

Harrison, John. "Reconstructing the Privileges or Immunities Clause." *Yale Law Journal* 101, no. 7 (May 1992): 1385–1474.

West, Robin. "Toward an Abolitionist Interpretation of the Fourteenth Amendment." *West Virginia Law Review* 94 (Fall 1991): 111–155.

■ Books

Benedict, Michael L. *The Blessings of Liberty: A Concise History of the Constitution of the United States.* 2nd ed. Boston: Houghton Mifflin, 2006.

Foner, Eric. *Reconstruction: America's Unfinished Revolution, 1863–1877.* New York: Harper and Row, 1988.

Hyman, Harold, and William M. Wiecek. *Equal Justice under Law: Constitutional Development, 1835–1875.* New York: Harper and Row, 1982.

James, Joseph B. *The Framing of the Fourteenth Amendment.* Urbana: University of Illinois Press, 1956.

———. *The Ratification of the Fourteenth Amendment.* Macon, Ga.: Mercer University Press, 1984.

Kendrick, Benjamin B. *The Journal of the Joint Committee of Fifteen on Reconstruction, 39th Congress, 1865–1867.* Vol. 67. New York: Columbia University Studies in History, 1914.

Nelson, William. *The Fourteenth Amendment: From Political Principle to Judicial Doctrine.* Cambridge, Mass.: Harvard University Press, 1988.

Perry, Michael J. *We the People: The Fourteenth Amendment and the Supreme Court.* New York: Oxford University Press, 1999.

TenBroek, Jacobus. *The Antislavery Origins of the Fourteenth Amendment.* Berkeley: University of California Press, 1951.

Urofsky, Melvin I. *A March of Liberty: A Constitutional History of the United States.* New York: Alfred A. Knopf, 1988.

■ Web Sites

"14th Amendment to the U.S. Constitution." Library of Congress "Primary Documents in American History" Web site. http://www.loc.gov/rr/program/bib/ourdocs/14thamendment.html.

—M. Philip Lucas

FOURTEENTH AMENDMENT TO THE U.S. CONSTITUTION

◆ Section 1.

All persons born or naturalized in the United States, and subject to the jurisdiction thereof, are citizens of the United States and of the State wherein they reside. No State shall make or enforce any law which shall abridge the privileges or immunities of citizens of the United States; nor shall any State deprive any person of life, liberty, or property, without due process of law; nor deny to any person within its jurisdiction the equal protection of the laws.

◆ Section 2.

Representatives shall be apportioned among the several States according to their respective numbers, counting the whole number of persons in each State, excluding Indians not taxed. But when the right to vote at any election for the choice of electors for President and Vice-President of the United States, Representatives in Congress, the Executive and Judicial officers of a State, or the members of the Legislature thereof, is denied to any of the male inhabitants of such State, being twenty-one years of age, and citizens of the United States, or in any way abridged, except for participation in rebellion, or other crime, the basis of representation therein shall be reduced in the proportion which the number of such male citizens shall bear to the whole number of male citizens twenty-one years of age in such State.

◆ Section 3.

No person shall be a Senator or Representative in Congress, or elector of President and Vice-President, or hold any office, civil or military, under the United States, or under any State, who, having previously taken an oath, as a member of Congress, or as an officer of the United States, or as a member of any State legislature, or as an executive or judicial officer of any State, to support the Constitution of the United States, shall have engaged in insurrection or rebellion against the same, or given aid or comfort to the enemies thereof. But Congress may by a vote of two-thirds of each House, remove such disability.

◆ Section 4.

The validity of the public debt of the United States, authorized by law, including debts incurred for payment of pensions and bounties for services in suppressing insurrection or rebellion, shall not be questioned. But neither the United States nor any State shall assume or pay any debt or obligation incurred in aid of insurrection or rebellion against the United States, or any claim for the loss or emancipation of any slave; but all such debts, obligations and claims shall be held illegal and void.

◆ Section 5.

The Congress shall have the power to enforce, by appropriate legislation, the provisions of this article.

Glossary

abridge	lessen or curtail
bounties	recruitment money for those volunteering for the army
due process of law	regular legal proceedings and customs
immunities	exemptions
jurisdiction	authority of a government power

Milton A. Candler (Library of Congress)

HENRY MCNEAL TURNER'S SPEECH ON HIS EXPULSION FROM THE GEORGIA LEGISLATURE

1868

"Am I not a man because I happen to be of a darker hue than honorable gentlemen around me?"

Overview

Henry McNeal Turner's speech to the Georgia legislature in September 1868 was a direct response to the expulsion by that body of twenty-seven African American state legislators. In the first elections initiated by Radical Reconstruction in July 1867, three African Americans were elected to the Georgia Senate and twenty-nine to the Georgia House of Representatives. These black legislators represented a Republican Party that hoped to rise to power in the Reconstruction South by creating a coalition among the newly enfranchised freedmen, sympathetic native southern whites, and northern whites who had come to the South seeking economic prosperity and political opportunities. As in most southern states, Georgia Republicans were riven by factional disputes. Democrats, hoping to take advantage of Republican factionalism, sought means to regain political power for conservative whites.

Years earlier, former governor Joseph E. Brown had suggested the expulsion of the recently elected black legislators on the ground of constitutional ineligibility. On August 6, 1868, a resolution from the House minority committee declared a mulatto representative ineligible. Soon after that, the Democratic state senator Milton A. Candler presented a motion to investigate the eligibility of African Americans to sit in the legislature. White Republicans in the Georgia legislature faced public pressure to attack the evils of "Negro government." By early September, enough Republicans joined with Georgia Democrats to pass resolutions removing African Americans from the legislature. The Senate voted twenty-four to eleven for these resolutions, specifically expelling the blacks Tunis G. Campbell and George Wallace as "ineligible to seats, on the ground that they are persons of color, and not eligible to office by the Constitution and laws of Georgia, nor by the Constitution and laws of the United States." White conservative strength was stronger in the state House of Representatives, where the final vote, cast on September 2, 1868, was eighty-three to twenty-three. In all, close to thirty Republicans in the Georgia legislature supported the measure either by voting for it or by abstaining.

The Republican governor Rufus Bullock defended the expelled blacks, claiming that "the framers of the Constitution made no distinction between electors or citizens on account of race or color, and neither can you." Bullock aimed his protest at the nation's capital, where, with support from black leaders in Georgia, Congress passed the Congressional Reorganization Act of 1869, reconvening the Georgia legislature of 1868 and reseating those black members who had been expelled.

The speech of Henry M. Turner was rooted in an experiment in biracial democracy that underlay Radical Reconstruction. It thus speaks to several important issues in African American political history and in the history of Reconstruction. It sheds illuminating light on the nature of black political leadership, the dynamics of Reconstruction politics in the South, and the ideology of African American leaders during Reconstruction.

Context

During the American Civil War and in its immediate aftermath in 1865, the president took responsibility for reconstructing the Union. In a number of moves made in 1863 and 1864, then President Abraham Lincoln had signaled a moderate approach to reuniting the nation. Lincoln placed his faith in former white Unionist leadership, though he did signal his willingness to see limited suffrage for some blacks. He also registered his opposition to the more radical extremes of Reconstruction by his veto of the Wade-Davis bill (1864), which would have required a prohibition on slavery and made former Confederate states' readmittance to the Union contingent on a majority vote of the so-called Ironclad Oath, which repudiated prior support for the Confederacy. After the Confederate surrender at Appomattox and Lincoln's assassination on April 14, 1865, President Andrew Johnson announced his own plan of Reconstruction. He promised amnesty to those who pledged allegiance to the United States and accepted emancipation, and he announced provisional governors for each of the former Confederate states and required them to ratify the Thirteenth Amendment abolishing slavery, nullify their secession ordinance, and repudiate the Confederate

1865

■ **June**
Presidential Reconstruction begins in Georgia when President Andrew Johnson names James Johnston provisional governor.

1867

■ **March 7**
Congress passes the first of four Reconstruction Acts, beginning the process of Radical, or Congressional, Reconstruction in Georgia and nine other southern states.

■ **May**
Georgia blacks organize into Republican Party.

■ **October**
Georgia votes to hold a constitutional convention.

■ **December–March**
The Georgia constitutional convention meets in Atlanta.

1868

■ **June**
Georgia fulfills the requirements of Congressional Reconstruction and is restored to the Union.

■ **September 3**
Turner is one of the delegates to be expelled from the Georgia legislature, prompting his speech.

■ **October**
Turner calls for a convention of black leaders in Macon.

■ **December**
President Grant and Congress reimplement military rule in Georgia.

1870

■ **December**
The Democrats defeat Republicans in state elections.

1871

■ **February**
Georgia is finally readmitted to the Union.

■ **October**
Republican governor Rufus Bullock resigns and leaves the state to avoid certain impeachment. A conservative government is reestablished in Georgia.

debt. Yet during the summer and fall of 1865, southerners exhibited a defiance that disturbed many northerners. They reelected former Confederates to office and passed a series of "Black Codes" that severely compromised the freedom and civil rights of former slaves. In December 1865, Congress refused to recognize these Johnsonian governments, moving Reconstruction into a new phase. The northern senators and representatives were dissatisfied with the readmission process that led to the election of these new southern members of Congress. In not seating them, they also served notice that Congress would make its own terms for Reconstruction.

The framing of Reconstruction policy now lay in the hands of Congress. Led by a Radical faction driven by antislavery idealism and by a commitment to black freedom and civil equality, Congressional Republicans passed a more stringent program of Reconstruction. They first moved to protect the rights of freedmen by extending the life of the Freedmen's Bureau. They also put through the Civil Rights Act of 1866, which asserted the power of the federal government to protect black rights by intervening in state affairs. In June 1866, Congress passed the Fourteenth Amendment (adopted July 9, 1868) that set the basis for citizenship. Still, ten former Confederate states refused to ratify the amendment. In response, Congress passed the first of four Reconstruction Acts on March 7, 1867, which divided ten southern states into five military districts and declared the existing state governments illegitimate and subject to military commanders. Georgia was part of the Third Military District commanded by Major General John Pope. The Reconstruction Acts called for a new registration of voters to elect delegates to constitutional conventions. They also allowed for freedmen to vote while proscribing certain groups of whites. Thus began the period of Congressional, or Radical, Reconstruction in the South.

The process of registration and elections spurred the creation of a Republican Party in the former Confederacy. In all southern states, the Republicans were an alliance of northern whites, native southern white supporters, and African Americans. While blacks constituted a majority of Republican voters in the southern states, they were only a majority of the population in two states, South Carolina and Mississippi. Although the extent of black domination of Reconstruction governments was exaggerated by those whites who opposed them, blacks did serve in the U.S. Congress, state executive and legislative positions, and local offices.

During 1865 and 1866, Freedmen Bureau agents helped initiate the rise of the Republican Party. They made speeches, encouraged organization, and supported the development of a partisan press. Henry M. Turner was a former army chaplain assigned to the bureau in Georgia. The bureau also supplied one of the key players in Georgia Reconstruction politics: John Emory Bryant, a former Union army officer from Maine, founded the Republican newspaper *Loyal Georgian* in Augusta, Georgia, and later served at the constitutional convention of 1867. Clergymen and missionaries from the Northern Methodist Church also assisted in the birth of the Republican

Party. In January 1866 a new organization, the Georgia Equal Rights Association, took the lead in spearheading efforts to mobilize support for Reconstruction. They received help from Union Leagues, pro-Union secret societies formed after the Civil War. The leagues were first popular in the Unionist strongholds in northern Georgia but did little to attract the interest of freedmen. In 1867, General Pope divided Georgia into registration districts to register voters to vote on a constitutional convention. Registration included 102,411 whites and 98,507 blacks. The Republican Party in Georgia was ready for the elections. By March they had a state executive committee and a party chairman.

As in other southern states in 1867, Republican freedmen and their southern and northern white allies were victorious in the elections calling for a constitutional convention. In Georgia, Republicans took advantage of Democratic disorganization and lethargy. Frustrated and discouraged white conservatives sat out the election; only 36,500 whites voted, of the more than 100,000 who had registered. The voters of Georgia approved a convention 102,282 to 4,127. The Georgia constitutional convention began on December 9, 1867. More than 80 percent of the delegates were white, a figure unusually high among southern states. The Radical Republicans, led by Bullock and Bryant, pushed for black suffrage and the disfranchisement of former Confederates. Other Republicans sought the support of white yeoman farmers by pressing the issue of debt relief. The Republican convention guaranteed basic civil and political rights to African Americans. Southern Republicans also created state-funded public school systems, asylums, and penitentiaries and promoted economic prosperity by funding railroad construction.

The constitutional conventions of 1867–1868 created new Republican governments that followed the agenda set forth by the conventions. Over the course of the next decade, however, Republican regimes in each state would succumb to both internal and external forces. Three major factors were responsible for the end of Radical Reconstruction. First, antiblack and anti-Republican violence seriously crippled Reconstruction efforts. Republican officeholders were attacked and often murdered. Second, internecine conflicts within the Republican coalition hampered their ability to rule effectively. In Georgia, the Macon newspaper editor and federal commissioner J. Clarke Swayze became a bitter opponent of fellow Republican Turner. It proved difficult to unite former Whigs and former Democrats. Within the black community, urban elites differed with rural freedmen over prioritizing civil rights or economic issues. Third, Reconstruction in the South was doomed by a growing lack of support among northern Republicans. The administration of President Ulysses S. Grant was crippled by scandals like Crédit Mobilier and the Whiskey Ring. (The former scandal led to the demise of Grant's first vice president; the latter involved Treasury Department agents, who received bribes from whiskey distillers in exchange for assisting distillers

Rufus Bullock (Library of Congress)

in tax evasion.) Economically, the Panic of 1873 led to the creation of a number of dissident parties, like Labor Reform and Greenbackers, that allied with Democrats to defeat incumbent Republicans. Among the northern population, the panic also led to growing concern with domestic financial issues.

In several ways, Reconstruction in Georgia followed this regional pattern. Like other states, internal dissensions within Republican ranks led to their defeat. Particularly challenging was the attempt to appeal to both the freedmen and the former Democrats of north Georgia. Georgia Republicans also had to contend with politically motivated terrorism. In March 1868 the Republican legislator George A. Ashburn was assassinated while visiting Columbus after receiving a warning from the Ku Klux Klan. According to Edmund Drago, "At least one-fourth of Georgia's black legislators were threatened, bribed, beaten, jailed or killed during the period." Yet Georgia Reconstruction was distinctive in other ways. Unlike Reconstruction in such states as South Carolina and Mississippi, Radical Reconstruction in Georgia was relatively short lived. And during its heyday, in protest of Congressional Reconstruction that enfranchised African American males, conservative southern white Democrats barred their admission into the Georgia legislature by declaring their ineligibility to holding office both in Georgia and the United States.

About the Author

Henry McNeal Turner was born in Newberry, South Carolina, to free black parents in 1834. As an apprentice to a local planter, Turner acquired the trades of blacksmith and carriage maker. He learned to read and write while working in a law office. Turner joined the African Methodist Episcopal Church in 1848 and became a licensed preacher in 1853. He traveled throughout the South as an itinerant evangelist and, in 1860, took a preaching position at Union Bethel Church in Baltimore, Maryland. In 1862 he moved to Washington, D.C., and, as pastor of Israel Bethel Church there, became a prominent leader in the black community. During the Civil War, President Abraham Lincoln appointed Turner as chaplain to the First Regiment, U.S. Colored Troops.

Turner moved to Georgia in 1865 with the Freedmen's Bureau. He soon became an influential figure in Reconstruction politics in that state. He organized Union Leagues that brought blacks into the Republican Party. Turner once boasted that he had traveled fifteen thousand miles and spoken five hundred times in Georgia. He served as a delegate to the 1866 Georgia black convention and worked for the Republican Congressional Committee in 1867. Turner was elected to the Georgia constitutional convention of 1867–1868. Voters then chose him for the Georgia House of Representatives in 1868. After his expulsion, Turner was reseated by order of Congress in 1870 and reelected in 1871. As a legislator, he submitted bills for an eight-hour day for laborers and to prohibit discrimination on public transportation (primarily streetcars), yet he was the only black member to support a literacy test for voting. Turner's political activism proved dangerous in Georgia in the late 1860s. Two attempts were made on his life, and his home was often protected by armed guards. In 1871 Turner was appointed by national Republicans as customs inspector in Savannah.

Turner was ordained a bishop in the African Methodist Episcopal Church in 1880 and became chancellor of Morris Brown College, an African American institution in Atlanta. He later joined the Prohibitionist Party. Besides publishing three religious periodicals, he became a leading advocate for black emigration from the United States. He met with President Benjamin Harrison to enlist his support in his colonization schemes. Turner served as the vice president of the American Colonization Society and even gave the benediction to the ship *Azor* as it left Charleston, South Carolina, for Africa in April 1878 with two hundred African Americans aboard. Turner made four trips to Africa during the 1890s. In 1894 the College of Liberia bestowed upon Turner the degree of Doctor of Canonical Law. He died in Windsor, Canada, in 1915.

Explanation and Analysis of the Document

Henry McNeal Turner's speech of September 3, 1868, to the Georgia legislature was essentially an impassioned attack on the injustice of his expulsion—an event he claimed in the first paragraph was "unparalleled in the history of the world." One reporter considered it "perhaps the best speech that had been made on his side." No legislator had ever been denied his office on the ground of race. Turner wanted to force his white listeners to look squarely at the fundamental contradiction between the principles of republicanism and racism. Attacking the pillars of white supremacy, he defends (in paragraph 4) the contributions of African Americans: "Who first rallied around the standard of Reconstruction? Who set the ball of loyalty rolling in the state of Georgia?" Turner then pursues the theme of white hypocrisy, pointing out the inconsistency of voting against the Constitution of 1867 while acting as current legislators to remove a black person.

Turner's speech was not as structured as a formal sermon or a political tract nor did it develop one sustained argument. Rather, he used several rhetorical strategies and made a number of points in his protest to the Georgia legislature. He opens his remarks in an essentially defiant tone. He would be defending his right to a seat in the legislature without apology: "I am here to demand my rights and to hurl thunderbolts at the men who would dare to cross the threshold of my manhood." In the next two paragraphs Turner drives home the novel and momentous nature of his case. Never, he claims, has a man been expelled from a governing body for no other offense than the color of his skin. He next reminds his fellow legislators of the political wisdom of giving former slaves political rights, calling it the "safest and best course for the interest of the state." In the fifth paragraph, he points out the irony that he is being expelled by sitting white legislators, many of whom did not even vote for the Georgia constitutional convention or originally recognize the legitimacy of the Radical government.

In paragraphs 6–8, Turner defends political equality between the races. He asks his listeners to remember the essential humanity of African Americans: "Am I a man? ... Have I a soul to save, as you have?" He also counters the old proslavery argument that blacks were of a different species and reminds his audience of the contributions of southern blacks. On the basis of this primary political equality, blacks should be able to speak for themselves: "It is very strange, if a white man can occupy on this floor *a seat created by colored votes*, and a black man cannot do it."

In the following three paragraphs, Turner counters the argument that Congress never gave blacks the right to hold office and insists that a biracial political order was the essence of Reconstruction. If this principle is in doubt, he suggests that the question of a black representative be submitted to the sitting Congress. Moreover, he begins to insist that former slaves deserve this change. White legislators do not realize "the dreadful hardships which these people have endured, and especially those who in any way endeavored to acquire an education."

To appeal to the white legislators, Turner reminds them in paragraphs 12 and 13 that during the Civil War and so far in the postwar period blacks have not behaved in any destructive fashion. He reminds them how few advantages the freed people have had, perhaps appealing to their sympathies as well. In speaking to both African

"I am here to demand my rights and to hurl thunderbolts at the men who would dare to cross the threshold of my manhood."

(Paragraph 1)

"Am I a man? If I am such, I claim the rights of a man. Am I not a man because I happen to be of a darker hue than honorable gentlemen around me?"

(Paragraph 6)

"We are willing to let the dead past bury its dead; but we ask you, now for our rights."

(Paragraph 13)

"Where have you ever heard of four millions of freemen being governed by laws, and yet have no hand in their making?"

(Paragraph 15)

American and white legislators, Turner then insists that black loyalty to the state depends on the state's loyalty to blacks: "Never lift a finger nor raise a hand in defense of Georgia, until Georgia acknowledges that you are men and invests you with the rights pertaining to manhood." Going back to his defense based on essentials (in paragraph 15), Turner argues that his expulsion contradicts a basic premise of republican government—the consent of the governed.

In paragraphs 16 and 17, Turner seems to reassure his audience, who were perhaps anxious about black radicalism. He repeats his earlier point that blacks will act within the boundaries of political behavior. He reminds white listeners that "we have built a monument of docility, of obedience, of respect, and of self-control, that will endure longer than the Pyramids of Egypt." He also presents himself as a political martyr, comparing his plight with other persecuted pioneers like the religious leader Martin Luther and the scientist Galileo. Finally, Turner warns the legislature that by their action to expel him, they will permanently alienate black voters. In his final paragraphs Turner closes with poetic and religious imagery, comparing the position of blacks to that of the ill-fated British cavalry charge (of October 25, 1854) against Russian forces in the Battle of Balaclava during the Crimean War and warning of providential revenge for "acts of the oppressor."

In his speech to the Georgia legislature, Turner echoed several themes of African American political thought during Reconstruction. First and primary was the fundamental commitment to Jeffersonian notions of independence and equality. Significantly, Turner quoted the Revolutionary premise that "government derives their just powers from the consent of the governed." A second theme was the use of religious principles and language to defend his cause.

Because God saw fit to make some red, and some white, and some black, and some brown, are we to sit here in judgment upon what God has seen fit to do? As well might one play with the thunderbolts of heaven as with that creature that bears God's image—God's photograph.

Like many Americans in the nineteenth century, Turner saw the scriptures as a political tract that taught the principles of justice.

Turner exhibits a curious mixture of militancy and conciliation in this speech. "I am here to demand my rights," he declares at one point, "and to hurl thunderbolts at the men who would dare to cross the threshold of my manhood." At other points, however, he assures his listeners that the freedman is not seeking retribution: "We are willing to let the dead past bury its dead; but we ask you, now for our *rights.*" Turner even urges his fellow freedmen to pay taxes and obey their employers. Turner's ambivalence might be explained by the nature of his audience. He undoubtedly had to appease the Radicals in the Republican ranks. At the same time, Georgia freedmen needed the support of white Republicans, who needed reassurance that Reconstruction would not turn the racial order upside down.

Audience

Turner was a self-acknowledged spokesman for the black community in Reconstruction Georgia. His role as preacher, Freedmen Bureau official, and state legislator illustrates the central place of black politicians during Reconstruction. After emancipation, African American men and women built community institutions like churches and schools. In Georgia, black leaders also founded newspapers such as the *Colored American* (1865) and organizations like the Georgia Equal Rights and Educational Association. As a central institution in the black community, the church became, according to Drago, "the focal point of black political life during Reconstruction." Preachers, especially those like Turner from the African Methodist Episcopal Church, entered into the political sphere. Of twenty-two African American delegates to the Georgia constitutional convention, seventeen were ministers. The antebellum free black urban elite contributed disproportionately to Reconstruction politics, providing the core of black leadership in Louisiana and South Carolina.

Congressional Republicans from the North were probably another intended audience of Turner's speech. The northern press kept a very close watch on Reconstruction events in the South. A number of papers, among them the *Cincinnati Commercial* and the *New York Tribune*, had southern correspondents. Northerners would have heard about the speech if they did not read it themselves. Radicals in the North, like Benjamin Butler of Massachusetts, spoke for the plight of black Republicans in the South. The correspondence of northern Republicans is filled with letters from the South describing the southerners' problems and seeking aid.

Impact

The expulsion of Henry McNeal Turner and other black delegates from the Georgia legislature heightened anti-black sentiment in the state. White conservatives passed several discriminatory laws against African Americans. One such law deprived them of the right to serve on juries. The Ku Klux Klan also escalated its violence on freed people. A group of blacks meeting in Macon claimed that the expulsion of Turner and other legislators gave support to the "murdering bands" of the Klan. Racial violence in Reconstruction Georgia culminated in September 1868 in a riot in the southern town of Camilla, in which at least seven blacks were killed during a political rally.

Turner's speech and his subsequent expulsion spurred black political leaders in Georgia to action, making them more militant and more willing to challenge the white leadership of the Republican Party. In October 1868, black leaders met in a convention in Macon, where they created the Civil and Political Rights Association to lobby Congress on behalf of southern blacks. They elected Turner as president. Republican losses during the presidential election of 1868 and political opposition led Governor Bullock to Washington, D.C., where he succeeded in receiving federal support for renewed Reconstruction measures. The action of white conservatives in expelling Georgia's black delegates was the kind of incident that incurred the wrath of Radical Republicans in Congress.

While the expulsion of the black delegates opened a breach between white and black Republicans, it did not lead to the formation of a separate black party. African American allegiance to the Republicans was shaken but not broken. The issue of black eligibility to hold elected office came before the Georgia Supreme Court in June 1869. In the case of *White v. Clements*, Justices Brown and McCay decided in favor of the African American delegates.

In early 1870 the rift widened between the Bullock and Bryant Republican factions on the extent of African American participation in Republican governments and over civil rights legislation. Moderate Republicans began to look for coalition with Democrats. In 1870 they joined with Democrats to support the candidacy of Bryant for Speaker of the House. Georgia Republicans eventually lost the support of Washington, as President Grant became increasingly disillusioned with the Bullock regime. When the 1870 election returned a Democratic majority to the legislature, Governor Bullock resigned his office. By October of 1871, a conservative government was in control of Georgia.

See also War Department General Order 143 (1863); Black Code of Mississippi (1865); Thirteenth Amendment to the U.S. Constitution (1865); Fourteenth Amendment to the U.S. Constitution (1868); Fifteenth Amendment to the U.S. Constitution (1870).

Further Reading

■ Articles

Armstrong, Thomas F. "From Task Labor to Free Labor: The Transition along Georgia's Rice Coast, 1820–1880." *Georgia Historical Quarterly* 64 (Fall 1980): 432–447.

Carson, Roberta F. "The Loyalty Leagues in Georgia." *Georgia Historical Society* 20 (June 1936): 125–153.

Cimbala, Paul A. "The Freedmen's Bureau, the Freedmen, and Sherman's Grant in Reconstruction Georgia, 1865–1867." *Journal of Southern History* 55 (November 1989): 597–632.

Coulter, E. Merton "Henry M. Turner: Georgia Negro Preacher-Politician during the Reconstruction Era." *Georgia Historical Quarterly* 48 (December 1964): 371–410.

Gottlieb, Manuel. "The Land Question in Georgia." *Science and Society* 3 (Summer 1939): 356–388.

Matthews, John M. "Negro Republicans in the Reconstruction of Georgia." *Georgia Historical Quarterly* 60 (Summer 1976): 145–164.

■ **Books**

Angell, Stephen Ward. *Bishop Henry McNeal Turner and African-American Religion in the South.* Knoxville: University of Tennessee Press, 1992.

Conway, Alan. *The Reconstruction of Georgia.* Minneapolis: University of Minnesota Press, 1966.

Drago, Edmund L. *Black Politicians and Reconstruction in Georgia: A Splendid Failure.* Baton Rouge: Louisiana State University Press, 1982.

Duncan, Russell. *Freedom's Shore: Tunis Campbell and the Georgia Freedman.* Athens: University of Georgia Press, 1986.

Fitzgerald, Michael W. "Reconstruction Politics and the Politics of Reconstruction." In *Reconstructions: New Perspectives of the Postbellum United States,* ed. Thomas J. Brown. New York: Oxford University Press, 2006.

Foner, Eric. *Reconstruction, America's Unfinished Revolution, 1863–1877.* New York: Harper and Row, 1988.

Nathans, Elizabeth S. *Losing the Peace: Georgia Republicans and Reconstruction, 1865–1871.* Baton Rouge: Louisiana State University Press, 1968.

Redkey, Edwin S. *Respect Black: The Writings and Speeches of Henry McNeal Turner.* New York: Arno Press, 1971.

Thompson, C. Mildred. *Reconstruction in Georgia: Economic, Social, Political, 1865–1872.* New York: Columbia University Press, 1915.

■ **Web Sites**

"Reconstruction: The Second Civil War." PBS "American Experience" Web site.
    http://www.pbs.org/wgbh/amex/reconstruction/index.html.

—Mitchell Snay

Questions for Further Study

1. Summarize the political climate surrounding Reconstruction after the Civil War. What were the political parties, both major and minor? What interests did they represent? Why was one faction of the Republican Party referred to as the Radical Republicans?

2. Why did the program for Reconstruction espoused by the Republican Party, especially the Radical Republicans, ultimately break down? What forces contributed to its demise?

3. What impact did Turner's expulsion have on the emergence of white supremacist groups such as the Ku Klux Klan?

4. If you had been in charge of the Reconstruction effort after the Civil War, what might you have done differently? Explain how your course of action might have altered the outcome of events.

5. Following the Civil War, numerous laws and constitutional amendments were passed to ensure the freedom and civil rights of African Americans. Among them were the Thirteenth, Fourteenth, and Fifteenth Amendments; the Ku Klux Klan Act; the Civil Rights Acts of 1866; and the Reconstruction Acts, as well as the funding of the Freedmen's Bureau. How were the southern states ultimately able to circumvent many of these laws?

Henry McNeal Turner's Speech on His Expulsion from the Georgia Legislature

Mr. Speaker: Before proceeding to argue this question upon its intrinsic merits, I wish the members of this House to understand the position that I take. I hold that I am a member of this body. Therefore, sir, I shall neither fawn nor cringe before any party, nor stoop to beg them for my rights. Some of my colored fellow members, in the course of their remarks, took occasion to appeal to the sympathies of members on the opposite side, and to eulogize their character for magnanimity. It reminds me very much, sir, of slaves begging under the lash. I am here to demand my rights and to hurl thunderbolts at the men who would dare to cross the threshold of my manhood. There is an old aphorism which says, "fight the devil with fire," and if I should observe the rule in this instance, I wish gentlemen to understand that it is but fighting them with their own weapon.

The scene presented in this House, today, is one unparalleled in the history of the world. From this day, back to the day when God breathed the breath of life into Adam, no analogy for it can be found. Never, in the history of the world, has a man been arraigned before a body clothed with legislative, judicial or executive functions, charged with the offense of being a darker hue than his fellow men. I know that questions have been before the courts of this country, and of other countries, involving topics not altogether dissimilar to that which is being discussed here today. But, sir, never in the history of the great nations of this world—never before—has a man been arraigned, charged with an offense committed by the God of Heaven Himself. Cases may be found where men have been deprived of their rights for crimes and misdemeanors; but it has remained for the state of Georgia, in the very heart of the nineteenth century, to call a man before the bar, and there charge him with an act for which he is no more responsible than for the head which he carries upon his shoulders. The Anglo-Saxon race, sir, is a most surprising one. No man has ever been more deceived in that race than I have been for the last three weeks. I was not aware that there was in the character of that race so much cowardice or so much pusillanimity. The treachery which has been exhibited in it by gentlemen belonging to that race has shaken my confidence in it more than anything that has come under my observation from the day of my birth.

What is the question at issue? Why, sir, this Assembly, today, is discussing and deliberating on a judgment; there is not a Cherub that sits around God's eternal throne today that would not tremble—even were an order issued by the Supreme God Himself—to come down here and sit in judgment on my manhood. Gentlemen may look at this question in whatever light they choose, and with just as much indifference as they may think proper to assume, but I tell you, sir, that this is a question which will not die today. This event shall be remembered by posterity for ages yet to come, and while the sun shall continue to climb the hills of heaven.

Whose legislature is this? Is it a white man's legislature, or is it a black man's legislature? Who voted for a constitutional convention, in obedience to the mandate of the Congress of the United States? Who first rallied around the standard of Reconstruction? Who set the ball of loyalty rolling in the state of Georgia? And whose voice was heard on the hills and in the valleys of this state? It was the voice of the brawny-armed Negro, with the few humanitarian-hearted white men who came to our assistance. I claim the honor, sir, of having been the instrument of convincing hundreds—yea, thousands—of white men, that to reconstruct under the measures of the United States Congress was the safest and the best course for the interest of the state.

Let us look at some facts in connection with this matter. Did half the white men of Georgia vote for this legislature? Did not the great bulk of them fight, with all their strength, the Constitution under which we are acting? And did they not fight against the organization of this legislature? And further, sir, did they not vote against it? Yes, sir! And there are persons in this legislature today who are ready to spit their poison in my face, while they themselves opposed, with all their power, the ratification of this Constitution. They question my right to a seat in this body, to represent the people whose legal votes elected me. This objection, sir, is an unheard-of monopoly of power. No analogy can be found for it, except it be the case of a man who should go into my house, take possession of my wife and children, and then tell me to walk out. I stand very much in the position of a criminal before your bar, because I dare to be the exponent of the views of those who sent me here. Or, in other words, we are told that if black men want to speak, they must speak through white trumpets; if black men want their sentiments expressed, they must be adulterated and sent through white messengers, who will quibble and equivocate and evade as rapidly as the pendulum of a clock. If this be not done, then the black men have committed an outrage, and then representatives must be denied the right, to represent their constituents.

The great question, sir, is this: Am I a man? If I am such, I claim the rights of a man. Am I not a man because I happen to be of a darker hue than honorable gentlemen around me? Let me see whether I am or not. I want to convince the House today that I am entitled to my seat here. A certain gentleman has argued that the Negro was a mere development similar to the orangoutang or chimpanzee, but it so happens that, when a Negro is examined, physiologically, phrenologically and anatomically, and I may say, physiognomically, he is found to be the same as persons of different color. I would like to ask any gentleman on this floor, where is the analogy? Do you find me a quadruped, or do you find me a man? Do you find three bones less in my back than in that of the white man? Do you find fewer organs in the brain? If you know nothing of this, I do; for I have helped to dissect fifty men, black and white, and I assert that by the time you take off the mucous pigment—the color of the skin—you cannot, to save your life, distinguish between the black man and the white. Am I a man? Have I a soul to save, as you have? Am I susceptible of eternal development, as you are? Can I learn all the arts and sciences that you can? Has it ever been demonstrated in the history of the world? Have black men ever exhibited bravery as white men have done? Have they ever been in the professions? Have they not as good articulative organs as you? Some people argue that there is a very close similarity between the larynx of the Negro and that of the orangoutang. Why, sir, there is not so much similarity between them as there is between the larynx of the man and that of the dog, and this fact I dare any member of this House to dispute. God saw fit to vary everything in nature. There are no two men alike—no two voices alike—no two trees alike. God has weaved and tissued variety and versatility throughout the boundless space of His creation. Because God saw fit to make some red, and some white, and some black, and some brown, are we to sit here in judgment upon what God has seen fit to do? As well might one play with the thunderbolts of heaven as with that creature that bears God's image—God's photograph.

The question is asked, "What is it that the Negro race has done?" Well, Mr. Speaker, all I have to say upon the subject is this: If we are the class of people that we are generally represented to be, I hold that we are a very great people. It is generally considered that we are the children of Canaan; and the curse of a father rests upon our heads, and has rested, all through history. Sir, I deny that the curse of Noah had anything to do with the Negro. We are not the Children of Canaan; and if we are, sir, where should we stand? Let us look a little into history. Melchizedek was a Canaanite; all the Phoenicians—all those inventors of the arts and sciences—were the posterity of Canaan; but, sir, the Negro is not. We are the children of Cush, and Canaan's curse has nothing whatever to do with the Negro. If we belong to that race, Ham belonged to it, under whose instructions Napoleon Bonaparte studied military tactics. If we belong to that race, Saint Augustine belonged to it. Who was it that laid the foundation of the great Reformation? Martin Luther, who lit the light of gospel truth—a light that will never go out until the sun shall rise to set no more; and, long ere then, Democratic principles will have found their level in the regions of Pluto and of Prosperpine....

The honorable gentleman from Whitfield [Mr. Shumate], when arguing this question, a day or two ago, put forth the proposition that to be a representative was not to be an officer—"it was a privilege that citizens had a right to enjoy." These are his words. It was not an office; it was a "privilege." Every gentleman here knows that he denied that to be a representative was to be an officer. Now, he is recognized as a leader of the Democratic party in this House, and generally cooks victuals for them to eat; makes that remarkable declaration, and how are you, gentlemen on the other side of the House, because I am an officer, when one of your great lights says that I am *not* an officer? If you deny my right—the right of my constituents to have representation here—because it is a "privilege," then, sir, I will show you that I have as many privileges as the whitest man on this floor. If I am not permitted to occupy a seat here, for the purpose of representing my constituents, I want to know how white men can be permitted to do so. How can a white man represent a colored constituency, if a colored man cannot do it? The great argument is: "Oh, we have inherited" this, that and the other. Now, I want gentlemen to come down to cool, common sense. Is the created greater than the Creator? Is man greater than God? It is very strange, if a white man can occupy on this floor *a seat created by colored votes,* and a black man cannot do it. Why, gentlemen, it is the most shortsighted reasoning in the world. A man can see better than that with half an eye; and even if he had no eye at all, he could forge one, as the Cyclops did, or punch one with his finger, which would enable him to see through that.

It is said that Congress never gave us the right to hold office. I want to know, sir, if the Reconstruction measures did not base their action on the ground that no distinction should be made on account of race, color or previous condition? Was not that the grand fulcrum on which they rested? And did not every reconstructed state have to reconstruct on the idea that no discrimination, in any sense of the term, should be made? There is not a man here who will dare say No. If Congress has simply given me a merely sufficient civil and political rights to make me a mere political slave for Democrats, or anybody else—giving them the opportunity of jumping on my back in order to leap into political power—I do not thank Congress for it. Never, so help me God, shall I be a political slave. I am not now speaking for those colored men who sit with me in this House, nor do I say that they endorse my sentiments, but assisting Mr. Lincoln to take me out of servile slavery did not intend to put me and my race into *political* slavery. If they did, let them take away my ballot—I do not want it, and shall not have it. I don't want to be a mere tool of that sort. I have been a slave long enough already.

I tell you what I would be willing to do: I am willing that the question should be submitted to Congress for an explanation as to what was meant in the passage of their Reconstruction measures, and of the Constitutional Amendment. Let the Democratic party in this House pass a resolution giving this subject that direction, and I shall be content. I dare you, gentlemen, to do it. Come up to the question openly, whether it meant that the Negro might hold office, or whether it meant that he should merely have the right to vote. If you are honest men, you will do it. If, however, you will not do that, I would make another proposition: Call together, again, the convention that framed the constitution under which we are acting; let them take a vote upon the subject, and I am willing to abide by their decision....

These colored men, who are unable to express themselves with all the clearness and dignity and force of rhetorical eloquence, are laughed at in derision by the Democracy of the country. It reminds me very much of the man who looked at himself in a mirror and, imagining that he was addressing another person, exclaimed: "My God, how ugly you are!"

These gentlemen do not consider for a moment the dreadful hardships which these people have endured, and especially those who in any way endeavored to acquire an education. For myself, sir, I was raised in the cotton field of South Carolina, and in order to prepare myself for usefulness, as well to myself as to my race, I determined to devote my spare hours to study. When the overseer retired at night to his comfortable couch, I sat and read and thought and studied, until I heard him blow his horn in the morning. He frequently told me with an oath, that if he discovered me attempting to learn, that he would whip me to death, and I have no doubt he would have done so, if he had found an opportunity. I prayed to Almighty God to assist me, and He did, and I thank Him with my whole heart and soul....

So far as I am personally concerned, no man in Georgia has been more conservative than I. "Anything to please the white folks" has been my motto; and so closely have I adhered to that course, that many among my own party have classed me as a Democrat. One of the leaders of the Republican party in Georgia has not been at all favorable to me for some time back, because he believed that I was too "conservative" for a Republican. I can assure you, however, Mr. Speaker, that I have had quite enough, and to spare, of such "conservatism." ...

But, Mr. Speaker, I do not regard this movement as a thrust at me. It is a thrust at the Bible—a thrust at the God of the Universe, for making a man and not finishing him; it is simply calling the Great Jehovah a fool. Why, sir, though we are not white, we have accomplished much. We have pioneered civilization here; we have built up your country; we have worked in your fields and garnered your harvests for two hundred and fifty years! And what do we ask of you in return? Do we ask you for compensation for the sweat our fathers bore for you—for the tears you have caused, and the hearts you have broken, and the lives you have curtailed, and the blood you have spilled? Do we ask retaliation? We ask it not. We are willing to let the dead past bury its dead; but we ask you, now for our *rights.* You have all the elements of superiority upon your side; you have our money and your own; you have our education and your own; and you have our land and your own too. We, who number hundreds of thousands in Georgia, including our wives and families, with not a foot of land to call our own—strangers in the land of our birth; without money, without education, without aid, without a roof to cover us while we live, nor sufficient clay to cover us when we die! It is extraordinary that a race such as yours, professing gallantry and chivalry and education and superiority, living in a land where ringing chimes call child and sire to the church of God—a land where Bibles are read and Gospel truths are spoken, and where courts of justice are presumed to exist; it is extraordinary that, with all these advantages on your side, you can make war upon the poor defenseless black man. You know we have no money, no railroads, no telegraphs, no advantages of any sort, and yet all manner of injustice is placed upon us. You know that the black people of this country acknowledge you as their superiors, by virtue of your education and advantages....

You may expel us, gentlemen, but I firmly believe that you will some day repent it. The black man cannot protect a country, if the country doesn't protect him; and if, tomorrow, a war should arise, I would not raise a musket to defend a country where my manhood is denied. The fashionable way in Georgia, when hard work is to be done, is for the white man to sit at his ease while the black man does the work; but, sir, I will say this much to the colored men of Georgia, as, if I should be killed in this campaign, I may have no opportunity of telling them at any other time: Never lift a finger nor raise a hand in defense of Georgia, until Georgia acknowledges that you are men and invests you with the rights pertaining to manhood. Pay your taxes, however, obey all orders from your employers, take good counsel from friends, work faithfully, earn an honest living, and show, by your conduct, that you can be good citizens.

Go on with your oppressions. Babylon fell. Where is Greece? Where is Nineveh? And where is Rome, the Mistress Empire of the world? Why is it that she stands, today, in broken fragments throughout Europe? Because oppression killed her. Every act that we commit is like a bounding ball. If you curse a man, that curse rebounds upon you; and when you bless a man, the blessing returns to you; and when you oppress a man, the oppression also will rebound. Where have you ever heard of four millions of freemen being governed by laws, and yet have no hand in their making? Search the records of the world, and you will find no example. "Governments derive their just powers from the consent of the governed." How dare you to make laws by which to try me and my wife and children, and deny me a voice in the making of these laws? I know you can establish a monarchy, an autocracy, an oligarchy, or any other kind of *ocracy* that you please; and that you can declare whom you please to be sovereign; but tell me, sir, how you can clothe me with more power than another, where all

are sovereigns alike? How can you say you have a republican form of government, when you make such distinction and enact such proscriptive laws?

Gentlemen talk a good deal about the Negroes "building no monuments." I can tell the gentlemen one thing: that is, that we could have built monuments of fire while the war was in progress. We could have fired your woods, your barns and fences, and called you home. Did we do it? No, sir! And God grant that the Negro may never do it, or do anything else that would destroy the good opinion of his friends. No epithet is sufficiently opprobrious for us now. I saw, sir, that we have built a monument of docility, of obedience, of respect, and of self-control, that will endure longer than the Pyramids of Egypt.

We are a persecuted people. Luther was persecuted; Galileo was persecuted; good men in all nations have been persecuted; but the persecutors have been handed down to posterity with shame and ignominy. If you pass this bill, you will never get Congress to pardon or enfranchise another rebel in your lives. You are going to fix an everlasting disfranchisement upon Mr. Toombs and the other leading men of Georgia. You may think you are doing yourselves honor by expelling us from this House; but when we go, we will do as Wickliffe and as Latimer did. We will light a torch of truth that will never be extinguished—the impression that will run through the country, as people picture in their mind's eye these poor black men, in all parts of this Southern country, pleading for their rights. When you expel us, you make us forever your political foes, and you will never find a black man to vote a Democratic ticket again; for, so help me God, I will go through all the length and breadth of the land, where a man of my race is to be found, and advise him to beware of the Democratic party. Justice is the great doctrine taught in the Bible. God's Eternal Justice is founded upon Truth, and the man who steps from Justice steps from Truth, and cannot make his principles to prevail.

I have now, Mr. Speaker, said all that my physical condition will allow me to say. Weak and ill, though I am, I could not sit passively here and see the sacred rights of my race destroyed at one blow. We are in a position somewhat similar to that of the famous "Light Brigade," of which Tennyson says, they had

Cannon to right of them,
Cannon to left of them,
Cannon in front of them,
Volleyed and thundered.

I hope our poor, downtrodden race may act well and wisely through this period of trial, and that they will exercise patience and discretion under all circumstances.

You may expel us, gentlemen, by your votes, to-day; but, while you do it, remember that there is a just God in Heaven, whose All-Seeing Eye beholds alike the acts of the oppressor and the oppressed, and who, despite the machinations of the wicked, never fails to vindicate the cause of Justice, and the sanctity of His own handiwork.

Fortieth Congress of the United States of America;

At the *third* Session,

Begun and held at the city of Washington, on Monday, the *seventh* day of *December*, one thousand eight hundred and *sixty-eight*.

A RESOLUTION

Proposing an amendment to the Constitution of the United States.

Resolved by the Senate and House of Representatives of the United States of America in Congress assembled, (two-thirds of both Houses concurring) That the following article be proposed to the legislatures of the several States as an amendment to the Constitution of the United States, which, when ratified by three-fourths of said legislatures shall be valid as part of the Constitution, namely:

Article XV.

Section 1. The right of citizens of the United States to vote shall not be denied or abridged by the United States or by any State on account of race, color, or previous condition of servitude —

Section 2. The Congress shall have power to enforce this article by appropriate legislation —

Schuyler Colfax
Speaker of the House of Representatives.

B. F. Wade
President of the Senate pro tempore.

Attest:
Ed. McPherson
Clerk of House of Representatives.

Geo. C. Gorham
Secy of Senate U.S.

The Fifteenth Amendment (National Archives and Records Administration)

Fifteenth Amendment to the U.S. Constitution

"The right ... to vote shall not be denied or abridged by the United States or by any State on account of race, color, or previous condition of servitude."

Overview

The Fifteenth Amendment (1870) was the third and last amendment adopted in the era immediate following the Civil War. It prohibited states from denying the right to vote to individuals on the basis of "race, color, or previous condition of servitude." Section 2 of the amendment further vested Congress with power to enforce it.

The Fifteenth Amendment bears elements of both continuity and discontinuity with earlier American history. Consistent with earlier history, it did not make voting an affirmative right for African Americans or other citizens, but rather it prohibited denying or abridging such groups the right to vote. Because it was the first specific prohibition to be incorporated into the Constitution, it served as a model for the Nineteenth Amendment (1920), which prohibited similar denials based on sex, and the Twenty-sixth Amendment (1971), which prohibited such denials to those who were eighteen years of age or older.

When Congress proposed the Fifteenth Amendment and the states ratified it, Congress was still attempting to "reconstruct" the southern states; this period of Reconstruction began in 1866 and ended in 1877. During this time, federal troops were posted in the South. Congress had forced states to adopt constitutions extending the right to vote to former slaves, and it had required southern states to ratify the Fourteenth Amendment as a condition for renewed representation in Congress.

Ironically, northern voters resisted some of the same requirements that they had imposed on the South. In his pathbreaking study of the Fifteenth Amendment, William Gillette observed that five jurisdictions rejected black suffrage in referendums in 1865. These votes, most of which were overwhelming, occurred in the Colorado Territory in September, in Connecticut in October, in Wisconsin and Minnesota in November, and in the District of Columbia in December. Similar votes rejected such suffrage in the Nebraska Territory in June 1866, in Kansas and Ohio in 1867, in Michigan and Missouri in 1868, and in New York in 1869. Minnesota reversed itself in November 1868, which was the same year Iowa also accepted such suffrage, but these states remained exceptions to the general rule.

Context

The United States transformed from thirteen separate colonies into thirteen states united and independent from Great Britain. Even though they vested powers in a central government, first under the Articles of Confederation from 1781 to 1789 and then under the Constitution that they created in 1787, the states retained numerous rights. Delegates to the Constitutional Convention, rejecting calls to impose a national property qualification on voters, left voting qualifications to the states, simply specifying in Article I, Section 2, of the Constitution that "the Electors [voters] in each State shall have the Qualifications requisite for Electors of the most numerous Branch of the State Legislature." Over time, most states eliminated voting qualifications based on church membership and religious belief—a common requirement in the early colonies—or property ownership; because property was more freely available in America than elsewhere, this qualification had rarely disenfranchised large numbers of voters. American history is commonly portrayed as progressively democratic, but in retrospect the movement was not always as forward as some think. Although its supporters claimed that the presidential election of 1828 ushered in a period of Jacksonian democracy, the emphasis continued to be on universal white male suffrage rather than on universal suffrage. Indeed, because the U.S. Constitution apportioned representation in the U.S. House of Representatives not simply according to white population but also according to "three-fifths" of such "other persons" (a euphemism for slaves), southern whites who were otherwise losing population compared with northerners and westerners continued to be overrepresented there.

Over time, southerners who once defended slavery only as a "necessary evil" came to defend it as a positive good. The South justified slavery on theories of human inequality that contradicted the nation's earlier articulation in the Declaration of Independence that "all men are created equal"; leading southerners argued that slavery both lifted what they regarded as the inferior race and provided leisure time for the superior race to cultivate itself. As southern attitudes hardened in justifying slavery, northern attitudes hardened against it. Not all northerners joined abolition-

Time Line

1776

■ **July 4**
Congress adopts the
Declaration of Independence,
which declares that "all men
are created equal."

1828

■ **November 3**
Andrew Jackson is elected
president; his election marks
the rise of the "common man,"
which is often associated with
universal white male suffrage.

1857

■ **March**
The U.S. Supreme Court
declares in the *Dred Scott*
decision that blacks are not
and cannot be U.S. citizens.

1860

■ **November 6**
Abraham Lincoln is narrowly
elected president.

1861

■ **April 12**
The Civil War begins when
southerners fire on Fort
Sumter in South Carolina.

1863

■ **January 1**
The Emancipation
Proclamation takes effect;
it proclaims the freedom
of black slaves behind
Confederate lines.

1865

■ **April 18**
The Confederate army
surrenders, ending the Civil
War.

■ **December 18**
The Thirteenth Amendment is
ratified, ending slavery.

1866

■ **June 13**
Congress proposes the
Fourteenth Amendment.

1868

■ **July 28**
The Fourteenth Amendment is
declared ratified.

■ **November 3**
Ulysses S. Grant is narrowly
elected president.

ists in favoring immediate emancipation, but an increasing number concluded that the institution was morally wrong and would have to be eliminated.

As slave states continued to lose power vis-à-vis the North, southerners increasingly feared that northern states would eventually strike at their "peculiar institution" of slavery. After the Republican Abraham Lincoln was narrowly elected president in 1860, eleven southern states chose to secede. Lincoln felt duty-bound to preserve the Union, and in 1861 the nation's bloodiest conflict, the Civil War, began. By the end of the war in 1865 Lincoln, who had long regarded slavery as a moral evil, had transformed its objective from that of simply preserving the Union to that of freeing the slaves. His Emancipation Proclamation, which initially applied as a war measure only behind enemy lines, was eventually secured by the ratification of the Thirteenth Amendment, which abolished chattel slavery throughout the nation.

Southern states attempted to limit the freedom of the newly freed slaves through legislation restricting movement and limiting other rights, Congress responded again by proposing the Fourteenth Amendment, which the states ratified in 1868. It overturned the notorious Supreme Court decision in *Dred Scott v. Sandford* (1857) and declared that all persons including blacks "born or naturalized" within the United States were citizens entitled to the privileges and immunities of U.S. citizens and to due process and equal protection. Ironically, by abolishing slavery, the Thirteenth Amendment increased southern representation in the House of Representatives by invalidating the three-fifths clause; Republicans thought they had to act to ensure that this increased southern representation did not actually work against African American rights. Section 2 of the Fourteenth Amendment, short of specifically prohibiting states from denying the vote to blacks, provided great anguish to advocates of woman's suffrage and allowed representation to be reduced in states that denied or abridged the right to vote to "any of the male inhabitants of such State, being twenty-one years of age, and citizens of the United States, except for rebellion, or other crime." Congress never reduced a state's representation based on this provision.

During the 1866 congressional elections President Andrew Johnson, who had become president in 1865 after John Wilkes Booth assassinated Lincoln, opposed ratification of the Fourteenth Amendment, which Congress had just proposed. Republicans picked up substantial support in this election, and Congress subsequently approved a bill over Johnson's veto on January 8, 1867, granting black suffrage in the District of Columbia. It followed up with a similar expansion of the franchise in the federal territories and required Nebraska to extend to blacks the right to vote as a condition of its admission into the Union. In the fifth section of the first Reconstruction Act of March 2, 1867, Congress further required southern states to enfranchise blacks as a condition of readmission into the Union and representation within Congress. Although the House of Representatives impeached President Johnson in 1868, the Senate fell a single vote shy of the two-thirds needed to convict him and remove him from office.

In the meantime, sentiment against African American voting outside the South continued to be strong, with Democrats picking up some seats that they had lost in 1866 in special elections. The Republican presidential platform that Ulysses S. Grant ran on in 1868 reflected the party's reluctance to extend the policies it had adopted in the South outside that region. Not surprisingly, Democrats praised President Johnson for opposing congressional Reconstruction and continued to advance the view that, despite the outcome of the Civil War, federalism left determination of the franchise to the states.

The Republican Ulysses S. Grant defeated the Democrat Horatio Seymour by only three hundred thousand votes in the 1868 election; he would have won the Electoral College but not the popular vote without the support of southern blacks whom Republicans had enfranchised. With most African Americans continuing to be grateful to Republicans for both their freedom and their civil and political rights, expanding the franchise to northern blacks presented a way to bolster Republican strength in the North.

Given its brevity, the Fifteenth Amendment is best understood in the context of possible alternatives. The Republican representative George S. Boutwell of Massachusetts initially sought simultaneously to introduce both a bill and an amendment to enfranchise northern blacks, but rights secured by a bill were less secure than those achieved by an amendment, and the fact that Boutwell thought an amendment might be desirable suggested that legislation might exceed existing federal powers. The version of the amendment that Boutwell introduced in the House of Representatives was close to the final version. Ohio's Republican representative Samuel Shellabarger had proposed a more detailed and radical version, while fellow Ohio Republican John A. Bingham had offered a similar proposal, which allowed states to establish a one-year residency requirement.

In the Senate, Nevada Republican William M. Stewart introduced an amendment on January 28, 1869, that would also have protected the rights of African Americans to hold office. Republican Representative Jacob Howard of Michigan proposed a similar amendment, which the Senate defeated on February 8, that would have made it permissible to exclude naturalized Chinese or Irish from balloting. The next day the Senate also rejected a proposal by Henry Wilson that would have abolished restrictions on voting or office holding based on factors including race, color, property, and education and that would thus presumably have precluded literacy tests and poll taxes. The Senate subsequently accepted a modified version of Wilson's amendment and an additional proposal by Indiana Senator Oliver P. Morton to reform the Electoral College.

The House considered the Senate amendment on February 15 but rejected it and requested a conference committee to resolve differences between the two proposals. The longtime abolitionist Wendell Phillips was among those who feared that the Senate's more utopian proposal stood little chance of ratification. Debate continued in both houses until they finally agreed to a conference committee consisting of House members Bing-

Time Line

1869	■ **February 26** Congress proposes the Fifteenth Amendment.
1870	■ **February 3** The states ratify the Fifteenth Amendment.
1965	■ **August 6** President Lyndon B. Johnson signs the historic Voting Rights Act, which Congress later reaffirms and extends.
1966	■ **March 7 and June 13** Relying largely on Section 2 of the Fifteenth Amendment, the U.S. Supreme Court upholds key provisions of the Voting Rights Act of 1965 in *South Carolina v. Katzenbach* and *Katzenbach v. Morgan*.

ham, Boutwell, and John A. Logan (Republican from Illinois) and Senate members Steward, Roscoe Conkling (Republican from New York), and George Edmunds (Republican from Vermont). This committee adopted the current version of the amendment. The House accepted this version by the necessary two-thirds vote on February 25, 1869, and the Senate agreed to it the next day. William Gillette, in his book on the subject, observes that the amendment sought two limited goals: "to enfranchise the northern Negro" and "to protect the southern Negro against disenfranchisement." He further attributed its passage largely to congressional moderates.

Nevada was the first state to ratify the amendment on March 1, 1869. During this process New York initially approved the amendment and then attempted to rescind its ratification, while Ohio first rejected it and then approved it. (Today's precedents, while still ambiguous, are more favorable to Ohio's actions than to New York's actions.) Congress required some southern states to approve it as a condition of resuming their place in Congress, and Secretary of State Hamilton Fish declared the amendment ratified on March 30, 1870. Southern states, dominated by Reconstruction governments, were most supportive of the amendment, which faced strong opposition in border states, tepid endorsement in the Middle Atlantic states, and considerable conflict in the Midwest. Kentucky, Delaware, California, Tennessee, Maryland, and Oregon all rejected ratification, though some later approved it.

Advocates of women's suffrage, who had called for women's suffrage at the Seneca Falls Convention of 1848 and who were already chafing over the use of the word *male* to describe voters in Section 2 of the Fourteenth Amendment, were very disappointed by the adoption of the Fif-

George S. Boutwell (Library of Congress)

teenth Amendment. Susan B. Anthony and Elizabeth Cady Stanton were among those who refused to endorse an amendment that extended suffrage to black men but not to women. When the American Equal Rights Association met in New York City in May 1869, it split into the National Woman Suffrage Association, led by Anthony and Stanton, and the American Woman Suffrage Association, led by Lucy Stone. These organizations continued to work apart until they were united in 1890 as the National American Woman Suffrage Association.

About the Author

Two-thirds majorities in both houses of Congress are needed to propose amendments, and approval by three-fourths of the states is required to ratify them. When Congress proposed the Fifteenth Amendment, it followed the procedures used for all previous amendments, sending the amendment to state legislatures rather than to state conventions (as it would later do in the case of the Twenty-first Amendment, repealing national Prohibition on alcohol) for ratification. Some opponents of the amendment in Congress had sought to send the amendment to special state conventions.

The first version of the Fifteenth Amendment, which Republican Representative George S. Boutwell of Massachusetts authored in the House of Representatives, ended up being close to the final version. Ohio representatives

Samuel Shellabarger and John A. Bingham, who was largely responsible for the wording of Section 1 of the Fourteenth Amendment, proposed more extensive amendments in the House. The initial version that the Senate considered, which was also broader than the one that Congress actually adopted, was largely the work of Henry Wilson, a Massachusetts Republican who would later serve as vice president under Ulysses S. Grant.

Ultimately, a congressional conference committee of six men proposed the existing Fifteenth Amendment. The committee focused not only on ironing out the differences between the House and Senate versions of the amendment but also on proposing language that was likely to gain the support of the necessary three-fourths of state legislatures.

Explanation and Analysis of the Document

The Fifteenth Amendment consists of two very brief sections. The first provides that "the right of citizens of the United States to vote shall not be denied or abridged by the United States or by any State on account of race, color, or previous condition of servitude." The second specifies that "Congress shall have the power to enforce this article by appropriate legislation." The scope of the Fifteenth Amendment is limited to U.S. citizens. Section 1 of the Fourteenth Amendment had established that all persons "born or naturalized in the United States" were citizens, but Congress had not yet extended such citizenship to Native Americans, and there was widespread opposition to naturalizing Chinese in the American West as well as Irish and other immigrants in other parts of the country. Whereas the Fourteenth Amendment extended some civil rights to all "persons," the Fifteenth Amendment intended to guard only "citizens" against deprivation of their votes.

In a continuation of federal principles, Section 1 of the Fifteenth Amendment does not positively confer the right to vote on anyone; it simply prohibits denying or abridging such rights based on "race, color, or previous condition of servitude." In contrast to this negative wording, Section 2 more positively vests Congress with enforcement powers, using language almost identical to that employed in Section 2 of the Thirteenth Amendment and Section 5 of the Fourteenth Amendment.

Audience

Once proposed and ratified by the required majorities, constitutional amendments join other parts of the Constitution as part of what Article VI of the Constitution calls "the supreme law of the land." The language of amendments thus speaks to the American people and to the world as a whole. Like the two previous amendments, the Fifteenth Amendment helped articulate American values and provide legal language that individuals can cite when they attempt to secure their rights in courts. Many Americans, including President Grant, who had favored

THE RESULT OF THE FIFTEENTH AMENDMENT,

And the Rise and Progress of the African Race in America and its final Accomplishment, and Celebration on May 19ᵗʰ A.D.1870.

This print from 1870 commemorates the celebration over the passage of the Fifteenth Amendment in Baltimore, Maryland. (Library of Congress)

its adoption, viewed it as the culmination of earlier provisions in the Thirteenth and Fourteenth Amendments and as a practical implementation of the principles articulated in the Declaration of Independence.

The Fifteenth Amendment arguably carried different messages for North and South. It required states in the North, which had previously rejected black suffrage, to accept it, while attempting to ensure that southern states, on which Congress had imposed such suffrage, would retain it. While the former hopes were largely fulfilled, the latter were dashed relatively quickly and did not reemerge for nearly a century.

Impact

Although the Fifteenth Amendment successfully enfranchised northern blacks, its long-term impact on African

Americans in the South for its first one hundred years was negligible. Congress initially adopted Enforcement Acts between 1866 and 1875 designed to prevent obstruction to federal voting, but once northern troops left the South in 1877, whites who had once supported the Confederacy struggled to regain their power. They effectively evaded the force of the Fifteenth Amendment through adoption of numerous stratagems left open when Congress omitted restrictions on property or educational qualifications. The Supreme Court decision in *Ex parte Yarbrough* (1884) was one of the few cases where the Court upheld federal laws restricting private actions aimed at denying African American voting rights.

Literacy tests, often administered in a highly discriminatory fashion, were used to keep both lower-class whites and blacks from voting. Many states further combined them with grandfather clauses, which the U.S. Supreme Court

"The right of citizens of the United States to vote shall not be denied or abridged by the United States or by any State on account of race, color, or previous condition of servitude."

(Section 1)

"If it be just, it should not be denied; if it be necessary, it should be adopted; if it be a punishment to traitors, they deserve it."

(Thaddeus Stevens, qtd. in Gillette, p. 31)

"I would sooner cut off my right hand than ask for the ballot for the black man and not for woman."

(Susan B. Anthony, qtd. in McFeely, p. 266)

"The question of suffrage is one which is likely to agitate the public so long as a portion of the citizens of the nation are excluded from its privileges in any State. It seems to be very desirable that this question should be settled now, and I entertain the hope and express the desire that it may be by the ratification of the fifteenth article of amendment to the Constitution."

(Ulysses S. Grant, First Inaugural Address, March 4, 1869)

did not invalidate until *Guinn v. United States* (1915); such clauses exempted individuals whose grandfathers had voted—at a time when only whites could vote—from such literacy tests. States also adopted poll taxes, which they sometimes made cumulative so that individuals who wanted to vote had to pay the tax not only for that year but also for previous years in which they had not voted. Other states added additional obstacles to voter registration. In still others, racist groups like the Ku Klux Klan used physical violence to intimidate black voters. As the Democratic Party increasingly dominated the South (so that the winners of the Democratic primary almost always won in general elections), it, too, cooperated in black disenfranchisement by excluding blacks until the Supreme Court finally outlawed the practice in *Smith v. Allwright* (1944).

Although the nation never returned to chattel slavery, judicial interpretations of the Thirteenth, Fourteenth, and Fifteenth Amendments were extremely limited by the end of the nineteenth century. In the Civil Rights Cases of 1883, the Court decided that the amendments covered only state as opposed to private actions. By 1896 the

Court used the doctrine of "separate but equal" to approve the developing system of racial segregation in *Plessy v. Ferguson*. The Court did not reverse course until its historic 1954 decision in *Brown v. Board of Education*, which finally began the long process of desegregation.

The Fifteenth Amendment proved so ineffective in its first century that Goldwin Smith, a British-born attorney who presented plans for reforming the Constitution in 1898, favorably cited a petition by Louisiana and other states to repeal it. Ironically, at about the same time, a number of attorneys unsuccessfully argued that the amendment had been so revolutionary and so contrary to American federalism that it had violated implicit constitutional limitations on the constitutional amending process.

However impotent it seemed, in time the amendment provided authority not only for some of the Supreme Court decisions that invalidated its evasions but also for congressional legislation. In 1957 Congress adopted the first of a number of civil rights acts designed to overcome the paucity of southern African American voters. These acts reached their high point with the adoption of the Voting Rights Act of 1965. Relying on congressional enforcement powers in Section 2 of the Fifteenth Amendment, this law suspended the use of literacy tests in seven southern states and used U.S. marshals to register voters. The law further prohibited states from adopting new laws that might restrict black suffrage without federal clearance. Justice Hugo Black was the only justice to object to this provision when the Supreme Court upheld this and other provisions in *South Carolina v. Katzenbach* (1966). Congress subsequently extended the Voting Rights Act in 1970, 1975, 1982, and 2006.

In 1964 the Twenty-fourth Amendment prohibited the imposition of poll taxes in federal elections. Relying chiefly on the equal protection clause of the Fourteenth Amend-

ment, the Supreme Court subsequently extended this ban to state elections in *Harper v. Virginia Board of Elections* (1966). Since the Supreme Court's decision in *Baker v. Carr* (1962) ruling that issues of state legislative apportionment are justiciable (that is, subject to judicial intervention), the Supreme Court has increasingly overseen state plans for legislative apportionment. In recent years, it has looked with increased suspicion at plans that used racial classifications to configure districts, sometimes even in cases where states used such plans to increase rather than to restrict minority representation. The Court has clearly understood the Fifteenth Amendment as giving it a broad mandate to oversee voting issues.

Questions for Further Study

1. When members of Congress debated the language of the Fifteenth Amendment, they had to decide whether to include protections for women as well as for African American men. Would it have been better for them to sponsor an amendment to protect the rights of both groups that might go down in defeat or for them to do what they chose to do? What do you think might have been the consequences of linking these two rights together?

2. Once federal troops withdrew in 1877 and southerners elected Democrats who opposed racial equality, the Fifteenth Amendment largely remained a virtual dead letter in the South. What, if anything, do you think the authors of the amendment might have done to preclude later evasions through literacy tests, all-white primaries, poll taxes, and the like?

3. Once the Nineteenth Amendment was adopted in 1920, women had few problems accessing the polls. How can you account for the relative success of the Nineteenth Amendment compared with the relative failure (especially in its early years) of the Fifteenth Amendment?

4. Literacy tests and poll taxes proved to be central obstacles to African American voting. Do you think it is possible to make a nonracist argument on behalf of one or both of these mechanisms? How would you make such an argument? Do you think it is convincing? Do you think literacy tests that are administered fairly might encourage people who would not otherwise do so to get an education?

5. Today laws restrict relatively few groups from voting. Restrictions vary from state to state, but they include limits on voting for felons, former felons, the mentally ill, noncitizens, and individuals under the age of eighteen. Do you think any of these restrictions should be lifted? If so, which ones? Explain.

6. The political landscape has changed considerably since the states ratified the Fifteenth Amendment in 1870. Do you think any existing state would seek to reimpose restrictions on African American voting if there was no such amendment today? Generally, do you think it more likely that the national government or the states might seek to restrict such rights?

7. Do you think it is permissible to apportion districts to maximize the likelihood that members of minority races will be able to elect members of their own race? Do you consider such apportionment essentially similar to or qualitatively different from attempting to maximize party advantage?

See also *Dred Scott v. Sandford* (1857); Emancipation Proclamation (1863); Black Code of Mississippi (1865); Thirteenth Amendment to the U.S. Constitution (1865); Fourteenth Amendment to the U.S. Constitution (1868); *Plessy v. Ferguson* (1896); *Guinn v. United States* (1915); *South Carolina v. Katzenbach* (1966).

Further Reading

■ Books

Amar, Akhil R. *America's Constitution: A Biography*. New York: Random House, 2005.

Bernstein, R. B. "Fifteenth Amendment." In *Constitutional Amendments: 1789 to the Present*, ed. Kris E. Palmer. Detroit: Gale Group, 2000.

Cogan, Neil H. *The Complete Reconstruction Amendments and Statutes*. 6 vols. New Haven, Conn.: Yale University Press, 2006.

Gillette, William. *The Right to Vote: Politics and the Passage of the Fifteenth Amendment*. Baltimore: Johns Hopkins University Press, 1965.

Grimes, Alan P. *Democracy and the Amendments to the Constitution*. Lexington, Mass.: Lexington Books, 1978.

Keyssar, Alexander. *The Right to Vote: The Contested History of Democracy in the United States*. New York: Basic Books, 2000.

Kyvig, David E. *Explicit and Authentic Acts: Amending the U.S. Constitution, 1776–1995*. Lawrence: University Press of Kansas, 1996.

Mathews, John M. *Legislative and Judicial History of the Fifteenth Amendment*. Baltimore: Johns Hopkins University Press, 1909.

McFeely, William S. *Frederick Douglass*. New York: W. W. Norton, 1991.

Pendergast, Tom, et al. *Constitutional Amendments: From Freedom of Speech to Flag Burning*. 3 vols. Detroit, Mich.: UXL, 2001.

Vile, John R. *Encyclopedia of Constitutional Amendments, Proposed Amendments, and Amending Issues, 1789–2002*. 2nd ed. Santa Barbara, Calif.: ABC-CLIO, 2003.

■ Web Sites

"First Inaugural Address of Ulysses S. Grant." Avalon Project at Yale Law School Web site.
    http://www.yale.edu/lawweb/avalon/presiden/inaug/grant1.htm.

Stanton, Elizabeth Cady. "Declaration of Sentiments and Resolutions, Seneca Falls Convention, 1848." Furman University Web site.
    http://facweb.furman.edu/~benson/seneca-falls.cmu.

"The Voting Rights Act of 1965." U.S. Department of Justice Web site.
    http://www.usdoj.gov/crt/voting/intro/intro_b.htm.

"Voting Rights Act: Timeline." American Civil Liberties Union Web site.
    http://www.votingrights.org/timeline/?year=1700.

—John R. Vile

FIFTEENTH AMENDMENT TO THE U.S. CONSTITUTION

A Resolution Proposing an amendment to the Constitution of the United States.

Resolved by the Senate and House of Representatives of the United States of America in Congress assembled, (two-thirds of both Houses concurring) that the following article be proposed to the legislature of the several States as an amendment to the Constitution of the United States which, when ratified by three-fourths of said legislatures shall be valid as part of the Constitution, namely:

♦ **Article XV**

Section 1. The right of citizens of the United States to vote shall not be denied or abridged by the United States or by any State on account of race, color, or previous condition of servitude—

Section 2. The Congress shall have the power to enforce this article by appropriate legislation.

Glossary

abridged	curtailed
servitude	slavery

Illustration from Harper's Weekly *of two Ku Klux Klan members in their disguises* (Library of Congress)

KU KLUX KLAN ACT

"Each and every person so offending shall be deemed guilty of a high crime."

Overview

During the Reconstruction era after the Civil War, the U.S. Congress passed four Civil Rights Acts, on April 9, 1866; May 31, 1870; April 20, 1871; and March 1, 1875. The third is also known as the Ku Klux Klan (KKK) Act. Collectively, these acts are sometimes called Enforcement Acts, for they were intended to create a more just and racially inclusive American culture by enforcing the Fourteenth and Fifteenth Amendments to the U.S. Constitution, which, together with the Thirteenth Amendment abolishing slavery, are often called the Reconstruction Amendments. While the Civil Rights Acts all shaped and protected the Fourteenth and Fifteenth Amendments, the KKK Act specifically aimed at violence and conspiracies perpetrated against black Americans.

Context

Postwar civil rights legislation represented a series of compromises between various factions within the Republican Party. Founded in 1854, the Republican Party was a coalition of several mid-nineteenth-century political organizations: Whigs, Free-Soilers, Know-Nothings, and even some pro-Union Democrats. Arriving at a political agenda or platform proved difficult, though by the time of Reconstruction most members of the party supported increased civil rights for blacks. Just what constituted "civil rights," however, was a matter of endless and evolving debate. For the radical minority of the party—the so-called Radical Republicans—civil rights included not only "life, liberty, and the pursuit of happiness" but also the full range of political and social rights, such as voting, jury participation, and equal access to public accommodations.

The Civil War brought an end to slavery in America, thus freeing over four million blacks. But Americans confronted two major challenges in the aftermath of war: the terms of readmission for southern states and the extent of assimilation for freedmen. Most white southerners resented punitive actions against them and resisted attempts to treat blacks as citizens. Southern legislatures passed oppressive laws, called Black Codes, which subjugated blacks in a manner essentially tantamount to slavery by prohibiting their right to vote, carry weapons in public places, work in certain occupations, and sit on juries and by limiting their right to testify against white people in court. Any effort to ensure peace and protect blacks through postwar military rule seemed as necessary to northerners as it was objectionable to southerners.

To assist freedmen to begin anew, Republicans in Congress established the Bureau of Refugees, Freedmen, and Abandoned Lands (more commonly called the Freedmen's Bureau) on March 3, 1865, hoping to destroy all remnants of the white power structure in the South. The bureau was largely intended to shield the lives, interests, and rights of black Americans. After the congressional election of 1866 and the further radicalization of the Republican Party, Congress passed four Reconstruction Acts in 1867 and 1868. Those acts created five military districts in the seceded states, required approval of new southern state constitutions by Congress, granted voting rights to all adult males in southern states, and forced southern states to ratify the Reconstruction Amendments.

Additionally, Congress passed a series of Civil Rights Acts. The first, passed April 9, 1866, consisted of ten sections and was titled "An Act to protect all Persons in the United States in their Civil Rights, and furnish the Means of their Vindication." Congress designed its legislation in conjunction with the Fourteenth Amendment in an effort to constitutionalize civil rights; it was this amendment that guaranteed to all citizens "due process" and "equal protection" under the law. The chief effect of the act was to confirm the citizenship of all persons born in the United States. To fortify black rights, Congress passed further legislation, reenacting sections of the previous act in the much longer Civil Rights Act of 1870, intended primarily to enforce the Fifteenth Amendment and the right of blacks to vote. This act established criminal penalties for anyone caught interfering with federal elections. Yet white southerners remained recalcitrant, forcing Congress to amend the act of 1870 with the Force Act of February 28, 1871. The Force Act stipulated that

Time Line

1865

■ **December 6**
The Thirteenth Amendment, abolishing slavery, is ratified.

■ **March 3**
The Freedmen's Bureau is established by Congress at the request of President Abraham Lincoln.

■ **December 24**
The Ku Klux Klan is formed in Pulaski, Tennessee.

1866

■ **April 9**
Congress passes the Civil Rights Act of 1866, making citizens of "all persons born in the United States."

1868

■ **July 9**
The Fourteenth Amendment, guaranteeing due process and equal protection under the law, is ratified.

1870

■ **May 31**
Congress passes the Civil Rights Act of 1870 (also called the Enforcement Act) to protect voting rights.

1871

■ **March**
South Carolina governor Robert Kingston Scott requests federal support to suppress the Ku Klux Klan, and President Ulysses S. Grant asks Congress for emergency relief.

■ **April 20**
Congress passes the Civil Rights Act of 1871—the KKK Act—to enforce the provisions of the Fourteenth Amendment.

■ **October 17**
President Grant suspends habeas corpus in nine counties in South Carolina, leading to mass arrests of Klansmen.

■ **November**
The first of two waves of trials of the Ku Klux Klan are conducted in Columbia, South Carolina; a second wave would begin in April 1872.

1875

■ **March 1**
President Grant signs the Civil Rights Act, guaranteeing equal treatment in "public accommodations."

---

all citizens of the United States who are or shall be otherwise qualified by law to vote at any election by the people in any State, Territory, district, county, city, parish, township, school district, municipality, or other territorial subdivision, shall be entitled and allowed to vote at all such elections, without distinction of race, color, or previous condition of servitude; any constitution, law, custom, usage, or regulation of any State or Territory, or by or under its authority, to the contrary notwithstanding.

Despite the ongoing efforts of Congress to peaceably readmit seceded states while simultaneously protecting freedmen, southern legislatures continued to write Black Codes and to impose literacy tests and poll taxes to prevent blacks from voting. At the same time, violence escalated even further throughout the South. Some southerners mounted a campaign of intimidation and murder against blacks and white Republicans in order to preserve white supremacy and prevent black citizenship. Whites were especially eager to inhibit black participation on juries and in elections.

In this environment, various white supremacist vigilante groups appeared, organized under banners such as the Men of Justice, the Pale Faces, the White Brotherhood, the Order of the Rose, and the Constitutional Union Guards. Perhaps the most egregious and methodical perpetrator of hostilities was the Ku Klux Klan, first organized by a group of six middle-class Confederate veterans from Pulaski, Tennessee, on December 24, 1865. Originally intended as a social group, the Klan became a paramilitary extension of the southern Democrats that quickly terrorized blacks throughout the South.

Within a year of its founding, the Klan consisted of several state organizations, each constituted as a Realm managed by a Grand Dragon, the entire organization led by Confederate general Nathan Forrest as Grand Wizard of the Empire. Klansmen (also called Ghouls), posing as ghosts of Confederate dead returned from the battlefield, dressed themselves and their horses in white robes and sheets. These horrifying disguises were employed during midnight rides of unlimited terror, usually intended to keep blacks from the election booths. They left thousands of dead blacks in their wake. In November 1868 alone, Louisiana residents killed 1,081 (mostly black) persons, a level of violence worse than the lynching spree of the late-nineteenth- and early-twentieth-century Jim Crow era. Although the KKK was disbanded during the 1870s, in 1915 the Klan reappeared in even larger numbers, reaching a peak membership of nearly five million by the mid-1920s.

By March 1871, violence against blacks had become sufficiently uncontrollable in South Carolina that Governor Robert Kingston Scott requested federal assistance to restore order. A former Union general and commissioner of the South Carolina Freedmen's Bureau, Scott was a Republican and the first governor of reconstructed South Carolina. As governor, Scott oversaw a massive increase in state debt (already quite large when he took office), thus provoking partisan-induced impeachment proceedings against him by the state assembly. Scott held on to his office, however, allowing him to wage war against the KKK.

Both the legislative and executive branches of the federal government responded to events in South Carolina and Scott's request. President Ulysses S. Grant had already created the Office of Solicitor General to assist the attorney general in prosecuting Klansmen, and Congress had passed the Judiciary Act of 1869 to increase the number of federal judges in the South. In March 1871, after hearing from Governor Scott, Grant asked Congress for emergency legislation, resulting in another enforcement act, namely the Civil Rights Act of 1871, also called the KKK Act. Congress also created the Department of Justice, which began operations on July 1, 1870, to help combat the KKK. Since so many southern police belonged to the Klan, Congress enabled the president to use federal troops in suppressing racial violence. The KKK Act also allowed the president to suspend habeas corpus, creating the possibility of mass arrests without individual charges or court proceedings. Following the act, President Grant issued a proclamation ordering the South Carolina KKK to disperse and surrender its weapons. When the Klan refused to submit to those orders, Grant suspended habeas corpus and sent federal troops to make arrests. Within two months, hundreds of Klansmen were arrested in South Carolina, while many others fled the state. Because the state judicial system could not handle the vast number of defendants, however, most of them were soon released.

About the Author

Among the radical leaders of the Republican Party was Benjamin Franklin Butler, the primary author of the KKK Act. Born in Deerfield, New Hampshire, on November 5, 1818, and named for the Founding Father Benjamin Franklin, Butler grew up in Lowell, Massachusetts, where his widowed mother ran a boardinghouse. After graduating from Waterville College (now Colby College) in Maine, Butler was admitted to the bar in Massachusetts. He began his political career as a Democrat and served in the Massachusetts legislature throughout the 1850s, which established his military rank of brigadier general at the start of the Civil War. Butler participated actively in the Democratic Convention of 1860, yet Republican president Abraham Lincoln was so impressed by the general's early and aggressive support for the Union that he appointed Butler as third-highest-ranking major general of the U.S. Volunteers. Nicknamed "Spoons" for his alleged habit of relieving southern homes of their silverware during his harsh administration of New Orleans after the Union recaptured it during the war (earning him, too, the nickname Butler the Beast), Butler also became famous at Virginia's Fort Monroe in 1861 for refusing to return escaped slaves to their masters and

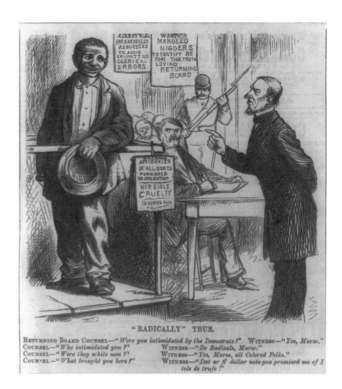

Caricature of Radical Republicans bribing African Americans to give false testimony of atrocities and intimidation by the Democrats (Library of Congress)

thereby creating the notion of slaves as "contraband" of war. After the war, Butler served in the U.S. House of Representatives (1867–1875 and 1877–1879) and as governor of Massachusetts in 1883–1884.

Despite his previous Democratic affiliation, Butler emerged from the Civil War as a devoted Republican; in fact, he could be counted among the more radical members of the party. Along with the U.S. senator of his state, Charles Sumner, Butler proposed the highly progressive Civil Rights Act of 1875, which banned racial discrimination in public accommodations. Butler had already demonstrated his dedication to civil rights, however, with the KKK Act.

During his career, Butler participated in many historic events. As a congressional representative he managed the impeachment trial of President Andrew Johnson in 1868, whereas as governor of Massachusetts he is remembered for having appointed the nation's first Irish American judge, the first African American judge (George Lewis Ruffin), and the first woman to executive office (Clara Barton). His shifting political affiliations, from antebellum Democrat to postwar Radical Republican to post-Reconstruction Greenback (a minor party that advocated the continued use of paper currency) to Democratic governor, are not unique and speak to the enormous social upheaval of the era. Butler died on January 11, 1893, in Washington, D.C.

Senator Benjamin Butler of Massachusetts (Library of Congress)

Explanation and Analysis of the Document

The KKK Act, written in dense, repetitive legislative language, consists of seven sections, the first of which is an unnumbered preamble of sorts, establishing the primary purpose of the act. It states that any person, even a person acting within the law of his state, who deprives a citizen of his or her rights as a citizen can be prosecuted in the U.S. federal courts. This section of the act, now codified as Section 1983 of the U.S. Code, remains the most influential portion of the KKK Act.

The longest section of the KKK Act, section 2, provided the core of this new legislation. Its focus is on conspiracies, that is, the effort by two or more persons to "conspire together to overthrow, or to put down, or to destroy by force the government of the United States." It goes on to list various ways in which this could be done, including the use of force or intimidation, delaying or hindering the execution of laws, seizing U.S. property, and in particular using force or intimidation to prevent a U.S. officer from executing his duty. Additionally, the section specifies any effort to "deter" a party from serving as a witness in court, using force or intimidation to prevent a juror from serving or to influence his verdict, preventing a person from holding public office, or impeding a person from exercising the right to vote. In a broader sense, it prohibited any conspiracy that would deprive a person of equal protection under the law. These offenses would be regarded as high crimes punishable by fines of not less than $500 and not more than $5,000 or imprisonment for not less than

six months or more than six years, possibly consisting of hard labor. Notice that the emphasis is on conspiracies, on the actions of "two or more persons." Clearly, the act was targeted at the KKK and similar organizations that conspired to do just the sorts of things this section of the act specifies. Although the KKK began as a fraternal organization, it quickly evolved into a terrorist one. Usually its victims were black leaders, such as ministers, politicians, teachers, or former soldiers. It used floggings, beatings, and rape to intimidate and undermine Reconstruction. In 1868, an election year, the KKK was behind as many as two thousand political assassinations throughout the South. Many of them were carried out with the approval and even support of the Democratic Party.

Section 3, after essentially repeating much of the material from the second section, begins to stipulate the powers the act grants to the president. In the event that a state is unable or unwilling to prevent the offenses from Section 2 (laboriously repeated so as not to leave any uncertainty), the president can call out the militia or the army and navy to enforce the act, with or without the state's request. Section 4 stipulates a further power: that if any of the "unlawful combinations" named in section 3 are organized and armed, "and so numerous and powerful as to be able … to either overthrow or set at defiance" the authorities, or when the threat to public safety is great, the president can suspend the writ of habeas corpus as part of the federal effort to suppress the insurgency. *Habeas corpus* is a Latin term used commonly in the law; its literal meaning is "you shall have the body," and it refers to the obligation of the government to specify charges against a person who has been arrested and to conduct a trial (and thus not to conduct secret arrests and detentions). By suspending habeas corpus, the authorities have the power to arrest and detain people indefinitely without bringing charges against them or bringing them to trial. Suspension of habeas corpus is an extreme measure that has been taken principally during wartime. Abraham Lincoln took the step during the Civil War, as did Woodrow Wilson during World War I. In the twenty-first century, the issue of habeas corpus has arisen in connection with the detention of suspected terrorists in facilities such as the U.S. base at Guantánamo Bay in Cuba.

The remaining sections of the act are relatively procedural by comparison to the previous ones. Section 5 states that conspirators of the sorts listed could not serve on a grand or petit jury hearing a case arising as a result of this act. A grand jury is one that determines whether there is enough evidence for a case to go to trial; it does not determine guilt or innocence. A petit jury is one that actually hears the case in open court. Additionally, jurors would be required to take an oath swearing that they had never participated in such conspiracies—which would prove to be a problem in South Carolina, where affiliation with the Klan was widespread. Section 6 states that any person who failed to report a KKK Act conspiracy could be treated as a participant to that conspiracy; this provision has been codified in Section 1986 of the U.S. Code. Finally, Section 7 defines the act as supporting, rather than repealing, any and all previous civil rights legislation.

"Be it enacted by the Senate and Home of Representatives of the United States of America in Congress assembled, *That any person who … shall subject, or cause to be subjected, any person within the jurisdiction of the United States to the deprivation of any rights, privileges, or immunities secured by the Constitution of the United States, shall … be liable to the party injured in any action at law.*"

(Paragraph 1)

"*Each and every person so offending shall be deemed guilty of a high crime.*"

(Section 2)

"*It shall be lawful for the President, and it shall be his duty to take such measures, by the employment of the militia or the land and naval forces of the United States, or of either, or by other means, as he may deem necessary for the suppression of such insurrection, domestic violence, or combinations.*"

(Section 3)

"*It shall be lawful for the President of the United States, when in his judgment the public safety shall require it, to suspend the privileges of the writ of habeas corpus.*"

(Section 4)

Audience

The first Enforcement Act (1870) failed to curtail racial violence in the South. Klansmen seemed particularly unimpressed by the law, prompting President Grant to send troops to South Carolina under the command of Major Lewis Merrill. Reacting to the spiraling violence throughout the region, Congress passed yet another enforcement act, tailored even more specifically toward the Klan. The KKK Act served as a stern rebuke and warning to all white supremacists in the South. Democrats and conservative Republicans complained that Congress exceeded its constitutional authority over individuals and dangerously enlarged presidential power. Radical Republicans, by contrast, worried more about the threat posed by paramilitary organizations, compelling them to send a definitive message to the Ku Klux Klan.

Impact

The KKK Act engendered a heroic, though brief, unfunded, and undermanned assault upon racial violence in the South. During Reconstruction, the KKK Act, in conjunction with federal troops (as opposed to state militias), helped suppress the Ku Klux Klan. Partly due to black jurors' presence in federal courts, numerous Klansmen were successfully prosecuted, fined, and imprisoned, most notably in South Carolina. After the KKK trials in South Carolina, the Klan effectively disappeared in America until 1915.

The South Carolina Ku Klux Klan trials stand out as a singular moment in the nineteenth-century campaign for civil rights. On October 12, 1871, President Grant declared nine counties of South Carolina in a state of rebellion and sent in federal troops. Yet Klan-related murders continued.

Thus, on October 17, he suspended habeas corpus in those counties, enabling mass arrests of Klansmen under the KKK Act. Grant's actions had the effect of emptying the streets while filling the jails of South Carolina.

Circuit Court Judge Hugh Lennox Bond of Maryland—recently appointed by President Grant because of his courageous commitment to civil rights—and District Judge George Seabrook Bryan of South Carolina presided over the KKK trials. Far from being an impartial jurist, Bond saw himself as part of a federal team of Klan busters. Bryan was a Democrat and former slaveholder appointed by President Andrew Johnson; his Carolina district court had acquitted most Klansmen. Democrats raised a substantial sum of money for the defense to hire the former U.S. senator from Maryland, Reverdy Johnson, and the former attorney general (under Andrew Johnson), Henry Stanbery, both vocal critics of Republican Reconstruction policy. David T. Corbin, a prominent South Carolina Republican who graduated from Dartmouth College before practicing law in Vermont, handled the prosecution.

The trials began on November 28, 1871, with both sides fully prepared for a major constitutional battle. The fact that the KKK Act required prospective jurors to swear they had never participated in the Klan partly explains the court's difficulty in forming a jury. Fifteen of the twenty-one grand jurors and two-thirds of the petit jurors were black, increasing both the probability of convictions and the animus of local whites.

More than simply deciding the fate of the Klan and the authority of the KKK Act, the court addressed the meaning of Reconstruction, the reach of the amended Constitution, and the fate of civil rights. The prosecution wanted a clear precedent for black rights, arguing that the Fourteenth and Fifteenth Amendments confirmed positive rights and applied the Bill of Rights against the states, while the defense sought to preserve federal-state relations, insisting that the Reconstruction Amendments did nothing to alter the existing federal system. Ultimately, the court heard many cases during its November 1871 and April 1872 terms; thousands of Klansmen were indicted, and over six hundred were convicted. In the first set of trials, the sentences—fines and imprisonment—were relatively light. In the second set the government concentrated on murder cases, and the court imposed eight- and ten-year prison sentences. Although the KKK Act penalties proved less harsh than criminal penalties for murder, it is unlikely that southern state courts would have found Klansmen guilty at all, so the sentences were regarded as better than nothing.

The KKK trials were more than the courts could handle. The sheer number of offenders was too great for an already stretched judiciary. It did not help that defendants were often wealthy whites while the victims were poor blacks. Klansmen cleverly admitted to their crimes in exchange for leniency, which was generally granted. To make matters worse, Democrats constantly criticized the government for partisan excess, militarily despotism, and executive tyranny. Indeed, even northern Democrats denied the existence of the Klan, suggesting it was a partisan fiction of the Republican Party. Despite success in South Carolina, Attorney General Amos Akerman admitted the inadequacy of the federal judiciary to end Klan violence. Thereafter the judiciary focused on ringleaders of the Klan, though prosecutions became increasingly difficult to achieve. By the spring of 1873, prosecutions under the KKK Act were discontinued. While the Klan was temporarily defeated, white supremacy and racial violence remained a fixture in southern life.

The Civil Rights Act of 1875 represents Congress's final attempt to secure civil rights for blacks. The act proved controversial from the moment it was proposed in 1870, not least for its attempt to eliminate segregation in all forms and for redefining civil rights to include what most Americans understood as "social rights." Even many Republicans objected to desegregation in schools, churches, and cemeteries. The notion that Congress could regulate private persons or companies was especially contentious, with Democrats and conservative Republicans repeatedly insisting that the law was unconstitutional and would never be upheld by the Supreme Court.

The 1875 act met with mixed treatment from federal circuit courts before being ruled unconstitutional by the Supreme Court. Hundreds of civil rights cases were tried and appealed during the late 1870s and early 1880s, with federal judges in Pennsylvania, Texas, Maryland, and Kentucky holding the act constitutional, while in New York, Tennessee, Missouri, Kansas, and other states, divided federal circuit courts sent the issue to the Supreme Court, where some of the act's provisions were ruled unconstitutional in the Civil Rights Cases of 1883.

Meanwhile, the Supreme Court impaired the effectiveness of the KKK Act by limiting the reach of the Fourteenth Amendment. In the Slaughter-House Cases (1873) the Court held that the Fourteenth Amendment protected the privileges and immunities only of national, not state, citizenship. Civil rights were thereafter deemed to be privileges of state citizenship and protected by the states. In *United States v. Reese* (1876), the Court held that Congress went beyond its constitutional authority in various parts of the Enforcement Acts. Since the KKK Act was intended to enforce the Fourteenth Amendment, those decisions rendered the act essentially obsolete. Subsequent Supreme Court decisions, including *United States v. Cruikshank* in 1876 and *Virginia v. Rives* in 1880, narrowed the Fourteenth Amendment even further, insisting that it applied only to state action. The Court's decision in *United States v. Harris* (1883) invalidated the criminal conspiracy section of the KKK Act for the same reason. Finally, when Democrats regained control of Congress later in the nineteenth century, they repealed certain elements of the Enforcement Acts.

Even today, however, federally codified portions of the KKK Act help protect the rights of U.S. citizens. The federal code allows people to sue for state and local violations of federal law and the Constitution. A very broad range of cases are litigated involving equal protection and due process rights as well as constitutional rights applied to the states by the Fourteenth Amendment and subsequent federal statutes. Also, the federal code allows citizens to sue if they are injured by conspiracies formed to prevent an officer of the United States from performing official duties, for obstructing justice, or for depriving others of the equal protection of the laws. The language of these statutes remains largely unchanged from the KKK Act of 1871.

See also Emancipation Proclamation (1863); Black Code of Mississippi (1865); Thirteenth Amendment to the U.S. Constitution (1865); Testimony before the Joint Committee on Reconstruction on Atrocities in the South against Blacks (1866); Fourteenth Amendment to the U.S. Constitution (1868); Fifteenth Amendment to the U.S. Constitution (1870); *United States v. Cruikshank* (1876); Civil Rights Cases (1883).

Further Reading

■ Articles

Kaczorowski, Robert J. "Federal Enforcement of Civil Rights during the First Reconstruction." *Fordham Urban Law Journal* 23 (Fall 1995): 155–186.

■ Books

Butler, Benjamin F. *Autobiography and Personal Reminiscences of Major-General Benj. F. Butler: Butler's Book.* Boston: A. M. Thayer, 1892.

Horn, Stanley F. *Invisible Empire: The Story of the Ku Klux Klan, 1866–1871.* Montclair, N.J.: Patterson Smith, 1939.

Ingalls, Robert P. *Hoods: The Story of the Ku Klux Klan.* New York: Putnam, 1979.

Schwartz, Bernard, ed. *Civil Rights: Statutory History of the United States.* New York: Chelsea House, 1970.

Trelease, Allen W. *White Terror: The Ku Klux Klan Conspiracy and Southern Reconstruction.* 1971. Reprint. Baton Rouge: Louisiana State University Press, 1995.

Williams, Lou Falkner. *The Great South Carolina Ku Klux Klan Trials, 1871–1872.* Athens: University of Georgia Press, 1996.

■ Web Sites

South Carolina Ku Klux Klan Trials: 1871–72. Law Library— American Law and Legal Information Web site.
http://law.jrank.org/pages/2615/South-Carolina-Ku-Klux-Klan-Trials-1871-72.html.

—R. Owen Williams

Questions for Further Study

1. What were the Black Codes, as exemplified by the Black Code of Mississippi (1865), and why did they make the Ku Klux Klan Act, along with the other Enforcement Acts, necessary in the post–Civil War period?

2. For decades after the Civil War, many people in the former Confederacy bitterly resented what they saw as the intrusion of the victorious North in southern affairs. Try to imagine a different set of historical circumstances in which the North approached the issue of Reconstruction differently. What do you think would have been the effect on newly freed slaves of your alternative version of history?

3. Habeas corpus is one of the fundamental liberties of Americans. What is habeas corpus, and under what circumstances might it be suspended? Do you see any similarity between the president's power to suspend habeas corpus under the Ku Klux Klan Act and the power of twenty-first-century presidents to do so in cases involving suspected terrorism? Explain.

4. For a period of time in the late nineteenth century the Ku Klux Klan was in eclipse, before its resurgence in the early twentieth century. What events led to a period of lessening Klan activity and influence?

5. Read this document in light of the 1876 U.S. Supreme Court case *United States v. Cruikshank.* In what sense did the Court's decision in that case have the effect of partially undermining the Ku Klux Klan Act?

Ku Klux Klan Act

♦ **Chap XXII—*An Act to enforce the Provisions of the Fourteenth Amendment to the Constitution of the United States, and for other Purposes.***

Be it enacted by the Senate and Home of Representatives of the United States of America in Congress assembled, That any person who, under color of any law, statute, ordinance, regulation, custom, or usage of any State, shall subject, or cause to be subjected, any person within the jurisdiction of the United States to the deprivation of any rights, privileges, or immunities secured by the Constitution of the United States, shall, any such law, statute, ordinance, regulation, custom, or usage of the State to the contrary notwithstanding, be liable to the party injured in any action at law, suit in equity, or other proper proceeding for redress; such proceeding to be prosecuted in the several district or circuit courts of the United States, with and subject to the same rights of appeal, review upon error, and other remedies provided in like cases in such courts, under the provisions of the act of the ninth of April, eighteen hundred and sixty-six, entitled "An act to protect all persons in the United States in their civil rights, and to furnish the means of their vindication"; and the other remedial laws of the United States which are in their nature applicable in such cases.

SEC. 2. That if two or more persons within any State or Territory of the United States shall conspire together to overthrow, or to put down, or to destroy by force the government of the United States, or to levy war against the United States, or to oppose by force the authority of the government of the United States, or by force, intimidation, or threat to prevent, hinder, or delay the execution of any law of the United States, or by force to seize, take, or possess any property of the United States contrary to the authority thereof, or by force, intimidation, or threat to prevent any person from accepting or holding any office or trust or place of confidence under the United States, or from discharging the duties thereof, or by force, intimidation, or threat to induce any officer of the United States to leave any State, district, or place where his duties as such officer might lawfully be performed, or to injure him in his person or property on account of his lawful discharge of the duties of his office, or to injure his person while engaged in the lawful discharge of the duties of his office, or to injure his property so as to molest, interrupt, hinder, or impede him in the discharge of his official duty, or by force, intimidation, or threat to deter any party or witness in any court of the United States from attending such court, or from testifying in any matter pending in such court fully, freely, and truthfully, or to injure any such party or witness in his person or property on account of his having so attended or testified, or by force, intimidation, or threat to influence the verdict, presentment, or indictment, of any juror or grand juror in any court of the United States, or to injure such juror in his person or property on account of any verdict, presentment, or indictment lawfully assented to by him, or on account of his being or having been such juror, or shall conspire together, or go in disguise upon the public highway or upon the premises of another for the purpose, either directly or indirectly, of depriving any person or any class of persons of the equal protection of the laws, or of equal privileges or immunities under the laws, or for the purpose of preventing or hindering the constituted authorities of any State from giving or securing to all persons within such State the equal protection of the laws, or shall conspire together for the purpose of in any manner impeding, hindering, obstructing, or defeating the due course of justice in any State or Territory, with intent to deny to any citizen of the United States the due and equal protection of the laws, or to injure any person in his person or his property for lawfully enforcing the right of any person or class of persons to the equal protection of the laws, or by force, intimidation, or threat to prevent any citizen of the United States lawfully entitled to vote from giving his support or advocacy in a lawful manner towards or in favor of the election of any lawfully qualified person as an elector of President or Vice-President of the United States, or as a member of the Congress of the United States, or to injure any such citizen in his person or property on account of such support or advocacy, each and every person so offending shall be deemed guilty of a high crime, and, upon conviction thereof in any district or circuit court of the United States or district or supreme court of any Territory of the United States having jurisdiction of similar offences, shall be punished by a fine not less than five hundred nor more than five thousand dollars, or by imprisonment, with or without hard labor, as the court may determine, for a period of not less than six months nor more than six years, as the court may determine, or by both such fine and imprisonment as the court shall determine. And if any one or more persons engaged in any such conspiracy shall do, or cause to be done, any act in furtherance of the object of such conspiracy, whereby any person shall be injured in his person or property, or deprived of having and exercising any right or privilege of a citizen of the United States, the person so injured or deprived of such rights and privileges may have and maintain an action for the recovery of damages occasioned by such injury or deprivation of rights and privileges against any one or more of the persons engaged in such conspiracy, such action to be prosecuted in the proper district or circuit court of the United States, with and subject to the same rights of appeal, review upon error, and other remedies provided in like cases in such courts under the provisions of the act of April ninth, eighteen hundred and sixty-six, entitled "An act to protect all persons in the United States in their civil rights, and to furnish the means of their vindication."

SEC. 3. That in all cases where insurrection, domestic violence, unlawful combinations, or conspiracies in any State shall so obstruct or hinder the execution of the laws thereof, and of the United States, as to deprive any portion or class of the people of such State of any of the rights, privileges, or immunities, or protection, named in the Constitution and secured by this act, and the constituted authorities of such State shall either be unable to protect, or shall, from any cause, fail in or refuse protection of the people in such rights, such facts shall be deemed a denial by such State of the equal protection of the laws to which they are entitled under the Constitution of the United States; and in all such cases, or whenever any such insurrection, violence, unlawful combination, or conspiracy shall oppose or obstruct the laws of the United States or the due execution thereof, or impede or obstruct the due course of justice under the same, it shall be lawful for the President, and it shall be his duty to take such measures, by the employment of the militia or the land and naval forces of the United States, or of either, or by other means, as he may deem necessary for the suppression of such insurrection, domestic violence, or combinations; and any person who shall be arrested under the provisions of this and the preceding sec-

tion shall be delivered to the marshal of the proper district, to be dealt with according to law.

SEC. 4. That whenever in any State or part of a State the unlawful combinations named in the preceding section of this act shall be organized and armed, and so numerous and powerful as to be able, by violence, to either overthrow or set at defiance the constituted authorities of such State, and of the United States within such State, or when the constituted authorities are in complicity with, or shall connive at the unlawful purposes of, such powerful and armed combinations; and whenever, by reason of either or all of the causes aforesaid, the conviction of such offenders and the preservation of the public safety shall become in such district impracticable, in every such case such combinations shall be deemed a rebellion against the government of the United States, and during the continuance, of such rebellion, and within the limits of the district which shall be so under the sway thereof, such limits to be prescribed by proclamation, it shall be lawful for the President of the United States, when in his judgment the public safety shall require it, to suspend the privileges of the writ of habeas corpus, to the end that such rebellion may be overthrown: *Provided*, That all the provisions of the second section of an act entitled "An act relating to habeas corpus, and regulating judicial proceedings in certain cases," approved March third, eighteen hundred and sixty-three, which relate to the discharge of prisoners other than prisoners of war, and to the penalty for refusing to obey the order of the court, shall be in full force so far as the same are applicable to the provisions of this section: *Provided further*. That the President shall first have made proclamation, as now provided by law, commanding such insurgents to disperse: *And provided also*, That the provisions of this section shall not be in force after the end of the next regular session of Congress.

SEC. 5. That no person shall be a grand or petit juror in any court of the United States upon any inquiry, hearing, or trial of any suit, proceeding, or prosecution based upon or arising under the provisions of this act who shall, in the judgment of the court, be in complicity with any such combination or conspiracy; and every such juror shall, before entering upon any such inquiry, hearing, or trial, take and subscribe an oath in open court that he has never, directly or indirectly, counselled, advised, or voluntarily aided any such combination or conspiracy; and each and every person who shall take this oath, and shall therein swear falsely, shall be guilty of perjury, and shall be subject to the pains and penalties declared against that crime, and the first section of the act entitled "An act defining additional causes of challenge and prescribing an additional oath for grand and petit jurors in the United States courts," approved June seventeenth, eighteen hundred and sixty-two, be, and the same is hereby, repealed.

SEC. 6. That any person or persons, having knowledge that any of the wrongs conspired to be done and mentioned in the second section of this act are about to be committed, and having power to prevent or aid in preventing the same, shall neglect or refuse so to do, and such wrongful act shall be committed, such person or persons shall be liable to the person injured, or his legal representatives, for all damages caused by any such wrongful act which such first-named person or persons by reasonable diligence could have prevented; and such damages may be recovered in an action on the case in the proper circuit court of the United States, and any number of persons guilty of such wrongful neglect or refusal may be joined as defendants in such action: *Provided*,

That such action shall be commenced within one year after such cause of action shall have accrued; and if the death of any person shall be caused by any such wrongful act and neglect, the legal representatives of such deceased person shall have such action therefor, and may recover not exceeding five thousand dollars damages therein, for the benefit of the widow of such deceased person, if any there be, or if there be no widow, for the benefit of the next of kin of such deceased person.

SEC. 7. That nothing herein contained shall be construed to supersede or repeal any former act or law except so far as the same may be repugnant thereto; and any offences heretofore committed against the tenor of any former act shall be prosecuted, and any proceeding already commenced for the prosecution thereof shall be continued and completed, the same as if this act had not been passed, except so far as the provisions of this act may go to sustain and validate such proceedings.

APPROVED, April 20, 1871.

Glossary

color	in legal terms, pretense
elector	a member of the Electoral College, which votes for the president and vice president of the United States
immunities	the concept that a state cannot deprive citizens from other states of their rights
petit juror	a juror in a trial court, as opposed to a grand juror
presentment	an accusation of a crime made by a grand jury on its own initiative
review upon error	an appeal to a higher court based on the argument that the lower court erred in its ruling
suit in equity	a civil suit, as opposed to a criminal proceeding
Territory	any of the areas formed under the authority of the U.S. government that had not yet been admitted to the Union as states
writ of habeas corpus	from the Latin for "we shall have the body," the requirement that the government openly specify the charges against and bring to trial a person accused of a crime

Morrison R. Waite (Library of Congress)

UNITED STATES V. CRUIKSHANK

"We may suspect that race was the cause of the hostility,

but it is not so averred."

Overview

United States v. Cruikshank et al. involved an effort to bring to justice three men accused of participating in the slaughter of some one hundred blacks in Colfax, Louisiana, on April 13, 1873, one of the most sensational incidents of Reconstruction political violence. During Reconstruction, the decade-long period after the Civil War, the federal government passed laws to protect blacks from violence and intimidation as they sought to exercise the right to vote. Nonetheless, in *Cruikshank*, the Supreme Court affirmed a lower federal court's decision to invalidate the result of a previous verdict of guilty and ordered the release of the defendants.

While the Court's decision rested in large part upon its criticism of a poorly drafted indictment, the narrow grounds upon which it based its decision hampered federal efforts to protect blacks from violence. Coupled with another Court decision, *United States v. Reese*, the *Cruikshank* decision marked a significant step in the federal government's retreat from Reconstruction. It would be nearly a century before new legislation reaffirmed the federal government's ability and will to protect African Americans in exercising their right to vote.

Context

In the five years following the end of the Civil War, Congress adopted several measures that together removed race as a barrier to African Americans' right to vote. The change was piecemeal in approach but revolutionary in impact. In March and July 1867 and March 1868, the Reconstruction Acts provided for the enfranchisement of African Americans so as to allow them to participate in fresh elections to establish new state constitutions in ten former Confederate states. African Americans also won election as delegates to these conventions, and the ten state constitutions that eventually emerged from this process secured their right to vote. In July 1868 the Fourteenth Amendment guaranteed citizenship for former slaves and equal protection under the law for all, and, while recognizing that the right of

suffrage remained one reserved to the states, it provided that a state's representation in the House of Representatives would be reduced in proportion to the state's restrictions upon suffrage. That year, over half a million African Americans voted in the presidential election, providing the Republican candidate Ulysses S. Grant with his popular majority—though he would have still claimed victory in the Electoral College had blacks not voted in such numbers.

Although Republicans achieved much with the enfranchisement of most southern blacks, blacks still could not vote in many other states, including key northern states such as Ohio and Pennsylvania. Republican efforts to secure suffrage for blacks in several northern states between 1865 and 1868 usually fell short of success. With Grant elected, Republicans turned to amending the Constitution once more, this time to remove barriers to voting for American citizens based on "race, color, or previous condition of servitude," as the Fifteenth Amendment would state. Such phrasing recognized that states remained the primary determiners of suffrage qualifications for their citizens but forbade those states from depriving black citizens of the right to vote based on their race. As constitutional amendments are ratified by state legislatures, not by popular vote, and the Republicans then controlled enough state legislatures for ratification, the Fifteenth Amendment became part of the Constitution in 1870.

Southern white supremacist terrorists first targeted black voters during the 1868 presidential contest. By 1870 Congress decided to take action, and on May 31 it passed the Enforcement Act of 1870, designed to provide federal protection for black voters and the means to prosecute white terrorists. In April 1871 another Enforcement Act, also known as the Ku Klux Klan Act, authorized President Grant to suspend the writ of habeas corpus in the effort to subdue such domestic terrorism: Grant used these powers to pursue the Klan in South Carolina in the fall of 1871. However, the Ku Klux Klan Act was of limited duration, and it expired in 1872. That year, a presidential election year, violence broke out in Louisiana during a closely contested local election whose results were disputed. Both Democrats and Republicans claimed victory; with Congress declining to count the state's electoral vote, it remained unclear for weeks which party would gain control of the state government, including

1870

■ **February 3**
The Fifteenth Amendment is ratified, guaranteeing African Americans' right to vote.

■ **May 31**
The Enforcement Act of 1870 is passed, protecting the right to vote as outlined in the Fifteenth Amendment.

1871

■ **February 28**
The 1870 Enforcement Act is amended to reduce registration fraud and allow for federal supervision of elections.

■ **April 20**
The Enforcement Act of 1871, also known as the Ku Klux Klan Act, is passed to punish the acts of white supremacist terrorists.

1873

■ **April 13**
Some one hundred African Americans gathered at the town courthouse are slaughtered in Colfax, Louisiana.

■ **June**
In the Colfax case, ninety-eight defendants are indicted by a federal grand jury, charged with violating the Enforcement Act of 1870.

1874

■ **February 23**
The first trial of nine Colfax defendants begins in federal court.

■ **April**
The first trial of the Colfax defendants ends in a mistrial for eight defendants and acquittal for the ninth.

■ **May 18**
The second trial of the eight remaining Colfax defendants begins.

■ **June 10**
The second Colfax trial ends with guilty verdicts for three defendants, William J. Cruikshank, John P. Hadnot, and William D. Irwin, on sixteen of thirty-two counts.

the governorship. Eventually the Republicans prevailed—but not without outbreaks of violence, the most sensational of which happened in Colfax, in Grant Parish.

Established in 1869 and named after the nation's eighteenth president, Grant Parish is located along the Red River, north of New Orleans, in the heart of Louisiana; the county seat located at Colfax is named after Grant's first vice president, Schuyler Colfax. It soon witnessed its share of political friction and violence: Both parties claimed victory in the 1872 elections. Clashes between blacks and whites subsequently increased, and in the early spring, blacks seeking protection began flocking to the shelter of the Colfax courthouse. Efforts to prevent a confrontation proved futile, and some three hundred whites gathered outside the courthouse. On Easter Sunday, April 13, 1873, the whites first demanded that the blacks surrender; when that proved unavailing, they allowed women and children to depart. Soon after, a firefight between the two sides commenced. Eventually the whites launched an assault on the courthouse, set it on fire, and tracked down those blacks who had fled from the building, killing some and capturing others. That night, the whites slaughtered the remaining black prisoners. Estimates of the dead for the entire day ranged from fifty to some four hundred black men; a federal investigation settling upon 105 known dead black men, with the fates of dozens more remaining unknown.

Federal officials indicted ninety-eight men under the terms of the Enforcement Act of 1870, among them, William J. Cruikshank, John P. Hadnot, and William D. Irwin, who, along with six other men, had been taken into custody by federal authorities. The nine men were tried in New Orleans before the U.S. circuit court judge William B. Woods. The prosecuting district attorney, James R. Beckwith, with a view to presenting a clean case, carefully narrowed the number of victims to two—Levi Nelson and Alexander Tillman, who had not been involved in resisting the whites by force. (Indeed, Nelson survived the massacre and testified for the government.) A first trial acquitted one defendant, while Woods declared a mistrial for the other eight defendants when the jury was unable to agree on a verdict. Those eight men underwent a second trial in May 1874, and on June 10 three men—Cruikshank, Hadnot, and Irwin—were found guilty of violating section 6 of the Enforcement Act of 1870, which stipulated that if two or more people conspired to violate the provisions of the act or to "oppress" any citizen by trying to prevent him from exercising his rights under federal law or the Constitution, such an act would be punished as a felony, with possible fines and imprisonment.

During the second trial, Judge Woods was joined for short periods of time by the Supreme Court associate justice Joseph P. Bradley, who appeared in New Orleans as part of his duties as a federal circuit-court judge—an onerous additional duty performed by all justices of the Supreme Court at the time. Woods was inclined to uphold the convictions, but Bradley dissented and was determined to explain why. His detailed opinion carefully defined federal power to enforce the Thirteenth, Fourteenth, and Fifteenth Amendments. He argued that while violence inflicted for racial reasons was well within the jurisdiction of federal law, that motive had to be proved: It was insufficient to argue simply that conflict between people of different races must be due to the racial difference. Unless race as a motive could be established, cases of criminal violence should be handled in state court. Turning to the case at hand, Bradley argued that as the indictment did not expressly specify that Nelson and Tillman's rights as U.S. citizens had been violated owing to their race, there was no justification to treat them under federal law. It was an opinion narrow in its reasoning but broad in its implications. As the district attorney who prosecuted the case later complained, "If the demolished indictment is not good, I am incompetent to frame a good one"; Bradley had come close to implying just that. As Bradley and Woods divided on the propriety of the convictions, the punishment was placed in abeyance, or "arrested," while the Supreme Court heard the case.

Between the time of the massacre at Colfax in April 1873 and the Supreme Court's release of its decision nearly three years later, Republican Reconstruction policy suffered a series of serious setbacks that all but doomed the federal government's efforts to protect African Americans as free people, as citizens, and as voters and officeholders. In several southern states, including Alabama, Arkansas, Mississippi, and Texas, Republicans lost their hold on power as the result of political circumstances, terrorism, and internal friction. In Louisiana and Mississippi, violence played a key role in Democrats' resurgence; although Republicans barely held on to power in Louisiana, they lost it in Mississippi, where the Democrats embraced as a slogan a pledge that they would regain power peaceably if they could and forcibly if they must. An economic depression in 1873 had long-term effects and, combined with debates over monetary policy and tales of Republican corruption and malfeasance, resulted in the Democrats' reclaiming control of the House of Representatives in 1874, shutting down any further efforts to pass legislation to protect black citizens from violence and intimidation.

Even President Grant, who had once expressed his willingness to protect black rights, allowed frustration to get the better of him. In a special message to the Senate in January 1875, he made specific reference to the Colfax massacre, "a butchery of citizens ... which in bloodthirstiness and barbarity is hardly surpassed by any acts of savage warfare." Nearly two years later, he declared that while critics of Reconstruction waxed eloquent about the missteps of southern Republican regimes, "every one of the Colfax miscreants goes unwhipped of justice, and no way can be found in this boasted land of civilization and Christianity to punish the perpetrators of this bloody and monstrous crime." Grant at length grew exasperated with the fractious behavior of southern Republicans and eroding support in the North for protecting the fruits of victory. When Mississippi's governor requested that federal troops be dispatched to his state in 1875, the president declined, explaining that "the whole public are tired out with these annual autumnal outbreaks in the South" and would no longer support such federal intervention policy. In fact, Grant himself had nom-

Time Line

1874

■ July
A federal circuit court in Louisiana "arrests" the Colfax convictions, opening the way for the Supreme Court to hear the case.

■ November
Democrats triumph in the midterm congressional elections, retaking control of the House of Representatives.

1875

■ January 13
President Ulysses S. Grant denounces the failure to bring the Colfax defendants to justice.

■ March 30–April 1
The Supreme Court hears the arguments in *United States v. Cruikshank*.

1876

■ March 27
The *Cruikshank* decision and opinions are released, overturning the convictions of Cruikshank, Hadnot, and Irwin.

inated Bradley to the Supreme Court in 1870, and it was his administration's Department of Justice, led by Attorney General George H. Williams, that did not seem equal to the task at hand, as much because of its lack of legal skill as a paucity of resources.

The chief justice when *Cruikshank* was argued from March 30 to April 1, 1875, was Morrison J. Waite, appointed by President Grant. Waite's eight associate justices, aside from Nathan Clifford, were all Republican appointees, though two, David Davis and Stephen J. Field (both Abraham Lincoln's nominees), could no longer be counted as Republicans themselves. Samuel F. Miller and Noah H. Swayne, both also Lincoln nominees, had each hoped to be tapped as the next chief justice; the remaining justices, Ward Hunt, William Strong, and Joseph P. Bradley, had been named by Grant. It was Bradley whose vote while on circuit-court duty in Louisiana brought *Cruikshank* to the Supreme Court, and he hoped his detailed 1874 opinion would guide the Court's decision and reasoning. Although ideally justices were to rise above their partisan roots, it was generally assumed that they would most often lean in the direction of their previous party affiliation and view cases in that light. When Congress passed legislation establishing an electoral commission to help resolve the disputed election of 1876, among the five commission members from the Court it was assumed that Clifford and Field would cast their votes for the Democratic case while Miller and Strong would side with the Republican claimant. When the sup-

A Harper's Weekly illustration of blacks hiding in the swamps of Louisiana in 1873 (Library of Congress)

posedly independent Davis stepped aside to accept election as U.S. senator from Illinois, Democrats wondered whether his replacement, none other than Bradley, would also favor the Republicans. Some Democrats believed otherwise, in part because of Bradley's actions in the course of events that brought the *Cruikshank* case before the Court, for he had thereby defied Republican preferences.

In 1873 all of the associate justices who heard the arguments in the *Cruikshank* case had participated in deciding what became known as the Slaughter-House Cases, with Miller delivering the opinion for a slim five-to-four majority on April 14, 1873—the day after the massacre at Colfax. The cases involved a series of suits testing the constitutionality of a Louisiana law that attempted to regulate the state's slaughterhouse industry by establishing a private corporation that would exercise sole control over the industry by allocating space to area slaughterhouses. The suits cited the Fourteenth Amendment in support of their claim that the legislation was invalid. Miller's opinion, allowing the Louisiana law and the controlling corporation to stand, argued that the Fourteenth Amendment's privileges and immunities clause affects only those rights a person holds as part of U.S. citizenship, not as citizens of a state; furthermore, the primary objective of that clause was rather to protect the federal rights of former slaves. Thus, the Four-

teenth Amendment did not protect the butchers' interests, namely, to freely pursue their chosen vocation, against the interests of the state. Miller's concept of dual citizenship would appear again in *Cruikshank*, this time as adverse to the former slaves. Clifford, Strong, Hunt, and Davis had agreed with Miller, while Field, Swayne, and Bradley dissented, along with Waite's predecessor, Salmon P. Chase.

While many members of the Court at first glance seemed sympathetic to the ends of Reconstruction policy, Bradley's circuit-court opinion on the Colfax massacre defendants, coming in the wake of Miller's reasoning in the Slaughter-House Cases, suggested that a majority of the justices were in favor of a strict and narrow explication of congressional legislation, which did not augur well for the prosecution. Moreover, the government's short brief for *Cruikshank* proved less than compelling in its argument, especially as it sidestepped Bradley's circuit-court opinion, failed to mention either African Americans or the Fifteenth Amendment, and mentioned the Enforcement Acts only in passing. It instead focused on just two counts of the indictment that concerned "conspiracy," arguing that an effort to conspire to deprive anyone of their constitutional rights was punishable under federal law. In contrast, the four briefs filed by the defense—including one by Justice Field's brother, David Dudley Field—argued at length that the pertinent

"To bring this case under the operation of the statute, therefore, it must appear that the right, the enjoyment of which the conspirators intended to hinder or prevent, was one granted or secured by the Constitution or laws of the United States. If it does not so appear, the criminal matter charged has not been made indictable by any act of Congress."

"The people of the United States resident within any State are subject to two governments—one State and the other National—but there need be no conflict between the two. The powers which one possesses the other does not. They are established for different purposes, and have separate jurisdictions. Together, they make one whole, and furnish the people of the United States with a complete government, ample for the protection of all their rights at home and abroad."

"Inasmuch, therefore, as it does not appear in these counts that the intent of the defendants was to prevent these parties from exercising their right to vote on account of their race, &c., it does not appear that it was their intent to interfere with any right granted or secured by the Constitution or laws of the United States."

"We may suspect that race was the cause of the hostility, but it is not so averred. This is material to a description of the substance of the offence, and cannot be supplied by implication. Everything essential must be charged positively, and not inferentially. The defect here is not in form, but in substance."

"The charge as made is really of nothing more than a conspiracy to commit a breach of the peace within a State. Certainly it will not be claimed that the United States have the power or are required to do mere police duty in the States."

sections of the Enforcement Act of 1870 were unconstitutional and that the Bill of Rights, far from conferring upon citizens specific rights, simply prohibited their infringement by the federal government and did not apply to state governments. The lawyer Field went so far as to attack the constitutionality of all postwar civil rights legislation, and he sought to bring his arguments before the public by publishing his brief.

All in all, by the time the Supreme Court heard the arguments in the *Cruikshank* case at the end of March 1875, the political foundations of Reconstruction, flawed as they were, were beginning to erode. By the time the Court released its opinion in March 1876, what had begun as a fighting withdrawal by Reconstruction's supporters was turning into a full-scale retreat to ensure the political survival of the Republican Party in the 1876 presidential contest.

About the Author

Chief Justice Morrison R. Waite composed the Court's opinion in *United States v. Cruikshank*. At first he had hoped to entrust Associate Justice Nathan Clifford with drafting the Court's opinion, but Clifford's draft, presented to the justices in November 1875, fell short of offering a comprehensive overview of the issues at stake and based the Court's ruling on narrow grounds.

The son of a judge, Waite, born on November 19, 1816, was a native of Connecticut and an 1837 graduate of Yale who moved to Ohio after graduation, eventually settling in Toledo. Originally a Whig in politics, he became a Republican, but his sole brush with political office came when he served a term in the Ohio Senate. In 1871 he served on the legal team that presented the United States' case at a Geneva tribunal convened to settle U.S. claims of damages caused by the CSS *Alabama*, built by Great Britain to serve the Confederacy. Three years later, in the wake of several frustrated attempts to nominate a new chief justice of the United States, President Grant settled upon Waite, who won confirmation despite critical commentary that he would not be up to the task. Along with *United States v. Reese*, *United States v. Cruikshank* provided Waite with his first substantial test as chief justice. After *Cruikshank*, Waite went on to serve twelve more years as chief justice. When he died on March 23, 1888, he left behind a solid but unspectacular record. If his performance surprised those critics who had criticized Grant for nominating a nonentity, it nevertheless fell short of the greatness achieved by other chief justices.

Explanation and Analysis of the Document

Waite's opinion outlines a concept of dual citizenship first developed by the Supreme Court in 1873 in the Slaughter-House Cases. A citizen owed allegiance to both the federal and state governments and, in turn, could expect those governments to protect the specific rights attributable to each jurisdiction. Under this construction it was left to the states to prosecute cases of murder, manslaughter, and homicide as well as most infringements of civil rights.

Although Waite argues that the Fifteenth Amendment in itself does not guarantee the right to vote, he concedes that the amendment's second section constructed a new constitutional right that could be protected by the federal government, namely, that voters not suffer discrimination "on account of race, color, or previous condition of servitude." Yet such wording, he contends, means that the fact that Cruikshank and his collaborators were charged with murdering black Republican voters was not sufficient to bring them under the scope of the Enforcement Act of 1870: Prosecutors had to charge—and prove—that the victims were murdered because of their race. The right not to be discriminated against as such was the only relevant right protected under federal law. But the prosecutors did not demonstrate violation of this right in this instance. The chief justice asserts that the indictments were so vague that they did not sufficiently meet the Fourth Amendment standard of informing the accused of the offense for which they were being tried. Had the indictment specified that race was the basis upon which the accused murdered the victims, then and only then would the actions of the accused have come under the Enforcement Acts.

Waite's opinion mentions the sixteen counts on which Cruikshank, Hadnot, and Irwin were convicted. The first eight counts charged that the defendants "banded together" to deprive Levi Nelson and Alexander Tillman of their rights, while the ninth through sixteenth counts charged, equivalently, that the defendants "conspired" to deprive Nelson and Tillman of their rights. The defendants were charged with seeking to deprive Nelson and Tillman of, in the first and ninth counts, the right to assemble peacefully; in the second and tenth counts, of the right to keep and bear arms; in the third and tenth counts, of the right to not be deprived of life and liberty without due process of law; in the fourth and twelfth counts, of equal rights and equal treatment under law; in the fifth and thirteenth counts, of their rights as citizens by reason of their race; in the sixth and fourteenth counts, of their right to vote; in the seventh and fifteenth counts, of the right to vote without suffering harm; and in the eighth and sixteenth counts, of the free exercise of their rights secured by federal law and the Constitution.

In his opinion, Waite carefully goes through the sixteen counts, which were framed with section 6 of the Enforcement Act of 1870 in mind. That section states that if two or more people "shall band or conspire together" to intimidate or harm "any citizen" to prevent that citizen from exercising his rights secured by the Constitution and federal law, those people could be found guilty of a felony and could be fined, imprisoned, or both. Citing the Slaughter-House Cases, Waite distinguishes between the rights of citizens protected by the federal government and those protected by state government. He reads the Bill of Rights as operating to restrain the federal government, not state governments, and thus quickly sets aside those charges dealing with the right to assemble peacefully and to bear arms. He rather summarily dismisses those counts that addressed the victims' right not to be deprived of life or liberty without due process, arguing that state governments were to protect those rights. Repeatedly he offers a narrow view of federal power based upon his interpretation of the Fourteenth Amendment; time and again, he argues that the victims needed to seek recourse at the state level.

Waite also criticizes the indictment as too vague in what it alleged. He rejects the fourth and twelfth counts, charging that they failed to claim race as the reason the defendants attempted to deprive Nelson and Tillman of their civil rights, even as he admits that the Fifteenth Amendment did establish a new right, that of exempting citizens from racial discrimination in their effort to exercise the right to vote. He employs the same justification as the reason the defendants attempted to deprive Nelson and Tillman of the right to vote, thus setting aside the sixth and fourteenth counts: He repeats that reasoning in dismissing the seventh and fifteenth counts, which charged the defendants with endangering Nelson and Tillman because they had voted.

This left two pairs of counts: the fifth and thirteenth, which concerned whether Tillman and Nelson had been deprived of their rights as citizens because of their race, and the eighth and sixteenth, which simply said that they had been deprived of their rights as U.S. citizens. Here Waite finds that section 6 of the Enforcement Act of 1870 went beyond the grant of authority extended to Congress in the Fifteenth Amendment by failing to specify race, rendering the section inappropriate; in turn, he finds the counts "too vague and general" and "so defective that no judgment of conviction should be pronounced upon them."

Waite's opinion develops the notion of federalism and dual sovereignty, reminding Americans that the Court would not nationalize all rights and grant them federal protection. Having failed to specify the federal right being violated as specified in the Enforcement Act of 1870, the indictment, in Waite's opinion, was insufficient and could not sustain a conviction. The Fourteenth Amendment offered minimal protection, as it called for federal intervention to remedy state inaction or violation of the Bill of Rights, but, again, the prosecution did not demonstrate the relevant unlawful activity, namely, any such inaction or violation on the part of the state. In sum, although Waite was willing to accept the responsibility of the federal government to protect a voter from finding his right to vote challenged or blocked owing to his race, the chief justice's decision placed a heavy burden of proof on prosecutors by requiring that they specify that motive and demonstrate it.

Audience

As might have been expected, Democrats celebrated the decision as a blow against Republican Reconstruction policy. They were aware that the decision weakened efforts to protect black voters by forcing prosecutors to prove that the motive of violence against them was their race. Given the limited resources of the Department of Justice, this would not be easy. Moreover, given Democratic control of the House of Representatives, it was extremely unlikely that new legislation would appear that would expand the protection offered black voters under law. However, many Republicans also spoke highly of the decision as responsible and dispassionate. By now, they wondered whether it was politically wise or even possible to protect black rights, given the growing opposition to federal intervention in southern affairs. African Americans and their allies might well have seen the decision as another step backward with a promise of worse to come, but even President Grant, who had been outspoken earlier in his comments on the case, chose to remain silent in the aftermath of the Court's decision.

Impact

The *Cruikshank* decision marked yet another milepost on the Republican retreat from Reconstruction. With the Democrats in control of the House of Representatives, there would be no chance for Republicans to pass new enforcement legislation. Meanwhile, by the time the decision appeared, the Grant administration was engulfed by charges of corruption involving cabinet members and the White House staff. Although the decision itself did not rule on the constitutionality of the Enforcement Act of 1870, the opinion ensured that its clauses would be construed strictly and narrowly. A second opinion released by the Court on the same day the *Cruikshank* decision was issued, *United States v. Reese*, bore more directly upon the Enforcement Act of 1870. In *Reese*, strictly interpreting the scope and meaning of that legislation, Waite found it insufficient to protect the right outlined in the Fifteenth Amendment, that is, the right to vote as not abridged due to race, color, or previous condition of servitude. The prosecution had charged that Kentucky election officials had violated the law in refusing to allow William Garner, an African American, to vote, but it could not be demonstrated that they did so because of Garner's race.

By March 1876, only three southern states remained under Republican rule: South Carolina, Louisiana, and Florida. Without the threat of federal prosecution, terrorist forces continued to target black voters, tipping the scale toward Democratic candidates. Had southern blacks been allowed to vote freely in the election of 1876, the Republican candidate Rutherford B. Hayes would have then secured the presidency. Instead, the Democratic candidate Samuel J. Tilden claimed a majority of the popular vote, falling just one electoral vote short of the presidency owing to disputed voting returns in the three Republican states still remaining in the South. Through the resulting Compromise of 1877, Hayes was awarded the disputed votes and the presidency in exchange for the promise that federal troops would be removed from the three southern Republican-led states. Grant and then Hayes duly removed the troops from Florida, South Carolina, and Louisiana, and by the summer of 1877 the southern states were all under Democratic rule. Not until the twentieth century would the federal government once more use force and the law to assure blacks their right to vote.

See also Thirteenth Amendment to the U.S. Constitution (1865); Fourteenth Amendment to the U.S. Constitution (1868); Fifteenth Amendment to the U.S. Constitution (1870); Ku Klux Klan Act (1871).

Further Reading

■ Books

Fairman, Charles. *Reconstruction and Reunion, 1864–88.* Cambridge, U.K.: Cambridge University Press, 2010.

Goldman, Robert M. *Reconstruction and Black Suffrage: Losing the Vote in Reese and Cruikshank.* Lawrence: University Press of Kansas, 2001.

Kaczorowski, Robert J. *The Politics of Judicial Interpretation: The Federal Courts, Department of Justice and Civil Rights, 1866–1876.* Dobbs Ferry, N.Y.: Oceana Publications, 1985.

Keith, LeeAnna. *The Colfax Massacre: The Untold Story of Black Power, White Terror, and the Death of Reconstruction.* New York: Oxford University Press, 2008.

Lane, Charles. *The Day Freedom Died: The Colfax Massacre, the Supreme Court, and the Betrayal of Reconstruction.* New York: Henry Holt, 2008.

Simpson, Brooks D. *The Reconstruction Presidents.* Lawrence: University Press of Kansas, 1998.

—Brooks D. Simpson

Questions for Further Study

1. In what way did the Court's decision in this case represent a retreat from Reconstruction and the protection of African Americans afforded by the Fourteenth and Fifteenth Amendments to the Constitution?

2. An ongoing source of dispute in the United States concerns the respective powers of the federal government and those of the states. How did *United States v. Cruikshank* reflect this struggle?

3. What events led to the Colfax massacre of 1873? Why did the Supreme Court become involved in what could have been regarded as a Louisiana matter?

4. What political consequences did the Court's decision in this case have? How might the history of Reconstruction and the post–Civil War South have been different if the Court had reached a different decision?

5. What could the U.S. government have done differently in enforcing the civil rights of African Americans in the post–Civil War South? If you had been president during the 1870s, what would you have done?

UNITED STATES V. CRUIKSHANK

Mr. Chief Justice Waite delivered the opinion of the court

This case comes here with a certificate by the judges of the Circuit Court for the District of Louisiana that they were divided in opinion upon a question which occurred at the hearing. It presents for our consideration an indictment containing sixteen counts, divided into two series of eight counts each, based upon sect. 6 of the Enforcement Act of May 31, 1870. That section is as follows:—

"That if two or more persons shall band or conspire together, or go in disguise upon the public highway, or upon the premises of another, with intent to violate any provision of this act, or to injure, oppress, threaten, or intimidate any citizen, with intent to prevent or hinder his free exercise and enjoyment of any right or privilege granted or secured to him by the Constitution or laws of the United States, or because of his having exercised the same, such persons shall be held guilty of felony, and, on conviction thereof, shall be fined or imprisoned, or both, at the discretion of the court—the fine not to exceed $5,000, and the imprisonment not to exceed ten years—and shall, moreover, be thereafter ineligible to, and disabled from holding, any office or place of honor, profit, or trust created by the Constitution or laws of the United States."

The question certified arose upon a motion in arrest of judgment after a verdict of guilty generally upon the whole sixteen counts, and is stated to be whether "the said sixteen counts of said indictment are severally good and sufficient in law, and contain charges of criminal matter indictable under the laws of the United States."

The general charge in the first eight counts is that of "banding," and in the second eight that of "conspiring" together to injure, oppress, threaten, and intimidate Levi Nelson and Alexander Tillman, citizens of the United States, of African descent and persons of color, with the intent thereby to hinder and prevent them in their free exercise and enjoyment of rights and privileges "granted and secured" to them "in common with all other good citizens of the United States by the Constitution and laws of the United States."

The offences provided for by the statute in question do not consist in the mere "banding" or "conspiring" of two or more persons together, but in their banding or conspiring with the intent, or for any of the purposes, specified. To bring this case under the operation of the statute, therefore, it must appear that the right, the enjoyment of which the conspirators intended to hinder or prevent, was one granted or secured by the Constitution or laws of the United States. If it does not so appear, the criminal matter charged has not been made indictable by any act of Congress.

We have in our political system a government of the United States and a government of each of the several States. Each one of these governments is distinct from the others, and each has citizens of its own who owe it allegiance and whose rights, within its jurisdiction, it must protect. The same person may be at the same time a citizen of the United States and a citizen of a State, but his rights of citizenship under one of these governments will be different from those he has under the other. *Slaughter-House Cases*, 16 Wall. 74.

Citizens are the members of the political community to which they belong. They are the people who compose the community, and who, in their associated capacity, have established or submitted themselves to the dominion of a government for the promotion of their general welfare and the protection of their individual as well as their collective rights. In the formation of a government, the people may confer upon it such powers as they choose. The government, when so formed, may, and when called upon should, exercise all the powers it has for the protection of the rights of its citizens and the people within its jurisdiction, but it can exercise no other. The duty of a government to afford protection is limited always by the power it possesses for that purpose.

Experience made the fact known to the people of the United States that they required a national government for national purposes. The separate governments of the separate States, bound together by the articles of confederation alone, were not sufficient for the promotion of the general welfare of the people in respect to foreign nations, or for their complete protection as citizens of the confederated States. For this reason, the people of the United States, "in order to form a more perfect union, establish justice, insure domestic tranquillity, provide for the common defence, promote the general welfare, and secure the blessings of liberty" to themselves and their posterity (Const. Preamble), ordained and established the government of the United States, and defined its powers by a Constitution, which they adopted as its fundamental law, and made its rule of action.

The government thus established and defined is to some extent a government of the States in their political capacity. It is also, for certain purposes, a government of the people. Its powers are limited in number, but not in degree. Within the scope of its powers, as enumerated and defined, it is supreme, and above the States; but beyond, it has no existence. It was erected for special purposes, and endowed with all the powers necessary for its own preservation and the accomplishment of the ends its people had in view. It can neither grant nor secure to its citizens any right or privilege not expressly or by implication placed under its jurisdiction.

The people of the United States resident within any State are subject to two governments—one State and the other National—but there need be no conflict between the two. The powers which one possesses the other does not. They are established for different purposes, and have separate jurisdictions. Together, they make one whole, and furnish the people of the United States with a complete government, ample for the protection of all their rights at home and abroad. True, it may sometimes happen that a person is amenable to both jurisdictions for one and the same act. Thus, if a marshal of the United States is unlawfully resisted while executing the process of the courts within a State, and the resistance is accompanied by an assault on the officer, the sovereignty of the United States is violated by the resistance, and that of the State by the breach of peace in the assault. So, too, if one passes counterfeited coin of the United States within a State, it may be an offence against the United States and the State: the United States because it discredits the coin, and the State because of the fraud upon him to whom it is passed. This does not, however, necessarily imply that the two governments possess powers in common, or bring them into conflict with each other. It is the natural consequence of a citizenship which owes allegiance to two sovereignties and claims protection from both. The citizen cannot complain, because he has voluntarily submitted himself to such a form of government. He owes allegiance to the two departments, so to speak, and, within their respective spheres, must pay the penalties which each exacts for disobedience to its laws. In return, he can demand protection from each within its own jurisdiction.

The Government of the United States is one of delegated powers alone. Its authority is defined and limited by the Constitution. All powers not granted to it by that instrument are reserved to the States or the people. No rights can be acquired under the Constitution or laws of the United States, except such as the Government of the United States has the authority to grant or secure. All that cannot be so granted or secured are left under the protection of the States. We now proceed to an examination of the indictment, to ascertain whether the several rights, which it is alleged the defendants intended to interfere with, are such as had been in law and in fact granted or secured by the Constitution or laws of the United States.

The first and ninth counts state the intent of the defendants to have been to hinder and prevent the citizens named in the free exercise and enjoyment of their "lawful right and privilege to peaceably assemble together with each other and with other citizens of the United States for a peaceful and lawful purpose."

The right of the people peaceably to assemble for lawful purposes existed long before the adoption of the Constitution of the United States. In fact, it is, and always has been, one of the attributes of citizenship under a free government. It "derives its source," to use the language of Chief Justice Marshall in 22 U. S. 211, "from those laws whose authority is acknowledged by civilized man throughout the world." It is found wherever civilization exists. It was not, therefore, a right granted to the people by the Constitution. The Government of the United States, when established, found it in existence, with the obligation on the part of the States to afford it protection. As no direct power over it was granted to Congress, it remains, according to the ruling in *Gibbons v. Ogden*, id., @ 22 U. S. 203, subject to State jurisdiction.

Only such existing rights were committed by the people to the protection of Congress as came within the general scope of the authority granted to the national government.

The first amendment to the Constitution prohibits Congress from abridging "the right of the people to assemble and to petition the government for a redress of grievances." This, like the other amendments proposed and adopted at the same time, was not intended to limit the powers of the State governments in respect to their own citizens, but to operate upon the National Government alone. *Barron v. The City of Baltimore*, 7 Pet. 250; *Lessee of Livingston v. Moore*, id., 551; *Fox v. Ohio*, 5 How. 434; *Smith v. Maryland*, 18 id. 76; *Withers v. Buckley*, 20 id. 90; *Pervear v. The Commonwealth*, 5 Wall. 479; *Twitchell v. The Commonwealth*,

7 id. 321; *Edwards v. Elliott*, 21 id. 557. It is now too late to question the correctness of this construction. As was said by the late Chief Justice, in *Twitchell v. The Commonwealth*, 7 Wall. 325, "the scope and application of these amendments are no longer subjects of discussion here." They left the authority of the States just where they found it, and added nothing to the already existing powers of the United States.

The particular amendment now under consideration assumes the existence of the right of the people to assemble for lawful purposes, and protects it against encroachment by Congress. The right was not created by the amendment; neither was its continuance guaranteed, except as against congressional interference. For their protection in its enjoyment, therefore, the people must look to the States. The power for that purpose was originally placed there, and it has never been surrendered to the United States.

The right of the people peaceably to assemble for the purpose of petitioning Congress for a redress of grievances, or for any thing else connected with the powers or the duties of the national government, is an attribute of national citizenship, and, as such, under the protection of, and guaranteed by, the United States. The very idea of a government republican in form implies a right on the part of its citizens to meet peaceably for consultation in respect to public affairs and to petition for a redress of grievances. If it had been alleged in these counts that the object of the defendants was to prevent a meeting for such a purpose, the case would have been within the statute, and within the scope of the sovereignty of the United States. Such, however, is not the case. The offence, as stated in the indictment, will be made out, if it be shown that the object of the conspiracy was to prevent a meeting for any lawful purpose whatever.

The second and tenth counts are equally defective. The right there specified is that of "bearing arms for a lawful purpose." This is not a right granted by the Constitution. Neither is it in any manner dependent upon that instrument for its existence. The second amendment declares that it shall not be infringed, but this, as has been seen, means no more than that it shall not be infringed by Congress. This is one of the amendments that has no other effect than to restrict the powers of the national government, leaving the people to look for their protection against any violation by their fellow citizens of the rights it recognizes, to what is called, in *The City of New York v. Miln*, 11 Pet. 139, the "powers which relate to merely municipal legislation, or what was, perhaps, more properly called internal police," "not surrendered or restrained" by the Constitution of the United States.

The third and eleventh counts are even more objectionable. They charge the intent to have been to deprive the citizens named, they being in Louisiana, "of their respective several lives and liberty of person without due process of law." This is nothing else than alleging a conspiracy to falsely imprison or murder citizens of the United States, being within the territorial jurisdiction of the State of Louisiana. The rights of life and personal liberty are natural rights of man. "To secure these rights," says the Declaration of Independence, "governments are instituted among men, deriving their just powers from the consent of the governed." The very highest duty of the States, when they entered into the Union under the Constitution, was to protect all persons within their boundaries in the enjoyment of these "unalienable rights with which they were endowed by their Creator." Sovereignty, for this purpose, rests alone with the States. It is no more the duty or within the power of the United States to punish for a conspiracy to falsely imprison or murder within a State, than it would be to punish for false imprisonment or murder itself.

The Fourteenth Amendment prohibits a State from depriving any person of life, liberty, or property without due process of law, but this adds nothing to the rights of one citizen as against another. It simply furnishes an additional guaranty against any encroachment by the States upon the fundamental rights which belong to every citizen as a member of society. As was said by Mr. Justice Johnson, in *Bank of Columbia v. Okely*, 4 Wheat. 244, it secures "the individual from the arbitrary exercise of the powers of government, unrestrained by the established principles of private rights and distributive justice."

These counts in the indictment do not call for the exercise of any of the powers conferred by this provision in the amendment.

The fourth and twelfth counts charge the intent to have been to prevent and hinder the citizens named, who were of African descent and persons of color, in "the free exercise and enjoyment of their several right and privilege to the full and equal benefit of all laws and proceedings, then and there, before that time, enacted or ordained by the said State of Louisiana and by the United States, and then and there, at that time, being in force in the said State and District of Louisiana aforesaid, for the security of their respective persons and property, then and there, at that time enjoyed at and within said State and District of Louisiana by white persons, being citizens of said State of Louisiana and the United States, for the protection of the persons and property of said white citizens."

There is no allegation that this was done because of the race or color of the persons conspired against. When stripped of its verbiage, the case as presented amounts to nothing more than that the defendants conspired to prevent certain citizens of the United States, being within the State of Louisiana, from enjoying the equal protection of the laws of the State and of the United States.

The Fourteenth Amendment prohibits a State from denying to any person within its jurisdiction the equal protection of the laws; but this provision does not, any more than the one which precedes it, and which we have just considered, add anything to the rights which one citizen has under the Constitution against another. The equality of the rights of citizens is a principle of republicanism. Every republican government is in duty bound to protect all its citizens in the enjoyment of this principle, if within its power. That duty was originally assumed by the States, and it still remains there. The only obligation resting upon the United States is to see that the States do not deny the right. This the amendment guarantees, but no more. The power of the national government is limited to the enforcement of this guaranty.

No question arises under the Civil Rights Act of April 9, 1866 (14 Stat. 27), which is intended for the protection of citizens of the United States in the enjoyment of certain rights, without discrimination on account of race, color, or previous condition of servitude, because, as has already been stated, it is nowhere alleged in these counts that the wrong contemplated against the rights of these citizens was on account of their race or color.

Another objection is made to these counts that they are too vague and uncertain. This will be considered hereafter, in connection with the same objection to other counts.

The sixth and fourteenth counts state the intent of the defendants to have been to hinder and prevent the citizens named, being of African descent, and colored, "in the free exercise and enjoyment of their several and respective right and privilege to vote at any election to be thereafter by law had and held by the people in and of the said State of Louisiana, or by the people of and in the parish of Grant aforesaid."

In @ 88 U. S. 214, we hold that the Fifteenth Amendment has invested the citizens of the United States with a new constitutional right, which is, exemption from discrimination in the exercise of the elective franchise on account of race, color, or previous condition of servitude. From this, it appears that the right of suffrage is not a necessary attribute of national citizenship, but that exemption from discrimination in the exercise of that right on account of race, &c., is. The right to vote in the States comes from the States, but the right of exemption from the prohibited discrimination comes from the United States. The first has not been granted or secured by the Constitution of the United States, but the last has been.

Inasmuch, therefore, as it does not appear in these counts that the intent of the defendants was to prevent these parties from exercising their right to vote on account of their race, &c., it does not appear that it was their intent to interfere with any right granted or secured by the Constitution or laws of the United States. We may suspect that race was the cause of the hostility, but it is not so averred. This is material to a description of the substance of the offence, and cannot be supplied by implication. Everything essential must be charged positively, and not inferentially. The defect here is not in form, but in substance.

The seventh and fifteenth counts are no better than the sixth and fourteenth. The intent here charged is to put the parties named in great fear of bodily harm, and to injure and oppress them, because, being and having been in all things qualified, they had voted "at an election before that time had and held according to law by the people of the said State of Louisiana, in said State, to-wit, on the fourth day of November, A.D. 1872, and at divers other elections by the people of the State, also before that time had and held according to law."

There is nothing to show that the elections voted at were any other than State elections, or that the conspiracy was formed on account of the race of the parties against whom the conspirators were to act. The charge as made is really of nothing more than a conspiracy to commit a breach of the peace within a State. Certainly it will not be claimed that the United States have the power or are required to do mere police duty in the States. If a State cannot protect itself against domestic violence, the United States may, upon the call of the executive, when the legislature cannot be convened, lend their assistance for that purpose. This is a guaranty of the Constitution (art. 4, sect. 4), but it applies to no case like this.

We are therefore of the opinion that the first, second, third, fourth, sixth, seventh, ninth, tenth, eleventh, twelfth, fourteenth, and fifteenth counts do not contain charges of a criminal nature made indictable under the laws of the United States, and that consequently they are not good and sufficient in law. They do not show that it was the intent of the defendants, by their conspiracy, to hinder or prevent the enjoyment of any right granted or secured by the Constitution.

We come now to consider the fifth and thirteenth and the eighth and sixteenth counts, which may be brought together for that purpose. The intent charged in the fifth and thirteenth is "to hinder and prevent the parties in their respective free exercise and enjoyment of the rights, privileges, immunities, and protection granted and secured to them respectively as citizens of the United States, and as citizens of said State of Louisiana ... for the reason that they, ... being then and there citizens of said State and of the United States, were persons of African descent and race, and persons of color, and not white citizens thereof;" and in the eighth and sixteenth, to hinder and prevent them "in their several and respective free exercise and enjoyment of every, each, all, and singular the several rights and privileges granted and secured to them by the Constitution and laws of the United States."

The same general statement of the rights to be interfered with is found in the fifth and thirteenth counts.

According to the view we take of these counts, the question is not whether it is enough, in general, to describe a statutory offence in the language of the statute, but whether the offence has here been described at all. The statute provides for the punishment of those who conspire "to injure, oppress, threaten, or intimidate any citizen, with intent to prevent or hinder his free exercise and enjoyment of any right or privilege granted or secured to him by the Constitution or laws of the United States."

These counts in the indictment charge, in substance that the intent in this case was to hinder and prevent these citizens in the free exercise and enjoyment of "every, each, all, and singular" the rights granted them by the Constitution, &c. There is no specification of any particular right. The language is broad enough to cover all.

In criminal cases, prosecuted under the laws of the United States, the accused has the constitutional right "to be informed of the nature and cause of the accusation." Amend. VI. In *United States v. Mills*, 7 Pet. 142, this was construed to mean that the indictment must set forth the offence "with clearness and all necessary certainty, to apprise the accused of the crime with which he stands charged;" and in *United States v. Cook*, 17 Wall. 174 that "every ingredient of which the offence is composed must be accurately

and clearly alleged." It is an elementary principle of criminal pleading that, where the definition of an offence, whether it be at common law or by statute, "includes generic terms, it is not sufficient that the indictment shall charge the offence in the same generic terms as in the definition, but it must state the species—it must descend to particulars."

The object of the indictment is, first, to furnish the accused with such a description of the charge against him as will enable him to make his defence, and avail himself of his conviction or acquittal for protection against a further prosecution for the same cause; and, second, to inform the court of the facts alleged, so that it may decide whether they are sufficient in law to support a conviction, if one should be had. For this, facts are to be stated, not conclusions of law alone. A crime is made up of acts and intent; and these must be set forth in the indictment, with reasonable particularity of time, place, and circumstances.

It is a crime to steal goods and chattels, but an indictment would be bad that did not specify with some degree of certainty the articles stolen. This because the accused must be advised of the essential particulars of the charge against him, and the court must be able to decide whether the property taken was such as was the subject of larceny. So, too, it is in some States a crime for two or more persons to conspire to cheat and defraud another out of his property, but it has been held that an indictment for such an offence must contain allegations setting forth the means proposed to be used to accomplish the purpose. This because, to make such a purpose criminal, the conspiracy must be to cheat and defraud in a mode made criminal by statute; and, as all cheating and defrauding has not been made criminal, it is necessary for the indictment to state the means proposed, in order that the court may see that they are in fact illegal. *State v. Parker*, 43 N. H. 83; *State v. Keach*, 40 Vt. 118; *Alderman v. The People*, 4 Mich. 414; *State v. Roberts*, 34 Me. 32. In Maine, it is an offence for two or more to conspire with the intent unlawfully and wickedly to commit any crime punishable by imprisonment in the State prison (*State v. Roberts*), but we think it will hardly be claimed that an indictment would be good under this statute which charges the object of the conspiracy to have been "unlawfully and wickedly to commit each, every, all, and singular the crimes punishable by imprisonment in the State prison." All crimes are not so punishable. Whether a particular crime be such a one or not is a question of law. The accused has, therefore, the right to have a specification of the charge against him in this respect in order that he may decide whether he should present his defence by motion to quash, demurrer, or plea, and the court that it may determine whether the facts will sustain the indictment. So here, the crime is made to consist in the unlawful combination with an intent to prevent the enjoyment of any right granted or secured by the Constitution, &c. All rights are not so granted or secured. Whether one is so or not is a question of law, to be decided by the court, not the prosecutor. Therefore, the indictment should state the particulars, to inform the court as well as the accused. It must be made to appear—that is to say, appears from the indictment, without going fur-ther—that the acts charged will, if proved, support a conviction for the offence alleged.

But it is needless to pursue the argument further. The conclusion is irresistible that these counts are too vague and general. They lack the certainty and precision required by the established rules of criminal pleading. It follows that they are not good and sufficient in law. They are so defective that no judgment of conviction should be pronounced upon them.

The order of the Circuit Court arresting the judgment upon the verdict is, therefore, affirmed; and the cause remanded, with instructions to discharge the defendants.

Glossary

articles of confederation	the initial constitution of the United States, replaced by the present Constitution because they gave too much power to the states and not enough to the federal government
Chief Justice Marshall	John Marshall, the early-nineteenth-century chief justice whose decisions defined many of the powers of the federal government
demurrer	a court pleading filed by a defendant stating that the facts of the case do not support the plaintiff's accusations
Enforcement Act of May 31, 1870	one of three federal laws passed to protect the civil rights of African Americans, especially the right to vote
Justice Johnson	Associate Justice William Johnson
quash	the action of voiding a legal proceeding or court decision

Richard Harvey Cain's "All That We Ask Is Equal Laws, Equal Legislation, and Equal Rights"

"We do not come here begging for our rights....

We come demanding our rights in the name of justice."

Overview

The South Carolina congressman Richard Harvey Cain's speech to the U.S. House of Representatives of January 10, 1874, given the title "All That We Ask Is Equal Laws, Equal Legislation, and Equal Rights," was one of two that he made in support of what became the Civil Rights Act of 1875. The legislation had been first introduced by Senator Charles Sumner and Congressman Benjamin Butler, both of Massachusetts, in 1870. The original all-encompassing bill would have prohibited segregation or discrimination in public accommodations, transportation, jury service, public schools, and churches. It languished in the Senate for five years, until Sumner begged on his deathbed that it be passed. His plea energized the bill's supporters, and it was approved by the Senate, minus, however, its provision banning discrimination in churches.

Despite its success in the Senate, most observers thought the bill would not get through the House. But impassioned speeches by the seven black members of Congress, including Cain, helped create momentum for the bill. All of the men related instances of personal discrimination against them even after their election to Congress. The oratory of Cain's fellow South Carolina congressman Robert Brown Elliott on behalf of the bill attracted national attention, but the powerful words of Cain's speech of January 1874 were little noticed by the press, even among sympathetic Republican newspapers in his home state. However, Cain's speech, together with the others, had ample impact where it counted. One Republican leader in Congress praised all the black congressmen for being more eloquent than their white brethren. Congress was impressed, and the bill became law on March 1, 1875, though it had been further amended to delete the coverage of public schools. Nevertheless, the bill's passage was a major step forward taken just in time, as soon thereafter a Democratic majority took over the House. The enactment of the public accommodations bill was in many ways the high-water mark for the Reconstruction-era Congress.

Context

After the Civil War, the United States attempted to reconstruct the war-ravaged South and lay a foundation for the broader democracy that would encompass both black and white citizens. Emancipation would result in long-term economic and social shifts, but how the law would be molded was the most critical question. When Richard H. Cain moved to South Carolina in 1865, the defeated former Confederates had assumed control of the state government and had enacted the Black Codes, which were modeled after slave codes and were designed to restrict the freedom of African Americans in every aspect of their lives. But South Carolina was a majority black state, and its freedmen did not simply acquiesce to the actions of the former Confederates. In 1865 the Colored People's Convention was held in Charleston to protest such laws. This was the first gathering of black men from throughout the state in South Carolina history, and Cain was among those attending. While the state legislature did not respond to the petition of the black convention to refrain from passing Black Codes, their protest was heard by others. In fact, the state was still under Union army control, and the military commander for South Carolina declared the Black Codes void.

In 1866 Congress passed its first Civil Rights Act, despite President Andrew Johnson's opposition. This act effectively overruled the Black Codes across the South and affirmed the actions of the military governor of South Carolina. The act declared that all Americans were citizens regardless of race and were guaranteed the right to contract, to sue and be sued, to give evidence in court, and to purchase and hold real and personal property. A year later, in March 1867, Congress began enacting a series of statutes known as the Reconstruction Acts. These laws imposed preconditions before congressmen from the southern states could be seated, the most significant of which required that the former Confederate states grant all men the right to vote. In states like South Carolina, this meant that a majority of the voting citizens were now black, and as elections came along black citizens began voting and making laws. Cain was elected a delegate to the state's constitutional convention in 1868. When the state's voters approved the constitution and elected a new legislature, the majority of

Time Line

1863

■ **January 1**
The Republican president
Abraham Lincoln signs the
Emancipation Proclamation,
freeing all slaves in the
rebelling states.

1865

■ **December 6**
Having been approved that
January, the Thirteenth
Amendment is ratified by the
states.

■ **April 9**
Robert E. Lee surrenders to
the Union general Ulysses
S. Grant on behalf of his
Confederate army.

1866

■ **April 9**
The first Civil Rights Act,
granting American citizenship
to freed slaves, is approved by
Congress.

■ **June 13**
The Fourteenth Amendment,
which will extend citizenship
to all those born in the United
States, is approved.

1867

■ **March–July**
Three Reconstruction Acts are
approved by Congress over
President Andrew Johnson's
vetoes.

■ **November**
Elections in which African
Americans vote for the first
time are held across the
South.

1868

■ **March 11**
The fourth Reconstruction Act
is passed by Congress.

■ **July 9**
The Fourteenth Amendment
is ratified.

1870

The first African Americans
are named to Congress,
through the election of
Hiram Revels as senator from
Mississippi and Joseph H.
Rainey as representative from
South Carolina.

---

those chosen were black, with Cain becoming one of the first black men elected to the state senate. A priority for these legislators was achieving civil rights for all citizens at the state level.

The Reconstruction Amendments to the U.S. Constitution had been approved by Congress and were being ratified by the states during this same period. These were the most important amendments to the Constitution since the Bill of Rights. The Thirteenth Amendment, ratified in 1865, abolished slavery. The Fourteenth Amendment extended citizenship to all those born in the United States and was ratified in 1868. The Fifteenth Amendment granted all men the right to vote and was ratified in 1870. Other than the Thirteenth Amendment, these amendments were not self-executing; federal and state legislation was needed to obtain enforcement, which was one purpose of the Reconstruction Acts—four statues enacted in 1867–1868—and the various civil rights acts. Imposing a system that ensured the participation of the freedmen in the body politic did not resolve the issue of their social equality. The civil rights bill introduced by Senator Sumner in 1870 attempted to address this by banning discrimination in all major areas of everyday life—in public accommodations, transportation, jury service, public schools, and churches. Southern whites by and large opposed any civil rights for the former slaves, and their opposition was often violent. Congress was compelled to pass the Enforcement Acts of 1870 and 1871 (the latter also known as the Ku Klux Klan Act) to protect black citizens from the outrages of these terrorists. Yet Sumner's bill was a much more radical concept. It was one thing to protect blacks from the Klan; it was quite another to mandate equal treatment for them at the hands of local governments and private citizens alike.

Sumner's bill languished for three sessions after its first introduction, but Sumner introduced it in the Senate yet again in December 1873, on the opening day of the second session of the Forty-third Congress. In the House, Congressman Butler did the same. Sumner died on March 11, 1874, and his deathbed request was that his bill be passed. Cain had been elected a U.S. congressman from South Carolina the previous year, and he made an impassioned speech in support of the bill in January 1874. In all, seven black representatives sat in the Forty-third Congress, and all spoke in support of Sumner's civil rights bill.

Speaking in opposition were a number of former Confederate soldiers and officers. Among them were Alexander Stephens, former vice president of the Confederacy and congressman from Georgia, and the Democratic congressman Robert B. Vance of North Carolina, who had been a brigadier general in the Confederate army. Clearly, Vance was proud of his military service and made clear that he and other southern whites considered themselves in all respects superior to blacks. His chief arguments against the bill were insulting and patronizing. He asserted that black men were asking for something they had not earned, their civil rights. But his major concern was one that would echo through the halls of Congress for decades. He argued that the bill would force whites to socialize with blacks.

He warned that forced socialization would destroy the kind relationship that southern whites had established with their freed slaves and that those former slaves could not survive without the help of their former masters.

About the Author

Richard Harvey Cain was born on April 12, 1825, of free black parents in Greenbrier County, Virginia (now in West Virginia). In 1831 the family moved to Gallipolis, Ohio. There he obtained an education through church school classes. In 1844 he was ordained in the Methodist Episcopal Church and assigned to Hannibal, Missouri, but the segregationist practices of the Methodists caused him to resign and join the African Methodist Episcopal Church (AME). He served an AME church in Iowa in the 1850s and then attended Wilberforce University, an AME school in Ohio. When the Civil War broke out, he and other Wilberforce students attempted to enlist but were turned away by the governor of Ohio. From 1861 to 1865, Cain was assigned to a church in Brooklyn, New York. While he was in New York he attended the National Convention of Colored Men, held in Syracuse in 1864.

Following the Civil War, Cain was sent to Charleston, South Carolina. There he reorganized Emanuel Church, which would grow to over four thousand members and become one of the most potent political organizations in the state. In 1867 Cain assumed control of a newspaper, the *Charleston Leader*, which fostered such important political figures as Alonzo Ransier and Robert Brown Elliott. From the outset of his arrival in Charleston, Cain was quite active in politics. When the Black Codes were proposed, the Colored People's Convention was held in Charleston in 1865 to object to them. The protest failed to dissuade the white legislature from approving the restrictive laws, but the convention's voice was successful in persuading the military commander of South Carolina, the Union general Daniel Sickles, to nullify the Black Codes.

Subsequently, Cain was elected as a delegate to the South Carolina Constitutional Convention of 1868. In the convention, he sponsored a resolution urging Congress to appropriate $1 million to purchase land in South Carolina for freedmen. Although it was not accepted, the idea was incorporated in the establishment of the state land commission. Cain was elected to the state senate from Charleston in 1868 and was a member of the committees on printing (1868–1870), incorporations (1868–1870), and railroads (1869–1870). He became known as "Daddy Cain" because of his leadership on the cause of civil rights for black South Carolinians as well as his influence among his fellow Republicans. He was chairman of the Charleston County Republican Party from 1870 to 1871 and a delegate to numerous state Republican conventions from 1867 to 1876. His political power was demonstrated with his election as the at-large representative from South Carolina to the Forty-third Congress, opening March 4, 1873.

Time Line

1871
- **April 20**
  The Ku Klux Klan Act is approved by Congress.

1872
- Six African Americans are elected to the House of Representatives, including Richard Harvey Cain.

1874
- **January 10**
  Cain delivers a speech in support of the pending civil rights bill.
- **March 1**
  The Civil Rights Act of 1875 is signed into law; a clause that would have led to integration of public schools is dropped from the final bill.

1876
- **November**
  Contested election results across the South lead to the Compromise of 1877 and the removal of federal troops from South Carolina and other southern states, effectively ending Reconstruction.

1883
- **October 15**
  In the Civil Rights Cases, the U.S. Supreme Court declares the Civil Rights Act of 1875 unconstitutional.

In Congress, Cain and other black congressmen gained national attention through their oratory in support of the civil rights bill that had been the last cause of Charles Sumner. The bill was all-encompassing, in that it proposed to ban segregation and racial discrimination in public accommodations, public schools, jury selection, cemeteries, transportation, and churches. In March 1874, the dying Sumner urged passage of the bill. After his death, the bill passed the Senate intact except for the proviso on churches. In the House, Cain was one of seven black members who spoke of their personal experiences with discrimination even as congressmen. Also among these men were his protégés Elliott and Ransier. In 1875 the bill passed the House, but without its ban on discrimination in public education.

Cain was not a candidate for renomination in 1874 but was elected to the Forty-fifth Congress, opening March 4, 1877. Cain's service in Congress ended in March 1879. The abandonment of the enforcement of civil rights in the South by the federal government coupled with the threats and violence by southern whites against blacks meant that

Group portrait of the senators of the Forty-third Congress (Library of Congress)

Reconstruction was over. Cain, like most African American public officials, exited the political arena and attempted to contribute in other fields. In 1880 he was named a bishop in the AME Church, to preside over the denomination's work in Louisiana and Texas. He was a founder of Paul Quinn College in Austin, Texas (the school later moved to Waco), and served as its president for four years. Cain moved to Washington, D.C., in 1883 and died there on January 18, 1887.

Explanation and Analysis of the Document

The chief theme of Cain's speech is that the black man merely wants "equal laws, equal legislation, and equal rights." While the speech was responsive to one by Representative Vance, it was independently a powerful and assertive oration on behalf of the civil rights bill. Cain made clear that African Americans had "come demanding our rights in the name of justice."

♦ The Rights of Citizenship

One of Cain's first points, made in the second paragraph, is that the Thirteenth, Fourteenth, and Fifteenth Amendments stand for the proposition that black people are "invested with all the rights of citizenship." Next, he addresses Vance's allegation that the civil rights bill would impose social relations. Cain retorts that the bill would simply place "the colored men of this country upon the same footing with every other citizen under the law, and will not at all enforce social relationship with any other class of persons in the country whatsoever." He counters Vance's claim that civil rights were already enjoyed by all people in North Carolina by using his own and other blacks' personal experiences there. Cain relates a story from his fellow South Carolina congressman Elliott: "My colleague … a few months ago entered a restaurant at Wilmington and sat down to be served, and while there a gentleman stepped up to him and said, 'You cannot eat here.'" Cain himself had eaten on the train rather than risk such a confrontation in a North Carolina restaurant, only to be accused of "putting on airs" in paying for dinner service on the train. He caustically ends this portion of his speech by saying, "Yet this was in the noble State of North Carolina."

Next Cain responds to Vance's argument that if the bill were to pass, the black man in the South would

Illustration depicting South Carolina representative Robert B. Elliot delivering one of several impassioned speeches in favor of the Civil Rights Act of 1875 (Library of Congress)

lose the friendship of the region's whites. Cain was attempting to appeal to more sympathetic whites, but in paragraph 7 his speech demonstrates a certain amount of naïveté in expressing the belief that the "higher class" of southern whites did not oppose the civil rights bill. Twice more in the speech, Cain exhibits optimism about the country and the age. In some of his most eloquent words, Cain states in paragraph 26, "Rapid as the weaver's shuttle, swift as the lightning's flash, such progress is being made that our rights will be accorded to us ere long."

◆ Equality in Education

Probably the most important provision of the bill to Cain was one that would have prohibited segregation in schools. Naturally, Vance had assaulted this proviso, by claiming that the state university in South Carolina had been destroyed by desegregation. But Cain easily repels this attack. Being from that state, he knew that the University of South Carolina had lost some faculty and students but was still operating and thriving. In fact, the college operated a law school that was soon to produce nearly a dozen black

lawyers. Beyond responding to the attack on the University of South Carolina, Cain expresses fervent belief in the value of education. He again asserts that the better class of whites in the South support African American equality, here declaring that they see the value of education for his people. He cites examples from Massachusetts, Rhode Island, and New York to buttress his claim that there would be little trouble in integrated schools. He also uses reports from California, Illinois, and Indiana to demonstrate that discrimination in education is a national problem, further proof of the need for the civil rights provision on education. Cain recognizes that the right to an education is the most paramount civil right. He entreats, "All we ask is that you, the legislators of the nation, shall pass a law so strong and so powerful that no one shall be able to elude it and destroy our rights under the Constitution and laws of our country." Later in the speech, in paragraph 23, he refers to education and jury service as "great palladiums of our liberty." At the end of his speech, Cain briefly returns to the subject of education to cite it as a device critical to civil rights and to declare his belief that the educational system ought not to discriminate against anyone.

"But since our emancipation, since liberty has come, and only since—
only since we have stood up clothed in our manhood, only since we have
proceeded to take hold and help advance the civilization of this nation—
it is only since then that this bugbear is brought up against us again."
(Paragraph 11)

"The gentleman from North Carolina [Mr. Vance] announced before he
sat down, in answer to an interrogatory by a gentleman on this side of the
House, that they went into the war conscientiously before God. So be it.
Then we simply come and plead conscientiously before God that those
are our rights, and we want them. We plead conscientiously before God,
believing that these are our rights by inheritance, and by the inexorable
decree of Almighty God."
(Paragraph 19)

"I want to say that we do not come here begging for our rights. We come
here clothed in the garb of American citizenship. We come demanding
our rights in the name of justice. We come, with no arrogance on
our part, asking that this great nation, which laid the foundations of
civilization and progress more deeply and more securely than any other
nation on the face of the earth, guarantee us protection from outrage."
(Paragraph 25)

"We come here, five millions of people—more than composed this whole
nation when it had its great tea-party in Boston Harbor, and demanded
its rights at the point of the bayonet—asking that unjust discriminations
against us be forbidden. We come here in the name of justice, equity, and
law, in the name of our children, in the name of our country, petitioning
for our rights."
(Paragraph 25)

"Inasmuch as we have toiled with you in building up this nation;
inasmuch as we have suffered side by side with you in the war; inasmuch
as we have together passed through affliction and pestilence, let there be
now a fulfillment of the sublime thought of our father—let all men enjoy
equal liberty and equal rights."
(Paragraph 28)

◆ Economic Justice

Another argument utilized effectively by Cain is a call for civil rights as a matter of economic justice. Throughout his speech Cain uses his eloquence and facility with language to express this firm belief. At times his words are poetic, such as when he notes, "We have been hewers of wood and drawers of water." He then adds,

If we have made your cotton-fields blossom as the rose; if we have made your rice-fields wave with luxuriant harvests; if we have made your corn-fields rejoice; if we have sweated and toiled to build up the prosperity the whole country by the productions of our labor, I submit, now that the war has made a change, now that we are free—I submit to the nation whether it is not fair and right that we should come in and enjoy to the fullest extent our freedom and liberty.

He reinforces this point by citing examples of patient service and sacrifice by his people for the nation. He reminds the assembly of the costs incurred by black men in the ranks of the Union army, especially citing their bravery on the battlefields of Fort Wagner, in South Carolina, and Vicksburg, Mississippi. Cain also adapts Vance's defensive affirmation that he had gone to war on behalf of the Confederacy "conscientiously before God" to offer his own prayer to "Almighty God" to grant "our rights by inheritance." Then Cain points out the clarion call of the Declaration of Independence whereby "all men ... are endowed by their Creator with certain inalienable rights, among which are life, liberty, and the pursuit of happiness."

◆ The Meaning of the Civil War

Cain next moves to respond to the critics of the bill who claimed it would usurp the rights of the states. He expresses astonishment that these congressmen could place states' rights above the rights of individuals. He points out that these same men had joined efforts to pass legislation in Congress in 1860 to save the Union and preserve slavery. Without explicitly stating as much, Cain makes the point that since the war for states' rights had already been lost and the war for civil rights had been won, the patriotic course of action would be to concede that the Reconstruction Amendments were the law of the land. These amendments and the Civil War should compel these "gentlemen" to accept civil rights for all people.

It is in paragraph 24 that Cain's most famous line, lending the speech its title, is uttered: "All that we ask is equal laws, equal legislation, and equal rights throughout the length and breadth of this land." Then Cain responds to Vance's remark that "the colored men" were begging Congress for their rights. Cain denies this by recasting the circumstances, asserting, "We come demanding our rights in the name of justice."

In concluding, Cain expresses an optimism that justice will prevail. His words are again powerful: "Let it be proclaimed that henceforth all the children of this land shall be free; that the stars and stripes, waving over all, shall secure to every one equal rights, and the nation will say 'amen.'" Cain calls on the nation's five million black people to sing a song of rejoicing, and he again emphasizes the toil and sacrifice they have made on behalf of the nation. Before his final words, Cain cites his own support for amnesty for former Confederates; in giving the speech, he turned to Vance and offered to shake hands as he affirmed his "desire to bury forever the tomahawk." Cain then turns his offer into a memorial for the "widows and orphans" of North and South and urges that in their name Congress "let this righteous act be done. I appeal to you in the name of God and humanity to give us our rights, for we ask nothing more."

Audience

The primary audience for Cain's speech was the Forty-third Congress. In addition, during some of the speeches by the black congressmen on behalf of the civil rights bill, the gallery of the House of Representatives was filled by African Americans. The failure of the press to report Cain's speech may suggest that his oration was otherwise little known at the time. But the bill Cain was supporting was especially important to many African Americans, and all Americans would be an audience for the Civil Rights Act of 1875 upon its passage.

Impact

The act imposed both criminal and civil penalties for its violation. Enforcement could be made either by an individual or through federal attorneys, marshals, and commissioners. As the historian John Hope Franklin has pointed out, many African Americans attempted to obtain accommodations, meals, drinks, haircuts, railway passage, and entry into theaters all across the country within days of the act's passage. However, white resistance was substantial. More important, legal enforcement was sporadic, uneven, and sometimes denied. Some cases made it to federal district court, but obtaining convictions by jury proved to be very difficult. When eighteen blacks sued a railroad for relegating them to a segregated car, for instance, the jury found for the railroad. A few federal judges declared the act constitutional, but a greater number of judges declared the law unconstitutional.

The 1875 Civil Rights Act was passed at a time when Reconstruction was both cresting and ebbing. That year, there were more black congressmen than at any other point in the era, but much of the South had fallen back into Democratic hands. South Carolina was one of only three states remaining in Republican control after the elections of 1874. Soon, Reconstruction ended. Violence against Republicans, and especially blacks, preceded the Democratic takeover of the South Carolina state government in 1877. The Compromise of 1877 decided the highly contested U.S. presidency and resulted in the abandonment of enforcement of civil rights in the South by the national Republican Party. Meanwhile, waning support for Reconstruction had already been seen on many fronts. In particular, the courts were proving unsympathetic to civil rights. The judicial retreat from Reconstruction began in 1873 when the Supreme Court in the Slaughter-House Cases held that national citizenship provided few "privileges and immunities." Federal prosecutions under the Enforcement Acts of 1870 and 1871 dropped dramatically across the South in 1875. In 1876 the Supreme Court held in *United States v. Cruikshank* that the federal government had no authority to prosecute individuals who deprived blacks of their civil rights. The Court said that blacks should instead look to state officials for protection. Of course, state officials in the South were the very people Congress had sought to protect blacks from.

Soon cases were being appealed to the Supreme Court. However, no opinion was issued until 1883, when, in the Civil Rights Cases, the Court declared the 1875 act unconstitutional as applied to public accommodations. The Court reasoned that the Fourteenth Amendment applied only to actions of the states, not private conduct, and that the refusal of service by a private individual did not violate the Thirteenth Amendment because such conduct did not constitute a badge of slavery. Like many of the accomplishments of Reconstruction, the Civil Rights Act of 1875 became a victim to the Jim Crow jurisprudence that would dominate the Supreme Court and the nation for decades to come.

See also Emancipation Proclamation (1863); Thirteenth Amendment to the U.S. Constitution (1865); Fourteenth Amendment to the U.S. Constitution (1868); Fifteenth Amendment to the U.S. Constitution (1870); Ku Klux Klan Act (1871); *United States v. Cruikshank* (1876); Civil Rights Cases (1883).

Further Reading

■ Books

Bailey, N. Louise, et al. *Biographical Directory of the South Carolina Senate, 1776–1985.* Columbia: University of South Carolina Press, 1986.

Black Americans in Congress, 1870–2007. Washington, D.C.: U.S. Government Printing Office, 2008.

Foner, Eric. *Reconstruction: America's Unfinished Revolution, 1863–1877.* New York: Harper & Row, 1988.

Franklin, John Hope. "The Enforcement of the Civil Rights Act of 1875." In *African Americans and the Emergence of Segregation, 1865–1900,* ed. Donald G. Nieman. New York: Garland, 1994.

Simmons, William J. *Men of Mark: Eminent, Progressive and Rising.* 1887. Reprint. New York: Arno Press, 1968.

■ Web Sites

"Richard Harvey Cain." Black Americans in Congress Web site: http://baic.house.gov/member-profiles/profile.html?intID=2.

—W. Lewis Burke

Questions for Further Study

1. Compare this document with George H. White's Farewell Address to Congress in 1901. Both speeches were made by black legislators, and both were addressed to their legislatures. What, if anything, changed between 1874 and 1901? Did the two speakers make similar arguments?

2. Describe the circumstances that led to the passage of the Civil Rights Act of 1875. What protections did the act afford that were not afforded by earlier legislation and the Civil Rights Amendments to the Constitution?

3. What were the chief arguments made against passage of the Civil Rights Act of 1875? How did Cain respond to these arguments?

4. What role did party politics play in the passage of the Civil Rights Act and in subsequent events? What were the origins of these party allegiances?

5. In the Civil Rights Cases of 1883, the U.S. Supreme Court declared the Civil Rights Act unconstitutional. Consult that document. On what basis did the Court reach its decision? How do you think Cain would have responded to the Court's reasoning?

RICHARD HARVEY CAIN'S "ALL THAT WE ASK IS EQUAL LAWS, EQUAL LEGISLATION, AND EQUAL RIGHTS"

Mr. CAIN. Mr. Speaker, I feel called upon more particularly by the remarks of the gentleman from North Carolina [Mr. Vance] on civil rights to express my views. For a number of days this question has been discussed, and various have been the opinions expressed as to whether or not the pending bill should be passed in its present form or whether it should be modified to meet the objections entertained by a number of gentlemen whose duty it will be to give their votes for or against its passage. It has been assumed that to pass this bill in its present form Congress would manifest a tendency to override the Constitution of the country and violate the rights of the States.

Whether it be true or false is yet to be seen. I take it, so far as the constitutional question is concerned, if the colored people under the law, under the amendments to the Constitution, have become invested with all the rights of citizenship, then they carry with them all rights and immunities accruing to and belonging to a citizen of the United States. If four, or nearly five, million people have been lifted from the thralldom of slavery and made free; if the Government by its amendments to the Constitution has guaranteed to them all rights and immunities, as to other citizens, they must necessarily therefore carry along with them all the privileges enjoyed by all other citizens of the Republic.

Sir, the gentleman from North Carolina [Mr. Vance] who spoke on the question stated some objections, to which I desire to address a few words of reply. He said it would enforce social rights, and therefore would be detrimental to the interests of both the whites and the blacks of the country. My conception of the effect of this bill, if it be passed into a law, will be simply to place the colored men of this country upon the same footing with every other citizen under the law, and will not at all enforce social relationship with any other class of persons in the country whatsoever. It is merely a matter of law. What we desire is that our civil rights shall be guaranteed by law as they are guaranteed to every other class of persons; and when that is done all other things will come in as a necessary sequence, the enforcement of the rights following the enactment of the law.

Sir, social equality is a right which every man, every woman, and every class of persons have within

their own control. They have a right to form their own acquaintances, to establish their own social relationships. Its establishment and regulation is not within the province of legislation. No laws enacted by legislators can compel social equality. Now, what is it we desire? What we desire is this: inasmuch as we have been raised to the dignity, to the honor, to the position of our manhood, we ask that the laws of this country should guarantee all the rights and immunities belonging to that proud position, to be enforced all over this broad land.

Sir, the gentleman states that in the State of North Carolina the colored people enjoy all their rights as far as the highways are concerned; that in the hotels, and in the railroad cars, and in the various public places of resort, they have all the rights and all the immunities accorded to any other class of citizens of the United States. Now, it may not have come under his observation, but it has under mine, that such really is not the case; and the reason why I know and feel it more than he does is because my face is painted black and his is painted white. We who have the color—I may say the objectionable color—know and feel all this. A few days ago, in passing from South Carolina to this city, I entered a place of public resort where hungry men are fed, but I did not dare—I could not without trouble—sit down to the table. I could not sit down at Wilmington or at Weldon without entering into a contest, which I did not desire to do. My colleague, the gentleman who so eloquently spoke on this subject the other day, [Mr. Elliott,] a few months ago entered a restaurant at Wilmington and sat down to be served, and while there a gentleman stepped up to him and said, "You cannot eat here." All the other gentlemen upon the railroad as passengers were eating there; he had only twenty minutes, and was compelled to leave the restaurant or have a fight for it. He showed fight, however, and got his dinner; but he has never been back there since. Coming here last week I felt we did not desire to draw revolvers and present the bold front of warriors, and therefore we ordered our dinners to be brought into the cars, but even there we found the existence of this feeling; for, although we had paid a dollar apiece for our meals, to be brought by the servants into the cars, still there was objection on the part of the railroad people to our eating our meals in the cars, because they said we were putting on airs. They refused us in the restaurant, and then did not desire that we should eat our meals in the cars, although we paid for them. Yet this was in the noble State of North Carolina.

Mr. Speaker, the colored men of the South do not want the adoption of any force measure. No; they do not want anything by force. All they ask is that you will give them, by statutory enactment under the fundamental law, the right to enjoy precisely the same privileges accorded to every other class of citizens.

The gentleman, moreover, has told us that if we pass this civil-rights bill we will thereby rob the colored men of the South of the friendship of the whites. Now, I am at a loss to see how the friendship of our white friends can be lost to us by simply saying we should be permitted to enjoy the rights enjoyed by other citizens. I have a higher opinion of the friendship of the southern men than to suppose any such thing. I know them too well. I know their friendship will not be lost by the passage of this bill. For eight years I have been in South Carolina, and I have found this to be the fact, that the higher class, comprising gentlemen of learning and refinement, are less opposed to this measure than are those who do not occupy so high a position in the social scale.

Sir, I think that there will be no difficulty. But I do think this that there will be more trouble if we do not have those rights. I regard it important, therefore, that we should make the law so strong that no man can infringe those rights.

But, says the gentleman from North Carolina, some ambitious colored man will, when this law is passed, enter a hotel or railroad car, and thus create disturbance. If it be his right, then there is no vaulting ambition in his enjoying that right. And if he can pay for his seat in a first-class car or his room in a hotel, I see no objection to his enjoying it. But the gentleman says more. He cited, on the school question, the evidence of South Carolina, and says the South Carolina University has been destroyed by virtue of bringing into contact the white students with the colored. I think not. It is true that a small number of students left the institution, but the institution still remains. The buildings are there as erect as ever; the faculty are there as attentive to their duties as ever they were; the students are coming in as they did before. It is true, sir, that there is a mixture of students now; that there are colored and white students of law and medicine sitting side by side; it is true, sir, that the prejudice of some of the professors was so strong that it drove them out of the institution; but

the philanthropy and good sense of others were such that they remained; and thus we have still the institution going on, and because some students have left, it cannot be reasonably argued that the usefulness of the institution has been destroyed. The University of South Carolina has not been destroyed.

But the gentleman says more. The colored man cannot stand, he says, where this antagonism exists, and he deprecates the idea of antagonizing the races. The gentleman says there is no antagonism on his part. I think there is no antagonism so far as the country is concerned. So far as my observation extends, it goes to prove this: that there is a general acceptance upon the part of the larger and better class of the whites of the South of the situation, and that they regard the education and the development of the colored people as essential to their welfare, and the peace, happiness, and prosperity of the whole country. Many of them, including the best minds of the South, are earnestly engaged in seeking to make this great system of education permanent in all the States. I do not believe, therefore, that it is possible there can be such an antagonism. Why, sir, in Massachusetts there is no such antagonism. There the colored and the white children go to school side by side. In Rhode Island there is not that antagonism. There they are educated side by side in the high schools. In New York, in the highest schools, are to be found, of late, colored men and colored women. Even old democratic New York does not refuse to give the colored people their rights, and there is no antagonism. A few days ago, when in New York, I made it my business to find out what was the position of matters there in this respect. I ascertained that there are, I think, seven colored ladies in the highest school in New York, and I believe they stand No. 1 in their class, side by side with members of the best and most refined families of the citizens of New York, and without any objection to their presence.

I cannot understand how it is that our southern friends, or a certain class of them, always bring back this old ghost of prejudice and of antagonism. There was a time, not very far distant in the past, when this antagonism was not recognized, when a feeling of fraternization between the white and the colored races existed, that made them kindred to each other. But since our emancipation, since liberty has come, and only since—only since we have stood up clothed in our manhood, only since we have proceeded to take hold and help advance the civilization of this nation—it is only since then that this bugbear is brought up against us again. Sir, the progress of the age demands that the colored man of this country shall be lifted by law into the enjoyment of every right, and that every appliance which is accorded to the German, to the Irishman, to the Englishman, and every foreigner, shall be given to him; and I shall give some reasons why I demand this in the name of justice.

For two hundred years the colored men of this nation have assisted in building up its commercial interests. There are in this country nearly five millions of us, and for a space of two hundred and forty-seven years we have been hewers of wood and drawers of water; but we have been with you in promoting all the interests of the country. My distinguished colleague, who defended the civil rights of our race the other day on this floor, set this forth so clearly that I need not dwell upon it at, this time.

I propose to state just this: that we have been identified with the interests of this country from its very foundation. The cotton crop of this country has been raised and its rice-fields have been tilled by the hands of our race. All along as the march of progress, as the march of commerce, as the development of your resources has been widening and expanding and spreading, as your vessels have gone on every sea, with the stars and stripes waving over them, and carried your commerce everywhere, there the black man's labor has gone to enrich your country and to augment the grandeur of your nationality. This was done in the time of slavery. And if, for the space of time I have noted, we have been hewers of wood and drawers of water; if we have made your cotton-fields blossom as the rose; if we have made your rice-fields wave with luxuriant harvests; if we have made your corn-fields rejoice; if we have sweated and toiled to build up the prosperity of the whole country by the productions of our labor, I submit, now that the war has made a change, now that we are free—I submit to the nation whether it is not fair and right that we should come in and enjoy to the fullest extent our freedom and liberty.

A word now as to the question of education. Sir, I know that, indeed, some of our republican friends are even a little weak on the school clause of this bill; but, sir, the education of the race, the education of the nation, is paramount to all other considerations. I regard it important, therefore, that the colored people should take place in the educational march of this nation, and I would suggest that there should be no discrimination. It is against discrimination in this particular that we complain.

Sir, if you look over the reports of superintendents of schools in the several States, you will find, I think, evidences sufficient to warrant Congress in passing the civil-rights bill as it now stands. The report of the commissioner of education of California shows that, under the operation of law and of prejudice, the colored children of that State are practically excluded from schooling. Here is a case where a large class of children are growing up in our midst in a state of ignorance and semi-barbarism. Take the report of the superintendent of education of Indiana, and you will find that while efforts have been made in some places to educate the colored children, yet the prejudice is so great that it debars the colored children from enjoying all the rights which they ought to enjoy under the law. In Illinois, too, the superintendent of education makes this statement: that, while the law guarantees education to every child, yet such are the operations among the school trustees that they almost ignore, in some places, the education of colored children.

All we ask is that you, the legislators of the nation, shall pass a law so strong and so powerful that no one shall be able to elude it and destroy our rights under the Constitution and laws of our country. That is all we ask.

But, Mr. Speaker, the gentleman from North Carolina [Mr. Vance] asks that the colored man shall place himself in an attitude to receive his rights. I ask, what attitude can we assume? We have tilled your soil, and during the rude shock of war, until our hour came, we were docile during that long, dark night, waiting patiently the coming day. In the Southern States during that war our men and women stood behind their masters; they tilled the soil, and there were no insurrections in all the broad lands of the South; the wives and daughters of the slaveholders were as sacred then as they were before; and the history of the war does not record a single event, a single instance, in which the colored people were unfaithful, even in slavery; nor does the history of the war record the fact that on the other side, on the side of the Union, there were any colored men who were not willing at all times to give their lives for their country. Sir, upon both sides we waited patiently. I was a student at Wilberforce University, in Ohio, when the tocsin of war was sounded, when Fort Sumter was fired upon, and I never shall forget the thrill that ran through my soul when I thought of the coming consequences of that shot. There were one hundred and fifteen of us, students at that university, who, anxious to vindicate the stars and stripes, made up a company, and offered our services to the governor of Ohio; and, sir, we were told that this was a white man's war and that the negro had nothing to do with it. Sir, we returned—docile, patient, waiting, casting our eyes to the heavens whence help always comes. We knew that there would come a period in the history of this nation when our strong black arms would be needed. We waited patiently; we waited until Massachusetts, through her noble governor, sounded the alarm, and we hastened then to hear the summons and obey it.

Sir, as I before remarked, we were peaceful on both sides. When the call was made on the side of the Union we were ready; when the call was made for us to obey orders on the other side, in the confederacy, we humbly performed our tasks, and waited patiently. But, sir, the time came when we were called for; and, I ask, who can say that when that call was made, the colored men did not respond as readily and as rapidly as did any other class of your citizens. Sir, I need not speak of the history of this bloody war. It will carry down to coming generations the valor of our soldiers on the battle-field. Fort Wagner will stand forever as a monument of that valor, and until Vicksburgh shall be wiped from the galaxy of battles in the great contest for human liberty that valor will be recognized.

And for what, Mr. Speaker and gentlemen was the great war made! The gentleman from North Carolina [Mr. Vance] announced before he sat down, in answer to an interrogatory by a gentleman on this side of the House, that they went into the war conscientiously before God. So be it. Then we simply come and plead conscientiously before God that those are our rights, and we want them. We plead conscientiously before God, believing that these are our rights by inheritance, and by the inexorable decree of Almighty God.

We believe in the Declaration of Independence, that all men are born free and equal, and are endowed by their Creator with certain inalienable rights, among which are life, liberty, and the pursuit of happiness. And we further believe that to secure those rights governments are instituted. And we further believe that when governments cease to subserve those ends the people should change them.

I have been astonished at the course which gentlemen on the other side have taken in discussing this bill. They plant themselves right behind the Constitution, and declare that the rights of the State ought not to be invaded. Now, if you will take the history of the war of the rebellion, as published by the Clerk of this House, you will see that in 1860 the whole country, each side, was earnest in seeking to make such amendments to the Constitution as would forever secure slavery and keep the Union together under the circumstances. The resolutions passed, and the sentiments expressed in speeches at that time, if examined by gentlemen, will be found to bear out all that I have indicated. It was felt in 1860 that anything that

would keep the "wayward sisters" from going astray was desirable. They were then ready and willing to make any amendments.

And now, when the civil rights of our race are hanging upon the issue, they on the other side are not willing to concede to us such amendments as will guarantee them; indeed, they seek to impair the force of existing amendments to the Constitution of the United States, which would carry out the purpose.

I think it is proper and just that the civil-rights bill should be passed. Some think it would be better to modify it, to strike out the school clause, or to so modify it that some of the State constitutions should not be infringed. I regard it essential to us and the people of this country that we should be secured in this if in nothing else. I cannot regard that our rights will be secured until the jury-box and the school-room, these great palladiums of our liberty, shall have been opened to us. Then we will be willing to take our chances with other men.

We do not want any discriminations to be made. If discriminations are made in regard to schools, then there will be accomplished just what we are fighting against. If you say that the schools in the State of Georgia, for instance, shall be allowed to discriminate against colored people, then you will have discriminations made against us. We do not want any discriminations. I do not ask any legislation for the colored people of this country that is not applied to the white people. All that we ask is equal laws, equal legislation, and equal rights throughout the length and breadth of this land.

The gentleman from North Carolina [Mr. Vance] also says that the colored men should not come here begging at the doors of Congress for their rights. I agree with him. I want to say that we do not come here begging for our rights. We come here clothed in the garb of American citizenship. We come demanding our rights in the name of justice. We come, with no arrogance on our part, asking that this great nation, which laid the foundations of civilization and progress more deeply and more securely than any other nation on the face of the earth, guarantee us protection from outrage. We come here, five millions of people—more than composed this whole nation when it had its great tea-party in Boston Harbor, and demanded its rights at the point of the bayonet—asking that unjust discriminations against us be forbidden. We come here in the name of justice, equity, and law, in the name of our children, in the name of our country, petitioning for our rights.

Our rights will yet be accorded to us, I believe, from the feeling that has been exhibited on this floor of the growing sentiment of the country. Rapid as the weaver's shuttle, swift as the lightning's flash, such progress is being made that our rights will be accorded to us ere long. I believe the nation is perfectly willing to accord this measure of Justice, if only those who represent the people here would say the word. Let it be proclaimed that henceforth all the children of this land shall be free; that the stars and stripes, waving over all, shall secure to every one equal rights, and the nation will say "amen."

Let the civil-rights bill be passed this day, and five million black men, women, and children, all over the land, will begin a new song of rejoicing, and the thirty-five millions of noble-hearted Anglo-Saxons will join in the shout of joy. Thus will the great mission be fulfilled of giving to all the people equal rights.

Inasmuch as we have toiled with you in building up this nation; inasmuch as we have suffered side by side with you in the war; inasmuch as we have together passed through affliction and pestilence, let there be now a fulfillment of the sublime thought of our fathers—let all men enjoy equal liberty and equal rights.

In this hour, when you are about to put the capstone on the mighty structure of government, I ask you to grant us this measure, because it is right. Grant this, and we shall go home with our hearts filled with gladness. I want to "shake hands over the bloody chasm." The gentleman from North Carolina has said he desires to have forever buried the memory of the recent war. I agree with him. Representing a South Carolina constituency, I desire to bury forever the tomahawk. I have voted in this House with a free heart to declare universal amnesty. Inasmuch as general amnesty has been proclaimed, I would hardly have expected there would be any objection on this floor to the civil-rights bill, giving to all men the equal rights of citizens. There should be no more contest. Amnesty and civil rights should go together. Gentlemen on the other side will admit that we have been faithful; and now, when we propose to bury the hatchet, let us shake hands upon this measure of justice; and if heretofore we have been enemies, let us be friends now and forever.

Our wives and our children have high hopes and aspirations; their longings for manhood and womanhood are equal to those of any other race. The same sentiment of patriotism and of gratitude, the same spirit of national pride that animates the hearts of other citizens, animates theirs. In the name of the dead soldiers of our race, whose bodies lie at Petersburgh and on other battle-fields of the South; in the name of the widows and orphans they have left behind; in the name of the widows of the confederate soldiers who fell upon the same fields, I conjure you let this righteous act be done. I appeal to you in the name of God and humanity to give us our rights, for we ask nothing more.

Glossary

Anglo-Saxons	the early Germanic tribes that subdued the British Isles; used loosely to refer to white northern Europeans
Fort Sumter	a fort in South Carolina, site of the opening hostilities of the Civil War in 1861
Fort Wagner	a fort in South Carolina, the scene of an assault in 1863 led by the Fifty-fourth Massachusetts Volunteer Infantry, one of the Union's first black units
immunities	in constitutional law, the concept that a person in one state enjoys the same legal protections in other states when he or she crosses the border
Mr. Elliott	Robert Brown Elliott, a congressional representative from South Carolina
Mr. Vance	Democratic congressman Robert B. Vance of North Carolina
Petersburgh	Petersburg, a city in Virginia, scene of one of the final campaigns of the Civil War
stars and stripes	the U.S. flag
tea-party in Boston Harbor	reference to an event that took place on December 16, 1773, when American colonists protested British taxation by boarding three British ships and dumping their cargos of tea into the harbor
tocsin	a warning bell
Vicksburgh	Vicksburg, a city in Mississippi, the site of a major Civil War battle in 1863

Joseph P. Bradley (Library of Congress)

CIVIL RIGHTS CASES

"It is ... scarcely just to say that the colored race has been the special favorite of the laws."

Overview

In the Civil Rights Cases decision of 1883, the U.S. Supreme Court limited the powers of Congress with its finding that the equal protection clause of the Fourteenth Amendment did not pertain to actions involving private parties. This case decided five similar discrimination cases that had been grouped together as the Civil Rights Cases when they were heard by the Supreme Court. These cases involved African Americans who had been denied access to whites-only facilities in railroads, hotels, and theaters. All five cases were related to the Civil Rights Act of 1875, which the majority of justices declared unconstitutional in the Civil Rights Cases decision. Nearly ninety years later, Congress would revive that legislation with the enactment of the Civil Rights Act of 1964. One of the most frequently examined decisions of the nineteenth century, the Civil Rights Cases decision dealt a dramatic blow to African Americans because it significantly narrowed the legal reach of the pivotal Fourteenth Amendment, which had provided for equal protection under the Constitution for African Americans.

Context

The American Civil War freed nearly four million slaves. While historians continue to debate the causes of the war, as President Abraham Lincoln made clear in his Second Inaugural Address, "These slaves constituted a peculiar and powerful interest. All knew that this interest was somehow the cause of the war." Eleven southern states seceded from the Union to form the Confederate States of America, nominally to protect "states' rights" but more specifically to preserve the institution of slavery. Even after four years of bloodshed, Confederate defeat, and the ratification of the Thirteenth Amendment abolishing slavery, southern states stubbornly resisted northern attempts to grant blacks civil, political, and social rights. Throughout the period known as Reconstruction (until the mid-1870s Republicans in Congress passed a great deal of legislation, and two more amendments to the Constitution (the Fourteenth and Fifteenth

Amendments), all with an eye toward expanding American citizenship to include former slaves. Of these many initiatives, none has had more positive or lasting effect than the Fourteenth Amendment, the five sections of which are notable for providing the "due process" and "equal protection" clauses that serve as the basis for over two-thirds of all cases that go before the Supreme Court today.

Under the leadership of such Radical Republicans from the Midwest and New England as John Bingham, Charles Sumner, and Thaddeus Stevens, Congress had passed the Civil Rights Act of 1866, which reversed the Supreme Court's decision in 1857 in *Dred Scott v. Sandford*, in which the Court had ruled that African Americans could not be considered citizens of the United States. The Civil Rights Act of 1866 deemed "all persons born in the United States" to be American citizens. Congress then established constitutional protection of that act with the Fourteenth Amendment, the ratification of which Congress demanded of former Confederate states before they could be readmitted to the Union. The equal protection clause of the Fourteenth Amendment's vital first section—"no state shall ... deny to any person within its jurisdiction equal protection of the laws"—enforced the Declaration of Independence's principle that "all men are created equal." The Fourteenth Amendment extended legal protection to African Americans and ensured both equality and protection of all U.S. citizens, although the meaning of the terms *equality* and *protection* would soon prove to be the focus of considerable debate.

The Civil Rights Act of 1875 was controversial from the moment Senator Charles Sumner of Massachusetts first proposed it in 1870. The original bill had attempted to eliminate all forms of segregation, which Sumner viewed as inherently discriminatory. Sumner's proposed legislation also sought to redefine what most Americans took to be "social rights" as civil rights. The concept that Congress could regulate the actions of individuals or privately held companies proved to be especially contentious; Democrats and Republicans alike insisted that such provisions were unconstitutional and would never be upheld by the Supreme Court. Many legislators objected to the bill's initial provisions for desegregation in schools, churches, and cemeteries, all of which were omitted from the final version passed by the lame-duck second session of the Forty-third Congress.

1857

■ **March 6**
The Supreme Court hands down its decision in *Dred Scott v. Sandford*, ruling that African Americans could not be considered citizens of the United States.

1865

■ **December 6**
The Thirteenth Amendment, which abolishes slavery, is ratified.

1866

■ **April 9**
Over the veto of President Andrew Johnson, Congress passes the Civil Rights Act of 1866, which makes "all persons born in the United States" American citizens.

1868

■ **July 9**
The Fourteenth Amendment is ratified, extending citizenship and guaranteeing legal equal protection to all persons born or naturalized in the United States, including African Americans who formerly were slaves.

1875

■ **March 1**
Congress passes the Civil Rights Act of 1875, barring racial discrimination in "public accommodations."

1883

■ **October 15**
The Supreme Court issues the Civil Rights Cases decision, ruling the Civil Rights Act of 1875 unconstitutional.

1964

■ **July 2**
President Lyndon B. Johnson signs the Civil Rights Act into law.

The Civil Rights Act of 1875 met with mixed treatment from federal circuit courts prior to being ruled unconstitutional by the Supreme Court in 1883. During the late 1870s and early 1880s, as many as one hundred cases related to the act's provisions were tried and appealed before federal judges in Pennsylvania, Texas, Maryland, and Kentucky—all of which ruled the act constitutional. Divided federal courts in New York, Tennessee, Missouri, Kansas, and other states referred issues arising from the act to the

Supreme Court. Although the Supreme Court had already considered the meaning of *equal protection* in three jury cases of 1880, it was not until the Civil Rights Cases ruling that the Court put forth the critically important doctrine of "state action," which limited federal guarantees of equal protection in favor of the laws and customs of individual states.

About the Author

All of the Supreme Court justices who heard the Civil Rights Cases had been appointed and confirmed under Republican presidential administrations. Two of Lincoln's appointees, Samuel Freeman Miller and Stephen Johnson Field, remained on the Court in 1883. Miller was the only Democrat on the nation's highest bench. Justice John Marshall Harlan had been a Democrat before the Civil War but had become a Republican during Reconstruction. The other judges included Chief Justice Morrison Remick Waite and, in order of seniority, William Burnham Woods, Stanley Matthews, Horace Gray, and Samuel Blatchford. Joseph P. Bradley wrote the majority opinion in the Civil Rights Cases decision, while Justice Harlan offered the lone dissent.

Joseph P. Bradley was born on March 14, 1813, in Berne, New York. He studied at Rutgers University before taking up the practice of law through various apprenticeships in Newark, New Jersey, where he passed the bar in 1839. Bradley married Mary Hornblower, the daughter of the chief justice of the New Jersey Supreme Court, and soon became a prominent patent and commercial lawyer. In 1862 he waged an unsuccessful campaign for Congress as a conservative Republican who refused to support either emancipation or civil rights for blacks, despite his aversion to slavery. While there was reason to suspect Bradley's views before his appointment to the Supreme Court under President Ulysses S. Grant in 1870, few could have anticipated the many anti–civil rights decisions in which Bradley's reasoning would prevail. By joining the majority, Bradley attacked the Enforcement Act of 1870 (which protected black voters) in *United States v. Reese* (1875) and *United States v. Cruikshank* (1876). In *United States v. Harris* (1883), Bradley again joined the Court's majority limiting the scope of the Ku Klux Klan Act of 1871, an attempt by Congress to outlaw conspiracies against African Americans. In his majority opinion for the Civil Rights Cases, Bradley pronounced the Civil Rights Act of 1875 unconstitutional. Bradley died on January 22, 1892.

John Marshall Harlan was born on June 1, 1833, into a Kentucky slaveholding family. In 1852 he graduated from Centre College in Danville and joined his father's law practice and then, in 1853, graduated from Transylvania University's law school in Lexington. Harlan was elected county judge of Franklin County, Kentucky, in 1858. In 1861, when the Civil War broke out, he enlisted in the Union army, rising to the rank of colonel. Leaving the army on the death of his father, Harlan took the post of attorney general of Kentucky. In 1877 he was appointed to the Supreme Court by President Rutherford B. Hayes and, because of his antebellum career as a border-state Democrat (though he had become a Republican in 1868), he endured a heated six-week confirmation process in Congress. Harlan, despite his Kentucky plantation heritage and antebellum opposition to emancipation, soon metamorphosed into the Court's chief opponent of compromise on civil rights. He stood out among the justices as the most resolute voice on behalf of blacks. Refusing to join the majority of justices in the *United States v. Harris* decision, Harlan argued instead for stronger federal enforcement of the Thirteenth, Fourteenth, and Fifteenth Amendments. In his dissent for *Plessy v. Ferguson* in 1896, which echoed his dissent in the Civil Rights Cases, Harlan famously insisted: "Our Constitution is color-blind.... In respect of civil rights, all citizens are equal before the law." While Harlan supported the legal equality of African Americans, he never abandoned prejudiced assumptions about racial difference. Harlan served on the nation's highest bench for thirty-four years. Besides his strong stances on civil rights, he was also a proponent of governmental regulation of the economy during a period when the Court began to develop a broader constitutional focus on matters of law and public policy. Harlan died on October 14, 1911.

Explanation and Analysis of the Document

The five cases consolidated in the Civil Rights Cases were *United States v. Stanley, United States v. Ryan, United States v. Nichols, United States v. Singleton,* and *Robinson &Wife v. Memphis and Charleston Railroad Company.* The Stanley and Nichols cases concerned indictments for denying access to inns or hotels; the Ryan and Singleton cases addressed access to theaters, one in San Francisco and the other in New York City. The Robinson case had originally been brought in Tennessee and involved the refusal of the Memphis and Charleston Railroad Company to allow Mrs. Robinson to travel in a ladies' train car. U.S. Solicitor General Samuel F. Phillips submitted all but the Robinson case as a group on November 7, 1882; briefs regarding the Robinson case were submitted on March 29, 1883.

The five related lawsuits in the Civil Rights Cases all had to do with Section 1 of the Civil Rights Act of 1875, which stated:

All persons within the jurisdiction of the United States shall be entitled to the full and equal enjoyment of the accommodations, advantages, facilities, and privileges of inns, public conveyances on land or water, theaters, or other places of public amusement; subject only to the conditions and limitations established by law, and applicable alike to citizens of every race and color, regardless of any previous condition of servitude.

Section 2 of the act stipulated:

Any person who shall violate [Section 1] ... shall ... forfeit and pay the sum of five hundred dollars to the person aggrieved thereby ... and shall also, for every

Senator Charles Sumner (Library of Congress)

such offense, be deemed guilty of a misdemeanor, and upon conviction thereof, shall be fined not less than five hundred nor more than one thousand dollars, or shall be imprisoned not less than thirty days nor more than one year.

♦ "Majority Opinion"

Writing for the majority of justices, Justice Bradley no longer argued for a broad view of the Fourteenth Amendment, which he had proposed in previous cases. With the Civil Rights Cases majority opinion, Bradley echoed the narrow position of the Slaughter-House Cases (1873) majority opinion, which held that state authority was primary and national authority was secondary or "corrective." He rejected the radical pro-nationalist, expansive-rights view and contended instead that the Civil Rights Act of 1875 was an impermissible attempt by Congress to regulate the private conduct of individuals with respect to racial discrimination. The act, Bradley wrote, "does not profess to be corrective of any constitutional wrong committed by the States." Regarding Section 4 of the act, he held that even private interference with such rights as voting, jury service, or appearing as witnesses in state court were not within Congress's control. Anyone faced with such interference had to look to state courts for relief.

The Court had two important missions in issuing this ruling: to contain the power of Congress in enacting

"It would be running the slavery argument into the ground to make it apply to every act of discrimination which a person may see fit to make as to guests he will entertain, or as to the people he will take into his coach or cab or car, or admit to his concert or theatre, or deal with in other matters of intercourse or business."

("Majority Opinion")

"It is, I submit, scarcely just to say that the colored race has been the special favorite of the laws."

("Dissenting Opinion")

"The one underlying purpose of congressional legislation has been to enable the black race to take the rank of mere citizens. The difficulty has been to compel a recognition of the legal right of the black race to take the rank of citizens, and to secure the enjoyment of privileges belonging, under the law, to them as a component part of the people for whose welfare and happiness government is ordained."

("Dissenting Opinion")

legislation and to safeguard states' rights. The first became a prerequisite for the second. With respect to the first, Bradley stipulated: "Legislation which Congress is authorized to adopt ... is not general ... but corrective legislation." To emphasize this point, Bradley repeated the word *corrective* ten more times. As for the second objective, Bradley almost buried the following point in the opinion's text: "Legislation cannot properly cover the whole domain of rights appertaining to life, liberty, and property, defining them and providing for their vindication.... It would be to make Congress take the place of the State legislatures and to supersede them." Federal limitation of state authority through acts of Congress was what the Court most wanted to prevent. While the Court's majority did not challenge the Fourteenth Amendment's applicability to state laws and actions, it also did not tolerate congressional oversight of what it considered private actions regulated under state laws.

Bradley argued that while private actors broke laws, their actions could not destroy civil rights; only states could do that. In other words, "civil rights ... cannot be impaired by the wrongful acts of individuals, unsupported by state authority in the shape of laws, customs, or ju-

dicial or executive proceedings. The wrongful act of an individual ... is simply a private wrong, or a crime of that individual." According to this reasoning, demonstrations of white supremacy and incidents of segregation and violence against blacks were wrongful private acts and did not generate anything akin to a state action, that is, the denial of civil rights, which could be remedied only by a corrective governmental action.

In the event confusion might persist on the distinction between wrongful private acts and deprivation of civil rights, Bradley provided several specific examples:

An individual cannot deprive a man of his right to vote, to hold property, to buy and sell, to sue in the courts, or to be a witness or a juror; he may, by force or fraud, interfere with the enjoyment of the right in a particular case; he may commit an assault against the person, or commit murder, or use ruffian violence at the polls, or slander the good name of a fellow citizen; but, unless protected in these wrongful acts by some shield of State law or State authority, he cannot destroy or injure the right; he will only render himself amenable to satisfaction or punishment ... [according to] the laws of the State where the wrongful acts are committed.

In sum, an individual's civil rights could not be destroyed by the acts of others. Any damage done had to be handled as a crime by the state where the offense had occurred.

Bradley also rejected the argument that the Thirteenth Amendment allowed Congress to pass the Civil Rights Act, since denial of access to public accommodations did not constitute slavery. According to the Court, such a broad construction of the Thirteenth Amendment would run "the slavery argument into the ground to make it apply to every act of discrimination." Bradley then went on to assert:

When a man has emerged from slavery, and by the aid of beneficent legislation has shaken off the inseparable concomitants of that state, there must be some stage in the progress of his elevation when he takes the rank of a mere citizen, and ceases to be the special favorite of the laws, and when his rights as a citizen, or a man, are to be protected in the ordinary modes by which other men's rights are protected.

Gone from the Civil Rights Cases majority opinion was the generous spirit of Bradley's circuit-court opinion in an antecedent to the Slaughter-House Cases. In 1870, three years before the Supreme Court struck down the privileges and immunities clause of the Fourteenth Amendment in the Slaughter-House Cases ruling, Bradley had issued judicial relief for a "flagrant case of violation of the fundamental rights of labor" in *Livestock Dealers' & Butchers Association v. Crescent City Live-Stock Landing & Slaughterhouse Co., et al.*, often called the Crescent City Case. Here he had reasoned that where the Constitution "has provided a remedy, we ought not to shrink from granting the appropriate relief." Gone, too, was Bradley's earlier view that Congress had been authorized to enforce the Fourteenth Amendment with "appropriate legislation." Gone was the perception that "those who framed the article were not themselves aware" of its breadth. Gone was the belief that the Fourteenth Amendment went beyond the "privileges and immunities" of the original Constitution and embraced potentially far more. Gone was the principle that "the privileges and immunities of all citizens shall be absolutely unabridged, unimpaired." Gone as well was the conviction of Bradley's opinion in *United States v. Cruikshank*, which stated "that Congress has the power to secure [the rights of blacks] not only as against the unfriendly operation of state laws, but against outrage ... on the part of individuals, irrespective of state laws."

♦ "Dissenting Opinion"

Justice John Marshall Harlan was the sole justice who dissented from the majority opinion. Although Justice Bradley had forsaken the pro–civil rights stance of his Crescent City Case opinion and Slaughter-House Cases dissent, Justice Harlan used Bradley's reasoning in those cases as a starting point for his dissent in the Civil Rights Cases.

While by the 1880s many Republicans had abandoned Radical Reconstruction and the extension of civil rights, Harlan had grown more committed to alleviating the plight of African Americans. Few, if any, nineteenth-century Supreme Court opinions have proved to be more prescient or memorable than Harlan's dissent in the Civil Rights Cases.

With a cherished pen and inkwell, the same pen that Chief Justice Roger Taney had used to write the majority opinion in *Dred Scott v. Sandford*, Harlan composed his dissent in the Civil Rights Cases. He forcefully rejected the majority opinion as "entirely too narrow and artificial," protesting that the Thirteenth Amendment gave Congress sufficient power to legislate beyond matters of bondage to address all "badges of slavery." At thirty-six pages and considerably longer than the majority opinion, Harlan's dissent characterized the Civil Rights Cases decision as at best tepid jurisprudential progress.

Harlan took aim at the Court majority's tandem mission with two goals of his own: a detailed critique of the view of congressional authority as "corrective" and recognition of "the enlarged powers conferred by the recent amendments upon the general government." He began his dissent with the observation that the Court had, in effect, sacrificed the recent Reconstruction Amendments (the Thirteenth, Fourteenth, and Fifteenth Amendments) to the Constitution and concluded, among other important points, that "the rights which Congress, by the act of 1875, endeavored to secure and protect are legal, not social rights."

Harlan stressed a number of Court decisions that conflicted with the majority opinion, particularly with respect to the Court's authority to overturn congressional legislation. In *Fletcher v. Peck*, the Court had maintained that to determine whether Congress had transgressed its constitutional power was "a question of much delicacy, which ought seldom, if ever, to be decided in the affirmative." In the Sinking Fund Cases—where railroad companies challenged a lower court injunction against them for trying to pay a stock dividend in alleged violation of recent legislation—the Court had held that declaring an act of Congress void "should never be made except in a clear case" and "every possible presumption is in favor of the validity of a statute." The Court's decision in *Prigg v. Commonwealth of Pennsylvania* held that "when the end is required the means are given" to Congress, though in that case "the end" had meant support for slavery and slaveholders. In *Ableman v. Booth*, the Court had sustained the constitutionality of the Fugitive Slave Act of 1850 "upon the implied power of Congress to enforce" the property claims of slaveholders. Harlan's point was that when slaveholders controlled the federal government, the Court had sustained the authority of Congress to legislate in favor of slavery; however, when it came to enforcement of the Constitution and civil rights in the years after Reconstruction, the Court was doing just the opposite—ruling to impede the legislative authority of Congress.

Perhaps the Court was at least a little embarrassed to be blocking civil rights legislation, especially once Harlan pointed out the litany of recent rulings that appeared to contradict the majority opinion. According to the Court in *Strauder v. West Virginia* and *Ex parte Virginia*, the purpose of the Reconstruction Amendments "was to raise the colored race from that condition of inferiority ... into perfect equality of civil rights." In both *United States v. Cruikshank* and *United States v. Reese*, the Court had held that the Fifteenth Amendment "invested the citizens of the United States with a new constitutional right, which is exemption from discrimination" and that "the right to vote comes from the States; but the right of exemption from the prohibited discrimination comes from the United States."

According to Harlan, "exemption from discrimination ... is a new constitutional right" conferred by the nation; Congress shall provide for the "form and manner" of protecting this right. Overwhelmed by the Court's contradictions and conservatism, Harlan posed this question: "Are the powers of the national legislature to be restrained in proportion as the rights and privileges, derived from the nation, are valuable?" One can sense Harlan's extreme frustration with the Court in his concluding comment:

> The one underlying purpose of congressional legislation has been to enable the black race to take the rank of mere citizens. The difficulty has been to compel a recognition of the legal right of the black race to take the rank of citizens, and to secure the enjoyment of privileges belonging, under the law, to them as a component part of the people for whose welfare and happiness government is ordained.

If the Court had wanted to protect civil rights, legal precedent already existed. In his presentation to the justices, Solicitor General Phillips brought up *Munn v. Illinois* (1876), in which the Court had held that government regulation of privately owned grain elevators was "necessary for the public good" and had also affirmed broad police powers for government: "Under the powers inherent in every sovereignty, a government may regulate the conduct of its citizens toward each other." In his Civil Rights Cases dissent, Justice Harlan likewise observed that in *Munn v. Illinois* the Court had ruled that private property is no longer only a private concern when it becomes "affected with a public interest." Accordingly, the Court might well have viewed inns and railroads as public enterprises and thus under the purview of Congress.

Moreover, the Court could have looked to the commerce clause of the Constitution (Article I, Section 8). Justice Harlan noted just that regarding the Robinson case: "Might not the act of 1875 be maintained in that case, as applicable at least to commerce between the States, notwithstanding [that] it does not ... profess to have been passed ... to regulate commerce?" When Salmon Chase was chief justice from 1864 to 1873, the Court did not alter the interpretation of the commerce clause. In the Civil Rights Cases majority opinion, Justice Bradley acknowledged that "Congress is clothed with direct and plenary powers of legislation" under the commerce clause. However, he did not appear to accept that the three Reconstruction Amendments bolstered Congress's legislative plenary powers. Thus, Bradley dismissed whether inns and public conveyances were encompassed under Congress's legislative authority under the commerce clause as "a question which is not now before us." Nevertheless, the Court could have found the Civil Rights Act of 1875 constitutional under the commerce clause, especially in light of its *Munn v. Illinois* ruling.

That Bradley interpreted the Fourteenth Amendment as merely "corrective" elicited Harlan's harshest criticism. Harlan observed that the entire amendment hardly assumed what Bradley claimed was an exclusively negative or "corrective" form simply because of the clause in Section 1 beginning with "no state shall." The historian Carter Woodson offered this candid assessment: "The court was too evasive or too stupid to observe that the first clause of this amendment was an affirmative.... Such sophistry deserves the condemnation of all fair-minded people." The Court also might have interpreted the Civil Rights Act and the Reconstruction Amendments in light of factors such as history and legislative intent. Or as Harlan put it, borrowing from an old adage: "It is not the words of the law but the internal sense of it that makes the law; the letter of the law is the body; the sense and reason of the law is the soul."

Audience

As with most Supreme Court decisions, the justices' audience included not only lawyers, lower court judges, and legislators at all levels but also in fact all Americans. The Civil Rights Cases decision had political significance for both the Republican and Democratic parties. Given the number of black lynchings in America throughout the late-nineteenth and early-twentieth centuries, it seems likely that groups such as the Ku Klux Klan interpreted the Civil Rights Cases decision as tacitly allowing local instances of racist mob rule.

Impact

The Civil Rights Cases decision closed the first chapter of the civil rights struggle in the United States. The majority ruling negated Section 5 of the Fourteenth Amendment, which had mandated Congress to enforce the amendment with "appropriate legislation." Yet again, the Court abrogated Congress's ability to protect and enforce civil liberties, as it had already previously ruled in the Reese, Cruikshank, and Harris cases. This ruling was as much a setback for Congress as it was for African Americans. With this fierce gesture, the Court applied the brakes on the development of national government and the extension of civil rights.

News of the Court's decision elicited a mixture of smugness and indifference to the principle of equal protection. The *Atlanta Constitution* reported:

> We do not hope to compass with words the deep and perfect satisfaction with which the decision of the United States Supreme Court on the Civil-Rights Bill will

be received throughout the South.... It was against the mischievous intrusion of the negro into places set apart for white people that we protested.

Frederick Douglass saw the mischief elsewhere: "The decision is to the direction and interest of the Old Calhoun doctrine of State rights as against Federal authority.... The decision has resulted largely from confusing social with civil rights." The *Chicago Tribune* agreed with Douglass: "The Constitution in its present shape does not warrant Congressional regulation of social affairs ... which individuals regulate to suit themselves." The *Washington Post* published statements attributed to Lee Nance, "an intelligent and well-informed colored resident of this city," who was quoted as having said, "'I would say that I am bothered more about where and how I can get enough money with which to pay for a good, square meal, than I am about where I will eat it.'" The *Post* then editorialized that "there are other issues of more concern to the colored people ... than the social and sentimental questions passed upon by the court." While acknowledging the existence of prejudice against African Americans, *Harper's Weekly* maintained: "Colored citizens ... need not regret the fate of the Civil Rights Bill. The wrongs under which they suffer are not to be remedied by law."

From the perspective of more than one well-respected editor, the Civil Rights Act of 1875 never had a chance. *The Nation* under the editor E. L. Godkin had championed civil rights for African Americans, but by 1883 Godkin, like much of the rest of America, had grown weary of the fight. On October 18, 1883, the magazine published this assessment:

The Act was forced through Congress.... It was as clear then as it is now to almost every candid-minded man, that the Fourteenth Amendment, on which the promoters of the Act professed to base it, was really directed against State legislation, and not against the acts of individuals.... The Civil Rights Act was really rather an admonition, or statement of moral obligation, than a legal command. Probably nine-tenths of those who voted for it knew very well that whenever it came before the Supreme Court it would be torn to pieces.

The *Cleveland Gazette* perhaps offered the most succinct, if solemn, pronouncement: The Civil Rights Bill "lingered unconsciously nearly nine years and died on the 15th of October, 1883."

The Court's narrow reading of the Fourteenth Amendment in the Civil Rights Cases decision destroyed movements toward integration and helped usher in racial segregation that would continue through the post–World War II years in much of the United States. That Justice Bradley and his colleagues did not view segregation as a "badge of slavery" brings up the question that if segregation is not such a badge, what is? The Court's ruling erased civil rights enforcement from the Republican agenda and mandated federal withdrawal from civil rights enforcement, a policy that would not begin to be reversed until well after World War II. Interestingly, when framing the Civil Rights Act of 1964, Congress relied on its powers under the commerce clause of the Constitution—one of the same arguments brought up by Justice Harlan in his famous dissent in the Civil Rights Cases. In passing the Civil Rights Act of 1964,

Questions for Further Study

1. In what ways did the Court's decision in the Civil Rights Cases undermine the protections the Fourteenth Amendment to the Constitution afforded African Americans?

2. Using this document alongside the Thirteenth Amendment to the U.S. Constitution, the Fourteenth Amendment to the U.S. Constitution, the Fifteenth Amendment to the U.S. Constitution, the Ku Klux Klan Act, and *United States v. Cruikshank*, prepare a time line of fifteen key events from 1865 to 1883 that affected African Americans. Be prepared to defend your choices.

3. What was the basis of the Court's reasoning in ruling as it did in the Civil Rights Cases?

4. On what basis did John Marshall Harlan dissent from the majority opinion in the Civil Rights Cases? Select five sentences that you believe express the core of his analysis.

5. What factors in the social, economic, or political environment might have led the Supreme Court to rule as it did in the Civil Rights Cases?

Congress circumvented not only the legal precedent of the Civil Rights Cases decision but also the Supreme Court's limitation on congressional power to enforce "equal protection" under the law.

See also *Prigg v. Pennsylvania* (1841); Fugitive Slave Act of 1850; Black Code of Mississippi (1865); Thirteenth Amendment to the U.S. Constitution (1865); Fourteenth Amendment to the U.S. Constitution (1868); Fifteenth Amendment to the U.S. Constitution (1870).

Further Reading

■ Articles

Frantz, Laurent B. "Congressional Power to Enforce the Fourteenth Amendment against Private Acts." *Yale Law Journal* 73, no. 8 (July 1964): 1353–1384.

Hartz, Louis. "John M. Harlan in Kentucky, 1855–1877: The Story of His Pre-Court Career." *Filson Club History Quarterly* 14 (January 1940): 17–40.

Lado, Marianne L. Engelman. "A Question of Justice: African-American Legal Perspectives on the 1883 Civil Rights Cases." *Chicago-Kent Law Review* 70 (1995): 1123–1195.

McPherson, James M. "Abolitionists and the Civil Rights Act of 1875." *Journal of American History* 52, no. 3 (December 1965): 493–510.

Scott, John Anthony. "Justice Bradley's Evolving Concept of the Fourteenth Amendment from the Slaughterhouse Cases to the Civil Rights Cases." *Rutgers Law Review* 25 (Summer 1971): 552–569.

Woodson, Carter. "Fifty Years of Negro Citizenship as Qualified by the United States Supreme Court." *Journal of Negro History* 6, no. 1 (January 1921): 1–53.

■ Books

Beatty, Jack. *Age of Betrayal: The Triumph of Money in America, 1865–1900.* New York: Alfred A. Knopf, 2007.

Elliott, Mark. *Color-Blind Justice: Albion Tourgée and the Quest for Racial Equality from the Civil War to Plessy v. Ferguson.* New York: Oxford University Press, 2006.

Garraty, John A., ed. *Quarrels That Have Shaped the Constitution.* New York: Harper & Row, 1964.

Miller, Loren. *The Petitioners: The Story of the Supreme Court of the United States and the Negro.* New York: Pantheon Books, 1966.

Urofsky, Melvin I., and Paul Finkelman. *A March of Liberty: A Constitutional History of the United States.* Vol. 1: *From the Founding to 1890.* 2nd ed. New York: Oxford University Press, 2002.

—R. Owen Williams

CIVIL RIGHTS CASES

Majority Opinion

Mr. Justice Bradley delivered the opinion of the court. After stating the facts in the above language, he continued:

It is obvious that the primary and important question in all the cases is the constitutionality of the law, for if the law is unconstitutional, none of the prosecutions can stand.

The sections of the law referred to provide as follows:

Sec. 1. That all persons within the jurisdiction of the United States shall be entitled to the full and equal enjoyment of the accommodations, advantages, facilities, and privileges of inns, public conveyances on land or water, theatres, and other places of public amusement, subject only to the conditions and limitations established by law and applicable alike to citizens of every race and color, regardless of any previous condition of servitude.

Sec. 2. That any person who shall violate the foregoing section by denying to any citizen, except for reasons by law applicable to citizens of every race and color, and regardless of any previous condition of servitude, the full enjoyment of any of the accommodations, advantages, facilities, or privileges in said section enumerated, or by aiding or inciting such denial, shall for every such offence, forfeit and pay the sum of five hundred dollars to the person aggrieved thereby, to be recovered in an action of debt, with full costs, and shall also, for every such offence, be deemed guilty of a misdemeanor, and, upon conviction thereof, shall be fined not less than five hundred nor more than one thousand dollars, or shall be imprisoned not less than thirty days nor more than one year, *Provided,* That all persons may elect to sue for the penalty aforesaid, or to proceed under their rights at common law and by State statutes, and having so elected to proceed in the one mode or the other, their right to proceed in the other jurisdiction shall be barred. But this provision shall not apply to criminal proceedings, either under this act or the criminal law of any State; *and provided further,* that a judgment for the penalty in favor of the party aggrieved, or a judgment upon an indictment, shall be a bar to either prosecution respectively.

Are these sections constitutional? The first section, which is the principal one, cannot be fairly understood without attending to the last clause, which qualifies the preceding part.

The essence of the law is not to declare broadly that all persons shall be entitled to the full and equal enjoyment of the accommodations, advantages, facilities, and privileges of inns, public conveyances, and theatres, but that such enjoyment shall not be subject to any conditions applicable only to citizens of a particular race or color, or who had been in a previous condition of servitude. In other words, it is the purpose of the law to declare that, in the enjoyment of the accommodations and privileges of inns, public conveyances, theatres, and other places of public amusement, no distinction shall be made between citizens of different race or color or between those who have, and those who have not, been slaves. Its effect is to declare that, in all inns, public conveyances, and places of amusement, colored citizens, whether formerly slaves or not, and citizens of other races, shall have the same accommodations and privileges in all inns, public conveyances, and places of amusement as are enjoyed by white citizens, and vice versa. The second section makes it a penal offence in any person to deny to any citizen of any race or color, regardless of previous servitude, any of the accommodations or privileges mentioned in the first section.

Has Congress constitutional power to make such a law? Of course, no one will contend that the power to pass it was contained in the Constitution before the adoption of the last three amendments. The power is sought, first, in the Fourteenth Amendment, and the views and arguments of distinguished Senators, advanced whilst the law was under consideration, claiming authority to pass it by virtue of that amendment, are the principal arguments adduced in favor of the power. We have carefully considered those arguments, as was due to the eminent ability of those who put them forward, and have felt, in all its force, the weight of authority which always invests a law that Congress deems itself competent to pass. But the responsibility of an independent judgment is now thrown upon this court, and we are bound to exercise it according to the best lights we have.

The first section of the Fourteenth Amendment (which is the one relied on), after declaring who shall be citizens of the United States, and of the several

States, is prohibitory in its character, and prohibitory upon the States. It declares that:

> No State shall make or enforce any law which shall abridge the privileges or immunities of citizens of the United States; nor shall any State deprive any person of life, liberty, or property without due process of law; nor deny to any person within its jurisdiction the equal protection of the laws.

It is State action of a particular character that is prohibited. Individual invasion of individual rights is not the subject matter of the amendment. It has a deeper and broader scope. It nullifies and makes void all State legislation, and State action of every kind, which impairs the privileges and immunities of citizens of the United States or which injures them in life, liberty or property without due process of law, or which denies to any of them the equal protection of the laws. It not only does this, but, in order that the national will, thus declared, may not be a mere *brutum fulmen,* the last section of the amendment invests Congress with power to enforce it by appropriate legislation. To enforce what? To enforce the prohibition. To adopt appropriate legislation for correcting the effects of such prohibited State laws and State acts, and thus to render them effectually null, void, and innocuous. This is the legislative power conferred upon Congress, and this is the whole of it. It does not invest Congress with power to legislate upon subjects which are within the domain of State legislation, but to provide modes of relief against State legislation, or State action, of the kind referred to. It does not authorize Congress to create a code of municipal law for the regulation of private rights, but to provide modes of redress against the operation of State laws and the action of State officers executive or judicial when these are subversive of the fundamental rights specified in the amendment. Positive rights and privileges are undoubtedly secured by the Fourteenth Amendment, but they are secured by way of prohibition against State laws and State proceedings affecting those rights and privileges, and by power given to Congress to legislate for the purpose of carrying such prohibition into effect, and such legislation must necessarily be predicated upon such supposed State laws or State proceedings, and be directed to the correction of their operation and effect. A quite full discussion of this aspect of the amendment may be found in *United Sates v. Cruikshank,* ... *Virginia v. Rives,* ... and *Ex parte Virginia....*

An apt illustration of this distinction may be found in some of the provisions of the original Constitution. Take the subject of contracts, for example. The Constitution prohibited the States from passing any law impairing the obligation of contracts. This did not give to Congress power to provide laws for the general enforcement of contracts, nor power to invest the courts of the United States with jurisdiction over contracts, so as to enable parties to sue upon them in those courts. It did, however, give the power to provide remedies by which the impairment of contracts by State legislation might be counteracted and corrected, and this power was exercised. The remedy which Congress actually provided was that contained in the 25th section of the Judiciary Act of 1789, 1 Stat. 8, giving to the Supreme Court of the United States jurisdiction by writ of error to review the final decisions of State courts whenever they should sustain the validity of a State statute or authority alleged to be repugnant to the Constitution or laws of the United States. By this means, if a State law was passed impairing the obligation of a contract and the State tribunals sustained the validity of the law, the mischief could be corrected in this court. The legislation of Congress, and the proceedings provided for under it, were corrective in their character. No attempt was made to draw into the United States courts the litigation of contracts generally, and no such attempt would have been sustained. We do not say that the remedy provided was the only one that might have been provided in that case. Probably Congress had power to pass a law giving to the courts of the United States direct jurisdiction over contracts alleged to be impaired by a State law, and under the broad provisions of the act of March 3d 1875, ch. 137, 18 Stat. 470, giving to the circuit courts jurisdiction of all cases arising under the Constitution and laws of the United States, it is possible that such jurisdiction now exists. But under that, or any other law, it must appear as well by allegation, as proof at the trial, that the Constitution had been violated by the action of the State legislature. Some obnoxious State law passed, or that might be passed, is necessary to be assumed in order to lay the foundation of any federal remedy in the case, and for the very sufficient reason that the constitutional prohibition is against *State laws* impairing the obligation of contracts.

And so, in the present case, until some State law has been passed, or some State action through its officers or agents has been taken, adverse to the rights of citizens sought to be protected by the Fourteenth Amendment, no legislation of the United States under said amendment, nor any proceeding under such legislation, can be called into activity, for the prohibitions of the amendment are against State laws and acts done under State authority. Of course, legislation may, and should, be provided in advance to meet the exigency when it arises, but it should be adapted to the mischief and wrong which the amendment was intended to provide against, and that is State laws, or State action of some kind, adverse to the rights of the citizen secured by the amendment. Such legislation cannot properly cover the whole domain of rights appertaining to life, liberty and property, defining them and providing for their vindication. That would be to establish a code of municipal law regulative of all private rights between man and man in society. It would be to make Congress take the place of the State legislatures and to supersede them. It is absurd to affirm that, because the rights of life, liberty, and property (which include all civil rights that men have) are, by the amendment, sought to be protected against invasion on the part of the State without due process of law, Congress may therefore provide due process of law for their vindication in every case, and that, because the denial by a State to any persons of the equal protection of the laws is prohibited by the amendment, therefore Congress may establish laws for their equal protection. In fine, the legislation which Congress is authorized to adopt in this behalf is not general legislation upon the rights of the citizen, but corrective legislation, that is, such as may be necessary and proper for counteracting such laws as the States may adopt or enforce, and which, by the amendment, they are prohibited from making or enforcing, or such acts and proceedings as the States may commit or take, and which, by the amendment, they are prohibited from committing or taking. It is not necessary for us to state, if we could, what legislation would be proper for Congress to adopt. It is sufficient for us to examine whether the law in question is of that character.

An inspection of the law shows that it makes no reference whatever to any supposed or apprehended violation of the Fourteenth Amendment on the part of the States. It is not predicated on any such view. It proceeds *ex directo* to declare that certain acts committed by individuals shall be deemed offences, and shall be prosecuted and punished by proceedings in the courts of the United States. It does not profess to be corrective of any constitutional wrong committed by the States; it does not make its operation to depend upon any such wrong committed. It applies equally to cases arising in States which have

the justest laws respecting the personal rights of citizens, and whose authorities are ever ready to enforce such laws, as to those which arise in States that may have violated the prohibition of the amendment. In other words, it steps into the domain of local jurisprudence, and lays down rules for the conduct of individuals in society towards each other, and imposes sanctions for the enforcement of those rules, without referring in any manner to any supposed action of the State or its authorities.

If this legislation is appropriate for enforcing the prohibitions of the amendment, it is difficult to see where it is to stop. Why may not Congress, with equal show of authority, enact a code of laws for the enforcement and vindication of all rights of life, liberty, and property? If it is supposable that the States may deprive persons of life, liberty, and property without due process of law (and the amendment itself does suppose this), why should not Congress proceed at once to prescribe due process of law for the protection of every one of these fundamental rights, in every possible case, as well as to prescribe equal privileges in inns, public conveyances, and theatres? The truth is that the implication of a power to legislate in this manner is based upon the assumption that, if the States are forbidden to legislate or act in a particular way on a particular subject, and power is conferred upon Congress to enforce the prohibition, this gives Congress power to legislate generally upon that subject, and not merely power to provide modes of redress against such State legislation or action. The assumption is certainly unsound. It is repugnant to the Tenth Amendment of the Constitution, which declares that powers not delegated to the United States by the Constitution, nor prohibited by it to the States, are reserved to the States respectively or to the people.

We have not overlooked the fact that the fourth section of the act now under consideration has been held by this court to be constitutional. That section declares that no citizen, possessing all other qualifications which are or may be prescribed by law, shall be disqualified for service as grand or petit juror in any court of the United States, or of any State, on account of race, color, or previous condition of servitude, and any officer or other person charged with any duty in the selection or summoning of jurors who shall exclude or fail to summon any citizen for the cause aforesaid, shall, on conviction thereof, be deemed guilty of a misdemeanor, and be fined not more than five thousand dollars.

In *Ex parte Virginia*, … it was held that an indictment against a State officer under this section for excluding persons of color from the jury list is sustainable. But a moment's attention to its terms will show that the section is entirely corrective in its character. Disqualifications for service on juries are only created by the law, and the first part of the section is aimed at certain disqualifying laws, namely, those which make mere race or color a disqualification, and the second clause is directed against those who, assuming to use the authority of the State government, carry into effect such a rule of disqualification. In the Virginia case, the State, through its officer, enforced a rule of disqualification which the law was intended to abrogate and counteract. Whether the statute book of the State actually laid down any such rule of disqualification or not, the State, through its officer, enforced such a rule, and it is against such State action, through its officers and agents, that the last clause of the section is directed. This aspect of the law was deemed sufficient to divest it of any unconstitutional character, and makes it differ widely from the first and second sections of the same act which we are now considering.

These sections, in the objectionable features before referred to, are different also from the law ordinarily called the "Civil Rights Bill," originally passed April 9th, 1866, 14 Stat. 27, ch. 31, and reenacted with some modifications in sections 16, 17, 18, of the Enforcement Act, passed May 31st, 1870, 16 Stat. 140, ch. 114. That law, as reenacted, after declaring that all persons within the jurisdiction of the United States shall have the same right in every State and Territory to make and enforce contracts, to sue, be parties, give evidence, and to the full and equal benefit of all laws and proceedings for the security of persons and property as is enjoyed by white citizens, and shall be subject to like punishment, pains, penalties, taxes, licenses and exactions of every kind, and none other, any law, statute, ordinance, regulation or custom to the contrary notwithstanding, proceeds to enact that any person who, under color of any law, statute, ordinance, regulation or custom, shall subject, or cause to be subjected, any inhabitant of any State or Territory to the deprivation of any rights secured or protected by the preceding section (above quoted), or to different punishment, pains, or penalties, on account of such person's being an alien, or by reason of his color or race, than is prescribed for the punishment of citizens, shall be deemed guilty of a misdemeanor, and subject to fine and imprisonment as specified in the act. This law is clearly corrective in its character, intended to counteract and furnish redress against State laws and proceedings, and customs having the force of law, which sanction the wrongful acts specified. In the Revised Statutes, it is true, a very important clause, to-wit, the words "any law, statute, ordinance, regulation or custom to the contrary notwithstanding," which gave the declaratory section its point and effect, are omitted; but the penal part, by which the declaration is enforced, and which is really the effective part of the law, retains the reference to State laws by making the penalty apply only to those who should subject parties to a deprivation of their rights under color of any statute, ordinance, custom, etc., of any State or Territory, thus preserving the corrective character of the legislation.… The Civil Rights Bill here referred to is analogous in its character to what a law would have been under the original Constitution, declaring that the validity of contracts should not be impaired, and that, if any person bound by a contract should refuse to comply with it, under color or pretence that it had been rendered void or invalid by a State law, he should be liable to an action upon it in the courts of the United States, with the addition of a penalty for setting up such an unjust and unconstitutional defence.

In this connection, it is proper to state that civil rights, such as are guaranteed by the Constitution against State aggression, cannot be impaired by the wrongful acts of individuals, unsupported by State authority in the shape of laws, customs, or judicial or executive proceedings. The wrongful act of an individual, unsupported by any such authority, is simply a private wrong, or a crime of that individual; an invasion of the rights of the injured party, it is true, whether they affect his person, his property, or his reputation; but if not sanctioned in some way by the State, or not done under State authority, his rights remain in full force, and may presumably be vindicated by resort to the laws of the State for redress. An individual cannot deprive a man of his right to vote, to hold property, to buy and sell, to sue in the courts, or to be a witness or a juror; he may, by force or fraud, interfere with the enjoyment of the right in a particular case; he may commit an assault against the person, or commit murder, or use ruffian violence at the polls, or slander the good name of a fellow citizen; but, unless protected in these wrongful acts by some shield of State law or State authority, he cannot destroy or injure the right; he will only render himself amenable to satisfaction or punishment, and amenable therefor to the laws of the State where the wrongful acts are committed. Hence, in all those cases where the Constitution seeks to protect the rights of the citizen against discriminative and unjust laws of the State by prohibiting such laws, it is not individual offences, but abrogation and denial of rights, which it denounces and for which it clothes the Congress with power to provide a remedy. This abrogation and denial of rights for which the States alone were or could be responsible was the great seminal and fundamental wrong which was intended to be remedied. And the remedy to be provided must necessarily be predicated upon that wrong. It must assume that, in the cases provided for, the evil or wrong actually committed rests upon some State law or State authority for its excuse and perpetration.

Of course, these remarks do not apply to those cases in which Congress is clothed with direct and plenary powers of legislation over the whole subject, accompanied with an express or implied denial of such power to the States, as in the regulation of commerce with foreign nations, among the several States, and with the Indian tribes, the coining of money, the establishment of post offices and post roads, the declaring of war, etc. In these cases, Congress has power to pass laws for regulating the subjects specified in every detail, and the conduct and transactions of individuals in respect thereof. But where a subject is not submitted to the general legislative power of Congress, but is only submitted thereto for the purpose of rendering effective some prohibition against particular State legislation or State action in reference to that subject, the power given is limited by its object, and any legislation by Congress in the matter must necessarily be corrective in its character, adapted to counteract and redress the operation of such prohibited State laws or proceedings of State officers.

If the principles of interpretation which we have laid down are correct, as we deem them to be (and they are in accord with the principles laid down in the cases before referred to, as well as in the recent case of *United States v. Harris* …), it is clear that the law in question cannot be sustained by any grant of legislative power made to Congress by the Fourteenth Amendment. That amendment prohibits the States from denying to any person the equal protection of the laws, and declares that Congress shall have power to enforce, by appropriate legislation, the provisions of the amendment. The law in question, without any reference to adverse State legislation on the subject, declares that all persons shall be entitled to equal accommodations and privileges of inns, public conveyances, and places of public amusement, and imposes a penalty upon any individual who shall deny to any citizen such equal accommodations and privileges. This is not corrective legislation; it is primary and direct; it takes immediate and absolute possession of the subject of the right of admission to inns, public conveyances, and places of amusement. It supersedes and displaces State legislation on the same subject, or only allows it permissive force. It ignores such legislation, and assumes that the matter is one that belongs to the domain of national regulation. Whether it would not have been a more effective protection of the rights of citizens to have clothed Congress with plenary power over the whole subject is not now the question. What we have to decide is whether such plenary power has been conferred upon Congress by the Fourteenth Amendment, and, in our judgment, it has not.

We have discussed the question presented by the law on the assumption that a right to enjoy equal accommodation and privileges in all inns, public conveyances, and places of public amusement is one of the essential rights of the citizen which no State can abridge or interfere with. Whether it is such a right or not is a different question which, in the view we have taken of the validity of the law on the ground already stated, it is not necessary to examine.

We have also discussed the validity of the law in reference to cases arising in the States only, and not in reference to cases arising in the Territories or the District of Columbia, which are subject to the plenary legislation of Congress in every branch of municipal regulation. Whether the law would be a valid one as applied to the Territories and the District is not a question for consideration in the cases before us, they all being cases arising within the limits of States. And whether Congress, in the exercise of its power to regulate commerce amongst the several States, might or might not pass a law regulating rights in public conveyances passing from one State to another is also a question which is not now before us, as the sections in question are not conceived in any such view.

But the power of Congress to adopt direct and primary, as distinguished from corrective, legislation on the subject in hand is sought, in the second place, from the Thirteenth Amendment, which abolishes slavery. This amendment declares that neither slavery, nor involuntary servitude, except as a punishment for crime, whereof the party shall have been duly convicted, shall exist within the United States, or any place subject to their jurisdiction, and it gives Congress power to enforce the amendment by appropriate legislation.

This amendment, as well as the Fourteenth, is undoubtedly self-executing, without any ancillary legislation, so far as its terms are applicable to any existing state of circumstances. By its own unaided force and effect, it abolished slavery and established universal freedom. Still, legislation may be necessary and proper to meet all the various cases and circumstances to be affected by it, and to prescribe proper modes of redress for its violation in letter or spirit. And such legislation may be primary and direct in its character, for the amendment is not a mere prohibition of State laws establishing or upholding slavery, but an absolute declaration that slavery or involuntary servitude shall not exist in any part of the United States.

It is true that slavery cannot exist without law, any more than property in lands and goods can exist without law, and, therefore, the Thirteenth Amendment may be regarded as nullifying all State laws which establish or uphold slavery. But it has a reflex character also, establishing and decreeing universal civil and political freedom throughout the United States, and it is assumed that the power vested in Congress to enforce the article by appropriate legislation clothes Congress with power to pass all laws necessary and proper for abolishing all badges and incidents of slavery in the United States, and, upon this assumption, it is claimed that this is sufficient authority for declaring by law that all persons shall have equal accommodations and privileges in all inns, public conveyances, and places of amusement, the argument being that the denial of such equal accommodations and privileges is, in itself, a subjection to a species of servitude within the meaning of the amendment. Conceding the major proposition to be true, that Congress has a right to enact all necessary and proper laws for the obliteration and prevention of slavery with all its badges and incidents, is the minor proposition also true, that the denial to any person of admission to the accommodations and privileges of an inn, a public conveyance, or a theatre does subject that person to any form of servitude, or tend to fasten upon him any badge of slavery? If it does not, then power to pass the law is not found in the Thirteenth Amendment.

In a very able and learned presentation of the cognate question as to the extent of the rights, privileges and immunities of citizens which cannot rightfully be abridged by state laws under the Fourteenth Amendment, made in a former case, a long list of burdens and disabilities of a servile character, incident to feudal vassalage in France, and which were abolished by the decrees of the National Assembly, was presented for the purpose of showing that all inequalities and observances exacted by one man from another were servitudes or badges of slavery which a great nation, in its effort to establish universal liberty, made haste to wipe out and destroy. But these were servitudes imposed by the old law, or by long custom, which had the force of law, and exacted by one man from another without the latter's consent. Should any such servitudes be imposed by a state law, there can be no doubt that the law would be repugnant to the Fourteenth, no less than to the Thirteenth, Amendment, nor any greater doubt that Congress has adequate power to forbid any such servitude from being exacted.

But is there any similarity between such servitudes and a denial by the owner of an inn, a public conveyance, or a theatre of its accommodations and privileges to an individual, even though the denial be founded on the race or color of that individual? Where does any slavery or servitude, or badge of either, arise from such an act of denial? Whether it might not be a denial of a right which, if sanctioned by the state law, would be obnoxious to the prohibitions of the Fourteenth Amendment is another question. But what has it to do with the question of slavery?

It may be that, by the Black Code (as it was called), in the times when slavery prevailed, the proprietors of inns and public conveyances were forbidden to receive persons of the African race because it might assist slaves to escape from the control of their masters. This was merely a means of preventing such escapes, and was no part of the servitude itself. A law of that kind could not have any such object now, however justly it might be deemed an invasion of the party's legal right as a citizen, and amenable to the prohibitions of the Fourteenth Amendment.

The long existence of African slavery in this country gave us very distinct notions of what it was and what were its necessary incidents. Compulsory service of the slave for the benefit of the master, restraint of his movements except by the master's will, disability to hold property, to make contracts, to have a standing in court, to be a witness against a white person, and such like burdens and incapacities were the inseparable incidents of the institution. Severer punishments for crimes were imposed on the slave than on free persons guilty of the same offences. Congress, as we have seen, by the Civil Rights Bill of 1866, passed in view of the Thirteenth Amendment before the Fourteenth was adopted, undertook to wipe out these burdens and disabilities, the necessary incidents of slavery constituting its substance and visible form, and to secure to all citizens of every race and color, and without regard to previous servitude, those fundamental rights which are the essence of civil freedom, namely, the same right to make and enforce contracts, to sue, be parties, give evidence, and to inherit, purchase, lease, sell and convey property as is enjoyed by white citizens. Whether this legislation was fully authorized by the Thirteenth Amendment alone, without the support which it afterward received from the Fourteenth Amendment, after the adoption of which it was reenacted with some additions, it is not necessary to inquire. It is referred to for the purpose of showing that, at that time (in 1866), Congress did not assume, under the authority given by the Thirteenth Amendment, to adjust what may be called the social rights of men and races in the community, but only to declare and vindicate those fundamental rights which appertain to the essence of citizenship, and the enjoyment or deprivation of which constitutes the essential distinction between freedom and slavery.

We must not forget that the province and scope of the Thirteenth and Fourteenth amendments are different: the former simply abolished slavery; the latter prohibited the States from abridging the privileges or immunities of citizens of the United States, from depriving them of life, liberty, or property without due process of law, and from denying to any the equal protection of the laws. The amendments are different, and the powers of Congress under them are different. What Congress has power to do under one it may not have power to do under the other. Under the Thirteenth Amendment, it has only to do with slavery and its incidents. Under the Fourteenth Amendment, it has power to counteract and render nugatory all State laws and proceedings which have the effect to abridge any of the privileges or immunities of citizens of the United States, or to deprive them of life, liberty or property without due process of law, or to deny to any of them the equal protection of the laws. Under the Thirteenth Amendment, the legislation, so far as necessary or proper to eradicate all forms and incidents of slavery and involuntary servitude, may be direct and primary, operating upon the acts of individuals, whether sanctioned by State legislation or not; under the Fourteenth, as we have already shown, it must necessarily be, and can only be, corrective in its character, addressed to counteract and afford relief against State regulations or proceedings.

The only question under the present head, therefore, is whether the refusal to any persons of the accommodations of an inn or a public conveyance or a place of public amusement by an individual, and

without any sanction or support from any State law or regulation, does inflict upon such persons any manner of servitude or form of slavery as those terms are understood in this country? Many wrongs may be obnoxious to the prohibitions of the Fourteenth Amendment which are not, in any just sense, incidents or elements of slavery. Such, for example, would be the taking of private property without due process of law, or allowing persons who have committed certain crimes (horse stealing, for example) to be seized and hung by the *posse comitatus* without regular trial, or denying to any person, or class of persons, the right to pursue any peaceful avocations allowed to others. What is called class legislation would belong to this category, and would be obnoxious to the prohibitions of the Fourteenth Amendment, but would not necessarily be so to the Thirteenth, when not involving the idea of any subjection of one man to another. The Thirteenth Amendment has respect not to distinctions of race or class or color, but to slavery. The Fourteenth Amendment extends its protection to races and classes, and prohibits any State legislation which has the effect of denying to any race or class, or to any individual, the equal protection of the laws.

Now, conceding for the sake of the argument that the admission to an inn, a public conveyance, or a place of public amusement on equal terms with all other citizens is the right of every man and all classes of men, is it any more than one of those rights which the states, by the Fourteenth Amendment, are forbidden to deny to any person? And is the Constitution violated until the denial of the right has some State sanction or authority? Can the act of a mere individual, the owner of the inn, the public conveyance or place of amusement, refusing the accommodation, be justly regarded as imposing any badge of slavery or servitude upon the applicant, or only as inflicting an ordinary civil injury, properly cognizable by the laws of the State and presumably subject to redress by those laws until the contrary appears?

After giving to these questions all the consideration which their importance demands, we are forced to the conclusion that such an act of refusal has nothing to do with slavery or involuntary servitude, and that, if it is violative of any right of the party, his redress is to be sought under the laws of the State, or, if those laws are adverse to his rights and do not protect him, his remedy will be found in the corrective legislation which Congress has adopted, or may adopt, for counteracting the effect of State laws or State action prohibited by the Fourteenth Amendment. It would be running the slavery argument into the ground to make it apply to every act of discrimination which a person may see fit to make as to the guests he will entertain, or as to the people he will take into his coach or cab or car, or admit to his concert or theatre, or deal with in other matters of intercourse or business. Innkeepers and public carriers, by the laws of all the States, so far as we are aware, are bound, to the extent of their facilities, to furnish proper accommodation to all unobjectionable persons who in good faith apply for them. If the laws themselves make any unjust discrimination amenable to the prohibitions of the Fourteenth Amendment, Congress has full power to afford a remedy under that amendment and in accordance with it.

When a man has emerged from slavery, and, by the aid of beneficent legislation, has shaken off the inseparable concomitants of that state, there must be some stage in the progress of his elevation when he takes the rank of a mere citizen and ceases to be the special favorite of the laws, and when his rights as a citizen or a man are to be protected in the ordinary modes by which other men's rights are protected. There were thousands of free colored people in this country before the abolition of slavery, enjoying all the essential rights of life, liberty and property the same as white citizens, yet no one at that time thought that it was any invasion of his personal status as a freeman because he was not admitted to all the privileges enjoyed by white citizens, or because he was subjected to discriminations in the enjoyment of accommodations in inns, public conveyances and places of amusement. Mere discriminations on account of race or color were not regarded as badges of slavery. If, since that time, the enjoyment of equal rights in all these respects has become established by constitutional enactment, it is not by force of the Thirteenth Amendment (which merely abolishes slavery), but by force of the Thirteenth and Fifteenth Amendments.

On the whole, we are of opinion that no countenance of authority for the passage of the law in question can be found in either the Thirteenth or Fourteenth Amendment of the Constitution, and no other ground of authority for its passage being suggested, it must necessarily be declared void, at least so far as its operation in the several States is concerned.

This conclusion disposes of the cases now under consideration. In the cases of the *United States v. Michael Ryan,* and of *Richard A. Robinson and Wife v. The Memphis & Charleston Railroad Company,* the judgments must be affirmed. In the other cases, the answer to be given will be that the first and second sections of the act of Congress of March 1st, 1875,

entitled "An Act to protect all citizens in their civil and legal rights," are unconstitutional and void, and that judgment should be rendered upon the several indictments in those cases accordingly.

And it is so ordered.

Dissenting Opinion

Mr. Justice Harlan dissenting.

The opinion in these cases proceeds, it seems to me, upon grounds entirely too narrow and artificial. I cannot resist the conclusion that the substance and spirit of the recent amendments of the Constitution have been sacrificed by a subtle and ingenious verbal criticism.

It is not the words of the law, but the internal sense of it that makes the law; the letter of the law is the body; the sense and reason of the law is the soul.

Constitutional provisions, adopted in the interest of liberty and for the purpose of securing, through national legislation, if need be, rights inhering in a state of freedom and belonging to American citizenship have been so construed as to defeat the ends the people desired to accomplish, which they attempted to accomplish, and which they supposed they had accomplished by changes in their fundamental law. By this I do not mean that the determination of these cases should have been materially controlled by considerations of mere expediency or policy. I mean only, in this form, to express an earnest conviction that the court has departed from the familiar rule requiring, in the interpretation of constitutional provisions, that full effect be given to the intent with which they were adopted.

The purpose of the first section of the act of Congress of March 1, 1875, was to prevent race discrimination in respect of the accommodations and facilities of inns, public conveyances, and places of public amusement. It does not assume to define the general conditions and limitations under which inns, public conveyances, and places of public amusement may be conducted, but only declares that such conditions and limitations, whatever they may be, shall not be applied so as to work a discrimination solely because of race, color, or previous condition of servitude. The second section provides a penalty against anyone denying, or aiding or inciting the denial, of any citizen, of that equality of right given by the first section except for reasons by law applicable to citizens of every race or color and regardless of any previous condition of servitude.

There seems to be no substantial difference between my brethren and myself as to the purpose of Congress, for they say that the essence of the law is not to declare broadly that all persons shall be entitled to the full and equal enjoyment of the accommodations, advantages, facilities, and privileges of inns, public conveyances, and theatres, but that such enjoyment shall not be subject to conditions applicable only to citizens of a particular race or color, or who had been in a previous condition of servitude. The effect of the statute, the court says, is that colored citizens, whether formerly slaves or not, and citizens of other races shall have the same accommodations and privileges in all inns, public conveyances, and places of amusement as are enjoyed by white persons, and vice versa.

The court adjudges, I think erroneously, that Congress is without power, under either the Thirteenth or Fourteenth Amendment, to establish such regulations, and that the first and second sections of the statute are, in all their parts, unconstitutional and void.

Whether the legislative department of the government has transcended the limits of its constitutional powers, "is at all times," said this court in *Fletcher v. Peck,* … a question of much delicacy which ought seldom, if ever, to be decided in the affirmative in a doubtful case…. The opposition between the Constitution and the law should be such that the judge feels a clear and strong conviction of their incompatibility with each other.

More recently, in *Sinking Fund Cases,* … we said:

It is our duty, when required in the regular course of judicial proceedings, to declare an act of Congress void if not within the legislative power of the United States, but this declaration should never be made except in a clear case. Every possible presumption is in favor of the validity of a statute, and this continues until the contrary is shown beyond a rational doubt. One branch of the government cannot encroach on the domain of another without danger. The safety of our institutions depends in no small degree on a strict observance of this salutary rule.

Before considering the language and scope of these amendments, it will be proper to recall the relations subsisting, prior to their adoption, between the national government and the institution of slavery, as indicated by the provisions of the Constitution, the legislation of Congress, and the decisions of this court. In this mode, we may obtain keys with which to open the mind of the people and discover the thought intended to be expressed.

In section 2 of article IV of the Constitution, it was provided that no person held to service or labor in one State, under the laws thereof, escaping into another, shall, in consequence of any law or regulation therein, be discharged from such service or labor, but shall be delivered up on claim of the party to whom such service or labor may be due.

Under the authority of this clause, Congress passed the Fugitive Slave Law of 1793, establishing a mode for the recovery of fugitive slaves and prescribing a penalty against any person who should knowingly and willingly obstruct or hinder the master, his agent, or attorney in seizing, arresting, and recovering the fugitive, or who should rescue the fugitive from him, or who should harbor or conceal the slave after notice that he was a fugitive.

In *Prigg v. Commonwealth of Pennsylvania,* … this court had occasion to define the powers and duties of Congress in reference to fugitives from labor. Speaking by Mr. Justice Story, it laid down these propositions:

That a clause of the Constitution conferring a right should not be so construed as to make it shadowy or unsubstantial, or leave the citizen without a remedial power adequate for its protection when another construction equally accordant with the words and the sense in which they were used would enforce and protect the right granted;

That Congress is not restricted to legislation for the execution of its expressly granted powers, but, for the protection of rights guaranteed by the Constitution, may employ such means, not prohibited, as are necessary and proper, or such as are appropriate, to attain the ends proposed;

That the Constitution recognized the master's right of property in his fugitive slave, and, as incidental thereto, the right of seizing and recovering him, regardless of any State law or regulation or local custom whatsoever; and,

That the right of the master to have his slave, thus escaping, delivered up on claim, being guaranteed by the Constitution, the fair implication was that the national government was clothed with appropriate authority and functions to enforce it.

The court said

The fundamental principle, applicable to all cases of this sort, would seem to be that, when the end is required the means are given, and when the duty is enjoined, the ability to perform it is contemplated to exist on the part of the functionary to whom it is entrusted.

Again,

It would be a strange anomaly and forced construction to suppose that the national government meant to rely for the due fulfillment of its own proper duties, and the rights which it intended to secure, upon State legislation, and not upon that of the Union. *A fortiori,* it would be more objectionable to suppose that a power which was to be the same throughout the Union should be confided to State sovereignty, which could not rightfully act beyond its own territorial limits.

The act of 1793 was, upon these grounds, adjudged to be a constitutional exercise of the powers of Congress.

It is to be observed from the report of Priggs' case that Pennsylvania, by her attorney general, pressed the argument that the obligation to surrender fugitive slaves was on the States and for the States, subject to the restriction that they should not pass laws or establish regulations liberating such fugitives; that the Constitution did not take from the States the right to determine the status of all persons within their respective jurisdictions; that it was for the State in which the alleged fugitive was found to determine, through her courts or in such modes as she prescribed, whether the person arrested was, in fact, a freeman or a fugitive slave; that the sole power of the general government in the premises was, by judicial instrumentality, to restrain and correct, not to forbid and prevent in the absence of hostile State action, and that, for the general government to assume primary authority to legislate on the subject of fugitive slaves, to the exclusion of the States, would be a dangerous encroachment on State sovereignty. But to such suggestions, this court turned a deaf ear, and adjudged that primary legislation by Congress to enforce the master's right was authorized by the Constitution.

We next come to the Fugitive Slave Act of 1850, the constitutionality of which rested, as did that of 1793, solely upon the implied power of Congress to enforce the master's rights. The provisions of that act were far in advance of previous legislation. They placed at the disposal of the master seeking to recover his fugitive slave substantially the whole power of the nation. It invested commissioners, appointed under the act, with power to summon the *posse comitatus* for the enforcement of its provisions, and commanded all good citizens to assist in its prompt and efficient execution whenever their services were required as part of the *posse comitatus.* Without going

into the details of that act, it is sufficient to say that Congress omitted from it nothing which the utmost ingenuity could suggest as essential to the successful enforcement of the master's claim to recover his fugitive slave. And this court, in *Ableman v. Booth,* ... adjudged it to be "in all of its provisions, fully authorized by the Constitution of the United States."

The only other case, prior to the adoption of the recent amendments, to which reference will be made, is that of *Dred Scott v. Sanford....* That case was instituted in a circuit court of the United States by Dred Scott, claiming to be a citizen of Missouri, the defendant being a citizen of another State. Its object was to assert the title of himself and family to freedom. The defendant pleaded in abatement that Scott—being of African descent, whose ancestors, of pure African blood, were brought into this country and sold as slaves—was not a citizen. The only matter in issue, said the court, was whether the descendants of slaves thus imported and sold, when they should be emancipated, or who were born of parents who had become free before their birth, are citizens of a State in the sense in which the word "citizen" is used in the Constitution of the United States.

In determining that question, the court instituted an inquiry as to who were citizens of the several States at the adoption of the Constitution and who at that time were recognized as the people whose rights and liberties had been violated by the British government. The result was a declaration by this court, speaking by Chief Justice Taney, that the legislation and histories of the times, and the language used in the Declaration of Independence, showed that neither the class of persons who had been imported as slaves nor their descendants, whether they had become free or not, were then acknowledged as a part of the people, nor intended to be included in the general words used in that instrument; that they had for more than a century before been regarded as beings of an inferior race, and altogether unfit to associate with the white race either in social or political relations, and so far inferior that they had no rights which the white man was bound to respect, and that the negro might justly and lawfully be reduced to slavery for his benefit; that he was "bought and sold, and treated as an ordinary article of merchandise and traffic, whenever a profit could be made by it;" and, that this opinion was at that time fixed and universal in the civilized portion of the white race. It was regarded as an axiom in morals, as well as in politics, which no one thought of disputing, or supposed to be open to dispute, and men in every grade and position in society daily and habitually acted upon it in their private pursuits, as well as in matters of public concern, without for a moment doubting the correctness of this opinion.

The judgment of the court was that the words "people of the United States" and "citizens" meant the same thing, both describing the political body who, according to our republican institutions, form the sovereignty and hold the power and conduct the government through their representatives; that they are what we familiarly call the "sovereign people," and every citizen is one of this people and a constituent member of this sovereignty; but that the class of persons described in the plea in abatement did not compose a portion of this people, were not "included, and were not intended to be included, under the word 'citizens' in the Constitution;" that, therefore, they could "claim none of the rights and privileges which that instrument provides for and secures to citizens of the United States;" that, on the contrary, they were at that time considered as a subordinate and inferior class of beings who had been subjugated by the dominant race and, whether emancipated or not, yet remained subject to their authority, and had no rights or privileges but such as those who held the power and the government might choose to grant them.

Such were the relations which formerly existed between the government, whether national or state, and the descendants, whether free or in bondage, of those of African blood who had been imported into this country and sold as slaves.

The first section of the Thirteenth Amendment provides that neither slavery nor involuntary servitude, except as a punishment for crime, whereof the party shall have been duly convicted, shall exist within the United States, or any place subject to their jurisdiction.

Its second section declares that "Congress shall have power to enforce this article by appropriate legislation." This amendment was followed by the Civil Rights Act of April 9, 1866, which, among other things, provided that all persons born in the United States, and not subject to any foreign power, excluding Indians not taxed, are hereby declared to be citizens of the United States.... The power of Congress, in this mode, to elevate the enfranchised race to national citizenship was maintained by the supporters of the act of 1866 to be as full and complete as its power, by general statute, to make the children, being of full age, of persons naturalized in this country, citizens of the United States without going through the process of naturalization. The act of 1866 in this respect was also likened to that of 1843, in which

Congress declared that the Stockbridge tribe of Indians, and each and every one of them, shall be deemed to be and are hereby declared to be, citizens of the United States to all intents and purposes, and shall be entitled to all the rights, privileges, and immunities of such citizens, and shall in all respects be subject to the laws of the United States.

If the act of 1866 was valid in conferring national citizenship upon all embraced by its terms, then the colored race, enfranchised by the Thirteenth Amendment, became citizens of the United States prior to the adoption of the Fourteenth Amendment. But, in the view which I take of the present case, it is not necessary to examine this question.

The terms of the Thirteenth Amendment are absolute and universal. They embrace every race which then was, or might thereafter be, within the United States. No race, as such, can be excluded from the benefits or rights thereby conferred. Yet it is historically true that that amendment was suggested by the condition, in this country, of that race which had been declared by this court to have had—according to the opinion entertained by the most civilized portion of the white race at the time of the adoption of the Constitution—"no rights which the white man was bound to respect," none of the privileges or immunities secured by that instrument to citizens of the United States. It had reference, in peculiar sense, to a people which (although the larger part of them were in slavery) had been invited by an act of Congress to aid in saving from overthrow a government which, theretofore, by all of its departments, had treated them as an inferior race, with no legal rights or privileges except such as the white race might choose to grant them.

These are the circumstances under which the Thirteenth Amendment was proposed for adoption. They are now recalled only that we may better understand what was in the minds of the people when that amendment was considered, and what were the mischiefs to be remedied and the grievances to be redressed by its adoption.

We have seen that the power of Congress, by legislation, to enforce the master's right to have his slave delivered up on claim was *implied* from the recognition of that right in the national Constitution. But the power conferred by the Thirteenth Amendment does not rest upon implication or inference. Those who framed it were not ignorant of the discussion, covering many years of our country's history, as to the constitutional power of Congress to enact the Fugitive Slave Laws of 1793 and 1850. When, therefore, it was determined, by a change in the fundamental law, to uproot the institution of slavery wherever it existed in the land and to establish universal freedom, there was a fixed purpose to place the authority of Congress in the premises beyond the possibility of a doubt. Therefore, *ex industria,* power to enforce the Thirteenth Amendment by appropriate legislation was expressly granted. Legislation for that purpose, my brethren concede, may be direct and primary. But to what specific ends may it be directed? This court has uniformly held that the national government has the power, whether expressly given or not, to secure and protect rights conferred or guaranteed by the Constitution. *United States v. Reese, … Strauder v. West Virginia.…* That doctrine ought not now to be abandoned when the inquiry is not as to an implied power to protect the master's rights, but what may Congress, under powers expressly granted, do for the protection of freedom and the rights necessarily inhering in a state of freedom.

The Thirteenth Amendment, it is conceded, did something more than to prohibit slavery as an *institution* resting upon distinctions of race and upheld by positive law. My brethren admit that it established and decreed universal *civil freedom* throughout the United States. But did the freedom thus established involve nothing more than exemption from actual slavery? Was nothing more intended than to forbid one man from owning another as property? Was it the purpose of the nation simply to destroy the institution, and then remit the race, theretofore held in bondage, to the several States for such protection, in their civil rights, necessarily growing out of freedom, as those States, in their discretion, might choose to provide? Were the States against whose protest the institution was destroyed to be left free, so far as national interference was concerned, to make or allow discriminations against that race, as such, in the enjoyment of those fundamental rights which, by universal concession, inhere in a state of freedom? Had the Thirteenth Amendment stopped with the sweeping declaration in its first section against the existence of slavery and involuntary servitude except for crime, Congress would have had the power, by implication, according to the doctrines of *Prigg v. Commonwealth of Pennsylvania,* repeated in *Strauder v. West Virginia,* to protect the freedom established, and consequently, to secure the enjoyment of such civil rights as were fundamental in freedom. That it can exert its authority to that extent is made clear, and was intended to be made clear, by the express grant of power contained in the second section of the Amendment.

That there are burdens and disabilities which constitute badges of slavery and servitude, and that the power to enforce by appropriate legislation the Thirteenth Amendment may be exerted by legislation of a direct and primary character for the eradication not simply of the institution, but of its badges and incidents, are propositions which ought to be deemed indisputable. They lie at the foundation of the Civil Rights Act of 1866. Whether that act was authorized by the Thirteenth Amendment alone, without the support which it subsequently received from the Fourteenth Amendment, after the adoption of which it was reenacted with some additions, my brethren do not consider it necessary to inquire. But I submit, with all respect to them, that its constitutionality is conclusively shown by their opinion. They admit, as I have said, that the Thirteenth Amendment established freedom; that there are burdens and disabilities, the necessary incidents of slavery, which constitute its substance and visible form; that Congress, by the act of 1866, passed in view of the Thirteenth Amendment, before the Fourteenth was adopted, undertook to remove certain burdens and disabilities, the necessary incidents of slavery, and to secure to all citizens of every race and color, and without regard to previous servitude, those fundamental rights which are the essence of civil freedom, namely, the same right to make and enforce contracts, to sue, be parties, give evidence, and to inherit, purchase, lease, sell, and convey property as is enjoyed by white citizens; that, under the Thirteenth Amendment, Congress has to do with slavery and its incidents, and that legislation, so far as necessary or proper to eradicate all forms and incidents of slaver and involuntary servitude, may be direct and primary, operating upon the acts of individuals, whether sanctioned by State legislation or not. These propositions being conceded, it is impossible, as it seems to me, to question the constitutional validity of the Civil Rights Act of 1866. I do not contend that the Thirteenth Amendment invests Congress with authority, by legislation, to define and regulate the entire body of the civil rights which citizens enjoy, or may enjoy, in the several States. But I hold that, since slavery, as the court has repeatedly declared, *Slaughterhouse Cases, … Strauder West Virginia,* … was the moving or principal cause of the adoption of that amendment, and since that institution rested wholly upon the inferiority, as a race, of those held in bondage, their freedom necessarily involved immunity from, and protection against, all discrimination against them, because of their race, in respect of such civil rights as belong to freemen of other races. Congress, therefore, under its express power to enforce that amendment by appropriate legislation, may enact laws to protect that people against the deprivation, *because of their race,* of any civil rights granted to other freemen in the same State, and such legislation may be of a direct and primary character, operating upon States, their officers and agents, and also upon at least such individuals and corporations as exercise public functions and wield power and authority under the State.

To test the correctness of this position, let us suppose that, prior to the adoption of the Fourteenth Amendment, a State had passed a statute denying to freemen of African descent, resident within its limits, the same right which was accorded to white persons of making and enforcing contracts and of inheriting, purchasing, leasing, selling and conveying property; or a statute subjecting colored people to severer punishment for particular offences than was prescribed for white persons, or excluding that race from the benefit of the laws exempting homesteads from execution. Recall the legislation of 1865–1866 in some of the States, of which this court in the *Slaughterhouse Cases* said that it imposed upon the colored race onerous disabilities and burdens; curtailed their rights in the pursuit of life, liberty and property to such an extent that their freedom was of little value; forbade them to appear in the towns in any other character than menial servants; required them to reside on and cultivate the soil, without the right to purchase or own it; excluded them from many occupations of gain, and denied them the privilege of giving testimony in the courts where a white man was a party.... Can there be any doubt that all such enactments might have been reached by direct legislation upon the part of Congress under its express power to enforce the Thirteenth Amendment? Would any court have hesitated to declare that such legislation imposed badges of servitude in conflict with the civil freedom ordained by that amendment? That it would have been also in conflict with the Fourteenth Amendment because inconsistent with the fundamental rights of American citizenship does not prove that it would have been consistent with the Thirteenth Amendment.

What has been said is sufficient to show that the power of Congress under the Thirteenth Amendment is not necessarily restricted to legislation against slavery as an institution upheld by positive law, but may be exerted to the extent, at least, of protecting the liberated race against discrimination in respect of legal rights belonging to freemen where such discrimination is based upon race.

It remains now to inquire what are the legal rights of colored persons in respect of the accommodations, privileges and facilities of public conveyances, inns, and places of public amusement?

First, as to public conveyances on land and water. In *New Jersey Steam Navigation Co. v. Merchants' Bank,* ... this court, speaking by Mr. Justice Nelson, said that a common carrier is in the exercise of a sort of public office, and has public duties to perform, from which he should not be permitted to exonerate himself without the assent of the parties concerned.

To the same effect is *Munn v. Illinois....* In *Olcott v. Supervisor,* ... it was ruled that railroads are public highways, established by authority of the State for the public use; that they are nonetheless public highways because controlled and owned by private corporations; that it is a part of the function of government to make and maintain highways for the convenience of the public; that no matter who is the agent, or what is the agency, the function performed is *that of the State;* that, although the owners may be private companies, they may be compelled to permit the public to use these works in the manner in which they can be used; that, upon these grounds alone have the courts sustained the investiture of railroad corporations with the State's right of eminent domain, or the right of municipal corporations, under legislative authority, to assess, levy and collect taxes to aid in the construction of railroads. So in *Township of Queensbury v. Culver,* ... it was said that a municipal subscription of railroad stock was in aid of the construction and maintenance of a public highway, and for the promotion of a public use. Again, in *Township of Pine Grove v. Talcott...* : "Though the corporation [railroad] was private, its work was public, as much so as if it were to be constructed by the State." To the like effect are numerous adjudications in this and the State courts with which the profession is familiar. The Supreme Judicial Court of Massachusetts, in *Inhabitants of Worcester v. The Western R.R. Corporation,* ... said in reference to a railroad:

The establishment of that great thoroughfare is regarded as a public work, established by public authority, intended for the public use and benefit, the use of which is secured to the whole community, and constitutes, therefore, like a canal, turnpike, or highway, a public easement.... It is true that the real and personal property, necessary to the establishment and management of the railroad is vested in the corporation, but it is in trust for the public.

In *Erie, Etc., R.R. Co. v. Casey*, … the court, referring to an act repealing the charter of a railroad, and under which the State took possession of the road, said:

It is a public highway, solemnly devoted to public use. When the lands were taken, it was for such use, or they could not have been taken at all…. Railroads established upon land taken by the right of eminent domain by authority of the commonwealth, created by her laws as thoroughfares for commerce, are her highways. No corporation has property in them, though it may have franchises annexed to and exercisable within them.

In many courts it has been held that, because of the public interest in such a corporation, the land of a railroad company cannot be levied on and sold under execution by a creditor. The sum of the adjudged cases is that a railroad corporation is a governmental agency, created primarily for public purposes and subject to be controlled for the public benefit. Upon this ground, the State, when unfettered by contract, may regulate, in its discretion, the rates of fares of passengers and freight. And upon this ground, too, the State may regulate the entire management of railroads in all matters affecting the convenience and safety of the public, as, for example, by regulating speed, compelling stops of prescribed length at stations, and prohibiting discriminations and favoritism. If the corporation neglect or refuse to discharge its duties to the public, it may be coerced to do so by appropriate proceedings in the name or in behalf of the State.

Such being the relations these corporations hold to the public, it would seem that the right of a colored person to use an improved public highway upon the terms accorded to freemen of other races is as fundamental, in the state of freedom established in this country, as are any of the rights which my brethren concede to be so far fundamental as to be deemed the essence of civil freedom. "Personal liberty consists," says Blackstone, in the power of locomotion, of changing situation, or removing one's person to whatever places one's own inclination may direct, without restraint unless by due course of law.

But of what value is this right of locomotion if it may be clogged by such burdens as Congress intended by the act of 1875 to remove? They are burdens which lay at the very foundation of the institution of slavery as it once existed. They are not to be sus-

tained except upon the assumption that there is, in this land of universal liberty, a class which may still be discriminated against, even in respect of rights of a character so necessary and supreme that, deprived of their enjoyment in common with others, a freeman is not only branded as one inferior and infected, but, in the competitions of life, is robbed of some of the most essential means of existence, and all this solely because they belong to a particular race which the nation has liberated. The Thirteenth Amendment alone obliterated the race line so far as all rights fundamental in a state of freedom are concerned.

Second, as to inns. The same general observations which have been made as to railroads are applicable to inns. The word "inn" has a technical legal signification. It means, in the act of 1875, just what it meant at common law. A mere private boarding house is not an inn, nor is its keeper subject to the responsibilities, or entitled to the privileges, of a common innkeeper.

To constitute one an innkeeper within the legal force of that term, he must keep a house of entertainment or lodging for all travelers or wayfarers who might choose to accept the same, being of good character or conduct.

Redfield on Carriers, etc., §7. Says Judge Story:

An innkeeper may be defined to be the keeper of a common inn for the lodging and entertainment of travelers and passengers, their horses and attendants. An innkeeper is bound to take in all travelers and wayfaring persons, and to entertain them, if he can accommodate them, for a reasonable compensation, and he must guard their goods with proper diligence…. If an innkeeper improperly refuses to receive or provide for a guest, he is liable to be indicted therefor…. They (carriers of passengers) are no more at liberty to refuse a passenger, if they have sufficient room and accommodations, than an innkeeper is to refuse suitable room and accommodations to a guest.

Story on Bailments §§475–476.

In *Rex v. Ivens*, 7 Carrington & Payne 213, 32 E.C.L. 49, the court, speaking by Mr. Justice Coleridge, said:

An indictment lies against an innkeeper who refuses to receive a guest, he having at the time room in his house and either the price of the guest's entertainment being tendered to him or such circumstances occurring as will dispense with that tender.

This law is founded in good sense. The innkeeper is not to select his guest. He has no right to say to one, you shall come to my inn, and to another, you shall not, as everyone coming and conducting himself in a proper manner has a right to be received, and, for this purpose innkeepers are a sort of public servants, they having, in return a kind of privilege of entertaining travelers and supplying them with what they want.

These authorities are sufficient to show that a keeper of an inn is in the exercise of a *quasi*-public employment. The law gives him special privileges. and he is charged with certain duties and responsibilities to the public. The public nature of his employment forbids him from discriminating against any person asking admission as a guest on account of the race or color of that person.

Third. As to places of public amusement. It may be argued that the managers of such places have no duties to perform with which the public are, in any legal sense, concerned, or with which the public have any right to interfere, and that the exclusion of a black man from a place of public amusement on account of his race, or the denial to him on that ground of equal accommodations at such places, violates no legal right for the vindication of which he may invoke the aid of the courts. My answer is that places of public amusement, within the meaning of the act of 1875, are such as are established and maintained under direct license of the law. The authority to establish and maintain them comes from the public. The colored race is a part of that public. The local government granting the license represents them as well as all other races within its jurisdiction. A license from the public to establish a place of public amusement imports in law equality of right at such places among all the members of that public. This must be so unless it be—which I deny—that the common municipal government of all the people may, in the exertion of its powers, conferred for the benefit of all, discriminate or authorize discrimination against a particular race solely because of its former condition of servitude.

I also submit, whether it can be said—in view of the doctrines of this court as announced in *Munn v. State of Illinois,* ... and reaffirmed in *Peik v. Chicago & N.W. Railway Co.,* ... that the management of places of public amusement is a purely private matter, with which government has no rightful concern? In the *Munn* case, the question was whether the State of Illinois could fix, by law, the maximum of charges for the storage of grain in certain warehouses in that State—the *private property of individual citizens.* After quoting a remark attributed to Lord Chief Justice Hale, to the effect that, when private property is "affected with a public interest, it ceases to be *juris privati*only," the court says:

> Property does become clothed with a public interest when used in a manner to make it of public consequence and affect the community at large. When, therefore, one devotes his property to a use in which the public has an interest, he, in effect, grants to the public an interest in that use, and must submit to be controlled by the public for the common good to the extent of the interest he has thus created. He may withdraw his grant by discontinuing the use, but, so long as he maintains the use, he must submit to the control.

The doctrines of *Munn v. Illinois* have never been modified by this court, and I am justified upon the authority of that case in saying that places of public amusement, conducted under the authority of the law, are clothed with a public interest because used in a manner to make them of public consequence and to affect the community at large. The law may therefore regulate, to some extent, the mode in which they shall be conducted, and, consequently, the public have rights in respect of such places which may be vindicated by the law. It is consequently not a matter purely of private concern.

Congress has not, in these matters, entered the domain of State control and supervision. It does not, as I have said, assume to prescribe the general conditions and limitations under which inns, public conveyances, and places of public amusement shall be conducted or managed. It simply declares, in effect, that, since the nation has established universal freedom in this country for all time, there shall be no discrimination, based merely upon race or color, in respect of the accommodations and advantages of public conveyances, inns, and places of public amusement.

I am of the opinion that such discrimination practised by corporations and individuals in the exercise of their public or *quasi*-public functions is a badge of servitude the imposition of which Congress may prevent under its power, by appropriate legislation, to enforce the Thirteenth Amendment; and consequently, without reference to its enlarged power under the Fourteenth Amendment, the act of March 1, 1875, is not, in my judgment, repugnant to the Constitution.

It remains now to consider these cases with reference to the power Congress has possessed since the adoption of the Fourteenth Amendment. Much that has been said as to the power of Congress under the Thirteenth Amendment is applicable to this branch of the discussion, and will not be repeated.

Before the adoption of the recent amendments, it had become, as we have seen, the established doctrine of this court that negroes, whose ancestors had been imported and sold as slaves, could not become citizens of a State, or even of the United States, with the rights and privileges guaranteed to citizens by the national Constitution; further, that one might have all the rights and privileges of a citizen of a State without being a citizen in the sense in which that word was used in the national Constitution, and without being entitled to the privileges and immunities of citizens of the several States. Still further, between the adoption of the Thirteenth Amendment and the proposal by Congress of the Fourteenth Amendment, on June 16, 1866, the statute books of several of the States, as we have seen, had become loaded down with enactments which, under the guise of Apprentice, Vagrant, and contract regulations, sought to keep the colored race in a condition, practically, of servitude. It was openly announced that whatever might be the rights which persons of that race had as freemen, under the guarantees of the national Constitution, they could not become citizens of a State, with the privileges belonging to citizens, except by the consent of such State; consequently, that their civil rights as citizens of the State depended entirely upon State legislation. To meet this new peril to the black race, that the purposes of the nation might not be doubted or defeated, and by way of further enlargement of the power of Congress, the Fourteenth Amendment was proposed for adoption.

Remembering that this court, in the *Slaughterhouse Cases,* declared that the one pervading purpose found in all the recent amendments, lying at the foundation of each and without which none of them would have been suggested, was the freedom of the slave race, the security and firm establishment of that freedom, and the protection of the newly made freeman and citizen from the oppression of those who had formerly exercised unlimited dominion over him—that each amendment was addressed primarily to the grievances of that race—let us proceed to consider the language of the Fourteenth Amendment.

Its first and fifth sections are in these words:

Sec. 1. All persons born or naturalized in the United States, and subject to the jurisdiction thereof, are citizens of the United States and of the State wherein they reside. No State shall make or enforce any law which shall abridge the privileges or immunities of citizens of the United States; nor shall any State deprive any person of life, liberty, or property, without due process of law; nor deny to any person within its jurisdiction the equal protection of the laws....

Sec. 5. That Congress shall have power to enforce, by appropriate legislation, the provisions of this article.

It was adjudged in *Strauder v. West Virginia,* ... and *Ex parte Virginia,* ... and my brethren concede, that positive rights and privileges were intended to be secured, and are, in fact, secured, by the Fourteenth Amendment.

But when, under what circumstances, and to what extent may Congress, by means of legislation, exert its power to enforce the provisions of this amendment? The theory of the opinion of the majority of the court—the foundation upon which their reasoning seems to rest—is that the general government cannot, in advance of hostile State laws or hostile State proceedings, actively interfere for the protection of my of the rights, privileges, and immunities secured by the Fourteenth Amendment. It is said that such rights, privileges, and immunities are secured by way of *prohibition* against State laws and State proceedings affecting such rights and privileges, and by power given to Congress to legislate for the purpose of carrying *such prohibition* into effect; also, that congressional legislation must necessarily be predicated upon such supposed State laws or State proceedings, and be directed to the correction of their operation and effect.

In illustration of its position, the court refers to the clause of the Constitution forbidding the passage by a State of any law impairing the obligation of contracts. That clause does not, I submit, furnish a proper illustration of the scope and effect of the fifth section of the Fourteenth Amendment. No express power is given Congress to enforce, by primary direct legislation, the prohibition upon State laws impairing the obligation of contracts. Authority is, indeed, conferred to enact all necessary and proper laws for carrying into execution the enumerated powers of Congress and all other powers vested by the Constitution in the government of the United States or in any department or officer thereof. And, as heretofore shown, there is also, by necessary implication, power in Congress, by legislation, to protect a right derived from the national Constitution. But a prohibition upon a State is not a power in *Congress* or *in the national government*. It is simply a *denial of power* to the State. And the only mode in which the inhibition upon State laws impairing the obligation of contracts can be enforced is indirectly, through the courts in suits where the parties raise some question as to the constitutional validity of such laws. The judicial power of the United States extends to such suits for the reason that they are suits arising under the Constitution. The Fourteenth Amendment presents the first instance in our history of the investiture of Congress with affirmative power, by *legislation,* to *enforce* an express prohibition upon the States. It is not said that the *judicial* power of the nation may be exerted for the enforcement of that amendment. No enlargement of the judicial power was required, for it is clear that, had the fifth section of the Fourteenth Amendment been entirely omitted, the judiciary could have stricken down all State laws and nullified all State proceedings in hostility to rights and privileges secured or recognized by that amendment. The power given is, in terms, by congressional legislation, to enforce the provisions of the amendment.

The assumption that this amendment consists wholly of prohibitions upon State laws and State proceedings in hostility to its provisions is unauthorized by its language. The first clause of the first section—

> All persons born or naturalized in the United States, and subject to the jurisdiction thereof, are citizens of the United States, and of the State wherein they reside

—is of a distinctly affirmative character. In its application to the colored race, previously liberated, it created and granted as well citizenship of the United States as citizenship of the State in which they respectively resided. It introduced all of that race whose ancestors had been imported and sold as slaves at once into the political community known as the "People of the United States." They became instantly citizens of the United States and of their respective States. Further, they were brought by this supreme act of the nation within the direct operation of that provision of the Constitution which declares that "the citizens of each State shall be entitled to all privileges and immunities of citizens in the several States." ...

The citizenship thus acquired by that race in virtue of an affirmative grant from the nation may be protected not alone by the judicial branch of the government, but by congressional legislation of a primary direct character, this because the power of Congress is not restricted to the enforcement of prohibitions upon State laws or State action. It is, in terms distinct and positive, to enforce "the *provisions of this article*" of amendment; not simply those of a prohibitive character, but the provisions—*all* of the provisions—affirmative and prohibitive, of the amendment. It is, therefore, a grave misconception to suppose that the fifth section of the amendment has reference exclusively to express prohibitions upon State laws or State action. If any right was created by that amendment, the grant of power through appropriate legislation to enforce its provisions authorizes Congress, by means of legislation operating throughout the entire Union, to guard, secure, and protect that right.

It is therefore an essential inquiry what, if any, right, privilege or immunity was given, by the nation to colored persons when they were made citizens of the State in which they reside? Did the constitutional grant of State citizenship to that race, of its own force, invest them with any rights, privileges and immunities whatever? That they became entitled, upon the adoption of the Fourteenth Amendment, "to all privileges and immunities of citizens in the several States," within the meaning of section 2 of article 4 of the Constitution, no one, I suppose, will for a moment question. What are the privileges and immunities to which, by that clause of the Constitution, they became entitled? To this it may be answered generally, upon the authority of the adjudged cases, that they are those which are fundamental in citizenship in a free republican government, such as are "common to the citizens in the latter States under their constitutions and laws by virtue of their being citizens." Of that provision it has been said, with the approval of this court, that no other one in the Constitution has tended so strongly to constitute the citizens of the United States one people. *Ward v. Maryland,* ... *Corfield v. Coryell,* ... *Paul v. Virginia,* ... *Slaughterhouse Cases.*...

Although this court has wisely forborne any attempt by a comprehensive definition to indicate all of the privileges and immunities to which the citizen of a State is entitled of right when within the jurisdiction of other States, I hazard nothing, in view of former adjudications, in saying that no State can sustain her denial to colored citizens of other States, while within her limits, of privileges or immunities fundamental in republican citizenship upon the ground that she accords such privileges and immunities only to her white citizens, and withholds them from her colored citizens. The colored citizens of other States, within the jurisdiction of that State, could claim, in virtue of section 2 of article 4 of the Constitution, every privilege and immunity which that State secures to her white citizens. Otherwise it would be in the power of any State, by discriminating class legislation against its own citizens of a particular race or color, to withhold from citizens of other States belonging to that proscribed race, when within her limits, privileges and immunities of the character regarded by all courts as fundamental in citizenship, and that too when the constitutional guaranty is that the citizens of each State shall be entitled to "all privileges and immunities of citizens of the several States." No State may, by discrimination against a portion of its own citizens of a particular race, in respect of privileges and immunities fundamental in citizenship, impair the constitutional right of citizens of other States, of whatever race, to enjoy in that State all such privileges and immunities as are there accorded to her most favored citizens. A colored citizen of Ohio or Indiana, while in the jurisdiction of Tennessee, is entitled to enjoy any privilege or immunity, fundamental in citizenship, which is given to citizens of the white race in the latter State. It is not to be supposed that anyone will controvert this proposition.

But what was secured to colored citizens of the United States—as between them and their respective States—by the national grant to them of State citizenship? With what rights, privileges, or immunities did this grant invest them? There is one, if there be no other—exemption from race discrimination in respect of any civil right belonging to citizens of the white race in the same State. That, surely, is their constitutional privilege when within the jurisdiction of other States. And such must be their constitutional right in their own State, unless the recent amendments be splendid baubles thrown out to delude those who deserved fair and generous treatment at the hands of the nation. Citizenship in this country necessarily imports at least equality of civil rights among citizens of every race in the same State. It is fundamental in American citizenship that, in respect of such rights, there shall be no discrimination by the State, or its officers, or by individuals or corporations exercising public functions or authority, against any citizen because of his race or previous condition of servitude. In *United States v. Cruikshank,* … it was said at page 555, that the rights of life and personal liberty are natural rights of man, and that "the equality of the rights of citizens is a principle of republicanism." And in *Ex parte Virginia,* … the emphatic language of this court is that one great purpose of these amendments was to raise the colored race from that condition of inferiority and servitude in which most of them had previously stood into perfect equality of civil rights with all other persons within the jurisdiction of the States.

So, in *Strauder v. West Virginia,* … the court, alluding to the Fourteenth Amendment, said:

> This is one of a series of constitutional provisions having a common purpose, namely, securing to a race recently emancipated, a race that, through many generations, had been held in slavery, all the civil rights that the superior race enjoy.

Again, in *Neal v. Delaware,* … it was ruled that this amendment was designed primarily to secure to the colored race, thereby invested with the rights, privileges, and responsibilities of citizenship, the enjoyment of all the civil rights that, under the law, are enjoyed by white persons.

The language of this court with reference to the Fifteenth Amendment adds to the force of this view. In *United States v. Cruikshank,* it was said:

> In *United States v. Reese,* … we held that the Fifteenth Amendment has invested the citizens of the United States with a new constitutional right, which is exemption from discrimination in the exercise of the elective franchise, on account of race, color, or previous condition of servitude. From this it appears that the right of suffrage is not a necessary attribute of national citizenship, but that exemption from discrimination in the exercise of that right on account of race, &c., is. The right to vote in the States comes from the States, but the right of exemption from the prohibited discrimination comes from the United States. The first has not been granted or secured by the Constitution of the United States, but the last has been.

Here, in language at once clear and forcible, is stated the principle for which I contend. It can scarcely be claimed that exemption from race discrimination, in respect of civil rights, against those to whom State citizenship was granted by the nation, is any less, for the colored race, a new constitutional right, derived from and secured by the national Constitution, than is exemption from such discrimination in the exercise of the elective franchise. It cannot be that the latter is an attribute of national citizenship, while the other is not essential in national citizenship or fundamental in State citizenship.

If, then, exemption from discrimination in respect of civil rights is a new constitutional right, secured by the grant of State citizenship to colored citizens of the United States—and I do not see how this can now be questioned—why may not the nation, by means of its own legislation of a primary direct character, guard, protect, and enforce that right? It is a right and privilege which the nation conferred. It did not come from the States in which those colored citizens reside. It has been the established doctrine of this court during all its history, accepted as essential to the national supremacy, that Congress, in the absence of a positive delegation of power to the State legislatures, may, by its own legislation, enforce and protect any right derived from or created by the national Constitution. It was so declared in *Prigg v. Commonwealth of Pennsylvania*. It was reiterated in *United States v. Reese*, ... where the court said that rights and immunities created by and dependent upon the Constitution of the United States can be protected by Congress. The form and manner of the protection may be such as Congress, in the legitimate exercise of its discretion, shall provide. These may be varied to meet the necessities of the particular right to be protected.

It was distinctly reaffirmed in *Strauder v. West Virginia*, ... where we said that a right or immunity created by the Constitution or only guaranteed by it, even without any express delegation of power, may be protected by Congress.

How then can it be claimed, in view of the declarations of this court in former cases, that exemption of colored citizens, within their States, from race discrimination in respect of the civil rights of citizens is not an immunity created or derived from the national Constitution?

This court has always given a broad and liberal construction to the Constitution, so as to enable Congress, by legislation, to enforce rights secured by that instrument. The legislation which Congress may enact in execution of its power to enforce the provisions of this amendment is such as may be appropriate to protect the right granted. The word appropriate was undoubtedly used with reference to its meaning, as established by repeated decisions of this court. Under given circumstances, that which the court characterizes as corrective legislation might be deemed by Con-

gress appropriate and entirely sufficient. Under other circumstances, primary direct legislation may be required. But it is for Congress, not the judiciary, to say that legislation is appropriate—that is, best adapted to the end to be attained. The judiciary may not, with safety to our institutions, enter the domain of legislative discretion and dictate the means which Congress shall employ in the exercise of its granted powers. That would be sheer usurpation of the functions of a coordinate department, which, if often repeated, and permanently acquiesced in, would work a radical change in our system of government. In *United States v. Fisher*, ... the court said that Congress must possess the choice of means, and must be empowered to use any means which are, in fact, conducive to the exercise of a power granted by the Constitution.... The sound construction of the Constitution, said Chief Justice Marshall, must allow to the national legislature that discretion, with respect to the means by which the powers it confers are to be carried into execution, which will enable that body to perform the high duties assigned to it in the manner most beneficial to the people. Let the end be legitimate, let it be within the scope of the Constitution, and all means which are appropriate, which are plainly adapted to that end, which are not prohibited, but consist with the letter and spirit of the Constitution, are constitutional. *McCulloch v. Maryland*....

Must these rules of construction be now abandoned? Are the powers of the national legislature to be restrained in proportion as the rights and privileges, derived from the nation, are valuable? Are constitutional provisions, enacted to secure the dearest rights of freemen and citizens, to be subjected to that rule of construction, applicable to private instruments, which requires that the words to be interpreted must be taken most strongly against those who employ them? Or shall it be remembered that a constitution of government, founded by the people for themselves and their posterity and for objects of the most momentous nature—for perpetual union, for the establishment of justice, for the general welfare, and for a perpetuation of the blessings of liberty—necessarily requires that every interpretation of its powers should have a constant reference to these objects? No interpretation of the words in which those powers are granted can be a sound one which narrows down their ordinary import so as to defeat those objects.

Story Const. §422.

The opinion of the court, as I have said, proceeds upon the ground that the power of Congress to legislate for the protection of the rights and privileges secured by the Fourteenth Amendment cannot be brought into activity except with the view, and as it may become necessary, to correct and annul State laws and State proceedings in hostility to such rights and privileges. In the absence of State laws or State action adverse to such rights and privileges, the nation may not actively interfere for their protection and security, even against corporations and individuals exercising public or *quasi*-public functions. Such I understand to be the position of my brethren. If the grant to colored citizens of the United States of citizenship in their respective States imports exemption from race discrimination in their States in respect of such civil rights as belong to citizenship, then to hold that the amendment remits that right to the States for their protection, primarily, and stays the hands of the nation until it is assailed by State laws or State proceedings is to adjudge that the amendment, so far from enlarging the powers of Congress—as we have heretofore said it did—not only curtails them, but reverses the policy which the general government has pursued from its very organization. Such an interpretation of the amendment is a denial to Congress of the power, by appropriate legislation, to enforce one of its provisions. In view of the circumstances under which the recent amendments were incorporated into the Constitution, and especially in view of the peculiar character of the new rights they created and secured, it ought not to be presumed that the general government has abdicated its authority, by national legislation, direct and primary in its character, to guard and protect privileges and immunities secured by that instrument. Such an interpretation of the Constitution ought not to be accepted if it be possible to avoid it. Its acceptance would lead to this anomalous result: that, whereas, prior to the amendments, Congress, with the sanction of this court, passed the most stringent laws—operating directly and primarily upon States and their officers and agents, as well as upon individuals—in vindication of slavery and the right of the master, it may not now, by legislation of a like primary and direct character, guard, protect, and secure the freedom established, and the most essential right of the citizenship granted, by the constitutional amendments. With all respect for the opinion of others, I insist that the national legislature may, without transcending the limits of the Constitution, do for human liberty and the fundamental rights of American citizenship what it did, with the sanction of this court, for the protection of slavery and the rights of the masters of fugitive slaves. If fugitive slave laws, providing modes and prescribing penal-

ties whereby the master could seize and recover his fugitive slave, were legitimate exercises of an implied power to protect and enforce a right recognized by the Constitution, why shall the hands of Congress be tied so that—under an express power, by appropriate legislation, to enforce a constitutional provision granting citizenship—it may not, by means of direct legislation, bring the whole power of this nation to bear upon States and their officers and upon such individuals and corporations exercising public functions as assume to abridge, impair, or deny rights confessedly secured by the supreme law of the land?

It does not seem to me that the fact that, by the second clause of the first section of the Fourteenth Amendment, the States are expressly prohibited from making or enforcing laws abridging the privileges and immunities of citizens of the United States furnishes any sufficient reason for holding or maintaining that the amendment was intended to deny Congress the power, by general, primary, and direct legislation, of protecting citizens of the several States, being also citizens of the United States, against all discrimination in respect of their rights as citizens which is founded on race, color, or previous condition of servitude.

Such an interpretation of the amendment is plainly repugnant to its fifth section, conferring upon Congress power, by appropriate legislation, to enforce not merely the provisions containing prohibitions upon the States, but all of the provisions of the amendment, including the provisions, express and implied, in the first clause of the first section of the article granting citizenship. This alone is sufficient for holding that Congress is not restricted to the enactment of laws adapted to counteract and redress the operation of State legislation, or the action of State officers, of the character prohibited by the amendment. It was perfectly well known that the great danger to the equal enjoyment by citizens of their rights as citizens was to be apprehended not altogether from unfriendly State legislation, but from the hostile action of corporations and individuals in the States. And it is to be presumed that it was intended by that section to clothe Congress with power and authority to meet that danger. If the rights intended to be secured by the act of 1875 are such as belong to the citizen in common or equally with other citizens in the same State, then it is not to be denied that such legislation is peculiarly appropriate to the end which Congress is authorized to accomplish, *viz.,* to protect the citizen, in respect of such rights, against discrimination on account of his race. Recurring to the specific prohibition in the Fourteenth Amendment upon the making or enforcing of State laws abridging the privileges of citizens of the United States, I remark that if, as held in the *Slaughterhouse Cases,* the privileges here referred to were those which belonged to citizenship of the United States, as distinguished from those belonging to State citizenship, it was impossible for any State prior to the adoption of that amendment to have enforced laws of that character. The judiciary could have annulled all such legislation under the provision that the Constitution shall be the supreme law of the land, anything in the constitution or laws of any State to the contrary notwithstanding. The States were already under an implied prohibition not to abridge any privilege or immunity belonging to citizens of the United States as such. Consequently, the prohibition upon State laws in hostility to rights belonging to citizens of the United States was intended—in view of the introduction into the body of citizens of a race formerly denied the essential rights of citizenship—only as an express limitation on the powers of the States, and was not intended to diminish in the slightest degree the authority which the nation has always exercised of protecting, by means of its own direct legislation, rights created or secured by the Constitution. Any purpose to diminish the national authority in respect of privileges derived from the nation is distinctly negatived by the express grant of power by legislation to enforce every provision of the amendment, including that which, by the grant of citizenship in the State, secures exemption from race discrimination in respect of the civil rights of citizens.

It is said that any interpretation of the Fourteenth Amendment different from that adopted by the majority of the court would imply that Congress had authority to enact a municipal code for all the States covering every matter affecting the life, liberty, and property of the citizens of the several States. Not so. Prior to the adoption of that amendment, the constitutions of the several States, without perhaps an exception, secured all *persons* against deprivation of life, liberty, or property otherwise than by due process of law, and, in some form, recognized the right of all *persons* to the equal protection of the laws. Those rights therefore existed before that amendment was proposed or adopted, and were not created by it. If, by reason of that fact, it be assumed that protection in these rights of persons still rests primarily with the States, and that Congress may not interfere except to enforce, by means of corrective legislation, the prohibitions upon State laws or State proceedings inconsistent with those rights, it does not at all follow that privileges which have been *granted by the*

nation may not be protected by primary legislation upon the part of Congress. The personal rights and immunities recognized in the prohibitive clauses of the amendment were, prior to its adoption, under the protection, primarily, of the States, while rights, created by or derived from the United States have always been and, in the nature of things, should always be, primarily under the protection of the general government. Exemption from race discrimination in respect of the civil rights which are fundamental in *citizenship* in a republican government, is, as we have seen, a new right, created by the nation, with express power in Congress, by legislation, to enforce the constitutional provision from which it is derived. If, in some sense, such race discrimination is, within the letter of the last clause of the first section, a denial of that equal protection of the laws which is secured against State denial to all persons, whether citizens or not, it cannot be possible that a mere prohibition upon such State denial, or a prohibition upon State laws abridging the privileges and immunities of citizens of the United States, takes from the nation the power which it has uniformly exercised of protecting, by direct primary legislation, those privileges and immunities which existed under the Constitution before the adoption of the Fourteenth Amendment or have been created by that amendment in behalf of those thereby made *citizens* of their respective States.

This construction does not in any degree intrench upon the just rights of the States in the control of their domestic affairs. It simply recognizes the enlarged powers conferred by the recent amendments upon the general government. In the view which I take of those amendments, the States possess the same authority which they have always had to define and regulate the civil rights which their own people, in virtue of State citizenship, may enjoy within their respective limits, except that its exercise is now subject to the expressly granted power of Congress, by legislation, to enforce the provisions of such amendments—a power which necessarily carries with it authority, by national legislation, to protect and secure the privileges and immunities which are created by or are derived from those amendments. That exemption of citizens from discrimination based on race or color, in respect of civil rights, is one of those privileges or immunities can no longer be deemed an open question in this court.

It was said of the case of *Dred Scott v. Sandford* that this court there overruled the action of two generations, virtually inserted a new clause in the Constitution, changed its character, and made a new departure in the workings of the federal government. I may be permitted to say that, if the recent amendments are so construed that Congress may not, in its own discretion and independently of the action or nonaction of the States, provide by legislation of a direct character for the security of rights created by the national Constitution, if it be adjudged that the obligation to protect the fundamental privileges and immunities granted by the Fourteenth Amendment to citizens residing in the several States rests primarily not on the nation, but on the States, if it be further adjudged that individuals and corporations exercising public functions or wielding power under public authority may, without liability to direct primary legislation on the part of Congress, make the race of citizens the ground for denying them that equality of civil rights which the Constitution ordains as a principle of republican citizenship, then not only the foundations upon which the national supremacy has always securely rested will be materially disturbed, but we shall enter upon an era of constitutional law when the rights of freedom and American citizenship cannot receive from the nation that efficient protection which heretofore was unhesitatingly accorded to slavery and the rights of the master.

But if it were conceded that the power of Congress could not be brought into activity until the rights specified in the act of 1875 had been abridged or denied by some State law or State action, I maintain that the decision of the court is erroneous. There has been adverse State action within the Fourteenth Amendment as heretofore interpreted by this court. I allude to *Ex parte Virginia, supra*. It appears in that case that one Cole, judge of a county court, was charged with the duty by the laws of Virginia of selecting grand and petit jurors. The law of the State did not authorize or permit him, in making such selections, to discriminate against colored citizens because of their race. But he was indicted in the federal court, under the act of 1875, for making such discriminations. The attorney general of Virginia contended before us that the State had done its duty, and had not authorized or directed that county judge to do what he was charged with having done; that the State had not denied to the colored race the equal protection of the laws, and that consequently the act of Cole must be deemed his individual act, in contravention of the will of the State. Plausible as this argument was, it failed to convince this court, and after saying that the Fourteenth Amendment had reference to the political body denominated a State "by whatever instruments or in whatever modes that action may be taken," and that a State acts by its legislative, executive, and judicial authorities, and can act in no other way, we proceeded:

The constitutional provision, therefore, must mean that no agency of the State or of the officers

Glossary

a fortiori	Latin for "with even stronger reason"
act of 1875	the Civil Rights Act of 1875
Black Code	any state or local law or set of laws intended to limit the rights or liberties of African Americans
Blackstone	Sir William Blackstone, a preeminent jurist in eighteenth-century England and the author of *Commentaries on the Laws of England*
brutum fulmen	Latin for "inert thunder," meaning an empty threat or display of force
Chief Justice Marshall	John Marshall, chief justice of the United States in the early nineteenth century, best known for his decisions strengthening the power of the federal government
Chief Justice Taney	Roger Taney, chief justice of the United States remembered primarily for delivering the majority opinion in *Dred Scott v. Sandford*
ex directo	a Latin expression meaning literally "from the direct"; directly, immediately
ex parte	Latin for "by (or for) one party," used in the law to refer to a legal proceeding brought by one party without the presence of the other being required
feudal vassalage	the state of being a serf, owing allegiance to a lord, under the medieval feudal system

or agents by whom its powers are exerted shall deny to any person within its jurisdiction the equal protection of the laws. Whoever, by virtue of public position under a State government, deprives another of property, life, or liberty without due process of law, or denies or takes away the equal protection of the laws, violates the constitutional inhibition; and, as he acts under the name and for the State, and is clothed with the State's power, his act is that of the State. This must be so, or the constitutional prohibition has no meaning. Then the State has clothed one of its agents with power to annul or evade it. But the constitutional amendment was ordained for a purpose. It was to secure equal rights to all persons, and, to insure to all persons the enjoyment of such rights, power was given to Congress to enforce its provisions by appropriate legislation. Such legislation must act upon persons, not upon the abstract thing denominated a State, but upon the persons who are the agents of the State in the denial of the rights which were intended to be secured. *Ex parte Virginia*....

In every material sense applicable to the practical enforcement of the Fourteenth Amendment, railroad corporations, keepers of inns, and managers of places of public amusement are agents or instrumentalities of the State, because they are charged with duties to the public and are amenable, in respect of their duties and functions, to governmental regulation. It seems to me that, within the principle settled in *Ex parte Virginia,* a denial by these instrumentalities of the State to the citizen, because of his race, of that equality of civil rights secured to him by law is a denial by the State within the meaning of the Fourteenth Amendment. If it be not, then that race is left, in respect of the civil rights in question, practically at the mercy of corporations and individuals wielding power under the States.

But the court says that Congress did not, in the act of 1866, assume, under the authority given by the Thirteenth Amendment, to adjust what may be called the social rights of men and races in the community. I agree that government has nothing to do with social, as distinguished from technically legal, rights of individuals. No government ever has brought, or ever can bring, its people into social intercourse against their wishes. Whether one person will permit or maintain social relations with another is a matter with which government has no concern. I agree

Judge Story	Joseph Story, an early-nineteenth-century U.S. Supreme Court justice and author of the legal treatise *Commentaries on the Law of Bailments*
juris private	Latin for "of private right" (as opposed to public right)
Lord Chief Justice Hale	Matthew Hale, Lord Chief Justice of England in the seventeenth century
Mr. Justice Coleridge	John Coleridge, the Lord Chief Justice of England in the late eighteenth century
"no rights which the white man was bound to respect"	an oft-quoted line from the Supreme Court's decision in *Dred Scott v. Sandford*
nugatory	of no value, trifling, ineffective
posse comitatus	Latin for "power of the county" and referring to a municipality's power to form a temporary police force, commonly called a posse
self-executing	a law that takes effect immediately under given conditions, without the need for any intervening court action
Territories	the western lands that would later become U.S. states
viz.	abbreviation of the Latin word *videlicet*, meaning "that is"
writ of error	a judicial writ from an appellate court ordering the court of record to produce the records of trial; an appeal

that, if one citizen chooses not to hold social intercourse with another, he is not and cannot be made amenable to the law for his conduct in that regard, for even upon grounds of race, no legal right of a citizen is violated by the refusal of others to maintain merely social relations with him. What I affirm is that no State, nor the officers of any State, nor any corporation or individual wielding power under State authority for the public benefit or the public convenience, can, consistently either with the freedom established by the fundamental law or with that equality of civil rights which now belongs to every citizen, discriminate against freemen or citizens in those rights because of their race, or because they once labored under the disabilities of slavery imposed upon them as a race. The rights which Congress, by the act of 1875, endeavored to secure and protect are legal, not social, rights. The right, for instance, of a colored citizen to use the accommodations of a public highway upon the same terms as are permitted to white citizens is no more a social right than his right under the law to use the public streets of a city or a town, or a turnpike road, or a public market, or a post office, or his right to sit in a public building with others, of whatever race, for the purpose of hearing the political questions of the day discussed. Scarcely a day passes without our seeing in this courtroom citizens of the white and black races sitting side by side, watching the progress of our business. It would never occur to anyone that the presence of a colored citizen in a courthouse, or courtroom, was an invasion of the social rights of white persons who may frequent such places. And yet such a suggestion would be quite as sound in law—I say it with all respect—as is the suggestion that the claim of a colored citizen to use, upon the same terms as is permitted to white citizens, the accommodations of public highways, or public inns, or places of public amusement, established under the license of the law, is an invasion of the social rights of the white race.

The court, in its opinion, reserves the question whether Congress, in the exercise of its power to regulate commerce amongst the several States, might or might not pass a law regulating rights in public conveyances passing from one State to another. I beg to suggest that that precise question was substantially presented here in the only one of these cases relating to railroads—*Robinson and Wife v. Memphis & Charleston Railroad Company.* In that case, it appears that Mrs. Robinson, a citizen of Mississippi, purchased a railroad ticket entitling her to be carried from Grand Junction, Tennessee, to Lynchburg, Virginia. Might not the act of 1875 be maintained in that case as applicable at least to commerce between the States, notwithstanding it does not, upon its face, profess to have been passed in pursuance of the power of Congress to regulate commerce? Has it ever been held that the judiciary should overturn a statute because the legislative department did not accurately recite therein the particular provision of the Constitution authorizing its enactment? We have often enforced municipal bonds in aid of railroad subscriptions where they failed to recite the statute authorizing their issue, but recited one which did not sustain their validity. The inquiry in such cases has been was there, in any statute, authority for the execution of the bonds? Upon this branch of the case, it may be remarked that the State of Louisiana, in 1869, passed a statute giving to passengers, without regard to race or color, equality of right in the accommodations of railroad and street cars, steamboats or other watercrafts, stage coaches, omnibuses, or other vehicles. But in *Hall v. De Cuir,* ... that act was pronounced unconstitutional so far as it related to commerce between the States, this court saying that, "if the public good requires such legislation, it must come from Congress, and not from the States." I suggest, that it may become a pertinent inquiry whether Congress may, in the exertion of its power to regulate commerce among the States, enforce among passengers on public conveyances equality of right, without regard to race, color or previous condition of servitude, if it be true—which I do not admit—that such legislation would be an interference by government with the social rights of the people.

My brethren say that, when a man has emerged from slavery, and by the aid of beneficent legislation has shaken off the inseparable concomitants of that state, there must be some stage in the progress of his elevation when he takes the rank of a mere citizen, and ceases to be the special favorite of the laws, and when his rights as a citizen or a man are to be protected in the ordinary modes by which other men's rights are protected. It is, I submit, scarcely just to say that the colored race has been the special favorite of the laws. The statute of 1875, now adjudged to be unconstitutional, is for the benefit of citizens of every race and color. What the nation, through Congress, has sought to accomplish in reference to that race is what had already been done in every State of the Union for the white race—to secure and protect rights belonging to them as freemen and citizens, nothing more. It was not deemed enough "to help the feeble up, but to support him after." The one underlying purpose of congressional legislation has been to enable the black race to take the rank of mere citizens. The difficulty has been to compel a recognition of the legal right of the black race to take the rank of citizens, and to secure the enjoyment of privileges belonging, under the law, to them as a component part of the people for whose welfare and happiness government is ordained. At every step in this direction, the nation has been confronted with class tyranny, which a contemporary English historian says is, of all tyrannies, the most intolerable, for it is ubiquitous in its operation and weighs perhaps most heavily on those whose obscurity or distance would withdraw them from the notice of a single despot.

Today it is the colored race which is denied, by corporations and individuals wielding public authority, rights fundamental in their freedom and citizenship. At some future time, it may be that some other race will fall under the ban of race discrimination. If the constitutional amendments be enforced according to the intent with which, as I conceive, they were adopted, there cannot be, in this republic, any class of human beings in practical subjection to another class with power in the latter to dole out to the former just such privileges as they may choose to grant. The supreme law of the land has decreed that no authority shall be exercised in this country upon the basis of discrimination, in respect of civil rights, against freemen and citizens because of their race, color, or previous condition of servitude. To that decree—for the due enforcement of which, by appropriate legislation, Congress has been invested with express power—everyone must bow, whatever may have been, or whatever now are, his individual views as to the wisdom or policy either of the recent changes in the fundamental law or of the legislation which has been enacted to give them effect.

For the reasons stated, I feel constrained to withhold my assent to the opinion of the court.

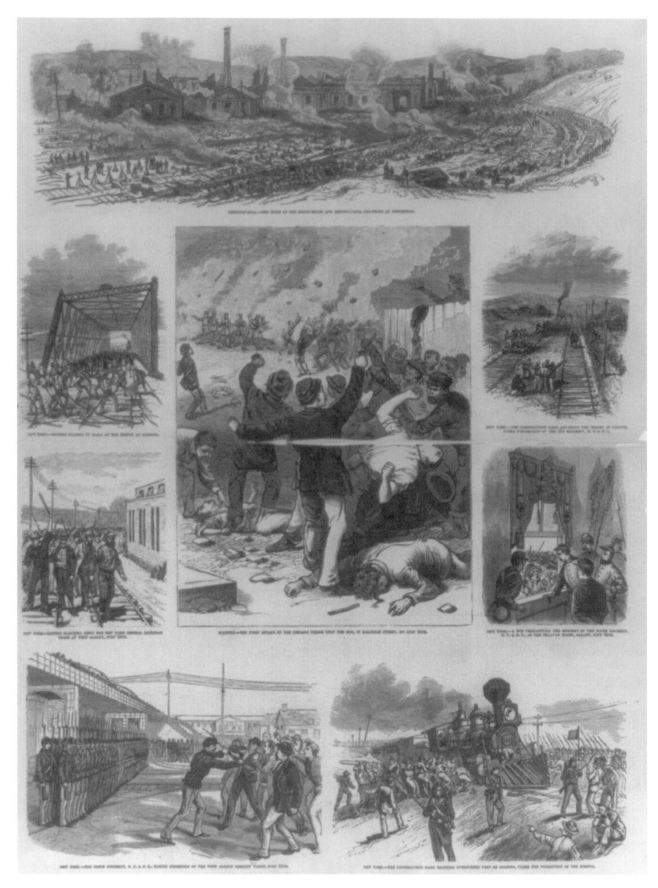

Scenes of the 1877 railroad strike, from Chicago, Illinois; Pittsburgh, Pennsylvania; and Corning and Albany, New York (Library of Congress)

T. Thomas Fortune: "The Present Relations of Labor and Capital"

"I abhor injustice and oppression wherever they are to be found."

Overview

T. Thomas Fortune's speech "The Present Relations of Labor and Capital" was an important statement of economic radicalism by a leading black writer, newspaper editor, and political activist of the late nineteenth century. The speech was given on April 20, 1886, and then first appeared in print on May 1—May Day—in Fortune's newspaper, the *New York Freeman*. Fortune was one of the few high-profile black leaders of the era to voice his support for the labor movement and to embrace Socialist principles. Fortune believed that industrial labor unions, concentrated in northern cities and western mining towns, ought to ally themselves with southern black agricultural laborers in common cause against monopolists of wealth and property. Fortune's position put him outside the mainstream political discourse, and he echoed some of the most radical elements of the labor movement.

Context

When the Civil War ended in 1865, Fortune was just eight years old. The Thirteenth Amendment to the Constitution, ratified later that year, permanently abolished slavery in the United States and marked the beginning of a new era. Fortune's generation of African Americans would be the first to grow up in the United States without the institution, and the next fifteen years would be characterized by political strife over the rights of former slaves. The policy of Reconstruction in the former slave states, directed by the Republican Party leaders in Congress, brought new constitutional rights for black Americans, including the guarantee of equality before the law, the rights to hold political office and serve on juries, and the right to manhood suffrage. The majority of white southerners vigorously opposed these policies, and some resorted to organized violence and terrorism to deprive blacks of their rights, joining shadowy groups like the Ku Klux Klan. While Republicans held on to power in the South for as long as fifteen years in some places, the white-supremacist-dominated Democratic

Party gained control of the governments in all the southern states by the late 1870s. The 1880s would be a period of transition in which white landowners would tighten their control over black laborers in the South while still professing to recognize their basic right to political and civil equality—though in practice many blacks were unable to exercise their rights freely.

Despite its downfall, Reconstruction brought new opportunities and aspirations for upward mobility to former slaves. Whereas slaves had been forbidden by law to be literate in the antebellum South, the post–Civil War South witnessed the rapid proliferation of schools for African Americans. Republican rule in the South during Reconstruction ushered in a new era of taxpayer-supported public schools and privately supported institutions of higher education, established by northern philanthropists and religious organizations. By the 1870s, a college-educated class of black leaders was emerging from the ranks of former slaves and their families. Newspapers owned and operated by African Americans also proliferated as black literacy grew and black political leadership established itself in the Reconstruction era. Since white-owned newspapers rarely spoke to the issues of the black community, black editors became natural leaders of their own community, addressing pressing issues and shaping public opinion.

African Americans suffered many bitter disappointments and frustrations through the resurgence of racial oppression and economic exploitation that prevailed in the South with the downfall of Reconstruction. Economically, the transition from slavery to a strictly capitalist economy stalled as the South failed to break up the cash-crop plantation system. The wealthiest landowners continued to invest in raising large crops of cotton, tobacco, and sugar—primarily cotton—despite overproduction that glutted the market and caused prices to fall. Black workers, meanwhile, continued to dominate the southern agricultural workforce, as they had as slaves, receiving now a share of the crop in lieu of wages. Because of falling prices, workers and often landowners as well found themselves falling further and further into debt. For blacks, the consequences of becoming debt ridden were dire, leaving them at the mercy of the landowners and merchants on whom they depended for credit. Debt-ridden blacks were tied to the land, forced to

1884

- **October**
The Federation of Organized Trades and Labor Unions declares that May 1, 1886, will be the beginning of the eight-hour workday and that May Day will be an International Workers' Day.

- **December**
Having published *Black and White: Land, Labor, and Politics in the South* earlier in the year, Fortune starts the *New York Freeman* newspaper.

1885

- Fortune publishes the pamphlet "The Negro in Politics."

1886

- **April 20**
Fortune delivers his speech "The Present Relations of Labor and Capital" to the Brooklyn Literary Union, in New York.

- **May 1**
"The Present Relations of Labor and Capital" is published in the *New York Freeman*. Hundreds of thousands of workers across the country demonstrate for an eight-hour workday.

- **May 4**
The demonstrations grow deadly in Chicago's Haymarket Square when a bomb explodes, sparking a riot and leading to the deaths of workers and police.

1887

- Fortune resigns as editor of the *New York Freeman* and launches the *New York Age*.

1890

- The National Afro-American League is formed in Chicago.

1895

- **September 18**
Booker T. Washington gives his Atlanta Exposition Address.

1900

- Fortune supports Booker T. Washington in the formation of the National Negro Business League and ghostwrites *A New Negro for a New Century* in Washington's name.

continue raising cash crops under increasingly harsh conditions while surrendering their shares to cover their debts.

While black southerners were fast becoming a landless peasantry in the South with no avenue for upward mobility, white and black laborers alike in the industrial North and West found themselves at the mercy of corporate monopolies. The financial depression of the mid-1870s rocked the country as a whole, leaving millions out of work and depleting the savings of the working classes through the bank failures of 1873–1874—including that of the Freedman's Saving and Trust Company, which lost millions of dollars saved by former slaves when the institution became insolvent in 1874. In 1877, the severe conditions led to a massive strike against the monopolistic railroad companies that were slashing wages repeatedly in the face of declining profits. Although it was violently repressed by federal and state troops, the great railroad strike of 1877 launched a national labor movement and convinced many reformers that an impending new "civil war" between labor and capital was imminent.

In the 1880s labor organizations of all stripes grew in strength and number across the nation. The Knights of Labor emerged as the most powerful national organization devoted to the issues of the working classes. The group sought to organize all workers—skilled and unskilled, men and women, white and black. By 1886, the Knights boasted over seven hundred thousand members. Although they predominantly focused on industrial labor, the Knights were willing to organize black agricultural laborers, making inroads among sugar plantation workers in Louisiana in the late 1880s. Calls for an eight-hour workday were among the most popular of their demands, but the Knights also opposed the convict-lease system, which addressed one of the most important issues facing the black community in the South. Blacks made up a disproportionately high number of the incarcerated population in the South, which state governments had begun to use as a source of cheap labor by leasing them to work for corporations and thus depressing both wages and the labor market. While progress toward an interracial movement was still embryonic, there was some reason for hope that the interests of African Americans would not be completely excluded in the industrial labor movement.

"The Present Relations of Labor and Capital" was given as a speech on April 20, 1886, and subsequently appeared in print on the significant date of May 1, 1886, in Fortune's newspaper, the *New York Freeman*. In 1884, the Federation of Organized Trades and Labor Unions had called for a shorter, eight-hour workday, to commence on May 1, 1886. Heeding this call, hundreds of thousands of workers across the country instituted a work stoppage on May 1, 1886, to demand an eight-hour workday and celebrate May Day as an International Workers' Day. In Chicago, over forty thousand workers went on strike that day, and over the next two days an even greater number of strikers joined the ranks. A clash between strikers and police in Haymarket Square on May 4 turned violent when a bomb exploded, killing a police officer. In retaliation, many workers in the crowd were shot and beaten by the police, who also accidentally fired upon each other; in the course of what became known as the Haymarket Riot, seven additional policemen and an unknown number of civilians were killed, and many more were wounded. After eight anarchists were put on trial for plotting the bomb attack, public opinion turned decisively against the strikers and the trade unions. Eventually, four men were executed for the bombing, and the Socialist ideas they represented received a devastating blow. May 1, 1886, was the apex of the nineteenth-century labor movement in America before its precipitous decline.

About the Author

T. Thomas Fortune was one of the leading black editors of the late nineteenth century, with a reputation for militancy and independence from major political parties. He was born a slave on October 3, 1856, in Marianna, Florida. During Reconstruction, his family moved to Jacksonville, Florida, in the wake of growing threats by the Ku Klux Klan. Fortune's father, Emanuel Fortune, was very active in Reconstruction politics and served as a Republican congressman in Florida's House of Representatives.

Fortune began working at newspapers as a printer's apprentice when he was still a teenager. In 1876 he briefly attended Howard University in Washington, D.C, but left for financial reasons. After marrying Carrie Smiley in 1877, he returned to Florida and taught school. The Fortunes moved to New York City in 1878, and Fortune began working for the *Weekly Witness*. Fortune then founded the *New York Globe*, which he edited from 1881 to 1884. When the *Globe* ceased publication, Fortune founded the *New York Freeman*, a newspaper that was published until 1887, when it became the *New York Age*. In the 1890s, the *New York Age* became perhaps the most distinguished and widely read black newspaper in the country.

In 1884 Fortune published his most important work, *Black and White: Land, Labor, and Politics in the South*, an influential volume that looked at the problems facing African Americans in the South. Receiving wide attention in the press, the book launched Fortune's career as a spokesperson for African American rights and an early civil rights activist. In *The Negro in Politics* (1885), Fortune split with the Republican Party, which he felt had abandoned blacks, and declared that blacks must not subordinate the interests of their race to those of any party. In 1888 he openly campaigned for the Democratic candidate Grover Cleveland, to the horror of many black leaders who remained loyal to the party of Abraham Lincoln and the Emancipation Proclamation—and who regarded the Democrats as the party of the Confederacy and the Ku Klux Klan. Later, Fortune begrudgingly rejoined the Republican Party after acknowledging the extent of Democratic support for white supremacy.

In the late 1880s, Fortune organized a national civil rights organization that became the National Afro-American League in 1890. He strongly supported the term *Afro-American* over other labels of identity, such as *Negro* or *colored*, as a term for Americans of African descent. In the 1890s, Fortune notably supported Ida B. Wells's antilynch-

Time Line

1907
- Fortune ghostwrites *The Negro in Business* for Washington but then breaks with Washington later that year.

1923
- Fortune becomes the editor of *Negro World*, Marcus Garvey's newspaper.

1928
- **June 2** Fortune dies in Philadelphia at the age of seventy-one.

ing campaign, publishing her articles in the *Age*, and he also sued and won an antidiscrimination case against a hotel for denying him service.

According to the historian John H. Bracey, Jr., there were three main phases of Fortune's ideological development. During the early phase, in which he wrote *Black and White* and "The Present Relations of Labor and Capital," Fortune tended to view the problems of African Americans in the South through the lens of radical labor theory. He retreated from this position by the mid-1890s, aligning himself, in Bracey's words, with "the group economic development or bourgeois nationalism of Booker T. Washington." Fortune often served as a ghostwriter for Washington and received substantial financial support in exchange. Finally breaking with Washington in 1907, Fortune turned toward militant black nationalism and became the editor of Marcus Garvey's *Negro World* in the last years of his life. Fortune died on June 2, 1928, in Philadelphia.

Explanation and Analysis of the Document

In "The Present Relations of Labor and Capital," Fortune echoes the primary Socialist argument of the 1880s: The consolidation of capital and land in the hands of the few is the root problem of modern society and the source of all conflict. In his 1884 book *Black and White*, Fortune looked at the oppression of African Americans in the South through the dual lens of race and class, contending that white racism and an exploitative economic system acted together to subjugate blacks. Two years later in this speech, he focused exclusively on the common plight of the laboring poor, regardless of their nationality or race. The discussion of white racism that informed *Black and White* was missing altogether from this piece, as Fortune emphasized the common oppression of workers across the world.

Very quickly in "The Present Relations of Labor and Capital," the reader understands that Fortune is making a fundamentally Socialist argument. He starts the essay by stating that the inequalities between rich and poor have led to global

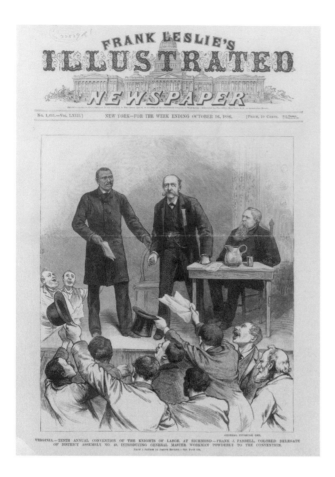

FRANK LESLIE'S ILLUSTRATED NEWSPAPER

At the tenth annual convention of the Knights of Labor, 1886, a black delegate (Frank J. Farrell) introduces the Knights leader, Terence Powderly. (Library of Congress)

unrest. He is not limiting his scope to African Americans or even to poor Americans. He speaks for all oppressed people, regardless of nation, creed, or race, and he warns that if there is not a return to egalitarian principles across the "civilized" world, violent upheaval will come about.

Stepping back from this apocalyptic warning, Fortune lays out the very basic needs that all people share: for food, water, clothing, shelter, and air. These needs are, as Fortune argues, "self evident" and not the subject of debate. He points to both early human history and the current practices of "savage people" to show that, in fact, these are natural rights. And yet, in the modern world, in "civilized" countries, these natural rights have been upended, as laws and practices conspire to place "the prime elements of human existence" into the hands of a fortunate few. Housing, food, and even freedom are doled out to the working masses sparingly, if at all, by the small wealthy minority. Fortune argues that society is organized, and its very laws orchestrated, for the sole purpose of maintaining and supplementing the wealth of a few at the expense of the majority. Implicit in his argument that the governments and laws of modern cultures are designed to continually repress the rights of workers is a call to action and rebellion. There can be no working within the system to achieve change if the system is corrupt.

This argument is made explicit when Fortune turns next to an analysis of the French Revolution. The rallying cry of the French Revolution (1789–1799) was "Liberté, Egalité, Fraternité" (Liberty, Equality, Brotherhood), and in this revolution that led to the overthrow of the monarchy, Fortune sees the "most memorable check" to the type of oppression that the working masses endure. In other words, it took a bloody revolution and the complete overthrow of the social order to shift the balance of power from the haves to the have-nots. The French Revolution also conjures images of the guillotine and the beheadings of many members of the French aristocracy, bringing home Fortune's opening point that if the economic and cultural system remains unchanged, the masses should be expected to revolt, and to revolt with violence.

Fortune next cites the slave rebellion in Haiti of 1791–1804, drawing a line from the ideals espoused in the French Revolution to this revolt. By doing so, he compares rebelling against slavery to rebelling against other forms of oppression; he places the slave revolt in Haiti in the same context as uprisings of white peasants, serfs, and the working poor. Fortune is implicitly arguing that whether agricultural laborers or factory workers, white or black, enslaved or free, the working masses should stand in solidarity against their oppressors—the landowners, the slave owners, the wealthy elite.

The slave revolt in Haiti, like the French Revolution, was known both for its extreme violence and for its success. The slaves secured their freedom and established the first black-ruled republic. Fortune references the Haitian leaders by name in the speech. Toussaint-Louverture, who had been born a slave in Saint Domingue (called Haiti after the revolt), was a free coachman when he became the leader of the revolt. Later, he established Haiti's constitution and was named governor-general for life. Fortune also names the "bloody Dessalines" and the "courtly Christophe." Jean-Jacques Dessalines, who was one of Toussaint-Louverture's lieutenants, eventually betrayed the revolutionary and named himself emperor of Haiti in 1805. He was assassinated in 1806. Henri Christophe, who plotted against Dessalines, was later the president and the king of Haiti. While these Haitian leaders, along with the leaders of the French Revolution, did not stay true to the Socialist principles that Fortune believes they originally stood for, they were notably successful at overthrowing entrenched social systems. These leaders emerged when their countries hit crises—when the slaves of Saint Domingue and the peasants of France could no longer tolerate the gulf between their conditions and those of the landed class. Their rebellions were bloody and ultimately short lived. In referring to these particular revolutions, Fortune is warning that another crisis has been reached, and he points to where the crisis might lead.

Fortune also cites the American Revolution as a crisis point and notes that the primary complaint then was against undue taxation. He believes that "bread and butter" were at the heart of the problem in all three of these revolutions and are at the heart of every crisis. Until there is balance between those who labor, those who supervise the laborers, and those who control the wealth (capital) that the laborers create, unrest and

Illustration of the Haymarket Riot, with portraits of seven policemen (Library of Congress)

revolution are inevitable. Under the current system, Fortune believes that in this "trinity," laborers are unfairly denied their rightful share of the wealth their sweat produces. And yet, without laborers, there can be no wealth. Fortune argues that if wealth itself is destroyed, it can and will be rebuilt through the work of laborers. The reverse is not true. Destroy the laborers, and no wealth can be produced.

Given this situation, Fortune argues, should we be surprised that labor is no longer satisfied? Modern culture has served to democratize and educate the masses, and they are no longer willing to sit silently as they are deprived while others amass fortunes. Fortune declares that the new crop of millionaires created in the past few decades offers more evidence that the system of laws is designed to create a minority of winners at the expense of the majority. These are the conditions that have led to the rising discontent of the working classes in America and Europe.

Fortune clearly states his own beliefs in equal rights for all men, regardless of their "caste or class." He believes that the laws that skew the division of wealth so unequally run counter to the laws of God. Divine law does not dictate that some men prosper while others suffer; the laws of man alone are responsible for inequity. By pointing to the example of miners in Siberia and poor black rice workers in the Carolinas, Fortune again implies that the working poor share a common oppression and should share common goals.

Fortune ends his piece by restating that the rising conflict between labor and capital is not new but has been ongoing for centuries. What has changed is that labor is rising and may now be in a position to meaningfully change a system that he sees as fundamentally oppressive. He points to England, where the monarchy has lost the absolute power it held in the time of Queen Elizabeth I, to show that the balance of power can change, if slowly. Equality for all may be possible.

Audience

As a speech, "The Present Relations of Labor and Capital" was given on April 20, 1886, to the Brooklyn Literary Union in Brooklyn, New York. This organization was originally founded by abolitionists as a youth self-help organization for African Americans. Established to promote literacy and spread knowledge, the group sought to be informed about the important literary and social issues of the day. Fortune printed his speech in his newspaper, the *New York Freeman*, on May 1, 1886. As with the literary union, the audience of the *Freeman* would have been an almost exclusively black audience. In both cases, Fortune conveyed a fairly straightforward Socialist analysis of labor and capital to an audience that probably had little familiarity with the works of Karl Marx and other Socialist thinkers.

"From the institution of feudalism to the present time the inspiration of all conflict has been that of capitalist, landowner and hereditary aristocracy against the larger masses of society the untitled, the disinherited proletariat of the world."

(Paragraph 6)

"Should we, therefore, be surprised that with the constantly growing intelligence and democratization of mankind labor should have grown discontented at the systematic robbery practiced upon it for centuries, and should now clamor for a more equitable basis of adjustment of the wealth it produces?"

(Paragraph 9)

Impact

The impact of Fortune's speech is difficult to determine. Many editorials and speeches like it were given on May 1, 1886, in the white newspapers, and they cumulatively inspired workers to demonstrate in New York and elsewhere on that day. Perhaps the Socialist militancy of these speeches also spread fear among opponents of the labor movement and heightened the fury of reactionaries. Since the Haymarket Riot occurred only days after "The Present Relations of Labor and Capital" was printed, the temper of the times subsequently changed drastically, and the essay's influence was short lived. Socialist ideas that might have been tolerated by many Americans in the days before Haymarket became intolerable afterward. The crackdown against labor radicals silenced many Socialists and drove opinions like those expressed in Fortune's speech underground. Fortune himself did not express Socialist views thereafter, turning his energies instead toward the founding of a black civil rights organization devoted to the protection of political and civil rights.

Within a few years of the Haymarket Riot, the Knights of Labor went defunct. Because the Knights had been one of the sponsors of the worker demonstration in Haymarket Square, the organization was unfairly depicted as a haven for Socialists, anarchists, and Communists who preached violent revolution—despite the fact that none of those accused of the bombing were members of the organization. Soon, the labor movement would be purged of its radical elements, and the more conservative American Federation of Labor—which excluded women, blacks, and unskilled labor—would become the mainstream voice of labor in the United States.

In general, black leaders turned away from radical ideas and civil rights protest movements by the mid-1890s. Concern for the labor movement was eclipsed by the rise of Jim Crow segregation as a new wave of white supremacist politics swept over the South in the 1890s. Partly in response to the growth of black agricultural labor organizations, a movement began among southern whites to legally disenfranchise African Americans and thus deprive them of power at the ballot box. This movement coincided with new segregation laws that enforced the separation of blacks and whites in public spaces and also with an outbreak of lynch mobs that victimized hundreds of southern blacks during this time. Confronted by this new tide of oppression, many black leaders sought a "truce" with white extremists by renouncing political agitation for equal rights.

Booker T. Washington epitomized what historians have called the "accommodationist" strategy in his speech before the Cotton States and International Exposition in Atlanta, Georgia, on September 18, 1895. Addressing an audience of white southerners—including political leaders—he suggested that racial harmony could be achieved if whites employed blacks as a faithful laboring class and blacks accepted a position of social inferiority for the time being. He proposed that blacks could improve themselves through hard work and financial thrift and eventually achieve middle-class status (though never social integration with whites). By accommodating white supremacy, Washington hoped to create economic opportunities that would enable blacks to build an independent economic base. In 1900 he founded the National Negro Business League, which promoted investment in black-owned businesses and sought to expand the black professional class of doctors, lawyers, and businessmen. By this time, Fortune was a supporter of Washington and was likewise urging the development of a black middle class.

Washington exerted a powerful influence in the years following his Atlanta speech. Enjoying extensive financial backing—especially by whites—he gained a following by bestowing patronage on individuals and institutions that supported his views. Many blacks hoped that Washington's work would stem the tide of white violence and dampen white fears about black revolution. But critics of Washington's work within the black community increased their objections as lynch mobs and white oppression failed to abate. By 1903 opponents of Washington began to be heard. In 1905, W. E. B. Du Bois and William Monroe Trotter established the Niagara Movement, which openly rejected the "accommodationist" strategy and announced a return to agitation for equal rights for blacks.

See also Emancipation Proclamation (1863); Thirteenth Amendment to the U.S. Constitution (1865); Booker T. Washington's Atlanta Exposition Address (1895); Niagara Movement Declaration of Principles (1905).

Further Reading

■ Books

Alexander, Shawn Leigh, ed. *T. Thomas Fortune, the Afro-American Agitator: A Collection of Writings, 1880–1928*. Gainesville: University Press of Florida, 2008.

Bracey, John H., Jr. Foreword to *Black and White: Land, Labor, and Politics in the South*, by T. Thomas Fortune. Chicago: Johnson Publishing, 1970.

Fortune, T. Thomas. *Black and White: Land, Labor, and Politics in the South*. 1884. Reprint. New York: Washington Square Press, 2007.

————. *The Negro in Politics*. N.p.: Ogilvie & Rowntree, 1885.

————. *Dreams of Life: Miscellaneous Poems*. 1905. Reprint. Miami: Mnemosyne Publishing, 1969.

Franklin, John Hope. *From Slavery to Freedom: A History of American Negroes*. New York: Alfred A. Knopf, 1947.

Franklin, John Hope, and August Meier, eds. *Black Leaders of the Twentieth Century*. Urbana: University of Illinois Press, 1981.

Marable, Manning, and Leith Mullings, eds. *Let Nobody Turn Us Around: Voices of Resistance, Reform, and Renewal; An African American Anthology*. Lanham, Md.: Rowman & Littlefield, 2000.

Smock, Raymond W. *Booker T. Washington: Black Leadership in the Age of Jim Crow*. Chicago: Ivan R. Dee, 2009.

Thornbrough, Emma Lou. *T. Thomas Fortune: Militant Journalist*. Chicago: University of Chicago Press, 1972.

■ Web Sites

"The Booker T. Washington Papers." History Cooperative Web site, University of Illinois Press.
 http://www.historycooperative.org/btw/index.html.

—Mark Elliott

Questions for Further Study

1. In what sense were Fortune's views considered "radical" in the late nineteenth century?

2. Describe the economic circumstances of black southern sharecroppers that impeded their economic development and that led to the kinds of views Fortune expressed.

3. Fortune did not restrict his analysis to black workers; his critique applied to workers of whatever race or color. Explain how Fortune's views transcended racial barriers.

4. Why do you believe Fortune and others who expressed similar views declined in popular acceptance in the late nineteenth and on into the twentieth centuries?

5. Compare this document with Booker T. Washington's Atlanta Exposition Address (1895). How did the economic views of the two writers differ?

T. Thomas Fortune: "The Present Relations of Labor and Capital"

I do not exaggerate the gravity of the subject when I say that it is now the very first in importance not only in the United States but in every country in Europe. Indeed the wall of industrial discontent encircles the civilized globe.

The iniquity of privileged class and concentrated wealth has become so glaring and grievous to be borne that a thorough agitation and an early readjustment of the relation which they sustain to labor can no longer be delayed with safety to society.

It does not admit of argument that every man born into the world is justly entitled to so much of the produce of nature as will satisfy his physical necessities; it does not admit of argument that every man, by reason of his being, is justly entitled to the air he must breathe, the water he must drink, the food he must eat and the covering he must have to shield him from the inclemency of the weather. These are self evident propositions, not disputed by the most orthodox advocate of excessive wealth on the one hand and excessive poverty on the other. That nature intended these as the necessary correlations of physical being is abundantly proved in the primitive history of mankind and in the freedom and commonality of possession which now obtain everywhere among savage people. The moment you deny to a man the unrestricted enjoyment of all the elements upon which the breath he draws is dependent, that moment you deny to him the inheritance to which he was born.

I maintain that organized society, as it obtains today, based as it is upon feudal conditions, is an outrageous engine of torture and an odious tyranny; that it places in the hands of a few the prime elements of human existence, regardless of the great mass of mankind; that the whole aim and necessity of the extensive and costly machinery of the law we are compelled to maintain grows out of the fact that this fortunate or favored minority would otherwise be powerless to practice upon the masses of society the gross injustice which everywhere prevails.

For centuries the aim and scope of all law have been to more securely hedge about the capitalist and the landowner and to repress labor within a condition wherein bare subsistence was the point aimed at.

From the institution of feudalism to the present time the inspiration of all conflict has been that of capitalist, landowner and hereditary aristocracy against the larger masses of society the untitled, the disinherited proletariat of the world.

This species of oppression received its most memorable check in the great French Revolution, wherein a new doctrine became firmly rooted in the philosophy of civil government that is, that the toiling masses of society possessed certain inherent rights which kingcraft, hereditary aristocracy, landlordism and usury mongers must respect. As a result of the doctrine studiously inculcated by the philosophers of the French Revolution we had the revolt of the blacks of Haiti, under the heroic Toussaint L'Ouverture, the bloody Dessalines and the suave, diplomatic and courtly Christophe, by which the blacks secured forever their freedom as free men and their independence as a people; and our own great Revolution, wherein the leading complaint was taxation by the British government of the American colonies without conceding them proportionate representation. At bottom in each case, bread and butter was the main issue. So it has always been. So it will continue to be, until the scales of justice are made to strike a true balance between labor on the one hand and the interest on capital invested and the wages of superintendence on the other. Heretofore the interest on capital and the wages of superintendence have absorbed so much of the wealth produced as to leave barely nothing to the share of labor.

It should be borne in mind that of this trinity labor is the supreme potentiality. Capital, in the first instance, is the product of labor. If there had never been any labor there would not now be any capital to invest. Again, if a bonfire were made of all the so called wealth of the world it would only require a few years for labor to reproduce it; but destroy the brawn and muscle of the world and it could not be reproduced by all the gold ever delved from the mines of California and Australia and the fabulous gems from the diamond fields of Africa. In short, labor has been and is the producing agency, while capital has been and is the absorbing or parasitical agency.

Should we, therefore, be surprised that with the constantly growing intelligence and democratization of mankind labor should have grown discontented at the systematic robbery practiced upon it for centuries, and should now clamor for a more equitable basis of adjustment of the wealth it produces?

I could name you a dozen men who have in the last forty or fifty years amassed among them a billion dollars, so that a millionaire has become as common a thing almost as a pauper. How came they by their millions? Is it possible for a man in his lifetime, under the most favorable circumstances, to amass a million dollars? Not at all! The constitution of our laws must be such that they favor one as against the other to permit of such a glaring disparity.

I have outlined for you the past and present relations of capital and labor. The widespread discontent of the labor classes in our own country and in Europe gives emphasis to the position here taken.

I abhor injustice and oppression wherever they are to be found, and my best sympathies go out freely to the struggling poor and the tyranny ridden of all races and lands. I believe in the divine right of man, not of caste or class, and I believe that any law made to perpetuate or to give immunity to these as against the masses of mankind is an infamous and not to be borne infringement of the just laws of the Creator, who sends each of us into the world as naked as a newly fledged jay bird and crumbles us back into the elements of Mother Earth by the same processes of mutation and final dissolution.

The social and material differences which obtain in the relations of mankind are the creations of man, not of God. God never made such a spook as a king or a duke; he never made such an economic monstrosity as a millionaire; he never gave John Jones the right to own a thousand or a hundred thousand acres of land, with their complement of air and water. These are the conditions of man, who has sold his birthright to the Shylocks of the world and received not even a mess of pottage for his inheritance. The thing would really be laughable, if countless millions from the rice swamps of the Carolinas to the delvers in the mines of Russian Siberia, were not ground to powder to make a holiday for some selfish idler.

Everywhere labor and capital are in deadly conflict. The battle has been raging for centuries, but the opposing forces are just now in a position for that death struggle which it was inevitable must come before the end was. Nor is it within the scope of finite intelligence to forecast the lines upon which the settlement will be made. Capital is entrenched behind ten centuries of law and conservatism, and controlled withal by the wisest and coolest heads in the world. The inequality of the forces joined will appear very obvious. Yet the potentiality of labor will be able to force concessions from time to time, even as the commoners of England have through centuries been able to force from royalty relinquishment of prerogative after prerogative, until, from having been among the most despotic of governments under Elizabeth, the England of today under Queen Victoria is but a royal shadow. So the time may come when the forces of labor will stand upon absolute equality with those of capital, and that harmony between them obtain which has been sought for by wise men and fools for a thousand years.

Glossary

the bloody Dessalines	Jean-Jacques Dessalines, one of Toussaint-Louverture's lieutenants who eventually betrayed him and named himself emperor of Haiti
Christophe	Henri Christophe, who plotted against Dessalines and was later president and then king of Haiti
Elizabeth	Queen Elizabeth I of England
mess of pottage	something of little value; a reference to Genesis 25:29–34, in which Esau sells his birthright to his brother, Jacob, for a meal of lentil stew
Shylocks of the world	a reference to the fictional character Shylock, a moneylender, in Shakespeare's play *The Merchant of Venice*
Toussaint L'Ouverture	Toussaint-Louverture, leader of the successful Haitian Revolution (1791–1803) who became governor-general of Haiti

A 2009 postage stamp honoring Anna Julia Cooper (AP/Wide World Photos)

Anna Julia Cooper's "Womanhood: A Vital Element in the Regeneration and Progress of a Race"

"'I am my Sister's keeper! should be the hearty response of every man and woman of the race."

Overview

Taken from Anna Julia Cooper's essay collection *A Voice from the South* (1892), the speech "Womanhood: A Vital Element in the Regeneration and Progress of a Race" sums up the main arguments of one of the most important black feminists of the late nineteenth century. A former slave, Cooper attained advanced education—eventually earning a doctorate in Paris—and spoke in favor of women's empowerment in the field of education, the church, and the home. Her book successfully engaged the white public dialogue on race and gender in the later nineteenth century and testified to the social advancement of black women in the South.

Context

Most feminists of the nineteenth century believed that men and women had different "natures" and inherent qualities that best suited each gender to "separate spheres" in society. For women, these qualities included a heightened sympathy, purity, religiosity, a capacity for moral instruction, and a devotion to child rearing. Sometimes dubbed the cult of "true womanhood," these qualities were expected of all "true" women. This concept of "womanhood" or femininity was most influential among the northern white middle classes. Although they accepted the notions of "true womanhood," feminists broke from mainstream views about "women's sphere" in arguing that women's roles in society were as important as men's. Rejecting claims of women's inferiority, they insisted that women were the intellectual equals of men and argued for an "expanded women's sphere" that included a greater role in public life, higher education for women, greater professional roles in "feminine" fields such as education and nursing, and the right to vote. On the issue of suffrage, feminists argued that women's greater capacity for morality and virtue demanded that they have a voice in politics (albeit a passive one as voters, not leaders).

For black women, the ideology of "separate spheres" and "true womanhood" was fraught with complications.

White abolitionists drew upon these ideas to criticize the institution of slavery before the Civil War. They argued that slavery corrupted both the white and black household by subverting the family and proper gender roles. Enslaved men were unable to perform the role of proper husbands to enslaved women, whose white masters provided for their sustenance and often exerted authority over their sexual life and relationships. The large numbers of children born to enslaved mothers whose fathers were unknown to them (often the children of white men) provided abolitionists with evidence of the damaging effects of slavery on "womanhood" and the family. In this scenario, the woman's purity was violated, the role of husband forsaken, and capacity of the mother to instill moral virtue compromised. Thus, while indicting slavery, abolitionists also brought attention to enslaved black women's inability to achieve the white middle-class ideal of womanhood.

During Reconstruction, in the aftermath of emancipation, white religious missionaries and teachers poured into the South to help former slaves establish schools and churches. These Protestant reformers preached the ideas of separate spheres and "true womanhood," and their ideas often received a warm reception among black women. Many black women felt that their dignity and self-worth, their relationships with men, and the sanctity of their home life would be protected by adherence to the principles of "true womanhood." They entered into teaching in large numbers and became active members of Protestant churches during this time. For many, the spread of "true womanhood" among black women became a measure of progress from the days of slavery and a means to counter negative racial stereotypes. By the late nineteenth century, it became common for black leaders to speak of the need for "uplift" of the black community into middle-class respectability.

Black women organized women's clubs to combat lynching and racism in the 1890s, just as white middle-class women organized reform groups to support causes such as suffrage and temperance. One factor in organizing their own clubs was that black women found themselves increasingly excluded from white women's organizations. Mary Church Terrell, who was a classmate of Anna Julia Cooper's at Oberlin College, established the National Association of Colored Women's Clubs in 1896, an umbrella organization

1858
- Anna Julia Cooper is born.

1868
- Cooper attends Saint Augustine's Normal School and Collegiate Institute, fighting and winning the right to take the more rigorous classical coursework reserved for male students.

1883
- Dr. Alexander Crummell, an influential Episcopal priest, publishes the pamphlet *The Black Woman of the South, Her Neglects and Needs.*

1884
- Cooper earns her BA degree from Oberlin College.

1886
- Cooper gives a lecture titled "Womanhood: A Vital Element in the Regeneration and Progress of a Race" to a group of black clergymen of the Protestant Episcopal Church in Washington, D.C.

1887
- Cooper earns an MA degree in mathematics from Oberlin.
- Cooper begins teaching at the M Street High School in Washington, D.C., the nation's first public high school for African Americans.

1892
- *A Voice from the South* is published and includes the 1886 lecture "Womanhood."
- **June**
  Cooper is a cofounder of the Colored Woman's League of Washington, D.C.

1893
- **May 18**
  Cooper delivers a talk titled "Women's Cause Is One and Universal" during the World's Congress of Representative Women in Chicago, held in conjunction with the Columbian Exposition.

for black women's clubs, whose official slogan was "Lifting as We Climb." Of the many mutual benefit societies, settlement houses, and schools dominated by black women, the vast majority were associated with Protestant churches such as the Baptists, Methodists, and Congregationalists. These organizations straddled the line between women's and men's "spheres," because they were unapologetically political while at the same time remaining within the accepted woman's realm of religion and moral improvement.

Anna Julia Cooper's 1892 collection of essays, *A Voice from the South*, gave expression to the most progressive form of "true womanhood" ideology among southern black women of the time. The sociologist Charles Lemert remarks in chapter 1 of his edition of her selected writing, "Cooper's ideas, though simply put, were an important link in the more-than-a-century-long evolution of black feminist social theory from Sojourner Truth's legendary 'Arn't I a Woman' speech in the mid-nineteenth century to the full expression of black feminist thought in the 1980s."

About the Author

Born a slave in 1858 in North Carolina to Hannah Haywood and her slave owner, Anna Julia Cooper became one of the most prominent African American educators of her time. She received an elite classical education, first at Saint Augustine's Normal School and Collegiate Institute, an Episcopal school in Raleigh, North Carolina, of which she is critical in "Womanhood: A Vital Element in the Regeneration and Progress of a Race." She married George Cooper at age nineteen but was widowed two years later. Soon after her husband's death, she applied to Oberlin College in Ohio and was one of three black women to graduate from that school in 1884. After returning to teach at Saint Augustine's, she earned her master's degree in mathematics from Oberlin in 1887. During this time, she made the address titled "Womanhood" to the black clergy of the Protestant Episcopal Church in Washington, D.C.

In 1887, Cooper began teaching at M Street High School in Washington, D.C., eventually rising to the post of principal. She was dismissed from this post in 1906 amid scandalous allegations that played out in the Washington press, in which she was accused of having an improper relationship with a younger teacher and her former ward, John Love. The rumor was not substantiated, and historians have posited that Cooper's dismissal was political, related to the fact that she was a strong proponent of a rigorous curriculum that emphasized college preparedness rather than vocational training. In any case, Cooper eventually returned to M Street as a teacher in 1910.

In the late nineteenth century and early twentieth century, Cooper was very active in promoting the cause of African Americans, first with the publication of the landmark *Voice from the South*, of which "Womanhood" is part, and later through speeches around the world. She, along with W. E. B. Du Bois, was one of a few African Americans present at the first Pan-African Conference in London. Devoted to education, Cooper also helped found organizations that helped further the education of African Americans, including the Colored Settlement House in Washington, D.C., and the D.C. branch of the Colored Young Women's Christian Association. In 1930 she became president of Frelinghuysen University, a black university in D.C.

Cooper is also notable as the fourth African-American woman to receive a doctorate. At the age of sixty-five, she earned her doctorate from the Sorbonne in Paris. Her dissertation examined French attitudes toward slavery. Cooper died in 1964 at the age of 105, having lived from the time of slavery to the height of the civil rights movement.

Explanation and Analysis of the Document

In "Womanhood: A Vital Element in the Regeneration and Progress of a Race," Anna Julia Cooper argues that black women are the key to the future success of African Americans, both male and female. Invoking the Victorian ideal of "true womanhood," Cooper stresses that women can exert influence through the home and that the most stable and progressive cultures share common values where women and home life are venerated. Originally delivered to an all-male audience of black clergy, this speech (later the first chapter in Cooper's book *Voice from the South*) is a call for support of African American women and the importance of their education.

◆ Opening

Cooper begins her essay by pointing to Christianity and the feudal system as the sources for the "noble and ennobling ideal of woman" that provides women with the agency to make a positive difference in their society. She contrasts this ideal of womanhood with the state of women in non-Western civilizations where women are oppressed. Cooper cites the state of women in China and under Muslim rule to make her point, arguing that a Chinese woman's spirit is as crushed as her foot (referring to the tradition of foot binding in China). Cooper is more expansive on the problems she sees with the state of Muslim women. Arguing that the home and home life lends strength to a people and society, Cooper decries the custom of the harem and quotes a writer who calls the "private life of the Turk ... vilest of the vile, unprogressive, unambitious, and inconceivably low." In thriving societies, Cooper believes, women are revered as wives, mothers, and sisters, and in her view, in the East, "the homelife is impure."

Cooper moves quickly from her condemnation of the state of women in the East and the weakness of Eastern society to a celebration of Western civilization in Europe and America. While Cooper believes that America has yet to fulfill its promise, she has confidence that society is moving in the correct direction. Cooper's optimism for America rests on the "homelife and the influence of good women in those homes" who serve as a moral guide for the family. Positing the importance of home life, Cooper makes the argument for women's centrality to the success of a society.

Time Line

1894
- An important realization of Cooper's call for women's leadership, the *Woman's Era* is launched as the official organ of the National Association of Colored Women, with Josephine St. Pierre Ruffin as editor.

1895
- Cooper is active in the first meeting of the National Conference of Colored Women.

1900
- Cooper delivers an address, "The Negro Problem in America," at the Pan-African Conference in London, England.

1906
- Cooper is forced to resign as principal of M Street High School in Washington, D.C., in part because of her insistence on an academically rigorous curriculum as opposed to vocational training.

◆ Woman's Influence on Society

A good portion of Cooper's text is devoted to surveying the progress of women in Europe and describing the role of Christianity and feudal society in advancing women. Cooper was classically educated, and she supports her argument by citing an ancient Roman historian (Tacitus), an eminent nineteenth-century British historian and statesman (Thomas Macaulay), and a nineteenth-century American philosopher (Ralph Waldo Emerson). She is echoing their perspective that, as Macaulay wrote (and Cooper quotes), "You may judge a nation's rank in the scale of civilization from the way they treat their women."

The chivalry that sprouted from feudal society, Cooper explains, was significant in defining the idealized perspective of women. However, chivalry had its limits. Too often, Cooper argues, chivalry meant that men respected only the "elect few" among whom they might expect to socialize or marry. Cooper fears that this limitation still exists. Greater respect for women—respect that transcends class and culture—can be found in Christianity, though Cooper notes that the Christian church has also been limited. She points specifically to problems with the Catholic Church's treatment of women in the Middle Ages and the sexual transgressions of priests. However, Christianity, if not always the formal practices of religion, has led to the betterment of women's condition. Specifically, Cooper points to Christ's teaching that imparted the same ethical code and standards for both men and women. In her reading of the tenets of

"Now the fundamental agency under God in the regeneration, the retraining of the race, as well as the ground work and starting point of its progress upward, must be the black woman."

(Vital Agency of Womanhood in the Regeneration and Progress of a Race)

"Only the Black Woman can say 'when and where I enter, in the quiet, undisputed dignity of my womanhood, without violence and without suing or special patronage, then and there the whole Negro race enters with me.'"

(Vital Agency of Womanhood in the Regeneration and Progress of a Race)

"'I am my Sister's keeper!' should be the hearty response of every man and woman of the race, and this conviction should purify and exalt the narrow, selfish and petty personal aims of life into a noble and sacred purpose."

(The Role for the Protestant Episcopal Church)

Christianity, men and women are equals, with the same moral responsibilities.

Cooper ends the first part of her argument by stating that now that she has shown examples from history that societies which venerate women are the same societies that have made the most advances, it is fair to state that "the position of woman in society determines the vital elements of its regeneration and progress." She then addresses women directly, emphasizing the importance of their position and the extent of their responsibility. The future of civilization rests on women's shoulders, and their education must be taken seriously.

♦ Vital Agency of Womanhood in the Regeneration and Progress of a Race

After making her historical survey and tracing the importance of women to the development of Western civilization, Cooper turns to the specific importance of her theory on African Americans. The address is being made to black clergymen, and Cooper explains that she is not simply engaging in an intellectual exercise. Rather, she is advocating for the better education of black women because in their social progress lies the progress of all African Americans. Cooper states that her task is doubly difficult both because her argument is obvious and because she is not the first to

raise these points. Cooper acknowledges that her topic has been addressed previously by Dr. Alexander Crummell, a black Episcopal pastor who wrote a pamphlet, *The Black Woman in the South*, that argued that the plight of black women under slavery was worse than that of men and called for the education and training of the newly freed black women in the rural South. Crummell was extremely influential in his time—Cooper refers to him as the "king." If such an influential black clergyman has not succeeded in raising the urgency of bettering black women, Cooper demurs, what chance does she have?

To Crummell's argument, Cooper also wishes to advocate for black girls of the South. These girls are at special risk because they often have no father or brother to protect them. Cooper herself never knew her white father, who had been her mother's owner during slavery. Without protectors, black girls are at risk of sexual exploitation by white men. These girls need to be "saved" and educated because they represent the "foundation stones of our future as a race." Cooper is unimpressed by the growing number of professional black men, because black women and girls are "subject to taint and corruption in the enemy's camp." In other words, black women will foster the future success of African Americans, but not if they are exploited, dismissed, and left uneducated.

Cooper was writing twenty-one years after the end of slavery. In her view, slavery caused two centuries of "compression and degradation" of African Americans. Any "weaknesses" evident in African Americans, Cooper says, are attributable to slavery. However, in a hundred years' time, she believes that any "weaknesses" will lie solely as the fault of African Americans. To make sure that African Americans are strong and productive in the future, Cooper turns again to the importance of educating black women. To judge the race as a whole, she argues, one must look at the strength of black families and not at the accomplishments of individuals. The achievement of one man does not speak to the success of his race. It is not until the "homes, average homes, homes of the rank and file" are "lighted and cheered by the good, the beautiful, and the true" that the African-American race will "be lifted into the sunlight."

In the most-quoted passage from this piece, Cooper asserts: "Only the Black Woman can say 'when and where I enter, in the quiet, undisputed dignity of my womanhood, without violence and without suing or special patronage, then and there the whole *Negro race enters with me.*'" In other words, when black women are assured of their rightful role without argument, then the entire race will be assured in its progress and development.

♦ **The Role for the Protestant Episcopal Church**

After describing the importance of black women to the future of the African American race, Cooper points to some direct action that the Protestant Episcopal Church, whose clergy she was addressing, could take to improve the lives of black women in the South. Cooper, who was educated by the Protestant Episcopal Church, was a strong critic of its limitations and what she saw as a retreat from what should be its mission in the South.

She turns first to an example of the opportunities that exist for her white counterparts. White girls are supported, are free from racial prejudice, and can look to organizations such as the White Cross League in England, says Cooper. This reference is important because the White Cross League, founded by the Christian feminist Jane Ellice Hopkins, was specifically established as a "social purity" organization for working-class girls. Cooper also looks to ways in which the English Anglican Church (of which the Episcopal Church in the United States is an offshoot) supports their "wronged sisters"—fallen women. Cooper in her veiled references to the "snares and traps" waiting for black girls in the South, is speaking directly to the need both for protecting the virginity of these girls and for sustaining black women who have "fallen."

Cooper thinks that the Protestant Episcopal Church needs to "missionize" black southerners. The Episcopal Church makes a poor showing in the South and among blacks. Methodists, Baptists, and Congregationalists are active in the South, whereas the Episcopalians can boast of only one black congregation in the South and less than two dozen black clergy in the entire country. Younger black Christians who might naturally be Episcopalians are finding a calling instead among different sects.

The fault lies, Cooper believes, in the fact that the Episcopal Church has not rightly respected black men. When gathering to discuss the best ways to further the development of African Americans, the church has neglected to invite black men to participate as equal partners. Second, and more directly to the point of Cooper's larger argument, the church has not worked directly to develop black women or seen the possibilities of using black women to draw others to the church. The church, Cooper believes, is out of touch with the daily lives of black Americans and until it "provides a clergy that can come in touch with our life and have a fellow feeling for our woes ... the good bishops are likely to continue 'perplexed' by the sparsity of colored Episcopalians." Cooper here gives an example of race prejudice still evident in the church—one black priest was asked by his bishop to sit in the back of a convention so as not to disturb the white clergymen.

Cooper is also disappointed that Dr. Alexander Crummell's call in his pamphlet for the formation of organizations specific to the education and training of black women was not heeded by the Episcopal Church and that no effort toward the establishment of church sisterhoods has been made. Other religions have gone further—founding colleges and universities, including Fisk, Hampton, Atlanta University, and Tuskegee. Cooper contrasts these schools with Saint Augustine's, the school she attended before moving to Oberlin, and the institution where the Episcopal "Church in the South ... mainly looks for the training of her colored clergy and for help of the 'Black Woman' and 'Colored Girl' of the South." Rather than producing a crop of "missionaries" to evangelize their fellow southern blacks, as have Fisk, Hampton, Atlanta, and Tuskegee, Saint Augustine's has managed to graduate only five women since its founding in 1868. Young men are being trained by Saint Augustine's, but poor women are simply not being trained and supported in meaningful numbers. Rather, the school educates primarily women who can pay their own way. The Episcopal Church, Cooper believes, is neglecting its duty to prepare girls "for the duties and responsibilities that await the intelligent wife, the Christian mother, the earnest, virtuous, helpful woman, at once the lever and the fulcrum for uplifting the race."

Cooper ends the speech with a direct call to her audience to take up the work of educating and supporting women: "Is it too much to ask you to step forward and direct the work for your race along those lines which you know to be of first and vital importance?" In this piece, Cooper grows ever more specific, moving from the importance of women to the advance of civilization, to the importance of black women to the progress of the African American race, to the importance of black women to the vitality of the Episcopal Church in the South. Cooper places black women in a continuum with white women of Europe and America, articulating that the treatment of women defines a society, a race, and a religion.

Audience

Originally delivered as a speech to the all-male black clergy of the Protestant Episcopal Church, this article often speaks specifically to the failings of the Episcopal Church in offering opportunities to women. Later, when it was republished as the first chapter of *A Voice from the South*, Cooper aimed to reach a much broader audience by using it to frame a book-length analysis of race and gender in the South. Her book addresses both black and white intellectuals and engages in a broad national dialogue.

Impact

A Voice from the South is considered by critics today to be a foundational text of modern black feminism. Many of Cooper's insights into the nexus of race and gender have been elaborated upon by later writers. In its own time, the book also drew wide attention and praise. Charles Lemert quotes the author of *The Work of the Afro-American Woman* (1894), Gertrude Bustill Mossell, who called Cooper's book *A Voice from the South* "one of the strongest pleas for the race and sex of the writer that ha[d] ever appeared."

Cooper and other feminist black writers were ignored by their male counterparts: The year that *A Voice from the South* was published (1892) the former slave and antislavery advocate Frederick Douglass was asked to provide the names of important black women for inclusion in an anthology of black writing, and he replied, "I have thus far seen no book of importance written by a negro woman and I know of no one among us who can appropriately be called famous." Within a short time, however, Cooper would leap to the front ranks of black leadership. In 1900, she spoke along with the civil rights activist W. E. B. Du Bois at the Pan-African Congress in London as representatives of the United States. However, her legacy was forgotten for many years and not resurrected until the 1980s. *A Voice from the South* was republished in 1990.

See also Josephine St. Pierre Ruffin's "Address to the First National Conference of Colored Women" (1895); Mary Church Terrell: "The Progress of Colored Women" (1898).

Further Reading

■ Books

Carby, Hazel. *Reconstructing Womanhood: The Emergence of the Afro-American Woman Novelist*. New York: Oxford University Press, 1987.

Collins, Patricia Hill. *Black Feminist Thought: Knowledge, Consciousness, and the Politics of Empowerment*. 2nd ed. New York: Routledge, 2000.

Cooper, Anna Julia. *A Voice from the South*, ed. Mary Helen Washington. New York: Oxford University Press, 1990.

Questions for Further Study

1. How do Cooper and her work illustrate the intersections of race, gender, and social class in late-nineteenth-century America?

2. In what ways does Cooper's essay prefigure more modern feminist thought, particularly black feminist thought?

3. Many prominent black writers and leaders tended to be pessimistic about American society because of its legacy of slavery and ongoing racism. Did Cooper share that pessimism? Why or why not?

4. Cooper wrote, "But weaknesses and malformations, which to-day are attributable to a vicious schoolmaster and a pernicious system, will a century hence be rightly regarded as proofs of innate corruptness and radical incurability." Focusing on her use of the word *rightly*, what do you believe Cooper's reaction to racial realities would have been at the end of the twentieth century and in the first years of the twenty-first?

5. Compare this document with one or more written by other prominent black women during this era; possibilities include Josephine St. Pierre Ruffin's "Address to the First National Conference of Colored Women" (1895); Mary Church Terrell's "The Progress of Colored Women" (1898); and Mary McLeod Bethune's "What Does American Democracy Mean to Me?" What similar arguments do the writers make? How are their views different?

Giddings, Paula. *When and Where I Enter: The Impact of Black Women on Race and Sex in America*. New York: Bantam, 1984.

Lemert, Charles, and Esme Bhan, eds. *The Voice of Anna Julia Cooper*. Lanham, Md.: Rowman and Littlefield, 1998.

Johnson, Karen A. *Uplifting the Women and the Race: The Lives, Educational Philosophies, and Social Activism of Anna Julia Cooper and Nannie Helen Burroughs*. New York: Garland, 2000.

■ **Web Sites**

"African American Women." Duke University Library "Digitized Collections" Web site.
    http://library.duke.edu/specialcollections/collections/digitized/african-american-women/.

African American Women Writers of the 19th Century Schomburg Center for Research in Black Culture's "Digitial Schomburg African American Women Writers of the 19th Century" Web site.
    http://digital.nypl.org/schomburg/writers_aa19/toc.html.

—Mark Elliott

ANNA JULIA COOPER'S "WOMANHOOD: A VITAL ELEMENT IN THE REGENERATION AND PROGRESS OF A RACE"

The two sources from which, perhaps, modern civilization has derived its noble and ennobling ideal of woman are Christianity and the Feudal System.

In Oriental countries woman has been uniformly devoted to a life of ignorance, infamy, and complete stagnation. The Chinese shoe of to-day does not more entirely dwarf, cramp, and destroy her physical powers, than have the customs, laws, and social instincts, which from remotest ages have governed our Sister of the East, enervated and blighted her mental and moral life.

Mahomet makes no account of woman whatever in his polity. The Koran, which, unlike our Bible, was a product and not a growth, tried to address itself to the needs of Arabian civilization as Mahomet with his circumscribed powers saw them. The Arab was a nomad. Home to him meant his present camping place. That deity who, according to our western ideals, makes and sanctifies the home, was to him a transient bauble to be toyed with so long as it gave pleasure and then to be thrown aside for a new one. As a personality, an individual soul, capable of eternal growth and unlimited development, and destined to mould and shape the civilization of the future to an incalculable extent, Mahomet did not know woman. There was no hereafter, no paradise for her. The heaven of the Mussulman is peopled and made gladsome not by the departed wife, or sister, or mother, but by *houri*—a figment of Mahomet's brain, partaking of the ethereal qualities of angels, yet imbued with all the vices and inanity of Oriental women. The harem here, and—"dust to dust" hereafter, this was the hope, the inspiration, the *summum bonum* of the Eastern woman's life! With what result on the life of the nation, the "Unspeakable Turk," the "sick man" of modern Europe can to-day exemplify.

Says a certain writer: "The private life of the Turk is vilest of the vile, unprogressive, unambitious, and inconceivably low." And yet Turkey is not without her great men. She has produced most brilliant minds; men skilled in all the intricacies of diplomacy and statesmanship; men whose intellects could grapple with the deep problems of empire and manipulate the subtle agencies which check-mate kings. But these minds were not the normal outgrowth of a healthy trunk. They seemed rather ephemeral excrescencies which shoot far out with all the vigor and promise, apparently, of strong branches; but soon alas fall into decay and ugliness because there is no soundness in the root, no life-giving sap, permeating, strengthening and perpetuating the whole. There is a worm at the core! The homelife is impure! and when we look for fruit, like apples of Sodom, it crumbles within our grasp into dust and ashes.

It is pleasing to turn from this effete and immobile civilization to a society still fresh and vigorous, whose seed is in itself, and whose very name is synonymous with all that is progressive, elevating and inspiring, viz., the European bud and the American flower of modern civilization.

And here let me say parenthetically that our satisfaction in American institutions rests not on the fruition we now enjoy, but springs rather from the possibilities and promise that are inherent in the system, though as yet, perhaps, far in the future.

"Happiness," says Madame de Stael, "consists not in perfections attained, but in a sense of progress, the result of our own endeavor under conspiring circumstances *toward* a goal which continually advances and broadens and deepens till it is swallowed up in the Infinite." Such conditions in embryo are all that we claim for the land of the West. We have not yet reached our ideal in American civilization. The pessimists even declare that we are not marching in that direction. But there can be no doubt that here in America is the arena in which the next triumph of civilization is to be won; and here too we find promise abundant and possibilities infinite.

Now let us see on what basis this hope for our country primarily and fundamentally rests. Can any one doubt that it is chiefly on the homelife and on the influence of good women in those homes? Says Macaulay: "You may judge a nation's rank in the scale of civilization from the way they treat their women." And Emerson, "I have thought that a sufficient measure of civilization is the influence of good women." Now this high regard for woman, this germ of a prolific idea which in our own day is bearing such rich and varied fruit, was ingrafted into European civilization, we have said, from two sources, the Christian Church and the Feudal System. For although the Feudal System can in no sense be said to have originated the idea, yet there can be no doubt that the habits of life and modes of thought to which Feudalism gave rise, materially fostered and developed it; for they gave us chivalry, than which no institution has more sensibly magnified and elevated woman's position in society.

Tacitus dwells on the tender regard for woman entertained by these rugged barbarians before they left their northern homes to overrun Europe. Old Norse legends too, and primitive poems, all breathe the same spirit of love of home and veneration for the pure and noble influence there presiding—the wife, the sister, the mother.

And when later on we see the settled life of the Middle Ages "oozing out," as M. Guizot expresses it, from the plundering and pillaging life of barbarism and crystallizing into the Feudal System, the tiger of the field is brought once more within the charmed circle of the goddesses of his castle, and his imagination weaves around them a halo whose reflection possibly has not yet altogether vanished.

It is true the spirit of Christianity had not yet put the seal of catholicity on this sentiment. Chivalry, according to Bascom, was but the toning down and softening of a rough and lawless period. It gave a roseate glow to a bitter winter's day. Those who looked out from castle windows revelled in its "amethyst tints." But God's poor, the weak, the unlovely, the commonplace were still freezing and starving none the less, in unpitied, unrelieved loneliness.

Respect for woman, the much lauded chivalry of the Middle Ages, meant what I fear it still means to some men in our own day—respect for the elect few among whom they expect to consort.

The idea of the radical amelioration of womankind, reverence for woman as woman regardless of rank, wealth, or culture, was to come from that rich and bounteous fountain from which flow all our liberal and universal ideas—the Gospel of Jesus Christ.

And yet the Christian Church at the time of which we have been speaking would seem to have been doing even less to protect and elevate woman than the little done by secular society. The Church as an organization committed a double offense against woman in the Middle Ages. Making of marriage a sacrament and at the same time insisting on the celibacy of the clergy and other religious orders, she gave an inferior if not an impure character to the marriage relation, especially fitted to reflect discredit on woman. Would this were all or the worst! but the Church by the licentiousness of its chosen servants invaded the household and established too often as vicious con-

nections those relations which it forbade to assume openly and in good faith. "Thus," to use the words of our authority, "the religious corps became as numerous, as searching, and as unclean as the frogs of Egypt, which penetrated into all quarters, into the ovens and kneading troughs, leaving their filthy trail wherever they went." Says Chaucer with characteristic satire, speaking of the Friars:

Women may now go safely up and doun,
In every bush, and under every tree,
Ther is non other incubus but he,
And he ne will don hem no dishonor.

It may help us under some of the perplexities which beset our way in "the one Catholic and Apostolic Church" to-day, to recall some of the corruptions and incongruities against which the Bride of Christ has had to struggle in her past history and in spite of which she has kept, through many vicissitudes, the faith once delivered to the saints. Individuals, organizations, whole sections of the Church militant may outrage the Christ whom they profess, may ruthlessly trample under foot both the spirit and the letter of his precepts, yet not till we hear the voices audibly saying "Come let us depart hence," shall we cease to believe and cling to the promise, "*I am with you to the end of the world.*"

"Yet saints their watch are keeping,
The cry goes up 'How long!'
And soon the night of weeping
Shall be the morn of song."

However much then the facts of any particular period of history may seem to deny it, I for one do not doubt that the source of the vitalizing principle of woman's development and amelioration is the Christian Church, so far as that church is coincident with Christianity.

Christ gave ideals not formulae. The Gospel is a germ requiring millennia for its growth and ripening. It needs and at the same time helps to form around itself a soil enriched in civilization, and perfected in culture and insight without which the embryo can neither be unfolded or comprehended. With all the strides our civilization has made from the first to the nineteenth century, we can boast not an idea, not a principle of action, not a progressive social force but was already mutely foreshadowed, or directly enjoined in that simple tale of a meek and lowly life. The quiet face of the Nazarene is ever seen a little way ahead, never too far to come down to and touch the life of the lowest in days the darkest, yet ever leading onward, still onward, the tottering childish feet of our strangely boastful civilization.

By laying down for woman the same code of morality, the same standard of purity, as for man; by refusing to countenance the shameless and equally guilty monsters who were gloating over her fall,—graciously stooping in all the majesty of his own spotlessness to wipe away the filth and grime of her guilty past and bid her go in peace and sin no more; and again in the moments of his own careworn and footsore dejection, turning trustfully and lovingly, away from the heartless snubbing and sneers, away from the cruel malignity of mobs and prelates in the dusty marts of Jerusalem to the ready sympathy, loving appreciation and unfaltering friendship of that quiet home at Bethany; and even at the last, by his dying bequest to the disciple whom he loved, signifying the protection and tender regard to be extended to that sorrowing mother and ever afterward to the sex she represented;—throughout his life and in his death he has given to men a rule and guide for the estimation of woman as an equal, as a helper, as a friend, and as a sacred charge to be sheltered and cared for with a brother's love and sympathy, lessons which nineteen centuries' gigantic strides in knowledge, arts, and sciences, in social and ethical principles have not been able to probe to their depth or to exhaust in practice.

It seems not too much to say then of the vitalizing, regenerating, and progressive influence of womanhood on the civilization of today, that, while it was foreshadowed among Germanic nations in the far away dawn of their history as a narrow, sickly and stunted growth, it yet owes its catholicity and power, the deepening of its roots and broadening of its branches to Christianity.

The union of these two forces, the Barbaric and the Christian, was not long delayed after the Fall of the Empire. The Church, which fell with Rome, finding herself in danger of being swallowed up by barbarism, with characteristic vigor and fertility of resources, addressed herself immediately to the task of conquering her conquerers. The means chosen does credit to her power of penetration and adaptability, as well as to her profound, unerring, all-compassing diplomacy; and makes us even now wonder if aught human can successfully and ultimately withstand her far-seeing designs and brilliant policy, or gainsay her well-earned claim to the word *Catholic*.

She saw the barbarian, little more developed than a wild beast. She forbore to antagonize and mystify his warlike nature by a full blaze of the heart searching and humanizing tenets of her great Head. She said little of the rule "If thy brother smite thee on one cheek, turn to him the other also;" but thought it sufficient for the needs of those times, to establish the so-called "Truce of God" under which men were bound to abstain from butchering one another for three days of each week and on Church festivals. In other words, she respected their individuality: non-resistance pure and simple being for them an utter impossibility, she contented herself with less radical measures calculated to lead up finally to the full measure of the benevolence of Christ.

Next she took advantage of the barbarian's sensuous love of gaudy display and put all her magnificent garments on. She could not capture him by physical force, she would dazzle him by gorgeous spectacles. It is said that Romanism gained more in pomp and ritual during this trying period of the Dark Ages than throughout all her former history.

The result was she carried her point. Once more Rome laid her ambitions hand on the temporal power, and allied with Charlemagne, aspired to rule the world through a civilization dominated by Christianity and permeated by the traditions and instincts of those sturdy barbarians.

Here was the confluence of the two streams we have been tracing, which, united now, stretch before us as a broad majestic river. In regard to woman it was the meeting of two noble and ennobling forces, two kindred ideas the resultant of which, we doubt not, is destined to be a potent force in the betterment of the world.

Now after our appeal to history comparing nations destitute of this force and so destitute also of the principle of progress, with other nations among whom the influence of woman is prominent coupled with a brisk, progressive, satisfying civilization,—if in addition we find this strong presumptive evidence corroborated by reason and experience, we may conclude that these two equally varying concomitants are linked as cause and effect; in other words, that the position of woman in society determines the vital elements of its regeneration and progress.

Now that this is so on *a priori* grounds all must admit. And this not because woman is better or stronger or wiser than man, but from the nature of the case, because it is she who must first form the man by directing the earliest impulses of his character.

Byron and Wordsworth were both geniuses and would have stamped themselves on the thought of their age under any circumstances; and yet we find the one a savor of life unto life, the other of death unto death. "Byron, like a rocket, shot his way upward with scorn and repulsion, flamed out in wild, explosive, brilliant excesses and disappeared in darkness made all the more palpable."

Wordsworth lent of his gifts to reinforce that "power in the Universe which makes for righteousness" by taking the harp handed him from Heaven and using it to swell the strains of angelic choirs. Two locomotives equally mighty stand facing opposite tracks; the one to rush headlong to destruction with all its precious freight, the other to toil grandly and gloriously up the steep embattlements to Heaven and to God. Who—who can say what a world of consequences hung on the first placing and starting of these enormous forces!

Woman, Mother,—your responsibility is one that might make angels tremble and fear to take hold! To trifle with it, to ignore or misuse it, is to treat lightly the most sacred and solemn trust ever confided by God to human kind. The training of children is a task on which an infinity of weal or woe depends. Who does not covet it? Yet who does not stand awestruck before its momentous issues! It is a matter of small moment, it seems to me, whether that lovely girl in whose accomplishments you take such pride and delight, can enter the gay and crowded salon with the ease and elegance of this or that French or English gentlewoman, compared with the decision as to whether her individuality is going to reinforce the good or the evil elements of the world. The lace and the diamonds, the dance and the theater, gain a new significance when scanned in their bearings on such issues. Their influence on the individual personality, and through her on the society and civilization which she vitalizes and inspires—all this and more must be weighed in the balance before the jury call return a just and intelligent verdict as to the innocence or banefulness of these apparently simple amusements.

Now the fact of woman's influence on society being granted, what are its practical bearings on the work which brought together this conference of colored clergy and laymen in Washington? "We come not here to talk." Life is too busy, too pregnant with meaning and far reaching consequences to allow you to come this far for mere intellectual entertainment.

The vital agency of womanhood in the regeneration and progress of a race, as a general question, is conceded almost before it is fairly stated. I confess one of the difficulties for me in the subject assigned lay in its obviousness. The plea is taken away by the opposite attorney's granting the whole question.

"Woman's influence on social progress"—who in Christendom doubts or questions it? One may as well be called on to prove that, the sun is the source of light and heat and energy to this many-sided little world.

Nor, on the other hand, could it have been intended that I should apply the position when taken and proven, to the needs and responsibilities of the women of our race in the South. For is it not written, "Cursed is he that cometh after the king?" and has not the King already preceded me in "The Black Woman of the South"?

They have had both Moses and the Prophets in Dr. Crummell and if they hear not him, neither would they be persuaded though one came up from the South.

I would beg, however, with the Doctor's permission, to add my plea for the *Colored Girls* of the South:—that large, bright, promising fatally beautiful class that stand shivering like a delicate plantlet before the fury of tempestuous elements, so full of promise and possibilities, yet so sure of destruction; often without a father to whom they dare apply the loving term, often without a stronger brother to espouse their cause and defend their honor with his life's blood; in the midst of pitfalls and snares, waylaid by the lower classes of white men, with no shelter, no protection nearer than the great blue vault above, which half conceals and half reveals the one Care-Taker they know so little of. Oh, save them, help them, shield, train, develop, teach, inspire them! Snatch them, in God's name, as brands from the burning! There is material in them well worth your while, the hope in germ of a staunch, helpful, regenerating womanhood on which, primarily, rests the foundation stones of our future as a race.

It is absurd to quote statistics showing the Negro's bank account and rent rolls, to point to the hundreds of newspapers edited by colored men and lists of lawyers, doctors, professors, D. D's, LL D's, etc., etc., etc., while the source from which the life-blood of the race is to flow is subject to taint and corruption in the enemy's camp.

True progress is never made by spasms. Real progress is growth. It must begin in the seed. Then, "first the blade, then the ear, after that the full corn in the ear." There is something to encourage and inspire us in the advancement of individuals since their emancipation from slavery. It at least proves that there is nothing irretrievably wrong in the shape of the black man's skull, and that under given circumstances his development, downward or upward, will be similar to that of other average human beings.

But there is no time to be wasted in mere felicitation. That the Negro has his niche in the infinite purposes of the Eternal, no one who has studied the history of the last fifty years in America will deny. That much depends on his own right comprehension of his responsibility and rising to the demands of the hour, it will be good for him to see; and how best to use his present so that the structure of the future shall be stronger and higher and brighter and nobler and holier than that of the past, is a question to be decided each day by every one of us.

The race is just twenty-one years removed from the conception and experience of a chattel, just at the age of ruddy manhood. It is well enough to pause a moment for retrospection, introspection, and prospection. We look back, not to become inflated with conceit because of the depths from which we have arisen, but that we may learn wisdom from experience. We look within that we may gather together once more our forces, and, by improved and more practical methods, address ourselves to the tasks before us. We look forward with hope and trust that the same God whose guiding hand led our fathers through and out of the gall and bitterness of oppression, will still lead and direct their children, to the honor of His name, and for their ultimate salvation.

But this survey of the failures or achievements of the past, the difficulties and embarrassments of the present, and the mingled hopes and fears for the future, must not degenerate into mere dreaming nor consume the time which belongs to the practical and effective handling of the crucial questions of the hour; and there can be no issue more vital and momentous than this of the womanhood of the race.

Here is the vulnerable point, not in the heel, but at the heart of the young Achilles; and here must the defenses be strengthened and the watch redoubled.

We are the heirs of a past which was not our fathers' moulding. "Every man the arbiter of his own destiny" was not true for the American Negro of the past: and it is no fault of his that he finds himself to-day the inheritor of a manhood and womanhood impoverished and debased by two centuries and more of compression and degradation.

But weaknesses and malformations, which to-day are attributable to a vicious schoolmaster and a perni-

cious system, will a century hence be rightly regarded as proofs of innate corruptness and radical incurability.

Now the fundamental agency under God in the regeneration, the re-training of the race, as well as the ground work and starting point of its progress upward, must be the *black woman*.

With all the wrongs and neglects of her past, with all the weakness, the debasement, the moral thralldom of her present, the black woman of to-day stands mute and wondering at the Herculean task devolving around her. But the cycles wait for her. No other hand can move the lever. She must be loosed from her bands and set to work.

Our meager and superficial results from past efforts prove their futility; and every effort to elevate the Negro, whether undertaken by himself or through the philanthropy of others, cannot but prove abortive unless so directed as to utilize the indispensable agency of an elevated and trained womanhood.

A race cannot be purified from without. Preachers and teachers are helps, and stimulants and conditions as necessary as the gracious rain and sunshine are to plant growth. But what are rain and dew and sunshine and cloud if there be no life in the plant germ? We must go to the root and see that it is sound and healthy and vigorous; and not deceive ourselves with waxen flowers and painted leaves of mock chlorophyll.

We too often mistake individuals' honor for race development and so are ready to substitute pretty accomplishments for sound sense and earnest purpose.

A stream cannot rise higher than its source. The atmosphere of homes is no rarer and purer and sweeter than are the mothers in those homes. A race is but a total of families. The nation is the aggregate of its homes. As the whole is sum of all its parts, so the character of the parts will determine the characteristics of the whole. These are all axioms and so evident that it seems gratuitous to remark it; and yet, unless I am greatly mistaken, most of the unsatisfaction from our past results arises from just such a radical and palpable error, as much almost on our own part as on that of our benevolent white friends.

The Negro is constitutionally hopeful and proverbially irrepressible; and naturally stands in danger of being dazzled by the shimmer and tinsel of superficials. We often mistake foliage for fruit and overestimate or wrongly estimate brilliant results.

The late Martin R. Delany, who was an unadulterated black man, used to say when honors of state fell upon him, that when he entered the council of kings the black race entered with him; meaning, I suppose, that there was no discounting his race identity and attributing his achievements to some admixture of Saxon blood. But our present record of eminent men, when placed beside the actual status of the race in America to-day, proves that no man can represent the race. Whatever the attainments of the individual may be, unless his home has moved on *pari passu*, he can never be regarded as identical with or representative of the whole.

Not by pointing to sun-bathed mountain tops do we prove that Phoebus warms the valleys. We must point to homes, average homes, homes of the rank and file of horny handed toiling men and women of the South (where the masses are) lighted and cheered by the good, the beautiful, and the true,—then and not till then will the whole plateau be lifted into the sunlight.

Only the Black Woman can say "when and where I enter, in the quiet, undisputed dignity of my womanhood, without violence and without suing or special patronage, then and there the whole *Negro race enters with me*." Is it not evident then that as individual workers for this race we must address ourselves with no half-hearted zeal to this feature of our mission. The need is felt and must be recognized by all. There is a call for workers, for missionaries, for men and women with the double consecration of a fundamental love of humanity and a desire for its melioration through the Gospel; but superadded to this we demand an intelligent and sympathetic comprehension of the interests and special needs of the Negro.

I see not why there should not be an organized effort for the protection and elevation of our girls such as the White Cross League in England. English women are strengthened and protected by more than twelve centuries of Christian influences, freedom and civilization; English girls are dispirited and crushed down by no such all-levelling prejudice as that supercilious caste spirit in America which cynically assumes "A Negro woman cannot be a lady." English womanhood is beset by no such snares and traps as betray the unprotected, untrained colored girl of the South, whose only crime and dire destruction often is her unconscious and marvelous beauty. Surely then if English indignation is aroused and English manhood thrilled under the leadership of a Bishop of the English church to build up bulwarks around their wronged sisters, Negro sentiment cannot remain callous and Negro effort nerveless in view of the imminent peril of the mothers of the next generation. "*I am my*

Sister's keeper!" should be the hearty response of every man and woman of the race, and this conviction should purify and exalt the narrow, selfish and petty personal aims of life into a noble and sacred purpose.

We need men who can let their interest and gallantry extend outside the circle of their aesthetic appreciation; men who can be a father, a brother, a friend to every weak, struggling unshielded girl. We need women who are so sure of their own social footing that they need not fear leaning to lend a hand to a fallen or falling sister. We need men and women who do not exhaust their genius splitting hairs on aristocratic distinctions and thanking God they are not as others; but earnest, unselfish souls, who can go into the highways and byways, lifting up and leading, advising and encouraging with the truly catholic benevolence of the Gospel of Christ.

As Church workers we must confess our path of duty is less obvious; or rather our ability to adapt our machinery to our conception of the peculiar exigencies of this work as taught by experience and our own consciousness of the needs of the Negro, is as yet not demonstrable. Flexibility and aggressiveness are not such strong characteristics of the Church to-day as in the Dark Ages.

As a Mission field for the Church the Southern Negro is in some aspects most promising; in others, perplexing. Aliens neither in language and customs, nor in associations and sympathies, naturally of deeply rooted religious instincts and taking most readily and kindly to the worship and teachings of the Church, surely the task of proselytizing the American Negro is infinitely less formidable than that which confronted the Church in the Barbarians of Europe. Besides, this people already look to the Church as the hope of their race. Thinking colored men almost uniformly admit that the Protestant Episcopal Church with its quiet, chaste dignity and decorous solemnity, its instructive and elevating ritual, its bright chanting and joyous hymning, is eminently fitted to correct the peculiar faults of worship—the rank exuberance and often ludicrous demonstrativeness of their people. Yet, strange to say, the Church, claiming to be missionary and Catholic, urging that schism is sin and denominationalism inexcusable, has made in all these years almost no inroads upon this semi-civilized religionism.

Harvests from this over ripe field of home missions have been gathered in by Methodists, Baptists, and not least by Congregationalists, who were unknown to the Freedmen before their emancipation.

Our clergy numbers less than two dozen priests of Negro, blood and we have hardly more than one self-supporting colored congregation in the entire Southland. While the organization known as the A. M. E. Church has 14,063 ministers, itinerant and local, 4,069 self-supporting churches, churches, 4,2754,275 Sunday-schools, with property valued at $7,772,284, raising yearly for church purposes $1,427,000.

Stranger and more significant than all, the leading men of this race (I do not mean demagogues and politicians, but men of intellect, heart, and race devotion, men to whom the elevation of their people means more than personal ambition and sordid gain—and the men of that stamp have not all died yet) the Christian workers for the race, of younger and more cultured growth, are noticeably drifting into sectarian churches, many of them declaring all the time that they acknowledge the historic claims of the Church, believe her apostolicity, and would experience greater personal comfort, spiritual and intellectual, in her revered communion. It is a fact which any one may verify for himself, that representative colored men, professing that in their heart of hearts they are Episcopalians, are actually working in Methodist and Baptist pulpits; while the ranks of the Episcopal clergy are left to be filled largely by men who certainly suggest the propriety of a "*perpetual* Diaconate" if they cannot be said to have created the necessity for it.

Now where is the trouble? Something must be wrong. What is it?

A certain Southern Bishop of our Church reviewing the situation, whether in Godly anxiety or in "Gothic antipathy" I know not, deprecates the fact that the colored people do not seem *drawn* to the Episcopal Church, and comes to the sage conclusion that the Church is not adapted to the rude untutored minds of the Freedmen, and that they may be left to go to the Methodists and Baptists whither their racial proclivities undeniably tend. How the good Bishop can agree that all-foreseeing Wisdom, and Catholic Love would have framed his Church as typified in his seamless garment and unbroken body, and yet not leave it broad enough and deep enough and loving enough to seek and save and hold seven millions of God's poor, I cannot see.

But the doctors while discussing their scientifically conclusive diagnosis of the disease, will perhaps not think it presumptuous in the patient if he dares to suggest where at least the pain is. If this be allowed, *a Black woman of the South* would beg to point out two possible oversights in this southern work which may indicate in part both a cause and a remedy for some failure. The first is *not calculating for the Black man's personality*; not having respect, if I may so express it, to his manhood or deferring at all to his conceptions of the needs of his people. When colored persons have been employed it was too often as machines or as manikins. There has been no disposition, generally, to get the black man's ideal or to let his individuality work by its own gravity, as it were. A conference of earnest Christian men have met at regular intervals for some years past to discuss the best methods of promoting the welfare and development of colored people in this country. Yet, strange as it may seem, they have never invited a colored man or even intimated that one would be welcome to take part in their deliberations. Their remedial contrivances are purely theoretical or empirical, therefore, and the whole machinery devoid of soul.

The second important oversight in my judgment is closely allied to this and probably grows out of it, and that is not developing Negro womanhood as an essential fundamental for the elevation of the race, and utilizing this agency in extending the work of the Church.

Of the first I have possibly already presumed to say too much since it does not strictly come within the province of my subject. However, Macaulay somewhere criticises the Church of England as not knowing how to use fanatics, and declares that had Ignatius Loyola been in the Anglican instead of the Roman communion, the Jesuits would have been schismatics instead of Catholics; and if the religious awakenings of the Wesleys had been in Rome, she would have shaven their heads, tied ropes around their waists, and sent them out under her own banner and blessing. Whether this be true or not, there is certainly a vast amount of force potential for Negro evangelization rendered latent, or worse, antagonistic by the halting, uncertain, I had almost said, *trimming* policy of the Church in the South. This may sound both presumptuous and ungrateful. It is mortifying, I know, to benevolent wisdom, after having spent itself in the execution of well conned theories for the ideal development of a particular work, to hear perhaps the weakest and humblest element of that work: asking "what doest thou?"

Yet so it will be in life. The "thus far and no farther" pattern cannot be fitted to any growth in God's kingdom. The universal law of development is "onward and upward." It is God-given and inviolable. From the unfolding of the germ in the acorn to reach the sturdy oak, to the growth of a human soul into the full knowledge and likeness of its Creator, the breadth and scope of the movement in each and all are too grand, too mysterious, too like God himself, to be encompassed and locked down in human molds.

After all the Southern slave owners were right: either the very alphabet of intellectual growth must be forbidden and the Negro dealt with absolutely as a chattel having neither rights nor sensibilities; or else the clamps and irons of mental and moral, as well as civil compression must be riven asunder and the truly enfranchised soul led to the entrance of that boundless vista through which it is to toil upwards to its beckoning God as the buried seed germ, to meet the sun.

A perpetual colored diaconate, carefully and kindly superintended by the white clergy; congregations of shiny faced peasants with their clean white aprons and sunbonnets catechised at regular intervals and taught to recite the creed, the Lord's prayer and the ten commandments—duty towards God and duty towards neighbor, surely such well tended sheep ought to be grateful to their shepherds and content in that station of life to which it pleased God to call them. True, like the old professor lecturing to his solitary student, we make no provision here for irregularities. "Questions must be kept till after class," or dispensed with altogether. That some do ask questions and insist on answers, in class too, must be both impertinent and annoying. Let not our spiritual pastors and masters however be grieved at such self-assertion as merely signifies we have a destiny to fulfill and as men and women we must *be about our Father's business.*

It is a mistake to suppose that the Negro is prejudiced against a white ministry. Naturally there is not a more kindly and implicit follower of a white man's guidance than the average colored peasant. What would to others be an ordinary act of friendly or pastoral interest he would be more inclined to regard gratefully as a condescension. And he never forgets such kindness.

Could the Negro be brought near to his white priest or bishop, he is not suspicious. He is not only willing but often longs to unburden his soul to this intelligent guide. There are no reservations when he is convinced that you are his friend. It is a saddening satire on American history and manners that it takes something to convince him. That our people are not "drawn" to a Church whose chief dignitaries they see only in the chancel, and whom they reverence as they would a painting or an angel, whose life never comes down to and touches theirs with the inspiration of an objective reality, may be "perplex-

ing" truly (American caste and American Christianity both being facts) but it need not be surprising. There must be something of human nature in it, the same as that which brought about that "the Word was made flesh and dwelt among us" that He might "draw" us towards God.

Men are not "drawn" by abstractions. Only sympathy and love can draw, and until our Church in America realizes this and provides a clergy that can come in touch with our life and have a fellow feeling for our woes, without being imbedded and frozen up in their "Gothic antipathies," the good bishops are likely to continue "perplexed" by the sparsity of colored Episcopalians.

A colored priest of my acquaintance recently related to me, with tears in his eyes, how his reverend Father in God, the Bishop who had ordained him, had met him on the cars on his way to the diocesan convention and warned him, not unkindly, not to take a seat in the body of the convention with the white clergy. To avoid disturbance of their godly placidity he would of course please sit back and somewhat apart. I do not imagine that that clergyman had very much heart for the Christly (!) deliberations of that convention.

To return, however, it is not on this broader view of Church work, which I mentioned as a primary cause of its halting progress with the colored people, that I am to speak. My proper theme is the second oversight of which in my judgment our Christian propagandists have been guilty: or, the necessity of church training, protecting and uplifting our colored womanhood as indispensable to the evangelization of the race.

Apelles did not disdain even that criticism of his lofty art which came from an uncouth cobbler; and may I not hope that the writer's oneness with her subject both in feeling and in being may palliate undue obtrusiveness of opinions here. That the race cannot be effectually lifted up till its women are truly elevated we take as proven. It is not for us to dwell on the needs, the neglects, and the ways of succor, pertaining to the black woman of the South. The ground has been ably discussed and an admirable and practical plan proposed by the oldest Negro priest in America, advising and urging that special organizations such as Church Sisterhoods and industrial schools be devised to meet her pressing needs in the Southland. That some such movements are vital to the life of this people and the extension of the Church among them, is not hard to see. Yet the pamphlet fell still-born from the press. So far as I am informed the Church has made no motion towards carrying out Dr. Crummell's suggestion.

The denomination which comes next our own in opposing the proverbial emotionalism of Negro worship in the South, and which in consequence like ours receives the cold shoulder from the old heads, resting as we do under the charge of not "having religion" and not believing in conversion—the Congregationalists—have quietly gone to work on the young, have established industrial and training schools, and now almost every community in the South is yearly enriched by a fresh infusion of vigorous young hearts, cultivated heads, and helpful hands that have been trained at Fisk, at Hampton, in Atlanta University, and in Tuskegee, Alabama.

These young people are missionaries actual or virtual both here and in Africa. They have learned to love the methods and doctrines of the Church which trained and educated them; and so Congregationalism surely and steadily progresses.

Need I compare these well known facts with results shown by the Church in the same field and during the same or even a longer time.

The institution of the Church in the South to which she mainly looks for the training of her colored clergy and for the help of the "Black Woman" and "Colored Girl" of the South, has graduated since the year 1868, when the school was founded, *five young women*; and while yearly numerous young men have been kept and trained for the ministry by the charities of the Church, the number of indigent females who have here been supported, sheltered and trained, is phenomenally small. Indeed, to my mind, the attitude of the Church toward this feature of her work, is as if the solution of the problem of Negro missions depended solely on sending a quota of deacons and priests into the field, girls being a sort of *tertium quid* whose development may be promoted if they can pay their way and fall in with the plans mapped out for the training of the other sex.

Now I would ask in all earnestness, does not this force potential deserve by education and stimulus to be made dynamic? Is it not a solemn duty incumbent on all colored churchmen to make it so? Will not the aid of the Church be given to prepare our girls in head, heart, and hand for the duties and responsibilities that await the intelligent wife, the Christian

Glossary

Achilles	a hero of the ancient Trojan War
A. M. E. Church	the African Methodist Episcopal Church
Apelles	an ancient Greek painter
Bascom	probably Henry Bidleman Bascom, an early-nineteenth-century American Congregationalist minister
Bethany	a biblical village near Jerusalem
Byron and Wordsworth	George Gordon, Lord Byron and William Wordsworth, prominent English Romantic poets in the early nineteenth century
"Byron, like a rocket, shot his way upward ..."	from Henry Bidleman Bascom's *Lectures on Mental and Moral Philosophy*
Catholic	traditionally, a reference to the universality of the Christian church, not to the Catholic denomination
Charlemagne	king of France and Holy Roman Emperor during the eighth and ninth centuries
Chaucer	Geoffrey Chaucer, a fourteenth-century British poet, author of *The Canterbury Tales*; the quotation is from the "Wife of Bath's Tale."
Chinese shoe	the Chinese practice of binding the feet of girls to prevent the feet from growing
Dr. Crummell	Alexander Crummell, a nineteenth-century pastor and abolitionist

mother, the earnest, virtuous, helpful woman, at once both the lever and the fulcrum for uplifting the race.

As Negroes and churchmen we cannot be indifferent to these questions. They touch us most vitally on both sides. We believe in the Holy Catholic Church. We believe that however gigantic and apparently remote the consummation, the Church will go on conquering and to conquer till the kingdoms of this world, not excepting the black man and the black woman of the South, shall have become the kingdoms of the Lord and of his Christ.

That past work in this direction has been unsatisfactory we must admit. That without a change of policy results in the future will be as meagre, we greatly fear. Our life as a race is at stake. The dearest interests of our hearts are in the scales. We must either break away from dear old landmarks and plunge out in any line and every line that enables us to meet the pressing need of our people, or we must ask the Church to allow and help us, untrammelled by the prejudices and theories of individuals, to work aggressively under her direction as we alone can, with God's help, for the salvation of our people.

The time is ripe for action. Self-seeking and ambition must be laid on the altar. The battle is one of sacrifice and hardship, but our duty is plain. We have been recipients of missionary bounty in some sort for twenty-one years. Not even the senseless vegetable is content to be a mere reservoir. Receiving without giving is an anomaly in nature. Nature's cells are all little workshops for manufacturing sunbeams, the product to be *given out* to earth's inhabitants in warmth, energy, thought, action. Inanimate creation always pays back an equivalent.

Now, *How much owest thou my Lord?* Will his account be overdrawn if he call for singleness of purpose and self-sacrificing labor for your brethren? Having passed through your drill school, will you refuse a general's commission even if it entail responsibility, risk and anxiety, with possibly some adverse criticism? Is it too much to ask you to step forward and direct the work for your race along those lines which you know to be of first and vital importance?

Will you allow these words of Ralph Waldo Emerson? "In ordinary," says he, "we have a snappish criticism which watches and contradicts the opposite party. We want the will which advances and dictates

Glossary

Emerson	Ralph Waldo Emerson, nineteenth-century American essayist and poet
Feudal System	the medieval social and economic system based on the relationship between landowners and their vassals
"first the blade, then the ear, after that the full corn in the ear"	from the biblical book of Mark, chapter 4, verse 28
houri	beautiful maidens who, in Islamic belief, live in Paradise
"How much owest thou my Lord?"	from the biblical book of Luke, chapter 16, verse 5
"I am with you to the end of the world"	loosely quoted from the biblical book of Matthew, chapter 28, verse 20
"If thy brother smite thee on one cheek …"	from the biblical book of Matthew, chapter 5, verse 39
Ignatius Loyola	sixteenth-century Spanish saint and founder of the Jesuit order of Catholic priests
"In ordinary …"	from Ralph Waldo Emerson's 1870 essay "Courage"
Koran	the sacred scripture of Islam; often spelled Qur'an
M. Guizot	François Guizot, a nineteenth-century French historian; "M" means "monsieur"

[acts]. Nature has made up her mind that what cannot defend itself, shall not be defended. Complaining never so loud and with never so much reason, is of no use. What cannot stand must fall; *and the measure of our sincerity and therefore of the respect of men is the amount of health and wealth we will hazard in the defense of our right."*

Glossary

Macaulay	Thomas Babington Macaulay, a nineteenth-century British historian
Madame de Stael	a Swiss author who lived in Paris and had a marked influence on French literature at the turn of the nineteenth century
Mahomet	an antique spelling of Muhammad, the prophet of Islam
Martin R. Delany	a black military officer in the Civil War
Mussulman	an antique variant of Muslim
Nazarene	Jesus Christ, from his birthplace at Nazareth
pari passu	Latin for "with equal step," often used to mean "hand in hand" or "part and parcel"
Phoebus	the sun
Sodom	an ancient biblical city believed to have been destroyed by God; often used as a metaphor for vice
summum bonum	Latin for "highest good"
Tacitus	Publius Cornelius Tacitus, an ancient Roman senator and historian
Wesleys	John and Charles Wesley, founders of Methodism in the eighteenth century
"Yet saints their watch are keeping ..."	from a hymn by Samuel John Stone

Illustration of Jim Crow (Library of Congress)

"There is no just reason why manly men of any race should allow themselves to be continually outraged and oppressed by their equals."

Overview

"Organized Resistance Is Our Best Remedy" may not be one of John Edward Bruce's most recognized works, but it is considered his most militant. The speech, which was delivered to an all-black audience on October 5, 1889, in Washington, D.C., directly addresses the violence against African Americans that was rampant in the southern United States in the late nineteenth century. Bruce, a longtime journalist and black rights activist, took it upon himself to directly confront the issues of racial inequality and violence facing African Americans.

Bruce's "Organized Resistance" speech identifies aggression and force against African Americans as the white solution to the so-called Negro problem. He argues that the only way African Americans can combat southern white aggression is with organized resistance. The address was given in the fall of 1889 in the nation's capital, but little else is known about its origins. Bruce's speech stands alone as a work of confrontational oratory, calling upon those in the African American community to assert themselves and defend their basic human rights against the violence inflicted by whites in the South. "Organized Resistance Is Our Best Remedy" is part of a collection of Bruce's manuscripts housed at the New York Public Library's Schomburg Center for Research in Black Culture.

Context

The end of the nineteenth century was a time of heightened racial tensions between blacks and whites, especially in the southern United States. Violence against African Americans was a daily occurrence, and the overwhelming tone of the time was for blacks to adopt an accommodationist philosophy, that is, to accept their fate as second-class citizens, learn to live with it, and find a way to fit into a white society. The four decades prior to 1889 set the stage for increased racial animosity and in turn paved the way for African American activists such as Bruce to empower the black community and promote racial pride.

By the middle of the nineteenth century, the United States was teetering on the brink of civil war. The Mexican-American War, fought between 1846 and 1848, had ended with the acquisition of a large amount of land by the United States. The North and the South clashed over whether the new land should outlaw slavery or allow it. Staunch opposition by the South to the exclusion of slavery in new territories led to the Compromise of 1850, which established something of a middle ground on the slavery issue and delayed the war between the states for another decade. The legislation bundled into the Compromise of 1850 allowed California to enter the Union as a free state and ended the slave trade in Washington, D.C. To pacify the South, however, the compromise left the decision on whether to allow slavery in the territory that would later become the states of New Mexico, Nevada, Arizona, and Utah to the people who lived there. Another attempt to appease the southern states was the passage of the Fugitive Slave Act as part of the Compromise of 1850. The Fugitive Slave Act required the return of runaway slaves to their owners and imposed stiff punishments on antislavery advocates who harbored or assisted fugitives.

In 1852 the white abolitionist Harriet Beecher Stowe published her controversial novel *Uncle Tom's Cabin*, which promoted abolitionist thought, primarily in the North, and angered supporters of slavery in the South. The book only increased tensions between the two regions, adding momentum to the conflict that would ultimately become the Civil War. Two years later, in May 1854, the Kansas-Nebraska Act was passed. Similar in spirit to parts of the Compromise of 1850, the act allowed popular sovereignty to determine whether or not a territory would allow the practice of slavery within its borders. Settlers flooded the territories to sway the vote, and violence ensued. The decision for Kansas to be admitted to the Union as a free state did not come easily. The North and antislavery supporters were desperate to keep slavery out of any new states, while the South was determined to expand slavery north of the 40th parallel (previously considered, by the repealed Missouri Compromise, a border that slavery could not cross). At least three elections took place to determine the fate of Kansas. The first election was won by proslavery supporters, but the election was considered fraudulent by antislavery advocates. Antislavery supporters called for another election, again with no viable

Time Line

1850

■ **September**
The Compromise of 1850 is passed in the hope of quelling tensions between the North and the South.

1852

■ Harriet Beecher Stowe publishes *Uncle Tom's Cabin*, an antislavery novel that helps bring the abolitionist movement to the forefront of American society.

1854

■ **May 30**
The Kansas-Nebraska Act is passed by Congress, allowing settlers to decide by popular vote if a territory is to allow slavery within its borders.

1856

■ **February 22**
John Edward Bruce is born to slave parents in Maryland.

1857

■ **March 6**
The decision in *Dred Scott v. Sandford* is handed down by the U.S. Supreme Court, stating that slaves are not citizens and therefore are not guaranteed any freedoms or protection under the Constitution.

1861

■ **April 12**
The first shots of the Civil War ring out over Fort Sumter at Charleston Harbor, South Carolina, signaling the start of a war that will have lasting effects on African American rights in the United States.

1865

■ **January 31**
The Thirteenth Amendment to the U.S. Constitution is passed by Congress, outlawing slavery in the United States; however, it is not ratified by all the states until December 6.

■ **April 9**
The Civil War ends with Confederate general Robert E. Lee's surrender to General Ulysses S. Grant at Appomattox Court House, Virginia.

---

outcome as no proslavery supporters voted. Another election was called, ending much like the first; it was not until 1861 that an antislavery population became the majority in the territory, admitting Kansas as a free state. Nebraska would not be admitted into the Union as a free state until after the close of the Civil War. The Kansas-Nebraska Act exacerbated the increasingly growing split between the supporters of abolition and the proponents of slavery.

Throughout the mid-1800s the rights of African Americans were hazy at best. On March 6, 1857, the questionable status of blacks in the United States was clarified temporarily by U.S. Chief Justice Roger Taney's decision in the case of *Dred Scott v. Sandford*—a decision that served as a major setback for every person of color living in the United States at the time. Dred Scott was a slave who had traveled extensively with his owner and lived for nine years in free territory. Scott argued that his freedom was ensured throughout the country, even in slave states, after those nine years, based on the "once free, always free" philosophy. Much to the dismay of antislavery advocates throughout the nation, Taney declared that Scott had never been free and that he was not and never would be a citizen of the United States; thus, he had no protection under federal law. The opinion further stated that Congress did not have the power to outlaw slavery in newly acquired American territories.

It is important to note that Chief Justice Taney was a former slaveholder from Maryland and that five of the nine justices on the Supreme Court in 1857 were slave owners. Following Taney's decision, abolitionist sentiment swelled. Northerners questioned the validity of a decision handed down by a predominantly southern court said to represent the entire United States. The majority of Americans at the time lived in the northern states and territories, but the Supreme Court's decision makers hailed mainly from the South. Taney's opinion sparked public outcries against the Supreme Court and called into question the constitutionality of decisions made by a court that represented the interests of the minority in America at the time—the slaveholders. Many historians consider *Dred Scott v. Sandford* a pivotal case in race relations that virtually guaranteed the outbreak of the Civil War four years later.

The Civil War was among the bloodiest wars in American history, with enormous losses on both sides. In all, more than two hundred thousand soldiers died in combat; another four hundred thousand lost their lives to disease. The postwar South was devastated both by battle and by the realization that slavery was no longer an acceptable practice for the Union. Southern states that had originally seceded from the Union were required to create new state constitutions in order to qualify for readmission. The new constitutions mandated, among other things, clauses granting civil liberties to former slaves. John Edward Bruce made his "Organized Resistance Is Our Best Remedy" speech in 1889, nearly twenty-five years after the Civil War ended. By that time, the decision in *Dred Scott v. Sandford* had been overturned by the passage of the Thirteenth and Fourteenth Amendments to the U.S. Constitution. The former, passed in 1865, made slavery illegal in the United States; the latter, ratified in 1868, guaranteed that any person born in the United States, regardless of color, was a natural American citizen whose rights could not be taken away—meaning that individual states in the South could no longer deny African Americans their freedom. Although the basic rights of freedom and citizenship seemed to be spelled out by these amendments, their impact was minimal.

The Reconstruction era, which lasted from the end of the war until 1877, brought several changes to the postwar South, including organizations such as the Freedmen's Bureau, with the intention of bettering the situation of formerly enslaved African Americans by providing basic necessities, health care, education, and work opportunities. Reconstruction was a relatively brief era in American history, and its conclusion was disastrous for African Americans, as it signaled the end of many social, political, and economic gains made by the black community. The presence of northern troops in the South after the Civil War was commonplace. It was the duty of Union troops to protect the rights of newly freed blacks and to suppress violence against blacks when local authorities failed to act.

In 1870 the Fifteenth Amendment was ratified, granting all men, regardless of race, the right to vote. Unfortunately, by the late 1890s states like Louisiana had created grandfather clauses that took away the voting rights of blacks who were not lineal descendants of men who had voting rights prior to 1867. The rights of blacks would experience another blow with the abolishment of the Freedmen's Bureau in 1872 and again five years later when federal troops began their withdrawal from the South. With the departure of northern troops, freed men and women no longer had federal protection of their civil rights or protection from race-motivated violence. With the exit of the last Union troops from the South, white supremacist leaders began their ruinous rise, taking over key political positions and influencing southern policies. It appeared as though the stigma of *Dred Scott v. Sandford* lingered in the South despite the passage of constitutional amendments to the contrary

The year 1877 ushered in the era of Jim Crow in the South, which would last until the 1960s. Jim Crow laws made up a discriminatory social code, backed up by legislation, through which blacks were deemed second-class citizens and racial segregation was considered necessary to maintain order. By the early 1880s documented violence against African Americans was becoming common, as Jim Crow laws were generally enforced by violence or the threat thereof by white authorities. Lynchings, burnings, and other random acts of terror were perpetrated against African Americans, and the number of these documented attacks increased into the twentieth century, with many more abuses never reported. It was against this backdrop of seemingly dashed hopes that John Edward Bruce gave his "Organized Resistance Is Our Best Remedy" speech. His goal was to rally African Americans toward self-defense and dispel the notion that people of color would always be second-class citizens in the United States.

Time Line

1868

■ July 9
The Fourteenth Amendment to the U.S. Constitution declares anyone of any color born in the United States to be an American citizen; along with the Thirteenth Amendment, this reverses the decision in the *Dred Scott* case.

1889

■ October 5
Bruce gives his speech "Organized Resistance Is Our Best Remedy" in Washington, D.C.

1897

■ March 5
Bruce cofounds the American Negro Academy (ANA) to protest accommodationism.

1901

■ Bruce publishes *The Blood Red Record: A Review of the Horrible Lynchings and Burning of Negroes by Civilized White Men in the United States.*

1911

■ In his greatest and most lasting achievement, Bruce cofounds the Negro Society for Historical Research with Arthur Schomburg.

1916

■ The Jamaican activist Marcus Garvey moves to the United States and establishes the Back to Africa movement and the Universal Negro Improvement Association; Bruce soon becomes one of Garvey's closest followers.

1924

■ August 7
Bruce dies.

About the Author

John Edward Bruce was born a slave on a plantation in Piscataway, Maryland, on February 22, 1856. His parents, Martha and Robert Bruce, were both slaves, and Robert was sold off to another owner when John was just a toddler, leaving a void in his son's life. Young Bruce, his mother, and his brother remained in bondage until 1861, when they moved to Washington, D.C. His brother died shortly thereafter. Bruce and his mother then lived for a short time in

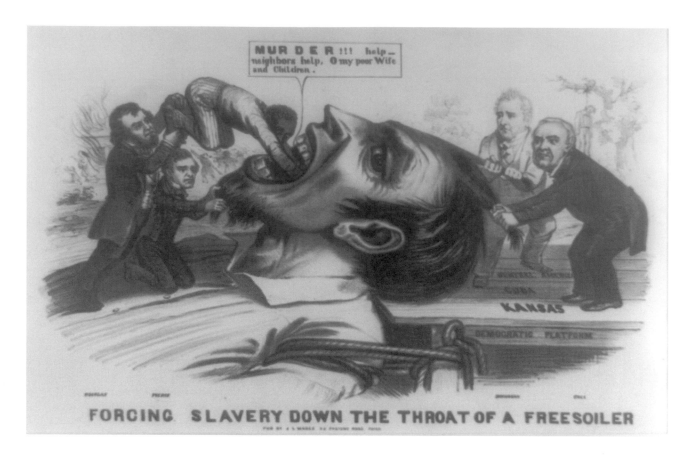

Politicians forcing slavery down the throat of a Free-Soiler (Library of Congress)

Connecticut, where Bruce attended an integrated school for approximately two years. The two returned to Washington sometime between 1867 and 1868. Upon their return, Bruce attended the Free Library School and other schools funded by two post–Civil War agencies: the Freedman's Aid Society and the Freedmen's Bureau. While in Washington, Bruce took on odd jobs to help support his mother. He worked variously in a café, as a doorman, and as a utility worker for the father-in-law of the Union general Ulysses S. Grant. It was in Washington that Bruce first developed his hatred of racism and condemned those who failed to confront the problem directly.

In 1874 Bruce began his journalism career as a messenger at the Washington, D.C., bureau of the *New York Times*. A year later he published his first piece in *Progressive American*. Between 1879 and 1882, Bruce started up a number of newspapers, including the *Argus Weekly*, the *Sunday Item*, and the *Republican*. Throughout his fifty-year-long career as a journalist, he wrote for more than forty periodicals; he also served as editor of the Baltimore, Maryland–based newspaper the *Commonwealth*. The influential black civil rights activist and *New York Globe* editor Timothy Thomas Fortune gave him the nickname "Bruce Grit" because of the tenacity and courage displayed in his writings. The new pen name stuck, and as "Bruce Grit," Bruce contributed a regular column to Fortune's *Globe* and in 1887 became a special correspondent for a later incarnation of the *Globe* called the *New York Age*.

Throughout his adult life Bruce Grit used his writings to advance African American interests; he also joined organizations—the first Afro-American League, founded by Fortune in 1887, among them—that promoted the interests of black Americans. Unable to agree with the widely circulated stance of accommodation (a philosophy advocating patience with the very slow and gradual assimilation of free black Americans into the white world rather than overt resistance to racial oppression), Bruce often found himself in opposition to other leading African American activists of the time, including Booker T. Washington, the renowned black educator and founder of Alabama's Tuskegee Institute.

In the fall of 1889 Bruce delivered the speech "Organized Resistance Is Our Best Remedy" to an unknown audience in Washington, D.C. A little more than two decades later, in 1911, Bruce and his close friend Arthur Schomburg established the Negro Society for Historical Research in Bruce's New York home. Bruce and Schomburg's goal for the society was to promote African achievement and create an intellectual center for African Americans.

Bruce's belief and zeal in improving the lives of blacks led him to follow the ideas of the Jamaican-born black activist Marcus Garvey. Although he was at first apprehensive regarding Garvey's true motives for settling in the United States, Bruce was swayed by a 1919 speech Garvey gave in Harlem, a predominantly black section of New York City known for its vibrant literary, artistic, and intellectual atmosphere. Bruce be-

"Agitation is a good thing, organization is a better thing."

(Paragraph 1)

"The man who will not fight for the protection of his wife and children is a coward and deserves to be ill treated. The man who takes his life in his hand and stands up for what he knows to be right will always command the respect of his enemy."

(Paragraph 1)

"Submission to the dicta of the Southern bulldozers is the basest cowardice, and there is no just reason why manly men of any race should allow themselves to be continually outraged and oppressed by their equals before the law."

(Paragraph 2)

"The Negro must not be rash and indiscreet either in action or in words but he must be very determined and terribly in earnest, and of one mind to bring order out of chaos and to convince Southern rowdies and cutthroats that more than two can play at the game with which they have amused their fellow conspirators in crime for nearly a quarter of a century."

(Paragraph 4)

"Organized resistance to organized resistance is the best remedy for the solution of the vexed problem of the century."

(Paragraph 4)

came a part of the Garvey movement and later became known by Garveyites as the "Duke of Uganda." The title was given to Bruce by Garvey, who had referred to himself within his own movement as "President" and gave titles to those who were closest to the inner workings of the movement and those he felt made worthy contributions to furthering the black race. Garvey is probably best known for establishing the Back to Africa movement and founding the Universal Negro Improvement Association; Bruce aligned himself with both and remained an active supporter of Garvey until his death in 1924. Upon his death, the Universal Negro Improvement Associa-

tion honored Bruce for his contributions to their cause by knighting him the Duke of Uganda. Bruce's funeral consisted of three ceremonies and was attended by over five thousand people, including Garvey, who gave the eulogy.

A militant African American journalist, Bruce left his mark on the literary world with his sharp, direct, and unapologetic writings and speeches on race in America. However, few people know about his speech titled "Organized Resistance Is Our Best Remedy"; it was delivered at an unspecified location in Washington, D.C., to what is believed to have been an all-black audience.

Explanation and Analysis of the Document

The speech "Organized Resistance Is Our Best Remedy" is brief but powerful. Historians note that Bruce's ideas on the practice of self-defense by African Americans were well thought out and his vocabulary carefully chosen. Delivered on October 5, 1889, at an unknown venue in Washington, D.C., the speech directly identifies the problem of violence against African Americans by southern aggressors and encourages the black community to fight organized resistance with organized resistance. Bruce acknowledges that there is strength in numbers among African Americans and foresees tangible progress in the movement for self-defense under the proper leadership. After arguing that force is a justified method of defense under ancient law, Bruce concludes his speech with great sincerity, stepping back from his impassioned plea to his audience and closing instead with a simple appeal to their rational side: "I submit this view of the question, ladies and gentleman, for your careful consideration."

By this time in his journalistic career, Bruce was well aware of the influence he wielded in the African American community. In the opening of his "Organized Resistance" speech, he tries to prepare his audience for the bold and shocking nature of what he is about to propose. He explains that the use of force, or "organized resistance," is justified in light of the white response to the "Negro problem." The term *Negro problem* refers to the dehumanizing and degrading view of freed blacks as nothing more than an ongoing source of difficulty for whites—a view shared by many of the nation's southern whites after the Civil War. Antiblack sentiment festered among parts of the white population in the South, leading especially violent whites to "deal" with the "Negro problem" by launching unprovoked attacks on African Americans. Barbaric terrorist tactics such as burnings and lynchings were continually perpetrated against black Americans to keep them from asserting their rights as full citizens of the United States. Bruce would take on the subject of lynching in his book *The Blood Red Record: A Review of the Horrible Lynchings and Burning of Negroes by Civilized White Men in the United States*, published in 1901.

Bruce anticipates opposition to his ideas by the audience. He notes that slaves were trained to be submissive; consequently, they often gave in to oppression from their owners, hoping for the situation to resolve itself. To these people, Bruce argues that African Americans have already tried the patient approach, to no avail. He then unveils his plan of organized resistance based on the concept of strength in numbers, pointing out that there must be millions of African Americans across the South, some known by government record and some unknown, since the southern states did not keep careful records of the numbers of African Americans within their borders. If millions of African Americans could be brought together under strong, well-directed leadership, explains Bruce, then black organized force against white organized force would produce "most beneficial results" for African Americans.

Beginning with the end of the first paragraph, Bruce addresses any naysayers opposed to the idea of using force to assert the natural rights of African Americans. Using language that almost chastises those who would fail to stand tall against their southern white aggressors, he states that those who are not willing to fight for their families are "cowards" who deserve harsh treatment. Bruce then appeals to the pride and honor of the men to whom he is speaking, stating that those who are willing to risk their lives for their beliefs will undoubtedly be respected. Bruce is calling upon blacks to stand united against southern hostilities, to risk death for their natural rights, and to bravely oppose their aggressors. This position is in direct defiance to the accommodationist stance taken by other African American activists of the time, most notably Booker T. Washington. Bruce is promoting aggressive action to achieve racial respect, rather than the widely circulated notion of merely accepting the circumstances that African Americans were forced to live with at this point in history.

The following two shorter paragraphs continue to provide justification for organized force as the only remaining option for African Americans. Bruce refers to the perpetrators of white oppression as "bulldozers" who use their self-proclaimed edicts to mow down people of color. He asserts that the very idea of African Americans being intimidated by southern attempts at coercion are ludicrous and reminds the audience that blacks and whites are equals under the law. The speech takes on a religious tone when Bruce states that "salvation" will be found only when African Americans come to terms with the idea of resistance. He notes that prospective leaders of the organized resistance must be "wise and discreet" and refers to the body of African Americans as one person, most likely to emphasize the unity inherent in an organized resistance movement.

In the last paragraph of the speech, Bruce gives his most tangible advice on implementing the call for resistance and provokes the audience with a plea for immediacy. Once again he emphasizes that African Americans must think and act as one in order to accomplish this most serious task of organized force. He also refers to the white antagonists in the speech as "rowdies and cutthroats." There is no doubt that these adjectives were chosen specifically to incite fury and disdain among the members of the audience, especially those who had been directly affected by white brutality. Bruce empowers his listeners by arguing that an organized African American resistance would be a formidable opponent to southern white aggressors who resort to terror and violence against law-abiding blacks.

Bruce includes additional justification in this last paragraph for the use of force against force. He cites the precedent of the biblical law of retribution, "an eye for an eye and a tooth for a tooth," stating that these laws were used in similar circumstances throughout history. It is at this point in the speech that Bruce's militant ideals become undeniable. According to Bruce, African Americans should demand equal justice for every wrong southern whites inflict upon them. The speech reaches its climax when he asserts that his formula for resistance will no doubt result in some bloodshed. Bruce then concludes "Organized Resistance Is Our Best Remedy" by asking his audience to carefully consider his proposition.

Audience

Bruce's speech was delivered to an unidentified audience—most likely all African American and predominantly male—at an undisclosed meeting place in the nation's capital. In keeping with the majority of his writings, the speech was geared solely toward the black community in an effort to discourage their acceptance of accommodationist thought. It is likely that some members of the audience were former slaves who had been inculcated with the notion that they would never be able to reach social equality with whites and instead should be content to be tolerated by the white world. Bruce's message was that oppression and violence against African Americans could no longer be tolerated in the United States and that it was up to the black community to assert itself through organized resistance against southern whites.

Impact

Bruce's speech did not have a direct or immediate documented impact at the time it was delivered; however, it stands as a testament to the fearlessness the speaker exemplified in his pursuit of African American interests. He did not cower at the notion of resistance against brutality; rather, he brought the reality of white oppression and violence against African Americans to the fore. Shortly after this speech, Bruce published *The Blood Red Record*, a pamphlet providing detailed accounts of brutality against African Americans, including names of lynching victims and the methods of violence used against them. Some historians argue that Bruce's writings were overlooked because he did not write for the white community; his works, it has been noted, had "little to do with white history." This is quite evident in Bruce's speech: He clearly addresses the issue of violence against African Americans, but he acknowledges the "white" southerner only at the very end of his speech. By minimizing the use of the word *white* and making the role of the white southerner secondary, Bruce does indeed keep his speech out of "white history." His revolutionary call to resistance can be viewed as an inspiration to future black activists and as a precursor to the civil rights movement that began in the United States in the mid-1950s.

See also Slavery Clauses in the U.S. Constitution (1787); Fugitive Slave Act of 1850; *Dred Scott v. Sandford* (1857); Thirteenth Amendment to the U.S. Constitution (1865); Fourteenth Amendment to the U.S. Constitution (1868); Fifteenth Amendment to the U.S. Constitution (1870).

Further Reading

■ Books

Foner, Philip S., and Robert J. Branham, eds. *Lift Every Voice: African American Oratory, 1787–1900*. Tuscaloosa: University of Alabama Press, 1998.

Gilbert, Peter. *The Selected Writings of John Edward Bruce: Militant Black Journalist*. New York: Arno Press, 1971.

Seraile, William. *Bruce Grit: The Black Nationalist Writings of John Edward Bruce*. Knoxville: University of Tennessee Press, 2003.

■ Web Sites

"Compromise of 1850." National Archives "Our Documents" Web site. http://www.ourdocuments.gov/doc.php?doc=27.

Questions for Further Study

1. Compare Bruce's proposals with the outlooks expressed by other African American writers of this era, such as Booker T. Washington, T. Thomas Fortune, John L. Moore, and, at the turn of the twentieth century, W. E. B. Du Bois.

2. Compare this document with the entry titled Ku Klux Klan Act. In what ways does the latter document reinforce Bruce's views?

3. In what ways did Bruce's speech foreshadow black militancy and the Black Power movement of the 1960s and 1970s (as represented, for example, by Stokely Carmichael's speech on Black Power at Berkeley or Eldridge Cleaver's "Education and Revolution")? What goals and methods did the movement share with Bruce?

"Dred Scott v. Sanford (1857)." National Archives "Our Documents" Web site.
   http://www.ourdocuments.gov/doc.php?flash=false&doc=29.

"Kansas-Nebraska Act." National Archives "Our Documents" Web site.
   http://www.ourdocuments.gov/doc.php?flash=false&doc=28.

—Kimberly R. Cook

John Edward Bruce's "Organized Resistance Is Our Best Remedy"

I fully realize the delicacy of the position I occupy in this discussion and know too well that those who are to follow me will largely benefit by what I shall have to say in respect to the application of force as one of the means to the solution of the problem known as the Negro problem. I am not unmindful of that fact that there are those living who have faith in the efficacy of submission, who are impregnated with the slavish fear which had its origin in oppression and the peculiar environments of the slave period. Those who are thus minded will advise a pacific policy in order, as they believe, to effect a settlement of this question, with which the statesmanship of a century has grappled without any particularly gratifying results. Agitation is a good thing, organization is a better thing. The million Negro voters of Georgia, and the undiscovered millions in other Southern states—undiscovered so far as our knowledge of their number exists—could with proper organization and intelligent leadership meet force with force with most beneficial results. The issue upon us cannot be misunderstood by those who are watching current events.... The man who will not fight for the protection of his wife and children is a *coward* and deserves to be ill treated. The man who takes his life in his hand and stands up for what he knows to be right will always command the respect of his enemy.

Submission to the *dicta* of the Southern bulldozers is the basest cowardice, and there is no just reason why manly men of any race should allow themselves to be continually outraged and oppressed by their equals before the law....

Under the present conditions of affairs the only hope, the only salvation for the Negro is to be found in a resort to force under wise and discreet leaders. He must sooner or later come to this in order to set at rest for all time to come the charge that he is a moral coward ....

The Negro must not be rash and indiscreet either in action or in words but he must be very determined and terribly in earnest, and of one mind to bring order out of chaos and to convince Southern rowdies and cutthroats that more than two can play at the game with which they have amused their fellow conspirators in crime for nearly a quarter of a century. Under the Mosaic dispensation it was the custom to require an eye for an eye and a tooth for a tooth under no less barbarous civilization than that which existed at that period of the world's history; let the Negro require at the hands of every white murderer in the South or elsewhere a life for a life. If they burn our houses, burn theirs, if they kill our wives and children, kill theirs, pursue them relentlessly, meet force with force everywhere it is offered. If they demand blood, exchange it with them, until they are satiated. By a vigorous adherence to this course the shedding of human blood by white men will soon become a thing of the past. Wherever and whenever the Negro shows himself to be a man he can always command the respect even of a cutthroat. Organized resistance to organized resistance is the best remedy for the solution of the vexed problem of the century, which to me seems practical and feasible, and I submit this view of the question, ladies and gentleman, for your careful consideration.

Glossary

Mosaic dispensation	the law of Moses

A caricature of Henry Cabot Lodge as a hedgehog with swords and bayonets labeled "U.S." replacing some of his bristles. (Library of Congress)

MILESTONE DOCUMENTS IN AFRICAN AMERICAN HISTORY

JOHN L. MOORE'S "IN THE LION'S MOUTH"

"We want protection at the ballot box, so that the laboring man may have an equal showing."

Overview

A letter to the editor written by the Reverend John L. Moore of the Colored Farmers' National Alliance and Cooperative Union appeared in the *National Economist* newspaper, published in Washington, D.C., on March 7, 1891. It was reprinted from a newspaper in Jacksonville, Florida, that had featured an attack on leaders of the Colored Farmers' National Alliance for its support of the Lodge election bill a proposed congressional bill that would provide for the federal supervision of elections in the South. Moore's letter is a testament to independent black leadership in the South during the post-Reconstruction period, a period often portrayed as a time of political inaction among southern African Americans. The letter, referred to here as "In the Lion's Mouth" (usually noted as simply "Moore's letter" in documents), is in reference to a metaphor used by Moore in which he saw African Americans and white independents increasingly placing themselves in a politically vulnerable situation by allowing professional politicians to represent their interests instead of fielding candidates of their own.

On June 26, 1890, the U.S. representative Henry Cabot Lodge of Massachusetts had introduced into Congress a federal elections bill that detractors quickly called the "force bill." Lodge's proposed legislation would allow federal authorities to oversee national elections if, in a district with at least five hundred people, fifty people signed a petition attesting to electoral fraud—such as tampering of ballot boxes, deliberately miscounting votes, or adding the votes of fictitious persons—all strategies regularly employed by officials to favor Democratic outcomes. Although the legislation technically applied only to federal elections, the bill would have also impinged upon state and local election practices. Given the history of Reconstruction in the South—in particular the strong federal control that white southerners felt they had been subjected to during that period of political and social recovery from the Civil War—the Lodge bill ignited fierce opposition among southern white Democrats, those most threatened by such federal supervision. Political opposi-

tion to the proposed bill included the Jacksonville newspaper editor to whom Moore addressed his letter. The House of Representatives passed the bill on July 2, 1890, but Democrats in the U.S. Senate, along with eight Republicans, would wind up defeating it the following year.

Context

The end of Reconstruction in 1877, marked by the withdrawal of a federal military presence in the South, saw black and white Republican legislators and officeholders systematically, sometimes brutally removed from office by white Democrats who sought to "redeem" the South from Republican authority. These "Redeemers," as they came to be known, also terrorized local black populations through paramilitary organizations such as the White Leagues and the Red Shirts, which served as adjuncts of the Democratic Party. Led by white planters, Democrats took office and reasserted their antebellum privileges and prerogatives. They would do so as the "Southern Democracy"—the network of courts, militias, sheriffs, and newspapers supporting redemption. Helping to ensure their control over black labor and much of the southern political economy was the system of sharecropping, a new economic arrangement in the region. Under this system, sharecroppers owed a share of their crop to landlords after each harvest, although cash rents were sometimes collected; in practice, the system led to debt peonage, de facto forced labor owing to the exorbitant interest rates applied to loans made by landowners to sharecroppers and tenants.

African Americans in the South would respond to their economic plight in various ways. Some sought to migrate to the West in search of new opportunities, while others attempted to fight back politically. Between 1886 and 1900—within a decade following the end of Reconstruction and before the consolidation of Jim Crow laws, which disenfranchised and segregated African Americans—tens of thousands of black farmers, sharecroppers, and agrarian workers mobilized to action. They demanded higher wages, debt relief, government regulation of railroads, a farmer subsidy program, the protection of civil and political rights, and electoral reform. The movement grew out

Time Line

1877
- Reconstruction ends with the removal from the South of the last federal troops stationed to enforce the era's legislation.

1883
- The Civil Rights Act of 1875, which guaranteed equal treatment in public accommodations, is ruled unconstitutional by the U.S. Supreme Court.

1886
- The Colored Farmers' National Alliance and Cooperative Union is formed in Houston County, Texas.

1890
- Several prolabor and profarmer Populist-oriented parties are established in the nation to compete against one or both of the major parties.

- **July 2**
The Lodge election bill is passed in the House of Representatives.

1891
- **January**
The Lodge bill is defeated in the Senate after a southern Democratic filibuster.

- **March 7**
The *National Economist* reprints a letter from the Reverend John L. Moore to the editor of a newspaper in Jacksonville, Florida, in which he responds to criticisms of the Colored Farmers' National; Alliance for its support of federal oversight of national elections.

1892
- **November**
In the presidential election, the People's (or Populist) Party candidate James B. Weaver receives over one million votes.

1894
- A Republican-Populist coalition wins control of the North Carolina state legislature.

of established networks of black benevolent associations, fraternal orders, and churches that served as centers for the recruitment, education, and leadership training of African Americans in the years following Reconstruction. Black Populism—a broad-based independent political movement that took shape to combat Jim Crow—gained more definitive organizational form with the creation of various mutual aid societies and labor unions, including the Colored Agricultural Wheels, the Knights of Labor, the Cooperative Workers of America, the Farmers Union, and the Colored Farmers' National Alliance.

In 1890 the movement began to shift toward the electoral arena as it became clear that electoral action was necessary to make the policy changes that were sought. African Americans helped to establish and then grow the People's (or Populist) Party in coalition with white independents in order to challenge Democratic Party domination in the South. African Americans also ran insurgent and independent candidates for office and participated in "fusion" campaigns with the Republican Party, whereby two parties would share a slate of candidates. Most African Americans were loyal to the Republican Party at this time; it was Abraham Lincoln's party, the party of emancipation. Some candidates backed by Black Populists won; certain concessions and reforms were even briefly put into place, including election reforms and greater funding for public education, as in North Carolina and eastern Texas.

Lodge, a conservative northern Republican, saw federal election oversight as a way for Republicans to compete more effectively against Democrats in the South. Leaders of the Colored Farmers' National Alliance saw the bill as an important way for African Americans to regain a political voice in the South. The *National Economist*, interested in disseminating reform-oriented press by republishing articles that appeared in newspapers with smaller circulations or by highlighting certain articles, would help spread one among these black leaders' views on the importance of the bill.

About the Author

The Reverend John L. Moore was an African Methodist Episcopal minister from Crescent City, in Putnam County, northern Florida. While Moore's date of birth is unknown, he states in his letter to the editor that he had lived in various parts of the South since 1863. He may have come from the North as a young man as part of Union army efforts to defeat the Confederacy during the Civil War. Moore may have been named after the American Revolutionary War veteran John Moore, who served as skipper of the sloop *Roebuck*. The skipper famously struck a British officer for insolent treatment and, as a result, served an eighteen-month prison sentence. The Black Populist Moore may have captured some of this same rebellious spirit in his letter.

Moore eventually settled in Crescent City, about sixty miles south of Jacksonville, where his letter first appeared. Crescent

City is notable for being the birthplace of the well-known black labor organizer and civil rights leader A. Philip Randolph, founder of the Brotherhood of Sleeping Car Porters—the first African American union chartered by the American Federation of Labor. Given the small size of the Crescent City black community, it is likely that Moore personally knew Randolph's parents and extended family. According to census records, there were 554 people living in Crescent City in 1890. Of the city's total population, over one-third, or approximately 190 people, were African American.

Like other key black leaders of the era, Moore cultivated his skills as an organizer, orator, and writer via the black church. Southern black churches not only served as seedbeds of African American political activity from the antebellum era through Reconstruction but also provided much of the organizational impetus and leadership training in political movements thereafter. In his time, Moore was joined by a number of other black ministers in the Black Populist movement, including the Reverends Walter A. Pattillo of North Carolina, Henry S. Doyle of Georgia, and John B. Rayner of Texas. Moore thus formed part of a post-Reconstruction black leadership that continued the struggle for black civil and political rights that had begun with the dispersion of Africans to North America since the early seventeenth century.

Moore was elected superintendent of the Putnam County Colored Farmers' Alliance in 1889, became a member of the Florida People's Party statewide executive committee, and served as a national delegate to the series of conventions leading up to the formation of the national People's Party in July 1892. As late as 1899, Moore served as secretary of the African Methodist Episcopal Church's conference held in Orlando, Florida. His political activities following the collapse of Black Populism and the advent of Jim Crow are unknown.

Explanation and Analysis of the Document

In this letter to the editor, Moore expresses his indignation at an electoral process in the South so fraudulent that federal supervision of elections is necessary. The proposed Lodge bill strongly united African Americans—black leaders of the Colored Farmers' National Alliance in particular—in opposition to southern Democrats, who largely controlled the electoral process in the region.

♦ Paragraph 1

Moore rejects the idea that the Colored Farmers' National Alliance (known as the "black Alliance") is seeking to perpetuate national "Republican rule"; rather, he emphasizes the need for election supervision across the nation. Moore uses an example provided by the national executive committee member Alonzo Wardall of the South Dakota white-led Southern Farmers' Alliance (termed the "white Alliance"). Wardall reported to the Colored Farmers' National Alliance at the separate meetings of black and white Alliances held in Ocala, Florida, in December 1890 on the kinds of election

Time Line

1896

■ **May 18**
The U.S. Supreme Court ruling in *Plessy v. Ferguson* establishes the "separate but equal" doctrine.

1898

■ **November 10**
In the Wilmington Insurrection, the North Carolina legislature is overtaken by white supremacist Democrats; other attacks of blacks by whites follow.

1900

■ Jim Crow policies are put into effect across much of the South to legally disfranchise and segregate African Americans.

fraud taking place in his Republican-majority state. If the Republicans, Moore suggests, were willing to carry out such egregious forms of vote miscounting in South Dakota with the advent of the People's Party (an excess of ten thousand votes counted in favor of Republicans over the number of people actually registered in the state), what kind of fraud would the Democratic Party commit in the South? Moore notes specific kinds of election manipulation already used by Democrats in the South, including the refusal by party-appointed election registrars to permit the inspection of ballot boxes and the notorious "eight-ballot box system," which required separately marked ballot boxes at the polls for each office. The eight-box law was designed to induce illiterate voters to cast their ballots incorrectly, thereby providing a legal pretext for invalidating many black votes.

Moore goes on to challenge the idea that federal supervision would not benefit African Americans. While he makes clear that the proposed bill is "not satisfactory to us throughout as it reads," he also asserts that black leaders are seeking "something guaranteeing every man a free vote and an honest count." Alliance delegates unanimously supported the bill at their Ocala conference. Meanwhile, Southern Farmers' Alliance delegates went on record strongly opposing the proposed bill. It was ultimately defeated in the Senate in January 1891.

♦ Paragraph 2

Moore raises an objection to the characterization that the Colored Farmers' National Alliance's support for the Lodge bill is an instance of their "antagonizing the races"—that is, creating animosity between black and white people. Here Moore turns the tables on white newspaper editors and accuses them of not speaking out against the provocative actions of southern white people who seek to create discord among black and white people: "I never hear you, Mr.

Thomas E. Watson of Georgia (Library of Congress)

Editor, nor any of the other leading journals, once criticise their action." Contrary to the accusation that he and other black leaders were provoking discord, Moore had actually been making overtures to white alliance delegates on the basis of shared economic concerns. As the minister notes, "We are aware of the fact that the laboring colored man's interests and the laboring white man's interests are one and the same." Black and white farmers shared concerns over high interest rates and transportation costs, while black and white agrarian laborers shared concerns over low wages.

The theme of shared economic interests between black and white southerners expressed by Colored Farmers' National Alliance leaders such as Moore prefigured the famous statement made by the white Georgia Populist Thomas E. Watson regarding the shared plight of black and white farmers. In October 1892 Watson would publish in the progressive monthly *Arena* an article titled "The Negro Question in the South," in which he declared, "You are kept apart that you may be separately fleeced of your earnings. You are made to hate each other because upon that hatred is rested the keystone of the arch of financial despotism which enslaves you both."

Making note of the significant number of African Americans who constitute the nation's workforce, especially those involved in "agricultural pursuits," Moore offers an independent political perspective, one which is distinctly nonparti-

san: Black Populists will vote for whoever will advance the interests of farmers and laborers, be they Republicans, Democrats, or People's Party candidates. He offers here a substantially nuanced view of black political intent and action, one which runs counter to the notion that African Americans solely supported Republican candidates. It is a more tactically sophisticated view than the one presupposed of African Americans reflexively following the Republican Party.

♦ **Paragraph 3**

In this paragraph Moore locates the contemporary struggles of African Americans within the larger historical framework. He notes the long struggle for black liberation, reminding his readers that Africans were initially brought to North America as slaves in the early seventeenth century, but is careful not to speak of violent forms of resistance to slavery. Instead, he uses more passive language and phrasing, stating, for instance, how four million African Americans were freed from the "yoke of bondage" by 1865, and discusses the ways in which black men and women cared for white southerners during the course of the Civil War. His emphasis is on African Americans' seeking or exercising their rights as citizens, and he takes a jab at those who labeled African Americans who asserted their rights during Reconstruction "desperadoes"—that is, criminals.

While Moore states that Reconstruction was a failure, he does so not merely for pragmatic purposes—to appeal to delicate southern white sensibilities—but to make the point that in Reconstruction's wake African Americans have become fully capable of the duties and responsibilities that come with rights such as to vote and to hold public office. In other words, Moore is not just appealing to white readers by calling Reconstruction a failure; he is pointing to the subsequent progress made by African Americans through black churches and education toward the end of creating an independent citizenry. He underscores the fact that "political advantages"—such as the privilege to vote—count for little "where the ballot is unprotected." In making this last point, he demonstrates the often fine line southern black leaders had to navigate between two very different worlds: one black and poor, the other white and rich.

♦ **Paragraph 4**

Moore's reference to Governor Benjamin Tillman of South Carolina speaks to the often contradictory position that black leaders of the Colored Farmers' National Alliance faced in dealing with political forces in the South. Although Tillman was an open opponent of black political rights—having himself led physical attacks on African Americans during Reconstruction—he nevertheless publicly spoke out against the lynching of African Americans in 1890. For this public condemnation of lynching, the Colored Farmers' National Alliance in South Carolina endorsed his gubernatorial candidacy, even as they sought other electoral options. Tillman won the election that year with the black Alliance's support; for a time, the governor even used his authority to curb lynching. However, as Moore notes, Tillman also spoke of the "natural and inevitable" nature of white supremacist violence.

Almost as a way of assuaging white fears of potential black interest in social equality, Moore makes plain that "we are not clamoring for social relations with the whites either. We do not want to eat at their tables, sleep in their beds, neither ride in the cars with them; but we do want as good fare as the whites receive for the same consideration." In other words, the minister, reflecting the wider views of Black Populists, sought political equality while leaving social equality aside.

Moore proceeds to present the words of the Missouri white Alliance leader R. M. Hawley to articulate the shared position between the Colored Farmers' National Alliance and the midwestern white Alliance on issues of election reform. The abolishment of party primaries was viewed as a key way of ridding "politics of party strife and all its concomitant evils" in order to "let in the clear light of the science of economical government." The language highlights the need to move toward a more transparent system of elections, one that not only accurately represents voters' interests but also poses a more efficient way of governing. For Moore, "non-partisanism"—where neither "party favorites" are protected nor "secret caucuses by members of Congress or members of the legislatures" permitted—was, in essence, the "natural" goal.

♦ **Paragraph 5**

Moore's religious outlook explicitly fuses with political commentary in the penultimate paragraph of his letter with his metaphor of "the lion's mouth." The reference is a biblical one, to the pastoral epistles. These epistles are addressed to the disciples and helpers of Paul, in this case, Timothy. The passage in question (2 Timothy 4:17–18) deals with the running of the Christian church and the care of the religion's faithful. Here, Paul conveys to Timothy that one should hold firmly to one's faith in order to endure suffering—to be "rescued from the lion's mouth" by the Lord.

While the metaphor Moore uses is directed at the Southern Farmers' Alliance's intransigence—specifically, their allowing exiting politicians to speak on behalf of the alliances (a form of political co-optation on the part of the major parties)—he is also warning of what could happen if reformers do not carve out a more independent political path. By conceding further to the Democratic Party in the South, in particular, Moore suggests, political reformers and their vision of a more democratic electoral process are likely to be destroyed.

♦ **Paragraph 6**

The final paragraph is a call for unity with those white Alliance members who may be open to working in political cooperation with Black Populists. Moore notes the numeric strength of the Colored Farmers' National Alliance in the South and its potential force at the ballot box should it be joined with the votes of white independents. Moore's tone turns decidedly reconciliatory here as he writes, "We are willing and ready to lay down the past." He ends by invoking a sweeping image of political reform for those across not only the South but the North and West as well. For Moore, at stake is nothing short of a more participatory

Henry Cabot Lodge (Library of Congress)

and representative electoral process in the South and in the nation as a whole. Only with such an open and equitable system can African Americans ultimately enjoy the achievement of "equal rights to all and special privileges to none"—that is, not only as a motto but, indeed, as a reality

Audience

Moore's letter to the editor reached both black and white reading and listening audiences (as newspapers were often read aloud in both black and white communities for the benefit of the illiterate). The letter was circulated first through the Jacksonville newspaper in which it originally appeared and then through the more widely circulating *National Economist*, which variously featured articles written by Black Populist leaders. Sections of the letter were then picked up by other publications, including in book form, as in the chapter "The Race Problem" by J. H. Turner, the national secretary and treasurer of the National Farmers' Alliance and Industrial Union, in *The Farmers' Alliance History and Agricultural Digest*, edited by Nelson A. Dunning. It is likely that parts of Moore's letter were also published in one or more of the Colored Farmers' Alliance's newspapers, including the *Texas National Alliance*, the *South Carolina Alliance Light*, or the *North Carolina Alliance Advocate*. However, none of these local papers has survived.

"In all the discussions of the whites ... I never hear you, Mr. Editor, nor any of the other leading journals, once criticise their action or say they are antagonizing the races .... But let the negro speak once, and what do we hear? Antagonizing races, negro uprising, negro domination, etc. Anything to keep the reading public hostile toward the negro."

(Paragraph 2)

"As members of the Colored Farmers Alliance we avowed that we were going to vote with and for the man or party that will secure for the farmer or laboring man his just rights.... We want protection at the ballot box, so that the laboring man may have an equal showing.... We are aware of the fact that the laboring colored man's interests and the laboring white man's interests are one and the same."

(Paragraph 2)

"I for one have fully decided to vote with and work for that party, or those who favor the workingmen, let them belong to the Democratic or Republican, or the People's party. I know I speak the sentiment of that convention, representing as we do one-fifth of the laborers of this country, seven-eighths of our race in this country being engaged in agricultural pursuits."

(Paragraph 2)

"We know and you know that neither of the now existing parties is going to legislate in the interest of the farmers or laboring men except so far as it does not conflict with their interest to do so."

(Paragraph 2)

"The action of the Alliance in this reminds me of the man who first put his hand in the lion's mouth and the lion finally bit it off; and then he changed to make the matter better and put his head in the lion's mouth, and, therefore, lost his head. Now, the farmers and laboring men ... lost their hands, so to speak; now organized in one body or head, if they give themselves over to the same power that took their hand, it will likewise take their head."

(Paragraph 5)

Impact

While it is unclear the extent to which Moore's letter had an impact on political circumstances at the time, his letter is an indication of the kind of forthright support that existed among African Americans for the Lodge bill. The Colored Farmers' National Alliance's support for the bill may have swayed some northern white Alliance members to lend their endorsement to the bill, while it likely antagonized southern white Alliance members further, as the latter came out strongly against endorsing the bill. Outside black and white Alliance circles, the letter may be best seen as one among a number of voices for and against the notion of federal supervision of elections in the South. Not until the Voting Rights Act of 1965 would such a federal measure be enacted.

Moore's letter demonstrates how African Americans demanded civil and political rights in the decades following the collapse of Reconstruction; it also shows the ways in which Black Populists reached out to their white counterparts based on mutual economic and political interests to carve out an independent political course of action. In the final decade of the nineteenth century, by voting for third-party candidates or insurgent candidates or by supporting individual independent candidates, Black Populists challenged political convention, which looked at African Americans in the South as passive bystanders or victims of white men (either white Democrats or white independents) struggling among themselves to gain or retain power in the region.

Moore's letter to the editor was expressive of, if not a key factor in, African Americans' continuing to build a movement of their own—that is, one separate yet tactically connected to the white-led Populist movement. Moore was among several leading Black Populists, including Pattillo

of North Carolina, Doyle of Georgia, Rayner of Texas, and William H. Warwick of Virginia, who figured prominently in establishing and helping to advance an independent political strategy. The concept of a national people's party had been forged at a meeting of black and white Alliances in St. Louis in December 1889. A series of national meetings followed over the next two and a half years, which included a number of reform-oriented and labor organizations. Meetings, most of which were attended by Moore, were held in Ocala in December 1890 as well as in Washington, D.C., in January 1891; Cincinnati, Ohio, in May 1891; and St. Louis again in February 1892. The series culminated in a national nominating convention for the newly established People's Party held in Omaha, Nebraska, on July 4, 1892.

Although historians have tended to view African Americans as a subcomponent of the white-led Populist movement of the same era, there is increasing consensus that black leaders formed their own movement, with its own organizations, particular tactics, and leadership, coming out of the experiences of African Americans in postemancipation society. However, by the late 1890s, and mostly under Democratic-led attacks—from propaganda campaigns that warned of "negro domination," as noted in Moore's letter to the editor, to outright physical attacks on and murder of black leaders—Black Populism would collapse. Among scholars of Populism, Moore's letter to the editor was initially seen (if at all) as an instance of African Americans' complaining about their mistreatment, albeit with an eye toward alliance making; it is now more readily seen as a letter that establishes the extent to which black leaders asserted their own independent voices in promoting the interests of African Americans in the South.

See also *Plessy v. Ferguson* (1896).

Questions for Further Study

1. Why were southern Democrats so vehemently opposed to the election bill introduced by Henry Cabot Lodge?

2. Summarize the conflict between Democrats and Republicans in the post-Reconstruction era. What impact did this conflict have on African Americans?

3. How did African Americans respond to the economic difficulties they faced in the post-Reconstruction era? What specific actions did they take? What role did the Colored Farmers' National Alliance play in fostering African American aspirations?

4. Moore wrote: "We are aware of the fact that the laboring colored man's interests and the laboring white man's interests are one and the same." To what extent is this view similar to that expressed by T. Thomas Fortune in "The Present Relations of Labor and Capital" (1886)? Do the views of the two writers differ in any significant ways?

5. Why did the Colored Farmers' National Alliance support the candidacy of Benjamin Tillman as governor of South Carolina despite Tillman's open racism?

Further Reading

■ Articles

Abramowitz, Jack. "The Negro in the Populist Movement." *Journal of Negro History* 38, no. 3 (July 1953): 257–289.

Watson, Thomas E. "The Negro Question in the South." *Arena* 6 (October 1892): 540–550.

■ Books

Ali, Omar H. *In the Lion's Mouth: Black Populism in the New South, 1886–1900.* (In press)

Gaither, Gerald H. *Blacks and the Populist Movement: Ballots and Bigotry in the New South.* Tuscaloosa: University of Alabama Press, 2005.

Humphrey, Richard M. "History of the Colored Farmers' National Alliance and Co operative Union." In *The Farmers' Alliance History and Agricultural Digest*, ed. Nelson A. Dunning. Washington, D.C.: Alliance Publishing Co., 1891.

Postel, Charles. *The Populist Vision.* New York: Oxford University Press, 2007.

■ Web Sites

"Black Populism in the New South." Towson University Web site. http://pages.towson.edu/oali/black_populism_in_the_new_south.htm.

—Omar H. Ali

John L. Moore's "In the Lion's Mouth"

March 7, 1891

Upon perusing said article I found it to be an attack upon the National Colored Farmers Alliance and Co-operative Union on their action while in session at Ocala, Fla., in passing resolutions asking Congress to pass the federal election bill now pending before the Senate of the United States. Now, as I was a member of that body, and you have taken us to task because of our action, I hereby reply and only ask that you will do me the kindness of publishing my reply, as it may be the means of you and others seeing us just as we are. I notice you, as others, call it the force bill, and you remarked, "How the force bill could benefit the negro even in the slightest degree passes comprehension. All its advocates expect of it is to help perpetuate Republican rule in this country." I can say you or any one else are sadly mistaken if you think the object of the National Colored Farmers Alliance was to perpetuate Republican rule in this country if that rule is to be as it has been in this county for several years. But our object was to have protection of the ballot boxes, because none sees the need of reform more than we do. How is that reform to be brought about while the present parties have control of the ballot boxes (unless it comes through the now existing parties, which is not likely if their past history argues anything)? The Hon. Alonzo Wardall, of Huron, South Dakota, informed us while at Ocala, that in his State the Republicans were 22,000 majority, but when the independent party sprang up and votes were counted at the last election there were 10,000 more votes than registered voters, which, of course, called for a contest, and when a contest comes up under those circumstances those who are in sympathy with their kind, and the other fellows must stay out. That was in a State largely Republican; and should the reformist begin to operate in our own sunny land of flowers, or in any State that can boast of her Democratic fidelity, they would meet with the eight-ballot box system and tickets spread on top at their proper places for the Democratic voters, and the other fellows would have to do the best they could; and if they voted right they would not be allowed a chance as inspectors at the ballot box, and the result would be increased Democratic majorities. And while the federal election bill is not satisfactory to us throughout as it reads, yet we want something guaranteeing every man a free vote and an honest count. The federal election bill being the only thing that ever emanated from our halls of legislation that pointed in that direction, we, in body assembled as representatives of our race, asked Congress to pass it.

In all the discussions of the whites in all the various meetings they attend and the different resolutions, remarks and speeches they make against the negro, I never hear you, Mr. Editor, nor any of the other leading journals, once criticise their action or say they are antagonizing the races, neither do you ever call a halt. But let the negro speak once, and what do we hear? Antagonizing races, negro uprising, negro domination, etc. Anything to keep the reading public hostile toward the negro, not allowing him the privilege to speak his opinion, and if that opinion be wrong show him by argument, and not at once make it a race issue. As to the race question, I do not care a fig. I work and attend to my own business. I desire, with the rest of my race who do the same, to have some rule to go upon (and I am quite colored), which is something many of my white brethren can not say, to which my race can easily testify from the number of tramps of the dominant race that frequent our doors. I can not say if many of the Republican members of Congress may be expecting to perpetuate their rule; we do not know; but as members of the Colored Farmers Alliance we avowed that we were going to vote with and for the man or party that will secure for the farmer or laboring man his just rights and privileges, and in order that he may enjoy them without experiencing a burden. We want protection at the ballot box, so that the laboring man may have an equal showing, and the various labor organizations to secure their just rights, we will join hands with them irrespective of party, "and those fellows will have to walk." We are aware of the fact that the laboring colored man's interests and the laboring white man's interests are one and the same. Especially is this true at the South. Anything that can be brought about to benefit the workingman, will also benefit the negro more than any other legislation that can be enacted. The Democratic party may get in power; the negroes may all vote with them; they may mete out to them offices according to representation (which I know they would not do). The educated and better living among the colored class would not only get favors (this would be right, as an ignoramus, white or black, has no business with an office). The majority would not be benefited. Or, if the Republican party remains in power and should come to do the same (which they never have, and I know never will do), the result would be the same. So I for one have fully decided to vote with and work for that party, or those who favor the workingmen, let them belong to the Democratic or Republican, or the People's party. I know I speak the sentiment of that convention, representing as we do one-fifth of the laborers of this country, seven-eighths of our race in this country being engaged in agricultural pursuits. Can you wonder why we have turned our attention from the few pitful offices a few of our members could secure, and turned our attention toward benefiting the mass of our race, and why we are willing to join our forces with those who are willing to legislate that this mass may be benefited? And we ask Congress to protect the ballot-box, so they may be justly dealt with in their effort to gain that power. We know and you know that neither of the now existing parties is going to legislate in the interest of the farmers or laboring men except so far as it does not conflict with their interest to do so.

I see, Mr. Editor, where you speak of negro domination in our Southland. I can say that I have been in the South for twenty-eight years and have lived in *six* different Southern States, and I have never found the negro in the majority, but the same docile creature, ready to bow to his old master under most every circumstance. The few who did claim rights as citizens of the United States under existing laws, were treated by the Southern white and the Northern white men who settled in the South, in too many instances, as desperadoes. Another question many Southern white men are forever agitating is that their wives and daughters are in danger in the South among the negroes. To this I say, Bah! Who looked after the white man's family in the South before the war when he was absent? Who was left at home to raise the product, do the affairs of the home and look after the families, while the master senior or master junior were battling to hold those rights which entitled them to keep those same obedient servants as bondsmen, to educate their children, cultivate their land, and do their bidding? Look, for instance, we were brought here. I want you to mark that point. "Brought here," never came of ourselves. In 1620 made slaves, and continued in that condition without a stroke of national legislation against it until 1863, and when the matter was finally settled in

1865 there were 4,000,000 of us turned loose from under the yoke of bondage, for which we give God praise. Yet we acknowledge that the reconstruction act was a failure. You might ask, why do I say so? Simply because it brought about an unnatural condition of things. Political influence placed weakness on the top of power, and power did what it always will do-shook it off. Now, we are procee[d]ing the right way. Starting at the bottom, we are laying a foundation in moral, intellectual and financial strength, and so sure as God is God and law is law—I mean natural law—whenever these come to the top we will have come to stay. According to my observation the church and the schoolhouse have the true solution of the destiny of our people, at least for present. There is never any trouble about recognizing and respecting those who, by proper acts, command recognition and respect. However long it requires to do this, it is the only way out of the difficulty. Political advantages can not count for much when the people are weak and dependent, and where the ballot is unprotected.

As to Governor Tillman's inaugural address, to which you referred, we have heard the like for years; yet we find the party in sympathy with the negroes from both parties always ends with the last sound of the inaugural address, while the hostile portion always remains in force. You further quoted Governor Tillman as saying, "retaliation and injustice had been practiced on the blacks by the whites; but said it was natural and inevitable," and that is the expression of our white brethren everywhere. Whatever is done to the negro is "natural and inevitable." Again in your editorial of the same issue headed, "The Last Struggle," your quotation reads: "The negroes North and South should be taught that this is always to be a country ruled by white men." We will never have anything against the white men for that; for according to our privileges I think we have helped the white men all they could expect under our condition; and we are not clamoring for social relations with the whites either. We do not want to eat at their tables, sleep in their beds, neither ride in the cars with them; but we do want as good fare as the whites receive for the same consideration. As to the Alliance, in the language of Hon. R. M. Hawley, of Missouri, we believe this to be its mission:

"No protection to party favorites; no force bills to keep up party and sectional prejudices; no secret caucuses by members of Congress or members of the legislatures to consider matters of legislation. Let these be abolished by law. Also abolish all party primary elections and party conventions for nominating candidates, and provide for a people's primary election, where every voter can write on his ticket the name of any person he prefers for any office from president down to constable. Let the proper county. State, and national officers, who shall be designated by law, receive the returns, count up and authorize the result, which shall be that the candidate receiving the highest number of votes and the one receiving the next highest number for each office shall be declared the contending candidates for final election. This would empty politics of party strife and all its concomitant evils, and lead to the representation of the leading industry of each district in Congress, and county in the State legislatures. Party blindness would be removed and let in the clear light of the science of economical government. I believe that nonpartisanism will not reach its full and natural results till these things are accomplished; and this I believe to be the mission of the Alliance."

But, Mr. Editor, can we do anything while the present parties have control of the ballot box, and we (the Alliance) have no protection? The greatest mistake, I see, the farmers are now making, is this: The wily politicians see and know that they have to do something, therefore they are slipping into the Alliance, and the farmers, in many instances, are accepting them

as leaders; and if we are to have the same leaders, we need not expect anything else but the same results. The action of the Alliance in this reminds me of the man who first put his hand in the lion's mouth and the lion finally bit it off; and then he changed to make the matter better and put his head in the lion's mouth, and, therefore, lost his head. Now, the farmers and laboring men know in the manner they were standing before they organized; they lost their hands, so to speak; now organized in one body or head, if they give themselves over to the same power that took their hand, it will likewise take their head.

Now, Mr. Editor, I wish to say, if the laboring men of the United States will lay down party issues and combine to enact laws for the benefit of the laboring man, I, as county superintendent of Putman county colored Farmers' Alliance, and member of the National Colored Farmers, know that I voice the sentiment of that body, representing as we did 750,000 votes, when I say we are willing and ready to lay down the past, take hold with them irrespective of party, race, or creed, until the cry shall be heard from the Heights of Abraham of the North, to the Everglades of Florida, and from the rockbound coast of the East, to the Golden Eldorado of the West, that we can heartily endorse the motto, "Equal rights to all and special privileges to none."

Glossary

Golden Eldorado of the West	a metaphor for a place where wealth, such as gold, could be acquired easily and quickly
Governor Tillman	Benjamin Tillman, the openly racist governor of South Carolina in the early 1890s and, later, a U.S. senator
Heights of Abraham of the North	a landform near Quebec, Canada
Hon. Alonzo Wardall	a member of the National Executive Committee of the Farmers' Alliance
"in the lion's mouth"	an allusion to 2 Timothy 4:17–18, where Paul conveys to Timothy that one should hold firmly to one's faith in order to endure suffering—to be "rescued from the lion's mouth" by the Lord
People's party	also known as the Populist Party, a short-lived political party in the late nineteenth century

JOSEPHINE ST. PIERRE RUFFIN'S "ADDRESS TO THE FIRST NATIONAL CONFERENCE OF COLORED WOMEN"

"We are women, American women, as intensely interested in all that pertains to us as such as all other American women."

Overview

Josephine St. Pierre Ruffin's "Address to the First National Conference of Colored Women" opened the proceedings for a group of one hundred African American women who met in Boston at the Charles Street African Methodist Episcopal Church in July 1895. Ruffin was the president of the Women's Era Club in Boston, founded two years previously, and it was her work with this group that inspired her to found the National Federation of Afro-American Women. She organized and convened the Boston conference with a view to bringing together African American club women from across the nation to join with her in that effort. Attending the conference as representatives from clubs around the nation, the participants convened to assert their position as a critical component of the women's movement, to discuss the issues and challenges facing black women, and to debate how best to move forward in light of those challenges. The "Address to the First National Conference of Colored Women" was a call to action. Ruffin's remarks were brief, but they served to inspire a generation of African American women to active involvement in the women's movement and as a challenge to women everywhere to "bring in a new era to the colored women of America."

Context

The decades following the Civil War were a time of major social transformation. This was the period of the labor movement, rapid industrialization, large influxes of immigrants from Europe and Asia, and sweeping sentiments for social reforms. The U.S. government had devised a plan for "reconstructing" the South that set in motion a series of events that would propagate segregation for another hundred years. Women saw an opportunity to continue the work of the 1848 Seneca Falls Convention for women's rights, and, in doing so, African American women saw their chance to improve their own condition. It was against this backdrop that Josephine St. Pierre Ruffin spoke to the National Conference of Colored Women.

The U.S. government's Reconstruction program created policies and procedures intended to rebuild a bitterly divided nation. These policies addressed reintegrating southern states into the political system, dealing with former Confederate leaders, and, most important, defining the status of millions of newly freed slaves. Opinions varied on how best to resolve these matters. Abraham Lincoln had favored a policy of conciliation with the defeated South, but strong dissent arose during the troubled administration of Andrew Johnson (1865–1869), and the policies of the ensuing administration of Ulysses S. Grant (1869–1887) were dominated by the Radical Republican faction that stood for strong military enforcement of equal rights for the former slaves. These "radical" policies allowed for the passage of the Thirteenth (1865), Fourteenth (1868), and Fifteenth (1870) Amendments to the U.S. Constitution and created military jurisdictions over former Confederate states. With full citizenship, African Americans during this period began participating in the political process, ushering in a few years of widespread black representation, including fifteen representatives and two senators in Congress. However, Reconstruction met with a backlash in the South, as political parties fractured, white supremacy grew, and federal military power was gradually withdrawn. Reconstruction was dealt a fatal blow with the election of Rutherford B. Hayes in 1876, whose hands-off policy included the withdrawal of federal troops from the South. Reconstruction and the progress made for African Americans had ended.

As the postwar economy improved, a period of rapid industrialization, fueled by the growing numbers of immigrants, served as the catalyst for the growth of the labor movement. Advances in iron and steel production, the invention of the Morse telegraph (1837) and the telephone (1876), and the completion of the transcontinental railroad (1869) improved the nation's infrastructure and connected distant parts of the country. The growing immigrant population found work in many of these industries. Between the 1840s and World War I, approximately thirty-seven million people migrated to the United States in search of land, fortune, and opportunity. As immigrant populations soared, cities and factories became overcrowded, and living and working conditions grew dire. The Progressive movement of the 1890s and early 1900s sought to improve these con-

1869

■ **November**
The American Woman Suffrage Association is founded in Boston as a result of a schism in the equal rights movement over the proposal to include woman suffrage in the proposed Fifteenth Amendment.

1875

■ **March 1**
The Civil Rights Act of 1875 grants everyone the same treatment in public accommodations, regardless of race, color, or previous condition of servitude.

1883

■ **October 15**
The Supreme Court declares the Civil Rights Act of 1875 unconstitutional on the grounds that Congress lacks the authority to legislate in issues relating to racial discrimination at the state level.

1884

■ Josephine St. Pierre Ruffin founds *Women's Era*, the first newspaper of its kind published by and for African American women.

1895

■ **July 29**
Ruffin offers the opening address at the First National Conference of Colored Women, where the National Federation of Afro-American Women is born.

1896

■ The National Federation of Afro-American Women merges with the Colored Women's League of Washington to form the National Association of Colored Women (later the National Association of Colored Women's Clubs).

■ **May 18**
In *Plessy v. Ferguson* the Supreme Court effectively legitimizes racial segregation under the doctrine of "separate but equal" treatment.

ditions as well as to break up corrupt political machines. The labor movement also saw rapid expansion at this time, as unions fought for improved working conditions, regulation of work hours and pay, and prohibition of child labor.

This swell of sentiment for social reform was also taken up by the emerging women's movement. After the 1848 Seneca Falls (New York) Convention, the movement grew in supporters, strength, and influence. Women like Elizabeth Cady Stanton, Susan B. Anthony, and Lucretia Mott were speaking, writing, and engaging people in conversation to further equality for women in education, employment, family life, religion, and public life. By 1869 the American Woman Suffrage Association had begun to include black women in the conversation, including Josephine St. Pierre Ruffin, an early member in Boston. When the Civil Rights Act passed in 1875, preventing discrimination in "public accommodation" on the basis of "race, color, or previous condition of servitude"—with no mention of gender—women in the club movement began to fragment. A division formed in the suffrage community, with many women refusing to support black men's voting rights at the expense of their own and preferring instead to focus solely on voting rights for women. Feeling isolated by this position from the white women's club movement, African American women formed their own clubs, such as the National Federation of Afro-American Women (1895) and, later, the National Association of Colored Women (NACW, 1896). African American women's clubs worked not only for women's rights but also for the rights and welfare of black men and children. The desire for social reform that characterized the Progressive era helped further the influence of many of these clubs, as they sought political gain and a general improvement of black women's social standing.

About the Author

Josephine St. Pierre was born on August 31, 1842, in Boston, to well-to-do parents of (white) English and Martinican-African descent. Her parents were highly respected in the African American community. Because they opposed Boston's segregated school system, they sent their daughter to several schools during her childhood, two just outside Boston and one in New York City. She completed her education at the Bowdoin School, a coeducational institution then located on Derne Street in the Beacon Hill section of Boston.

In 1858, at the age of sixteen, Josephine St. Pierre married George Lewis Ruffin, a prominent attorney from Richmond, Virginia, and the first African American to graduate from Harvard Law School. George Ruffin, the first African American man elected to Boston's City Council, also served in the Massachusetts state legislature during the early 1870s. In 1883 he would became the first black judge in the United States. The Ruffins settled in the elite Beacon Hill neighborhood and eventually had five children. During the Civil War, they participated in the war effort, serving with the Sanitary Commission. It was during this period that Josephine became involved with suffrage and the women's movement.

After the war, St. Pierre Ruffin began working with several leaders of the suffrage movement, including Elizabeth Cady Stanton, Susan B. Anthony, and Julia Ward Howe. In 1869, together with Howe and Lucy Stone, she helped form the American Women Suffrage Association. By this time, she had begun writing for the black weekly newspaper in Boston, the *Courant*, which involved her in another organization, the New England Women's Press Association. Later, Ruffin integrated the New England Women's Club, and in 1894 she organized the Women's Era Club, specifically for African American women. Her work in these clubs focused specifically on how African American women could work to improve the conditions of all African Americans.

When George Ruffin died in 1886, Josephine's experience at the *Courant* prompted her to start her own newspaper with money from her husband's estate. The *Women's Era* newspaper became the first paper published for and by African American women. Financial stability allowed her to increase her involvement with the women's club movement, and in 1895 Ruffin organized the First National Conference of Colored Women, with a view to forming a national organization to unite the African American women's clubs of America. Delegates from clubs all across the United States attended. It was to these women that Ruffin spoke. Within the year, the National Federation of Afro-American Women was a reality and, in 1896, merged with the Colored Women's League of Washington to form the NACW, an organization that is still active today as the National Association of Colored Women's Clubs. Ruffin continued in community service and was especially involved in advancing African American women's rights. By 1910 she had helped to found the National Association for the Advancement of Colored People. Upon her death on March 13, 1924, Josephine St. Pierre Ruffin was widely honored for her skills as a journalist, activist, and pioneer in the African American women's rights movement.

Explanation and Analysis of the Document

Although the "Address to the First National Conference of Colored Women" is quite short, it had a resounding impact on the future of the African American women's movement. The address had one primary purpose: to convince black women of the necessity of creating their own national organization. Ruffin saw an opportunity for black women's groups to coalesce in the hope of creating a strong national voice for women everywhere. It is this point that makes Ruffin's address singular: She spoke not only to African American women but also to black men and white women. It was her hope to improve the lives of African Americans through their own efforts and through the efforts of white people as well. Ruffin's speech was widely celebrated, and only a year later Ruffin and Mary Church Terrell, founder of the Colored Women's League of Washington and a well-

Time Line

1900	■ **June 4–9** Ruffin, representing three separate organizations, is denied admittance to the General Federation of Women's Clubs' national meeting in Milwaukee, Wisconsin, because one of the groups (the New Era Club) is all black.
1918	■ Membership in the NACW numbers almost one hundred thousand.

known suffragist and journalist, combined their organizations to form the NACW.

Ruffin's address falls into three distinct sections. The first paragraph concerns the meeting itself—how the various groups came together, the rise of women's clubs, and the message that such a meeting would send to society. The main section (paragraphs 2–5) deals with the reasons for holding the conference. This is the lengthiest section, and it is where the heart of her argument lies. The last section is a very brief call to action, wherein Ruffin firmly states "the absolute necessity of a national organization of our women."

Ruffin opens by citing the need for black women to meet for a "good talk." With no national organization representing black women, this would be the opportunity to come together, regardless of geography, and discuss important issues. To Ruffin, the particular situation of black women, the hardships they faced, and the deprivations they endured because of their race and gender spoke to this need. Although the conference was put together rather rapidly, the leaders had been thinking for some time about convening all the regional women's clubs. Such clubs had been appearing all across the country, for both white and black women. Ruffin credits their work as the inspiration for the conference and for the desired creation of a national organization. Five years prior to the conference, there had been no clubs for African American women. By 1895 representatives from twenty such clubs were in attendance. Ruffin cites their history and their willingness to do their part as evidence that they, too, are "truly American women."

Ruffin turns next to the reasons for convening. First, she mentions how much courage and inspiration would be drawn from women meeting other women who shared the same goals. Next, she lays out the practical matters they should discuss, including the education of their children, the mental and intellectual elevation of all black people, and the ways in which to make the best of their situations, given their limited resources and social standing. Ruffin also speaks of the need to discuss the issues of the day, such as temperance, higher education, and domesticity. The end of the second paragraph sums up these initial reasons for meeting: "Surely we, with everything to pull

Julia Ward Howe (Library of Congress)

us back, to hinder us in developing, need to take every opportunity and means for the thoughtful consideration which shall lead to wise action."

Ruffin then notes the unfortunate prevailing belief regarding the general nature of black women, which, she says, is that they are "for the most part, ignorant and immoral, some exceptions, of course, but these don't count." She considers this attitude—that progressive black women of considerable talent, morals, education, and skill were being regarded nationwide as second-rate—to be the strongest reason for coming together. Women's opportunities were limited, even foreclosed, by this blatant racism. If such women were given even a small chance to improve the conditions of their lives, Ruffin believed they could create improvements in the lives of all other African Americans.

How, then, could this small chance be created? Ruffin's answer in paragraph 4 is one of the most passionate sections of her address. She understood that the women to whom she was speaking were some of the most affluent, educated, and privileged African Americans in the country. The changes Ruffin here envisions for African Americans were already in progress among her peers. It was for those less fortunate—the large body of African Americans—that opportunities needed to be created. To Ruffin, the issues were not merely improved education, rewarding employment, and the chance to travel. She viewed the matter in broader terms: The dignity of the race demanded that she

and women like her "stand forth and declare ourselves and our principles." To be seen as good, intelligent, hardworking people, these women had to show the world collective, and not merely individual, action. This was a platform from which black women could act as paragons, opening the eyes of the world to their shining example.

Central to this argument is a point that provides a good deal of insight into the mind-set from which these women were operating. Ruffin implies that up to this point black women had fallen silent when bearing witness to the hardships they all faced. They were also silent in the face of the "unholy charges" made against them. Her call to speak out represented a tangible shift in policy for African American social action. Ruffin admits that she herself had yielded to prevailing attitudes, first by publicly accepting her circumstances and then by simply joining individual women's clubs and attempting to leverage their resources to make headway. However, as the larger women's movement increasingly came to focus on the issue of suffrage, the unfortunate side effect was neglect for the broader rights of African American women. Black women like Ruffin therefore began to push for their own representation, their own groups. The 1895 Boston conference declared that black women, at the expense of their dignity, could no longer accept this disparity of treatment. However, in stepping into the public forum, these women recognized that their actions, words, and deeds would be scrutinized. As Ruffin put it, "Now with an army of organized women standing for purity and mental worth, we … open the eyes of the world." Serving as the standard for all African Americans weighed heavily on their minds, and this understanding informed the decisions and actions of the expanding African American women's club movement. Certainly the importance of their decisions was apparent throughout Ruffin's address.

At this point in her speech, Ruffin makes some interesting rhetorical choices, which for modern readers should serve as clues to the particular circumstances of black women at the time. The first is her refusal to discuss certain claims made against African American women by the white women's organizations. She alludes to situations where southern women had protested the admission of black women into historically white women's clubs, thus propagating racist stereotypes of the "immoral" black woman. Yet Ruffin declines to mention any of these protestations specifically. She says, in paragraph 4, that many of the claims of white women were so humiliating that they moved black women to "mortified silence." Her refusal to discuss this slander in her address points to the degrading nature of the allegations as well as to a desire to elevate the discourse above nasty rhetoric. By meeting the protestations with dignity and respect, Ruffin hoped that the character of these African American club women would attest to their virtue. In what would henceforth become the tone of the language of African American women's clubs, the struggle to overcome humiliation and exclusion would always depend on virtue and strength of character.

The second rhetorical choice that Ruffin makes in this latter part of her address is to assign the challenge specifically to black women: "For many and apparent reasons it is especially fitting that the *women* of the race take the lead in this movement." Nothing further needed to be said for those present that afternoon, but modern readers may benefit from a brief discussion of her remarks. Ruffin's choice relates to the complete subjugation of African American males during this period. Black males were seen by much of the white population in terms of stereotypes—"lazy," "violent," "insolent," and "stupid." This was the period when lynchings were becoming a common response to any black assertiveness. While black women were not much better off than their men folk, they were more able to step onto a public platform without being perceived as a threat to the structure of white society.

Ruffin makes it clear that it would be African American women's strength of character that would help all African Americans persevere and flourish, and this sentiment pervades the end of the address. Her closing words are poignant. Here she moves beyond the bounds of the room and addresses the wider women's movement. She acknowledges the desire to include women and men, regardless of color. The idea of creating a universal movement had divided white women working toward suffrage in the 1870s. But for Ruffin, a movement for one was already a movement for all. She demonstrated her commitment to this universal principle at the conference most clearly at the start of her final paragraph, which she begins by calling for "union and earnestness."

In her final paragraph, Ruffin lays out her paramount hope for the outcome of the conference: to see the creation of a national all-black women's organization. She believed that in order for African American women to achieve the hoped-for change, women from all areas of the country, in all walks of life, would have to band together: "From this will spring an organization that will in truth bring in a new era to the colored woman of America."

Audience

Josephine St. Pierre Ruffin's address was given in front of a group of one hundred African American women who wanted to come together as a strong voice of encouragement, inspiration, and guidance to the country and yet were deliberately excluded from the national scene of white women's clubs specifically because of their race. These women were an elite group, highly educated and fairly well off, being the wives and daughters of some of the most prominent men in the black community. In addition to this immediate audience, Ruffin addressed both black men and white women, asking that everyone avoid drawing the color line, an indication that she recognized the importance of working together to effect change.

Impact

The impact of Ruffin's address was felt immediately by the African American community. Her newly established Na-

General Federation of Women's Clubs headquarters
(Library of Congress)

tional Federation of Afro-American Women was paralleled by organizations such as the Colored Women's League of Washington, which had been founded two years earlier by Helen Cook. The year following the conference saw the organization of the NACW, which merged Ruffin's federation and the Colored Women's League of Washington. It became clear after this address that the only way African American women were going to be able to achieve any measure of standing was by banding together as one cohesive group. Indeed, the 1933 publication of *Lifting as They Climb* by the NACW member Elizabeth Lindsay Davis included a direct reprinting of the "Call to Conference," the list of attendees, the conference program schedule, and Ruffin's address in their entirety, owing to their significance in the formation of the first national club for African American women.

In the years and months after her remarks, Ruffin held the position of vice president of the NACW while maintaining her membership in the New England Women's Club and the New Era Club, desegregating both clubs. In 1900 Ruffin attended a meeting of the General Federation of Women's Clubs, where she was denied a seat on the floor after refusing to renounce her membership in the NACW. Ruffin was promptly excused from the meeting proceedings. This event became known as the "Ruffin incident," gaining national notoriety for both Ruffin and the NACW national.

Not all African Americans were pleased with this attention. Several well-respected people offered Ruffin their support following the incident, but the black orator Booker

"Five years ago we had no colored women's club outside of those formed for special work; today, with little over a month's notice, we are able to call representatives from more than twenty clubs. It is a good showing. It stands for much. It shows that we are truly American women, with all the adaptability, readiness to seize and possess our opportunities, willingness to do our part for good as other American women."

(Paragraph 1)

"For the sake of our own dignity, the dignity of our race, and the future good name of our children, it is 'mete, right and our bounden duty' to stand forth and declare ourselves and principles, to teach an ignorant and suspicious world that our aims and interests are identical with those of all good aspiring women."

(Paragraph 4)

"It is to break this silence, not by noisy protestations of what we are not, but by a dignified showing of what we are and hope to become that we are impelled to take this step, to make of this gathering an object lesson to the world."

(Paragraph 4)

"We want, we ask the active interest of our men, and, too, we are not drawing the color line; we are women, American women, as intensely interested in all that pertains to us as such as all other American women; we are not alienating or withdrawing, we are only coming to the front, willing to join any others in the same work and cordially inviting and welcoming any others to join us."

(Paragraph 5)

T. Washington was not one of them. In September of 1895, speaking just a few months after Ruffin gave her address, the Tuskegee Institute educator addressed an audience at the Cotton States and International Exposition in Atlanta, Georgia. Recognizing the social realities of his day, Washington felt that the only way for African Americans to succeed was through accommodation and industrial education, instead of focusing on immediately achieving civil rights. In his Atlanta Exposition Address, he proposed a compromise between asking for civil rights and receiving education and skills.

The differing viewpoints within the African American community began to come to a head, with those advocating for equality and civil rights and those advocating accommodation standing in stark contrast to each other. A few years later, an organization arose to work for civil rights and justice for all people of color. Founded in 1909, the National Association for the Advancement of Colored People, headed by the Harvard-trained historian and sociologist, W. E. B. Du Bois, was formed in opposition to the accommodationist viewpoints of Washington. Josephine St. Pierre Ruffin was an early member and leader within this organization.

See also Thirteenth Amendment to the U.S. Constitution (1865); Fourteenth Amendment to the U.S. Constitution (1868); Fifteenth Amendment to the U.S. Constitution (1870); Booker T. Washington's Atlanta Exposition Address (1895); *Plessy v. Ferguson* (1896); Mary Church Terrell: "The Progress of Colored Women" (1898); W. E. B. Du Bois: *The Souls of Black Folk* (1903).

Further Reading

■ Articles

Jones, Beverly W. "Mary Church Terrell and the National Association of Colored Women, 1896–1901." *Journal of Negro History* 67, no. 1 (Spring 1982): 20–33.

Lerner, Gerda. "Early Community Work of Black Club Women." *Journal of Negro History* 59, no. 2 (April 1974): 158–167.

■ Books

Davis, Elizabeth Lindsay. *Lifting as They Climb*, ed. Henry Louis Gates, Jr. New York: G. K. Hall, 1996.

Foner, Philip S., and Robert James Branham, eds. *Lift Every Voice: African-American Oratory 1787–1900*. Tuscaloosa: University of Alabama Press, 1998.

Streitmatter, Rodger. "Josephine St. Pierre Ruffin: A Nineteenth-Century Journalist of Boston's Black Elite Class." In *Women of the Commonwealth: Work, Family, and Social Change in Nineteenth-Century Massachusetts*, ed. Susan L. Porter. Amherst: University of Massachusetts Press, 1996.

———. *Raising Her Voice: African-American Journalists Who Changed History*. Lexington: University Press of Kentucky, 2009.

■ Web Sites

"History of the National Association of Colored Women's Clubs, Inc." National Association of Colored Women's Clubs Web Site. http://www.nacwc.org/about/history.php.

"Josephine St. Pierre Ruffin." MassHumanities Statehouse Women's Leadership Project Web Site. http://www.masshumanities.org/shwlp/honorees/ruffin.html.

"Josephine St. Pierre Ruffin." National Women's Hall of Fame "Women of the Hall" Web Site. http://www.greatwomen.org/women.php?action=viewone&id=132.

—Katherine M. Johnson

Questions for Further Study

1. What factors caused the women's movement to fragment in the later decades of the nineteenth century?

2. Ruffin's address bears obvious comparison with Mary Church Terrell's address "The Progress of Colored Women," delivered three years later. How were the women's backgrounds similar? What vision did the two share? Were there any marked differences in their views or outlook?

3. During the last decade of the nineteenth century, there was a flurry of activity by women that bore on women's rights and on the condition of African Americans. What social, economic, and political developments do you think may have contributed to this swell of activity?

4. In what ways, if any, do you think the women's club movement of the late nineteenth century was a precursor of the modern feminist movement?

5. What was the "Ruffin incident," and what implications did it have for African Americans at the time? How did others respond to the incident?

JOSEPHINE ST. PIERRE RUFFIN'S "ADDRESS TO THE FIRST NATIONAL CONFERENCE OF COLORED WOMEN"

It is with especial joy and pride that I welcome you all to this, our first conference. It is only recently that women have waked up to the importance of meeting in council, and great as has been the advantage to women *generally*, and important as it is and has been that they should confer, the necessity has not been nearly so great, matters at stake not nearly so vital, as that *we*, bearing peculiar blunders, suffering under especial hardships, enduring peculiar privations, should meet for a "good talk" among ourselves. Although rather hastily called, you as well as I can testify how long and how earnestly a conference has been thought of and hoped for and even prepared for. These women's clubs, which have sprung up all over the country, built and run upon broad and strong lines, have all been a preparation, small conferences in themselves, and their spontaneous birth and enthusiastic support have been little less than inspirational on the part of our women and a general preparation for a large union such as it is hoped this conference will lead to. Five years ago we had no colored women's clubs outside of those formed for special work; today, with little over a month's notice, we are able to call representatives from more than twenty clubs. It is a good showing. It stands for much. It shows that we are truly American women, with all the adaptability, readiness to seize and possess our opportunities, willingness to do our part for good as other American women.

The reasons why we should confer are so apparent that it would seem hardly necessary to enumerate them, and yet there are none of them but demand our serious consideration. In the first place we need to feel the cheer and inspiration of meeting each other; we need to gain the courage and fresh life that comes from the mingling of congenial souls, of those working for the same ends. Next, we need to talk over those things that are of especial interest to us as *colored women*, the training of our children, openings for our boys and girls, how they can be prepared for occupations and occupations may be found or opened for them, what *we* especially can do in the moral education and physical development, the home training it is necessary to give our children in order to prepare them to meet the peculiar conditions in which they shall find themselves, how to make the most of our own, to some extent, limited opportunities. Besides these are the general questions of the day, which we cannot afford to be indifferent to: temperance, morality, the higher education, hygienic and domestic questions. If these things need the serious consideration of women more advantageously placed by reason of all the aid to right thinking and living with which they are surrounded, surely we, with everything to pull us back, to hinder us in developing, need to take every opportunity and means for the thoughtful consideration which shall lead to wise action.

I have left the strongest reason for our conferring together until the last. All over America there is to be found a large and growing class of earnest, intelligent, progressive colored women, women who, if not leading full, useful lives, are only waiting for the opportunity to do so, many of them warped and cramped for lack of opportunity, not only to do more but to *be* more; and yet, if an estimate of the colored women of America is called for, the inevitable reply, glibly given is, "For the most part ignorant and immoral, some exceptions of course, but these don't count."

Now for the sake of the thousands of self-sacrificing young women teaching and preaching in lonely southern backwoods for the noble army of mothers who have given birth to these girls, mothers whose intelligence is only limited by their opportunity to get at books, for the sake of the fine cultured women who have carried off the honors in school here and often abroad, for the sake of our own dignity, the dignity of our race, and the future good name of our children, it is "meet, right and our bounden duty" to stand forth and declare ourselves and principles, to teach an ignorant and suspicious world that our aims and interests are identical with those of all good aspiring women. Too long have we been silent under unjust and unholy charges; we cannot expect to have them removed until we disprove them through *ourselves*. It is not enough to try to disprove unjust charges through individual effort, that never goes any further. Year after year southern women have protested against the admission of colored women into any national organization on the ground of the immorality of these women, and because all refutation has only been tried by individual work the charge has never been crushed, as it could and should have been at the first. Now with an army of organized women standing for purity and mental worth, we in ourselves deny the charge and open the eyes of the world to a state of affairs to which they have been blind, often willfully so, and the very fact that the charges, audaciously and flippantly made, as they often are, are of so humiliating and delicate a nature, serves to protect the accuser by driving the helpless accused into mortified silence. It is to break this silence, not by noisy protestations of what we are not, but by a dignified showing of what we are and hope to become that we are impelled to take this step, to make of this gathering an object lesson to the world. For many and apparent reasons it is especially fitting that the *women* of the race take the lead in this movement, but for all this we recognize the necessity of the sympathy of our husbands, brothers and fathers.

Our woman's movement is woman's movement in that it is led and directed by women for the good of women and men, for the benefit of *all* humanity, which is more than any one branch or section of it. We want, we ask the active interest of our men, and, too, we are not drawing the color line; we are women, American women, as intensely interested in all that pertains to us as such as all other American women; we are not alienating or withdrawing, we are only coming to the front, willing to join any others in the same work and cordially inviting and welcoming any others to join us.

If there is any one thing I would especially enjoin upon this conference it is union and earnestness. The questions that are to come before us are of too much import to be weakened by any trivialities or personalities. If any differences arise let them be quickly settled, with the feeling that we are all workers to the same end, to elevate and dignify colored American womanhood. This conference will not be what I expect if it does not show the wisdom, indeed the absolute necessity of a national organization of our women. Every year new questions coming up will prove it to us. This hurried, almost informal convention does not begin to meet our needs, it is only a beginning, made here in dear old Boston, where the scales of justice and generosity hang evenly balanced, and where the people "dare be true" to their best instincts and stand ready to lend aid and sympathy to worthy struggles. It is hoped and believed that from this will spring an organization that will in truth bring in a new era to the colored women of America.

"meet, right and our bounden duty"	a quote from a Christian prayer, "It is very meet, right, and our bounden duty, that we should at all times, and in all places, give thanks unto thee, O Lord, Holy Father, Almighty, Everlasting God."

DRESS BY BOOKER T. WASHINGTON, PRINCIPAL

RMAL AND INDUSTRIAL INSTITUTE, TUSKEGEE, ALABAMA,

AT OPENING OF ATLANTA EXPOSITION,

Sept. 18th, 1895.

- - - - - -

Gentlemen of the Board of Directors and Citizens:

of the population of the South is of the Negro

rprise seeking the material, civil or moral welfare

n can disregard this element of our population and

est success. I but convey to you, Mr. President and

e sentiment of the masses of my race, when I say that

the value and manhodd of the American Negro been

and generously recognized, than by the managers of

nt Exposition at every stage of its progress. It is

which will do more to cement the friendship of the

any occurrence since the dawn of our freedom.

this, but the opportunity here afforded will awaken

era of industrial progress. Ignorant and inexper-

not strange that in the first years of our new life

he top instead of the bottom, that a seat in Congress

Legislature was more sought t an real-estate or indus-

that the political convention, or stump speaking had

ns that starting a dairy farm or truck garden.

A s

vessel.

signal: '

friendly

you are."

ran up fr

bucket wh

was answe

of the di

down his

the mouth

bettering

the import

white man

your bucke

manly way

Cast it do

service an

to bear in

upon to be

is in the

commercial

than in em

the great

that the ma

Booker T. Washington's Speech at the Atlanta Exposition (Library of Congress)

BOOKER T. WASHINGTON'S ATLANTA EXPOSITION ADDRESS

"In all things that are purely social we can be as separate as the fingers, yet one as the hand in all things essential to mutual progress."

Overview

Late on an unseasonably hot mid-September afternoon in 1895, Booker T. Washington delivered a short speech to a standing-room-only crowd packed into the auditorium in Atlanta's Exposition Park during the opening ceremonies of the Cotton States and International Exposition. The address, which ran a little over ten minutes, propelled the previously unknown principal of Tuskegee Institute, a small black college in rural Alabama, into the national spotlight. By almost any measure, it (along with Martin Luther King, Jr.'s, 1963 "I Have a Dream" Speech) was one of the most important speeches presented by an African American. The immediate response, both in Atlanta and across the country, was overwhelmingly positive, but over time both Washington and his address have been sharply criticized, especially by other African American intellectuals and leaders. These critics termed the Atlanta address the "Atlanta Compromise" and made Washington a symbol of accommodation and acquiescence to southern racism, segregation, and the political disenfranchisement of African Americans. Throughout much of the twentieth century Washington and his famous (or infamous) address were a defining element in the African American political debate.

The assessment of Washington's Atlanta Exposition Address is clouded by the problem that Washington's actual words are less known than the responses and the analysis of those words by Washington's allies and especially by his opponents. As soon as the news of Washington's triumph at Atlanta spread across the country, friends and foes began to dissect his words and to interpret various phrases or images that he utilized. As a result, the speech itself quickly faded from memory, while discrete segments of the speech became permanently imbedded in American racial discourse, both within the African American community and among white Americans. The original context of the address, as well as its complex and nuanced arguments, gave way to the overly simplified and largely inaccurate view that Washington had surrendered the rights that African Americans had won during the Civil War and Reconstruction. By the time of Washington's death twenty years later, African American leadership was divided into Bookerite (pro-Washington) and anti-Bookerite factions, and Washington's opponents increasingly dominated the debate.

Context

The 1890s was a difficult decade for African Americans. Many of the gains they had achieved in securing their political and civil rights and in attaining a measure of physical security gave way to an assault on their rights as citizens and on their personal safety. During Reconstruction three constitutional amendments (the Thirteenth, Fourteenth, and Fifteenth Amendments) and the Civil Rights Acts of 1866 and 1875 had secured African American freedom and equal rights. The military occupation of the former Confederate States and federal legislation like the Civil Rights Act of 1871 (also known as the Ku Klux Klan Act) greatly diminished organized violence against blacks and their white political allies. In the late 1870s and 1880s these gains began to unravel. In the aftermath of the disputed presidential election of 1876, the last federal troops were withdrawn from the South. In 1883 the Supreme Court ruled in the Civil Rights Cases that the Fourteenth Amendment did not protect against discrimination by individuals or businesses, and three years later, for the first time in U.S. history, more blacks than whites were the victims of lynching.

In the 1890s racial conditions in the United States continued to deteriorate. In *Plessy v. Ferguson*, the Supreme Court legitimized state-sponsored segregation as long as "separate but equal" facilities were provided for blacks, and in 1898 the Court ruled that literacy tests and other similar methods of restricting the right to vote did not violate the Fifteenth Amendment. The 1890s witnessed more lynchings of blacks than any other decade in U.S. history. As the decade came to an end, race riots broke out in Wilmington, North Carolina (1898); New Orleans, Louisiana (1900); and New York (1900) as violence against blacks escalated. African Americans struggled to respond to this new wave of discrimination and violence without much success. The federal government, on which African Americans had depended during Reconstruction, was no longer a reliable ally. The Democrats had regained control of southern state

1856

■ **April 5**
Booker T. Washington is born into slavery on the farm of James Burroughs near Hale's Ford in the foothills of the Blue Ridge Mountains in Franklin County, Virginia.

1865

■ **August**
Freed by the defeat of the South in the Civil War, Washington and his family move to Malden, West Virginia.

1872

■ **October 5**
Washington leaves home and enrolls in Hampton Institute.

1881

■ **July 4**
Washington opens the Tuskegee Institute in Tuskegee, Alabama, modeling the school's curriculum on that of the Hampton Institute.

1895

■ **February 20**
Frederick Douglass, the most prominent African American leader of his generation, dies in Washington, D.C.

■ **September 18**
Washington delivers his Atlanta Exposition Address during the opening ceremonies of the Cotton States and International Exposition.

1896

■ **May 18**
In *Plessy v. Ferguson*, the Supreme Court rules that a Louisiana law segregating passengers on railroads is legal because it provides "separate but equal" facilities; this ruling validates a number of laws that segregate African Americans.

1898

■ **April 25**
In *Williams v. State of Mississippi*, the Supreme Court rules that a Mississippi law allowing poll taxes and literacy tests to be used as voter qualifications is legal, legitimizing the tactics used by southern states to deny African Americans the right to vote.

governments in the 1870s and won the presidency in 1884 and again in 1892. The Republican Party's commitment to civil rights also had waned. Frederick Douglass, who led the struggle against slavery and was an outspoken advocate of equal rights, died in February 1895, depriving African Americans of their best-known and most effective leader at this very crucial time.

Against this background Atlanta businessmen conceived of an international exposition, a small-scale world's fair, which would highlight the emergence of a "New South," promote the city and the entire region as a progressive area, and attract new business and investment capital. They hoped to capture some of the positive press coverage and economic benefits that Chicago had received with the 1893 Columbian Exposition. In the spring of 1894 Washington and several other African Americans were asked to join a delegation of prominent southerners to lobby Congress for an appropriation to support the Atlanta Exposition. Congress appropriated the funding, and as planning for the event proceeded, Washington was consulted again on the issue of the "Negro" exhibits. At some point, and after some controversy, exposition officials decided to involve African Americans in the opening ceremonies. On August 23, 1895, about three weeks before opening day, organizers of the exposition asked Washington to represent African Americans at this event.

The decision to involve African Americans so prominently in the exposition was interesting. Two years earlier black leaders had been unhappy with the way they were treated at the World's Columbian Exposition in Chicago. Their exhibits were segregated in Negro buildings, and blacks felt that as exhibitors at and visitors to the fair they had faced broken promises and discrimination. Consequently, a number of African American leaders were reluctant to support the Negro exhibits at this much smaller provincial event. Washington, however, cooperated with the organizers and urged others to do likewise, even though blacks had to fund their own exhibits and these exhibits would be housed in a separate building. Appreciation of Washington's assistance with Congress and his support of the event brought him to the podium on opening day.

About the Author

Booker Taliaferro Washington was born on a farm near Hale's Ford in the foothills of the Blue Ridge Mountains in Franklin County, Virginia. While his exact birth date is not clear, most authorities place it on April 5, 1856. Washington spent the first eight years of his childhood as a slave. Following emancipation he moved with his mother, brother, and sister to join his stepfather, who had found employment in the saltworks in Malden, West Virginia. Emancipation did not significantly raise the economic well-being of the family. The young Washington alternated between working in the saltworks and attending school. In 1867 his situation improved dramatically when he took a job in the home of General Lewis Ruffner, one of Malden's wealthiest citizens, serving as houseboy and companion for Viola Ruffner, the general's New England wife. Washington later credited Mrs. Ruffner for much of his early education and especially with preparing him for college.

At age sixteen Washington left home to further his education at Hampton Institute, which allowed impoverished black students to work at the school to pay the costs of their education. Three years later he graduated as one of its top students. After a short stint as a schoolteacher in Malden, he returned to Hampton to teach and to acquire additional education. During his time as a student and then as a teacher at Hampton, Washington became a protégé of General Samuel C. Armstrong and a student of Armstrong's theory of industrial education. In May 1881 the board of a recently authorized Alabama state normal school for black students asked Armstrong to recommend a white educator to serve as its principal. Armstrong recommended his prize student. After hesitation and with reluctance, the board accepted Washington to head the school.

When Washington arrived in Tuskegee, he discovered that the school existed only on paper—he had to find land, build buildings, and recruit faculty. It is to Washington's credit that despite his youth and inexperience, he mastered the political, administrative, and financial skills he needed to create a black institution in the inhospitable hills of northern Alabama. By the early 1890s Tuskegee had become a success, and Washington was beginning to address the broader political and economic issues that confronted African Americans.

The Atlanta Exposition Address transformed Washington from a southern educator to the most influential and powerful African American in the United States. He consulted with presidents and corporate leaders, and headed a political machine that dispersed funds from white philanthropists and political patronage throughout the black community. In the early twentieth century opposition to Washington's leadership increased, especially that organized around Du Bois. The founding of the National Association for the Advancement of Colored People in 1910 and Du Bois's prominent role in that organization deflected some white support from Washington. During the last years of Washington's life the African American leadership was increasingly divided into pro-Washington and pro–Du Bois/National Association for the Advancement of Colored People camps. Nevertheless, at the time of his death in November 1915, Washington was still the most widely known and respected African American leader in the United States.

Explanation and Analysis of the Document

Washington's Atlanta Exposition Address was presented in the auditorium on the exposition grounds. The auditorium was packed, mostly with whites, but there was also a segregated Negro section. Washington was one of two blacks seated on the stage, but he was the only one to speak. The speech itself was brief. In written form it is eleven paragraphs; Washington delivered it in about ten minutes.

Time Line

1901

■ **March**
Washington publishes his best-known autobiography, *Up from Slavery*.

■ **July 16**
Controversy arises after Washington dines at the White House while consulting President Theodore Roosevelt about political appointments in the South.

1903

■ **April 18**
W. E. B. Du Bois begins his criticism of Washington's leadership with the publication of the essay "Of Mr. Booker T. Washington and Others" in his book *The Souls of Black Folk.*

1905

■ **July 10**
Twenty-nine African Americans, including Du Bois, meet in Fort Erie, Ontario, to create a civil rights organization. The resulting Niagara Movement directly challenges Washington's leadership and policies.

1910

■ **May 14**
The biracial National Negro Conference officially gives birth to the National Association for the Advancement of Colored People, the oldest civil rights organization in the United States.

1915

■ **November 14**
Washington dies at home in Tuskegee.

In the first paragraph Washington notes the significance of the occasion. First, he emphasizes the significance of African Americans to the South—"One-third of the population of the South is of the Negro race"—and observes that no enterprise for the development of the South that ignores that element of the population will "reach the highest success." In this sentence, Washington introduces the major theme of his address: that the destinies and well-being of African American southerners and white southerners are inextricably linked. He returns to this theme again and again. Washington concludes this paragraph by praising the leaders of the exposition for recognizing the "value and manhood of the American Negro" throughout the planning and staging of the event. This statement is often viewed as obsequious; however, the role afforded African Ameri-

Booker T. Washington (Library of Congress)

cities that twenty years later became the black migration, or follow those who advocated immigration to a black-governed country, such as Haiti or Liberia. As discrimination and racial violence intensified, many considered Washington's advice to be misguided, binding blacks to a new slavery. Washington, however, argued that African Americans must work with their white neighbors—but without surrendering their dignity: "'Cast down your bucket where you are'—cast it down in making friends *in every manly way* of all the people of all races by whom we are surrounded" (emphasis added).

The next paragraph continues this argument. Still addressing the African Americans in the audience, Washington continues: "Cast it down in agriculture, mechanics, in commerce, in domestic service, and in the professions." Here Washington is laying out his economic agenda. While he is usually cited for promoting only low-skilled, working-class, and agricultural labor for blacks, here he is quite specific—his list of occupations includes commerce and the professions. Washington acknowledges that initially, lacking skills, capital, and education, most blacks will survive by the labor "of [their] hands," and he warns blacks not to denigrate the dignity and importance of this type of work. He also warns blacks not to sacrifice the habits of thrift and the accumulation of property and real wealth by conspicuous consumption and the superficial trappings of opulence. He notes that "there is as much dignity in tilling a field as in writing a poem," not to criticize poets but to recognize the importance of farmers. Finally, he warns blacks not to let discrimination and injustice blind them to the opportunities that surround them. In other words, if they focus only on their victimization, they will not succeed.

In paragraph 5, Washington shifts his focus to the white portion of his audience. Very carefully he lays out what white southerners must do, always recognizing that if he pushes too hard or too far he will fail and that failure would jeopardize Tuskegee and possibly his own safety. He begins with the very gentle phrase, "were I permitted I would repeat what I say to my own race"; then he tells white southerners to "'Cast down your bucket where you are.' Cast it down among the eight millions of Negroes whose habits you know, whose fidelity and love you have tested in days when to have proved treacherous meant the ruin of your firesides." Washington is telling white southerners to employ African Americans, not the immigrants who are pouring into the country from southern and eastern Europe; his reference to "strikes and labour wars" refers to the turmoil of recent clashes between unions and factory owners, such as the Homestead strike (1892) among steelworkers and the Pullman strike (1894) of factory workers. In his reference to the testing of black fidelity and love, he is referring to the Civil War and reminding whites that at the time they were most vulnerable, with most men off at war, blacks did not strike down the families they left behind. In discussing the contributions of blacks to the development of the South, Washington refers to both tilling the fields and building the cities, and

cans, from the lobbying efforts, the planning of the black exhibits, and Washington's participation in the opening ceremonies, contrasted considerably with blacks' roles in the World's Columbian Exposition of 1893 as well as other previous expositions.

The second paragraph contains the type of language that most irritated Washington's critics. After the rather serious opening, Washington feeds negative racial stereotypes when he essentially apologizes for the ignorance and inexperience that led newly emancipated blacks to make unwise choices, seeking political office rather than land or industrial skills and prizing political activity over entrepreneurship. Critics cite this paragraph as evidence that Washington acquiesced to white efforts to deprive blacks of their political rights. In truth, Washington consistently opposed both publicly and privately the disenfranchisement of southern blacks. However, Washington did feel that blacks should place greater emphasis on their economic betterment.

The third paragraph centers on one of Washington's best-known homilies. This is the story of the ship lost at sea, its crew dying of thirst and sending out a desperate cry for water, only to be told, "Cast down your bucket where you are." Washington uses this story to admonish the blacks in his audience to "cast down your bucket where you are," that is, to remain in the South rather than attempt to better their condition in a "foreign land." Washington consistently advised African Americans not to follow the Exodusters west, join the trickle to northern

The Cotton States and International Exposition (Library of Congress)

for the future he depicts blacks buying land, making waste areas blossom, and running factories. Throughout this section Washington softens his message with references to the African American people as law-abiding, unresentful, loyal, and faithful, and he reminds his audience that blacks have nursed whites' children, cared for their aged, and mourned their dead.

Washington concludes paragraph 5 with his most famous statement: "In all things that are purely social we can be as separate as the fingers, yet one as the hand in all things essential to mutual progress." This sentence is at the heart of the criticism of Washington and the Atlanta Exposition Address. Looked at out of context, it seems to acquiesce to "separate but equal" segregation. However, the sentence was spoken in a context that leaves the meaning less clear. Immediately preceding it, Washington spoke of blacks "interlacing our industrial, commercial, civil, and religious life with yours in a way that shall make the interests of both races one," picking up the theme introduced in the

first paragraph that the destinies of black and white southerners are intertwined.

In the very short sixth paragraph, Washington continues to discuss the connectedness of blacks and whites, observing that the security of both races requires the "highest intelligence and development of all" and urging whites to invest in the advancement of African Americans for the betterment of all.

In paragraph 7, Washington breaks the narrative and quotes from the poem "At Port Royal," written by the abolitionist poet John Greenleaf Whittier in 1862 to celebrate the November 1861 Union victory over the South and the occupation of the Port Royal area on the Georgia and South Carolina coasts. This battle was significant because the Union army liberated a number of slaves. It was one of the earliest steps toward emancipation. Quoting the most celebrated abolitionist poet to a largely white audience in Atlanta was very daring of Washington. Washington's message is one of oppressor and oppressed, bound together,

"'Cast down your bucket where you are.' Cast it down among the eight millions of Negroes whose habits you know, whose fidelity and love you have tested in days when to have proved treacherous meant the ruin of your firesides."

(Paragraph 5)

"In all things that are purely social we can be as separate as the fingers, yet one as the hand in all things essential to mutual progress."

(Paragraph 5)

"We shall contribute one-third to the business and industrial prosperity of the South, or we shall prove a veritable body of death, stagnating, depressing, retarding every effort to advance the body politic."

(Paragraph 8)

"The wisest among my race understand that the agitation of questions of social equality is the extremest folly, and that progress in the enjoyment of all the privileges that will come to us must be the result of severe and constant struggle rather than of artificial forcing."

(Paragraph 10)

"No race that has anything to contribute to the markets of the world is long in any degree ostracized."

(Paragraph 10)

"The opportunity to earn a dollar in a factory just now is worth infinitely more than the opportunity to spend a dollar in an opera-house."

(Paragraph 10)

confronting one fate. It is very likely that most whites in the audience knew the poem.

For those in the audience who might not know the poem or understand its message, Washington repeats it in very clear, unambiguous language in paragraph 8. Either blacks and whites cooperate for the betterment of the South, or blacks will work against whites and retard progress; either blacks will constitute one-third of the South's "intelligence and progress" and one-third of its "business and industrial prosperity," or "we shall prove a veritable body of death, stagnating, depressing, retarding every effort to advance the body politic." Washington threatens white southerners with economic and social catastrophe unless they are willing to work with blacks and allow blacks to share appropriately in southern progress and development.

After stating this grim warning, Washington turns to humor to defuse the tension. He begins paragraph 9 with a reference that caters to the white stereotype of blacks as petty thieves—much to the dismay of his critics. The rest of the paragraph is conciliatory. Washington describes the advances and accomplishments that African Americans had made in the thirty years since emancipation and the assistance from southern states and northern philanthropists that made this progress possible.

Paragraph 10 consists of three often-quoted sentences. In the first Washington asserts that "agitation of questions of social equality is the extremest folly" but that progress toward equality will result from "severe and constant struggle" rather than from "artificial forcing." Here again Washington is ambiguous, on the one hand denouncing agitation and on the other advocating prolonged struggle. The difference may lie in the term *social equality*, which some scholars suggest southerners equated with intermarriage. The second sentence reflects Washington's conviction that economic prosperity would erase racial prejudice. Washington ends this paragraph by asserting that at the current time, it is more important that blacks achieve the right to work in a factory than to buy a seat in the opera house. Again Washington expresses his belief that in the short term, economic prosperity should be the highest priority for African Americans. His critics accused him of again accepting segregation.

In the final paragraph, Washington ends where he began, praising the organizers of the exhibition and observing the tremendous progress blacks and whites have made, the former starting as slaves with nothing and the latter coming out of a war in which they lost everything. He again links the destiny of the two races and adds a religious component. It is God who has laid before the South the task of creating a just society, free of "sectional differences and racial animosities and suspicions." If whites, with the support of blacks, resolve this problem, they will bring into the South a "new heaven and a new earth," a reference drawn from Revelation 21:1. Left unspoken is the alternative described in Revelation 21:8 and known to most listeners. The failure to create a just society (a new heaven and a new earth) will be a fate shared by all southerners—the "lake which burneth with fire and brimstone: which is the second death."

Audience

The initial audience that Washington addressed was a few thousand southerners gathered in Atlanta for the opening of the exposition. Louis Harlan, Washington's principal biographer, describes the auditorium as "packed with humanity from bottom to top"; outside were "thousands more ... unable to get in." Still, this was a relatively small but important audience. The majority were white southerners, a very difficult audience for Washington to face. In 1895 few white southerners would have tolerated being lectured to by a black man. Washington had to make his points both gently and diplomatically without surrendering his dignity or his convictions. Also present in the audience were black southerners, fewer in number, attracted to the auditorium by the unusual opportunity to see a black man address an audience of prominent whites. Washington could also expect that his words, at least in part, would be reported throughout the black community. What Washington did not anticipate was the much larger national audience that his speech would reach. Within a few days his Atlanta Exposition Address was reported in whole or in part in newspapers across the land. Washington would quickly become the most widely known African American in the country, and passages from his speech would become fixed in popular culture and American memory.

Impact

The immediate response to the speech was phenomenal. In the auditorium the audience burst into thunderous applause the moment Washington finished speaking; the former governor of Georgia, who had presided over the proceedings, rushed forward to congratulate Washington. Newspapers around the country reported the address and reprinted the speech. Perhaps none did so as effusively as Joseph Pulitzer's *New York World*, with headlines announcing that "A Negro Moses Spoke for a Race." The reporter described Washington facing the crowd with the sun in his eyes, his "whole face lit up with the fire of prophecy.... It electrified the audience, and the response was as if it had come from the throat of a whirlwind." Within days, letters and telegrams poured in praising Washington and his speech, anointing Washington as the successor to the recently deceased Frederick Douglass, and comparing the speech to Lincoln's Gettysburg Address. One who sent his congratulations was Du Bois, who telegraphed, "Let me heartily congratulate you on your phenomenal success in Atlanta—it was a word fitly spoken." He followed it up with a letter to the *New York Age*, praising the Atlanta speech as a basis for a real settlement of the racial problems in the South. There was also some opposition, especially among northern blacks. The *Washington Bee* published a very critical editorial depicting the speech as a surrender to whites. Others rejected the comparison of Washington to Douglass, while still others cringed at Washington's use of stereotyped images of blacks as a source of humor. On the whole, however, public comment, black and white, was very favorable. The real criticism would come later.

The Atlanta Exposition Address made Washington a national figure and the most influential and powerful African American in the United States. In 1898 President William McKinley visited Tuskegee, affirming Washington's new prominence, and in 1901 Washington dined with President Roosevelt in the White House. Less publicly but even more significantly, President McKinley, President Roosevelt, and President William Taft regularly consulted with Washington on issues of significance to African Americans and on their appointments of both blacks and many white southerners to federal positions. Washington, in turn, developed a powerful political machine with allies among most prominent black Republicans and many black newspaper editors. Parallel to his expanding political power, Washington established close contacts among many of the most powerful white business leaders. In the process, he expanded his already effective fund-raising operation for Tuskegee into an economic machine that effectively controlled the distribution of white philanthropy into the black community.

History, however, has not been kind to Washington or his Atlanta address. By 1910 Du Bois and most northern black intellectuals either viewed the Atlanta speech as a surrender to white racism or blamed Washington and the policies enunciated in Atlanta for the deterioration of African American rights and the rise in racial violence. Within the black community this negative view persisted throughout most of the twentieth century. Finally, the Atlanta address, accurately or inaccurately, has become a symbol of a dichotomy in African American political thought—the division between those advocating a nonconfrontational economic and community-building approach to America's racial problems and those who push a more militant program of integration and immediate civil and political rights.

See also Thirteenth Amendment to the U.S. Constitution (1865); Fourteenth Amendment to the U.S. Constitution (1868); Fifteenth Amendment to the U.S. Constitution (1870); Ku Klux Klan Act (1871); Civil Rights Cases (1883); *Plessy v. Ferguson* (1896); Martin Luther King, Jr.: "I Have a Dream" (1963).

Further Reading

■ **Books**

Brundage, W. Fitzhugh, ed. *Booker T. Washington and Black Progress: Up from Slavery 100 Years Later*. Gainesville: University of Florida Press, 2003.

Harlan, Louis R. *Booker T. Washington: The Making of a Black Leader, 1856–1901*. New York: Oxford University Press, 1972.

———. *Booker T. Washington: The Wizard of Tuskegee, 1901–1915*. New York: Oxford University Press, 1983.

———, et al., eds. *The Booker T. Washington Papers*. 14 vols. Urbana: University of Illinois Press, 1972–1989.

Meier, August. *Negro Thought in America, 1880–1915: Racial Ideologies in the Age of Booker T. Washington*. Ann Arbor: University of Michigan Press, 1968.

Questions for Further Study

1. Critics of Washington and his Atlanta Exposition Address have accused him of betraying African Americans by giving in to southern perceptions of the racial inferiority of African Americans and accepting segregation and the loss of the African American political rights and the right to vote. To what extent is this criticism valid? To what extent is it not valid?

2. What rights does Washington assert for African Americans in the Atlanta address? How do these rights differ from those championed by the organizers of the Niagara Movement in their 1905 Declaration of Principles?

3. Washington delivered this speech in Atlanta, Georgia, in 1895. How did the location of the speech affect what Washington said? How might the speech have been different had Washington delivered it in New York rather than Atlanta?

4. One theme that Washington develops in this speech is the concept that the destinies of black southerners and white southerners are intertwined. How does Washington argue this point? What is the significance of this argument? Explain whether this argument is an effective basis for resolving racial problems in the South.

Moore, Jacqueline H. *Booker T. Washington, W. E. B. Du Bois, and the Struggle for Racial Uplift.* Wilmington, Del.: Scholarly Resources, 2003.

Washington, Booker T. *An Autobiography: The Story of My Life and Work.* Chicago: J. L. Nichols, 1900.

———. *Up from Slavery: An Autobiography.* New York: Doubleday, 1901.

West, Michael Rudolph. *The Education of Booker T. Washington: American Democracy and the Idea of Race Relations.* New York: Columbia University Press, 2006.

Wolters, Raymond. *Du Bois and His Rivals.* Columbia: University of Missouri Press, 2002.

■ **Web Sites**

"The Booker T. Washington Papers." University of Illinois Press Web site.
http://www.historycooperative.org/btw/info.html.

"South's New Epoch." *New York World*, September 19, 1895. University of Illinois Press Web site.
http://www.historycooperative.org/btw/Vol.4/html/3.html.

—Cary D. Wintz

Booker T. Washington's Atlanta Exposition Address

Mr. President and Gentlemen of the Board of Directors and Citizens:

One-third of the population of the South is of the Negro race. No enterprise seeking the material, civil, or moral welfare of this section can disregard this element of our population and reach the highest success. I but convey to you, Mr. President and Directors, the sentiment of the masses of my race when I say that in no way have the value and manhood of the American Negro been more fittingly and generously recognized than by the managers of this magnificent Exposition at every stage of its progress. It is a recognition that will do more to cement the friendship of the two races than any occurrence since the dawn of our freedom.

Not only this, but the opportunity here afforded will awaken among us a new era of industrial progress. Ignorant and inexperienced, it is not strange that in the first years of our new life we began at the top instead of at the bottom; that a seat in Congress or the state legislature was more sought than real estate or industrial skill; that the political convention or stump speaking had more attractions than starting a dairy farm or truck garden.

A ship lost at sea for many days suddenly sighted a friendly vessel. From the mast of the unfortunate vessel was seen a signal, "Water, water; we die of thirst!" The answer from the friendly vessel at once came back, "Cast down your bucket where you are." A second time the signal, "Water, water; send us water!" ran up from the distressed vessel, and was answered, "Cast down your bucket where you are." And a third and fourth signal for water was answered, "Cast down your bucket where you are." The captain of the distressed vessel, at last heeding the injunction, cast down his bucket, and it came up full of fresh, sparkling water from the mouth of the Amazon River. To those of my race who depend on bettering their condition in a foreign land or who underestimate the importance of cultivating friendly relations with the Southern white man, who is their next-door neighbor, I would say: "Cast down your bucket where you are"—cast it down in making friends in every manly way of the people of all races by whom we are surrounded.

Cast it down in agriculture, mechanics, in commerce, in domestic service, and in the professions. And in this connection it is well to bear in mind that whatever other sins the South may be called to bear, when it comes to business, pure and simple, it is in the South that the Negro is given a man's chance in the commercial world, and in nothing is this Exposition more eloquent than in emphasizing this chance. Our greatest danger is that in the great leap from slavery to freedom we may overlook the fact that the masses of us are to live by the productions of our hands, and fail to keep in mind that we shall prosper in proportion as we learn to dignify and glorify common labour, and put brains and skill into the common occupations of life; shall prosper in proportion as we learn to draw the line between the superficial and the substantial, the ornamental gewgaws of life and the useful. No race can prosper till it learns that there is as much dignity in tilling a field as in writing a poem. It is at the bottom of life we must begin, and not at the top. Nor should we permit our grievances to overshadow our opportunities.

To those of the white race who look to the incoming of those of foreign birth and strange tongue and habits for the prosperity of the South, were I permitted I would repeat what I say to my own race, "Cast down your bucket where you are." Cast it down among the eight millions of Negroes whose habits you know, whose fidelity and love you have tested in days when to have proved treacherous meant the ruin of your firesides. Cast down your bucket among these people who have, without strikes and labour wars, tilled your fields, cleared your forests, builded your railroads and cities, and brought forth treasures from the bowels of the earth, and helped make possible this magnificent representation of the progress of the South. Casting down your bucket among my people, helping and encouraging them as you are doing on these grounds, and to education of head, hand, and heart, you will find that they will buy your surplus land, make blossom the waste places in your fields, and run your factories. While doing this, you can be sure in the future, as in the past, that you and your families will be surrounded by the most patient, faithful, law-abiding, and unresentful people that the world has seen. As we have proved our loyalty to you in the past, in nursing your children, watching by the sick-bed of your mothers and fathers, and often following them with tear-dimmed eyes to their graves, so in the future, in our humble way, we shall stand by you with a devotion that no foreigner can approach, ready to lay down our lives, if need be, in defense of yours, interlacing our industrial, commercial, civil, and religious life with yours in a way that shall make the interests of both races one. In all things that are purely social we can be as separate as the fingers, yet one as the hand in all things essential to mutual progress.

There is no defense or security for any of us except in the highest intelligence and development of all. If anywhere there are efforts tending to curtail the fullest growth of the Negro, let these efforts be turned into stimulating, encouraging, and making him the most useful and intelligent citizen. Effort or means so invested will pay a thousand per cent interest. These efforts will be twice blessed—blessing him that gives and him that takes. There is no escape through law of man or God from the inevitable:

The laws of changeless justice bind
Oppressor with oppressed;
And close as sin and suffering joined
We march to fate abreast...

Nearly sixteen millions of hands will aid you in pulling the load upward, or they will pull against you the load downward. We shall constitute one-third and more of the ignorance and crime of the South, or one-third [of] its intelligence and progress; we shall contribute one-third to the business and industrial prosperity of the South, or we shall prove a veritable body of death, stagnating, depressing, retarding every effort to advance the body politic.

Gentlemen of the Exposition, as we present to you our humble effort at an exhibition of our progress, you must not expect overmuch. Starting thirty years ago with ownership here and there in a few quilts and pumpkins and chickens (gathered from miscellaneous sources), remember the path that has led from these to the inventions and production of agricultural implements, buggies, steam-engines, newspapers, books, statuary, carving, paintings, the management of drug stores and banks, has not been trodden without contact with thorns and thistles. While we take pride in what we exhibit as a result of our independent efforts, we do not for a moment forget that our part in this exhibition would fall far short of your expectations but for the constant help that has come to our educational life, not only from the Southern states, but especially from Northern philanthropists, who have made their gifts a constant stream of blessing and encouragement.

The wisest among my race understand that the agitation of questions of social equality is the extremest folly, and that progress in the enjoyment of all the privileges that will come to us must be the result of severe and constant struggle rather than of artificial forcing. No race that has anything to contribute to the markets of the world is long in any degree ostracized. It is important and right that all privileges of the law be ours, but it is vastly more important that we be prepared for the exercise of these privileges. The opportunity to earn a dollar in a factory just now is worth infinitely more than the opportunity to spend a dollar in an opera-house.

In conclusion, may I repeat that nothing in thirty years has given us more hope and encouragement, and drawn us so near to you of the white race, as this opportunity offered by the Exposition; and here bending, as it were, over the altar that represents the results of the struggles of your race and mine, both starting practically empty-handed three decades ago, I pledge that in your effort to work out the great and intricate problem which God has laid at the doors of the South, you shall have at all times the patient, sympathetic help of my race; only let this be constantly in mind, that, while from representations in these buildings of the product of field, of forest, of mine, of factory, letters, and art, much good will come, yet far above and beyond material benefits will be that higher good, that, let us pray God, will come, in a blotting out of sectional differences and racial animosities and suspicions, in a determination to administer absolute justice, in a willing obedience among all classes to the mandates of law. This, coupled with our material prosperity, will bring into our beloved South a new heaven and a new earth.

Glossary

body politic	the people as a whole in a state or a nation
letters	literature
mandates	authoritative demands or requirements
sectional	related to one part or state of a country over another

Supreme Court of the United States,

No. 210 , October Term, 1895.

Homer Adolph Plessy
Plaintiff in Error,

vs.

J. H. Ferguson, Judge of Section "A" Criminal District Court for the Parish of Orleans.

In Error to the Supreme Court of the State of Louisiana

This cause came on to be heard on the transcript of the record from the Supreme Court of the State of Louisiana, and was argued by counsel.

On consideration whereof, It is now here ordered and adjudged by this Court that the judgment of the said Supreme Court, in this cause, be, and the same is hereby, Affirmed with costs.

Per Mr. Justice Brown,
May 18, 1896.

Dissenting:
Mr. Justice Harlan

Plessy v. Ferguson (National Archieves and Records Administration)

PLESSY V. FERGUSON

1896

"If one race be inferior to the other socially, the constitution of the United States cannot put them upon the same plane."

Overview

Plessy v. Ferguson, argued on April 13, 1896, and decided on May 18, 1896, is probably best known for giving the United States the "separate but equal" doctrine. The case probably ranks close to *Dred Scott v. Sandford* (1857) as one of the most influential and thoroughly repudiated cases the Supreme Court has ever decided. The majority opinion was written by Justice Henry Billings Brown of Massachusetts, and it gained the assent of six additional justices. That opinion provided a legal imprimatur to segregation and the Jim Crow system of laws that flourished from the late nineteenth century through much of the twentieth century. *Plessy* held that notwithstanding the Reconstruction Amendments (the Thirteenth, Fourteenth, and Fifteenth Amendments), which were passed in the wake of the Civil War to grant equal citizenship to African Americans and promised the equal protection of the laws to all persons, the United States Constitution allowed states to segregate their black and white citizens when traveling on intrastate railroads. The separate but equal doctrine was applied to more than just railroads and supported segregation until it was largely repudiated, though not explicitly overruled, in *Brown v. Board of Education of Topeka* (1954).

Justice John Marshall Harlan of Kentucky wrote the sole dissent in *Plessy*, which provided much of the rhetorical support for the twentieth-century civil rights movement. Justice Harlan argued that the Reconstruction Amendments' guarantees of equality were so incompatible with segregation that segregation was unconstitutional. Justice David Brewer did not participate in the case.

Context

Although the Civil War ended just over thirty years before *Plessy v. Ferguson* was decided, the case was yet a result of the lingering conflict that existed after the war. During the decade following the Civil War, known as the Reconstruction era, America was a place of great change with respect to race relations. During the five years following the end of the war,

the Thirteenth, Fourteenth, and Fifteenth Amendments (collectively known as the Civil War or Reconstruction Amendments) were passed. The Thirteenth Amendment outlawed slavery. The Fourteenth Amendment was passed after it became clear that the Thirteenth Amendment could not guarantee that individual states would grant the full equality that many had believed would result from the end of slavery. The Fifteenth Amendment, which stated that voting rights could not be abridged based on race, color, or previous condition of servitude, was ratified to guarantee political equality for African American men. Taken together, these amendments were designed to make African Americans (former slaves and free blacks) full and equal participants in American society. In addition, Congress passed a number of laws designed to protect the newly won civil rights of black citizens and allow the full enjoyment of equal citizenship. For example, Congress passed the Civil Rights Act of 1875, which required that black citizens be provided the same access to public accommodations, such as railroads, theaters, and inns, as white citizens.

Although race relations were hardly smooth after the Civil War, Congress made clear that equality under the law was to be the order of the day. However, the presidential election of 1876 changed the course of the country. Rutherford Hayes and Samuel Tilden ran a very close election that had to be decided in the House of Representatives. In exchange for support to become president, Hayes agreed to end the Reconstruction era in the South and withdraw the remaining federal troops there. The withdrawal of troops signaled the psychological end to Reconstruction and the coming of a Jim Crow society based on racial separation and racial caste.

Louisiana's story tracks that of the South, though New Orleans had always enjoyed more racial mixing than other parts of the South. For example, just after the end of the Civil War, Louisiana enacted its Black Code. However, in 1868 Louisiana ratified a state constitution that provided equal rights to African Americans. Around this time, Louisiana also desegregated its schools. As with the rest of the South, however, the end of Reconstruction triggered the arrival of Jim Crow laws. Both Louisiana and New Orleans slid toward state-mandated segregation.

The segregationists consolidated power through the 1870s and the 1880s. In the 1880s many southern states

PLESSY V. FERGUSON

837

Time Line

1875

- **March 1**
  The Civil Rights Act of 1875 is passed, barring racial discrimination in public accommodations, including public conveyances.

1877

- The Compromise of 1877 allows Rutherford B. Hayes to become president on the condition that Hayes remove remaining federal troops from the South.

1880s

- Some southern states begin to require segregated railroad cars.

1883

- **October 16**
  The Supreme Court decides that the Civil Rights Cases deeming the Civil Rights Act of 1875 unconstitutional are outside congressional scope of power.

1890s

- Southern states revise constitutions in large part to disenfranchise African Americans and limit other civil rights.

1890

- The Supreme Court decides *Louisville, New Orleans & Texas Railway Co. v. Mississippi*, which denies an interstate commerce–based challenge to Mississippi's Separate Car Act.

- **July 10**
  Louisiana passes the Separate Car Act, which Home Plessy eventually challenges.

1892

- **June 7**
  Homer Plessy is arrested after boarding a train and refusing to sit in the car assigned for colored people.

1893

- The Panic of 1893 triggers an economic depression in the United States.

1895

- **September 18**
  Booker T. Washington gives his Atlanta Exposition Address, arguing for accommodation to segregation and urging focus on economic self-determination rather than on integration.

began to pass laws requiring the segregation of railroad cars. In 1890 Louisiana joined those states in passing the Separate Car Act of 1890. As a result of the legislation, a number of African Americans created the Citizens' Committee to Test the Constitutionality of the Separate Car Act to challenge the law and to attempt to protect the gains won for African Americans during the Reconstruction era. Homer Plessy's case was a test case designed specifically to challenge the Separate Car Act and the coming of the Jim Crow laws. The case had the potential to either stem the tide of racial separatism or drive a nail in the coffin of racial equality and reconciliation.

About the Author

Justice Henry Billings Brown wrote the majority opinion in *Plessy v. Ferguson*. Brown was born on March 2, 1836, in South Lee, Massachusetts. After graduating from Yale College, he studied law at Yale Law School and Harvard Law School. He served as a U.S. deputy marshal, assistant U.S. attorney, and federal judge of the Eastern District of Michigan for fifteen years before being confirmed to the U.S. Supreme Court in 1890. He retired from the Court in 1906 and died on September 4, 1913.

Justice John Marshall Harlan wrote the sole dissenting opinion in *Plessy v. Ferguson*. Harlan was born on June 1, 1833, in Boyle County, Kentucky. After graduating from Centre College, he studied law at Transylvania University. Although he was a former slaveholder, Harlan fought for the Union army in the Civil War. Harlan opposed abolition before the war and full equality for blacks just after the war. However, in the wake of the Civil War, Harlan joined the Republican Party and reversed his view of slavery and many racial equality issues. Harlan was confirmed to the Court on November 29, 1877. In addition to the *Plessy* dissent, he dissented in the Civil Rights Cases (1883), arguing that the Civil Rights Act of 1875 was constitutional and should have been held to legally require equal public accommodations for those of all races. Harlan served on the Court until his death on October 14, 1911.

Explanation and Analysis of the Document

♦ Statement of the Case

The case begins with a recitation of the facts of the case and its legal posture. On June 7, 1892, Plessy, the defendant also known as the plaintiff in error, paid for a first-class train ticket on the East Louisiana Railway headed from New Orleans to Covington, Louisiana, and sat down in an empty seat in the railroad car reserved for whites. He was "of seven-eighths Caucasian and one-eighth African blood" and had such a light complexion that one could not tell that he had any African ancestry. However, Plessy had already decided to challenge the law before boarding the train. Thus, after sitting down, Plessy informed the conductor that he was of mixed blood. He was told he had to move to the section for nonwhites or get off the train. Plessy was "forcibly ejected from said coach" and taken to jail after he refused to move.

Plessy was charged with violating an act of the Louisiana legislature commonly known as the Separate Car Act of 1890. In response to the charge, Plessy asserted that the act violated the U.S. Constitution. The Louisiana trial court disagreed and, according to the statement of the case as noted in the *Plessy* decision, stated that unless "the judge of the said court be enjoined by a writ of prohibition from further proceeding in such case, the court will proceed to fine and sentence petitioner to imprisonment." Plessy sought a writ of prohibition that would stop the court from enforcing the act. The Louisiana Supreme Court determined that the Separate Car Act was constitutional and denied the writ of prohibition. Consequently, Plessy "prayed for a writ of error from this court" and the case came to the U.S. Supreme Court.

◆ Majority Opinion of Justice Henry Billings Brown

Brown's opinion for the Court follows the recitation of facts. It begins by noting that the key issue is "the constitutionality of an act of the general assembly of the state of Louisiana, passed in 1890, providing for separate railway carriages for the white and colored races." The opinion then describes the content of the statute. The first section of the statute requires that railway companies other than street railroads provide "equal but separate accommodations for the white, and colored races," either by providing separate train cars or by erecting partitions in a single railcar that separates the races. The second section of the statute requires that the companies segregate their passengers by race. Train conductors and other company employees were required to assign passengers to respective accommodations by race. Passengers who refused to go to their assigned accommodations and train employees who intentionally assigned passengers to the wrong accommodations were liable for a fine of $25 or up to twenty days in jail. A railway company could refuse to carry a passenger who refused to sit in his or her assigned car, and no damages would arise based on the refusal. The third section of the act provides penalties for employees of the railway company who refuse to comply with the act, but it excepts "nurses attending children of the other race." According to Brown, the fourth section of the act is immaterial.

The opinion repeats facts from the statement of the case: that Plessy was of seven-eighths Caucasian and one-eighth African blood, that one could not tell that he was part African by looking at him, that he sat down in a vacant seat in the coach assigned for whites, that he did not move when he was told to move, that he was removed from the train, and that he was taken to the parish jail. Brown notes that Plessy claims that the Separate Car Act is unconstitutional under both the Thirteenth and Fourteenth Amendments. Brown quickly addresses the Thirteenth Amendment claim and then spends the rest of the opinion addressing the Fourteenth Amendment claim.

Brown explains that the Thirteenth Amendment addresses slavery and like conditions such as "Mexican peon-

Time Line	
1896	■ **May 18** *Plessy v. Ferguson* is decided.
1897	■ **January 11** Plessy pleads guilty to violating the Separate Car Act and pays a $25 fine.
1898	■ Louisiana holds a constitutional convention that effectively disenfranchises its African American citizens.
1909	■ **February 12** The National Association for the Advancement of Colored People is formed.

age or the Chinese coolie trade." In addition, the amendment applies to attempts to place people into involuntary servitude or to place badges of slavery on former slaves. However, says Brown, the Thirteenth Amendment is not applicable to this case. The statute at issue makes a distinction between the races based on color but does not seek to "destroy the legal equality of the two races, or re-establish a state of involuntary servitude." Brown notes that in cases like this one where a law allows or requires discrimination, if any amendment were to apply, it would be the Fourteenth, not the Thirteenth. This is because the Fourteenth Amendment was passed to address race-based distinctions that some believed effectively devalued the freedom given by the Thirteenth Amendment.

Brown begins his explanation of the applicability of the Fourteenth Amendment with an elucidation of its scope and limitations. He notes that the purpose of the amendment is "to establish the citizenship of the negro, to given definitions of citizenship of the United States and of the states, and to protect from the hostile legislation of the states the privileges and immunities of citizens of the United States, as distinguished from those of citizens of the states." Simply, the amendment provides equality of the races before the law. Equality before the law is not necessarily inconsistent with making race-based distinctions or even segregating the races, however. Brown notes that school segregation was allowed even in jurisdictions that scrupulously provided equal political rights between the races, citing Justice Lemuel Shaw's opinion in the 1849 case *Roberts v. City of Boston*. Although that case was decided before the Civil War and the passage of the Fourteenth Amendment and could not be deemed binding on any construction of the Fourteenth Amendment, Brown's point appears to be that there is a distinction between requiring equality before the law and requiring what he believes constituted social equality. In making his point, Brown previews an argument, which he would use later in the opinion, that enforced separation of the races does not suggest the inferiority of either race.

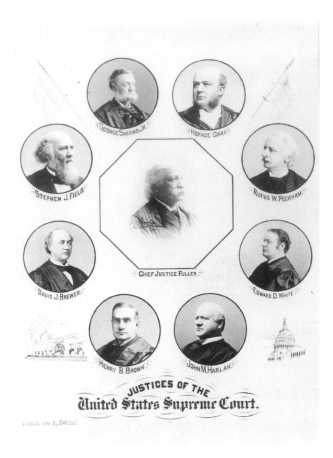

Supreme Court Justices in 1896 (Library of Congress)

Brown argues that the Fourteenth Amendment is a limitation on states when political or civil equality is at stake, rather than a mandate to allow Congress to grant positive rights to support notions of equality. For example, the Fourteenth Amendment requires that blacks and whites be treated equally when civil rights such as the ability to serve on a jury are at issue. Conversely, when social equality issues are at stake, such as conditions of travel, the Fourteenth Amendment leaves those matters to the states to regulate so long as no other constitutional provisions are violated. For example, when Louisiana sought to regulate racial aspects of how passengers were to be treated when traveling through the state in interstate travel, it would have been able to do so had the law not been related to interstate commerce, the regulation of which is left to Congress under the Constitution. That the Fourteenth Amendment generally leaves state prerogatives to regulate intact was made clear when the Court passed on the Civil Rights Act of 1875 in the Civil Rights Cases. There, the Court indicated that the Fourteenth Amendment does not give Congress the power to pass legislation that provides positive rights in areas of state prerogative such as the public accommodation of the races with respect to private businesses. Simply, the Fourteenth Amendment does not provide positive rights; it merely limits the kind of legislation states can pass.

Brown then directly addresses the constitutionality of the Separate Car Act. Although the act forced segregation, Brown finds that it does not harm the rights of African Americans because it "neither abridges the privileges or immunities of the colored man, deprives him of his property without due process of law, nor denies him the equal protection of the laws, within the meaning of the fourteenth amendment." The act had the potential to harm the rights of whites, however. If, as Plessy argues in the claim, the reputation of being a white person in a mixed-race community is like property, the act may have gone too far in protecting a conductor who improperly assigns whites to the black car and therefore damages the property value of the white person. Brown notes that this problem is of no moment to Plessy's claim, because a black man like Plessy loses no property value in his reputation by being improperly categorized as a white person.

In response to the argument that allowing racial separation opens the door to allowing the state to create other arbitrary distinctions based on race, Brown answers that the exercise of the state's police power itself has to be reasonable. The question is whether the Separate Car Act is reasonable based on "the established usages, customs, and traditions of the people, and with a view to the promotion of their comfort, and the preservation of the public peace and good order." Based on that standard, it is unclear that the segregation here is any worse than school segregation that, according to Brown, most courts appear to agree is constitutional.

After determining that the act is constitutional, Brown attempts to explain why the rule itself treats the races equally. He reprises his argument that forced segregation does not suggest the inferiority of either race and states that any inferiority that black citizens may feel comes from the spin blacks give to the act and not from the act itself. Indeed, he suggests that if a majority-black legislature had passed the act, whites would not feel inferior to blacks. Oddly, Brown then explains that voluntary mingling between the races is acceptable, but forced mingling by the state is not required. Given that the statute at issue stops voluntary mingling, Brown's argument is somewhat nonsensical. Brown ends the argument by suggesting that formal civil and political equality is as far as the Constitution does and can go. If the races are social unequals, the Constitution cannot remedy that situation. Brown ends his opinion by noting that it is unclear how much African blood makes one black for purposes of segregation statutes, but he leaves that issue to the individual states to decide.

♦ **Dissenting Opinion of Justice John Marshall Harlan**

Harlan begins by highlighting a few of the statute's salient points. He notes that the statute requires strict separation of the races with the exception of a nurse caring for a child of a different race. Indeed, a personal attendant could not attend to the needs of her employer if the attendant and employer were of different races unless the attendant wished to be held criminally liable. However, he notes, regardless of the fairness of the statute, the question for the Court is whether the statute's explicit regulation based on race is constitutional.

MILESTONE DOCUMENTS IN AFRICAN AMERICAN HISTORY

"We consider the underlying fallacy of the plaintiff's argument to consist in the assumption that the enforced separation of the two races stamps the colored race with a badge of inferiority. If this be so, it is not by reason of anything found in the act, but solely because the colored race chooses to put that construction upon it."

(Justice Henry Billings Brown, Majority Opinion)

"If the two races are to meet upon terms of social equality, it must be the result of natural affinities, a mutual appreciation of each other's merits, and a voluntary consent of individuals."

(Justice Henry Billings Brown, Majority Opinion)

"If the civil and political rights of both races be equal, one cannot be inferior to the other civilly or politically. If one race be inferior to the other socially, the constitution of the United States cannot put them upon the same plane."

(Justice Henry Billings Brown, Majority Opinion)

"The white race deems itself to be the dominant race in this country. And so it is, in prestige, in achievements, in education, in wealth, and in power. So, I doubt not, it will continue to be for all time.... But in view of the constitution, in the eye of the law, there is in this country no superior, dominant, ruling class of citizens.... Our constitution is color-blind, and neither knows nor tolerates classes among citizens."

(Justice John Marshall Harlan, Dissenting Opinion)

"In my opinion, the judgment this day rendered will, in time, prove to be quite as pernicious as the decision made by this tribunal in the Dred Scott Case."

(Justice John Marshall Harlan, Dissenting Opinion)

"What can more certainly arouse race hate ... than state enactments which, in fact, proceed on the ground that colored citizens are so inferior and degraded that they cannot be allowed to sit in public coaches occupied by white citizens?"

(Justice John Marshall Harlan, Dissenting Opinion)

Harlan provides the general structure of his argument. The civil rights of all citizens are to be protected equally. Consequently, there is no reason for the government to consider the race of any person when regulating civil rights. When a government considers race when legislating regarding civil rights, not only does it improperly provide civil rights, it also improperly affects the liberty of all U.S. residents.

Harlan then indicates the purpose of the Reconstruction Amendments The Reconstruction Amendments provide a broad protection for the rights of all citizens. The Thirteenth Amendment abolishes slavery, "prevents the imposition of any burdens or disabilities that constitute badges of slavery or servitude," and "decreed universal civil freedom in this country." But the Thirteenth Amendment was not strong enough to fully protect the rights of former slaves. Consequently, the Fourteenth Amendment was ratified to ensure that the freedom provided by the Thirteenth Amendment could be fully exercised. By explicitly making African Americans citizens and by stopping states from regulating rights based on race, the Fourteenth Amendment "added greatly to the dignity and glory of American citizenship, and to the security of personal liberty." In combination, the Thirteenth and Fourteenth Amendments were supposed to guarantee that "all the civil rights that pertain to freedom and citizenship" would be protected. The Fifteenth Amendment, which states that the right to vote is not provided on the basis of race, color, or previous condition of servitude, was added to guarantee that all citizens could participate "in the political control of his country." As a group, the Reconstruction Amendments were designed to guarantee that African Americans enjoyed the same rights as whites in the eyes of the law.

The Reconstruction Amendments were meant to ensure that blacks and former slaves were to be equal with whites and would enjoy the same rights. Even though the Fourteenth Amendment does not give positive rights, it does stop state governments from treating blacks badly merely because of their skin color. Indeed, the Supreme Court has made clear that with respect to civil and political rights, "all citizens are equal before the law." In concrete terms, this means that blacks cannot, for example, be kept from serving on juries. Harlan notes that the Supreme Court had decided so in *Strauder v. West Virginia* (1880)

Harlan then begins his attack on the majority's opinion by noting that the statute is clearly designed to keep blacks away from whites and that anyone who claims otherwise is lacking in candor. Then, rather than focusing directly on the equality issue, he suggests that the statute imperils liberty interests. That is, if people of different races want to sit together on a train, they are not allowed to do so under the statute without breaking the law. Harlan next suggests that allowing the law to stand could lead to ludicrous results, such as requiring that blacks use one side of the street and whites use the other side or requiring that blacks use one side of the courtroom and whites use the other side. Harlan's suggestion that blacks and whites might be segregated in the jury box is particularly biting, given that the Court had made clear in prior cases that blacks had a right to serve on integrated juries. How an integrated jury in a segregated jury box might work is anyone's guess.

Harlan then challenges the majority's notion that reasonableness is a ground on which to determine the constitutionality of a statute. He suggests that reasonableness is an issue for the legislature when passing a law. Constitutionality is an issue for the Court when reviewing legislation. It may be acceptable to consider reasonableness when determining how a statute will be interpreted consistent with legislative intent, but it is not acceptable to consider it when determining whether the legislature is allowed to pass a certain statute under the Constitution.

Harlan next begins a discussion that, through the years, would overtake the majority opinion in significance. First, he asserts that the Constitution is color-blind. Harlan, making his point in terms that are harsh to twenty-first-century ears, notes that the white race is dominant in America and that it likely would continue to be so. However, he states that the dominance of the white race does not mean that there is a caste system in America. Indeed, he argues that notwithstanding the relative position of the races, individuals must be treated as equals under the law. He states that the most powerful has no greater rights than the least powerful has and that the Court does a disservice when it claims otherwise. Harlan suggests, in fact, that the Court's vision is so troubling and antithetical to equality that the *Plessy* decision would become as nettlesome as the *Dred Scott* decision.

The effect of the *Plessy* decision, so suggests Harlan, would be to encourage some to create a caste system that would be antithetical to the Reconstruction Amendments. The decision is likely to cause great harm, given that blacks and whites need to learn to live together. Harlan suggests that laws like Louisiana's, which imply that blacks are "so inferior and degraded that they cannot be allowed to sit in public coaches occupied by white citizens," would elicit discord, distrust, and hate between the races.

Harlan then attacks the notion that the case is about social equality. The statute at issue relates to allowing people to sit in the same train car. Social equality is no more relevant to that issue than it is to the issue of having citizens of different races share the same street, share the same ballot box, or stand together at a political assembly. Indeed, Harlan notes, it is odd that one would raise the social equality issue in this context, given that the Chinese are considered so different from Americans that they are not allowed to become citizens. Although the Chinese cannot become citizens, they are allowed to ride in the same car as whites. Given that blacks are supposed to have equal rights as citizens, that they have fought in wars to preserve the Union, and that they have the right to share political control of the country, it is odd that they would not be allowed to share the same railway car with whites. In fact, Harlan argues, "the arbitrary separation of citizens, on the basis of race, while they are on a public highway, is a badge of servitude wholly inconsistent with the civil freedom and the equality before the law established by the constitution. It cannot be justified upon any legal grounds."

Harlan suggests that any harm that might come from having blacks and whites share railcars pales in comparison to the problems that would arise from denying civil rights by separating the races. If separation is appropriate, it is unclear why separation would not be appropriate when blacks are exercising rights that the Court agrees they must be allowed to exercise. He again suggests that, under the reasoning of *Plessy*, there would be nothing unconstitutional in a state's forcing jury boxes to be partitioned on the basis of race.

As he moves toward the conclusion of the dissent, Harlan argues that the cases that Brown cites to support segregation are from a bygone, pre–Civil War era during which inequality and slavery ruled. Given the mind-set of those who passed the laws and the absence of the Reconstruction Amendments, such cases are inapplicable to this situation and should be ignored. The question is not how to think about rights in an era of admitted inequality but what to do in an era when free blacks and former slaves are citizens and must be provided equal rights.

Harlan finishes by arguing that the law at issue is an affront to the liberty of all citizens and is inconsistent with the Constitution. He notes that if similar laws were passed by states and localities, trouble would ensue. Last, he indicates that if the right to provide rights unequally to citizens is allowed, black citizens who are full members in society would be placed "in a condition of legal inferiority." For the aforementioned reasons, Harlan notes, he is required to dissent.

Audience

Although the *Plessy* opinion was of particular use to Congress and the state legislatures that were beginning to impose the Jim Crow laws, the intended audience for the case was the country as a whole. Given that this was a decision of the Supreme Court, it is unclear that it should be taken as a call to action. Rather, it can be taken as an exposition on the meaning of the U.S. Constitution that might have the effect of emboldening state legislatures or cowing Congress but probably not as a case that was intended to have that effect.

Impact

The effect of *Plessy v. Ferguson* on the first half of the twentieth century cannot be overstated. Although the *Plessy* Court was not the first Court to provide a cramped reading of the Fourteenth Amendment, the context in which the reading occurred was important. Before *Plessy*, the Supreme Court decided that the Reconstruction Amendments could not be used to allow Congress to provide many positive rights to African Americans, notwithstanding the enforcement power provided to Congress in Section 5 of the amendment. However, *Plessy* limited the use of the Reconstruction Amendments by the courts to block state legislation that provided unequal rights to African Americans. Given the Fourteenth Amendment's equal protection clause, the blocking function was arguably the narrowest and most essential function the Reconstruction Amendments could have had. Without the broad availability of the Reconstruction Amendments to stop attempts to limit participation of African Americans in as much of American life as possible, the proponents of Jim Crow laws had a largely open field. *Plessy* simply helped extend and legitimize the Jim Crow era, during which blacks would lose many of the gains made in the South since the end of the Civil War. It allowed for years of poor treatment of blacks at the hands of state legislatures rather than merely at the hands of private actors.

The separate but equal doctrine was the *Plessy* Court's lasting legacy. The doctrine was simple and effective. It provided segregationists with a simple tool and a constitutional imprimatur to regulate out of existence many rights thought to be protected by the Fourteenth Amendment. That doctrine provided constitutional protection to those who sought to limit the equality of African Americans. Segregationists were not simply allowed to make black citizens somewhat invisible through segregation; they were also emboldened to push the envelope of disenfranchisement and inequality as far as possible, knowing that the Supreme Court likely would not act to protect the equality of African Americans. Indeed, a number of southern states, including Louisiana, reworked their constitutions in the late nineteenth century to implicitly or explicitly take rights away from African Americans. Although some of these attempts predated *Plessy*, the results of some of those actions were effectively immunized by *Plessy*. *Plessy* simply made a caste system legally enforceable under a Constitution that guaranteed due process and equal protection.

Plessy was not a radical decision that took the country in a shockingly new direction. However, it did confirm a type of legislation that had been of questionable constitutionality in light of the Fourteenth Amendment. At the time of its passage, *Plessy* was not overly controversial to any of the justices save Harlan and possibly Brewer, who took no part in the decision. Indeed, the decision was not a widely cited constitutional case at its time or for a number of ensuing decades. Until the notion of separate but equal was challenged through cases brought by the National Association for the Advancement of Colored People and others, *Plessy* was standard constitutional law fare.

Over time, the majority opinion in *Plessy* fell out of favor, though many held on to the notion that separate but equal was a reasonable goal. The doctrine was the touchstone for segregationists for years. Segregationists, however, tended to adhere to the separate part of the doctrine but not the equal part. The claims of separate but equal facilities rang hollow when various groups documented the separate and unequal conditions that tended to exist in the South. The arguments eventually became too strong for the doctrine to resist. The doctrine was discarded in a string of Supreme Court cases throughout the middle part of the twentieth century, including *Brown v. Board of Education of Topeka*.

The eventual discarding of the majority opinion means that Harlan's dissent is far more well known and arguably more important than the majority opinion is today. The dissent not only predicted the racial discord that would follow *Plessy*; it also gave us the notion of a color-blind Constitution. The phrase *color-blind Constitution* was a slogan used to argue for an end to segregation and other racist laws. However, it has been used recently by some to argue that affirmative action and other race-conscious laws and remedies are inconsistent with constitutional doctrine. That battle continues to rage and is unlikely to be resolved any time soon.

See also *Roberts v. City of Boston* (1850); *Dred Scott v. Sandford* (1857); Black Code of Mississippi (1865); Thirteenth Amendment to the U.S. Constitution (1865); Fourteenth Amendment to the U.S. Constitution (1868); Fifteenth Amendment to the U.S. Constitution (1870); Civil Rights Cases (1883); *Brown v. Board of Education* (1954).

Further Reading

■ Books

Fireside, Harvey. *Separate and Unequal: Homer Plessy and the Supreme Court Decision That Legalized Racism*. New York: Carroll & Graf, 2004.

Klarman, Michael J. *From Jim Crow to Civil Rights: The Supreme Court and the Struggle for Racial Equality*. New York: Oxford University Press, 2004.

Lofgren, Charles A. *The Plessy Case: A Legal-Historical Interpretation*. New York: Oxford University Press, 1987.

Medley, Keith Weldon. *We as Freemen: Plessy v. Ferguson*. Gretna, La.: Pelican, 2003.

Meyer, Howard N. *The Amendment That Refused to Die: Equality and Justice Deferred, A History of the Fourteenth Amendment*. Lanham, Md.: Madison Books, 2000.

Patrick, John J. *The Young Oxford Companion to the Supreme Court of the United States*. New York: Oxford University Press, 1998.

Woodward, C. Vann. "The Case of the Louisiana Traveler." In *Quarrels That Have Shaped the Constitution* ed. John A. Garraty. New York: Harper & Row, 1987.

—Henry L. Chambers, Jr.

Questions for Further Study

1. Compare the majority opinions in *Plessy v. Ferguson* and *Dred Scott v. Sandford*. Many claim that both were riddled with factual and logical errors. However, taking the facts as the authors of the majority opinions claimed them to be, were either, both, or neither consistent with the Constitution as it was then written?

2. Compare *Plessy v. Ferguson* with *Brown v. Board of Education of Topeka*. Is the key distinction between them that the *Brown* Court took the harms of segregation seriously while the *Plessy* Court did not, or are there other distinctions that explain why the cases were decided so differently? How could each opinion have garnered such large majorities of the Court's justices? How could both cases be consistent with the Constitution?

3. Did *Plessy v. Ferguson* effectively gut the Reconstruction Amendments in general or the Fourteenth Amendment in particular?

4. Should the legacy of Jim Crow laws be placed at Justice Brown's feet, as he was the writer of the *Plessy v. Ferguson* majority opinion?

5. What would a world governed by Harlan's dissent in *Plessy v. Ferguson* have looked like twenty years after the case was decided?

PLESSY V. FERGUSON

This was a petition for writs of prohibition and certiorari originally filed in the supreme court of the state by Plessy, the plaintiff in error, against the Hon. John H. Ferguson, judge of the criminal district court for the parish of Orleans, and setting forth, in substance, the following facts:

That petitioner was a citizen of the United States and a resident of the state of Louisiana, of mixed descent, in the proportion of seven-eighths Caucasian and one-eighth African blood; that the mixture of colored blood was not discernible in him, and that he was entitled to every recognition, right, privilege, and immunity secured to the citizens of the United States of the white race by its constitution and laws; that on June 7, 1892, he engaged and paid for a first-class passage on the East Louisiana Railway, from New Orleans to Covington, in the same state, and thereupon entered a passenger train, and took possession of a vacant seat in a coach where passengers of the white race were accommodated; that such railroad company was incorporated by the laws of Louisiana as a common carrier, and was not authorized to distinguish between citizens according to their race, but, notwithstanding this, petitioner was required by the conductor, under penalty of ejection from said train and imprisonment, to vacate said coach, and occupy another seat, in a coach assigned by said company for persons not of the white race, and for no other reason than that petitioner was of the colored race; that, upon petitioner's refusal to comply with such order, he was, with the aid of a police officer, forcibly ejected from said coach, and hurried off to, and imprisoned in, the parish jail of New Orleans, and there held to answer a charge made by such officer to the effect that he was guilty of having criminally violated an act of the general assembly of the state, approved July 10, 1890, in such case made and provided.

The petitioner was subsequently brought before the recorder of the city for preliminary examination, and committed for trial to the criminal district court for the parish of Orleans, where an information was filed against him in the matter above set forth, for a violation of the above act, which act the petitioner affirmed to be null and void, because in conflict with the constitution of the United States; that petitioner interposed a plea to such information, based upon the unconstitutionality of the act of the general assembly, to which the district attorney, on behalf of the state, filed a demurrer; that, upon issue being joined upon such demurrer and plea, the court sustained the demurrer, overruled the plea, and ordered petitioner to plead over to the facts set forth in the information, and that, unless the judge of the said court be enjoined by a writ of prohibition from further proceeding in such case, the court will proceed to fine and sentence petitioner to imprisonment, and thus deprive him of his constitutional rights set forth in his said plea, notwithstanding the unconstitutionality of the act under which he was being prosecuted; that no appeal lay from such sentence, and petitioner was without relief or remedy except by writs of prohibition and certiorari. Copies of the information and other proceedings in the criminal district court were annexed to the petition as an exhibit.

Upon the filing of this petition, an order was issued upon the respondent to show cause why a writ of prohibition should not issue, and be made perpetual, and a further order that the record of the proceedings had in the criminal cause be certified and transmitted to the supreme court.

To this order the respondent made answer, transmitting a certified copy of the proceedings, asserting the constitutionality of the law, and averring that, instead of pleading or admitting that he belonged to the colored race, the said Plessy declined and refused, either by pleading or otherwise, to admit that he was in any sense or in any proportion a colored man.

The case coming on for hearing before the supreme court, that court was of opinion that the law under which the prosecution was had was constitutional and denied the relief prayed for by the petitioner (Ex parte Plessy, 45 La. Ann. 80, 11 South. 948); whereupon petitioner prayed for a writ of error from this court, which was allowed by the chief justice of the supreme court of Louisiana.

Mr. Justice Harlan dissenting.

A. W. Tourgee and S. F. Phillips, for plaintiff in error.

Alex. Porter Morse, for defendant in error.

Justice Brown's Opinion of the Court

This case turns upon the constitutionality of an act of the general assembly of the state of Louisiana, passed in 1890, providing for separate railway carriages for the white and colored races. Acts 1890, No. 111, p. 152.

The first section of the statute enacts "that all railway companies carrying passengers in their coaches in this state, shall provide equal but separate accommodations for the white, and colored races, by providing two or more passenger coaches for each passenger train, or by dividing the passenger coaches by a partition so as to secure separate accommodations: provided, that this section shall not be construed to apply to street railroads. No person or persons shall be permitted to occupy seats in coaches, other than the ones assigned to them, on account of the race they belong to."

By the second section it was enacted "that the officers of such passenger trains shall have power and are hereby required to assign each passenger to the coach or compartment used for the race to which such passenger belongs; any passenger insisting on going into a coach or compartment to which by race he does not belong, shall be liable to a fine of twenty-five dollars, or in lieu thereof to imprisonment for a period of not more than twenty days in the parish prison, and any officer of any railroad insisting on assigning a passenger to a coach or compartment other than the one set aside for the race to which said passenger belongs, shall be liable to a fine of twenty-five dollars, or in lieu thereof to imprisonment for a period of not more than twenty days in the parish prison; and should any passenger refuse to occupy the coach or compartment to which he or she is assigned by the officer of such railway, said officer shall have power to refuse to carry such passenger on his train, and for such refusal neither he nor the railway company which he represents shall be liable for damages in any of the courts of this state."

The third section provides penalties for the refusal or neglect of the officers, directors, conductors, and employees of railway companies to comply with the act, with a proviso that "nothing in this act shall be construed as applying to nurses attending children of the other race." The fourth section is immaterial.

The information filed in the criminal district court charged, in substance, that Plessy, being a passenger between two stations within the state of Louisiana, was assigned by officers of the company to the coach used for the race to which he belonged, but he insisted upon going into a coach used by the race to which he did not belong. Neither in the information nor plea was his particular race or color averred.

The petition for the writ of prohibition averred that petitioner was seven-eighths Caucasian and one-eighth African blood; that the mixture of colored blood was not discernible in him; and that he was entitled to every right, privilege, and immunity secured to citizens of the United States of the white race; and that, upon such theory, he took possession of a vacant seat in a coach where passengers of the white race were accommodated, and was ordered by the conductor to vacate said coach, and take a seat in another, assigned to persons of the colored race, and, having refused to comply with such demand, he was forcibly ejected, with the aid of a police officer, and imprisoned in the parish jail to answer a charge of having violated the above act.

The constitutionality of this act is attacked upon the ground that it conflicts both with the thirteenth amendment of the constitution, abolishing slavery, and the fourteenth amendment, which prohibits certain restrictive legislation on the part of the states.

1. That it does not conflict with the thirteenth amendment, which abolished slavery and involuntary servitude, except a punishment for crime, is too clear for argument. Slavery implies involuntary servitude, a state of bondage; the ownership of mankind as a chattel, or, at least, the control of the labor and services of one man for the benefit of another, and the absence of a legal right to the disposal of his own person, property, and services. This amendment was said in the Slaughter-House Cases, 16 Wall. 36, to have been intended primarily to abolish slavery, as it had been previously known in this country, and that it equally forbade Mexican peonage or the Chinese coolie trade, when they amounted to slavery or involuntary servitude, and that the use of the word "servitude" was intended to prohibit the use of all forms of involuntary slavery, of whatever class or name. It was intimated, however, in that case, that this amendment was regarded by the statesmen of that day as insufficient to protect the colored race from certain laws which had been enacted in the Southern states, imposing upon the colored race onerous disabilities and burdens, and curtailing their rights in the pursuit of life, liberty, and property to such an extent that their freedom was of little value; and that the fourteenth amendment was devised to meet this exigency.

So, too, in the Civil Rights Cases, 109 U.S. 3, 3 Sup. Ct. 18, it was said that the act of a mere individual, the owner of an inn, a public conveyance or place of amusement, refusing accommodations to colored people, cannot be justly regarded as imposing any badge of slavery or servitude upon the applicant, but only as involving an ordinary civil injury, properly cognizable by the laws of the state, and presumably subject to redress by those laws until the contrary appears. "It would be running the slavery question into the ground," said Mr. Justice Bradley, "to make it apply to every act of discrimination which a person may see fit to make as to the guests he will entertain, or as to the people he will take into his coach or cab or car, or admit to his concert or theater, or deal with in other matters of intercourse or business."

A statute which implies merely a legal distinction between the white and colored races—a distinction which is founded in the color of the two races, and which must always exist so long as white men are distinguished from the other race by color—has no tendency to destroy the legal equality of the two races, or re-establish a state of involuntary servitude. Indeed, we do not understand that the thirteenth amendment is strenuously relied upon by the plaintiff in error in this connection.

2. By the fourteenth amendment, all persons born or naturalized in the United States, and subject to the jurisdiction thereof, are made citizens of the United States and of the state wherein they reside; and the states are forbidden from making or enforcing any law which shall abridge the privileges or immunities of citizens of the United States, or shall deprive any person of life, liberty, or property without due process of law, or deny to any person within their jurisdiction the equal protection of the laws.

The proper construction of this amendment was first called to the attention of this court in the Slaughter-House Cases, 16 Wall. 36, which involved, however, not a question of race, but one of exclusive privileges. The case did not call for any expression of opinion as to the exact rights it was intended to secure to the colored race, but it was said generally that its main purpose was to establish the citizenship of the negro, to give definitions of citizenship of the United States and of the states, and to protect from the hostile legislation of the states the privileges and immunities of citizens of the United States, as distinguished from those of citizens of the states. The object of the amendment was undoubtedly to enforce the absolute equality of the two races before the law, but, in the nature of things, it could not have been intended to abolish distinctions based upon color, or to enforce social, as distinguished from political, equality, or a commingling of the two races upon terms unsatisfactory to either. Laws permitting, and even requiring, their separation, in places where they are liable to be brought into contact, do not necessarily imply the inferiority of either race to the other, and have been generally, if not universally, recognized as within the competency of the state legislatures in the exercise of their police power. The most common instance of this is connected with the establishment of separate schools for white and colored children, which have been held to be a valid exercise of the legislative power even by courts of states where the political rights of the colored race have been longest and most earnestly enforced.

One of the earliest of these cases is that of *Roberts v. City of Boston*, 5 Cush. 198, in which the supreme judicial court of Massachusetts held that the general school committee of Boston had power to make provision for the instruction of colored children in separate schools established exclusively for them, and to prohibit their attendance upon the other schools. "The great principle," said Chief Justice Shaw, "advanced by the learned and eloquent advocate for the plaintiff [Mr. Charles Sumner], is that, by the constitution and laws of Massachusetts, all persons, without distinction of age or sex, birth or color, origin or condition, are equal before the law.... But, when this great principle comes to be applied to the actual and various conditions of persons in society, it will not warrant the assertion that men and women are legally clothed with the same civil and political powers, and that children and adults are legally to have the same functions and be subject to the same treatment; but only that the rights of all, as they are settled and regulated by law, are equally entitled to the paternal consideration and protection of the law for their maintenance and security." It was held that the powers of the committee extended to the establishment of separate schools for children of different ages, sexes and colors, and that they might also establish special schools for poor and neglected children, who have become too old to attend the primary school, and yet have not acquired the rudiments of learning, to enable them to enter the ordinary schools. Similar laws have been enacted by congress under its general power of legislation over the District of Columbia (sections 281–283, 310, 319, Rev. St. D. C.), as well as by the legislatures of many of the states, and have been generally, if not uniformly, sustained by the courts. *State v. McCann*, 21 Ohio St. 210; *Lehew v. Brummell* (Mo. Sup.) 15 S. W. 765; *Ward v. Flood*, 48 Cal. 36; *Bertonneau v. Directors of City Schools*, 3 Woods, 177, Fed. Cas. No. 1,361; *People v. Gallagher*, 93 N. Y. 438; *Cory v. Carter*, 48 Ind. 337; *Dawson v. Lee*, 83 Ky. 49.

Laws forbidding the intermarriage of the two races may be said in a technical sense to interfere with the freedom of contract, and yet have been universally recognized as within the police power of the state. *State v. Gibson*, 36 Ind. 389.

The distinction between laws interfering with the political equality of the negro and those requiring the separation of the two races in schools, theaters, and railway carriages has been frequently drawn by this court. Thus, in *Strauder v. West Virginia*, 100 U.S. 303, it was held that a law of West Virginia limiting to white male persons 21 years of age, and citizens of the state, the right to sit upon juries, was a discrimination which implied a legal inferiority in civil society, which lessened the security of the right of the colored race, and was a step towards reducing them to a condition of servility. Indeed, the right of a colored man that, in the selection of jurors to pass upon his life, liberty, and property, there shall be no exclusion of his race, and no discrimination against them because of color, has been asserted in a number of cases. *Virginia v. Rivers*, 100 U.S. 313; *Neal v. Delaware*, 103 U.S. 370; *Bush v. Com.*, 107 U.S. 110, 1 Sup. Ct. 625; *Gibson v. Mississippi*, 162 U.S. 565, 16 Sup. Ct. 904. So, where the laws of a particular locality or the charter of a particular railway corporation has provided that no person shall be excluded from the cars on account of color, we have held that this meant that persons of color should travel in the same car as white ones, and that the enactment was not satisfied by the company providing cars assigned exclusively to people of color, though they were as good as those which they assigned exclusively to white persons. *Railroad Co. v. Brown*, 17 Wall. 445.

Upon the other hand, where a statute of Louisiana required those engaged in the transportation of passengers among the states to give to all persons traveling within that state, upon vessels employed in that business, equal rights and privileges in all parts of the vessel, without distinction on account of race or color, and subjected to an action for damages the owner of such a vessel who excluded colored passengers on account of their color from the cabin set aside by him for the use of whites, it was held to be, so far as it applied to interstate commerce, unconstitutional and void. *Hall v. De Cuir*, 95 U.S. 485. The court in this case, however, expressly disclaimed that it had anything whatever to do with the statute as a regulation of internal commerce, or affecting anything else than commerce among the states.

In the Civil Rights Cases, 109 U.S. 3, 3 Sup. Ct. 18, it was held that an act of congress entitling all persons within the jurisdiction of the United States to the full and equal enjoyment of the accommodations, advantages, facilities, and privileges of inns, public con-

veyances, on land or water, theaters, and other places of public amusement, and made applicable to citizens of every race and color, regardless of any previous condition of servitude, was unconstitutional and void, upon the ground that the fourteenth amendment was prohibitory upon the states only, and the legislation authorized to be adopted by congress for enforcing it was not direct legislation on matters respecting which the states were prohibited from making or enforcing certain laws, or doing certain acts, but was corrective legislation, such as might be necessary or proper for counter-acting and redressing the effect of such laws or acts. In delivering the opinion of the court, Mr. Justice Bradley observed that the fourteenth amendment "does not invest congress with power to legislate upon subjects that are within the domain of state legislation, but to provide modes of relief against state legislation or state action of the kind referred to. It does not authorize congress to create a code of municipal law for the regulation of private rights, but to provide modes of redress against the operation of state laws, and the action of state officers, executive or judicial, when these are subversive of the fundamental rights specified in the amendment. Positive rights and privileges are undoubtedly secured by the fourteenth amendment; but they are secured by way of prohibition against state laws and state proceedings affecting those rights and privileges, and by power given to congress to legislate for the purpose of carrying such prohibition into effect; and such legislation must necessarily be predicated upon such supposed state laws or state proceedings, and be directed to the correction of their operation and effect."

Much nearer, and, indeed, almost directly in point, is the case of the Louisville, *N. O. & T. Ry. Co. v. State*, 133 U.S. 587, 10 Sup. Ct. 348, wherein the railway company was indicted for a violation of a statute of Mississippi, enacting that all railroads carrying passengers should provide equal, but separate, accommodations for the white and colored races, by providing two or more passenger cars for each passenger train, or by dividing the passenger cars by a partition, so as to secure separate accommodations. The case was presented in a different aspect from the one under consideration, inasmuch as it was an indictment against the railway company for failing to provide the separate accommodations, but the question considered was the constitutionality of the law. In that case, the supreme court of Mississippi (66 Miss. 662, 6 South. 203) had held that the statute applied solely to commerce within the state, and, that being the construction of the state statute by its highest court, was accepted as conclusive. "If it be a matter," said the court (page 591, 133 U. S., and page 348, 10 Sup. Ct.), "respecting commerce wholly within a state, and not interfering with commerce between the states, then, obviously, there is no violation of the commerce clause of the federal constitution. ... No question arises under this section as to the power of the state to separate in different compartments interstate passengers, or affect, in any manner, the privileges and rights of such passengers. All that we can consider is whether the state has the power to require that railroad trains within her limits shall have separate accommodations for the two races. That affecting only commerce within the state is no invasion of the power given to congress by the commerce clause."

A like course of reasoning applies to the case under consideration, since the supreme court of Louisiana, in the case of *State v. Judge*, 44 La. Ann. 770, 11 South. 74, held that the statute in question did not apply to interstate passengers, but was confined in its application to passengers traveling exclusively within the borders of the state. The case was decided largely upon the authority of Louisville, N. O. & T. Ry. Co. v. State, 66 Miss. 662, 6 South, 203, and affirmed by this court in 133 U.S. 587, 10 Sup. Ct. 348. In the present case no question of interference with interstate commerce can possibly arise, since the East Louisiana Railway appears to have been purely a local line, with both its termini within the state of Louisiana. Similar statutes for the separation of the two races upon public conveyances were held to be constitutional in *Railroad v. Miles*, 55 Pa. St. 209; *Day v. Owen* 5 Mich. 520; *Railway Co. v. Williams*, 55 Ill. 185; *Railroad Co. v. Wells*, 85 Tenn. 613; 4 S. W. 5; *Railroad Co. v. Benson*, 85 Tenn. 627, 4 S. W. 5; The Sue, 22 Fed. 843; *Logwood v. Railroad Co.*, 23 Fed. 318; *McGuinn v. Forbes*, 37 Fed. 639; *People v. King* (N. Y. App.) 18 N. E. 245; *Houck v. Railway Co.*, 38 Fed. 226; *Heard v. Railroad Co.*, 3 Inter St. Commerce Com. R. 111, 1 Inter St. Commerce Com. R. 428.

While we think the enforced separation of the races, as applied to the internal commerce of the state, neither abridges the privileges or immunities of the colored man, deprives him of his property without due process of law, nor denies him the equal protection of the laws, within the meaning of the fourteenth amendment, we are not prepared to say that the conductor, in assigning passengers to the coaches according to their race, does not act at his peril, or that the provision of the second section of the act that denies to the passenger compensation in damages for a refusal to receive him into the coach in which he properly belongs is a valid exercise of the legislative power. Indeed, we understand it to be conceded by the state's attorney that such part of the act as exempts from liability the railway company and its officers is unconstitutional. The power to assign to a particular coach obviously implies the power to determine to which race the passenger belongs, as well as the power to determine who, under the laws of the particular state, is to be deemed a white, and who a colored, person. This question, though indicated in the brief of the plaintiff in error, does not properly arise upon the record in this case, since the only issue made is as to the unconstitutionality of the act, so far as it requires the railway to provide separate accommodations, and the conductor to assign passengers according to their race.

It is claimed by the plaintiff in error that, in an mixed community, the reputation of belonging to the dominant race, in this instance the white race, is "property," in the same sense that a right of action or of inheritance is property. Conceding this to be so, for the purposes of this case, we are unable to see how this statute deprives him of, or in any way affects his right to, such property. If he be a white man, and assigned to a colored coach, he may have his action for damages against the company for being deprived of his so-called "property." Upon the other hand, if he be a colored man, and be so assigned, he has been deprived of no property, since he is not lawfully entitled to the reputation of being a white man.

In this connection, it is also suggested by the learned counsel for the plaintiff in error that the same argument that will justify the state legislature in requiring railways to provide separate accommodations for the two races will also authorize them to require separate cars to be provided for people whose hair is of a certain color, or who are aliens, or who belong to certain nationalities, or to enact laws requiring colored people to walk upon one side of the street, and white people upon the other, or requiring white men's houses to be painted white, and colored men's black, or their vehicles or business signs to be of different colors, upon the theory that one side of the street is as good as the other, or that a house or vehicle of one color is as good as one of another color. The reply to all this is that every exercise of the police power must be reasonable, and extend only to such laws as are enacted in good faith for the promotion of the public good, and not for the annoyance or oppression of a particular class. Thus, in *Yick Wo v. Hopkins*, 118 U.S. 356, 6 Sup. Ct. 1064, it was held by this court that a municipal ordinance of the city of San Francisco, to regulate the carrying on of public laundries within the limits of the municipality, violated the provisions of the constitution of the United States, if it conferred upon the municipal authorities arbitrary power, at their own will, and without regard to discretion, in the legal sense of the term, to give or withhold consent as to persons or places, without regard to the competency of the persons applying or the propriety of the places selected for the carrying on of the business. It was held to be a covert attempt on the part of the municipality to make an arbitrary and unjust discrimination against the Chinese race. While this was the case of a municipal ordinance, a like principle has been held to apply to acts of a state legislature passed in the exercise of the police power. *Railroad Co. v. Husen*, 95 U.S. 465; *Louisville & N. R. Co. v. Kentucky*, 161 U.S. 677, 16 Sup. Ct. 714, and cases cited on page 700, 161 U. S., and page 714, 16 Sup. Ct.; *Daggett v. Hudson*, 43 Ohio St. 548, 3 N. E. 538; *Capen v. Foster*, 12 Pick. 485; *State v. Baker*, 38 Wis. 71; *Monroe v. Collins*, 17 Ohio St. 665; *Hulseman v. Rems*, 41 Pa. St. 396; *Osman v. Riley*, 15 Cal. 48.

So far, then, as a conflict with the fourteenth amendment is concerned, the case reduces itself to the question whether the statute of Louisiana is a reasonable regulation, and with respect to this there must necessarily be a large discretion on the part of the legislature. In determining the question of reasonableness, it is at liberty to act with reference to the established usages, customs, and traditions of the people, and with a view to the promotion of their comfort, and the preservation of the public peace and good order. Gauged by this standard, we cannot say that a law which authorizes or even requires the separation of the two races in public conveyances is unreasonable, or more obnoxious to the fourteenth amendment than the acts of congress requiring separate schools for colored children in the District of Columbia, the constitutionality of which does not seem to have been questioned, or the corresponding acts of state legislatures.

We consider the underlying fallacy of the plaintiff's argument to consist in the assumption that the enforced separation of the two races stamps the colored race with a badge of inferiority. If this be so, it is not by reason of anything found in the act, but solely because the colored race chooses to put that construction upon it. The argument necessarily assumes that if, as has been more than once the case, and is not unlikely to be so again, the colored race should become the dominant power in the state legislature, and should enact a law in precisely similar terms, it would thereby relegate the white race to an inferior position. We imagine that the white race, at least, would not acquiesce in this assumption. The argument also assumes that social prejudices may be overcome by legislation, and that equal rights cannot be secured to the negro except by an enforced commingling of the two races. We cannot accept this proposition. If the two races are to meet upon terms of social equality, it must be the result of natural affinities, a mutual appreciation of each other's merits, and a voluntary consent of individuals. As was said by the court of appeals of New York in *People v. Gallagher*, 93 N. Y. 438, 448: "This end can neither be accomplished nor promoted by laws which conflict with the general sentiment of the community upon whom they are designed to operate. When the government, therefore, has secured to each of its citizens equal rights before the law, and equal opportunities for improvement and progress, it has accomplished the end for which it was organized, and performed all of the functions respecting social advantages with which it is endowed." Legislation is powerless to eradicate racial instincts, or to abolish distinctions based upon physical differences, and the attempt to do so can only result in accentuating the difficulties of the present situation. If the civil and political rights of both races be equal, one cannot be inferior to the other civilly or politically. If one race be inferior to the other socially, the constitution of the United States cannot put them upon the same plane.

It is true that the question of the proportion of colored blood necessary to constitute a colored person, as distinguished from a white person, is one upon which there is a difference of opinion in the different states; some holding that any visible admixture of black blood stamps the person as belonging to the colored race (*State v. Chavers*, 5 Jones [N. C.] 1); others, that it depends upon the preponderance of blood (*Gray v. State*, 4 Ohio, 354; *Monroe v. Collins*, 17 Ohio St. 665); and still others, that the predominance of white blood must only be in the proportion of three-fourths (*People v. Dean*, 14 Mich. 406; *Jones v. Com.*, 80 Va. 544). But these are questions to be determined under the laws of each state, and are not properly put in issue in this case. Under the allegations of his petition, it may undoubtedly become a question of importance whether, under the laws of Louisiana, the petitioner belongs to the white or colored race.

The judgment of the court below is therefore affirmed.

Mr. Justice BREWER did not hear the argument or participate in the decision of this case.

Mr. Justice Harlan Dissenting

By the Louisiana statute the validity of which is here involved, all railway companies (other than street-railroad companies) that carry passengers in that state are required to have separate but equal accommodations for white and colored persons, "by providing two or more passenger coaches for each passenger train, or by dividing the passenger coaches by a partition so as to secure separate accommodations." Under this statute, no colored person is permitted to occupy a seat in a coach assigned to white persons; nor any white person to occupy a seat in a coach assigned to colored persons. The managers of the railroad are not allowed to exercise any discretion in the premises, but are required to assign each passenger to some coach or compartment set apart for the exclusive use of is race. If a passenger insists upon going into a coach or compartment not set apart for persons of his race, he is subject to be fined, or to be imprisoned in the parish jail. Penalties are prescribed for the refusal or neglect of the officers, directors, conductors, and employees of railroad companies to comply with the provisions of the act.

Only "nurses attending children of the other race" are excepted from the operation of the statute. No exception is made of colored attendants traveling with adults. A white man is not permitted to have his colored servant with him in the same coach, even if his condition of health requires the constant personal assistance of such servant. If a colored maid insists upon riding in the same coach with a white woman whom she has been employed to serve, and who may need her personal attention while traveling, she is subject to be fined or imprisoned for such an exhibition of zeal in the discharge of duty.

While there may be in Louisiana persons of different races who are not citizens of the United States, the words in the act "white and colored races" necessarily include all citizens of the United States of both races residing in that state. So that we have before us a state enactment that compels, under penalties, the separation of the two races in railroad passenger coaches, and makes it a crime for a citizen of either race to enter a coach that has been assigned to citizens of the other race.

Thus, the state regulates the use of a public highway by citizens of the United States solely upon the basis of race.

However apparent the injustice of such legislation may be, we have only to consider whether it is consistent with the constitution of the United States.

That a railroad is a public highway, and that the corporation which owns or operates it is in the exercise of public functions, is not, at this day, to be disputed. Mr. Justice Nelson, speaking for this court in *New Jersey Steam Nav. Co. v. Merchants' Bank*, 6 How. 344, 382, said that a common carrier was in the exercise "of a sort of public office, and has public duties to perform, from which he should not be permitted to exonerate himself without the assent of the parties concerned." Mr. Justice Strong, delivering the judgment of this court in *Olcott v. Supervisors*, 16 Wall. 678, 694, said: "That railroads, though constructed by private corporations, and owned by them, are public highways, has been the doctrine of nearly all the courts ever since such conveniences for passage and transportation have had any existence. Very early the question arose whether a state's right of eminent domain could be exercised by a private corporation created for the purpose of constructing a railroad. Clearly, it could not, unless taking land for such a purpose by such an agency is taking land for public use. The right of eminent domain nowhere justifies taking property for a private use. Yet it is a doctrine universally accepted that a state legislature may authorize a private corporation to take land for the construction of such a road, making compensation to the owner. What else does this doctrine mean if not that building a railroad, though it be built by a private corporation, is an act done for a public use?" So, in *Township of Pine Grove v. Talcott*, 19 Wall. 666, 676: "Though the corporation [a railroad company] was private, its work was public, as much so as if it were to be constructed by the state." So, in *Inhabitants of Worcester v. Western R. Corp.*, 4 Metc. (Mass.) 564: "The establishment of that great thoroughfare is regarded as a public work, established by public authority, intended for the public use and benefit, the use of which is secured to the whole community, and constitutes, therefore, like a canal, turnpike, or highway, a public easement." "It is true that the real and personal property, necessary to the establishment and management of the railroad, is vested in the corporation; but it is in trust for the public."

In respect of civil rghts, common to all citizens, the constitution of the United States does not, I think, permit any public authority to know the race of those entitled to be protected in the enjoyment of such rights. Every true man has pride of race, and under appropriate circumstances, when the rights of others, his equals before the law, are not to be affected, it is his privilege to express such pride and to take such action based upon it as to him seems proper. But I deny that any legislative body or judicial tribunal may have regard to the race of citizens when the civil rights of those citizens are involved. Indeed, such legislation as that here in question is inconsistent not only with that equality of rights which pertains to citizenship, national and state, but with the personal liberty enjoyed by every one within the United States.

The thirteenth amendment does not permit the withholding or the deprivation of any right necessarily inhering in freedom. It not only struck down the institution of slavery as previously existing in the United States, but it prevents the imposition of any burdens or disabilities that constitute badges of slavery or servitude. It decreed universal civil freedom in this country. This court has so adjudged. But, that amendment having been found inadequate to the protection of the rights of those who had been in slavery, it was followed by the fourteenth amendment, which added greatly to the dignity and glory of American citizenship, and to the security of personal liberty, by declaring that "all persons born or naturalized in the United States, and subject to the jurisdiction thereof, are citizens of the United States and of the state wherein they reside," and that "no state shall make or enforce any law which shall abridge the privileges or immunities of citizens of the United States; nor shall any state deprive any person of life, liberty or property without due process of law, nor deny to any person within its jurisdiction the equal protection of the laws." These two amendments, if enforced according to their true intent and meaning, will protect all the civil rights that pertain to freedom and citizenship. Finally, and to the end that no citizen should be denied, on account of his race, the privilege of participating in the political control of his country, it was declared by the fifteenth amendment that "the right of citizens of the United States to vote shall not be denied or abridged by the United States or by any state on account of race, color or previous condition of servitude."

These notable additions to the fundamental law were welcomed by the friends of liberty throughout the world. They removed the race line from our governmental systems. They had, as this court has said, a common purpose, namely, to secure "to a race recently emancipated, a race that through many generations have been held in slavery, all the civil rights that the superior race enjoy." They declared, in legal effect, this court has further said, "that the law in the states shall be the same for the black as for the white; that all persons, whether colored or white, shall stand equal before the laws of the states; and in regard to the colored race, for whose protection the amendment was primarily designed, that no discrimination shall be made against them by law because of their color." We also said: "The words of the amendment, it is true, are prohibitory, but they contain a necessary implication of a positive immunity or right, most valuable to the colored race, the right to exemption from unfriendly legislation against them distinctively as colored; exemption from legal discriminations, implying inferiority in civil society, lessening the security of their enjoyment of the rights which others enjoy; and discriminations which are steps towards reducing them to the condition of a subject race." It was, consequently, adjudged that a state law that excluded citizens of the colored race from juries, because of their race, however well qualified in other respects to discharge the duties of jurymen, was repugnant to the fourteenth amendment. *Strauder v. West Virginia*, 100 U.S. 303, 306, 307 S.; *Virginia v. Rives*, Id. 313; Ex parte Virginia, Id. 339; *Neal v. Delaware*, 103 U.S. 370, 386; *Bush v. Com.*, 107 U.S. 110, 116, 1 S. Sup. Ct. 625. At the present term, referring to the previous adjudications, this court declared that "underlying all of those decisions is the principle that the constitution of the United States, in its present form, forbids, so far as civil and political rights are concerned, discrimination by the general government or the states against any citizen because of his race. All citizens are equal before the law." *Gibson v. State*, 162 U.S. 565, 16 Sup. Ct. 904.

The decisions referred to show the scope of the recent amendments of the constitution. They also show that it is not within the power of a state to prohibit colored citizens, because of their race, from participating as jurors in the administration of justice.

It was said in argument that the statute of Louisiana does not discriminate against either race, but prescribes a rule applicable alike to white and colored citizens. But this argument does not meet the difficulty. Every one knows that the statute in question had its origin in the purpose, not so much to exclude white persons from railroad cars occupied by blacks, as to exclude colored people from coaches occupied by or assigned to white persons. Railroad corporations of Louisiana did not make discrimination among whites in the matter of accommodation for travelers. The thing to accomplish was, under the guise of giving equal accommodation for whites and blacks, to compel the latter to keep to themselves while traveling in railroad passenger coaches. No one would be so wanting in candor as to assert the contrary. The fundamental objection, therefore, to the statute, is that it interferes with the personal freedom of citizens. "Personal liberty," it has been well said, "consists in the power of locomotion, of changing situation, or removing one's person to whatsoever places one's own inclination may direct, without imprisonment or restraint, unless by due course of law." 1 Bl. Comm. 134. If a white man and a black man choose to occupy the same public conveyance on a public highway, it is their right to do so; and no government, proceeding alone on grounds of race, can prevent it without infringing the personal liberty of each.

It is one thing for railroad carriers to furnish, or to be required by law to furnish, equal accommodations for all whom they are under a legal duty to carry. It is quite another thing for government to forbid citizens of the white and black races from traveling in the same public conveyance, and to punish officers of railroad companies for permitting persons of the two races to occupy the same passenger coach. If a state can prescribe, as a rule of civil conduct, that whites and blacks shall not travel as passengers in the same railroad coach, why may it not so regulate the use of the streets of its cities and towns as to compel white citizens to keep on one side of a street, and black citizens to keep on the other? Why may it not, upon like grounds, punish whites and blacks who ride together in street cars or in open vehicles on a public road or street? Why may it not require sheriffs to assign whites to one side of a court room, and blacks to the other? And why may it not also prohibit the commingling of the two races in the galleries of legislative halls or in public assemblages convened for the consideration of the political questions of the day? Further, if this statute of Louisiana is consistent with the personal liberty of citizens, why may not the state require the separation in railroad coaches of native and naturalized citizens of the United States, or of Protestants and Roman Catholics?

The answer given at the argument to these questions was that regulations of the kind they suggest would be unreasonable, and could not, therefore, stand before the law. Is it meant that the determination of questions of legislative power depends upon the inquiry whether the statute whose validity is questioned is, in the judgment of the courts, a reasonable one, taking all the circumstances into consideration? A statute may be unreasonable merely because a sound public policy forbade its enactment. But I do not understand that the courts have anything to do with the policy or expediency of legislation. A statute may be valid, and yet, upon grounds of public policy, may well be characterized as unreasonable. Mr. Sedgwick correctly states the rule when he says that, the legislative intention being clearly ascertained, "the courts have no other duty to perform than to execute the legislative will, without any regard to their views as to the wisdom or justice of the particular enactment." Sedg. St. & Const. Law, 324. There is a dangerous tendency in these latter days to enlarge the functions of the courts, by means of judicial interference with the will of the people as expressed by the legislature. Our institutions have the distinguishing characteristic that the three departments of government are co-ordinate and separate. Each must keep within the limits defined by the constitution. And the courts best discharge their duty by executing the will of the law-making power, constitutionally expressed, leaving the results of legislation to be dealt with by the people through their representatives. Statutes must always have a reasonable construction. Sometimes they are to be construed strictly, sometimes literally, in order to carry out the legislative will. But, however construed, the intent of the legislature is to be respected if the particular statute in question is valid, although the courts, looking at the public interests, may conceive the statute to be both unreasonable and impolitic. If the power exists to enact a statute, that ends the matter so far as the courts are concerned. The adjudged cases in which statutes have been held to be void, because unreasonable, are those in which the means employed by the legislature were not at all germane to the end to which the legislature was competent.

The white race deems itself to be the dominant race in this country. And so it is, in prestige, in achievements, in education, in wealth, and in power. So, I doubt not, it will continue to be for all time, if it remains true to its great heritage, and holds fast to the principles of constitutional liberty. But in view of the constitution, in the eye of the law, there is in this country no superior, dominant, ruling class of citizens. There is no caste here. Our constitution is color-blind, and neither knows nor tolerates classes among citizens. In respect of civil rights, all citizens are equal before the law. The humblest is the peer of the most powerful. The law regards man as man, and takes no account of his surroundings or of his color when his civil rights as guaranteed by the supreme law of the land are involved. It is therefore to be regretted that this high tribunal, the final expositor of the fundamental law of the land, has reached the conclusion that it is competent for a state to regulate the enjoyment by citizens of their civil rights solely upon the basis of race.

In my opinion, the judgment this day rendered will, in time, prove to be quite as pernicious as the decision made by this tribunal in the Dred Scott Case.

It was adjudged in that case that the descendants of Africans who were imported into this country, and sold as slaves, were not included nor intended to be included under the word "citizens" in the constitution, and could not claim any of the rights and privileges which that instrument provided for and secured to citizens of the United States; that, at time of the adoption of the constitution, they were "considered as a subordinate and inferior class of beings, who had been subjugated by the dominant race, and, whether emancipated or not, yet remained subject to their authority, and had no rights or privileges but such as those who held the power and the government might choose to grant them." 17 How. 393, 404. The recent amendments of the constitution, it was supposed, had eradicated these principles from our institutions. But it seems that we have yet, in some of the states, a dominant race—a superior class of citizens—which assumes to regulate the enjoyment of civil rights, common to all citizens, upon the basis of race. The present decision, it may well be apprehended, will not only stimulate aggressions, more or less brutal and irritating, upon the admitted rights of colored citizens, but will encourage the belief that it is possible, by means of state enactments, to defeat the beneficent purposes which the people of the United States had in view when they adopted the recent amendments of the constitution, by one of which the blacks of this country were made citizens of the United States and of the states in which they respectively reside, and whose privileges and immunities, as citizens, the states are forbidden to abridge. Sixty millions of whites are in no danger from the presence here of eight millions of blacks. The destinies of the two races, in this country, are indissolubly linked together, and the interests of both require that the common government of all shall not permit the seeds of race hate to be planted under the sanction of law. What can more certainly arouse race hate, what more certainly create and perpetuate a feeling of distrust between these races, than state enactments which, in fact, proceed on the ground that colored citizens are so inferior and degraded that they cannot be allowed to sit in public coaches occupied by white citizens? That, as all will admit, is the real meaning of such legislation as was enacted in Louisiana.

The sure guaranty of the peace and security of each race is the clear, distinct, unconditional recognition by our governments, national and state, of every right that inheres in civil freedom, and of the equality before the law of all citizens of the United States,

Glossary

averring	asserting
chattel	property
coolie	manual laborer, usually of Chinese descent, who was brought to United States to help build railroads (now considered a racial slur)
damages	monies paid for harm caused
defendant in error	the party that is defending the lower court's ruling
demurrer	contention by the defendant that although the facts put forward by the plaintiff may be true, they do not entitle the plaintiff to prevail in the lawsuit
due process	the appropriate procedures that are necessary to affect a person's right to life, liberty, or property
eminent domain	the right of a jurisdiction to take property for a public purpose if adequate compensation is paid
equal protection of the laws	the requirement that all persons be provided the same rights under the law and be granted equal treatment by the laws

without regard to race. State enactments regulating the enjoyment of civil rights upon the basis of race, and cunningly devised to defeat legitimate results of the war, under the pretense of recognizing equality of rights, can have no other result than to render permanent peace impossible, and to keep alive a conflict of races, the continuance of which must do harm to all concerned. This question is not met by the suggestion that social equality cannot exist between the white and black races in this country. That argument, if it can be properly regarded as one, is scarcely worthy of consideration; for social equality no more exists between two races when traveling in a passenger coach or a public highway than when members of the same races sit by each other in a street car or in the jury box, or stand or sit with each other in a political assembly, or when they use in common the streets of a city or town, or when they are in the same room for the purpose of having their names placed on the registry of voters, or when they approach the ballot box in order to exercise the high privilege of voting.

There is a race so different from our own that we do not permit those belonging to it to become citizens of the United States. Persons belonging to it are, with few exceptions, absolutely excluded from our country. I allude to the Chinese race. But, by the statute in question, a Chinaman can ride in the same passenger coach with white citizens of the United States, while citizens of the black race in Louisiana, many of whom, perhaps, risked their lives for the preservation of the Union, who are entitled, by law, to participate in the political control of the state and nation, who are not excluded, by law or by reason of their race, from public stations of any kind, and who have all the legal rights that belong to white citizens, are yet declared to be criminals, liable to imprisonment, if they ride in a public coach occupied by citizens of the white race. It is scarcely just to say that a colored citizen should not object to occupying a public coach assigned to his own race. He does not object, nor, perhaps, would he object to separate coaches for his race if his rights under the law were recognized. But he does object, and he ought never to cease objecting, that citizens of the white and black races can be adjudged criminals because they sit, or claim the right to sit, in the same public coach on a public highway. The arbitrary separation of citizens, on the basis of race, while they are on a public highway, is a badge of servitude wholly inconsistent with the civil freedom and the equality before the law established by the constitution. It cannot be justified upon any legal grounds.

If evils will result from the commingling of the two races upon public highways established for the

immunity	exemption
information	a substitute for a grand jury indictment issued directly by a prosecutor
intermarriage	interracial marriage
liability	responsibility for causing harm
naturalized	made a citizen without being born a citizen
parish	in some regions, a political subdivision or county
peonage	a style of forced labor generally associated with Mexico
petitioner	the party filing for relief in court
plaintiff in error	the party that has appealed a lower court's ruling
prayed	asked
respondent	party defending against a suit
writ of error	an order of an appellate court requesting the records of a lower court so the appellate court can examine the record for mistakes that may affect the lower court's judgment
writ of prohibition	an order from a court directing a lower court to refrain from prosecuting a case

benefit of all, they will be infinitely less than those that will surely come from state legislation regulating the enjoyment of civil rights upon the basis of race. We boast of the freedom enjoyed by our people above all other peoples. But it is difficult to reconcile that boast with a state of the law which, practically, puts the brand of servitude and degradation upon a large class of our fellow citizens, our equals before the law. The thin disguise of "equal" accommodations for passengers in railroad coaches will not mislead any one, nor atone for the wrong this day done.

The result of the whole matter is that while this court has frequently adjudged, and at the present term has recognized the doctrine, that a state cannot, consistently with the constitution of the United States, prevent white and black citizens, having the required qualifications for jury service, from sitting in the same jury box, it is now solemnly held that a state may prohibit white and black citizens from sitting in the same passenger coach on a public highway, or may require that they be separated by a "partition" when in the same passenger coach. May it not now be reasonably expected that astute men of the dominant race, who affect to be disturbed at the possibility that the integrity of the white race may be corrupted, or that its supremacy will be imperiled, by contact on public highways with black people, will endeavor to procure statutes requiring white and black jurors to be separated in the jury box by a "partition," and that, upon retiring from the court room to consult as to their verdict, such partition, if it be a movable one, shall be taken to their consultation room, and set up in such way as to prevent black jurors from coming too close to their brother jurors of the white race. If the "partition" used in the court room happens to be stationary, provision could be made for screens with openings through which jurors of the two races could confer as to their verdict without coming into personal contact with each other. I cannot see but that, according to the principles this day announced, such state legislation, although conceived in hostility to, and enacted for the purpose of humiliating, citizens of the United States of a particular race, would be held to be consistent with the constitution.

I do not deem it necessary to review the decisions of state courts to which reference was made in argu-ment. Some, and the most important, of them, are wholly inapplicable, because rendered prior to the adoption of the last amendments of the constitution, when colored people had very few rights which the dominant race felt obliged to respect. Others were made at a time when public opinion, in many localities, was dominated by the institution of slavery; when it would not have been safe to do justice to the black man; and when, so far as the rights of blacks were concerned, race prejudice was, practically, the supreme law of the land. Those decisions cannot be guides in the era introduced by the recent amendments of the supreme law, which established universal civil freedom, gave citizenship to all born or naturalized in the United States, and residing here, obliterated the race line from our systems of governments, national and state, and placed our free institutions upon the broad and sure foundation of the equality of all men before the law.

I am of opinion that the [law of the] state of Louisiana is inconsistent with the personal liberty of citizens, white and black, in that state, and hostile to both the spirit and letter of the constitution of the United States. If laws of like character should be enacted in the several states of the Union, the effect would be in the highest degree mischievous. Slavery, as an institution tolerated by law, would, it is true, have disappeared from our country; but there would remain a power in the states, by sinister legislation, to interfere with the full enjoyment of the blessings of freedom, to regulate civil rights, common to all citizens, upon the basis of race, and to place in a condition of legal inferiority a large body of American citizens, now constituting a part of the political community, called the "People of the United States," for whom, and by whom through representatives, our government is administered. Such a system is inconsistent with the guaranty given by the constitution to each state of a republican form of government, and may be stricken down by congressional action, or by the courts in the discharge of their solemn duty to maintain the supreme law of the land, anything in the constitution or laws of any state to the contrary notwithstanding.

For the reason stated, I am constrained to withhold my assent from the opinion and judgment of the majority.

Phillis Wheatley (Library of Congress)

Mary Church Terrell: "The Progress of Colored Women"

"Colored women ... are everywhere baffled and

mocked on account of their race."

Overview

On February 18, 1898, at a meeting of the National American Woman Suffrage Association (NAWSA), Mary Church Terrell delivered an address titled "The Progress of Colored Women." She states in the address that the occasion marks the fiftieth anniversary of the NAWSA, but this is only partly true. This meeting of the association was held in conjunction with the fiftieth anniversary of the Seneca Falls Convention of 1848 in New York, which many historians regard as the official start of the women's suffrage movement in the United States. In part as a result of the Seneca Falls Convention, various suffrage organizations were formed, including the National Woman Suffrage Association and the American Woman Suffrage Association. The NAWSA in turn had been formed in 1890 as a merger of the two organizations. Terrell, one of the nation's first African American women to earn a college degree, was active in the NAWSA and numerous other organizations. In 1896, for example, she had cofounded the National Association of College Women, which later became the National Association of University Women, an organization that has continued to this day. That year, too, she was named as the first president of the National Association of Colored Women's Clubs (NACWC). This group, known more simply as the National Association of Colored Women (the name Terrell uses in her address), united the National Federation of Afro-American Women, the Women's Era Club of Boston, and the Colored Women's League of Washington, D.C., as well as other groups that had taken part in the African American women's club movement. Thus, she was eminently qualified to speak about the status of African American women, and her speech was later published as a pamphlet.

Context

In the early decades of the nineteenth century, the issue of slavery dominated political discussion. While entrenched economic interests in the South labored to preserve the institution of slavery, numerous abolitionist organizations arose, primarily in the North, with the goal of driving a stake through the heart of the slave system. At the same time, the issue of rights for women, particularly the right to vote, began to simmer, especially after the Seneca Falls Convention, held in 1848 in upstate New York, published its Declaration of Sentiments, which called for equal rights for women. The women's rights and antislavery movements had overlapping concerns. Both represented a class of Americans who were being denied fundamental civil rights, and both believed that there was a synergy in the two movements that was mutually beneficial.

The Civil War put an end to the issue of slavery but not to the issue of equal rights for African Americans. At the same time, women were still denied the right to vote. In response to these concerns, Susan B. Anthony, Lucy Stone, Elizabeth Cady Stanton, and others formed the American Equal Rights Association in 1866, believing that such an organization could harness the energies of both the women's suffrage movement and the abolitionist movement. Almost immediately, though, tensions began to surface in the association. Those whose primary concern was women's suffrage were coming to reject the American political party system, believing that neither Democrats nor Republicans were interested in women's issues. In contrast, those whose primary concern was equal rights for African Americans were coming to ally themselves more firmly with the Republican Party, the party of Abraham Lincoln and the Emancipation Proclamation and also the party that was enforcing Reconstruction in the South after the war. Suffragist leaders were hopeful that the Fifteenth Amendment to the U.S. Constitution, which granted voting rights to African Americans, would extend the same rights to women—and were bitterly disappointed that it did not. Lucretia Mott, in particular, was outspoken about her resentment that black men were getting the vote but white women were not. She expressed the belief that black men would be every bit as oppressive in their attitudes toward women as white men were.

The result of these tensions was a split in the association in 1869. Those who supported the Fifteenth Amendment, believing that it would not be ratified if it included a provision for universal suffrage, formed the American Woman Suffrage Association under the leadership of Lucy Stone. This organization would continue to focus its energies en-

1863

- **September 23**
Mary Eliza Church, known after her marriage to Robert Terrell in 1891 as Mary Church Terrell, is born in Memphis, Tennessee.

1866

- **May 10**
Susan B. Anthony, Lucy Stone, Elizabeth Cady Stanton, and others form the American Equal Rights Association.

1869

- **May 15**
Susan B. Anthony and Elizabeth Cady Stanton found the National Woman Suffrage Association.

- **November**
Lucy Stone and Henry Blackwell found the American Woman Suffrage Association.

1884

- Terrell earns a bachelor's degree from Oberlin College in Ohio, one of the first African American women to earn a college degree.

1888

- Terrell earns a master's degree from Oberlin College.

1890

- The National American Woman Suffrage Association is formed from a merger of the National Woman Suffrage Organization and the American Woman Suffrage Association.

1896

- Terrell becomes the first president of the National Association of Colored Women's Clubs; that same year, she also cofounds the National Association of College Women, later known as the National Association of University Women.

1897

- **February 17**
The National Congress of Mothers, forerunner of the Parent-Teacher Association, is founded.

1898

- **February 18**
Terrell delivers the address "The Progress of Colored Women" at a meeting of the National American Woman Suffrage Association.

tirely on the issue of women's suffrage. Anthony and Stanton, dubbed the "irreconcilables," opposed the Fifteenth Amendment precisely because it did not provide universal suffrage. They formed the more militant National Woman Suffrage Association, which, unlike the American Woman Suffrage Association, admitted only women and focused attention on other social issues—though even this was a source of some tension, for Anthony wanted to focus entirely on women's suffrage while others in the organization preferred to devote attention to other issues affecting women.

Throughout the 1870s and 1880s, the two rival organizations worked separately and often at cross-purposes. During the 1880s, however, it was becoming apparent to both organizations that a united front would be more effective. After protracted negotiations, the two organizations merged in 1890 to form the NAWSA. For the next two decades, the NAWSA was the preeminent women's rights organization in the country. The efforts of this and other organizations finally bore fruit in 1920 with the ratification of the Nineteenth Amendment, which extended suffrage to women.

Mary Church Terrell, as an African American woman, in effect bridged the concerns of the two streams of thought. Although she had enjoyed a comfortable, affluent upbringing, she came of age at the end of the Reconstruction era and was witness to the collapse of the hopes of African Americans after the Civil War as the Democratic Party regained ascendancy in the South, the Civil Rights Act of 1875 was declared unconstitutional, and state legislatures passed Jim Crow laws mandating segregation. Just two years before her speech, in 1896, the U.S. Supreme Court had issued its landmark ruling in *Plessy v. Ferguson*, which entrenched racial segregation by establishing the separate-but-equal doctrine. African American women were in a double bind, for they experienced discrimination and slights because of both their race and gender.

Terrell had come to believe that the best hope for progress among African American women was the women's club movement, particularly because of the emergence of a black middle class that had acquired some measure of education and wealth and thus was able to help the less fortunate. In 1893 the journalist and antilynching activist Ida B. Wells-Barnett formed one of the first such clubs. During the years from 1890 to 1920 the number of these clubs exploded; Chicago, for example, was home to over one hundred fifty black women's clubs. Throughout the nation African American women's clubs established kindergartens, day nurseries, reading rooms, settlement houses, youth clubs, children's camps, and homes for dependent and orphaned children, the elderly, and young working women. For example, in 1890 Emma Frances Grayson Merritt established the first U.S. kindergarten for African American students, and that same year Janie Porter Barrett founded the Locust Street Settlement House in Hampton, Virginia. In alliance with other black community institutions, African American clubwomen were deeply involved in politics and municipal reform. Women's clubs pressed for women's suffrage, fought discrimination in movie theaters and other public facilities, and promoted the passage of antilynching laws. They also raised money to support community institutions by sponsoring theatrical presentations, concerts, picnics, raffles, charity balls, and dances. It was from this background that Mary Church Terrell rose to address the NAWSA on "The Progress of Colored Women" in 1898.

About the Author

Mary Eliza Church was born in Memphis, Tennessee, on September 23, 1863. Her mother was Louisa Ayres Church; her father was Robert Church. Both were former slaves, but in the years after the Civil War the family was upwardly mobile. Robert Church was the owner of a successful saloon, and in the late 1870s he purchased enough land and property to become the first black millionaire in Memphis. Meanwhile, Louisa Church operated a successful hair salon. Although the couple divorced when Mary was three years old, her father continued to support the family and worked to ensure that Mary received the best education possible for a black girl at that time. She attended Antioch College's Model School in Yellow Springs, Ohio, and then went on to earn a bachelor's degree in 1884 from Ohio's Oberlin College, an institution that had been in the forefront of the abolition movement and had admitted African Americans as far back as 1835.

At Oberlin, she refused to take what was often called the "ladies' course," a two-year degree in literary studies. Instead, she opted for the more challenging classical or "gentlemen's course," that is, a four-year degree. In 1885 she taught at Wilberforce College (now Wilberforce University) in Ohio, and in 1886 she taught at what was then called M Street High School, or the Preparatory High School for Colored Youth (now Dunbar High School), in Washington, D.C. During this period she also fulfilled the master of arts requirements for Oberlin College, earning the degree in 1888. She then went on a two-year tour from 1888 to 1890, during which she visited major European cities. While in Europe, she became fluent in German, Italian, and French; her language skills would later enable her to speak at European suffrage meetings. In 1891 Church married Robert Terrell, a lawyer she had met while teaching at M Street High School who would become the first black judge for the District of Columbia. They had one surviving child, Phillis, whom they named after the eighteenth-century poet Phillis Wheatley. At the time of her marriage, she had considered abandoning social activism. It was her good friend Frederick Douglass who persuaded her otherwise.

In the 1890s Terrell started a lifelong career as a social activist. In 1895 she was appointed to the board of education in the District of Columbia, the first African American woman to hold such as position. In 1895 she was one of the founding members of the National Federation of Afro-American Women, an umbrella organization for black women's clubs. In 1896 the federation merged with the Women's Era Club of Boston, the Colored Women's League of Washington, D.C., and several other groups to form the NACWC, and Terrell served as that organization's first president. That same year, she also cofounded the National

Association of College Women (later renamed the National Association of University Women). Additionally, she pursued a career as a journalist, writing under the pen name Euphemia Kirk for a number of newspapers, both white and black, about the African American women's club movement. Later, in 1909, she was one of only two black women asked to sign the "Call" inviting people to take part in the organizational meeting of the National Association for the Advancement of Colored People, making her a founding member of that organization.

For the next forty years, Terrell remained active in the fight for justice and equality. She published her autobiography, *A Colored Woman in a White World*, in 1940. In 1950 she led a successful effort to desegregate restaurants and retail stores in the District of Columbia, working in tandem with a group that had mounted a legal challenge forcing the district to enforce antidiscrimination laws. Even past the age of eighty, she continued to take part in boycotts, picket lines, and sit-ins to protest segregation. She died on July 24, 1954, after having lived just long enough to witness the U.S. Supreme Court's landmark ruling in *Brown v. Board of Education* just two months earlier.

Explanation and Analysis of the Document

Terrell begins by noting that fifty years earlier, at the time of the Seneca Falls Convention, it would have been regarded as an impossibility that a national women's organization would convene in the nation's capital, let alone that someone such as she, the descendant of a former slave, would be addressing the gathering. She looks forward not only to the enfranchisement of women but also to the emancipation of her race through the efforts of such notables in the women's rights movement as Ernestine Rose, Lucretia Mott, Elizabeth Cady Stanton, Lucy Stone, and, of course, Susan B. Anthony. Terrell makes reference to the opening of colleges to women who, earlier in their lives, lived under a system where in many states it had been a crime to teach a black person to read. She points to the many ways in which blacks and women were fettered, unable to own property and lacking any control over their own bodies. She calls attention, though, to the number of African American women who have been able to surmount such obstacles through education, despite the "cruel, unreasonable prejudice which neither their merit

Elizabeth Cady Stanton (seated) and Susan B. Anthony (standing) (Library of Congress)

nor their necessity seems able to subdue." She notes that the number of professional avocations open to African American women have remained few, and those that have been open paid low wages because of the sheer number of people competing for similar or the same jobs. In spite of these obstacles, women have made "herculean" efforts that have led to progress. She pays tribute to her alma mater, Oberlin College in north-central Ohio, the first college to admit African Americans. She also pays tribute to eastern women's colleges such as Vassar and Wellesley as well as to Cornell University and the University of Michigan at Ann Arbor (called Ann Arbor in the address). During the late nineteenth century, the University of Chicago (called Chicago University in the address) was in the forefront of providing opportunities in higher education to African Americans.

With the second paragraph, Terrell turns to the efforts of black women's clubs born of an "ardent desire to do good in the world." Many African American women who have been able to ameliorate their condition through education, she says, have "hastened to dispense these blessings to the less fortunate of their race." She notes that probably 90 percent of the teachers of black youth are women. It is noteworthy that Terrell emphasizes morality as much as education as a path to elevation of the race. She makes reference to the NACWC, pointing out that "homes, more homes, better homes, purer homes is the text upon which our sermons have been and will be preached." She then states that one of the most useful activities of the NAC-WC has been instruction in the art of raising children. She

makes reference to the "Mothers' Congress"—that is, the National Congress of Mothers. This organization, formed in 1897, would later become the Parent-Teacher Association, commonly referred to by the initials PTA.

In the third paragraph, Terrell begins to point to specific examples of the work of women. She refers to the Tuskegee, Alabama, branch of the NACWC, where, in the shadow of Booker T. Washington's Tuskegee Institute, "the work of bringing the light of knowledge and the gospel of cleanliness to their benighted sisters on the plantations has been conducted with signal success." In the fourth paragraph, she turns to the matter of domestic arts, noting that NACWC clubs have been teaching women to maintain standards of cleanliness and have also sponsored "talks on social purity and the proper method of rearing children." She notes that the crowded conditions of African American homes have made "maidenly youth and innocence" difficult, but she also argues that statistics have shown immorality among African American women to have been less prevalent than among women of various European countries.

With the fifth paragraph, Terrell becomes even more specific, pointing to a mission that had been established in New York City and was offering a kindergarten, classes for women, meetings for mothers as well as for men, and manual training for boys. She also points to similar successful organizations in Washington, D.C., Kansas City, Missouri, and Boston. She praises the contributions of the Phyllis Wheatley Club in New Orleans, named in honor of the eighteenth-century slave poet, Phillis Wheatley (Phyllis is a common misspelling of the name; later in the address, Terrell makes specific reference to Wheatley and her 1773 book of poems). In fact, there were numerous Phyllis Wheatley Clubs throughout the United States. The one in New Orleans operated a sanatorium and a training school for nurses.

In the sixth paragraph Terrell describes some of the successes of the medical facilities in New Orleans, which provided treatment for poor people and whose nurses had been in constant requisition during a yellow fever epidemic the year before. (Yellow fever had been a scourge throughout the nineteenth century, killing up to one hundred fifty thousand Americans.) In light of today's onerous health care costs, it is striking that this facility in New Orleans could operate for its first eight months on donations amounting to $1,000 and an appropriation from the city of $240. Terrell goes on to call attention to other charitable organizations throughout the country in such places as Montgomery, Alabama; Atlanta, Covington, and Augusta, Georgia; Boston; Memphis, Tennessee; and Lexington, Kentucky. In the seventh paragraph, Terrell calls attention to another example of an organization working to improve the lives of African Americans, the Mount Meigs Institute in rural Alabama. The Mount Meigs Institute was founded in 1888 by E. N. Pierce, of Plainfield, Connecticut. He had acquired a large plantation in Alabama and wanted to provide a school for blacks. He contacted Booker T. Washington at the nearby Tuskegee Institute and asked him to recommend a teacher. Washington recommended Cornelia Bowen, who formerly had taught at the Tuskegee Institute—the "one good woman" to whom Terrell refers.

"Nothing, in short, that could degrade or brutalize the womanhood of the race was lacking in that system from which colored women then had little hope of escape."

(Paragraph 1)

"Not only are colored women with ambition and aspiration handicapped on account of their sex, but they are everywhere baffled and mocked on account of their race."

(Paragraph 1)

"With tireless energy and eager zeal, colored women have, since their emancipation, been continuously prosecuting the work of educating and elevating their race, as though upon themselves alone devolved the accomplishment of this great task."

(Paragraph 2)

"Homes, more homes, better homes, purer homes is the text upon which our sermons have been and will be preached."

(Paragraph 2)

"And so, lifting as we climb, onward and upward we go, struggling and striving, and hoping that the buds and blossoms of our desires will burst into glorious fruition ere long.... Seeking no favors because of our color, nor patronage because of our needs, we knock at the bar of justice, asking an equal chance."

(Paragraph 11)

Terrell touches on the legal status of African Americans in the eighth paragraph. She notes that women's clubs have petitioned state legislatures to repeal "Jim Crow Car" laws, which required separate passenger cars for blacks and whites on railroads. Additionally, she observes that black women have tried to end the "Convict Lease System" in Georgia, a program by which the state of Georgia leased out prisoners, most of them black, to perform labor for private companies. At the same time, black women have been active in the cause of the Woman's Christian Temperance Union, an organization whose goal was to moderate the use of alcohol.

In addition to efforts on the legal front, black women have enjoyed successes in business. Terrell cites the example of a "milling and cotton business" in Alabama that was owned by a black woman and employed seventy-five men. Similarly in the arts, black women had been gaining respect. She makes reference to a black sculptor, though it is unclear whom she means. One possibility was Edmonia Lewis, an artist of African American and Native American descent who achieved considerable prominence as a sculptor in the late nineteenth and early twentieth centuries. She refers to the sculptor as "Bougerean's pupil." Bougerean is a misspelling of the name of Adolphe-William Bouguereau, a French academic painter (that is, a traditionalist rather than an innovator). Bouguereau took on numerous American students during his career.

Terrell then turns to education, particularly to the need for kindergartens, many of which already had been established to "counteract baleful influences on innocent victims." She notes the high incidence of crime in black communities and attributes it to poverty, lack of positive role models, ignorance, and the "pernicious example" of elders. Indeed, Terrell makes an impassioned argument for early childhood education and states that the "special mission" of the NACWC was to be the establishment of kindergartens. Terrell ends her speech on a note of soaring rhetoric. "Lifting as we climb, onward and upward we go." She looks forward with optimism to the day when "our desires will burst into glorious fruition." Black women, she says, seek neither special favors nor patronage but they "knock at the bar of justice, asking an equal chance."

Audience

The audience for "The Progress of Colored Women" consisted of those attending the meeting of the NAWSA held at the Columbia Theatre in Washington, D.C., from February 13 to 19, 1898. In attendance would have been such luminaries of the women's suffrage movement as the NAWSA's honorary president, Elizabeth Cady Stanton; its president, Susan B. Anthony; its vice president, the Reverend Anna Howard Shaw; various state presidents, who had come from as far away as California; and others who chaired or worked with the organization's various committees, most notably Carrie Chapman Catt. The conference included reports from various organizational officials on concerns such as the progress of legislative efforts to achieve suffrage both on the federal and state levels, civil rights, the economic status of women, marriage, fund-raising, and the progress of women in such fields as law and the church. Terrell was scheduled to give her address sometime after eight o'clock in the evening on February 18. In the NAWSA's published proceedings, the following notice was included:

> "The Progress of Colored Women" was set forth in an eloquent address by Mary Church Terrell, of the District, the President of the National Association of Colored Women. Mrs. Terrell has the orator's gift and interested her audience deeply. Though so impassioned in manner, the matter of her address was temperate and kindly in spirit.

Impact

Gauging the impact of a particular speech given to an audience of like-minded people is a difficult undertaking. Terrell's address to the NAWSA is of interest less for any particular impact it had at the time and more for the window it opens into race relations and racial progress at the end of the nineteenth century. On the one hand, while Terrell was the daughter of former slaves, she herself had grown up in affluent surroundings, received a college education, and continued to enjoy a comfortable life in Washington, D.C., with her attorney husband, who himself had graduated from the prestigious Groton Academy, Harvard University, and the

Howard University Law School, where he had been class valedictorian. She had come to know the abolitionist Frederick Douglass largely because they both had summer homes in Highland Beach, Maryland, and were neighbors there. Thus, Terrell had not experienced firsthand the privations to which many African Americans had been subjected. On the other hand, she used her talents and time to work tirelessly to improve the condition of women and African Americans. For her efforts, she was the recipient of many awards, including an honorary doctorate in 1948 from Oberlin College, which named her one of the college's one hundred most distinguished alumni. Her house in the nation's capital was named a National Historic Landmark in 1975, and as recently as 2009 she was one of just twelve civil rights pioneers featured on a series of U.S. Postal Service stamps.

Terrell's viewpoint was very much in the tradition of Booker T. Washington, whom she knew personally. Washington's stance on the advancement of African Americans presented a sharp contrast with that of W. E. B. Du Bois, whose landmark book, *The Souls of Black Folk*, would come out just five years after her address. During these years, differing strains of the early civil rights movement contended for the soul of African Americans. At the Tuskegee Institute, which he founded, Washington developed a program emphasizing industrial education. He trained brick masons, carpenters, and other artisans, who constructed several of Tuskegee's buildings while they were still students. Women were trained in the domestic arts. Tuskegee's program was based on Washington's belief that black students would be served best by training for vocations rather than professions, a view that he expressed in his famous and controversial Atlanta Exposition Address in 1895. On the other side of the divide was Du Bois, who argued that Washington's program amounted to submission and, in essence, accepted that blacks were inferior. Washington, in Du Bois's view, had abrogated the demands of African Americans for equality as citizens, political power, civil rights, and higher education to instead concentrate on industrial education and the accumulation of wealth. The third chapter of Du Bois's *The Souls of Black Folk* was given over to a refutation of Washington's views.

Terrell's address steered clear of these political considerations, yet it was clear that she was less interested in the political abstractions of Du Bois, the intellectual, and more interested in the day-to-day lives of African American women. She hoped that these women would be able, through their own efforts, to ameliorate their condition. In her address, she expressed this hope in her statement that "colored women are everywhere reaching out after the waifs and strays, who without their aid may be doomed to lives of evil and shame." While Du Bois was interested in universities, Terrell was interested in kindergartens, as well as "waifs and strays." Du Bois's approach was one of manly assertion of rights, while Terrell worked for women's suffrage. While Du Bois was interested in abstract political rights, Terrell was content with concrete steps along the path of advancement, such as the Mount Meigs Institute in Alabama, where "instruction ... is of the kind best suited to the needs of those people for whom it was established. Along with their scholastic training, girls are taught everything pertaining to the management of a home, while boys learn practical farming, carpentering, wheel-wrighting, blacksmithing, and have some military training." Both Terrell and Du Bois had an impact on the early civil rights movement, and both were founding members of the National Association for the Advancement of Colored People, which suggests that the tent was big enough for widely differing views and approaches to issues of importance to African Americans.

See also Emancipation Proclamation (1863); Fifteenth Amendment to the U.S. Constitution (1870); Booker T. Washington's Atlanta Exposition Address (1895); *Plessy v. Ferguson* (1896); Ida B. Wells-Barnett's "Lynch Law in America" (1900); W. E. B. Du Bois: *The Souls of Black Folk* (1903); *Brown v. Board of Education* (1954).

Further Reading

■ Articles

Jones, Beverly Washington. "Mary Church Terrell and the National Association of Colored Women: 1986–1901." *Journal of Negro History* 67 (1982): 20–33.

Nash, Margaret A. "'Patient Persistence': The Political and Educational Values of Anna Julia Cooper and Mary Church Terrell." *Educational Studies* 35 (April 2004): 122–136.

■ Books

Fradin, Dennis B., and Judith Bloom Fradin. *Fight On! Mary Church Terrell's Battle for Integration*. New York: Clarion Books, 2003.

Jones, Beverly Washington. *Quest for Equality: The Life and Writings of Mary Eliza Church Terrell, 1863–1954*. New York: Carlson Publishing, 1990.

Proceedings of the Thirtieth Annual Convention of the National American Woman Suffrage Association. Philadelphia: Alfred J. Harris, 1898.

Sterling, Dorothy. *Black Foremothers: Three Lives*. 2nd ed. New York: Feminist Press, 1988.

Terrell, Mary Church. *A Colored Woman in a White World*. New York: G. K. Hall, 1996.

■ Web Sites

Jones, Beverley W. "Mary Eliza Church Terrell, 1863–1954." Tennessee Encyclopedia of History and Culture Web site. http://tennesseeencyclopedia.net/imagegallery. php?EntryID=T081.

—Michael J. O'Neal

Questions for Further Study

1. The abolitionist movement and the women's rights movement at times collaborated and at other times were at odds with each other. What goals did the two movements share? Why did the movements fall out with each other after the Civil War?

2. Shirley Chisholm, who in 1968 became the first African American woman elected to Congress, was known to say that she experienced more discrimination from being a woman than from being black. Do you think that Terrell would have agreed? Why or why not?

3. What was the women's club movement? What were its goals? How successful do you imagine the club movement was?

4. Read the excerpt from W. E. B. Du Bois: *The Souls of Black Folk*. Now imagine a meeting between Terrell and Du Bois, perhaps over a cup of coffee, at the organizational meeting that led to the founding of the National Association for the Advancement of Colored People in 1909. Script an imaginary conversation that you think might have taken place.

5. Terrell came from a comfortable, even affluent background. She was a college graduate, and her attorney husband was a graduate of Harvard University. Comment on how you think these factors may have influenced Terrell's thinking about the issues she discussed. Do you think they may have somehow disqualified her to discuss the poverty of black communities? Explain.

MARY CHURCH TERRELL: "THE PROGRESS OF COLORED WOMEN"

Fifty years ago a meeting such as this, planned, conducted and addressed by women would have been an impossibility. Less than forty years ago, few sane men would have predicted that either a slave or one of his descendants would in this century at least, address such an audience in the Nation's Capital at the invitation of women representing the highest, broadest, best type of womanhood, that can be found anywhere in the world. Thus to me this semi-centennial of the National American Woman Suffrage Association is a double jubilee, rejoicing as I do, not only in the prospective enfranchisement of my sex but in the emancipation of my race. When Ernestine Rose, Lucretia Mott, Elizabeth Cady Stanton, Lucy Stone and Susan B. Anthony began that agitation by which colleges were opened to women and the numerous reforms inaugurated for the amelioration of their condition along all lines, their sisters who groaned in bondage had little reason to hope that these blessings would ever brighten their crushed and blighted lives, for during those days of oppression and despair, colored women were not only refused admittance to institutions of learning, but the law of the States in which the majority lived made it a crime to teach them to read. Not only could they possess no property, but even their bodies were not their own. Nothing, in short, that could degrade or brutalize the womanhood of the race was lacking in that system from which colored women then had little hope of escape. So gloomy were their prospects, so fatal the laws, so pernicious the customs, only fifty years ago. But, from the day their fetters were broken and their minds released from the darkness of ignorance to which for more than two hundred years they had been doomed, from the day they could stand erect in the dignity of womanhood, no longer bond but free, till tonight, colored women have forged steadily ahead in the acquisition of knowledge and in the cultivation of those virtues which make for good. To use a thought of the illustrious Frederick Douglass, if judged by the depths from which they have come, rather than by the heights to which those blessed with centuries of opportunities have attained, colored women need not hang their heads in shame. Consider if you will, the almost insurmountable obstacles which have confronted colored women in their efforts to educate and cultivate

themselves since their emancipation, and I dare assert, not boastfully, but with pardonable pride, I hope, that the progress they have made and the work they have accomplished, will bear a favorable comparison at least with that of their more fortunate sisters, from whom the opportunity of acquiring knowledge and the means of self-culture have never been entirely withheld. For, not only are colored women with ambition and aspiration handicapped on account of their sex, but they are everywhere baffled and mocked on account of their race. Desperately and continuously they are forced to fight that opposition, born of a cruel, unreasonable prejudice which neither their merit nor their necessity seems able to subdue. Not only because they are women, but because they are colored women, are discouragement and disappointment meeting them at every turn. Avocations opened and opportunities offered to their more favored sisters have been and are tonight closed and barred against them. While those of the dominant race have a variety of trades and pursuits from which they may choose, the woman through whose veins one drop of African blood is known to flow is limited to a pitiful few. So overcrowded are the avocations in which colored women may engage and so poor is the pay in consequence, that only the barest livelihood can be eked out by the rank and file. And yet, in spite of the opposition encountered, and the obstacles opposed to their acquisition of knowledge and their accumulation of property, the progress made by colored women along these lines has never been surpassed by that of any people in the history of the world. Though the slaves were liberated less than forty years ago, penniless, and ignorant, with neither shelter nor food, so great was their thirst for knowledge and so herculean were their efforts to secure it, that there are today hundreds of negroes, many of them women, who are graduates, some of them having taken degrees from the best institutions of the land. From Oberlin, that friend of the oppressed, Oberlin, my dear alma mater, whose name will always be loved and whose praise will ever be sung as the first college in the country which was just, broad and benevolent enough to open its doors to negroes and to women on an equal footing with men; from Wellesley and Vassar, from Cornell and Ann Arbor, from the best high schools throughout the North, East and West, colored girls have been graduated with honors, and have thus forever settled the question of their capacity and worth. But a few years ago in an examination in which a large number of young women and men competed for a scholarship, entitling the successful competitor to an entire course through the Chicago University, the only colored girl among them stood first and captured this great prize. And so, wherever colored girls have studied, their instructors bear testimony to their intelligence, diligence and success.

With this increase of wisdom there has sprung up in the hearts of colored women an ardent desire to do good in the world. No sooner had the favored few availed themselves of such advantages as they could secure than they hastened to dispense these blessings to the less fortunate of their race. With tireless energy and eager zeal, colored women have, since their emancipation, been continuously prosecuting the work of educating and elevating their race, as though upon themselves alone devolved the accomplishment of this great task. Of the teachers engaged in instructing colored youth, it is perhaps no exaggeration to say that fully ninety per cent are women. In the back-woods, remote from the civilization and comforts of the city and town, on the plantations, reeking with ignorance and vice, our colored women may be found battling with evils which such conditions always entail. Many a heroine, of whom the world will never hear, has thus sacrificed her life to her race, amid surroundings and in the face of privations which only martyrs can tolerate and bear. Shirking responsibility has never been a fault with which colored women might be truthfully charged. Indefatigably and conscientiously, in public work of all kinds they engage, that they may benefit and elevate their race. The result of this labor has been prodigious indeed. By banding themselves together in the interest of education and morality, by adopting the most practical and useful means to this end, colored women have in thirty short years become a great power for good. Through the National Association of Colored Women, which was formed by the union of two large organizations in July, 1896, and which is now the only national body among colored women, much good has been done in the past, and more will be accomplished in the future, we hope. Believing that it is only through the home that a people can become really good and truly great, the National Association of Colored Women has entered that sacred domain. Homes, more homes, better homes, purer homes is the text upon which our sermons have been

and will be preached. Through mothers' meetings, which are a special feature of the work planned by the Association, much useful information in everything pertaining to the home will be disseminated. We would have heart-to-heart talks with our women, that we may strike at the root of evils, many of which lie, alas, at the fireside. If the women of the dominant race with all the centuries of education, culture and refinement back of them, with all their wealth of opportunity ever present with them—if these women feel the need of a Mothers' Congress that they may be enlightened as to the best methods of rearing children and conducting their homes, how much more do our women, from whom shackles have but yesterday fallen, need information on the same vital subjects? And so throughout the country we are working vigorously and conscientiously to establish Mothers' Congresses in every community in which our women may be found.

Under the direction of the Tuskegee, Alabama branch of the National Association, the work of bringing the light of knowledge and the gospel of cleanliness to their benighted sisters on the plantations has been conducted with signal success. Their efforts have thus far been confined to four estates, comprising thousands of acres of land, on which live hundreds of colored people, yet in the darkness of ignorance and the grip of sin, miles away from churches and schools. Under the evil influences of plantation owners, and through no fault of their own, the condition of the colored people is, in some sections to-day no better than it was at the close of the war. Feeling the great responsibility resting upon them, therefore, colored women, both in organizations under the National Association, and as individuals are working with might and main to afford their unfortunate sisters opportunities of civilization and education, which without them, they would be unable to secure.

By the Tuskegee club and many others all over the country, object lessons are given in the best way to sweep, dust, cook, wash and iron, together with other information concerning household affairs. Talks on social purity and the proper method of rearing children are made for the benefit of those mothers, who in many instances fall short of their duty, not because they are vicious and depraved, but because they are ignorant and poor. Against the one-room cabin so common in the rural settlements in the South, we have inaugurated a vigorous crusade. When families of eight or ten, consisting of men, women and children, are all huddled together in a single apartment, a condition of things found not only in the South, but among our poor all over the land, there is little hope of inculcating morality or modesty. And yet, in spite of these environments which are so destructive of virtue, and though the safeguards usually thrown around maidenly youth and innocence are in some sections withheld from colored girls, statistics compiled by men, not inclined to falsify in favor of my race, show that immorality among *colored women* is *not* so great as among women in countries like Austria, Italy, Germany, Sweden and France.

In New York City a mission has been established and is entirely supported by colored women under supervision of the New York City Board. It has in operation a kindergarten, classes in cooking and sewing, mothers' meetings, mens' meetings, a reading circle and a manual training school for boys. Much the same kind of work is done by the Colored Woman's League and the Ladies Auxiliary of this city, the Kansas City League of Missouri, the Woman's Era Club of Boston, the Woman's Loyal Union of New York, and other organizations representing almost every State in the Union. The Phyllis Wheatley Club of New Orleans, another daughter of the National Association, has in two short years succeeded in establishing a Sanatorium and a Training School for nurses. The conditions which caused the colored women of New Orleans to choose this special field in which to operate are such as exist in many other sections of our land. From the city hospitals colored doctors are ex-

cluded altogether, not even being allowed to practice in the colored wards, and colored patients—no matter how wealthy they are—are not received at all, unless they are willing to go into the charity wards. Thus the establishment of a Sanatorium answers a variety of purposes. It affords colored medical students an opportunity of gaining a practical knowledge of their profession, and it furnishes a well-equipped establishment for colored patients who do not care to go into the charity wards of the public hospitals.

The daily clinics have been a great blessing to the colored poor. In the operating department, supplied with all the modern appliances, two hundred operations have been performed, all of which have resulted successfully under the colored surgeon-in-chief. Of the eight nurses who have registered, one has already passed an examination before the State Medical Board of Louisiana, and is now practicing her profession. During the yellow fever epidemic in New Orleans last summer, there was a constant demand for Phyllis Wheatley nurses. By indefatigable energy and heroic sacrifice of both money and time, these noble women raised nearly one thousand dollars, with which to defray the expenses of the Sanatorium for the first eight months of its existence. They have recently succeeded in securing from the city of New Orleans an annual appropriation of two hundred and forty dollars, which they hope will soon be

Glossary

Ann Arbor	the University of Michigan in the city of Ann Arbor
Bougerean	a misspelling of the name of Adolphe-William Bouguereau, a French painter who took on numerous American students during his career
Convict Lease System	a program by which the state of Georgia leased out prisoners, most of them black, to perform labor for private companies
Ernestine Rose, Lucretia Mott, Elizabeth Cady Stanton, Lucy Stone and Susan B. Anthony	all prominent leaders of the women's rights and women's suffragist movement; Stanton was the NAWSA's honorary president, and Anthony was president.
Frederick Douglass	a former slave and the most prominent nineteenth-century American abolitionist
Great Teacher	Jesus Christ
"Jim Crow Car" laws	laws that required separate passenger cars for blacks and whites on railroads
Mothers' Congress	the National Congress of Mothers, the organization formed in 1897 that would later become the Parent-Teacher Association, or PTA

increased. Dotted all over the country are charitable organizations for the aged, orphaned and poor, which have been established by colored women; just how many, it is difficult to state. Since there is such an imperative need of statistics, bearing on the progress, possessions, and prowess of colored women, the National Association has undertaken to secure this data of such value and importance to the race. Among the charitable institutions, either founded, conducted or supported by colored women, may be mentioned the Hale Infirmary of Montgomery, Alabama; the Carrie Steel Orphanage of Atlanta; the Reed Orphan Home of Covington; the Haines Industrial School of Augusta in the State of Georgia; a Home for the Aged of both races at New Bedford and St. Monica's Home of Boston in Massachusetts; Old Folks' Home of Memphis, Tenn.; Colored Orphan's Home, Lexington, Ky., together with others of which time forbids me to speak.

Mt. Meigs Institute is an excellent example of a work originated and carried into successful execution by a colored woman. The school was established for the benefit of colored people on the plantations in the black belt of Alabama, because of the 700,000 negroes living in that State, probably 90 per cent are outside of the cities; and Waugh was selected because in the township of Mt. Meigs, the population is practically all colored. Instruction given in this school is of the kind best suited to the needs of those people for whom it was established. Along with their scholastic training, girls are taught everything pertaining to the management of a home, while boys learn practical farming, carpentering, wheel-wrighting, blacksmithing, and have some military training. Having started with almost nothing, only eight years ago, the trustees of the school now own nine acres of land, and five buildings, in which two thousand pupils have received instruction—all through the courage, the industry and sacrifice of one good woman. The Chicago clubs and several others engage in rescue work among fallen women and tempted girls.

Questions affecting our legal status as a race are also constantly agitated by our women. In Louisiana and Tennessee, colored women have several times petitioned the legislatures of their respective States to repeal the obnoxious "Jim Crow Car" laws, nor will any stone be left unturned until this iniquitous and unjust enactment against respectable American citizens be forever wiped from the statutes of the South. Against the barbarous Convict Lease System of Georgia, of which negroes, especially the female prisoners, are the principal victims, colored women are waging a ceaseless war. By two lecturers, each of whom, under the Woman's Christian Temperance Union has been National Superintendent of work among colored people, the cause of temperance has for many years been eloquently espoused.

Glossary

Mt. Meigs Institute	a school for blacks in Alabama founded in 1888 by E. N. Pierce, of Plainfield, Connecticut
National Association of Colored Women	more formally, the National Association of Colored Women's Clubs
Oberlin	Oberlin College in north-central Ohio, the first college to admit African Americans
one good woman	Cornelia Bowen, who taught at Booker T. Washington's Tuskegee Institute before joining Mount Meigs Institute
Phyllis Wheatley	Phillis Wheatley, a Boston slave who published *Poems on Various Subjects, Religious and Moral* in 1773
semi-centennial of the National American Woman Suffrage Association	a reference to the fiftieth anniversary of the Seneca Falls Convention of 1848 in New York; the National American Woman Suffrage Association was formed from the merger of the National Woman Suffrage Association and the American Woman Suffrage Association in 1890
woman upon whose chisel	possibly Edmonia Lewis, a prominent sculptor of African American and Native American descent in the late nineteenth and early twentieth centuries
Woman's Christian Temperance Union	an organization whose goal was to moderate the consumption of alcohol

In business, colored women have had signal success. There is in Alabama a large milling and cotton business belonging to and controlled entirely by a colored woman who has sometimes as many as seventy-five men in her employ. In Halifax, Nova Scotia, the principal ice plant of the city is owned and managed by one of our women. In the professions we have dentists and doctors, whose practice is lucrative and large. Ever since the publication, in 1773, of a book entitled "Poems on Various Subjects, Religious and Moral," by Phyllis Wheatley, negro servant of Mr. John Wheatley of Boston, colored women have from time to time given abundant evidence of literary ability. In sculpture we are represented by a woman upon whose chisel Italy has set her seal of approval; in painting, by Bougerean's pupil, whose work was exhibited in the last Paris Salon, and in Music by young women holding diplomas from the first conservatories in the land.

And, finally, as an organization of women nothing lies nearer the heart of the National Association than the children, many of whose lives, so sad and dark, we might brighten and bless. It is the kindergarten we need. Free kindergartens in every city and hamlet of this broad land we must have, if the children are to receive from us what it is our duty to give. Already during the past year kindergartens have been established and successfully maintained by several organizations, from which most encouraging reports have come. May their worthy example be emulated, till in no branch of the Association shall the children of the poor, at least, be deprived of the blessings which flow from the kindergarten alone. The more unfavorable the environments of children, the more necessary is it that steps be taken to counteract baleful influences on innocent victims. How imperative is it then that as colored women, we inculcate correct principles and set good examples for our own youth, whose little feet will have so many thorny paths of prejudice temptation, and injustice to tread. The colored youth is vicious we are told, and statistics showing the multitudes of our boys and girls who crowd the penitentiaries and fill the jails appall and dishearten us. But side by side with these facts and figures of crime I would have presented and pictured the miserable hovels from which these youthful criminals come. Make a tour of the settlements of colored people, who in many cities are relegated to the most noisome sections permitted by the municipal government, and behold the mites of humanity who infest them. Here are our little ones, the future representatives of the race, fairly drinking in the pernicious example of their elders, coming in contact with nothing but ignorance and vice, till at the age of six, evil habits are formed which no amount of civilizing or Christianizing can ever completely break. Listen to the cry of our children. In imitation of the example set by the Great Teacher of men, who could not offer himself as a sacrifice, until he had made an eternal plea for the innocence and helplessness of childhood, colored women are everywhere reaching out after the waifs and strays, who without their aid may be doomed to lives of evil and shame. As an organization, the National Association of Colored Women feels that the establishment of kindergartens is the special mission which we are called to fulfill. So keenly alive are we to the necessity of rescuing our little ones, whose noble qualities are deadened and dwarfed by the very atmosphere which they breathe, that the officers of the Association are now trying to secure means by which to send out a kindergarten organizer, whose duty it shall be both to arouse the conscience of our women, and to establish kindergartens, wherever the means therefore can be secured.

And so, lifting as we climb, onward and upward we go, struggling and striving, and hoping that the buds and blossoms of our desires will burst into glorious fruition ere long. With courage, born of success achieved in the past, with a keen sense of the responsibility which we shall continue to assume, we look forward to a future large with promise and hope. Seeking no favors because of our color, nor patronage because of our needs, we knock at the bar of justice, asking an equal chance.

An illustration showing a man representing the White League shaking hands with a Ku Klux Klan member over an African American couple with a dead baby. In the background, a lynched man hangs from tree. (Library of Congress)

IDA B. WELLS-BARNETT'S "LYNCH LAW IN AMERICA"

"Brave men do not gather by thousands to torture and murder a single individual."

Overview

"Lynch Law in America" appeared in the January 1900 issue of *Arena*, a Boston-based magazine with a broad audience of white Progressives and former abolitionists. "Lynch Law in America" sums up the arguments of the nation's leading antilynching activist of the late nineteenth century, Ida B. Wells-Barnett. In this article, she discusses the misinformation about lynching that has deceived the public, and she provides counterevidence that reveals the real motivations and gruesome practices that lynching entails. Her article makes an urgent appeal for white Americans to reassess the wave of antiblack violence across the country and consider its implications for America's international standing and devotion to the rule of law.

Context

Organized white violence against African Americans has had a long history in the United States. Slavery involved systematic violence against blacks on many levels. During the era of slavery, nonslaveholding whites often belonged to "slave patrols" that were called out to track down fugitive slaves and put down slave revolts. Organized like militias, these patrols fostered white solidarity and maintained the institution of slavery through community action. Community participation in slave patrols was a precursor to the organized violence against blacks in the postslavery period.

At the same time, white mob violence was also common in northern cities, particularly in the form of antiabolitionist riots. Mobs that attacked abolitionists and broke up abolitionist meetings beginning in the 1830s often targeted blacks individually. It was not uncommon for northern whites to lynch or beat an innocent African American to death. One of the worst incidents of U.S. racial violence came during the Civil War, when draft riots broke out in 1863 in northern cities, including New York, and turned into race riots, with dozens of blacks being murdered in the streets.

With emancipation, a new era of racial violence was inaugurated. The congressional policy of Reconstruction of the former Confederate states instituted new constitutional rights for black Americans, including the guarantee of equality before the law and the rights to hold political office, to serve on juries, and to vote. The majority of white southerners vigorously opposed these policies, and some resorted to organized violence and terrorism to prevent blacks from exercising them. White militias were formed—such as the Red Shirts of South Carolina or the White Leagues of Louisiana and Mississippi—and used force and intimidation to prevent blacks from voting or attending political meetings. These groups were often responsible for atrocities like the slaughter of between seventy and one hundred fifty black men, women, and children in Colfax, Louisiana, in 1873. Secret societies like the Ku Klux Klan and the Knights of the White Camellia pursued similar goals but operated in disguise and undertook a variety of misdeeds under the cover of darkness. Mutilation, torture, and sexual assault were common by such groups. Over four hundred lynchings of blacks in the South are estimated to have occurred between 1868 and 1871 alone.

With the collapse of the Reconstruction governments in the late 1870s, the political incentive for white violence diminished, but the violence itself persisted, taking on new forms. White supremacist governments were firmly entrenched in each of the former Confederate states, and relatively few blacks attempted to exercise political power in the post-Reconstruction period. Southern white violence against blacks began to fade as an issue of national concern, with major incidents becoming less frequent for a few years. Incidents of white mob lynchings of individual black victims, however, began to rise again steadily in the mid- to late 1880s. The word *lynching* itself, which once had no racial connotations, began to refer strictly to white mob actions directed against blacks. Prior to the late 1880s, lynching had usually been practiced as a form of vigilante justice in isolated, typically rural regions of the country against accused criminals of all races. In these cases, victims most often stood accused of a serious crime, especially rape or murder, that had aroused the ire of the community. Community anger, coupled with isolation from legal institutions, overrode the constitutional rights of the accused to a fair trial. But 1885 was the last year in which more whites than blacks were executed by lynch mobs. After that, the "lynch law" came to apply primarily against blacks accused of a

Time Line

1862
- July 16
Ida Bell Wells is born in Holly Springs, Mississippi.

1866
- The Ku Klux Klan is formed in Tennessee and begins its campaign of political violence against blacks in the former Confederate states.

1868
- The Fourteenth Amendment is ratified, guaranteeing all citizens, regardless of race, equal protection of the laws and the right to due process.

1870
- The Fifteenth Amendment is ratified, guaranteeing that the right to vote will not be infringed because of race, color, or previous condition of servitude.

1884
- Wells sues a Tennessee railroad company for denying her service in the "Ladies Car" and wins (but the Tennessee Supreme Court later overturns the decision).

1888
- The white radical Albion W. Tourgée begins to address the crime of lynching in his weekly editorial for the white-owned Radical Republican newspaper *Chicago Daily Inter-Ocean.*

1889
- Wells becomes co-owner and editor of the Memphis *Free Speech and Headlight.*

1892
- Three of Wells's close friends are murdered by a white mob, and she is forced to flee Memphis after publishing an editorial titled "Eight Men Lynched."

- Wells publishes a series of articles about lynching in the *New York Age* and a pamphlet titled *Southern Horrors: Lynch Law in All Its Phases.*

crime in the South, and these incidents occurred often with the approval and assistance of police and legal authorities.

The peak year for lynchings in the United States came in 1892, with over 230 incidents documented nationwide, 161 of which involved black victims. The lynching of blacks also took on increasingly ritualized, predictable forms. Once a lynch mob was raised, police authorities would hand the accused over to the mob and disclaim responsibility for the victim's fate. The victim would often be tortured and mutilated—castration was common—before being shot or hung. The body was often burned, and pieces were taken as souvenirs. Authorities never brought charges against participants in lynch mobs, and these murders were invariably classified as having been carried out "by persons unknown."

At first, there was little outcry over these acts and scant press coverage. It was widely rumored that such acts were done exclusively in response to the crime of rape, or attempted rape, of white women by black men (although, in fact, these accusations were present in only one-quarter of all cases of lynching). Because of the sensitive nature of rape—euphemistically known as the "nameless" or "unspeakable" crime—few black leaders or newspaper editors were willing to defend the victims who had been accused of it. Beginning in 1889, however, a white novelist and Radical Republican, Albion W. Tourgée, began denouncing lynchings in his weekly column in the *Chicago Daily Inter-Ocean*, and he detailed incidents of lynchings in which rape was not an issue and the "crimes" of the accused were based on flimsy accusations. The journalist Ida B. Wells-Barnett became the first black writer to systematically address the issue of lynching, in her articles for the *New York Age* in 1892.

Led by Wells, the campaign against lynching grew in prominence in the 1890s. Antilynching activists demanded that due process and the right to a fair trial be respected, no matter what the nature of the crimes alleged. Beginning in 1896 in Ohio, a few states began to adopt antilynching laws that brought punishment to the perpetrators of lynchings and the communities in which they occurred. Nevertheless, lynching continued to occur with impunity, especially in the southern states, and this became a major factor in the "great migration" of blacks out of the South beginning in the 1890s.

After the *Plessy v. Ferguson* case of 1896, in which the U.S. Supreme Court ruled segregation to be consistent with the Fourteenth Amendment and the U.S. Constitution generally, the movement for protection of African American rights suffered a devastating setback. The decade that followed has been described by historians as the "nadir" of the black experience in America because of the sense of hopelessness and despair. In 1898 the whites of Wilmington, North Carolina, massacred black leaders and publicists in a violent overthrow of the local government that had previously respected black voting rights. Allegations that black leaders had encouraged the rape of white women served as the primary cause for the white violence. Everywhere in the South, whites moved to disenfranchise black voters by law or by force. Some black leaders, such as Booker T. Washington, appeared ready to give up on political protest in favor of equal rights, while others, such as Wells-Barnett, continued the struggle.

In 1908 a bloody race riot in Springfield, Illinois, began when a police sheriff refused to turn over two black prisoners to a lynch mob. The event became the catalyst for a new civil rights organization: An alliance of black and white radicals—including Wells-Barnett—formed the National Association for the Advancement of Colored People (NAACP) with a mission to reverse the spread of racism and antiblack violence in the country.

In 1919 the NAACP published *Thirty Years of Lynching in the United States, 1889–1918*, which publicized many incidents of lynching and investigated the truth behind them. The NAACP also sponsored a national antilynching law—the Dyer bill—that would make lynching a federal crime and allow federal investigation and prosecution of its perpetrators. Although the Dyer bill was blocked by filibuster in the Senate, its proposal marked the beginning of a sharp decline in lynching across the nation. Total national lynchings dropped into the single digits, with eight incidents in 1936, and remained at that level for the next thirty years. Effective publication and condemnation of the practice by the NAACP and other groups were a major factor in turning the tide.

About the Author

Ida B. Wells was born in 1862 in Holly Springs, Mississippi, to a carpenter, James Wells, and a cook, Elizabeth Wells. Her parents were active supporters of the Republican Party during Reconstruction in Mississippi. When she was sixteen, her parents and a younger sibling died in an epidemic of yellow fever that swept through the community. To prevent the breakup of her remaining family, Wells dropped out of school to obtain a teaching position and became the primary provider for her five younger siblings.

In 1880, Wells accepted an aunt's invitation and moved to Memphis, Tennessee, with two of her younger sisters. Continuing to work as a schoolteacher, she became involved in politics after she was forcibly removed from the "Ladies Car" on a Tennessee rail line and was ordered to move to the smoking car. She sued the company and wrote her first newspaper editorial, for the *Living Way*, about her case, which she won in the local court. The Tennessee Supreme Court later overturned the ruling. Wells soon published a regular column in the *Living Way* under the pen name "Iola." In 1889 she launched her own newspaper, which she edited and co-owned, titled the Memphis *Free Speech and Headlight*.

On March 9, 1892, Wells's life changed dramatically when three of her close friends were found murdered, rumored to be the victims of a lynch mob. Wells was shocked when she determined that the cause of their murder derived from the business rivalry between a white-owned grocery store and the store jointly owned by the three black murder victims. She began to publish investigative journalist articles about the causes of lynching. Her editorial of May 21, 1892, titled "Eight Men Lynched," prompted angry whites to attack her newspaper office and destroy her printing equipment.

Time Line	
1893	■ Wells undertakes a speaking tour of Great Britain and joins with Frederick Douglass in a protest against the exclusion of blacks from the Chicago World's Fair.
1894	■ Wells undertakes a second speaking tour of Great Britain and publishes a serial account of her trip in the *Chicago Daily Inter-Ocean*.
1895	■ Wells publishes *A Red Record* and marries the *Chicago Conservator* editor, Ferdinand L. Barnett.
1900	■ **January** Wells-Barnett publishes "Lynch Law in America" in the journal *Arena* and later in her pamphlet *Mob Rule in New Orleans*.
1909	■ Wells-Barnett is a founding member of the National Association for the Advancement of Colored People (NAACP).
1931	■ **March 25** Wells-Barnett dies in Chicago.
1970	Wells-Barnett's autobiography, *A Crusade for Justice: The Autobiography of Ida B. Wells*, is published posthumously by her daughter Alfreda M. Duster.

Wells learned of the attack and of a threat made on her life while she was out of town on business, and she determined never to return to Memphis.

In New York, Wells was hired to write editorials for T. Thomas Fortune's *New York Age*, the leading black newspaper of the day. Her sensational antilynching editorials led to a pamphlet, *Southern Horrors: Lynch Law in All of Its Phases*, published later in 1892. A testimonial dinner was held in her honor in June, announcing her arrival as a leading national voice for civil rights.

In 1893, Wells joined with Frederick Douglass and other prominent leaders to protest the exclusion and demeaning portrayal of blacks at the Chicago World's Fair. Wells took the lead in preparing a pamphlet titled *Why the Colored American*

An African-American orphanage is destroyed in the New York draft riots of 1863 (AP/Wide World Photos)

Is Not in the World's Columbian Exposition, which discussed a variety of racial injustices facing black Americans, from lynching to convict labor. Two thousand copies of the pamphlet were distributed at the fair. That same year, Wells received an invitation from British activists to speak on the subject of lynching in Great Britain. Her first tour brought international pressure upon the white community of the South, particularly in Memphis, where white newspapers were forced to respond to Wells's accusations and disclaim the practice of lynching. A second tour of Great Britain in 1894 was sponsored by the *Chicago Daily Inter-Ocean*, a leading Republican newspaper, which published Wells's accounts of her stay in a regular column titled "Ida B. Wells Abroad." By enlisting the international community to condemn lynching, Wells helped bring about a more honest public discourse on lynching in America, and her claims began to be taken more seriously.

In 1895, Wells married the Chicago lawyer and newspaper editor Ferdinand L. Barnett. Wells made the bold and unusual decision to keep her maiden name but to hyphenate it with Barnett's. The newly rechristened "Wells-Barnett" and her husband had four children; like her decision about her name, her approach to motherhood was equally unusual for the time: She continued to work and often brought her children along on speaking engagements. Wells-Barnett also became deeply involved in editing and writing for Barnett's paper, the *Chicago Conservator*. Wells-Barnett published two more antilynching pamphlets: *A Red Record* (1895) and *Mob Rule in New Or-*

leans (1900). She was also active in many civil rights organizations and women's clubs. The Ida B. Wells Club, for women, was named in her honor in Chicago in 1893. In 1909 she became a founding member of the NAACP. Her antilynching work continued for the rest of her life. She left an autobiography incomplete at her death in 1931, which her daughter later edited and published posthumously.

Explanation and Analysis of the Document

In "Lynch Law in America," Wells-Barnett declares that lynching has become a national crime to which all sections of the country have contributed and must bear responsibility. She begins the article by discussing the origin and evolution of lynching in the United States and the transformation of the practice into a tool of racist terror in the South. She describes the current situation with respect to the widespread incidents of lynching and the various excuses offered for it. Finally, she urges Americans to take action against the crime of lynching.

Lynching, according to Wells-Barnett, began in the far West, where settlers had no access to courts or the legal system. She refers to the communal justice of the frontier as following the "unwritten law." This custom, as she describes it, was harsh and severe and usually resulted in immediate hanging from the nearest tree. Facing hardships of a rough existence, there was little time to give prison-

> *"The negro has suffered far more from the commission of this crime [rape] against the women of his race by white men than the white race has ever suffered through his crimes. Very scant notice is taken of the matter when this is the condition of affairs. What becomes a crime deserving capital punishment when the tables are turned is a matter of small moment when the negro woman is the accusing party."*
>
> (Paragraph 13)

> *"Our watchword has been 'the land of the free and the home of the brave.' Brave men do not gather by thousands to torture and murder a single individual, so gagged and bound he cannot make even feeble resistance or defense."*
>
> (Paragraph 15)

ers constitutionally guaranteed rights, such as trial by jury, sworn testimony, right to a defense, or the right of appeal. Verdicts were immediately carried out (for the lack of jails perhaps), and judgments were final. But as "civilization spread into the Territories," and the apparatus of administered law became available, the practice of lynching "gradually disappeared from the West."

In its next phase, Wells-Barnett argues, the practice of lynching arose in the southern states and reflected a spirit of lawlessness that infected southerners during Reconstruction. When the Fourteenth and Fifteenth Amendments conferred equal citizenship and the right of suffrage on the former slaves in the South, many white southerners refused to accept those changes. In defiance of the law, and the constitutional rights of blacks, unreconstructed Confederates began to form into vigilante groups. Secret societies such as the Red Shirts and the Ku Klux Klan inaugurated a campaign of violence that aimed to "beat, exile, and kill negroes" in opposition to the Reconstruction laws. The excuse for this outbreak of racist violence was that black suffrage would result in "negro domination"—a term that southerners used to refer to a government in which blacks made up an important constituency of the majority party and thus possessed political power. During this time, the excuse for killing blacks derived from the assertion of their rights, whether voting rights or contract rights or the right of self-defense.

After Reconstruction collapsed in the face of white violence, a new excuse for antiblack violence in the South appeared: the protection of white women. Wells-Barnett calls this justification a new "statute in the unwritten law." Wells-Barnett argues that when a white women accuses a black man of improper behavior toward her, including a mere insult, it has become accepted that a white mob must be raised and the man put to death. Unlike the violence of the Ku Klux Klan during Reconstruction, the practice of lynching has achieved, as Wells-Barnett shows, universal acceptance and approval by whites throughout the country. The theory that white womanhood is in imminent danger from the uncontrollable urges of black men is an unproven accusation, in Wells-Barnett's estimation, since it has not been subjected to the rule of law or proper criminal investigation. By connecting the "justified" racist violence of lynching to the widely reviled, politically motivated violence of Reconstruction, Wells-Barnett not only shows the continuity of this behavior of white southerners but also casts suspicion on the new excuse for it.

Wells-Barnett goes on to describe the kinds of violence that have become ritually incorporated into the act of "lynching." Great publicity and offers of rewards usually precede the act itself. When the accused is caught, a public ceremony is held. A holiday is sometimes declared by local authorities so that schoolchildren can witness the event and onlookers from afar can be given time to travel by rail to it. Without any trial or testimony, the accused is tortured and often burned alive. Dismemberment of the body is common, with the mob taking home souvenirs in the form of fingers, toes, and ears. Wells-Barnett compares these barbarities to the tortures of the Middle Ages and the Spanish Inquisition. The word *lynching* hardly encompasses all of the kinds of violence perpetrated by white mobs in these brutal events.

In the next section of the article, Wells-Barnett discusses some of the misconceptions about lynching and points to facts about the accused that have been ignored. First, she says that lynching has not been confined to the southern states but that it has begun to spread into the North and West as well. Second, she remarks that the widespread belief that lynchings have been enacted only in cases of threats or assaults on white women is untrue. Less than one-third of all cases of lynching involved accusations by white women against black men. In many of those cases, the accusations were later recanted or shown to have no merit. Some cases involved the lynching of women and children, rather than men. Statistics also show that a wide variety of accused crimes have resulted in lynchings, and, in some cases, no accusation at all had been leveled at the victims. Wells-Barnett cites the case of Sam Hose, who was burned alive in Georgia. The charge of rape was falsely proclaimed in the press in the days leading up to the lynching, but afterward it was shown to have been an unfounded rumor and that Hose's "crime" was, in fact, an act of self-defense against his employer.

Wells-Barnett concludes her article by offering four reasons to oppose the practice of lynching: consistency, economy, national honor, and patriotism. Her four reasons have a common theme: Each refers to America's reputation in the eyes of the world. First, she points out that the practice of lynching conflicts with the democratic traditions of the nation. Throughout the article, she has referred to the violation of the rule of law and the Constitution. She goes further and alludes to the fact that the United States has presented itself to the world as a beacon of freedom. Indeed, Americans have denounced the injustices of other nations around the world to their oppressed minorities. She cites Turkish oppression of the Armenian Christians, Russian oppression of the Jews, English oppression of the Irish, Indian oppression of women, and Spanish oppression of Cubans as examples of causes Americans have taken up. Unless Americans confront their own oppression of blacks in tolerating the practice of lynching, she suggests, their criticism of other nations will appear as rank hypocrisy to the rest of the world.

Second, she points out that several instances of foreign nationals being lynched have caused the United States to pay hefty indemnities to other nations. By admitting that the U.S. government cannot protect "said subjects" of other nations or bring the participants of a mob to justice, these payments are "humiliating in the extreme." Third, and related to this point, America's inability to maintain the rule of law puts its government on a par with the least "civilized" and respected nations of the world. She compares the triumph of "savagery" in the American South with the cannibalism of the South Sea Islands and the brutality of American Indian warriors. Their acts, Wells-Barnett suggests, can be explained by the lack of familiarity of these nations with Christianity, but the United States cannot use that excuse. National honor, therefore, demands that America reject lynching so as to live up to its own laws and moral principles.

Finally, Wells-Barnett appeals to American patriotism. If the world does not respect the United States, no American citizen can expect to travel abroad or participate in discussions on international affairs without inviting ridicule. The pride of the country is at stake, she implies. She concludes by citing a French newspaper that scoffed at American criticism of the French judicial system (which had been criticized widely for anti-Semitism in the treason case of Captain Alfred Dreyfus) by suggesting that Americans attend to their own lynching problem before criticizing others.

Perhaps the most interesting aspect of Wells-Barnett's article is her use of the concept of "civilization" and her invocation of world opinion and America's international standing to support her case. In her use of "civilization," Wells-Barnett turns the tables on racists who insist upon the "savagery" of black men. Control of primal urges (sexual ones especially) were considered a mark of "civilized" people in the nineteenth century. White women were in peril, supposedly, because black men could not control their sexual urges. Wells-Barnett, however, points out that white men have sexually transgressed the color line far more often than black men. But the crime of rape or sexual assault against a black woman by a white man has never been punished. Furthermore, the orgy of blood and murder that she describes in the practice of lynching suggests that white men have given in to the most primal forms of bloodlust and revenge. By the standards of "civilization," southern whites have more to answer for than blacks, as they seem unable to control their basest passions.

In 1893 and 1894, Wells-Barnett had undertaken two speaking tours of the British Isles to publicize her investigations into the practice of lynching. These extremely successful tours managed to create greater international awareness of the situation for southern blacks and initiate an international dialogue about it. British criticism stung Americans and put apologists for lynching on the defensive in the United States. Wells-Barnett clearly intends to press this strategy in the conclusion of "Lynch Law in America." By emphasizing the negative consequences of lynching on America's reputation on the world stage, she hits upon an effective strategy that puts pressure on white Americans regardless of their sympathy for black victims of lynching. It is in America's best interest to curb these embarrassing episodes and to follow the rule of law for all citizens, regardless of race, she maintains. Wells-Barnett takes every opportunity to remind her readers that America's response to lynching is being observed from abroad.

Audience

Wells-Barnett published "Lynch Law in America" in the January 1900 issue of *Arena*, a Progressive Boston-based magazine devoted to raising awareness of injustices against the poor and powerless. Through this magazine she reached an influential white audience that was not likely to read her pamphlets or newspaper articles.

Impact

Although she was one of the few black leaders who made lynching a top focus for concern in the 1890s—a decade in which blacks also faced the imposition of disenfranchisement and Jim Crow segregation—Wells-Barnett's antilynching campaign succeeded in bringing the issue to national attention. Heightened awareness outside the South about the pervasiveness of this practice and the dubiousness of the public excuses for it eventually flowered into broad public disapproval. The response to mob violence in Springfield, Illinois, in 1908 that launched the NAACP reflected a changed opinion among Progressive northerners, who saw the spread of lynching as a moral concern of the first order. No doubt Wells-Barnett's campaign deserves a great deal of credit for this change in opinion.

See also Emancipation Proclamation (1863); Fourteenth Amendment to the U.S. Constitution (1868); Fifteenth Amendment to the U.S. Constitution (1870); *Plessy v. Ferguson* (1896); Walter F. White: "The Eruption of Tulsa" (1921).

Further Reading

■ Articles

Karcher, Carolyn L. "Ida B. Wells and Her Allies against Lynching: A Transnational Perspective." *Comparative American Studies* 3, no. 2 (June 2005): 131–151.

———. "The White 'Bystander' and the Black Journalist 'Abroad:'" Albion W. Tourgée and Ida B. Wells as Allies against Lynching." *Prospects* 29 (October 2005): 85–119.

■ Books

Bay, Mia. *To Tell the Truth Freely: The Life of Ida B. Wells.* New York: Hill and Wang, 2009.

Davidson, James West. *"They Say": Ida B. Wells and the Reconstruction of Race.* New York: Oxford University Press, 2007.

Giddings, Paula J. *Ida: A Sword among Lions.* New York: HarperCollins/Amistad, 2008.

Hendricks, W. A. *Gender, Race, and Politics in the Midwest.* Bloomington: Indiana University Press, 1998.

McMurry, Linda O. *To Keep the Waters Troubled: The Life of Ida B. Wells.* New York: Oxford University Press, 1998.

Schechter, Patricia A. *Ida B. Wells-Barnett and American Reform, 1880–1930.* Chapel Hill: University of North Carolina Press, 2001.

Wells, Ida B. *Southern Horrors and Other Writings: The Anti-Lynching Campaign of Ida B. Wells, 1892–1900,* ed. Jacqueline Jones Royster. New York: Bedford Books, 1997.

■ Web Sites

"Behind the Veil: Documenting African American Life in the Jim Crow South." Center for Documentary Studies at Duke University Web site.
http://cds.aas.duke.edu/btv/index.html.

PBS's "The Rise and Fall of Jim Crow" Web site.
http://www.pbs.org/wnet/jimcrow/index.html.

—Mark Elliott

Questions for Further Study

1. To what extent did the conditions Wells-Barnett described contribute to the race riot in Tulsa, Oklahoma, detailed in Walter White's "The Eruption of Tulsa"?

2. Summarize the arguments Wells-Barnett makes in opposition to lynching. How, in her view, did it conflict with Christianity and with the democratic traditions of the country? What impact did the prevalence of lynching have on America's reputation abroad?

3. In the decades that followed, efforts to pass a federal antilynching bill were unsuccessful. Does this mean that Wells-Barnett's article was in some sense a failure by not influencing public opinion?

4. What role did the Ku Klux Klan and other white supremacist and paramilitary organizations play in the growth of lynching?

5. In what way did her personal experience contribute to Wells-Barnett's campaign against lynching?

IDA B. WELLS-BARNETT'S
"LYNCH LAW IN AMERICA"

Our country's national crime is *lynching*. It is not the creature of an hour, the sudden outburst of uncontrolled fury, or the unspeakable brutality of an insane mob. It represents the cool, calculating deliberation of intelligent people who openly avow that there is an "unwritten law" that justifies them in putting human beings to death without complaint under oath, without trial by jury, without opportunity to make defense, and without right of appeal. The "unwritten law" first found excuse with the rough, rugged, and determined man who left the civilized centers of eastern States to seek for quick returns in the gold-fields of the far West. Following in uncertain pursuit of continually eluding fortune, they dared the savagery of the Indians, the hardships of mountain travel, and the constant terror of border State outlaws. Naturally, they felt slight toleration for traitors in their own ranks. It was enough to fight the enemies from without; woe to the foe within! Far removed from and entirely without protection of the courts of civilized life, these fortune-seekers made laws to meet their varying emergencies. The thief who stole a horse, the bully who "jumped" a claim, was a common enemy. If caught he was promptly tried, and if found guilty was hanged to the tree under which the court convened.

Those were busy days of busy men. They had no time to give the prisoner a bill of exception or stay of execution. The only way a man had to secure a stay of execution was to behave himself. Judge Lynch was original in methods but exceedingly effective in procedure. He made the charge, impaneled the jurors, and directed the execution. When the court adjourned, the prisoner was dead. Thus lynch law held sway in the far West until civilization spread into the Territories and the orderly processes of law took its place. The emergency no longer existing, lynching gradually disappeared from the West.

But the spirit of mob procedure seemed to have fastened itself upon the lawless classes, and the grim process that at first was invoked to declare justice was made the excuse to wreak vengeance and cover crime. It next appeared in the South, where centuries of Anglo-Saxon civilization had made effective all the safeguards of court procedure. No emergency called for lynch law. It asserted its sway in defiance of law and in favor of anarchy. There it has flourished ever since, marking the thirty years of its existence with the inhuman butchery of more than ten thousand men, women, and children by shooting, drowning, hanging, and burning them alive. Not only this, but so potent is the force of example that the lynching mania has spread throughout the North and middle West. It is now no uncommon thing to read of lynchings north of Mason and Dixon's line, and those most responsible for this fashion gleefully point to these instances and assert that the North is no better than the South.

This is the work of the "unwritten law" about which so much is said, and in whose behest butchery is made a pastime and national savagery condoned. The first statute of this "unwritten law" was written in the blood of thousands of brave men who thought that a government that was good enough to create a citizenship was strong enough to protect it. Under the authority of a national law that gave every citizen the right to vote, the newly-made citizens chose to exercise their suffrage. But the reign of the national law was short-lived and illusionary. Hardly had the sentences dried upon the statute-books before one Southern State after another raised the cry against "negro domination" and proclaimed there was an "unwritten law" that justified any means to resist it.

The method then inaugurated was the outrages by the "red-shirt" bands of Louisiana, South Carolina, and other Southern States, which were succeeded by the Ku-Klux Klans. These advocates of the "unwritten law" boldly avowed their purpose to intimidate, suppress, and nullify the negro's right to vote. In support of its plans the Ku-Klux Klans, the "red-shirt" and similar organizations proceeded to beat, exile, and kill negroes until the purpose of their organization was accomplished and the supremacy of the "unwritten law" was effected. Thus lynchings began in the South, rapidly spreading into the various States until the national law was nullified and the reign of the "unwritten law" was supreme. Men were taken from their homes by "red-shirt" bands and stripped, beaten, and exiled; others were assassinated when their political prominence made them obnoxious to their political opponents; while the Ku-Klux barbarism of election days, reveling in the butchery of thousands of colored voters, furnished records in Congressional investigations that are a disgrace to civilization.

The alleged menace of universal suffrage having been avoided by the absolute suppression of the negro vote, the spirit of mob murder should have been satisfied and the butchery of negroes should have ceased. But men, women, and children were the victims of murder by individuals and murder by mobs, just as they had been when killed at the demands of the "unwritten law" to prevent "negro domination." Negroes were killed for disputing over terms of contracts with their employers. If a few barns were burned some colored man was killed to stop it. If a colored man resented the imposition of a white man and the two came to blows, the colored man had to die, either at the hands of the white man then and there or later at the hands of a mob that speedily gathered. If he showed a spirit of courageous manhood he was hanged for his pains, and the killing was justified by the declaration that he was a "saucy nigger." Colored women have been murdered because they refused to tell the mobs where relatives could be found for "lynching bees." Boys of fourteen years have been lynched by white representatives of American civilization. In fact, for all kinds of offenses—and, for no offenses—from murders to misdemeanors, men and women are put to death without judge or jury; so that, although the political excuse was no longer necessary, the wholesale murder of human beings went on just the same. A new name was given to the killings and a new excuse was invented for so doing.

Again the aid of the "unwritten law" is invoked, and again it comes to the rescue. During the last ten years a new statute has been added to the "unwritten law." This statute proclaims that for certain crimes or alleged crimes no negro shall be allowed a trial; that no white woman shall be compelled to charge an assault under oath or to submit any such charge to the investigation of a court of law. The result is that many men have been put to death whose innocence was afterward established; and to-day, under this reign of the "unwritten law," no colored man, no matter what his reputation, is safe from lynching if a white woman, no matter what her standing or motive, cares to charge him with insult or assault.

It is considered a sufficient excuse and reasonable justification to put a prisoner to death under this "unwritten law" for the frequently repeated charge that these lynching horrors are necessary to prevent crimes against women. The sentiment of the country has been appealed to, in describing the isolated condition of white families in thickly populated negro districts; and the charge is made that these homes are in as great danger as if they were surrounded by wild beasts. And the world has accepted this theory without let or hindrance. In many cases there has been open expression that the fate meted out to the victim was only what he deserved. In many other instances there has been a silence that says more forcibly than words can proclaim it that it is right and proper that a human being should be seized by a mob and burned to death upon the unsworn and the uncorroborated charge of his accuser. No matter that our laws presume every man innocent until he is proved guilty; no matter that it leaves a certain class of individuals completely at the mercy of another class; no matter that it encourages those criminally disposed to blacken their faces and commit any crime in the calendar so long as they can throw suspicion on some negro, as is frequently done, and then lead a mob to take his life; no matter that mobs make a farce of the law and a mockery of justice; no matter that hundreds of boys are being hardened in crime and schooled in vice by the repetition of such scenes before their eyes—if a white woman declares herself insulted or assaulted, some life must pay the penalty, with all the horrors of the Spanish Inquisition and all the barbarism of the Middle Ages. The world looks on and says it is well.

Not only are two hundred men and women put to death annually, on the average, in this country by mobs, but these lives are taken with the greatest publicity. In many instances the leading citizens aid and abet by their presence when they do not participate, and the leading journals inflame the public mind to the lynching point with scare-head articles and offers of rewards. Whenever a burning is advertised to take place, the railroads run excursions, photographs are taken, and the same jubilee is indulged in that characterized the public hangings of one hundred years ago. There is, however, this difference: in those old days the multitude that stood by was permitted only to guy or jeer. The nineteenth century lynching mob cuts off ears, toes, and fingers, strips off flesh, and distributes portions of the body as souvenirs among the crowd. If the leaders of the mob are so minded, coal-oil is poured over the body and the victim is then roasted to death. This has been done in Texarkana and Paris, Tex., in Bardswell, Ky., and in Newman, Ga. In Paris the officers of the law delivered the prisoner to the mob. The mayor gave the school children a holiday and the railroads ran excursion trains so that the people might see a human being burned to death. In Texarkana, the year before, men and boys amused themselves by cutting off strips of flesh and thrusting knives into their helpless victim. At Newman, Ga., of the present year, the mob tried every conceivable torture to compel the victim to cry out and confess, before they set fire to the faggots that burned him. But their trouble was all in vain—he never uttered a cry, and they could not make him confess.

This condition of affairs were brutal enough and horrible enough if it were true that lynchings occurred only because of the commission of crimes against women—as is constantly declared by ministers, editors, lawyers, teachers, statesmen, and even by women themselves. It has been to the interest of those who did the lynching to blacken the good name of the helpless and defenseless victims of their hate. For this reason they publish at every possible opportunity this excuse for lynching, hoping thereby not only to palliate their own crime but at the same time to prove the negro a moral monster and unworthy of the respect and sympathy of the civilized world. But this alleged reason adds to the deliberate injustice of the mob's work. Instead of lynchings being caused by assaults upon women, the statistics show that not one-third of the victims of lynchings are even charged with such crimes. The Chicago *Tribune*, which publishes annually lynching statistics, is authority for the following:

In 1892, when lynching reached high-water mark, there were 241 persons lynched. The entire number is divided among the following States:

Alabama: 22
Arkansas: 25
California: 3
Florida: 11
Georgia: 17
Idaho: 8
Illinois: 1
Kansas: 3
Kentucky: 9
Louisiana: 29
Maryland: 1
Mississippi: 16
Missouri: 6
Montana: 4
New York: 1
North Carolina: 5
North Dakota: 1
Ohio: 3
South Carolina: 5
Tennessee: 28
Texas: 15
Virginia: 7
West Virginia: 5
Wyoming: 9
Arizona Ter[ritory]: 3
Oklahoma: 2

Of this number, 160 were of negro descent. Four of them were lynched in New York, Ohio, and Kansas; the remainder were murdered in the South. Five of this number were females. The charges for which they were lynched cover a wide range. They are as follows:

Rape: 46
Murder: 58
Rioting: 3
Race Prejudice: 6
No cause given: 4
Incendiarism: 6
Robbery: 6
Assault and battery: 1
Attempted rape: 11
Suspected robbery: 4
Larceny: 1
Self-defense: 1
Insulting women: 2
Desperadoes: 6
Fraud: 1
Attempted murder: 2
No offense stated, boy and girl: 4

In the case of the boy and girl above referred to, their father, named Hastings, was accused of the murder of a white man. His fourteen-year-old daughter and sixteen-year-old son were hanged and their bodies filled with bullets; then the father was also lynched. This occurred in November, 1892, at Jonesville, La.

Indeed, the record for the last twenty years shows exactly the same or a smaller proportion who have been charged with this horrible crime. Quite a number of the one-third alleged cases of assault that have been personally investigated by the writer have shown that there was no foundation in fact for the charges; yet the claim is not made that there were no real culprits among them. The negro has been too long associated with the white man not to have copied his vices as well as his virtues. But the negro resents and utterly repudiates the efforts to blacken his good name by asserting that assaults upon women are peculiar to his race. The negro has suffered far more from the commission of this crime against the women of his race by white men than the white race has ever suffered through *his* crimes. Very scant notice is taken of the matter when this is the condition of affairs. What be-

Document Text

comes a crime deserving capital punishment when the tables are turned is a matter of small moment when the negro woman is the accusing party.

But since the world has accepted this false and unjust statement, and the burden of proof has been placed upon the negro to vindicate his race, he is taking steps to do so. The Anti-Lynching Bureau of the National Afro-American Council is arranging to have every lynching investigated and publish the facts to the world, as has been done in the case of Sam Hose, who was burned alive last April at Newman, Ga. The detective's report showed that Hose killed Cranford, his employer, in self-defense, and that, while a mob was organizing to hunt Hose to punish him for killing a white man, not till twenty-four hours after the murder was the charge of rape, embellished with psychological and physical impossibilities, circulated. That gave an impetus to the hunt, and the Atlanta *Constitution's* reward of $500 keyed the mob to the necessary burning and roasting pitch. Of five hundred newspaper clippings of that horrible affair, nine-tenths of them assumed Hose's guilt—simply because his murderers said so, and because it is the fashion to believe the negro peculiarly addicted to this species of crime. All the negro asks is justice—a fair and impartial trial in the courts of the country. That given, he will abide the result.

But this question affects the entire American nation, and from several points of view: First, on the ground of consistency. Our watchword has been "the land of the free and the home of the brave." Brave men do not gather by thousands to torture and murder a single individual, so gagged and bound he cannot make even feeble resistance or defense. Neither do brave men or women stand by and see such things done without compunction of conscience, nor read of them without protest. Our nation has been active and outspoken in its endeavors to right the wrongs of the Armenian Christian, the Russian Jew, the Irish Home Ruler, the native women of India, the Siberian exile, and the Cuban patriot. Surely it should be the nation's duty to correct its own evils!

Second, on the ground of economy. To those who fail to be convinced from any other point of view touching this momentous question, a consideration of the economic phase might not be amiss. It is generally known that mobs in Louisiana, Colorado, Wyoming, and other States have lynched subjects of other countries. When their different governments demanded satisfaction, our country was forced to confess her inability to protect said subjects in the several States because of our State-rights doctrines,

or in turn demand punishment of the lynchers. This confession, while humiliating in the extreme, was not satisfactory; and, while the United States cannot protect, she can pay. This she has done, and it is certain will have to do again in the case of the recent lynching of Italians in Louisiana. The United States already has paid in indemnities for lynching nearly a half million dollars, as follows:

Paid China for Rock Springs (Wyo.) massacre: $147,748.74
Paid China for outrages on Pacific Coast: 276,619.75
Paid Italy for massacre of Italian prisoners at New Orleans: 24,330.90
Paid Italy for lynchings at Walsenburg, Col[orado]: 10,000.00
Paid Great Britain for outrages on James Bain and Frederick Dawson: 2,800.00

Third, for the honor of Anglo-Saxon civilization. No scoffer at our boasted American civilization could say anything more harsh of it than does the American white man himself who says he is unable to protect the honor of his women without resort to such brutal, inhuman, and degrading exhibitions as characterize "lynching bees." The cannibals of the South Sea Islands roast human beings alive to satisfy hunger. The red Indian of the Western plains tied his prisoner to the stake, tortured him, and danced in fiendish glee while his victim writhed in the flames. His savage, untutored mind suggested no better way than that of wreaking vengeance upon those who had wronged him. These people knew nothing about Christianity and did not profess to follow its teachings; but such primary laws as they had they lived up to. No nation, savage or civilized, save only the United States of America, has confessed its inability to protect its women save by hanging, shooting, and burning alleged offenders.

Finally, for love of country. No American travels abroad without blushing for shame for his country on this subject. And whatever the excuse that passes current in the United States, it avails nothing abroad. With all the powers of government in control; with all laws made by white men, administered by white judges, jurors, prosecuting attorneys, and sheriffs; with every office of the executive department filled by white men—no excuse can be offered for exchanging the orderly administration of justice for barbarous lynchings and "unwritten laws." Our country should be placed speedily above the plane of confessing herself a failure at self-government. This cannot be until Americans of every section, of broadest patriotism and best and wisest citizenship, not only see the defect in our country's armor but take the necessary steps to remedy it. Although lynchings have steadily increased in number and barbarity during the last twenty years, there has been no single effort put forth by the many moral and philanthropic forces of the country to put a stop to this wholesale slaughter. Indeed, the silence and seeming condonation grow more marked as the years go by.

A few months ago the conscience of this country was shocked because, after a two-weeks trial, a French judicial tribunal pronounced Captain Dreyfus guilty. And yet, in our own land and under our own flag, the writer can give day and detail of one thousand men, women, and children who during the last six years were put to death without trial before any tribunal on earth. Humiliating indeed, but altogether unanswerable, was the reply of the French press to our protest: "Stop your lynchings at home before you send your protests abroad."

Glossary

Anglo-Saxon	a reference to the Germanic tribes that invaded and settled Great Britain; more generally, Anglo-American civilization
Captain Dreyfus	Alfred Dreyfus, a Jewish French military officer who was at the center of a scandal that divided France in the 1890s after he was falsely convicted of treason
Irish Home Ruler	an Irish person who wanted an Ireland independent from the United Kingdom
"jumped" a claim	the practice of stealing someone's mining property
Mason and Dixon's line	a line surveyed in the eighteenth century to settle border disputes in the American colonies, more generally referring to the boundary between the North and the South in the United States
Spanish Inquisition	a tribunal established in fifteenth-century Spain to enforce Catholic orthodoxy; used often as a symbol of cruelty because of its use of torture and extreme punishments